College writing skills in a real-world context

Real Essays

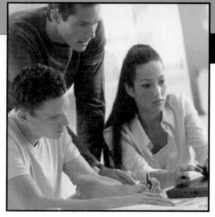

with Readings

Writing Projects
for College,
Work, and
Everyday Life

SUSAN ANKER

Connecting college writing skills to

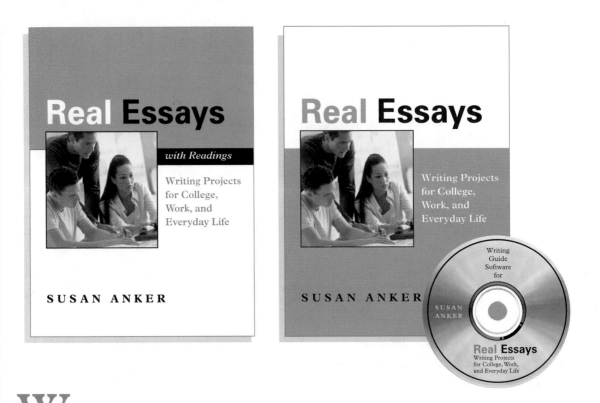

W ritten by the author of *Real Writing,* the most successful new developmental textbook published in a decade, **Real Essays** builds and strengthens the writing and editing skills that students need to succeed in college, at work, and in everyday life. *Real Essays*

- ■ teaches writing, reading, and editing as practical and essential processes

- ■ includes clear models and step-by-step guidance for writing nine types of essays

- ■ covers all grammar topics — with an emphasis on fragments, run-ons, subject-verb agreement, and problems with verb forms

- ■ fosters critical reading skills that help students comprehend, analyze, and respond to readings

Real Essays with Readings
2003 Paperbound 816 pages
ISBN 0–312–39915–4

Real Essays
2003 Paper 720 pages
ISBN 0–312–39914–6

Instructor's Annotated Edition
ISBN 0–312–39916–2

Writing Guide Software
ISBN 0–312–40487–5

bedfordstmartins.com/realessays

real-world success

The Anker Series

Beginning with the publication of *Real Writing: Paragraphs and Essays for College, Work, and Everyday Life* in 1998, the Anker Series was the first to put writing in a real-world context and to cement the connection between what students learn in their college composition course and how they live their lives. The Series helps students succeed because of its thorough, practical writing instruction and the message that writing well is both an essential and achievable skill. Featuring photos, quotes, profiles, and advice, Susan Anker's texts are infused with the voices and concerns of developmental writing instructors and their students. Bedford/St. Martin's is proud to present *Real Essays,* the second in a two-book series that meets the needs and acknowledges the challenges faced by students and instructors who live in the real world.

An author with a unique perspective

Susan Anker (B.A., M.Ed., Boston University) brings a unique perspective to the teaching of developmental writing. Talking and working extensively with hundreds of developmental writing instructors from across the country has been the single common denominator in a rich and varied professional career. Her revolutionary real-world approach to writing instruction is the culmination of her work as a teacher of English and developmental writing; an editor of English, ESL, and other humanities texts; and co-founder of Anker Publishing Company, publisher of professional development materials for higher education instructors and administrators.

> " This text challenges students to reach beyond what they have been told they can achieve. I like that very much."
> — **Anne Gervasi,** *DeVry University*

Motivates students with a real-world

■ **Profiles of Success show that success is within reach.** Interviews with and photographs of former developmental writing students who have achieved success in the real world open the writing chapters in Part Two. By describing the kinds of work-related writing they do and showing how they actually use the type of writing covered in the chapter, these individuals show students just how valuable writing skills are in and beyond college.

■ **Real-world models of writing.** Unique to *Real Essays*, all nine writing chapters in Part Two include three essay-length samples — one each from college, work, and everyday life — with guidance and activities for analyzing the structure of the model and opportunities to write similar essays.

■ **Assignments that emphasize purpose and audience.** Writing chapters give students opportunities to apply their skills to a document written with a real purpose and targeted to a real audience, putting the writing that they do in a real-world context.

> *Real Essays* shows students examples of how writing is used in the real world through the success stories in the chapters in Part Two. So often students don't see how any of this applies to them or their lives, and the Profiles of Success show them that connection."
> — **Leigh Adams,**
> *Southwest Missouri State University*

Profile of Success

Daigo Fujiwara

Daigo Fujiwara, Assistant Art Director

BACKGROUND: *Daigo came to the United States from Japan as an exchange student when he was a senior in high school. After graduation he remained — against the wishes of his parents — to continue his education. Although he wanted to go to college, his English language test scores were low, so he took writing courses in English as a second language at Becker Junior College and then enrolled there. Although he could speak English fairly well, his writing skills were still poor. Through continuing on with ESL writing courses, Daigo improved his skills and graduated first from Becker and then from Northeastern University. In addition to his job as an assistant art director, Daigo is a photographer and plays bass in a band.*

EMPLOYER: *Inc. magazine*

COLLEGE(S)/DEGREES: *Becker Junior College (A.A.), Northeastern University (B.A.)*

TYPES OF WRITING ON THE JOB: *Summaries of articles for illustrators, memos to illustrators, follow-up letters to illustrators, notes about layout, directions for interns, forms describing necessary changes in artwork*

HOW DAIGO USES DESCRIPTION: *Daigo has to write*

detailed descriptions of what he needs for the magazine's art program. These descriptions, called specifications, are written for freelance artists. For an example of Daigo's use of description, see p.97.

COMPUTER SKILLS: *Word processing, photo imaging software (Photoshop), illustration software, internet*

TEAMWORK ON THE JOB: *Daigo works with the Inc.'s director and editor to develop a concept, to decide whether to use photographs or illustrations for each article, and to make individual selections.*

FUTURE GOAL: *Daigo hopes, first, to remain interested in whatever he's doing by learning new skills and, second, to continue his bass playing.*

19

---

2. DESCRIPTION IN THE WORKPLACE

The following is an example of the kind of description that Daigo writes in his job as graphic artist and assistant art director. Although the memo to the photo researcher is not in standard essay form, it is a clear example of description in the workplace.

May 8, 2002

TO: Jonathan Kuvicek, Photo Researcher

FR: Daigo Fujiwara, Assistant Art Director

RE: Photographs to accompany article

As we discussed earlier today, we need four photographs to accompany the article on innovative workspaces. Overall, the photos should be colorful, upbeat, and somewhat playful, demonstrating the positive attributes of the spaces.

The photographs should include people working in them. We would like to have a representative group of people: a variety of racial and ethnic groups balanced by gender. Probably most of the people will be younger, since the companies piloting these innovative spaces tend to attract younger employees. As we discussed, the opening photo might contrast a traditional cubicle arrangement with the newer arrangements.

All photographs should be in full color. The opening photograph will be sized at 3" x 6"; the other three will be 5" x 4". When you submit photos for our consideration, please indicate any cropping suggestions.

As we agreed, you will submit a group of photographs for our consideration by May 20.

emphasis

17
Solving Problems
Case Studies for Writing and Teamwork

Understand What Problem-Solving Is
Understand What Teamwork Is
Solve Problems from Real-World Case Studies

Understand What Problem-Solving Is

IDEA JOURNAL
Write about a problem that you have encountered at work or in your personal life.

DEFINITION: Problem-solving is the process of identifying the problem and discovering a reasonable solution.

Think of the situations in your life that you might classify as problems. Perhaps you're falling behind in one of your courses. Or maybe you are managing a sales staff that hasn't met its quota for the third straight month. It could be that your child's day care center is having trouble retaining quality staff. While they often disrupt our lives, problems give us opportunities to tackle difficult situations with confidence. Being able to find reasonable solutions to problems is critical to success in every arena of life.

Problem-solving includes several basic steps.

THE PROBLEM-SOLVING PROCESS

1. Identify the problem. You should be able to say or write it in a brief statement.
2. List people, information, and other resources that can help you solve the problem.
3. Identify possible solutions.
4. Evaluate each possible solution.
5. Identify the steps the solution would require.

■ Unique to *Real Essays*, a full chapter introduces students to the process of problem solving. Five real-life scenarios form the core of a chapter that immerses students in a collaborative problem-solving process — identifying a problem, listing possible solutions, evaluating possible solutions, and choosing and defending a workable solution — and guides them as they write an essay that proposes a solution to one problem. The chapter also supplies ample support for working in teams.

Solve Problems from Real-World Case Studies

Using the problem-solving process and working as part of a team, you will suggest a reasonable solution to a real-life problem presented in one of the following case studies. Once you have chosen or been assigned a case, read the case carefully. Then the team can meet to start working through the process of problem-solving.

CASE STUDIES

1. Network Administrator

You are a network administrator for a large corporation and have the ability, though not the authority, to read all email messages sent to and from employees using company email. Your company has a strict policy that safeguards the privacy of personal email, and the last network administrator was fired for reading other employees' mail. During one of your routine monitoring sessions, you notice an unusually large number of messages being sent from one internal email address to another. Out of curiosity, you open and read some of these email messages. The messages are from the boss's son to his girlfriend (both of whom are employees of the company) and are threatening in nature. In his email, he talks about hurting his girlfriend, and each message is more threatening than the one before it. What do you do?

2. College Ice Hockey Coach

It is two nights before an important conference game—the game that will decide whether your team advances to the championship playoffs or ends its season short of a championship. You learn that four key players have violated their curfew. Curfews are an important part of the discipline program created by the coaching staff. Both the rules of the curfew and the school's zero-tolerance policy for rulebreaking are clearly established during pre-season training. The punishment for breaking curfew is a one-game suspension. The group of players facing punishment includes the team's leading scorers. The team, which includes fourteen other young women, has worked hard all season to achieve the school's best record in more than two decades. What do you do?

Presents writing in logical, manageable

■ **A focus on the key elements of each mode promotes successful writing.** Every chapter in Part Two opens with a list of four basic features of the type of writing covered — the "Four Basics." This presentation, which highlights the essential elements needed to understand and use a rhetorical strategy, organizes and simplifies the writing instruction. The Writing Guide (see below), the questions following the chapter readings, and the chapter-ending Final Check work together to reinforce the importance of the Four Basics.

Understand What Narration Is

DEFINITION: **Narration** is writing that tells a story of an event or experience.

▪▪ Four Basics of Good Narration

1. It reveals something of importance to you (your main point).
2. It includes all of the major events of the story.
3. It uses details to bring the story to life for your audience.
4. It presents the events in a clear order, usually according to when they happened.

Sharing stories is one important way in which we communicate with one another. Whether they are serious or humorous, stories provide information and examples that can show, explain, or prove a point. To sh~~ow~~ how a story is funny, you give example~~s~~ ~~t~~o explain that you were ~~t~~ ~~per~~son, you give details; to ~~~~ ~~y~~ou have experie~~nced~~ ~~t~~hat experi~~ence~~

■ **Step-by-step Writing Guides offer real help.** Each chapter in Part Two, the core writing instruction, includes a Writing Guide that breaks down the process for a mode into a series of manageable tasks. Each step is accompanied by clear advice for completing each task and checklist items that guide students as they write the essay and help them to keep track of their progress.

WRITING ESSAYS
122   PartTwo • Writing Different Kinds of Essays

Writing Guide   **Narration**

Follow the steps in this Writing Guide to help you prewrite, write, revise, and edit your narration. Check off each step as you complete it

THINKING CRITICALLY ABOUT NARRATION

FOCUS   Think about who will read your narration and what point you want your readers to understand from your story.

ASK
- What experience or series of events do I want to write about?
- What is important about the story from my point of view?
- What main point do I want to make with this story?
- To make that point, what major events do I need to include?
- What details, examples, and facts will bring these events to life and show the reader what the point is and why it is important?
- Should I include conversation (something that was said)?

PREWRITE TO EXPLORE YOUR TOPIC

Prewriting for narration involves considering several possible experiences or stories to retell and deciding on the one that you can bring to life for your readers and that reveals something important.

For more on purpose and audience, see Chapter 1.
_____ Determine your purpose for writing.
.... Identify the audience for your essay.
_____ Decide what story you want to tell.

For more on prewriting techniques, see Chapter 2.
_____ Use a prewriting technique (brainstorming, freewriting, questioning, discussing, clustering) to explore your impressions and thoughts about what happened, how it affected you or others, and what the story shows, explains, or proves.

❝ *Real Essays* includes outstanding step-by-step guidance for producing well-written, supported, and organized essays."
— **Jeffrey Siddall,** *College of DuPage*

increments

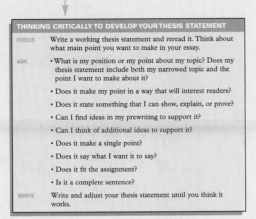

THINKING CRITICALLY TO DEVELOP YOUR THESIS STATEMENT

FOCUS	Write a working thesis statement and reread it. Think about what main point you want to make in your essay.
ASK	• What is my position or my point about my topic? Does my thesis statement include both my narrowed topic and the point I want to make about it? • Does it make my point in a way that will interest readers? • Does it state something that I can show, explain, or prove? • Can I find ideas in my prewriting to support it? • Can I think of additional ideas to support it? • Does it make a single point? • Does it say what I want it to say? • Does it fit the assignment? • Is it a complete sentence?
WRITE	Write and adjust your thesis statement until you think it works.

■ Critical Thinking guides teach college-level thinking skills.

Three-part critical thinking guides throughout the text prompt students to *focus* on a task, *ask* themselves basic questions about it, and then *write* or *edit* after thinking through the questions.

■ Helps students use technology to become better writers.
"Use a Computer" sections present brief tips and basic strategies for writing with computers. Essay options in Part Two prompt students to investigate specific Web sites or types of sites in preparation for writing an essay.

■ Two chapters make the research essay manageable.
The first chapter teaches key research skills such as searching databases, taking notes, and avoiding plagiarism. The second presents the process for writing a research essay in seven stages. A continuous student example and the student's final MLA-style essay are included.

WRITING ESSAYS
Chapter 8 • Narration   123

WRITE A THESIS STATEMENT

The thesis statement in narration includes the topic and the main point you want to make about it.

For more on writing a thesis statement, see Chapter 3.

Topic	+	Main point	=	Thesis statement

Skydiving	is the most thrilling experience I have ever had.
The details of my accident	will indicate that the truck driver was at fault.

_____ Decide what is important about the story you will tell from your point of view. Imagine telling your story and someone says, "So what?" How would you respond?

For more on point of view in narration, See p. 200.

_____ What point do you want your readers to understand from this narrative?

SUPPORT YOUR POINT

Your support in narration includes the major events in your story and the supporting details that explain the events for readers.

_____ List all of the major events in the story.

_____ Review your working thesis statement, and drop any events that do not help to explain, show, or prove your main point. Make your thesis more specific.

_____ Choose at least three major events that will help your reader understand your main point.

_____ Add supporting details about each event that will help your reader to experience it as you did. It might help to think about how familiar your readers are with your topic and what details would bring your major events to life for them.

MAKE A PLAN

For more on making a plan, see Ch. 5.

Narration usually tells a story in chronological (time) order, presenting events in the order in which they happened.

❝ I like that the chapters on writing the research essay emphasize that it is an 'essay' students are writing. The very phrase 'research paper' connotes this huge monster that students fear. However, writing an essay is something that they have done many times over."
— **Rick Dollieslager,** *Thomas Nelson Community College*

Helps students become better editors

■ **Helps students overcome the four most serious errors — and more.** Rather than giving all errors equal weight, *Real Essays* concentrates first, with fuller coverage and plenty of practice, on the errors identified by teachers across the country as the most serious: fragments, run-ons, subject–verb agreement problems, and verb form problems. These topics, pulled together in Part Four, lead off the Editing section of the text. This unique approach teaches students to concentrate on a limited number of major sentence problems as a first step to becoming better editors of their own writing. The remaining chapters include thorough coverage of all standard grammar, usage, punctuation, and mechanics topics — with hundreds of practice items.

■ **Links to Exercise Central provide more opportunities for skill practice.** Marginal references throughout the editing chapters direct students to Exercise Central for additional exercises. The largest online bank of editing exercises, Exercise Central offers two levels of skill practice, customized feedback, and instructor monitoring tools.

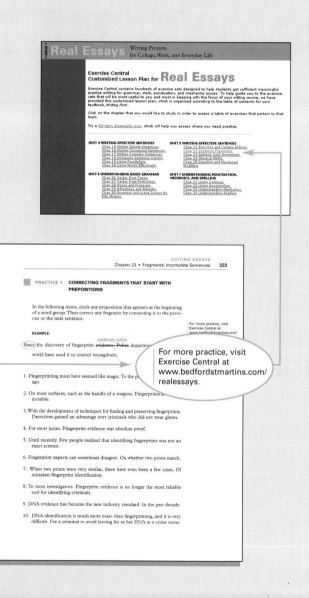

# of their own writing

■ Quick Review Charts present key information visually. For students who are visual learners, grammar concepts and editing strategies are presented in chapter-ending flow charts for quick comprehension and practical application.

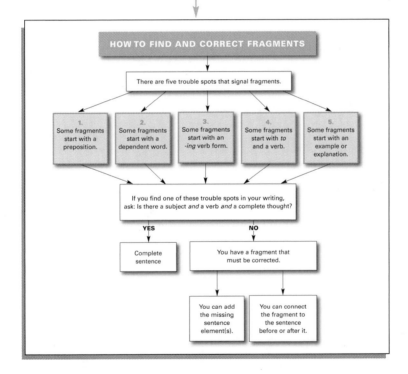

HOW TO FIND AND CORRECT FRAGMENTS

There are five trouble spots that signal fragments.

1. Some fragments start with a preposition.

2. Some fragments start with a dependent word.

3. Some fragments start with an -*ing* verb form.

4. Some fragments start with *to* and a verb.

5. Some fragments start with an example or explanation.

If you find one of these trouble spots in your writing, ask: Is there a subject *and* a verb *and* a complete thought?

YES

NO

Complete sentence

You have a fragment that must be corrected.

You can add the missing sentence element(s).

You can connect the fragment to the sentence before or after it.

> Grammar topics are presented in a clear and methodical way, and Susan Anker's explanations of why grammar proficiency is important make sense to my students."
> — Robin Havenick, *Linn-Benton Community College*

Easy to use

■ **Key chapter elements are clear, accessible, and predictable.** The help students need to write their papers — step-by-step writing guides, critical thinking guides, models, practices, checklists, and computer tips — is clearly labeled and easy to use. The chapters follow a consistent three-part organization, and key chapter elements are consistently designed.

■ **Marginal references direct students to useful information.** To help students navigate, the design features easy-to-read references in the margins to other material in the text, on the companion Web site, and in the Writing Guide Software.

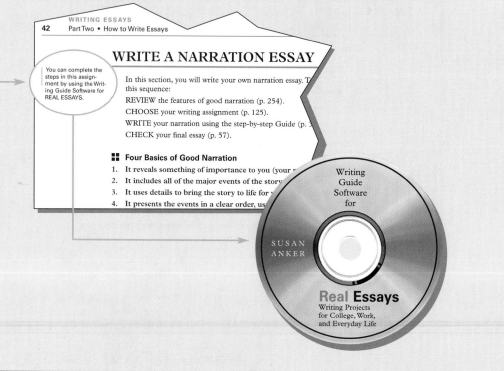

Five Tips for Writing on a Computer

1. *Save your work as you write.* It is very frustrating to lose your work at any stage of the writing process. Saving your work at regular intervals while you are writing-say, every 15 minutes-is the best way to keep from losing what you have written if there is a power failure or some other interruption on the computer. (In Microsoft Word 2002, you can set autosave functions by going to the Tools menu, selecting Options, clicking on the Save tab, and checking the boxes to get the functions you want.)

2. *Save your work at the end of every session.* When you are finished using the computer, save your work in two places, if possible:
   • Save it on the hard drive of the computer (usually the C: drive).
   • Save it on a disk.
   One serves as a backup for the other-computers can "crash," and disks can break or malfunction. A plastic carrying case will help you protect and organize your disks.

3. *Name your files so you can find them easily.* Developing an easy-to-remember file naming system will help you manage your writing projects. College students usually use course names or numbers, assignment dates, and key words to help them track and manage the many files and drafts they create. If you are working on a draft of a paper for English 100, naming it "English 100 draft" may help you find it when you return to revise it. What happens when you write your second assignment, though-your second "English 100 draft"? Be specific in naming your files by using a key "favorite place first draft 9-..." or ... be a favorite place, for ex-... create new files-such as ... ious draft

WRITE A NARRATION ESSAY

> You can complete the steps in this assignment by using the Writing Guide Software for REAL ESSAYS.

In this section, you will write your own narration essay. T... this sequence:

REVIEW the features of good narration (p. 254).

CHOOSE your writing assignment (p. 125).

WRITE your narration using the step-by-step Guide (p. ...

CHECK your final essay (p. 57).

■■ Four Basics of Good Narration

1. It reveals something of importance to you (your ...
2. It includes all of the major events of the story ...
3. It uses details to bring the story to life for ...
4. It presents the events in a clear order, us...

Writing Guide Software for

SUSAN ANKER

Real Essays
Writing Projects for College, Work, and Everyday Life

More reviewer praise...

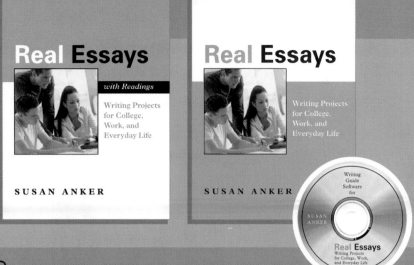

Thorough Coverage

I admit to being a perfectionist and having high standards for a textbook. Therefore, when I say that I cannot think of a single concept, example, or process that is missing from *Real Essays,* I am as surprised as you are."

—**Tamara Shue,** *Georgia Perimeter College*

Unique Treatment of Problem Solving

The description of the problem-solving process is accurate and thorough. It sums up very well what I have taken a week to get across in class."

— **Terrance Millet,** *Linn-Benton Community College*

Excellent Readings

The readings from the workplace are well chosen and excellent examples of good professional writing. The questions and exercises provided are illuminating and informative."

— **Nadan Choksi,** *Art Institute of Florida*

A wide array of print and new media

Electronic Ancillaries
Give Students More Practice and More Help with Writing

■ **Exercise Central.** With over 7,000 items, this is the largest online collection of grammar exercises available. Exercise Central is thorough, easy to use, and convenient for both students and instructors. Multiple exercise sets on every topic, at a variety of levels, ensure that students have as much practice as they need. Customized feedback for all answers assures that skills practice becomes a learning experience, and a reporting feature allows both students and instructors to monitor and assess student progress.

■ **Writing Guide Software.** Developed specifically for *Real Essays,* this software leads students step-by-step through the process of writing each of the types of essays covered in the text. Also included are critical reading guides, diagnostic tests, grammar tutorials, and a customizable error log that links to Exercise Central. ISBN 0–312–40487–5.

■ **Book Companion Site.** The companion Web site for *Real Essays* provides additional resources for instructors as well as links to Exercise Central and the English Research Room, an online resource for research writers.

www.bedfordstmartins.com/realessays

resources

Print Ancillaries
Take Instructors' Busy Lives into Account

■ **Instructor's Annotated Edition of**
Real Essays. Gives practical page-by-page advice on teaching with *Real Essays,* with five types of marginal tips — written by Susan Anker and by Susan Naomi Bernstein (University of Houston – Downtown) — including discussion prompts, collaborative activities, strategies for teaching ESL students and speakers of non-standard dialects, and more. Also contains answers to all exercises and suggestions for using the other ancillaries. ISBN 0–312– 39916–2.

■ **Practical Suggestions for Teaching** *Real Essays,* Eddye Gallagher, Tarrant County College. Contains information and advice on working with basic writers, bringing the real world into the classroom, building critical thinking skills, using computers, teaching ESL students and speakers of non-standard dialects (with a special contribution from James May of Valencia Community College), and assessment (with a special contribution from Karen Eisenhauer of Brevard Community College). Tips for new instructors and ideas for making the most of *Real Essays* are also included. ISBN 0–312–39917–0.

■ **Additional Resources to Accompany**
Real Essays, Susan Anker and Eddye S. Gallagher, Tarrant County College. Supplements the instructional materials in the text with a variety of transparency masters and other reproducibles for classroom use. ISBN 0–312–40488–3.

■ **Teaching Developmental Writing:**
Background Readings. A Bedford/St. Martin's Professional Resource, Susan Naomi Bernstein, University of Houston — Downtown. Includes 35 professional essays by Mina Shaughnessy, Mike Rose, Rei Noguchi, and others on topics of interest to basic writing instructors, along with useful editorial apparatus pointing out practical applications for the classroom. ISBN 0–312–25815–1.

More help for students

■ *Real Essays* **Quick Reference Card.** This laminated four-page card, which can be stood up next to a student's computer monitor, includes editing advice, tips on evaluating Web sources, and useful word processing tips. ISBN 0–312–40490–5.

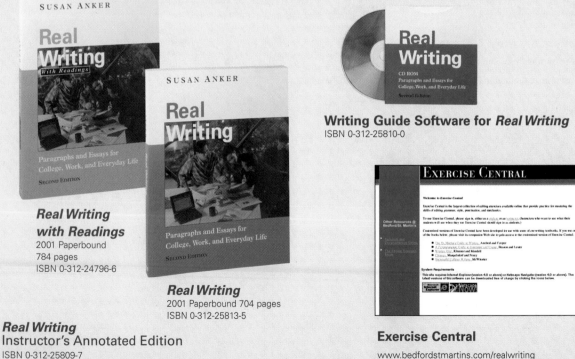

Real Essays
with Readings

Writing Projects for College,
Work, and Everyday Life

Real Essays

with Readings

Writing Projects for College, Work, and Everyday Life

Susan Anker

BEDFORD/ST. MARTIN'S   *Boston ◆ New York*

To Isabel Willey, who gave me the love of language

For Bedford/St. Martin's

Developmental Editors: Michelle M. Clark, Beth Castrodale
Production Editors: Karen Baart, Deborah Baker
Senior Production Supervisor: Dennis Conroy
Marketing Manager: Brian Wheel
Editorial Assistant: Karin Halbert
Copyeditor: Janet Renard
Text Design: Claire Seng-Niemoeller
Cover Design: Billy Boardman
Cover Art: © Photonica, New York, NY.
Composition: Stratford Publishing Services
Printing and Binding: R. R. Donnelley & Sons Company

President: Joan E. Feinberg
Editorial Director: Denise B. Wydra
Editor in Chief: Karen S. Henry
Director of Marketing: Karen Melton
Director of Editing, Design, and Production: Marcia Cohen
Managing Editor: Elizabeth M. Schaaf

Library of Congress Control Number: 2002112253

For information, write: Bedford/St. Martin's, 75 Arlington Street, Boston, MA 02116
(617-399-4000)

ISBN: 0–312–39914–6 (*Real Essays*)
       0–312–39915–4 (*Real Essays with Readings*)
       0–312–39916–2 (*Instructor's Annotated Edition*)

Acknowledgments
Christine Aziz. "The Lion of Kabul." From the *New Internationalist*, November 1996. Reprinted by permission of the New Internationalist, Toronto, Ontario, M5V 3A8, Canada.
Dave Barry. "The Ugly Truth about Beauty." From the *Miami Herald*, February 1, 1998. Originally titled "Beauty and the Beast." Copyright © 1998 Dave Barry. Reprinted by permission.

Preface for Instructors

Too often, students perceive their writing course as a pesky, creaking gate they must pass through in order to move on to "content" courses that, when completed, serve as the way to a good job. The aim of *Real Essays*, as indicated by its subtitle, *Writing Projects for College, Work, and Everyday Life*, is to show students that their writing course is a crucial gateway to success in every arena of their lives. To achieve this aim, *Real Essays* casts writing and editing skills as practical and valuable. Further, it sends the message that strengthening these skills is worth the effort because all the roles students will play in their lives—college student, employee, parent, consumer, community member—require that they write often and well.

Real Essays shares an overarching purpose with its companion, *Real Writing: Paragraphs and Essays for College, Work, and Everyday Life*: to put writing in a real-world context. This two-book series links writing skills to students' own goals in and beyond college. What's more, these books motivate students with photographs, quotes, profiles, and advice from current and former students—people like themselves who have struggled with writing, who have wondered why it was important, and who are learning that good writing is not a mysterious, divinely inspired gift but a skill that can be learned by any person who is willing to pay attention and practice. Together, these books form a foundation for success in the real world based on skills learned in the writing classroom.

Organization

Real Essays is divided into two major sections: writing essays and editing essays. Section I has three parts: "How to Write Essays" (Chapters 1–7); "Writing Different Kinds of Essays" (Chapters 8–16, covering narration, illustration, description, process analysis, classification, definition, comparison and contrast, cause and effect, and argument); and "Writing in College and at Work" (Chapters 17–21). Section II has four parts: "The Four Most Serious Errors" (Chapters 22–26, which includes a basic overview of editing); "Other Grammar Concerns" (Chapters 27–33); "Word

Use" (Chapters 34–36); and "Punctuation and Capitalization" (Chapters 37–41). The longer version of *Real Essays* also includes a final section, "Readings for Writers" (Chapters 42–51), with an introduction to the reading process; twenty high-interest, rhetorically organized readings; and prompts designed to help students comprehend, analyze, and respond to the readings. *Real Essays* ends with three useful appendices that give guidelines for writing email and memos; résumés and letters of application; and for making oral presentations.

These chapters are flexible, allowing you to use them in whatever order suits your course structure and your students' needs.

Features

Real Essays not only presents the information students need but also shows students how and why writing is relevant to them—connecting them to writing, to the content of the book, and to the course. *Real Essays* keeps things practical and lets students in on the fact that not all writing and grammar concepts are of equal importance. The text doesn't mislead students into thinking that writing is a simple process; instead, it presents material in meaningful and manageable chunks.

Motivates Students with a Real-World Emphasis

- **"Profiles of Success."** The writing chapters in Part Two open with photographs of and interviews with former students who have achieved success in the real world. By describing the kinds of work-related writing they do and showing how they actually use the type of writing covered in the chapter, these individuals show students just how valuable writing skills are, both in and beyond college. The "Profiles of Success" also describe how these individuals use technology and teamwork skills in their profession.

- **Real-world models of writing.** Unique to *Real Essays*, all nine writing chapters in Part Two include three essay-length samples—one each from college, work, and everyday life—with guidance and activities for analyzing the structure of the model and opportunities to write similar essays.

- **Problem-solving strategies.** Five real-life scenarios form the core of a unique chapter (Chapter 17) that immerses students in a collaborative problem-solving process—identifying a problem, listing possible solutions, evaluating possible solutions, and choosing and defending a workable solution—and guides them as they write an essay that proposes a solution to one problem. Chapter 17 also provides ample support for working in teams.

- **Assignments that emphasize purpose and audience.** Writing chapters give students opportunities to apply their skills to a document written with a real purpose and targeted to a real audience, putting the writing they do in a real-world context.

Presents Writing in Logical, Manageable Increments

- **A focus on the four basics of each mode promotes successful writing.** Each chapter in Part Two, "Writing Different Kinds of Essays," opens with a list (indicated by this symbol: ▪▪) of four basic features of the type of writing covered. This presentation, which highlights the essential elements needed to understand and use a rhetorical strategy, organizes and simplifies the writing instruction. The writing guide, the questions following the chapter readings, and the chapter-ending Final Check each reinforce the importance of these four basic elements.

- **Step-by-step "Writing Guides" offer real help.** Each chapter in Part Two, the core writing instruction, includes a "Writing Guide" that breaks down the process for a mode into a series of manageable tasks. Each step is accompanied by clear, concise advice for completing the task, and a series of checklist items that guide students as they write the essay and help them keep track of their progress.

- **"Thinking Critically" guides teach college-level thinking skills.** Three-part "Thinking Critically" boxes throughout the text prompt students to *focus* on the basic elements of the task, *ask* themselves some basic questions about it, and then *write* or *edit* after thinking through the questions. These guides help students avoid rushing through a writing, revising, or editing task.

- **Two chapters make the research essay manageable.** Chapter 20 teaches key research skills such as searching databases, taking notes, and avoiding plagiarism. Chapter 21 presents the process for writing a research essay in seven stages. A continuous student example and the student's final MLA-style essay are included.

- **"Use a Computer" sections in Part One ("How to Write Essays") help students use technology to become better writers.** These sections present brief tips and basic strategies for writing with computers. In addition, essay options in Part Two prompt students to investigate specific Web sites or types of sites in preparation for writing an essay. For example, in Chapter 8, "Narration," students are assigned to search a consumer complaint database for samples of written complaints, and write their own essay about a bad experience with a service or product.

Presents Editing in Logical, Manageable Increments

- **The editing section helps students overcome the four most serious errors—and more.** Rather than giving all errors equal weight, *Real Essays* concentrates first, with full coverage and plenty of practice, on the errors identified by teachers across the country as the most serious: fragments, run-ons, subject-verb agreement problems, and verb form problems. These topics, pulled together in Part Four, lead off the editing section of the text. This unique approach teaches students to concentrate on a limited number of major sentence problems as a first step to becoming better editors of their own writing. The remaining chapters include thorough coverage of all standard grammar, usage, punctuation, and mechanics topics—with hundreds of practice items.

- **Reference to Exercise Central provide more opportunities for skill practice.** Marginal references throughout the editing section direct students to Exercise Central for additional exercises. The largest online bank of editing exercises (with more than seven thousand items), Exercise Central offers two levels of skill practice, customized feedback, and instructor monitoring tools.

- **"Quick Review Charts" at the end of each grammar chapter present key information visually.** For students who are visual learners, the editing section presents concepts and strategies in chapter-ending flowcharts for quick comprehension and practical application.

Is Easy to Use

- **"Introduction for Students" offers a quick orientation.** A brief introduction walks students through the text's organization and key features, with sample pages and clear descriptions. It also describes features that students can use while writing and editing their own papers. The introduction ends with an inventory of students' goals and a worksheet that helps students articulate their goals for the writing course.

- **Key chapter elements are clear, accessible, and predictable.** Various elements designed to help students write their papers—step-by-step "Writing Guides," "Critical Thinking" guides, models, practices, checklists, and computer tips—are clearly labeled and easy to use. The chapters follow a consistent three-part organization: *Understand—Read and Analyze—Write* in the writing chapters, and *Understand—Practice—Edit* in the grammar chapters.

- **Marginal references direct students to useful information.** To help students find the assistance they need, *Real Essays* features easy-to-read references in the margins to other material in the text, to the book's companion Web site, and to the "Writing Guide" software.

Ancillaries

Real Essays is complemented by a wide range of useful support materials for both students and instructors. These are all practical tools designed to give real help to busy people.

Print Resources

Instructor's Annotated Edition of Real Essays. Gives practical page-by-page advice on teaching with *Real Essays*, with five types of marginal tips—written by Susan Anker and Susan Naomi Bernstein (University of Houston)—including discussion prompts, strategies for teaching ESL students, and more. Also contains answers to all exercises and suggestions for using the other ancillaries.

Practical Suggestions for Teaching Real Essays by Eddye S. Gallagher, Tarrant County College. Contains information and advice on working with basic writers, bringing the real world into the classroom, building critical-thinking skills, using computers, teaching ESL students and speakers of nonstandard dialects (with a special contribution by James May of Valencia Community College), and assessment (with a special contribution by Karen Eisenhauer of Brevard Community College). Also includes tips for new instructors and ideas for making the most of *Real Essays*.

Additional Resources to Accompany Real Essays by Susan Anker and Eddye S. Gallagher, Tarrant County College. Supplements the instructional materials in the text with a variety of transparency masters and other reproducibles for classroom use.

Teaching Developmental Writing: Background Readings, a Bedford/St. Martin's Professional Resource, by Susan Naomi Bernstein, University of Houston. Offers thirty-five professional essays by Mina Shaughnessy, Mike Rose, Rei Noguchi, and others on topics of interest to basic writing instructors, along with a useful editorial apparatus pointing out practical applications for the classroom.

Real Essays Quick Reference Card. This four-page laminated card, which students can stand up next to their computer monitor, includes editing advice, help with Web searches, and useful word processing tips. (To order this card packaged with your students' copies of *Real Essays with Readings,* use the ISBN 0–312–40751–3. To order the card with the shorter version of *Real Essays,* use the ISBN 0–312–40773–4.)

Media Resources

"Writing Guide" software. Developed specifically to support *Real Essays*, this software leads students step-by-step through the process of writing each of the types of essays covered in the text. Also included are critical reading guides, diagnostic tests, grammar tutorials, and a personalized error log with built-in links to Exercise Central.

Exercise Central <www.bedfordstmartins.com/realessays>. With more than seven thousand items, this is the largest online collection of grammar exercises available. Exercise Central is thorough, easy to use, and convenient for both students and instructors. Multiple exercise sets on every topic, at a variety of levels, ensure that students have as much practice as they need. Customized feedback for all answers assures that skills practice becomes a learning experience, and a reporting feature allows both students and instructors to monitor and assess student progress.

Book companion site <www.bedfordstmartins.com/realessays>. The companion Web site for *Real Essays* provides additional resources for instructors as well as links to Exercise Central and the English Research Room, an online resource for research writers.

Acknowledgments

Real Essays was shaped by cadres of individuals around the country, not by a single voice. A textbook that is workable with diverse populations is, of necessity, the product of vast amounts of input, advice, and hard work on the part of many, and I am grateful to those individuals and groups who participated.

Reviewers

Because we drew upon the philosophy, structure, and content of *Real Writing,* I also want to acknowledge, once again, the many people who helped craft the vision and development of both editions of that book. I first thought to name those friends here, including the individuals who served on the Editorial Advisory Board for each edition, but—given space constraints—I'll just say that you know who you are, and you are as much a part of *Real Essays* as of *Real Writing.* Thank you, thank you.

    The following reviewers helped shape *Real Essays* by offering thoughtful comments and specific suggestions for meeting their students' challenges: Leigh Adams, Southwest Missouri State University–West Plains;

Mary Alexander, University of Phoenix; James Allen, College of DuPage; Cathryn Amdahl, Harrisburg Area Community College; Mark Amdahl, Montgomery County Community College; Mary Ann Bernal, San Antonio College; Jan Bone, Roosevelt University; Carol Ann Britt, San Antonio College; Lorraine Page Cadet, Grambling State University; Nandan Choksi, Art Institute of Fort Lauderdale; Sandra Chumchal, Blinn College; Laurie Coleman, San Antonio College; Nancy Davies, Miami-Dade Community College; Rick Dollieslager, Thomas Nelson Community College; Karen Eisenhauer, Brevard Community College; Linda Elaine, College of DuPage; Eileen Eliot, Broward County Community College; Melanie Fahlman-Reid, Capilano College; Katherine Finch, North Shore Community College; Anne Gervasi, DeVry University; Laura Gray-Rosendale, Northern Arizona University; Barbara L. Hamilton, Jones County Junior College; Earl Hawley, College of DuPage; Suzanne R. Hess, Florida Community College at Jacksonville; Lesa Hildebrand, Triton College; Kaaren Holum, University of the District of Columbia; Lennie Irvin, San Antonio College; Florence Johnson, North Dakota State College of Science; Gail Lighthipe, Bloomfield College; Jose Macia, Broward County Community College; Patricia A. Malinowski, Finger Lakes Community College; Gerald McCarthy, San Antonio College; David Merves, Miami-Dade Community College; Terrance Millet, Linn-Benton Community College; Katona Mulholland, Blue River Community College; Kimme Nuckles, Baker College; Amy Penne, Parkland College; Verlene Lee Pierre, Southeastern Louisiana University; Peggy Riley, Las Positas College; P. C. Scheponik, Montgomery County Community College; Tamara Shue, Georgia Perimeter College; Jeff Siddall, College of DuPage; Norman Stephens, Cerro Coso Community College; Denton Tulloch, Miami-Dade Community College; Priscilla Underwood, Quinsigamond Community College; Gail Upchurch, Olive Harvey College; Paul Vantine, Cameron University; Maria C. Villar-Smith, Miami-Dade Community College; Dorothy Voyles, Parkland College; Ted Walkup, Clayton College and State University; Michael Weiser, Thomas Nelson Community College; and Peggy Wogen, Kishwaukee College.

I would also like to thank Jim Rice and Marilyn Martin, both of Quinsigamond Community College, for graciously allowing me to "audit" courses.

Students

Many current and former students have contributed to this book. The nine former students who are "Profiles of Success" and who contributed examples of their real-world writing are Giovanni Bohorquez, Pamela O'Berry Evans, Daigo Fujiwara, Jolanda Jones, Gary Knoblock, Maureen Letendre, Patty Maloney, Salvador Torres, and Wayne Whitaker. I asked for a good deal of these people's time, and I very much appreciate their giving of it willingly and patiently.

Other students and former students contributed model essays to the book: Florence Bagley, Gene Boroski, Emma Brennan, Edna Crespo, Lindsey Ducharme, Roberta Fair, Elena Feltus, Danny Fitzgerald, Jessica Foote, James Freeman, Anna Griffith, George Hanson, Jason Knox, Susan Robinson, Janine Ronzo, and Karron Tempesta.

We asked a number of students to review various parts of the manuscript, and they gave us valuable comments. These students are Michael Joe Blalock, Jean Calixte, Roseann Castillo, Tina Colucci, Mark Coronado, Sandra Curatola, Theresa Dresser, Peggy L. Gamble, Angie Gonzales, Geri Hollinshed, Lizette Iverson, Monet Lasha, Ryan Olson, Michelle Perez, Eric Reese, Yolanda Robinson, Mark E. Skinner, Brenda Sotelo, Travis Tennison, Noel Vargas, and Diana L. Watie.

Contributors

Carolyn Lengel created interesting and grammatically sound exercises — in my mind, the work of a true wizard. Karin Halbert helped greatly with the selection of readings and the author headnotes, and Katie Finch crafted questions and writing prompts to accompany the readings. Marcia Muth edited raw manuscript, line-by-line, smoothing out sharp edges and awkward angles.

Eddye Gallagher (Tarrant County College) wrote the original manuscript for *Practical Suggestions,* a wonderfully savvy and useful guide for instructors, which was updated by Joanne Diaz (Boston University), Karen Eisenhauer (Brevard Community College), and James May (Valencia Community College). Susan Naomi Bernstein (University of Houston) contributed annotations for the *Instructor's Annotated Edition,* bringing to bear her fine sense of classroom practice. She also wrote the popular volume that accompanies the book: *Teaching Developmental Writing: Background Readings.*

Finally, Will Hochman (Southern Connecticut State University) contributed his expert and accessible advice on using computers in the writing process.

Bedford/St. Martin's

With every book I write for Bedford/St. Martin's, I am struck nearly dumb by the unparalleled resources they offer. The people there — to a one — are incredibly intelligent, articulate, and patient. Each also has an active sense of humor. And with the preface of each book, I try to be more succinct in my praise of them. It doesn't always work, but I'm trying.

In her role as editorial assistant, Karin Halbert, mentioned above as a contributor, also ably managed a vast and endless array of projects, including the very extensive review program. She is entirely reliable and competent.

Janet Renard copyedited the manuscript with an enviable ability to see straight to a problem and craft a solution, keeping us consistent throughout many hundreds of pages of manuscript.

The work of the New Media team does not go unnoticed. For their efforts to produce fine electronic resources, I thank Nick Carbone, Harriet Wald, and Coleen O'Hanley.

For the second time, I have been lucky to have Karen Baart to oversee the production process. She is grace under pressure personified and is skillfully devoted to getting things done right, and I appreciate her great worth. Deborah Baker succeeded Karen in this role and ably kept the book on track. I am also thankful to Claire Seng-Niemoeller for designing a student-friendly interior and to Billy Boardman for designing an attractive cover, and for having a kindred sense of humor. Finally, many thanks to Suzi Meyers for photo research and to Sandy Schechter for coordinating permissions.

As always, the talents and input of an array of marketing and sales managers accounted for changes throughout the process. This time, getting a title we could all live with was a Herculean feat. Thanks to Karen Melton, Brian Wheel, Tom Scotty, Bill Soeltz, Steve Patrick, Doug Bolton, John Hunger, Kate Nurre, Guy Geraghty, Rory Baruth, Mike Krotine, and Stacey Luce.

I am forever grateful to and in awe of the talents of Chuck Christensen and Joan Feinberg. During the development of this book, Chuck handed over the reins to Joan, who is now president of Bedford/St. Martin's. Joan brings her own gracious leadership style, and Bedford will forever bear the brand of her and Chuck's joint vision. Karen Henry, editor in chief, ensures that that vision infuses Bedford/St. Martin's publications, including both *Real Writing* and *Real Essays*.

Finally, I thank Michelle Clark, my editor, for her good advice, collaborative spirit, and consistent energy and enthusiasm, which endured through some challenging pressures. She is a terrific help. Beth Castrodale kindly and competently stepped in toward the end of the project and fleetly carried Michelle's baton without missing a beat.

This book would never have been completed without the support of my husband, Jim Anker. Together this year, we have weathered too much sadness. We're both standing, and *Real Essays* is a reality. I couldn't have managed either without him.

EDITING ESSAYS

Part Four. The Four Most Serious Errors   *343*

22. The Basic Sentence: An Editing Overview   345

23. Fragments: Incomplete Sentences   353

24. Run-Ons: Two Sentences Joined Incorrectly   373

25. Problems with Subject-Verb Agreement: When Subjects and Verbs Don't Match   387

READINGS

Introduction for Students

How to Use *Real Essays*

Why Should You Read This Introduction First?

These few pages will explain how to use this book. You've just spent a fair amount of money to buy it, so make sure you get your money's worth. This brief introduction will pitch to you the importance of this course and describe *Real Essays: Writing Projects for College, Work, and Everyday Life:* how it is organized, how to find information in it, and how to use certain features that will help you improve your writing. Reading this section will take you no more than twenty minutes—and it'll be worth it.

TEACHING TIP
This introduction provides a valuable orientation to *Real Essays* and includes a motivational message from the author. Consider working through it during the first class meeting. It may be helpful for students to examine the text in teams and then take some time during class to complete the writing questionnaire.

Why This Course Should Be Important to You

Your life is busy. You attend school, and you may even work full-time while taking classes. Maybe you're also a parent or have other pressing family or community commitments. You have bills to pay and goals to achieve.

And then there's this writing course.

You may be tempted to think of the course as just a nuisance to get through with a passing grade. However, it may be one of your best opportunities to develop the writing skills you need—whatever your current obligations or future plans are.

Here's a true story. When the first book in this series, *Real Writing*, was published, I proudly distributed my author copies to a few friends and relatives. I never thought they'd do much more than look at the pictures and think, "That's my daughter" or "That's my best friend." In fact they did say these things, but soon I started getting emails from people who had seen the book, had actually looked through it, and wanted to know how they could buy a copy. The first request I took as a fluke and wondered why anyone would want to buy this book when they were out of college and already employed in a good position. But the requests kept coming — from people in various occupations, ranging from a police officer to a manager at Verizon to a marketing specialist at IBM to a high-level computer whiz who tests government security programs. Each of them said basically the same thing: "Everyone in this office needs to write, and we're never sure whether what we're writing is right. We're dying for something that will help us, and we like this because it's not just about college writing but about the kinds of writing we really do."

As the title of this book, *Real Essays: Writing Projects for College, Work, and Everyday Life,* indicates, your need to write will not end with this course or with graduation from college. Every one of you will need to write competently for the rest of your life: to continue in college, to get a job and succeed in it, and to get by in your personal life. This course is for you, not for your instructor.

How This Book Is Organized

Real Essays is organized into seven parts:

- Part One (Chapters 1–7) describes the process you use to write any kind of essay for various purposes and audiences.

- Part Two (Chapters 8–16) gives concrete instruction about how to write nine common types of essays — the ones most often assigned in college courses — and guidance about how to apply those same skills to work-related and everyday writing tasks.

- Part Three (Chapters 17–21) presents strategies for completing other kinds of college, workplace, and everyday writing tasks such as taking tests, writing summaries and reports, proposing solutions, and writing from sources.

- Part Four (Chapters 22–26) includes chapters on each of the four most serious grammar errors, the ones that people most often notice: sentence fragments, run-ons, subject-verb agreement problems, and problems with verb forms.

- Part Five (Chapters 27–33) gives you instruction and practice in other areas of grammar, which are important in addition to the four

most serious errors: The book just presents the most important
things first.

- Part Six (Chapters 34–36) includes chapters about words: choosing the right word, not confusing words that sound or look alike, and spelling them correctly.
- Part Seven (Chapters 37–41) covers punctuation — using commas, apostrophes, and quotation marks, for example — and capitalization.

These basic matters are followed by useful appendices with specific advice about and examples of how to write email, memos, résumés, and letters of application, and how to give a good oral presentation.

In addition, your book may have a section called "Readings for Writers," which includes an introduction to critical reading followed by twenty readings on topics such as the use of foul language in our culture and the debate about whether competition is good for children. In addition to giving you practice in reading and — I hope — some enjoyment, these essays and articles will show you how professional writers use the strategies presented in the first two parts of *Real Essays*.

How to Find Information in *Real Essays*

Information is easy to find in *Real Essays*. Knowing where to look is a key first step.

Table of Contents

If you want to find a particular chapter, use the brief table of contents printed on the inside front cover. If you're looking for specific information within a chapter, try the detailed table of contents (pp. xv–xxvi), which lists chapter titles and major headings.

Index

If you want to find a particular topic, you can also use the index (p. I-1). Topics are listed alphabetically. To find information on using apostrophes in contractions, look under "apostrophes" and find the subentry "in contractions." The page number will direct you to the right information.

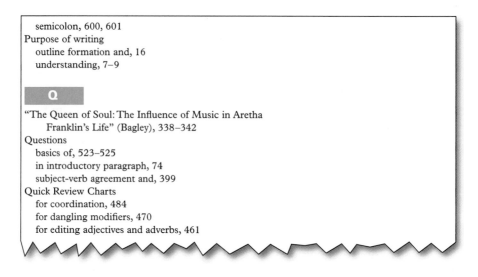

Chart of Correction Symbols

If your instructor uses symbols to indicate grammar, spelling, or punctuation errors in your writing, you can use the chart at the back of the book to get the meaning for each symbol and a chapter reference for more help.

Headings at the Tops of Pages

When you want to know where you are in the book, look at the headings that run along the tops of the pages. The left page gives you the name of the part of the book you're in (for example, Part Seven • Punctuation and Capitalization), and the right page tells you which chapter you're in (for example, Chapter 38 • Apostrophes).

List of Useful Charts and Reference Tools

Turn to the inside back cover for a list of all kinds of review and summary information in the book, with page numbers given so that you can easily access what you need—a checklist, a diagram, a reference chart—without flipping through the whole book or reading the whole table of contents.

References in the Margin

Real Essays includes helpful tips and references printed right in the margin. These direct you to additional information or resources in the book or on the book's companion Web site.

erline the subject of the verb *be*, *have*, or *do*, and circle
he verb.

(has)/ have) an important role in many children's

olved in Little League during fifth and sixth grades.

were) happy to cheer at most of the games.

) a Little Leaguer of my own, my daughter Tina.

not a natural athlete.

m / is / are) usually a lot of fun for her.

For more practice,
visit Exercise
Central at <www
.bedfordstmartins
.com/realessays>.

How to Use the Features of *Real Essays* to Improve Your Writing

Real Essays is designed to help you to become a better writer. Here are descriptions of charts, checklists, and other helpful features—some with samples from the book.

Thinking Critically Guides

Many chapters include short guides that help you focus on a writing or editing task in order to do it well. These guides make completing the task easier and give you useful practice in thinking about key issues before acting—something you need to do in college but, even more important, in your everyday lives and at work.

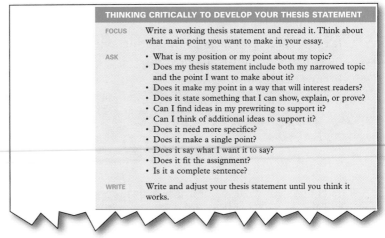

THINKING CRITICALLY TO DEVELOP YOUR THESIS STATEMENT	
FOCUS	Write a working thesis statement and reread it. Think about what main point you want to make in your essay.
ASK	• What is my position or my point about my topic? • Does my thesis statement include both my narrowed topic and the point I want to make about it? • Does it make my point in a way that will interest readers? • Does it state something that I can show, explain, or prove? • Can I find ideas in my prewriting to support it? • Can I think of additional ideas to support it? • Does it need more specifics? • Does it make a single point? • Does it say what I want it to say? • Does it fit the assignment? • Is it a complete sentence?
WRITE	Write and adjust your thesis statement until you think it works.

Writing Guide **Narration**

Follow the steps in this Writing
and edit your narration. Check

THINKING CRITICALLY ABO

FOCUS   Think about who w
        you want your reade

Writing Guides

Each chapter in Part Two,
"Writing Different Kinds of
Essays," includes a concrete
step-by-step guide that you
can follow as you write your
essay.

Four Basics of Writing

Each of the chapters in Part Two starts off with a list of the four basic
features of the kind of writing covered in the chapter. As you read how a
particular kind of writing is developed, keep these four basics in mind. As
you do the writing assignments, you can refer to these four basics before,
during, and after you write. Focusing on just four key elements for each
type of writing will make the assignments easier to manage.

■■ Four Basics of Good Argument

1. It takes a strong and definite position on an issue or advises a
   particular action.
2. It gives good reasons and supporting evidence to defend the
   position or recommended action.
3. It considers opposing views.
4. It has enthusiasm and energy from start to finish.

   The chapter on writing summaries and reports also provides you with
the list of basics, as does the appendix on writing emails and memos.

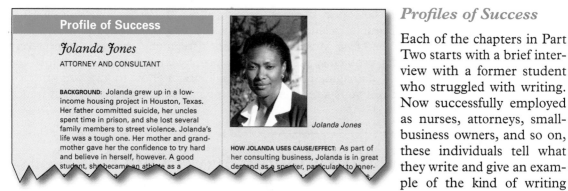

Profile of Success

Jolanda Jones
ATTORNEY AND CONSULTANT

BACKGROUND: Jolanda grew up in a low-income housing project in Houston, Texas. Her father committed suicide, her uncles spent time in prison, and she lost several family members to street violence. Jolanda's life was a tough one. Her mother and grandmother gave her the confidence to try hard and believe in herself, however. A good student, she became an athlete as a

Jolanda Jones

HOW JOLANDA USES CAUSE/EFFECT: As part of her consulting business, Jolanda is in great demand as a speaker, particularly to inner-

Profiles of Success

Each of the chapters in Part Two starts with a brief interview with a former student who struggled with writing. Now successfully employed as nurses, attorneys, small-business owners, and so on, these individuals tell what they write and give an example of the kind of writing they really do — every day. Their stories emphasize the importance of writing skills, computer skills, and the ability to work as part of a team.

Quick Review Charts

The chapters in Parts Four, Five, and Six end with "Quick Review" charts, which enable you, at a glance, to see what to do when you are editing your own writing for a particular type of grammar problem. These are like flowcharts in a how-to manual.

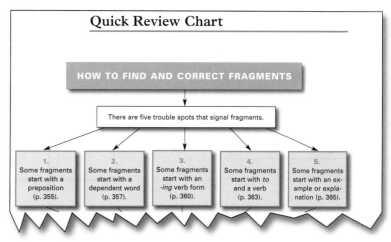

Quick Review Chart

HOW TO FIND AND CORRECT FRAGMENTS

There are five trouble spots that signal fragments.

1.	2.	3.	4.	5.
Some fragments start with a preposition (p. 355).	Some fragments start with a dependent word (p. 357).	Some fragments start with an *-ing* verb form (p. 360).	Some fragments start with *to* and a verb (p. 363).	Some fragments start with an example or explanation (p. 365).

Useful Appendices

At the end of the book are three very practical appendices: How to write email and memos (p. 719); how to write a résumé and a letter of application (p. 726); and how to give a good oral presentation (p. 736). Even if your instructor does not assign the appendices for class, read and save this material. It will come in handy on the job.

Remember the Number Four

Sometimes when you are writing, it may seem as if there is just too much to remember. To make things a little easier on you, remember the number *four;* it's important in this book. Part One covers *four* basic steps in the writing process: prewrite, draft, revise, and edit. Part Two includes a list of *four* key features, called the "Four Basics," for each type of writing. Part Four presents the "*Four* Most Serious Errors" (fragments, run-ons, subject-verb agreement problems, and verb form problems), the most noticeable and potentially damaging errors. *Real Essays*, in an effort to give you practical help, focuses your attention first on the most basic and important issues.

What Do You Want from This Course?

As I said earlier, this course is for you: You need the information and practice it provides if you want to pass the course, succeed in other courses, get a job, or be able to stand up for yourself in your everyday life. As you begin the course, decide what you want to gain from it.

First, what are some of your real-world goals? For example, what kind of job or career do you hope to have? What do you want to do in your everyday life: Find a nice place to live? Buy a car? Travel? Get your money back when you've been overcharged? Make new friends? Do some thinking about your real-life goals and list at least five, the more concrete and specific the better. ("To be happy" may be too general, for example.)

Once you have some real-world goals in mind, particularly the job or career ones, try to link those goals to the writing skills you want to learn or improve in this course. Carefully complete the worksheet that follows.

WRITING QUESTIONNAIRE

NAME ⎯⎯⎯⎯⎯⎯⎯⎯⎯⎯⎯⎯⎯⎯⎯⎯⎯⎯⎯⎯⎯⎯⎯⎯⎯⎯⎯⎯⎯⎯

COURSE ⎯⎯⎯⎯⎯⎯⎯⎯⎯⎯⎯⎯⎯⎯⎯⎯⎯⎯ **DATE** ⎯⎯⎯⎯⎯⎯⎯⎯⎯⎯⎯⎯⎯

Real-World Goals

Use the spaces below to list at least five specific goals you have set for yourself.

⎯⎯

⎯⎯

⎯⎯

⎯⎯

⎯⎯

Course Goals

Think about your writing and comments you have received about it in the past. What do you think your major problems with writing are? What should you work on improving? List a few answers to these questions in the spaces that follow.

⎯⎯

⎯⎯

⎯⎯

⎯⎯

⎯⎯

When you have jotted down a few ideas, list three writing skills you want to learn or practice. Be as specific as possible. For example, "Learn to write better" is too general to mean anything much or to help you focus on the areas you want to improve. Based on your answers to the questions above, write three specific skills you want to address and improve during this course.

1. ⎯⎯⎯⎯⎯⎯⎯⎯⎯⎯⎯⎯⎯⎯⎯⎯⎯⎯⎯⎯⎯⎯⎯⎯⎯⎯⎯⎯⎯⎯⎯⎯⎯⎯⎯⎯⎯⎯⎯

2. ⎯⎯⎯⎯⎯⎯⎯⎯⎯⎯⎯⎯⎯⎯⎯⎯⎯⎯⎯⎯⎯⎯⎯⎯⎯⎯⎯⎯⎯⎯⎯⎯⎯⎯⎯⎯⎯⎯⎯

3. ⎯⎯⎯⎯⎯⎯⎯⎯⎯⎯⎯⎯⎯⎯⎯⎯⎯⎯⎯⎯⎯⎯⎯⎯⎯⎯⎯⎯⎯⎯⎯⎯⎯⎯⎯⎯⎯⎯⎯

Real Essays
with Readings

Writing Projects for College,
Work, and Everyday Life

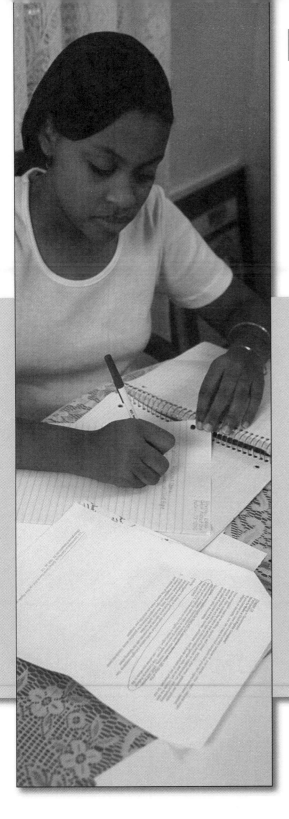

PART ONE

How to Write Essays

1

The Writing Process

An Overview

You Know This
You already know how to use many processes in your own life.
- You follow simple steps when you get ready for work or school.
- You manage complex processes such as buying a car or searching for a new job that you like.
- You perform many tasks at work or at school, moving from one step or stage to the next.

Understand Paragraph and Essay Form

TEACHING TIP Many chapters in this book begin by asking students to think about how the chapter content builds on something they already know. Add your own examples to the "You Know This" box to help make the point.

DEFINITION: A **paragraph** is a group of sentences that work together to make a point. A good paragraph has three necessary parts—the topic sentence, the body, and the concluding sentence—which serve specific purposes.

PARAGRAPH PART	PURPOSE OF THE PARAGRAPH PART
1. The **topic sentence**	states the **main point**. The topic sentence is often the first sentence of the paragraph.
2. The **body**	supports (shows, explains, or proves) the main point. It usually contains three to six **support sentences**, which present facts and details that develop the main point.

3

3. The **concluding sentence** reminds readers of the main point and often makes an observation.

Read the paragraph that follows. Standard parts of the paragraph are labeled.

Topic sentence —

Body made up of support sentences —

Concluding sentence —

Asking your boss for a raise doesn't have to be painful if you plan the conversation well. First, think about how you will introduce the subject when you talk with your boss. Then make a list of reasons why you deserve the raise. Be prepared to give specific examples of your achievements. When your plan is ready, make an appointment to meet with your boss. Your plan will allow you to be confident and will increase your chance of success.

DEFINITION: An **essay** is a piece of writing with more than one paragraph. A short essay may be three hundred to six hundred words long with four or five paragraphs. A long essay is six paragraphs or more; the length depends on what the essay needs to accomplish—persuading someone to do something, using research to make a point, or explaining a complex concept.

An essay has three necessary parts: an introduction, a body, and a conclusion.

ESSAY PART	PURPOSE OF THE ESSAY PART
1. The **introduction**	states the **main point** or **thesis**, generally in a single strong statement. The introduction may be a single paragraph or multiple paragraphs.
2. The **body**	supports (shows, explains, or proves) the main point. It generally has at least three **support paragraphs**, each containing facts and details that develop the main point. Each support paragraph begins with a **topic sentence** that supports the thesis statement.
3. The **conclusion**	reminds readers of the main point. It may summarize and reinforce the support in the body paragraphs, or it may make an observation based on that support. Whether it is a single paragraph or more, the conclusion should relate back to the main point of the essay.

The parts of an essay correspond to the parts of a paragraph:

- The **thesis** of an essay is like the **topic sentence** of a paragraph.
- The **support paragraphs** in the body of an essay are like the **support sentences** of a paragraph.
- The **conclusion** of an essay is like the **concluding sentence** of a paragraph.

TEACHING TIP
Have students inter-
view a second- or
third-year student in
their major to find out
what kind of writing
that person does for
his or her classes.

RELATIONSHIP BETWEEN PARAGRAPHS AND ESSAYS

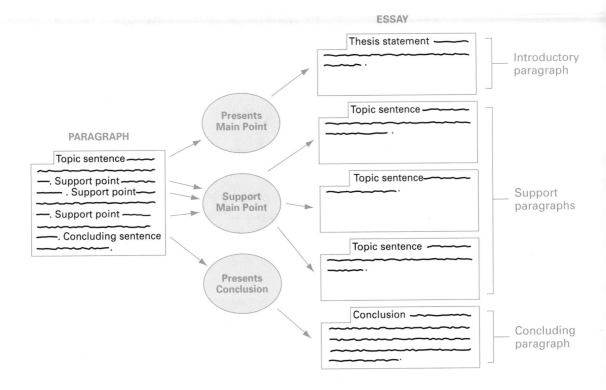

Read the following sample essay, in which the parts are underlined and labeled. It is on the same topic as the paragraph on page 4, but because it is an essay, it goes into greater detail on the topic.

TEACHING TIP
For some students, it
helps to present visual
analogies. Explain that
just as a skyscraper
needs more substantial
support than a three-
story apartment
building, an essay
needs more detailed
support than a
paragraph.

Introductory
paragraph

*Thesis
statement*

At one point or another, you will probably feel that you are entitled to get paid more for your work, but you may not have a clue about how to ask for a raise. Several simple but effective techniques will increase your chances of success.

Topic sentence

Support
paragraph 1

First, you must ask for the raise; don't expect your employer to take the initiative. Before you confront your employer, stand in front of the mirror and rehearse, "I *deserve* a raise." Never say, "May I have a raise?," "Could I have a raise?," or "Is it time for my raise?" Always say, "I *deserve* a raise." You need to believe that before you can convince your employer.

Topic sentence

Support
paragraph 2

Make a list of the reasons why you deserve a raise. Write down exactly what you have done to deserve the raise. Use concrete, observable achievements that cannot be disputed, and be ready with specific examples. If a dollar value in savings to the company has resulted from your work, make sure you have documentation confirming this.

Body

Topic sentence

Support
paragraph 3

You must also consider the amount of the raise you will ask for. Always ask for more than you think you deserve. The key word here is *more*. Rehearse this higher amount while standing in front of a mirror so you won't hesitate or stutter when you ask your boss for the raise. Too many people ask for a modest raise, unaware that this simple request may have negative side effects. When a worker asks for an unusually small raise, the employer has a tendency to devalue the employee, in the same way that people may be skeptical about buying something that is priced too low.

Concluding
paragraph

*Concluding
sentence*

Asking for a reasonably higher raise than you expect may trigger a new thought process in your employer's head. The new thought that you are worth more makes the employer more open to an honest assessment of your value to the company. If you give well-documented reasons why you are valuable to the company, your boss may see you in a new, more positive light. You may not get quite as much as you requested, but your boss is likely to act in some way on the new, positively revised image of you as an employee.

—Adapted from Perry W. Buffington (1996). *Cheap Psychological Tricks: What to Do When Hard Work, Honesty, and Perseverance Fail* (Atlanta, GA: Peachtree Press, 1996), pp. 25–27.

Understand Audience and Purpose

DEFINITION: The **purpose** for a piece of writing is your reason for writing it. In college, your purpose for writing is usually to show something, to explain something, or to create a convincing argument.

DEFINITION: The **audience** for a piece of writing is the person or people who read it, think about it, and respond to it. In college, your audience may be your teacher or your classmates. In order to have an effect on your readers, try to write for real people and address what they need or want to know.

Everything that you write has a **purpose**. Everything you write also has an **audience**. Consider both before you begin to write and at every step along the way.

TEACHING TIP
Bring in or have students find a letter to the editor from a newspaper or magazine. As a class, discuss the letter writer's original audience, and then ask how the letter might have to be changed for various different audiences. Choose one of these and have students form small groups to revise the letter with this audience in mind.

▰ PRACTICE 1   UNDERSTANDING AUDIENCE AND PURPOSE

Read the following description of a writing situation and the notes written in response for two different audiences. Then answer the questions.

TEACHING TIP
You may want to do this practice as a whole group. Read the situation and letters aloud, and ask students to respond orally.

SITUATION: Janine Ronzo wakes up and realizes her alarm didn't ring and so she has overslept. She is now going to be late for an interview with Ms. Farina, a supervisor at her company who has a job opening that interests Janine. She leaves a quick note (A) for her roommate, Pat. When she gets to the interview a half hour late, she writes a note (B) for Ms. Farina, who has already left the office to attend a two-day meeting.

A.

   AUDIENCE: Janine's roommate, Pat
   PURPOSE: To explain

   Pat — overslept and am late for work. Cldn't clean up from last nite or feed Sparky. Sorry. J.

B.

   AUDIENCE: Ms. Farina
   PURPOSE: To explain

   Dear Ms. Farina:

   I am very sorry that I missed our meeting today. Unfortunately, my usually reliable alarm chose not to go off this morning. When I awoke on my own, I immediately realized that it was later than usual and did everything I could to get here on time. However, I was a half hour late, and I missed our meeting.

Normally I am very prompt for work, a fact you can verify with my supervisor, Candy Silfer. I hope that we can reschedule our interview as I am very interested in discussing the position with you and I believe I am a strong candidate. I look forward to hearing from you, and I apologize again for inconveniencing you today. I will set a foolproof alarm system before our next meeting.

Sincerely,

Janine Ronzo

Answers may vary but should be similar to those supplied.

1. How does the note to Ms. Farina differ from the one to Pat? *The note to Ms. Farina is more formal than the one to Pat.*

2. How do the different audiences affect what the notes say (the content) and how they say it (the tone)? *Ms. Farina, a business associate, should be addressed in businesslike tone and language. Pat is a roommate, so the note can be casual. What each of them needs to know is different, too.*

3. Which note has more detail? *The one to Ms. Farina* Why? *The explanation has to be more thorough.*

4. What three words in the note to Pat would have been edited had the note been to Ms. Farina? *Cldn't, nite, J.*

THINKING CRITICALLY ABOUT PURPOSE AND AUDIENCE

	PURPOSE	AUDIENCE
FOCUS	Remember that you are writing for a reason.	Remember that someone will read what you write.
ASK	• What is my assignment? • What topic will I be writing about?	• Who will be reading this? • What does my audience already know about the topic?

	PURPOSE	AUDIENCE
ASK	• What point do I want to make about my topic?	• What does my audience want or need to know about my topic?
	• What do I want my audience to think about my topic?	• Does my audience have a particular attitude or opinion about my topic? Do I need to address that specifically?
WRITE	Always write with your purpose and your audience in mind.	

Understand the Writing Process

DEFINITION: The **writing process** consists of a series of steps: exploring ideas, planning, drafting, revising, and editing.

Whenever you are first learning to do something—play a sport, drive a car, ride a bicycle—the steps seem complicated and hard to remember. But after you practice them for a while, they seem to blend together. You no longer have to concentrate to remember the individual steps; you just do them. The same thing will happen as you practice the steps in the writing process.

> **TEACHING TIP**
> Invite students to describe a process related to their college experiences, such as applying for admission or financial aid, registering for classes, or purchasing textbooks.

WRITING ASSIGNMENT

Write an essay on one of the following topics or one of your own choice. Before or as you write, follow a student, Roberta Fair, through the writing process, starting on page 11 and continuing to page 22. Chapters 2 through 7 explain each step of the process in more detail.

A personal goal

How I get through hard times

My biggest responsibility

Something I'm really good at

Everyone in my family _____

I am the only one in my family _____

The Writing Process

EXPLORE IDEAS TO MAKE AND SUPPORT A POINT

Ask: What is my purpose in writing? Who will read my essay? What does my audience need to know?

- Find and explore your topic (Chapter 2).
- Make your point by stating your thesis (Chapter 3).
- Support your point with details and topic sentences (Chapter 4).

PLAN   Ask: How can I organize my ideas effectively for my reader?

- Make a plan and arrange your ideas (Chapter 5).

DRAFT   Ask: How can I show my reader what I mean?

- State your main point or thesis (Chapter 3).
- Write topic sentences for your body paragraphs (Chapter 6).
- Fill out your draft with details and support (Chapter 6).
- Add an interesting introduction, a strong conclusion, and a title (Chapter 6).

REVISE   Ask: How can I make my draft clearer or more convincing to my reader?

- Relate ideas or drop ideas that do not fit (Chapter 7).
- Add more detailed support to make ideas convincing and easy to understand (Chapter 7).
- Make connections with transitions and key words so that ideas flow smoothly (Chapter 7).

EDIT   Ask: What errors could confuse my readers and weaken my point?

- Find and correct errors in grammar (Chapters 22–33). Focus first on finding sentence fragments (Chapter 23), run-on sentences (Chapter 24), mismatched subjects and verbs (Chapter 25), and problems with verbs (Chapter 26).
- Look for errors in word use and spelling (Chapters 34–36) and in punctuation and capitalization (Chapters 37–41).

USE THE WRITING PROCESS: A STUDENT WRITER AT WORK

Each step of the writing process is illustrated in this section as student writer Roberta Fair moves from finding an idea to drafting and revising an essay. Chapters 2 through 7 provide more examples and practices for each step as well as additional writing assignments.

Step 1: Narrow and Explore Your Topic

DEFINITION: To **narrow** a topic is to focus on the smaller parts of a general topic until you find a more limited topic or an angle that is interesting, familiar, and specific.

> For more on finding and exploring a topic, see Chapter 2.

    DEFINITION: To **explore** a topic is to investigate what you already know about your narrowed topic in order to decide what you want to say. One way to explore a topic is to use a prewriting technique.

    DEFINITION: Prewriting techniques are strategies you can use to come up with ideas at any point during the writing process: to find a topic, to get ideas for what you want to say about that topic, and to support your ideas.

    In the first week of her college writing course, Roberta Fair was given this assignment:

Write an essay about a personal goal.

Her first step was to narrow the general topic, finding a specific idea. She started with the words *personal goals* and made a list of specific personal goals.

NARROWING A TOPIC

> <u>Personal Goals</u>
>
> lose some weight
>
> get a better job
>
> get a college degree
>
> get better on the computer
>
> stay patient with my kids
>
> take vitamins
>
> don't argue with my mother

Roberta then read her list and considered each item as a topic for her essay by asking, "Is this narrowed topic important to me?" Roberta decided that her most important personal goal was to get a college degree.

TOPIC	NARROWED TOPIC
a personal goal	*getting a college degree*

For detailed examples of these prewriting techniques, see Chapter 2.

Roberta considered using one of five common prewriting techniques to explore her narrowed topic.

COMMON PREWRITING TECHNIQUES

1. Freewrite
2. List/brainstorm
3. Question
4. Discuss
5. Cluster

ESL
You may want to invite your ESL students to prewrite in their native language. At the prewriting stage, the fluency of ideas is more important than linguistic fluency or correctness.

Roberta chose to explore her topic by freewriting. For five minutes, she wrote nonstop, writing everything she could think of about her topic without correcting her grammar or crossing anything out.

For a full description of freewriting and another example, see page 28.

ROBERTA'S FREEWRITING

Narrowed Topic: Getting a college degree

I don't know, I don't think about goals more than just handling every day—I don't have time. The kids, my job, laundry, food, school, it's a lot. So I just get by day by day but I know that won't get me or my kids anywhere. I really do wish I could get a better job that was more interesting and I sure wish I could make more money, and get my kids better stuff and live in a better place and not be worried all the time about money and our apartment and all that. I really do need to get that degree cause I know we'd have a better chance then. I know I need to finish college.

TEACHING TIP
Give students the opportunity to experiment with at least one of the prewriting techniques that is new to them or one that has previously not been effective. Encourage them to take a risk as they approach this new writing project.

ASSIGNMENT STEP 1   **NARROW AND EXPLORE YOUR TOPIC**

For more examples showing how to narrow and explore a topic, see Chapter 2.

Narrow one of the general topics in the writing assignment (p. 9) or one of your own choice. Jot down a list of possible topics that are narrower and more specific before choosing one to write about. Then freewrite or use another prewriting technique to explore your narrowed topic.

Step 2: Make a Point

DEFINITION: The **main point** of a piece of writing is the message or key idea you want to get across about your topic. Your **thesis** announces your main point or position on your topic to your reader.

For more on making a point and stating a thesis, see Chapter 3.

Roberta reread her freewriting, trying to figure out what main point she wanted to make. She circled her most important ideas about getting a college degree as she looked for her strongest message.

ROBERTA'S REREADING OF HER FREEWRITING

> I don't know, I don't think about goals more than just handling every day—I don't have time. The kids, my job, laundry, food, school, it's a lot. (So I just get by) day by day but I know that (won't get me or my kids anywhere.) I really do (wish I could get a better job) that was (more inter-esting) and I sure wish I could (make more money,) and (get my kids better stuff) and (live in a better place) and (not be worried all the time about money) and our apartment and all that. I really do need to get that degree cause I know we'd have a better chance then. I know I (need to finish college.)

Roberta's most important ideas made an overall point: Getting a college degree would help her get a good job, which would allow her to improve her life in other ways. Although this specific sentence wasn't in her freewriting, the ideas she circled added up to that point. Roberta stated her point in a working thesis statement, a first-try version of the sentence that would state her main point and let her readers know what she would be writing about.

ROBERTA'S WORKING THESIS

> Getting a college degree will help me build a better life for myself and my children.

ASSIGNMENT STEP 2   MAKE A POINT

Reread your freewriting or other prewriting work, and decide what main point you want to make about your narrowed topic. Look for your strongest message, and write a working thesis statement. (Don't worry if it

For more examples showing how to develop a thesis, see Chapter 3.

doesn't cover every idea you wrote down; you may modify your thesis as you write.)

Step 3: Support Your Point

For more on supporting a point, see Chapter 4.

DEFINITION: **Support** is the collection of evidence, examples, or facts that show, explain, or prove your thesis. **Support points** are the major ideas developed in the paragraphs that make up the body of your essay. **Supporting details** are the specifics you provide to explain your major support points to your readers.

Once Roberta had a working thesis for her essay, she began to think about what information would support her point and get it across to her audience. She asked herself a key question: How will getting a college degree help me? She made a list of possible support points; then she reread the list to drop unrelated points or weak ideas.

ROBERTA'S LIST OF IDEAS TO SUPPORT HER THESIS STATEMENT

Thesis: Getting a college degree will help me build a better life for myself and my children.

Key question: How?

make more money

only have one job, won't be so tired

it won't be so boring

more options about jobs

could get that red dress

more respect

move to a better place

feel better about myself

my kids will look up to me, and they're more likely to stay in school

meet guys in class

get kids some clothes they want

might lose weight because I wouldn't have time to eat

When Roberta reviewed her list, she discovered that she could combine her ideas about how a college degree would improve her life into three groups:

Group 1: Getting a better job

Group 2: Providing things for her children

Group 3: Feeling better about herself

She numbered her ideas according to these three groups.

ROBERTA'S GROUPING OF IDEAS

1	make more money	2	move to a better place
1	only have one job, won't be so tired	3	feel better about myself
1	it won't be so boring	3	my kids will look up to me, and they're more likely to stay in school
1	more options about jobs		
3	more respect	2	get kids some clothes they want

Roberta listed her groups as major support points. Then she noted supporting details, more specific information about each support point.

ROBERTA'S MAJOR SUPPORT POINTS	ROBERTA'S SUPPORTING DETAILS
1. Could get a better job	Make more money
	Work one job, not two jobs
	Have more options for jobs
	Get a less boring job
2. Provide for my children	Live in a better place
	Get them some things they want
	Be a good role model for them
3. Feel better about myself	Achieve a goal
	Get respect from others
	Respect myself

As she wrote her essay, Roberta continued to add supporting details to help her readers understand her main point and to bring to life her support points.

ASSIGNMENT STEP 3 **SUPPORT YOUR POINT**

Using Roberta's steps as a model, find three major support points for your working thesis. Then add three supporting details to each of the major support points.

For more examples showing how to support a point, see Chapter 4.

Step 4: Plan and Make an Outline

For more on planning and outlining, see Chapter 5.

DEFINITION: In writing, **order** means the sequence in which you present your ideas: what comes first, what comes next, and so on. Three common ways of ordering ideas are **chronological order** (by the sequence of time in which events happened), **spatial order** (by the physical arrangement of objects or features), and **order of importance** (by the significance of the ideas or reasons).

There is no one right order for any essay: It depends on your topic and the point you are making about that topic. Ask these two questions as you begin to organize your ideas:

1. Purpose: Why am I writing?
2. Audience: Who will be reading this?

Your answers will help arrange your ideas so that they have the most impact on your readers or so that your readers are most likely to understand your point.

Once Roberta had a body of ideas to work with, she began to plan how to organize them into her essay. Here are her answers to the two questions.

ROBERTA'S RESPONSES TO QUESTIONS ABOUT PURPOSE AND AUDIENCE

1. *Purpose: Why am I writing this?* For an assignment, but also for myself. If I have to spend time writing, I might as well get something out of it. So I'm writing to help me figure out what personal goal is important to me—and why it's important.

2. *Audience: Who will be reading this?* My professor, who doesn't know me at all. She has a college degree, so she probably agrees that getting one is important, but she'll be grading my writing based on the reasons I give and the way I write. I think I should build up to the most important reason for wanting to get a college degree. But what is that?

And also, sometimes professors read essays aloud, so it might be that other students in the class will hear what I've written. I don't want to feel like a fool in front of the class or my professor, so I want to give serious reasons.

Roberta decided to organize her ideas by order of importance, building up to the most important point. Because all of her points were important, she needed to decide which of her reasons for wanting to get a college degree were most important to her. She then put her ideas into outline form so that she had a clear blueprint to use as she wrote her essay.

ROBERTA'S OUTLINE

> **Thesis:** *Getting a college degree will help me build a better life for myself and my children.*
>
> 1. *Major support, body paragraph #1: Could get a better job*
>   *Supporting details:*
>   a. *Get a less boring job*
>   b. *Have more options for jobs*
>   c. *Make more money and work one job, not two jobs*
> 2. *Major support, body paragraph #2: Provide for my children*
>   *Supporting details:*
>   a. *Spend more time with them because I don't have to work two jobs*
>   b. *Get them some things they want*
>   c. *Live in a better place*
>   d. *Be a good role model for them*
> 3. *Major support, body paragraph #3: Feel better about myself*
>   *Supporting details:*
>   a. *Get respect from others*
>   b. *Respect myself because I achieved an important goal*
>   c. *Go on to achieve other goals*
>   *Possible Point for Concluding Paragraph: Won't be easy, but worth the time and effort involved.*

TEAMWORK
After students have written an outline, have them trade outlines with a classmate and comment on the clarity and effectiveness of their partner's work. Ask students to identify any gaps, detours, or shifts in logic.

To make her outline, Roberta used the supporting details she had listed earlier. She also added ideas such as 3c (Go on to achieve other goals) and her concluding point (Won't be easy, but worth the time and effort involved).

■ **ASSIGNMENT STEP 4   MAKE A PLAN**

Consider your purpose for writing and the likely audience for your writing as you decide how you want to organize your support. Then make an outline that will serve as a blueprint for your draft.

For more examples showing how to plan and outline, see Chapter 5.

Step 5: Write a Draft

DEFINITION: A **draft** is the first whole version of all your ideas put together in a piece of writing.

Once Roberta had a working outline, she was ready to write a draft of her essay, getting all her ideas on paper in related paragraphs. Roberta used the major support points from her outline to write topic sentences for the paragraphs in the body of her essay.

TEACHING TIP
Before students begin their draft, suggest that they leave room between their thesis statement and each support point (hard copy or electronic). Then they will have plenty of space to work on each paragraph.

For more on writing a draft, see Chapter 6.

ROBERTA'S SUPPORT POINTS	ROBERTA'S SUPPORT POINTS AS TOPIC SENTENCES
1. Could get a better job	1. With a college degree, I could get a better job.
2. Provide for my children	2. Having a college degree and a good job would also help me be a better provider for my children.
3. Feel better about myself	3. Having a college degree would make me feel better about myself.

Roberta began writing her draft. Her **introductory paragraph** included her thesis statement and other sentences to interest her readers and give them a preview of what her essay would discuss. Her **concluding paragraph** reminded readers of her main point and made a further observation based on the ideas in the essay. She also wrote a title that fit the topic of her essay.

ROBERTA'S DRAFT ESSAY

A Goal to Live By

Thesis statement — Getting a college degree will help me build a better life for myself and my children. When I think of a personal goal, that is definitely the most important to me. It's not just the degree itself that is important, but also the ways in which it could improve things.

Topic sentence followed by supporting details — With a college degree, I could get a better job. I would have more job options than I do now. That would give me an opportunity to get a job that isn't as boring as the one I have now. It would also mean that I could make more money in one job and wouldn't have to have two.

Topic sentence followed by supporting details — Having a college degree and a good job would also help me be a better provider for my children. I could spend more time with them because I wouldn't have to work two jobs. I could get them some of the things they want so badly. We could move to a better neighborhood that's safer.

Topic sentence followed by supporting deails — Having a college degree would make me feel better about myself. I'd get more respect from others. I'd feel good about myself because I'd achieved an important and hard goal.

> Although it won't be easy, getting my college degree will be worth the time and effort involved. With that degree, I will be able to build a better life and will have the self-esteem that I want for both myself and my children. You have to feel good about yourself.

Concluding sentence

■ **ASSIGNMENT STEP 5   WRITE A DRAFT**

Using your outline from Step 4, write a draft essay.

For more examples showing how to write an introduction, a conclusion, and a full draft, see Chapter 6.

Step 6: Revise Your Draft

DEFINITION: Revising is changing your ideas to make your writing clearer, stronger, and more convincing. When revising, you might add, cut, re-arrange, or change words and phrases, whole sentences, or paragraphs. It's your chance to move things around and make them work better to get your main point across to your readers.

Roberta put her draft aside for a day or two and then came back to it. She reread it and made some notes about how to improve it. She also visited the writing center at school, where she asked the tutor to read her draft and give her feedback she could use to make her essay more effective. Then she made more notes on her draft, following the tutor's suggestions.

TEACHING TIP
If your school has a writing center, arrange either for your students to take a tour or for a peer tutor to come to class to explain to students what the writing center has to offer and to work with students in a rough-draft session.

For more on revising—including unity, detail, and coherence—see Chapter 7.

ROBERTA'S NOTES ON HER DRAFT

> Getting a college degree will help me build a better life for myself and my children. When I think of a personal goal, that is definitely the most important to me. It's not just the degree itself that is important, but also the ways in which it could improve things. ———
>
> With a college degree, I could get a better job. I would have more job options than I do now. That would give me an opportunity to get a job that isn't as boring as the one I have now. It would also mean that I could make more money in one job and wouldn't have to have two.
>
> Having a college degree and a good job would also help me be a better provider for my children. I could spend more time with them ———

What things? Add specific details.

Say what I do now.

Tell what's boring about my job.

Say what I mean by "better provider."

(continued)

Like what? ———————

because I wouldn't have to work two jobs. I could get them some of the things they want so badly. We could move to a better neighborhood that's safer.

Add more detail here; how would I feel, and why would that be new to me?

Having a college degree would make me feel better about myself. I'd get more respect from others. I'd feel good about myself because I'd achieved an important and hard goal.

More; this just seems boring and weak

Although it won't be easy, getting my college degree will be worth the time and effort involved. With that degree, I will be able to build a better life and will have the self-esteem that I want for both myself and my children. You have to feel good about yourself.

Other ideas: doesn't seem to flow very well. It jumps from one paragraph to another. Try making it smoother by adding transitions, both in the paragraph and between paragraphs. Maybe add "most important" to last paragraph?

ROBERTA'S REVISED ESSAY with her changes in bold

A Goal to Live By

Clearer wording ———

Getting a college degree will help me build a better life for myself and my children. **Although I have a number of goals in life,** that is definitely the most important to me. **The degree itself is just a piece of paper, but it promises concrete, real rewards that I want and am ready to work for.**

Added stronger sentence

With a college degree, I could get a better job. I would have more job options than I do now. **I'm a waitress at a restaurant that doesn't even have good tips, and I want to be an assistant manager. The owner said I am a great worker, but an assistant manager has to have a degree. With a degree, I could look for management training programs in many fields.** That would give me an opportunity to get a job that isn't as boring as the one I have now, **where I take orders, warm up food in the microwave, and deliver the orders. I actually look forward to folding napkins, just because it's something different!** Being a manager would also

Added detail in new sentences

More specific information

mean that I could make more money in one job and wouldn't have to have two. **Right now, in addition to my waitress job, I work at Wal-Mart, but even two minimum-wage jobs don't cover all our expenses. I come up short every month.**

    Also, having a college degree and a good job would help me be a better provider for my children. **For example,** I could spend more time with them because I wouldn't have to work two jobs. **I could make sure they do their homework and eat right.** I could get them some of the things they want so badly. **They don't ask for much, but Jilly has wanted a special pair of jeans for months, and Carl's backpack is about to give out.** We could also move to a better neighborhood that's safer. **It worries me that there are gangs, and I want to get Carl, especially, away from them. There's too much easy crime here.**

    Most important, having a college degree would make me feel better about myself. I'd get more respect from others, **like the teachers and the tutors at Jilly and Carl's school. When I was in for a conference and the teacher found out I was a waitress, she acted as if Carl's low grades were to be expected from the son of an uneducated single parent. I know I'm smart, but people assume I must be dumb, and that wouldn't happen if I had a degree and a better job.** I'd feel good about myself because I'd achieved an important and hard goal. **Sometimes I feel as if I'm just letting life run me, and I want to take more control of it. It's my life, right? I need to respect myself before anyone else will.**

    Although it won't be easy, getting my college degree will be well worth the time and effort involved: **It will pay off big-time, both financially and psychologically.** With that degree, I will be able to build a better life and will have the self-esteem that I want for both myself and my children. **Most important of all, I will have choices, and I will be more in charge of my life. As they say, "You only go through once; you should make the most of it." I will.**

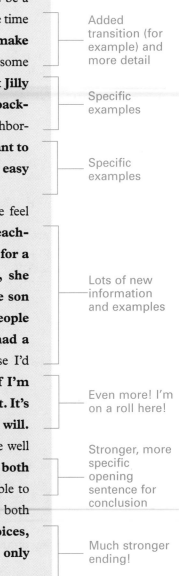

For advice on editing a draft, see Chapters 22–41.

Added transition (for example) and more detail

Specific examples

Specific examples

Lots of new information and examples

Even more! I'm on a roll here!

Stronger, more specific opening sentence for conclusion

Much stronger ending!

Roberta completed her essay by working through the following steps of the writing process: exploring ideas, planning, drafting, and revising. Her final step was to edit her paper for correctness in grammar, word use, spelling, punctuation, and mechanics (see Parts 4–7).

■ ASSIGNMENT STEP 6   **REVISE YOUR DRAFT**

For more examples showing how to revise a draft, see Chapter 7.

Revise your draft essay, looking for ways to make it stronger, clearer, and more convincing. Think about how you can make your major support points meaningful to your readers. Guide your readers through your ideas so that you accomplish your purpose.

Use a Computer to Write

You may have already used a computer to write. If not, you may be required to do so in this course. With a computer, you will find that a word processing program makes writing much easier than writing everything out by hand. If you are new to computers, ask your teacher or writing center tutor for guidance about how you can quickly learn to use your school's hardware and software. Also, ask other students about how they use computers at school.

In Chapters 2 through 7 you will be practicing the stages of the writing process, and in each chapter you will find tips for practicing that particular stage using word processing software like Microsoft Word or WordPerfect. Here are a few general tips for writing with a computer.

Five Tips for Writing on a Computer

1. *Save your work as you write.* It is very frustrating to lose your work at any stage of the writing process. Saving your work at regular intervals while you are writing—say, every fifteen minutes—is the best way to keep from losing what you have written if there is a power failure or some other interruption on the computer. (In Microsoft Word 2002, you can set Autosave functions by going to the Tools menu, selecting Options, clicking on the Save tab, and checking the boxes to get the functions you want.)

2. *Save your work at the end of every session.* When you are finished using the computer, save your work in two places, if possible:

- Save it on the hard drive of the computer (usually the C: drive if you are on a Windows machine).
- Save it on a disk.

One serves as a backup for the other—computers can crash, and disks can break or malfunction. A plastic carrying case will help you protect and organize your disks. When you are working on a computer in your home, back up your important files once a week. Back it up on the same day each week: That will help you remember to perform this important task.

3. *Name your files so you can find them easily.* Developing an easy-to-remember file naming system will help you make sense of your writing. College students usually use course names or numbers, assignment dates, and key words to help them track the many files and drafts they create. If you are working on a draft of a paper for English 100, naming it "English 100 draft" may help you find it when you return to revise it. What happens when you work on your second assignment, though—your second "English 100 draft"? It's always better to be specific in naming your files by using key words in your file name. Try "Favorite Place first draft 9-28-02" for an essay in which you describe a favorite place, for example. Selecting Save As allows you to create new files—such as "Favorite Place second draft 10-6-02"—from previous drafts so that you won't overwrite anything. Being able to track your drafts will help both you and your instructor see the development of your work.

4. *Label your disks.* If you work regularly on a computer, you may have several different disks that hold your work. On each disk label, write the contents of that disk. If you work on several different computers—at home, at work, and at school, for example—make sure you have disks that are compatible with all of those computers.

5. *Print out your work.* Even though you are saving the electronic version of your writing in two places, also print out your work. Having a paper copy, called a *hard copy,* gives you extra protection against electronic glitches. You may also find it easier to revise and edit on hard copy.

Finding and Exploring Your Topic

Choosing Something to Write About

WRITING AS YOU LEARN

Choose one of the following topics and focus on a specific aspect of it with which you are familiar. (For example, focus on one specific pet peeve you have, one specific story about yourself, or one specific event that has affected you personally.)

Something I find very annoying

A pet peeve

A story about myself

Male/female relationships

An event that affected me personally

With this topic in mind, read this chapter and complete all of the practice activities. When you finish the chapter, you will have found a good topic to write about and explored ideas related to that topic.

GUIDING QUESTIONS

- **PURPOSE:** Why am I writing this essay? What kinds of ideas will help me achieve my purpose?
- **AUDIENCE:** Who are my readers for this essay?

Understand What a Good Topic Is

DEFINITION: A **topic** is who or what you are writing about. A **good topic** is one that interests you, that you know something about, and that you can get involved in.

Any topic that you choose to write about should pass the following test.

FOUR-PART TEST FOR A TOPIC

1. **Does this topic interest me? If so, why do I care about it?**

   It's important that your answer to the first question is yes, because you may have a hard time figuring out what to say about a topic in which you have no interest. If the topic is assigned, you should try to find some interesting element. If you can choose the topic, make sure that it is of interest to you and that you can explain why you care about it.

2. **Do I know something about it? Do I want to know more?**

   Although you can learn about a topic as you write, begin with one that is at least familiar to you and that you want to explore further.

3. **Can I get involved with some part of it?**

   Choose a topic that motivates you to take some kind of action or that is otherwise relevant to your life.

4. **Is it specific enough for a short essay?**

   Look for a topic specific enough that you can make some point about it in a few paragraphs, but not so specific that there is nothing to say about it. If it seems too broad, decide whether you need to break it down into smaller parts; if it seems too narrow, look for a general idea to which it relates.

PRACTICE 1   **FINDING A GOOD TOPIC**

Put the writing assignment topic you have chosen to the four-part test. Review your answers and either keep the topic, modify it, or choose another one.

MY TOPIC: _Answers will vary._

TEACHING TIP
Tell students that the word *topic* is often used interchangeably with the word *subject*. Make clear to students what you mean when you use each of these terms.

Narrow Your Topic

TEACHING TIP
To give students an example of what narrowing a topic is like, use a photography analogy. The general topic is similar to what you can see through a camera's wide-angle lens. Narrowing it is like zooming in closer so that you can focus on smaller elements of the subject.

DEFINITION: To **narrow** a topic is to focus on the smaller parts of a general topic until you find a more limited topic or an angle that is interesting, familiar, and specific.

There are several ways to narrow the topic you have chosen.

1. Divide a general category into subcategories.

   GENERAL TOPIC: Cheating

   SUBCATEGORIES: Cheating on a school assignment

   Cheating in a game or sport

   Cheating on a diet

2. Think of specific examples.

   GENERAL TOPIC: Workplace survival skills

   EXAMPLES: Teamwork

   Public speaking

   Communicating by email

3. Focus on events from the last week or day.

   GENERAL TOPIC: Invasions of privacy

   EVENTS: The instructor read aloud parts of our journals that were supposed to be written just for him.

   The person interviewing me asked many very personal questions.

   An email message from a company whose products I'd never bought said that, based on my buying habits, I'd like what it had to offer.

A student, Jason Knox, was given the assignment to write an essay on the general topic of "A memorable accident."

First, he listed some examples of accidents he had experienced:

falling off my bicycle

a car crash on Route 495

dropping a tray of drinks

my first car accident

running a stop sign

falling out of a tree

Then, he asked himself key questions that helped him choose a narrowed topic.

KEY QUESTIONS TO CHOOSE A NARROWED TOPIC

1. Which of the narrowed topics is the most important to me?
2. Is it the right size for a short essay? Is it broad enough that I can make at least several major points about it? Is it narrow enough that I can tell the whole story in detail in a short essay?

Jason chooses "My first car accident" as his narrowed topic.

For an example of another student writer narrowing a topic, see Chapter 1, page 9.

> **PRACTICE 2   NARROWING A TOPIC**

Use one of the three methods on page 26 to narrow your topic. Then ask yourself the key questions above for choosing a narrowed topic. Write your narrowed topic below.

NARROWED TOPIC: *Answers will vary.* _____

Explore Your Topic

DEFINITION: To **explore** a topic is to investigate what you already know about your narrowed topic in order to decide what you want to say. You can use one of several prewriting techniques to explore a topic, or you can keep a journal.

> **DEFINITION:** **Prewriting techniques** are strategies you can use to come up with ideas at any point during the writing process: to find a topic, to get ideas for what you want to say about the topic, and to support your ideas.

Ask yourself: What interests me about this topic? Why do I care about it? What do I know? What do I want to say? Then use prewriting techniques to find the answers.

USE COMMON PREWRITING TECHNIQUES

You can explore your narrowed topic using one or more of five common prewriting techniques. Writers generally don't use all of these at once; instead, they choose the ones that work best for them after considering their assignment, their purpose for writing, and their narrowed topic.

1. Freewrite
2. List/brainstorm
3. Question
4. Discuss
5. Cluster

When using prewriting techniques, don't judge your ideas as you write. Later you can decide whether they're good or not. At this point, your goal is to come up with as many ideas as possible, so don't say "Oh, that's stupid" or "I'm not sure about that." Just get your brain working by writing down all the possibilities.

Student writer Jason Knox uses each of the common prewriting techniques to get ideas about his topic, "My first car accident."

Freewrite

Freewriting is like having a conversation with yourself, on paper. To freewrite, just start writing everything you can think of about your topic. Write nonstop for at least five minutes. Don't go back and cross anything out, and don't worry about using correct grammar or spelling; just write.

FREEWRITING EXAMPLE

So my first accident, what a jerk. I'd just gotten my license that day and was cruising around showing off. I saw my girlfriend, she came over while i was stopped at a red light. The car in back of me honked when the light turned green. My car started rolling back, and instead of hitting the brake I stomped on the gas and ran into the car in front of me. And then I rolled back and hit the car in back. disaster! what an idiot!

List/Brainstorm

List all the ideas about your topic that you can think of. Write as fast as you can for five minutes without stopping.

LISTING/BRAINSTORMING EXAMPLE

Topic: My first car accident

first day with my license

distracted by my girlfriend at a red light

someone behind me honked and startled me

I panicked

car started rolling back

I tried to stomp on the brake, but hit the gas pedal by mistake

plowed into the car in front of me

Ask a Reporter's Questions

Ask yourself questions to start getting ideas. The following questions, which reporters use, give you different angles on a narrowed topic: Who? What? Where? When? Why? How?

QUESTIONING EXAMPLE

Topic: My first car accident

<u>Who?</u> me, age 16

<u>What?</u> a guy with a new license feeling pretty cool gets into a stupid accident

<u>Where?</u> downtown, at the light on the hill

<u>When?</u> 4 years ago, on the same day I got my license

<u>Why?</u> because I was showing off and not paying attention

<u>How?</u> by pounding on the gas pedal instead of the brake and hitting two cars

Discuss

Many people find it helpful to discuss ideas with someone else before they write. As they talk, they get more ideas and they get immediate feedback from the other person.

    Team up with another person. If you both have writing assignments, first explore one person's topic, then the other's. The person whose topic is being explored is the interviewee; the other person is the interviewer. The interviewer should ask questions about anything that seems confusing or unclear and should let the interviewee know what sounds interesting. The interviewee should give thoughtful answers and keep an open mind. It is a good idea to take notes when you are the interviewee. If you are writing on a computer, record the notes in your prewriting file.

DISCUSSING EXAMPLE

Jason: I guess I'll write about this car accident.

Tim: What about it?

Jason: Well, it was really stupid.

Tim: Why?

Jason: On the very first day I got my license, I had an accident with two cars. It was my fault, and it wouldn't have happened if I'd been paying attention and not trying to show off.

Tim: What did you do?

Jason: I was stopped at a light on a steep hill and I saw my girlfriend. She came over to the car and I was showing off and stuff because I had a license. The car in back of me honked because the light had turned green, so I took my foot off the brake to go. But then I started rolling back, so I tried to press the brake again really hard to keep from hitting the car in back of me, but I pressed the gas instead. I rammed into the car in front of me and then rolled back and hit the car that had honked. And my girlfriend was standing there the whole time.

Tim: That sounds rough. Sure makes a good story, though.

Jason: Yeah, but too bad I got my license suspended.

Cluster

Clustering, also called mapping, is like listing except that you arrange your ideas in a more visual way. Using a blank sheet of paper, write your narrowed topic in the center and circle it. Then ask yourself some questions, such as *What about this topic is important to me? What do I know about it?* Write your ideas around the narrowed topic, drawing lines from your topic to the ideas and circling them in turn. Add more lines and circles to connect additional ideas, as shown in Jason's example.

CLUSTERING EXAMPLE

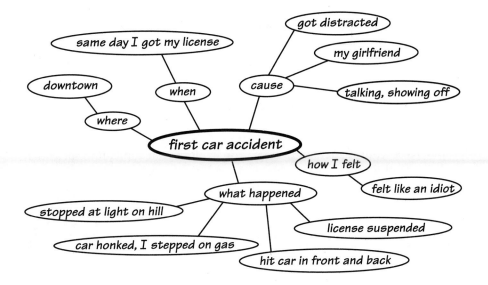

KEEP A JOURNAL

Another good way to explore ideas and topics for writing is to keep a journal. Set aside a few minutes a day or decide on some other regular schedule to write in your journal, which can take the form of a traditional notebook or a word processing file. Your journal will be a great source of ideas when you need to find something to write about.

You can use a journal in many ways:

TEACHING TIP
Give guidelines for what the physical journal should be: a notebook, pieces of paper, computer files, something of students' own choice, and so on.

- To record and explore your personal thoughts and feelings
- To comment on things that happen either to you or in politics, in the neighborhood, at work, at your college, and so on
- To list ideas to see what you know and think about them
- To examine situations you don't understand (as you write, you may figure them out)

JOURNAL ENTRY EXAMPLE

> I remember this car accident like it was yesterday. It was one of the dumbest things I've ever done. I'd just gotten my driver's license and was cruising around downtown feeling like a real big shot. While I was stopped at a light on a pretty steep hill, I saw my girlfriend and waved her over. Instead of paying attention to the light, I was just talking with her. The

car in back of me honked when the light turned green. I took my foot off the brake to go, but then started rolling back, so I tried to step on the brake but I pressed the gas, hard, instead, and plowed into the car in front of me. Then I rolled back and hit the car in back. And then I lost my license.

PRACTICE 3   PREWRITING

TEACHING TIP
Some students will need to complete more than two prewriting activities in order to fully explore a topic.

Choose *two* prewriting techniques, and use them to explore your narrowed topic. Keep your readers in mind as you explore your topic; find ideas that will be effective not only for your purpose but also for your readers' understanding.

Use a Computer to Find and Explore Your Topic

Try using a computer as you find and explore your topic. First, open a blank word processor file and write a list of topics that interest you. After testing each one with the Four-Part Test for a Topic on page 25, use your word processing program's drag-and-drop or copy-and-paste feature to bring the most promising topic farther down in your document. Label that topic "General Topic," and then narrow it using the strategies from page 26.

Next, select a specific example, event, or subcategory of your topic, and begin a new section of your document, again using the drag-and-drop or cut-and-paste feature. Choose a prewriting strategy from those listed on page 28, and begin to explore your topic. If you find yourself being concerned with grammar or spelling as you freewrite or brainstorm, for example, darken your monitor or turn it off so that you can't see what you're writing. Save your document so that you can use ideas and information from your prewriting later in your process.

3
Making a Point
Writing Your Thesis Statement

WRITING AS YOU LEARN

Using your topic and ideas from Chapter 2, develop a strong thesis for your essay.

The explanations, examples, and practices in this chapter will help you write a strong thesis statement. You can either write a thesis now and revise it after working through the chapter, or you can read the chapter and use what you've learned to write a strong thesis.

GUIDING QUESTIONS

- **PURPOSE**: What do I want to show or explain about my topic?

- **AUDIENCE**: What point can I make that would make an impression on my readers?

Understand What a Thesis Is

DISCUSSION
Write on the board five familiar song or movie titles. Ask students to write down the main point of each song or movie. Compare notes to see if everyone agrees on the main points. If not, give students an oppor-tunity to discuss their different inter-pretations briefly.

DEFINITION: The **thesis** of a piece of writing states the main point or idea you want to get across about your topic. It is your position on whatever you are writing about. The basic structure of a thesis is this:

Narrowed topic + Main point/position = Thesis

Eating disorders are caused by both cultural and psychological factors. A strong thesis has four basic features.

FOUR BASICS OF A STRONG THESIS

1. It focuses on a single main point or position about the topic.
2. It is neither too broad nor too narrow.
3. It is specific, not vague, and prepares readers for what is to come.
4. It is a forceful statement written in confident, firm language.

A strong, clearly stated thesis is essential to most good essays. In fact, everything else you write in your essay should be there because it supports the thesis, helping you get your main point across to your readers.

Early in your writing process, you may develop a *working thesis*, a first-try version of the sentence that will state your main point. You can revise the working thesis into a final thesis statement later in the writing process.

Practice Developing a Thesis

The following three-step sequence sets an essay in motion:

1. Narrow the general topic

   GENERAL TOPIC: Public safety

   NARROWED TOPIC: Airport security

2. Determine what point you want to make about the topic. (Use a prewriting technique.)

   WORKING THESIS: Allowing the federal government to take charge of airport security is a good idea.

3. Rewrite your thesis to make it more specific so that you can explain, show, or prove it with concrete evidence.

   THESIS: Allowing the federal government to take charge of airport security screening is a practical way to make air travel safer.

Once you have chosen your topic and used a prewriting technique to generate some ideas about it, the next step is to determine the point you want to make: You need to develop a thesis. The practices in the next part

TEACHING TIP
Emphasize that the main point of a piece of writing should include an opinion, not simply state a fact. If students don't see the difference between "I have two brothers" and "My two brothers have totally opposite personalities," have the class discuss what makes the first statement a fact and the second an opinion.

ESL
Some cultures avoid making direct points in writing. You may need to explain that, in academic writing in English, the rhetorical convention is that the writer make a clear, direct point. Ask students if writing conventions in their first languages approach the main point differently.

For examples of prewriting techniques, see pages 28–31.

DISCUSSION
Have the class discuss the possibilities for developing this thesis. Write specific suggestions on the board.

of this chapter will help you write thesis statements that have the four basics of a strong thesis.

1. WRITE A THESIS THAT STATES A SINGLE MAIN POINT

Your thesis should focus on only one main point. If you try to include more than one main point in a single essay, you will probably not have room to provide adequate support for all of the points. Inadequate support will likely confuse your readers.

THESIS STATEMENT WITH TWO MAIN POINTS

In the next decade, many schools will have a drastic shortage of teachers, and teachers should have to take competency tests.

The two points are underlined. The writer would need both to explain why there will be a shortage of teachers and to give reasons why teachers should have to take competency tests. These are both meaty points, and any writer would have trouble supporting them equally in a single essay.

THESIS STATEMENT WITH ONE MAIN POINT

In the next decade, many schools will have a drastic shortage of teachers.

OR

Teachers should have to take competency tests.

By choosing only one main point, the writer can focus on supporting that point and the essay will be more effective.

PRACTICE 1   IDENTIFY THE MAIN POINT

TEAMWORK
This practice works well as a small-group activity.

In each of the following thesis statements, underline the topic and double-underline the main point.

EXAMPLE: The smell of apples always reminds me of fall at home.

1. A visit to New York City will bring many surprises.

2. Many people don't know that this town has lots of free entertainment.

3. Going to the movies <u>is by no means cheap entertainment</u>.

4. Men and women <u>have very different communication styles</u>.

5. People <u>will buy almost anything if it is marked "Clearance."</u>

6. Consignment stores <u>offer an alternative shopping experience</u>.

7. Losing a job <u>can have numerous unexpected results</u>.

8. Executive perks <u>range from the small to the astounding</u>.

9. Being a driver education teacher <u>can make a person crazy</u>.

10. Elder care <u>is the field of the future</u>.

2. WRITE A THESIS THAT IS NEITHER TOO BROAD NOR TOO NARROW

Your thesis should be manageable; that is, it should fit the size of the essay assignment. If it is either too broad or too narrow, it will be hard for you to write an effective essay because you will not be able to show, explain, or prove your thesis with concrete ideas.

A thesis that is too broad is impossible to support fully in a short essay—there is just too much to cover well.

TOO BROAD   Family is an essential part of life.

[Both *family* and *life* are broad concepts, and the thesis would be impossible to explain in a short essay.]

REVISED   Time spent with my children is a welcome balance to time spent at work.

A thesis that is too narrow leaves the writer with little to show, explain, or prove. It can also make the reader think, "So what?"

TOO NARROW   My family members all have the same middle name.

[Once the writer says what the middle name is, there isn't much more to say, *unless* there's an interesting family story explaining why everyone has it.]

REVISED   An interesting event from long ago explains why my family members all have the same middle name.

■ **PRACTICE 2   IDENTIFY THESIS STATEMENTS THAT ARE TOO BROAD OR TOO NARROW**

Read the following thesis statements and decide whether they are too broad, too narrow, or the right size for a short essay. For statements that are too broad, write "B" in the space to the left; for statements that are too narrow, write "N"; and for statements that are the right size, write "OK."

EXAMPLE: _N_ My dog will be ten years old next month.

_B_   1. Hinduism is a fascinating religion.

_B_   2. I am a vegetarian.

_OK_   3. Being a vegetarian offers a wide range of food choices.

_B_   4. There are many vegetarians in this country.

_N_   5. Another gourmet coffee shop opened last week, the third one on a single block.

TEAMWORK
In small groups, have students identify the thesis statements in two or three of the readings at the back of the book and then discuss how well they meet the criteria for good thesis statements. Gould's "The People Next Door" (p. 666) and Beck's "Struggling for Perfection" (p. 686), both available in the version of the text with readings, have clear, identifiable thesis statements.

3. WRITE A SPECIFIC THESIS STATEMENT THAT PREPARES THE READER FOR WHAT'S TO COME

A strong thesis statement prepares readers by giving them a specific preview of what you will cover in your essay.

GENERAL   I have to write in my job.

[So what? Lots of people do. Why would anyone be interested in that statement?]

SPECIFIC   As a nurse, I take care of people, but my job requires good writing skills.

[Tells the reader that the essay will discuss the amount and probably the type of writing a nurse does.]

MORE SPECIFIC   As a nurse, my ability to write clearly is essential in documents such as patient reports, status notes to nurses on other shifts, and emails to other hospital staff.

[Tells the reader what kinds of writing the essay will discuss.]

██ **PRACTICE 3**   **WRITE SPECIFIC THESIS STATEMENTS**

Rewrite each of the following thesis statements by adding at least two specific details.

> **EXAMPLE:** Electronic devices in high schools can be a huge problem. <u>Wireless phones</u> that ring during a high school class <u>disrupt students' concentration and learning</u>.

1. I have a lot of useful skills.

   Answers will vary.

   _____

2. Tara's new puppy is adorable.

   _____

   _____

3. I have always had trouble writing.

   _____

   _____

4. Children have more allergies now than in the past.

   _____

   _____

5. After I was robbed, I had many feelings.

   _____

   _____

4. WRITE A THESIS STATEMENT THAT IS FORCEFUL

A strong thesis statement should be forceful and definite; a weak one leaves the reader thinking, "So what?" Avoid writing a thesis statement that begins, "In this essay I will show . . ." Don't say you will make a point. Just make it.

WEAK	In this essay, I will prove that high school dropouts have a difficult time in life.
FORCEFUL	High school dropouts can expect to face surprising hardships in life.
WEAK	I think you have to be careful when buying a used car.
FORCEFUL	Before buying a used car, get some basic information so that you don't pay more than you need to.

One way of writing a thesis statement is to announce the number of ideas you will discuss.

THESIS STATEMENT: Before buying a car, get information in three basic areas.

The writer of this thesis statement would go on to identify the three areas and discuss each in a paragraph. The outline of the essay might look like this:

THESIS STATEMENT: Before buying a car, get information in three basic areas.

TOPIC SENTENCE, PARAGRAPH 1: The first area that is important to research is . . .

TOPIC SENTENCE, PARAGRAPH 2: The second area that is important to research is . . .

TOPIC SENTENCE, PARAGRAPH 3: The third area that is important to research is . . .

Note, however, that although this approach ensures that the thesis statement and essay will be organized, it may also make them dull. Before sticking with this kind of thesis statement and topic sentence structure, try to make the thesis more forceful and interesting. For instance, in the thesis statement above, the writer might tell the reader why it is important to get information before buying a car.

PRACTICE 4   WRITE FORCEFUL THESIS STATEMENTS

Rewrite the weak thesis statements that follow to make them more forceful.

EXAMPLE: My dog is great.

My dog, Kayla, understands me better than any human being does.

1. I will explain some examples of history repeating itself.

   Answers will vary.

   _____

2. This college should provide better parking facilities, I think.

   _____

   _____

3. My new boss is really nice.

   _____

   _____

4. The drug Ecstasy is used by lots of people.

   _____

   _____

5. Working while going to college isn't easy.

   _____

   _____

The four practices you have already completed in this chapter have focused on the four basics of strong thesis statements. The next two practices will help you develop a thesis from prewriting or by narrowing the topic.

PRACTICE 5   DEVELOP A THESIS FROM PREWRITING

Read each example of a narrowed topic with prewriting, and write a possible thesis statement. There is no one right answer.

1. **NARROWED TOPIC**: The popularity of television shows like *Survivor* and *Temptation Island*

   FREEWRITING ON THE TOPIC

   These shows are popular because they're real, not some stupid sitcom. People are really out there, and you feel like they could be you and you know *there's no script, it's really happening and you're watching it. It's like <u>Do You Want to Be a Millionaire?</u> Someone just like me could win a lot of money but sometimes they don't know the easiest answers and then you feel smarter than they are. But still you're rooting for all the people on these shows because they are like you.*

THESIS: *Answers will vary.*

_____

2. **NARROWED TOPIC:** State proficiency tests required for high school graduation

BRAINSTORMING ON THE TOPIC

Not fair to kids who don't pass

Very tough tests

Sometimes tests aren't good

Teachers teach only what students need to pass test

I couldn't pass one now

Lots of class time spent on tests

What happens to kids who don't pass?

Can students sue the school if they fail?

THESIS: _____

_____

3. **NARROWED TOPIC:** Lack of privacy on the Internet

CLUSTERING ON THE TOPIC

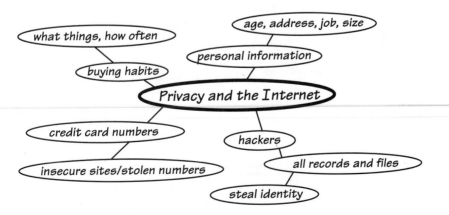

THESIS: _____

_____

PRACTICE 6   DEVELOPING A THESIS BY NARROWING A TOPIC

First, narrow each general topic listed below, and write your answer in the numbered space to its right. Then, in the lettered spaces that follow, write a possible thesis—something you might want to support in an essay—for each narrowed topic.

GENERAL TOPIC	NARROWED TOPIC
Weather	How sun affects people

POSSIBLE THESIS: When the sun is shining, people's moods improve.

GENERAL TOPIC	NARROWED TOPIC
1. Vacations	1. _Answers will vary._ _____
2. Hospitals	2. _____
3. Family problems	3. _____
4. Anger	4. _____
5. Love	5. _____
6. Partnerships	6. _____
7. Cars	7. _____
8. Food	8. _____
9. Parents or parenting	9. _____
10. Holidays	10. _____

POSSIBLE THESIS

a. _Answers will vary. All should include the narrowed topic and one main point._

b. _____

c. _____

d. _____

e. _____

f. _____

g. _____

h. _____

i. _____

j. _____

PRACTICE 7   REVISING A THESIS

Writers almost always need to revise their working thesis statements to make them more specific and more forceful. In the spaces provided below, rewrite each of the possible thesis statements you wrote in Practice 6, making them stronger. Again, think of a statement that you would be interested in writing about. You may want to add more information to your thesis statements to make them more specific and forceful, but short, punchy thesis statements also can be very powerful.

POSSIBLE THESIS: When the sun is shining, people's moods improve.

REVISED THESIS: Bright sunshine dramatically improves people's moods.

1. *Answers will vary depending on the answers in Practice 6.*

2. _____

3. _____

4. _____

5. _____

6. _____

7. _____

8. _____

9. _____

10. _____

If you have already written a thesis statement for the writing assignment at the beginning of this chapter, revise it now. If you have waited to write a thesis until you completed the practices, write one now, using the Thinking Critically guide that follows.

THINKING CRITICALLY TO DEVELOP YOUR THESIS STATEMENT

FOCUS Write a working thesis statement and reread it. Think about what main point you want to make in your essay.

ASK
- What is my position or my point about my topic?
- Does my thesis statement include both my narrowed topic and the point I want to make about it?
- Does it make my point in a way that will interest readers?
- Does it state something that I can show, explain, or prove?
- Can I find ideas in my prewriting to support it?
- Can I think of additional ideas to support it?
- Does it need more specifics?
- Does it make a single point?
- Does it say what I want it to say?
- Does it fit the assignment?
- Is it a complete sentence?

WRITE Write and adjust your thesis statement until you think it works.

Use a Computer to Write a Thesis Statement

As you review your prewriting, you can practice filtering the ideas you've come up with into possible thesis sentences. You may find it helpful to consider several options before choosing one to build on. To do this, open the document that includes your best prewriting about your topic and narrowed topic, and then save it as a new file with a new name (using Save As in the File menu). This preserves the original file and gives you a new file to use for thesis shaping.

Look through your prewriting in the new file to find several phrases or sentences that come close to stating the main point you want to make. Isolate your best phrases or sentences by putting several spaces between them, and use boldface type to identify any support points. Determine which combinations of words best capture the main point.

Next, use your word processing program's drag-and-drop or copy-and-paste feature to take the best parts of each phrase or sentence to build the thesis statement. When you make your ideas visible on the screen, it will be easier for you to adjust the focus of your working thesis so that your thinking isn't too narrow or too broad. After you draft a thesis statement, read it aloud. Does it sound like a strong, well-thought-out sentence that includes a single main point and is manageable, specific, and forceful?

4

Supporting Your Point

Finding Details, Examples, and Facts

WRITING AS YOU LEARN

Develop support for the thesis you wrote in Chapter 3. First, write your thesis here:

THESIS: _____

Then, after working through the chapter, apply what you have learned by writing out three support points and several supporting details for each point.

GUIDING QUESTIONS

- **PURPOSE:** What do I want to accomplish with this essay?

- **AUDIENCE:** In order to accomplish that purpose, what do I need to tell my readers? What do I know about my readers that will help me present support that will be convincing to them? What do they already know or think? What do they need to know in order to grasp my point?

Understand What Support for a Thesis Is

DEFINITION: Support is the collection of evidence, examples, or facts that show, explain, or prove your main point. **Support points** are the major ideas developed in the paragraphs that make up the body of your essay. **Supporting details** are the specifics you provide to explain your major support points to your readers.

Without support, you *state* the main point, but you don't *make* the main point. Consider the following statements:

> I didn't break the plates.
>
> I don't deserve an F on this paper.
>
> My telephone bill is wrong.

The statements may be true, but without support they are not convincing. Perhaps you sometimes get papers back with the comment "You need to support (or develop) your ideas"; this chapter will show you how to do so.

Writers sometimes confuse repetition with support. Using the same idea several times in different words is not support: It is just repetition.

REPETITION, NOT SUPPORT: My telephone bill is wrong. The amount is incorrect. It shouldn't be this much. It is an error.

SUPPORT: My telephone bill is wrong. There are four duplicate charges for the same time and the same number. The per minute charge is not the one my plan offers. I did not call Antarctica at all, much less three times.

As you develop support for your thesis, make sure that each point has the following three basic features.

THREE BASICS OF GOOD SUPPORT

1. **It relates to your main point.** The purpose of support is to show, explain, or prove your main point, so the support you use must be directly related to that main point.

2. **It considers your readers.** Aim your support at the people who will read your writing. Supply information that will convince or inform them.

3. **It is detailed and specific.** Give readers enough detail, particularly through examples, so that they can see what you mean.

TEACHING TIP
Emphasize that support points must be factual; an opinion alone will not convince readers. If students use an opinion, they should immediately support it with factual evidence.

Practice Supporting a Thesis Statement

A short essay usually has between three and five major points that support the thesis statement. Each major support point becomes the topic sentence in its own paragraph. In turn, each paragraph presents supporting details to back up that major support point.

Follow this sequence to develop support for a thesis:

1. Prewrite to find support.
2. Drop unrelated ideas.
3. Select the best support points.
4. Add supporting details.
5. Write topic sentences for your support points.

For an example of a student writer's use of this sequence, see pages 14–15.

1. PREWRITE TO FIND SUPPORT

Reread your thesis and imagine your readers asking, "What do you mean?" Use one or two prewriting techniques to come up with as many ideas as you can to answer that question and support your thesis. As you prewrite, just get your ideas down on paper or on screen; don't judge them yet.

TEACHING TIP
Because support is essential, yet often difficult to find, walk students through each step of the sequence using a very simple thesis statement about something familiar— the classroom, the college, the town (for example, "Parking on this campus is inadequate").

To review prewriting techniques, see pages 27–31.

TEAMWORK
Practice 1 works well in pairs or small groups if you have students choose listing or discussing as their prewriting technique.

▮ PRACTICE 1   PREWRITE TO FIND SUPPORT

Choose one of the following sentences or one of your own, and write for five minutes using one prewriting technique (freewriting, listing/brainstorming, questioning, discussing, clustering). You will need a good supply of ideas from which to choose support points for your thesis. Try to find at least a dozen different ideas.

SUGGESTED THESIS STATEMENTS

1. Valentine's Day gifts can range from the simple and inexpensive to the lavish and costly.
2. Online dating services offer some obvious advantages.
3. Online dating services involve some obvious disadvantages.

4. Discrimination comes in many forms.

5. My parents still don't know about some things I did as a child (teenager).

NOTE: Imagine your reader asking, "What do you mean?"

2. DROP UNRELATED IDEAS

After finishing your prewriting, remind yourself of your main point, as expressed in your thesis statement. Then review your prewriting carefully, and drop any ideas that are not directly related to your main point. (You may want to write the dropped ideas in your journal—in case you want to use them later as writing topics.) Also, cross out any ideas that would confuse your readers or seem meaningless to them. If new ideas occur to you, write them down.

For more on keeping a journal, see pages 31–32.

TEACHING TIP
Remind students that just because they find a point interesting doesn't necessarily mean that it belongs in the essay. The point must support the thesis statement.

PRACTICE 2   DROP UNRELATED IDEAS

Each thesis statement below is followed by a list of possible support points. Cross out the unrelated ideas in each list. Be ready to explain your choices.

For an example of a student writer dropping unrelated ideas from prewriting, see page 14.

1. **THESIS STATEMENT**: Written communication must be worded precisely and formatted clearly.

POSSIBLE SUPPORT POINTS

use bulleted lists for important short points

~~once I wrote a ridiculous memo to my boss but never sent it~~

try to keep it to no more than a single page

write the date

~~get it done by the end of the day~~

read it over before sending

~~hate to put things in writing~~

~~takes too much time~~

make a copy

~~getting 40 emails in a day is too many~~

2. **THESIS STATEMENT**: Just this year, I experienced a day that was perfect in every way.

POSSIBLE SUPPORT POINTS

weather was beautiful

on vacation

~~we'd had a great meal the night before~~

slept late

cold but inside fire was burning hot

new snow, all white

~~the year before we lost electricity~~

sky cloudless and bright blue

snow shimmering in the sunlight

perfect snow for skiing

no one else on the ski trail, very quiet

~~next Tuesday the ski resort would close for the season~~

3. **THESIS STATEMENT**: I know from experience that sometimes the customer is wrong.

POSSIBLE SUPPORT POINTS

work at supermarket

customers often misread sale flyer

they choose something like the item on sale but not it

get mad and sometimes get nasty

~~why do people bring screaming kids to the supermarket?~~

~~they don't have any right to be rude but they are~~

~~want to argue but I can't~~

customers steal food like eating grapes that are sold by the pound

~~sometimes they eat a whole box of cookies and bring up the empty box~~

~~then the kids are always grabbing at the candy and whining, sometimes~~
~~they just rip the candy open or put it in their mouths~~

customers misread the signs like ones that say "save $1.50" and think the
item is on sale for $1.50

~~should get a different job~~

cereal's the worst

3. SELECT THE BEST SUPPORT POINTS

Review your remaining ideas and select the best points to use. Consider
which ones will be clearest and most convincing to your readers. As noted
earlier, short essays usually have three to five major support points. They
will become the topic sentences for your support paragraphs.

TEACHING TIP
Encourage students
to get in the habit of
asking themselves
the kinds of basic
questions their read-
ers will ask: *Such as?*
In what way? For
example? If a student's
support points answer
those questions, his or
her readers should
understand the main
point.

▓ **PRACTICE 3   SELECT THE BEST SUPPORT POINTS**

For each item, circle the three points you would use to support the thesis
statement. Be ready to explain your answers.

For an example of a
student writer
choosing the best
support points, see
pages 14–15.

1. **THESIS STATEMENT**: A college degree should not be the only factor in
   hiring decisions.

   POSSIBLE SUPPORT POINTS

   (job experience)

   (motivation and enthusiasm)

   friends who work at the company

   appearance

   age

   (reliability and honesty)

good transportation

artistic talents

2. **THESIS STATEMENT**: People have a variety of learning styles.

   POSSIBLE SUPPORT POINTS

   (learn by doing)

   not interested in learning anything new

   (learn by seeing)

   don't bring their books to class

   disrupt the class

   (learn by working with others)

   get bored

   bad learners

   gifted students

3. **THESIS STATEMENT**: The beauty and grandeur of the cathedral astonished me.

   POSSIBLE SUPPORT POINTS

   (400 feet high)

   hundreds of tourists

   (white, pink, and green marble gleaming in the sun)

   junky gift shops in the circle around it

   interior very plain

   beautiful warm day

   built hundreds of years ago

   (intricate carving on all sides)

4. ADD SUPPORTING DETAILS

Once you have chosen your major support points, you will need to add details to explain or demonstrate each of those points. These supporting details can be examples, facts, or evidence. As the following example shows, a supporting detail is always more specific than a major support point.

> **THESIS STATEMENT:** I try to eat sensibly, but some foods are just too good to pass up.

> **SUPPORT POINT:** Chocolate in any form is a major temptation for me.
>
> > **SUPPORTING DETAIL:** Peanut M&M's are especially tempting—I could eat a whole pound bag in one sitting.
> >
> > **SUPPORTING DETAIL:** Canned chocolate frosting is great; I can eat it with a spoon right from the can.
> >
> > **SUPPORTING DETAIL:** Big fat truffles with the creamy centers just melt on my tongue.

> **SUPPORT POINT:** Freshly baked bread calls to me from the supermarket shelves.
>
> > **SUPPORTING DETAIL:** I can smell it as soon as I walk in the store.
> >
> > **SUPPORTING DETAIL:** Sometimes it's still warm and soft, with steam on the wrapping.
> >
> > **SUPPORTING DETAIL:** It reminds me of my grandmother making rolls for Thanksgiving dinners at her house in upstate New York.

> **SUPPORT POINT:** I tell myself never to buy boxes of cheese crackers, but sometimes my hand doesn't listen to me.
>
> > **SUPPORTING DETAIL:** Cheddar's my favorite, with lots of salt and shaped in little bite-sized squares.
> >
> > **SUPPORTING DETAIL:** Once I open the box, they'll be gone within a day, maybe even within a couple of hours, especially if I'm working at home.
> >
> > **SUPPORTING DETAIL:** I start by eating one at a time, but I get into handfuls as I go along.

For an example of a student adding supporting details, see pages 20–21.

TEAMWORK
Have students work in pairs to read their topic sentences aloud and share possible support points. Together, partners can select the three best points. Suggest that they refer to the Three Basics of Good Support (p. 47) when generating and selecting support points.

PRACTICE 4   ADD SUPPORTING DETAILS

For each major support point, again imagine your readers asking, "What do you mean?" Add specific details to answer that question.

THESIS STATEMENT: I am an excellent baker.

SUPPORT POINT: My chocolate chip cookies are particularly good.

SUPPORTING DETAIL: I bake with the **extra-large double chocolate chips** that are **soft, gooey, and darkly sweet** when they are baked.

In the space indicated, write the points you chose in Practice 3, item 1 (see p. 51), as the best support. Then in the space to the right, add three details that would explain, show, or prove each support point.

THESIS STATEMENT: A college degree should not be the only factor in hiring decisions. *Answers will vary.*

SUPPORT POINT

_____

SUPPORTING DETAILS

_____

_____

_____

SUPPORT POINT

_____

SUPPORTING DETAILS

_____

_____

_____

SUPPORT POINT

_____

SUPPORTING DETAILS

_____

_____

_____

5. WRITE TOPIC SENTENCES FOR YOUR SUPPORT POINTS

For an illustration of the parts of an essay, see pages 4–5.

Your major support points form the topic sentences for the paragraphs that support your thesis statement. Each topic sentence should clearly relate to and support (explain, show, or prove) your thesis by explaining what you mean. In your essay, each topic sentence will begin a new paragraph, and the paragraph will consist of details that explain the topic sentence.

THESIS STATEMENT: Playing a team sport taught me more than how to play the game.

TOPIC SENTENCE (1ST PARAGRAPH): I learned the importance of regular, committed practice.

TOPIC SENTENCE (2ND PARAGRAPH): I also realized that, in order to succeed, I had to work with other people.

TOPIC SENTENCE (3RD PARAGRAPH): Most important of all, I learned the importance of responsibility to others.

A topic sentence should clearly express an idea, one that supports the thesis and can in turn be supported by other details. As you develop major support points for your thesis, it is important to express your ideas in complete, clear topic sentences. Once you have developed your thesis statement and topic sentences, the rest of your essay involves filling in the details to bring your support to life for your readers.

For an example of a student writing topic sentences for her support points, see pages 17–18.

PRACTICE 5   WRITE TOPIC SENTENCES

Using the support points you generated in Practice 4, write topic sentences that support the thesis statement. Then, in the space under each topic sentence, list the details you selected. When you have completed this practice, you will have developed support for an essay.

THESIS STATEMENT: A college degree should not be the only factor in hiring decisions. *Answers will vary.*

TOPIC SENTENCE (SUPPORT POINT 1): _____

_____

    SUPPORTING DETAILS: _____

_____

_____

TOPIC SENTENCE (SUPPORT POINT 2): _____

_____

    SUPPORTING DETAILS: _____

_____

_____

TOPIC SENTENCE (SUPPORT POINT 3): _____

_____

SUPPORTING DETAILS: _____

_____

_____

THINKING CRITICALLY ABOUT SUPPORT FOR YOUR THESIS STATEMENT

FOCUS   Think about the main point you intend to make in your thesis statement.

ASK
- What support can I include that will show, explain, or prove what I mean?
- What do my readers need to know or understand in order to be convinced?
- What examples come to mind?
- What have I experienced myself?
- What major points could I make to convince or inform my readers?
- What details could I use to strengthen the support?
- Do I have enough details to support each major point?
- What could I add?

WRITE   Write for five minutes using a prewriting technique to find as many support points as you can.

For examples of prewriting techniques, see pages 27–31.

Use a Computer to Support Your Point

Open your working thesis statement document and use Save As to create the next document in your writing process—your list of major support points and supporting details. To gather possible support for your thesis thinking, freewrite responses to the questions in the Thinking Critically guide above. Review your freewriting; then use the Comment tool (on the Insert menu in Microsoft Word) to write notes to yourself about which ideas can be used as major support points and which can be supporting details.

In addition to freewriting, try a quick search of World Wide Web resources by going to Google (**<www.google.com>**) and typing your thesis sentence in the Search field. If you find useful details, examples, and facts in any of the links, remember to mention each source by noting its title, author, and Web address — and the date you found the source in your document. Even if you don't find specific details, examples, and facts, the kinds of information your online search produces may help you think more clearly about the support you need for your thesis.

You Know This
You have experience in planning.
- You make a list of things you need to do and put the most important things first.
- You write down what you need at a grocery store according to where the items are in the store.
- You keep track of your appointments or meetings for the day, arranged in sequence from morning to afternoon.

5

Making a Plan

Arranging Your Ideas

WRITING AS YOU LEARN

Write a plan that includes the thesis and support you have developed so far for your essay.

The explanations, examples, and practices in this chapter will help you to write a plan for your essay. Such a plan is also called an outline.

GUIDING QUESTIONS

TEACHING TIP
Have students respond to these questions by writing in their journals. This preliminary work will help prepare them for the activities in this chapter.

- **PURPOSE**: Based on what I want to accomplish with this essay, how should I arrange and present the points I plan to make?
- **AUDIENCE**: What sequence of my ideas will work most effectively so that my readers will understand or be convinced of my main point?

Understand Ways of Ordering Ideas

DEFINITION: In writing, **order** means the sequence in which you present your ideas: what comes first, second, third, and so on. Three common ways of ordering your ideas are **chronological order** (by the sequence of time in which events happened), **spatial order** (by the physical arrangement of objects or features), and **order of importance** (by the significance of the ideas or reasons).

After considering the questions about purpose and audience, the next step in planning your essay is to decide how to arrange, or order, your ideas.

CHRONOLOGICAL ORDER

Use **chronological order** (time order) to arrange points according to when they happened. Time order works well when you are telling the story of an event or explaining how an event happened. Usually, you go from what happened first to what happened last; in some cases, though, you can work back from what happened last to what happened first.

EXAMPLE USING CHRONOLOGICAL (TIME) ORDER

The cause of the fire that destroyed the apartment building was human carelessness. The couple in apartment 2F had planned a romantic dinner to celebrate the woman's raise at work. They lit candles all over the apartment and then shared a bottle of wine and ate a delicious meal. After dinner, they decided to go out to a club to continue the celebration. Unfortunately, they forgot to blow out all of the candles, and one of them was too close to a window curtain, which caught fire. First the blaze burned slowly, but because the curtain was not flame retardant, the fire picked up force and spread quickly. It engulfed the apartment and then spread to other floors of the building. By the time another resident smelled smoke, the fire was uncontrollable. Before it was all over, the building was destroyed. Fortunately, rescuers were able to save everyone who was in the building. But all of the tenants lost their homes and most of their possessions. Human carelessness caused much human misery in this situation.

TEAMWORK Have students break into pairs or small groups. Assign each pair or group one of the three sample paragraphs on pages 59–60 to rewrite using a different type of organization. After about 25 minutes, come back together as a class to see how the small groups fared. Ask each group to talk about which order they tried and about how the story changed with a new organization.

How does the writer use chronological order to arrange information?

The writer orders events from first to last.

SPATIAL ORDER

Use **spatial order** (space order) to arrange ideas so that your readers see your topic as you do. Space order works well when you are writing about a physical object, a place, or a person's appearance. Using the sequence that will give your readers the best picture of what your topic looks like, you can move from top to bottom, bottom to top, near to far, far to near, left to right, right to left, back to front, or front to back.

EXAMPLE USING SPATIAL (SPACE) ORDER

I stood watching in horror while all-powerful flames devoured an entire building, including my apartment and everything I owned. The first few floors looked normal, except that firefighters were racing into the front entry. They wore the long slickers and the helmets that I'd seen on television. They focused only on the building and the fire. A couple of floors up, windows were breaking, and gray, foul-smelling smoke was billowing out, as if to escape the building. I could see shadows of the firefighters moving in and out of the apartments. But my eyes were quickly drawn to the top two floors, where flames of orange and white darted out the windows and flickered in the background. A lone dog with brown and white spots barked furiously from the rooftop. Until you have actually witnessed a severe fire, you can't imagine how engulfing it is and how powerless you feel in its presence.

What type of spatial order does the writer use? *bottom to top*

ORDER OF IMPORTANCE

Use **order of importance** to arrange points according to their significance, interest, or surprise value. Usually, save the most important point for last. Then you can build up to it as you explain or convince readers to accept your position on a topic.

EXAMPLE USING ORDER OF IMPORTANCE

Fires caused by human carelessness often have disastrous effects on many people's lives. In a recent incident, when an apartment building was completely destroyed by a fire, the owner and tenants had no homes to return to. They also lost all of their possessions: furniture, clothing, and treasured personal items that could never be replaced. Worse than that, however, was that the owner and many of the tenants had no insurance to help them find new housing and replace their possessions. Many had to depend completely on relatives, friends, and a fund that was started for them by neighbors. They would not soon have their own places to live, nor could they buy clothing to replace what they had lost. The most disastrous effect of the fire was that a firefighter lost his life. The thirty-year-old man had a wife and three young children who were robbed of their loved one. Carelessness has no place around fire, as it has the power to destroy.

What is this writer's most important point about the effects of fires?
Fires can cause loss of life.

Practice Ordering Your Ideas

As you arrange your ideas, consider using chronological order, spatial order, or order of importance.

PURPOSE	TYPE OF ORDER
To describe an experience as it happened	Chronological (time)
To help your reader see a person, place, or object as you see it	Spatial (space)
To persuade or convince someone of the significance of your points	Importance

PRACTICE 1   USE CHRONOLOGICAL ORDER TO ARRANGE IDEAS

Arrange the support for each of the thesis statements that follow according to chronological order. Indicate the sequence of ideas by writing a number in the blank at the left. (A number 1 indicates what would happen first, a number 2 indicates what would happen second, and so on.)

1. **THESIS:** Ordering out for pizza is the easiest way to get a good meal, fast.

   2   Decide on what kind of toppings you want.

   3   Call in the order.

   1   Take out the menu for your favorite pizza shop.

   5   Pay the delivery person.

   6   Eat!

   4   Wait for the buzzer and open the door.

2. **THESIS:** Using the following steps will improve your chances of doing well on a test.

   3   When you are ready to begin, read the instructions carefully.

   4   Answer the easy questions first.

   6   Review your answers.

___2___   Before beginning, preview the whole test, noting which parts have the most points.

___1___   Listen to the professor's instructions when you receive the test.

___5___   Allow enough time to answer the hardest, longest items with the most points.

3. **THESIS**: Janeen's experience getting stuck in an elevator was frightening.

___1___   The elevator began to go up but jolted to a stop between floors.

___4___   First the security person told her to press the release button, but nothing happened.

___2___   Janeen waited for a few minutes and then pressed the alarm button.

___7___   Finally, the elevator repair people arrived and got the elevator going again.

___3___   A security person answered through the speaker, and Janeen explained that the elevator had stopped.

___6___   Again, nothing happened.

___5___   Then the security person tried to fix the problem internally.

PRACTICE 2   USE SPATIAL ORDER TO ARRANGE IDEAS

Arrange the support for each of the following thesis statements according to spatial order. Indicate the sequence of ideas by writing a number in the blank to the left. Then indicate the type of spatial arrangement you are using on the line at the end of each item (top to bottom, bottom to top, near to far, far to near, left to right, right to left, back to front, front to back).

1. **THESIS**: Sal wanted to make sure that he looked professional.

___5___   didn't wear one of his baseball caps

___1___   shoes clean and polished

___3___   dress shirt that he had ironed and tucked in carefully

___4___   hair neatly combed and pulled back

___2___   pants belted and not too baggy

TYPE OF SPATIAL ORDER: *bottom to top (Students who used top to bottom should have numbers in this order: 1, 5, 3, 2, 4.)*

2. **THESIS:** In the movie *Cast Away*, Tom Hanks looked as if he'd been marooned for a long time.

   3   a bare chest and a torso that was thin and wiry

   1   hair that was very long, wavy, and tangled

   5   feet that were dry and blistered

   2   a long beard, bleached by the sun to different colors

   4   ragged, shredded pants

TYPE OF SPATIAL ORDER: *top to bottom (Students who used bottom to top should have numbers in this order: 3, 5, 1, 4, 2.)*

3. **THESIS:** Just outside of my hotel door was a tropical paradise.

   3   beside the bar, a band playing island music

   1   first a row of palm trees swaying in the breeze

   4   twenty steps to the rows of beach chairs lined up near the water

   2   a few steps beyond the trees, a small bar serving drinks and snacks

   5   as far as the eye could see, sparkling greenish blue ocean with a gentle surf

TYPE OF SPATIAL ORDER: *near to far*

PRACTICE 3   USE ORDER OF IMPORTANCE TO ARRANGE IDEAS

Arrange the support for each of the thesis statements that follow according to order of importance, starting with the *least* important. Indicate the sequence of ideas by writing the number in the blank at the left.
Answers may vary. The following are suggested answers.

1. **THESIS:** Paying for a class and not getting the most from it is ridiculous.

   1   You're less likely to try it again.

   3   You lose the money you paid.

TEAMWORK
Practice 3 works particularly well in small groups because students have to discuss why they think one idea is more important than another. Point out that each person will have his or her own ideas about how to order the items. Be sure to mention that it's easier for students to make decisions about order of importance in their own writing than in an exercise.

    5   Worst of all is that you have no one to blame but yourself.

    4   You don't get the credit or the information from the class.

    2   You're worse off than before because you've spent money.

2. **THESIS**: People who have a drinking problem should attend Alcoholics Anonymous meetings.

    3   They're more willing to try to change their behavior.

    2   They talk with others who haven't had a drink for a while.

    1   They realize that others have similar problems.

    6   They may save themselves from great tragedy or death.

    5   They can take positive steps to change their lives.

    4   They are assigned a mentor or partner who can help at any time and who understands.

3. **THESIS**: Voting is a right that every U.S. citizen should take advantage of.

    3   It makes you feel more a part of the community and country.

    1   It doesn't take very much time.

    2   It's one of the many rights granted by the Constitution.

    5   Every vote really does count, as we saw in the 2000 presidential election between Al Gore and George W. Bush.

    4   Voting gives you a voice in deciding who will shape the government.

TEACHING TIP
If students have difficulty outlining their essays, encourage them to try a visual approach—writing their outline as a cluster diagram (with the thesis as the center circle, main support points extending out from the center, and supporting details extending still further) or as a flowchart.

Practice Making a Plan

Writing a draft essay is much easier if you work from a written plan than if you just start writing off the top of your head. When you have decided how to order your ideas, make a written plan—an **outline**—starting with your thesis statement. Then state each of your main support points as a topic sentence for one of the body paragraphs of the essay. Add each supporting detail in a sentence that develops or explains the topic sentence for that paragraph. Your plan should also include a possible main point for the concluding paragraph.

Although your outline serves as a good guide or blueprint for you as you draft your essay, don't think of it as inflexible. You can always modify your plan as you draft your essay.

Your outline for your draft essay should look like the one that follows. In this outline, student writer Gene Boroski has written both the support points for the body paragraphs and the supporting details in complete sentences. If you want to use fragments or phrases in your outline and wait to write the complete sentences while you draft, that's fine. Many people, however, find it useful to write complete sentences as they plan so that their outline is a more complete blueprint for the essay.

For a diagram of the relationship between paragraphs and essays, see page 5.

ESL
For practice, suggest that ESL students write two separate outlines, using two different types of order. Have students review each outline with you or with a writing center tutor in order to decide which outline will create the most coherent essay.

THESIS STATEMENT: As a distance education student, I should not have to pay student activities fees.

1. All of my courses are offered online. — Support point #1

   a. The courses do not exist in real time. — Supporting details

   b. I log on to the course whenever it is convenient for me.

   c. My interaction with the teacher and other students is only through email.

2. Even though I do not go to campus, my tuition is the same as for on-site — Support point #2 students.

   a. This seems reasonable to me because I am getting the same kind of — Supporting details instruction and knowledge.

   b. My tuition helps pay the professors' salaries, which I believe is fair.

   c. Unfortunately, because the courses are online, I am not eligible for academic assistance as on-site students are.

3. I don't use campus facilities, so why should I have to pay for the — Support point #3 services?

   a. I don't use facilities such as the cafeteria. — Supporting details

   b. I also don't need student health services, parking, or campus security.

   c. The computer network is already installed, so there is no extra cost involved for online courses.

POSSIBLE POINT FOR CONCLUDING PARAGRAPH: The college doesn't pay for my online service provider fees or for the electricity I use taking the course online, so why should I pay for services that I don't use?

For an example of a student writer making an outline for her essay, see page 17.

■ **PRACTICE 1** **OUTLINING MAJOR SUPPORT POINTS AND SUPPORTING DETAILS**

Arrange the major support points and supporting details in the spaces provided, as illustrated in the example below.

THESIS STATEMENT: Being a good customer service representative in a retail store requires several important skills.

ORDER OF IMPORTANCE

PURPOSE AND AUDIENCE: To explain part of the job to someone who is interested in a job as a customer service representative

Filling out paperwork

Looking at person

Listening carefully

Making notes

Asking questions

Being pleasant and polite

Smiling, saying hello

Figuring out how to solve the problem

Calling the right people

Major support points ⎯⎯⎯⎯ 1. Being pleasant and polite

a.   Smiling, saying hello

Supporting details ⎯⎯⎯ b.   Looking at person

2. Listening carefully

a.   Making notes

b.   Asking questions

3. Figuring out how to solve the problem

a.   Calling the right people

b.   Filling out paperwork

1. **THESIS STATEMENT:** I didn't think I was college material.

   ORDER OF IMPORTANCE

   PURPOSE AND AUDIENCE: To explain to a college admissions officer why you took time off after high school before applying to college.

   No one in my family had gone to college.

   I'd goofed off in high school.

   I didn't know anyone who could tell me what college was like.

   I've been out of high school for a while.

   My sister said college was a waste of time and money.

   I forgot what school was like.

   I didn't have good high school grades.

   I didn't care about school.

   I'm older than other students.

   Answers will vary.

2. **THESIS STATEMENT:** Be careful of telephone con artists.

   CHRONOLOGICAL ORDER

   PURPOSE AND AUDIENCE: To warn a friend about not getting scammed on the phone.

   Ask questions.

   Be realistic.

   What is your address?

Can I call you back?

Personal income is private.

Don't reveal personal information.

Nothing's free.

There's always a catch.

Your social security number can be misused.

1. _____

    a. _____

    b. _____

2. _____

    a. _____

    b. _____

3. _____

    a. _____

    b. _____

PRACTICE 2   OUTLINING AN ESSAY

Outline the essay that follows. Underline the thesis statement, and underline the main point in the concluding paragraph. Double-underline the topic sentences, and put a check mark next to each supporting detail.

We all know people who seem to fall in love, over and over. They love being in love. But others have different patterns. Some people seem to fall in love once and stay there. Others avoid long-term commitment. Until now, we had no way to figure out why some people were steady lovers and others not. <u>Some researchers now believe that the amount and type of certain hormones in a person's brain may determine a person's patterns of love.</u>

<u><u>Using mice as subjects, the researchers found that when two particular hormones (oxytocin and vasopressin) exist in the pleasure centers of the brain, they produce individuals with a pattern of long-lasting love.</u></u>

✓ Male mice with these hormones in their pleasure centers were faithful to

their partners. They stayed with their female mouse partners through ✓
pregnancy and the raising of offspring.

In contrast, when those same hormones existed outside of the pleasure
center, the male mice sought constant sources of new love. They did not
have steady partners and did not stick around when a female mouse ✓
became pregnant. The mice with hormones in this location were the ones ✓
who ran from commitment.

Unfortunately, the research did not deal with the most common love
pattern: individuals involved in relationships that last for some time but not
for life. In this pattern, people have a series of serious relationships that ✓
are often broken off when one person wants a formal commitment and
the other doesn't. Perhaps this research will come next, as it is in these ✓
relationships where much of the pain of love exists.

Though these behaviors may be built into the brain, scientists are
working on ways to modify the effects. They hope to find a balance so that
love patterns can be modified. One humorous researcher suggested that
before we select our mates, we should ask them to have a brain scan to determine whether they're likely to stay or go.

THINKING CRITICALLY WHILE MAKING A PLAN

FOCUS	Reread your thesis statement and support points.
ASK	• What would be the best way to organize my support points? (Time? Space? Importance?) • What point should come first? Next? After that? Last? • What supporting details will show, explain, or prove each of my main points? • Does this organization help me get my main point (my position) across? Will it help my readers follow my essay?
WRITE	Write a plan (an outline) that shows how you want to arrange your points.

Use a Computer to Make a Plan

After deciding on an order of organization (chronological, spatial, or importance), you can use your word processing program to help you arrange your ideas. In the View menu, click on Outline View. Notice that a toolbar appears with various arrows (right, left, up, down). Begin your outline with your working thesis statement, and then type in your major support points and supporting details, using the right arrow (→) to indent for details. You can use the left arrow (←) to bring your text back out to the margin.

You'll notice as you type that Outline View formats each level of detail in a different way. In the example shown here, the major support is in large boldface type, supporting details are in italic type, and even finer details are in normal type.

As you create your outline, you'll be able to scan your text for gaps in support. If you decide you want to rearrange the order of your ideas, use the up arrow (↑) and down arrow (↓) to do so.

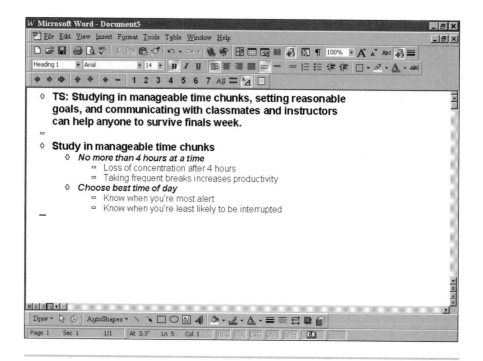

6

Writing a Draft

Putting Your Ideas Together

▓ WRITING AS YOU LEARN

Write a draft of the essay you are working on. Using the outline you created in Chapter 5, concentrate first on drafting the body paragraphs that support the thesis statement. (You may want to add support or details or change the order.) Then, write the full introductory paragraph and the conclusion.

Before writing your draft, read all of this chapter. It explains and illustrates effective introductory and concluding paragraphs. It also provides a student example, showing how to move from an outline to a draft.

GUIDING QUESTIONS

- **PURPOSE:** What are all my ideas supposed to add up to? What do I want to accomplish? Why am I writing this?

- **AUDIENCE:** How can I put myself in my readers' place? Will the facts, information, and reasons I've chosen make an impression on them?

Understand What a Draft Is

TEACHING TIP
Suggest to students
that a draft is similar to
a dress rehearsal
before a play or a
scrimmage before a
big game. In addition,
require students to
turn in their drafts with
their final papers

DEFINITION: A **draft** is the first whole version of all your ideas put together in a piece of writing.

You have been generating and organizing ideas for your draft. Now you need to put them together into essay form. Do the best job you can in drafting, but remember that you will have more chances to make changes. Think of your draft as a dress rehearsal for your final paper.

SIX BASICS OF A GOOD DRAFT

1. It has a thesis statement that presents the main point.

2. Its main support points are stated in topic sentences that develop or explain the thesis statement. (Often, the topic sentences begin each body paragraph.)

3. Its supporting details develop or explain the topic sentence in each body paragraph.

TEACHING TIP
Encourage students to
visit your school's
writing center (if there
is one) and meet the
staff. If possible,
arrange for a writing
tutor to come to your
class to stage a mock
tutorial session in
which you play the role
of student

4. Its introduction captures the readers' interest and lets them know what the essay is about.

5. Its conclusion reinforces the main point and makes an observation.

6. It follows standard essay form (introduction, body paragraphs, conclusion) and uses complete sentences.

Practice Writing a Draft

1. WRITE AN INTRODUCTION

TEACHING TIP
In the inverted-pyramid
structure, the intro-
ductory paragraph
starts with a general
statement and narrows
to the thesis statement.

The introduction to your essay should capture your readers' interest and present the main point. Think of your introductory paragraph as a marketing challenge. Ask yourself: How can I get my readers to want to continue reading?

THREE BASICS OF A GOOD INTRODUCTION

1. It should catch readers' attention.

2. It should present the essay's thesis statement (narrowed topic + main point).

3. It should give readers a good idea of what the essay will cover.

For more on thesis
statements, see
Chapter 3.

The thesis statement is often either the first or the last sentence in the introductory paragraph, though you may find essays in which the main point or thesis statement is in the middle of the introductory paragraph.

Here are examples of common kinds of introductions that spark readers' interest.

Start with a Surprising Fact or Idea

Surprises capture people's attention. The more unexpected and surprising something is, the more likely people are to take notice of it and read on.

ESL
Remind nonnative speakers that it is a convention of academic English to present the main point in the first paragraph, stated explicitly.

> Sex sells. This truth is a boon for marketing gurus and the pornography industry but a rather unfortunate situation for women. Every issue of *Playboy*, every lewd poster and even the Victoria's Secret catalog transform real women into ornaments, valued exclusively for their outward appearance. These publications are responsible for defining what is sexy and reinforce the belief that aesthetic appeal is a woman's highest virtue.
> —Amy Beck, "Struggling for Perfection"

Open with a Quotation

A good short quote can definitely get people interested. It must lead naturally into your main point, however, and not just be stuck there. If you start with a quote, make sure that you tell the reader who the speaker or writer is.

TEACHING TIP
Invite students to write several different introductions that respond to at least three of these suggestions. Have volunteers read their introductions aloud to the class and discuss the differences in writing process and product.

> It's "premature to push for federal legislation" to ban cell phone use while driving. That's according to Robert Shelton, executive director of the National Highway Traffic Safety Administration, in congressional testimony this spring. To that, we respond, "Oh, bullfeathers, Robert!"
> —Tom Magliozzi and Ray Magliozzi, "Protecting Its People: Let Our Government Do Its Job"

Give an Example or Tell a Story

People like stories, so opening an essay with a brief story or illustration often draws them in.

> Oh, those oranges arriving in the midst of the North Dakota winters of the forties—the mere color of them, carried through the door in a net bag or a crate from out of the white winter landscape. Their appearance was enough to set my brother and me to thinking that it might be about time to develop an illness, which was the surest way of receiving a steady supply of them. "Mom, we think we're getting a cold."
> —Larry Woiwode, "Ode to an Orange"

Offer a Strong Opinion

The stronger the opinion, the more likely it is that people will pay attention.

> If you're a man, at some point a woman will ask you how she looks. "How do I look?" she'll ask.
>
> You must be careful how you answer this question. The best technique is to form an honest yet sensitive opinion, then collapse on the floor with some kind of fatal seizure. Trust me, this is the easiest way out. You will never come up with the right answer.
>
> —Dave Barry, "The Ugly Truth about Beauty"

Ask a Question

A question needs an answer. If you start your introduction with a question, you engage your readers by inviting them to answer it.

> Is a girl called Gloria apt to be better-looking than one called Bertha? Are criminals more likely to be dark than blond? Can you tell a good deal about someone's personality from hearing his voice briefly over the phone? Can a person's nationality be pretty accurately guessed from his photograph? Does the fact that someone wears glasses imply that he is intelligent?
>
> The answer to all these questions is obviously, "No."
>
> Yet, from all the evidence at hand, most of us believe these things.
>
> —Robert L. Heilbroner, "Don't Let Stereotypes Warp Your Judgments"

TEAMWORK
Practice 1 works well in pairs or small groups.

PRACTICE 1   **IDENTIFY STRONG INTRODUCTIONS**

In a newspaper, a magazine, a catalog, an advertisement—anything written—find a strong introduction. Explain, in writing, why you think it is a strong introduction.

Answers will vary.

TEAMWORK
Practice 2 works well in pairs or small groups. Students should be prepared to explain their choices to the rest of the class.

PRACTICE 2   **MARKET YOUR MAIN POINT**

As you know from watching and reading advertisements, a good writer can make just about anything sound interesting. For each of the following topics, write an introductory statement using the technique indicated. Make that statement punchy and intriguing enough to motivate your readers to stay with you as you explain or defend it. Even if you wouldn't choose to write about the topics given in this practice, try to make fascinating, provocative statements about them.

1. **TOPIC**: Mandatory use of seat belts

   TECHNIQUE: Ask a question.

   Answers will vary. _____

2. **TOPIC**: Teenage suicide

   TECHNIQUE: Present a surprising fact or idea (you can make one up for this exercise).

   _____

3. **TOPIC**: Free access to music on the Internet

   TECHNIQUE: Give a strong opinion.

   _____

4. **TOPIC**: The quality of television shows

   TECHNIQUE: Use a quotation (you can make up a good one for this exercise).

   _____

5. **TOPIC**: Blind dates

   TECHNIQUE: Give an example or tell a brief story (you can just sum it up).

   _____

2. WRITE A CONCLUSION

Your conclusion should build energy and match the force of your thesis statement; it is your last chance to drive your main point home. Fading out with a weak conclusion is like slowing down at the end of a race: You lose ground. In writing, as in sports and other activities, you need to keep up the pace right to the very end. In fact, you should give yourself a last push at the end because people usually remember best what they see, hear, or read last. A good conclusion creates a sense of completion: It not only brings readers back to where they started but also shows them how far they have come.

THREE BASICS OF A GOOD CONCLUSION

1. It should refer to your thesis or main point.

2. It should sum up the support points you have developed in the essay.

3. It should make a further observation or point.

One of the best ways to end an essay is to refer directly to something in the introduction.

TEACHING TIP
If you use the inverted pyramid for introductions, explain conclusions in terms of a regular pyramid. The paragraph moves from the tip of the pyramid (the narrowest point) to the most general point: the basic idea that the writer wants the readers to remember.

- If you asked a question, ask it again and answer it based on what you've said in your essay.

- If you started a story, finish it.

- If you used a quotation, use another one — by the same person or by another person on the same topic.

- If you stated a surprising fact or idea, go back to it and comment on it, using what you have written in the body of the essay.

- Repeat key words that you used in your introduction to remind your reader of your original point.

Look again at two of the introductions you read earlier, each shown here with its conclusion.

Start with an Example or Tell a Story

INTRODUCTION A:

Oh, those oranges arriving in the midst of the North Dakota winters of the forties — the mere color of them, carried through the door in a net bag or a crate from out of the white winter landscape. Their appearance was enough to set my brother and me to thinking that it might be about time to develop an illness, which was the surest way of receiving a steady supply of them. "Mom, we think we're getting a cold."

CONCLUSION A:

"Mom, we think we're getting a cold."

"You mean you want an orange?"

This is difficult to answer or dispute or even to acknowledge, finally with the fullness that the subject deserves, and that each orange bears, within its own makeup, into this hard-edged yet insubstantial, incomplete, cold, wintry world.

— Larry Woiwode, "Ode to an Orange"

Start with a Strong Opinion or Position

INTRODUCTION B:

If you're a man, at some point a woman will ask you how she looks. "How do I look?" she'll ask.

You must be careful how you answer this question. The best technique is to form an honest yet sensitive opinion, then collapse on the floor with some kind of fatal seizure. Trust me, this is the easiest way out. You will never come up with the right answer.

CONCLUSION B:

To go back to my main point: If you're a man, and a woman asks you how she looks, you're in big trouble. Obviously, you can't say she looks bad. But you also can't say that she looks great, because she'll think you're lying, because she has spent countless hours, with the help of the multibillion-dollar beauty industry, obsessing about the differences between herself and Cindy Crawford. Also, she suspects that you're not qualified to judge anybody's appearance. This is because you have shaving cream in your hair.

—Dave Barry, "The Ugly Truth about Beauty"

PRACTICE 3   ANALYZE CONCLUSIONS

After reading the paired introductions and conclusions above, indicate the techniques used in each conclusion to refer back to its introduction.

A. Technique used to link introduction and conclusion: *Repetition of a*

quotation

B. Technique used to link introduction and conclusion: *Repetition of key*

words and restatement of main idea

PRACTICE 4   IDENTIFY GOOD INTRODUCTIONS AND CONCLUSIONS

TEAMWORK
Scramble the examples students bring in and have them work in small groups to match introductions and conclusions.

In a newspaper, magazine, or any other written material, find a piece of writing that has both a strong introduction and a strong conclusion. Answer the following questions about the introduction and conclusion.

Answers will vary.

1. What method of introduction is used? _____

   _____

2. What does the conclusion do? Does it restate the main idea? Sum up

   the points made in the piece? Make an observation? _____

   _____

3. How are the introduction and the conclusion linked? _____

   _____

PRACTICE 5   WRITE A CONCLUSION

Read the following introductory paragraphs, and then write a possible conclusion for each one. Your conclusions can be brief, but they should each include the features of a good conclusion and consist of several sentences.

1. **INTRODUCTION:** When it comes to long-term love relationships, I very much believe Anton Chekhov's statement, "Any idiot can face a crisis; it's the day-to-day living that wears you out." When faced with a crisis, couples often pull together. A crisis is a slap in the face that reminds you of who and what is important in your life. It is the routine necessities of living that can erode a relationship as couples argue over who does the laundry, who does the cleaning, or cooking, or bill paying. The constant skirmishes over day-to-day living can do more serious damage over the long term than a crisis.

   CONCLUSION: *Answers will vary.* _____

   _____

   _____

   _____

_____

_____

_____

2. **INTRODUCTION:** Why do so many people feel that they must be available at all times and in all places? Until recently, the only way you could reach someone was by telephone or by mail. Now if you don't have a cell phone, an email account, a beeper, and call waiting, people trying to reach you get annoyed. To me this is just a loss of privacy. I don't want to be available twenty-four hours a day.

CONCLUSION: _Answers will vary._ _____

_____

_____

_____

_____

_____

3. WRITE A DRAFT

Chapter 5 included an outline by student writer Gene Boroski. This outline is reproduced below, followed by the draft Gene wrote from it. Note that while Gene stays close to his outline as he writes his first-try draft, he makes some changes and additions along the way; he isn't just directly copying his outline into essay form.

TEAMWORK
Have students share their own drafts in small groups, exchanging comments and suggestions with group members. Students can use the Thinking Critically guide (p. 83) as a prompt for discussing their drafts.

GENE'S OUTLINE

THESIS STATEMENT: As a distance education student, I should not have to pay student activities fees.

1. All of my courses are offered online. ——————————— Support point #1

 a. The courses do not exist in real time. ————————
 Supporting
 b. I log on to the course whenever it is convenient for me. ———— details

 c. My interaction with the teacher and other students is only through email.

Support point #2 —— 2. Even though I do not go to campus, my tuition is the same as for on-site students.

Supporting details

    a.   This seems reasonable to me because I am getting the same kind of instruction and knowledge.

    b.   My tuition helps pay the professors' salaries, which I believe is fair.

    c.   Unfortunately, because the courses are online, I am not eligible for academic assistance as on-site students are.

Support point #3 —— 3. I don't use campus facilities, so why should I have to pay for the services?

Supporting details

    a.   I don't use facilities such as the cafeteria.

    b.   I also don't need student health services, parking, or campus security.

    c.   The computer network is already installed, so there is no extra cost involved for online courses.

POSSIBLE POINT FOR CONCLUDING PARAGRAPH: The college doesn't pay for my online service provider fees or for the electricity I use taking the course online, so why should I pay for services that I don't use?

GENE'S DRAFT

DISCUSSION
Discuss the main points and the supporting points of Gene's draft essay. Do students agree with his points? Are there other points that Gene neglected to consider? How does he organize his points? Is this the most effective means of organization? Why or why not?

For an example of another student writer's draft, see page 18.

    As a distance education student, I should not have to pay student activities fees. Distance education via computer is relatively new, and I think that college administrators have not adequately thought about what this means for student activities fees, for one thing. In some ways we are like on-site students and should be charged as they are, but I draw the line at student activities fees that benefit only the on-site students.

    All of my courses are offered online, so I never come to the campus. The courses don't even exist in real time, so I may log on to the course at 11:00 at night if that's the time that's most convenient for me. I do not interact face-to-face with my professor, but we communicate well, and often, by email. I can also interact with other distance education students that way. It is a very different way of taking classes, but it works well for people like me who can't get to campus during regularly scheduled classes.

    Even though I do not go to the campus, my tuition is the same as for on-site students. This seems reasonable to me because I am getting the same kind of instruction and knowledge. My tuition helps pay professors' salaries, which I believe is fair whether I'm taking their classes in the classroom or at a distance. Unfortunately, though, because the courses are online, I am not eligible for academic assistance as on-site students are. There are differences between on-site education and distance education, at least in some people's minds, probably because distance education is so new.

Distance education students do not use campus facilities, so why should we pay for them? For example, I don't use expensive facilities such as the cafeteria, campus health, campus security, or parking. Yes, I use the computer network, but that's already in place; it doesn't cost more to run a course online.

It is time to realize that there are differences in the college "experience" of on-site and distance education students. I don't ask the college to support my online service provider fees or the electricity I use because I am taking the course online, so why should I be asked to pay for services that I don't use?

4. TITLE YOUR ESSAY

Even if your title is the *last* part of the essay you write, it is the *first* thing that readers read. Use your title to get your readers' attention and to tell them what your essay is about. Use concrete, specific words.

THREE BASICS OF A GOOD ESSAY TITLE

1. It makes readers want to read the essay.
2. It does not repeat the same wording in your thesis statement.
3. It may hint at the main point but does not necessarily state it outright.

One way to find a good title is to consider the type of essay you are writing. If you are writing an argument (as you will in Chapter 16), state your position in your title. If you are telling your readers how to do something (as you will in Chapter 11), try using the term *steps* or *how to* in the title. This way, your readers will know immediately both what you are writing about and how you will present it. For example, "Five Steps to Financial Independence" may be a more inviting and more accurate title for a process analysis essay than "Financial Independence."

PRACTICE 6   WRITE A TITLE

Reread the following introductory paragraphs, and write a possible title for the essay each one begins. The first one is done as an example. Be prepared to explain why you worded each title as you did.

EXAMPLE

Sex sells. This truth is a boon for marketing gurus and the pornography industry but a rather unfortunate situation for women. Every issue of *Playboy,* every lewd poster and even the Victoria's Secret catalog transform real women into ornaments, valued exclusively for their outward appearance. These publications are responsible for defining what is sexy and reinforce the belief that aesthetic appeal is a woman's highest virtue.

POSSIBLE TITLE: *Sex Sells — Women Pay the Price*

1. It's "premature to push for federal legislation" to ban cell phone use while driving. That's according to Robert Shelton, executive director of the National Highway Traffic Safety Administration, in congressional testimony this spring. To that, we respond, "Oh, bullfeathers, Robert!"

POSSIBLE TITLE: *Answers will vary.*

2. Oh, those oranges arriving in the midst of the North Dakota winters of the forties — the mere color of them, carried through the door in a net bag or a crate from out of the white winter landscape. Their appearance was enough to set my brother and me to thinking that it might be about time to develop an illness, which was the surest way of receiving a steady supply of them. "Mom, we think we're getting a cold."

POSSIBLE TITLE: _____

3. If you're a man, at some point a woman will ask you how she looks. "How do I look?" she'll ask.

   You must be careful how you answer this question. The best technique is to form an honest yet sensitive opinion, then collapse on the floor with some kind of fatal seizure. Trust me, this is the easiest way out. You will never come up with the right answer.

POSSIBLE TITLE: _____

4. Is a girl called Gloria apt to be better-looking than one called Bertha? Are criminals more likely to be dark than blond? Can you tell a good deal about someone's personality from hearing his voice briefly over the phone? Can a person's nationality be pretty accurately guessed from his photograph? Does the fact that someone wears glasses imply that he is intelligent?

   The answer to all these questions is obviously, "No."

   Yet, from all the evidence at hand, most of us believe these things.

POSSIBLE TITLE: _____

THINKING CRITICALLY ABOUT WRITING A DRAFT

FOCUS   Reread your outline for the essay.

ASK
- Have I stated my main point or position in a thesis statement?
- Have I written topic sentences for each body paragraph?
- Do I have enough supporting details for each topic sentence?
- Have I arranged my support points as effectively as I can?
- What introductory technique will get my readers' attention and make my point stand out?
- How can I use the conclusion for one last chance to make my point?
- How can I link my conclusion to my introduction? What is the strongest or most interesting part of the introduction that I might refer back to in my conclusion?
- Will my title make readers want to read my essay?

WRITE   Write a draft essay.

Use a Computer to Write Your Draft

You may want to open the file in which you saved your outline and use Save As (in the File menu) to change the file name of your outline and then to begin to draft from it. (This preserves the original outline, and it gives you a new file—the draft file—to work with.) Alternatively, you may want to print your outline and put it next to the computer and begin to write a draft.

You can have multiple documents open in your word processing program—for example, your prewriting, your outline, and your draft—and use the Window menu, checking the appropriate file name, to go back and forth between them. In the example shown on the next page, the writer has a prewriting document open but can easily access an outline or draft by selecting the file name from the drop-down menu.

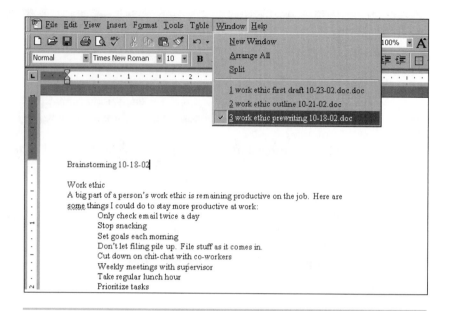

7

Revising Your Draft

Improving Your Essay

> **You Know This**
> You already revise in your everyday life.
> - You get dressed and then change certain items because they don't look right together.
> - You plan what you're going to say to someone, changing your "script" to make it more effective.
> - You rework your job application letter and résumé each time you look for a better position.

■ **WRITING AS YOU LEARN**

Revise your draft essay. To prepare yourself to revise your essay, read this entire chapter and work through each of the Practices.

GUIDING QUESTIONS

- **PURPOSE**: How can I better accomplish my purpose in this essay — explaining something, showing something, convincing my reader of something, or presenting my position on an issue?

- **AUDIENCE**: How are my readers likely to react to each point I make? What additional support points or supporting details would help them react positively to what I am telling them? What changes can I make so that my main point is stronger, clearer, or more convincing to my readers?

Understand What Revision Is

DEFINITION: **Revising** is focusing on your ideas and looking for ways to make them clearer, stronger, and more convincing. When revising, you might add, cut, move, or change whole sentences or paragraphs.

> **TEACHING TIP**
> Stress to students that revision is not just copying a draft over neatly—it is, instead, a reworking of ideas that comes from analyzing the draft. For students who need an analogy, revision is more like renovating a kitchen than cleaning it.

DEFINITION: **Editing** is finding and correcting problems with grammar, style, usage, and punctuation. While editing, you usually add, cut, or change words and phrases instead of whole sentences or paragraphs (as you might while revising).

Revising and editing are two different ways to improve a paper. Most writers find it difficult to do both at once. It is easier to look first at the ideas in your essay (revising) and then to look at the individual words and sentences (editing). Revising is covered in this chapter, and editing is covered in Chapters 22–41. As you revise, set three goals for yourself.

THREE REVISION GOALS

1. Search for ideas that do not fit (revise for unity, pp. 88–91).

2. Search for ideas that are not as specific or complete as they could be (revise for support and detail, pp. 91–93).

3. Search for ways to connect ideas so that they flow smoothly from one to the next (revise for coherence, pp. 93–101).

Revising—thinking through the ideas in your essay—is a key step in the writing process. It is essential in any kind of writing that you do for college, at work, or in your everyday life. No one gets everything right in one draft, so do not skip the revising stage. Commit yourself to making at least five changes in any draft essay.

FIVE REVISION TIPS

1. Give yourself a break from your draft—set it aside for a few hours or a whole day.

2. Read your draft aloud and listen to what you have written.

3. Imagine yourself as one of your readers.

4. Get feedback from a friend, a classmate, or a colleague (see the following section of this chapter).

5. Get help from a tutor at your college writing center or lab.

To revise your writing, you will need to try to be objective about it. You may need to read what you have written several times before deciding what changes would improve it. Remember to consider your audience (those who will read your essay) and your purpose (your reason for writing it). As you revise, focus on three areas of possible improvement: unity, detail, and coherence.

The following section of this chapter discusses one way for you to gain objectivity—the peer review. The next three sections then give advice on practicing revision.

Understand What Peer Review Is

DEFINITION: **Peer review** is getting feedback on your writing from another person or giving feedback to a fellow student, colleague, or friend.

Other people can look at your work with a fresh perspective and see things that you might not—parts that are good as well as parts that need more explanation or evidence. To say "It's great" without further comment doesn't help you improve your paper. The best reviewers are honest about what could be better, but also sensitive to the writer's feelings.

FOUR BASICS OF USEFUL FEEDBACK

1. It is given in a positive way.
2. It is specific.
3. It offers suggestions.
4. It may be given orally and in writing.

To get useful feedback in your writing class, you can find a partner and exchange papers. Each partner should read the other's paper and jot down a few comments. You may also be able to form a small group, in which you take turns reading the papers aloud while the group members make notes. Then the members of the group should offer comments that will help the writer improve the paper. The first time someone comments on what you

TEAMWORK
To model peer review, bring in a short paragraph or essay, and have students form small groups to answer the eight questions in the box below, with one person acting as recorder. Monitor carefully to make sure each group understands the process. Then discuss the answers as a class. If possible, invite a writing center peer tutor to class to help facilitate discussion.

Questions for Peer Reviewers

1. What is the main point?
2. After reading the introductory paragraph, do you have an idea of what the essay will cover, and why?
3. How could the introduction be more interesting?
4. Is there enough support for the main point? Where might the writer add support?
5. Are there confusing places where you have to reread something in order to understand it? How might the writer make the points, the organization, or the flow of ideas clearer or smoother?
6. How could the conclusion be more forceful?
7. What do you most like about the essay? Where could it be better? What would you do if it were your essay?
8. What other comments or suggestions do you have?

have written, you may feel a little embarrassed or awkward, but you are likely to feel better about the process once you see how your writing benefits from the comments.

It is useful for peer reviewers to ask or answer a few questions to guide their feedback. Some of these may come from the writer, questions such as "Does my introduction get your attention?" or "What about support for my main point—do I have enough, and is it convincing?" See the box on the previous page for questions peer reviewers might consider as they read through a draft.

Practice Revising for Unity

DEFINITION: **Unity** in writing means that all the points you make are related to your main point; they are *unified* in support of your main point.

As you draft an essay, you might drift away from your main point into something that isn't directly related to it, as the writer of the following paragraph did with the underlined sentences. The diagram after the paragraph shows where readers might get confused.

Just a few years ago online dating services were viewed with great suspicion, but they now have millions of subscribers who say the services offer many advantages over searching for a partner on your own. With an online dating service, people set up their own dates and don't have to cruise the bars. Many people do not like the bar scene, which they describe as a "meat market." Online dating services also give users the opportunity to screen individuals and contact only those who interest them. That screening saves time and also helps people avoid many awkward first dates. Subscribers can exchange email messages to see how they communicate before arranging a meeting. It's almost like the movie *You've Got Mail*. I love Meg Ryan, though she should never have hooked up with that Russell Crowe. With people spending so much time working, it's hard to meet anyone outside of work, so online dating services expand the possibilities greatly. The opportunity to "meet" a wide range of people without leaving your home and to screen out obvious mismatches is, for a growing number of people, the only way to play the dating game.

TOPIC SENTENCE: Just a few years ago online dating services were viewed with great suspicion, but they now have millions of subscribers who say the services offer many advantages over searching for a partner on your own.

SUPPORT POINT 1: With an online dating service, people set up their own dates and don't have to cruise the bars.

SUPPORT POINT 2: Online dating services also give users the opportunity to screen individuals and contact only those who interest them.

DETOUR

OFF MAIN POINT: It's almost like the movie *You've Got Mail*. I love Meg Ryan, though she should never have hooked up with that Russell Crowe.

SUPPORT POINT 3: With people spending so much time working, it's hard to meet anyone outside of work, so online dating services expand the possibilities greatly.

CONCLUDING SENTENCE: The opportunity to "meet" a wide range of people without leaving your home and to screen out obvious mismatches is, for a growing number of people, the only way to play the dating game.

Drifting away from your main point shifts your readers' focus and can be confusing. Your essay is much less likely to be effective if the flow of ideas goes off course.

PRACTICE 1   REVISE FOR UNITY

Each of the following essays includes sentences that are off the main point. Underline those sentences. The main point in each of the essays is in bold-face type.

1. Look for four off-the-point sentences.

  Oprah Winfrey is one of the most influential people of our times, but that doesn't mean that life is easy for her. As a child in rural Mississippi, she was dirt-poor and sexually abused. Somehow, she

TEACHING TIP
Choose a student to read these essays aloud to the class and ask the rest of the class to stop the reader as soon as the essay detours from the main point.

managed to climb out of that existence and become successful. But because she is now a superstar, every aspect of her life is under the media spotlight, and she is frequently criticized for everything from her weight to her attempts to help people spiritually.

Oprah's roller-coaster weight profile is always news. Every supermarket tabloid, every week, seems to have some new information about Oprah and her weight. I can relate to how humiliating that must be. She looked like a balloon in a recent picture I saw, even fatter than my Aunt Greta.

Oprah is also criticized for her wealth, estimated to be at about $800 million. You never hear about the charitable work she does, only about how much money she has. She has a fabulous apartment overlooking Lake Michigan in Chicago. While many businesspeople are as wealthy, few are criticized as often — or as publicly as Oprah.

Even Oprah's book club and magazine, *O,* bring unwarranted negativity. "Who is she to recommend books?" say some, and "What does she know about publishing?" say others. I especially liked the book *She's Come Undone.* But what could possibly be wrong with recommending books and championing literacy?

Oprah Winfrey, despite her wealth and fame, does not have an easy life. Her critics feel free to cut her down at every turn. Instead, why not celebrate her personal and professional achievements? She deserves respect, not ridicule.

2. Look for three off-the-point sentences.

A recent survey of the places students prefer to study revealed some strange results. We would expect the usual answers, such as the library, a bedroom, a desk, the kitchen, and the survey respondents did in fact name such areas. But apparently some people prefer less traditional places.

One unusual place cited was a church. The respondent said it was a great spot to study when services weren't taking place because it was always quiet and not crowded. Some churches are locked during the day because of vandalism. Other churches have had big problems with theft.

Another unusual study area was the locker room during a football game. Except for half-time, the large area was empty. The person who studies here claims that there's a high energy level in the locker room that, combined with the quiet, helps him concentrate. I wonder what the smell is like, however.

Possibly the most surprising study preference was in the pool area of a gym, sitting up in the bleachers. The light was good, said the student, she loved the smell of chlorine, and the sound of water was soothing.

The results may seem strange—a church, a locker room, and a pool—but they do share some characteristics: quiet, relative solitude, and no interruptions, other than half-time. Perhaps we should all think about new places that might help us study.

Practice Revising for Support and Detail

DEFINITION: Support is the collection of evidence, examples, or facts that show, explain, or prove your main point. **Support points** are the major ideas developed in the paragraphs that make up the body of your essay. **Supporting details** are the specifics you provide to explain your major support points to your readers.

For more on support points and supporting details, see Chapter 4.

When you read your draft essay, imagine yourself as the reader and look carefully at the major support points (topic sentences) and the supporting details you have developed. Do you have enough information to understand the main point? Does the writer present enough evidence to convince you of that point? Look for places where you could add more support and detail.

Read the two paragraphs that follow and note the support and details that the writer added to the second one. Notice that she didn't simply add to the paragraph; she also deleted some words and rearranged others to make the story clearer to readers. The additions are underlined; the deletions are crossed out.

TEACHING TIP
Try reading these or ~~other examples out~~ loud, removing any transitional words and phrases. Then discuss how the lack of transitions makes it difficult for the reader to connect ideas in logical order.

This morning I learned that my local police respond quickly and thoroughly to 911 calls. I meant to dial 411 for directory assistance, but by mistake I dialed 911. I hung up after only one ring because I realized what I'd done. A few seconds after I hung up, the phone rang, and it was the police. She said she'd received a 911 call from my number and was checking. I explained what happened and she said she had to send a cruiser over anyway. Within a minute, the cruiser pulled in, and I explained what happened. I apologized and felt very stupid, but I thanked him. I am glad to know that if I ever need to call 911, the police will be there.

REVISED TO ADD SUPPORT AND DETAIL

This morning I tested the 911 emergency system and found that it worked flawlessly. Unfortunately, the test was a mistake. ~~learned that my local police respond quickly and thoroughly to 911 calls.~~ I meant to dial 411 for directory assistance, but without thinking ~~by mistake~~ I dialed 911. I frantically pushed the disconnect button ~~hung up~~ after only one ring because I realized my error. ~~what I'd done.~~ As I reached for the phone to try again for the 411, ~~few seconds after I hung up,~~ it rang like an alarm. ~~the phone rang, and it was the police.~~ The police dispatcher crisply announced ~~She said~~ that she'd received a 911 call from this number. ~~and was checking.~~ I laughed weakly and explained what happened, hoping she would see the humor or at least the innocent human error. Instead, the crispness of her voice became brittle as she said that a cruiser was on its way. I went to meet my fate. Within a minute, the cruiser pulled in, and a police officer swaggered toward me. I explained what had happened, apologized, and thanked him very humbly. I felt guilty of stupidity, at the very least. ~~and felt very stupid, but I thanked him.~~ We learn from our mistakes, and in this case I am glad to know that if I ever need to call 911, the police will be there.

■   **PRACTICE 2   REVISE FOR DETAIL AND SUPPORT**

Read the following essay, and write in the space provided at least one additional support point or detail for each body paragraph and for the conclusion. Indicate where the added material should go in the paragraph by writing in a caret (^).

If it's leather, I love it. Anything made of leather makes me want to spend some time admiring it. This appeal is not just limited to coats and jackets but includes furniture, bags, gloves, boots, and any other leather product I find. To me it's an all-around wonderful experience.

The smell of leather is intoxicating. It seems to hang in the air, inviting me to take a big whiff. I smell the leather, especially soft leather, and it is wonderful. I'd like to bury my nose in a soft leather jacket for hours.

Answers will vary.

Leather also feels wonderful to the touch. It is smooth and silky. It feels soothing against my cheek and hands. When I'm wearing a leather jacket, I have to stop myself from running my hands up and down the sides and sleeves because it just feels so smooth and soft.

Finally, leather is comfortable, whatever form it comes in. A leather coat or jacket doesn't just look good—it's also very warm. Pull on a pair of leather gloves, and your hands won't be cold. And, best of all, sink into a soft, buttery leather easy chair. I guarantee it will relax you.

Just writing this essay about leather makes me want to put on a leather jacket and some soft leather slippers, and find a great leather chair to curl up in. It's my kind of heaven.

Practice Revising for Coherence

DEFINITION: **Coherence** in writing means that all your points and details connect to form a whole. In other words, even when the points and details are assembled in an order that makes sense, they still need "glue" to connect them.

A piece of writing that lacks coherence can sound choppy, like a string of unrelated statements. Revising for coherence improves your essay by helping readers see how one point leads to another. Individual ideas should be so well arranged and connected that they flow easily and leave readers with a clear overall impression. Two major devices can help you increase coherence in your essay.

TWO DEVICES THAT IMPROVE COHERENCE

1. Transitional words, phrases, and sentences that connect one idea to the next

2. Key words that are related to your main point and repeated throughout the essay

1. ADD TRANSITIONS

DEFINITION: Transitions are words, phrases, and sentences that connect your ideas so that your writing moves smoothly from one point to another. Transitions can be used to connect sentences and ideas within a paragraph and also to help readers move smoothly from one paragraph to another.

The following paragraphs show how transitional words and phrases are used to join sentences within the same paragraph. The first paragraph includes few transitions. In the second paragraph, added transitions are underlined.

I thought I would never make it to work today. My alarm clock didn't go off. I realized that my only clean shirt was missing two buttons right in front. After finding a sweater that would go over it, I ran for the bus, only to discover that the buses were running late. The one that came was painfully slow and seemed to make stops about every ten feet. The heat was blasting, and I was sweating but couldn't take off my sweater because my shirt was gaping open. I got to work, but the elevator was out of service, so I had to walk. I got to my desk, and I knew that the hardest part of the day was behind me.

TRANSITIONAL WORDS AND PHRASES JOINING IDEAS IN THE SAME PARAGRAPH

I thought I would never make it to work today. <u>First,</u> my alarm clock didn't go off. <u>Then</u> I realized that my only clean shirt was missing two buttons right in front. After finding a sweater that would go over it, I ran for the bus, only to discover that the buses were running late. <u>When one finally came,</u> it was painfully slow and seemed to make stops about every ten feet. <u>To make matters worse,</u> the heat was blasting, and I was sweating but couldn't take off my sweater because my shirt was gaping open. <u>Finally,</u> I got to work, but the elevator was out of service, so I had to walk. <u>By the time</u> I got to my desk, I knew that the hardest part of the day was behind me.

Transitions are also important when you are moving from one paragraph to another. Transitional sentences can connect two paragraphs in an essay. A transitional sentence tells readers, "I'm done with that point, and I'm moving to the next," without saying those words.

Read the following examples to see how transitions are used to move smoothly from one paragraph to the next. The first example includes few transitions. In the second example, added transitions are underlined.

When you are frustrated because you have called the plumber three times and he hasn't come to fix the big leak in your shower, stay calm. Even though you are paying for the service, the leak will not be fixed if you are rude.

Start by saying you know how busy plumbers are and how hard they work. Tell the plumber that you marvel at how he manages to keep track of all his work, and to do it so professionally as well.

Try to find a funny story to tell about the leaky shower and the problems it is causing. Here you might need to stretch the truth a little, but humor helps in most situations.

Say you can be available anytime, at his convenience, to let him in. You just need to know when so you can be there. You are in his hands, at his service. Given that wide window of time, he'd look foolish not booking a time.

Even if you had to work at being nice, you achieved the end result you wanted. If he still doesn't show up, call someone else, and be polite. It works most of the time.

TRANSITIONAL SENTENCES JOINING IDEAS IN DIFFERENT PARAGRAPHS

When you are frustrated because you have called the plumber three times and he hasn't come to fix the big leak in your shower, stay calm. Even though you are paying for the service, the leak will not be fixed if you are rude. Instead, try being polite and friendly.

Start by saying you know how busy plumbers are and how hard they work. Tell the plumber that you marvel at how he manages to keep track of all his work, and to do it so professionally as well. If he is like most people, this opening will soften him up a bit because you are building his ego and being nice.

Now that he feels good, try to find a funny story to tell about the leaky shower and the problems it is causing. Here you might need to stretch the truth a little, but humor helps in most situations. At this point, the plumber is feeling pretty friendly and relaxed—he's in a good mood.

It's time to close the deal. Say you can be available anytime, at his convenience, to let him in. You just need to know when so you can be there. You are in his hands, at his service. Given that wide window of time, he'd look foolish not booking a time.

As a result of your strategy, you are *almost* assured of getting your shower leak fixed. Even if you had to work at being nice, you achieved the end result you wanted. If he still doesn't show up, call someone else, and be polite. It works most of the time.

In the box on page 97 are some, though not all, of the common transitional words and phrases that often are used to indicate time, space, importance, and other relationships between ideas.

■ PRACTICE 3   **ADD TRANSITIONAL WORDS**

TEAMWORK
Practice 3 works well in pairs. Have the pairs try to find at least two transitional words to fill each blank and then discuss which word seems more appropriate and why.

Read the following paragraphs. In each blank, add a transition that would smoothly connect the ideas. In each case, there is more than one right answer.

EXAMPLE

Today, many workers are members of labor unions that exist to protect worker rights. _However,_ until the 1930s, unions did not exist. In the 1930s, Congress passed laws that paved the way for unions. _After that,_ workers had the right to organize, bargain, and strike. _Today,_ unions are a powerful force in American politics.

Suggested answers follow.

1. The modern-day parking meter is based on an invention by a Greek scientist named Hero, who lived in the first century A.D. The machine that he invented required that the user insert a coin. _When or After_ the coin fell, it hit a lever. _Then_ out came the desired product: a cup of holy water.

2. Jackie Robinson is considered by many to be the world's greatest baseball player. He got his big start playing for the University of California while he was in college. _First_, he was signed by the Brooklyn Dodgers to play second base. _Then or Later_, in 1995, the Dodgers won the World Series.

3. Robert Goddard is largely responsible for our ability to travel in space. In 1926, Goddard launched the first liquid-fuel rocket in

Auburn, Massachusetts. __*Before*__ Goddard's launch, rockets used solid fuels that required oxygen to burn. __*However or In contrast*__ , liquid fuel needs no oxygen. __*As a result or Therefore*__ , it can operate rockets beyond the Earth's atmosphere, where there is no oxygen.

Common Transitional Words and Phrases

SPACE

above	below	inside	to the left
across	beside	near	to the right
at the bottom	beyond	next to	to the side
at the top	farther	opposite	under
behind	further	over	where

TIME

after	eventually	meanwhile	soon
as	finally	next	then
at last	first	now	when
before	last	second	while
during	later	since	

IMPORTANCE

above all	in fact	more important	most
best	in particular	most important	worst
especially			

EXAMPLE

for example	for instance	for one thing	one reason

AND

additionally	and	as well as	in addition
also	another	furthermore	moreover

(continued)

BUT			
although	in contrast	nevertheless	still
but	instead	on the other hand	yet
however			

SO			
as a result	finally	so	therefore
because			

■ **PRACTICE 4   ADD TRANSITIONAL SENTENCES**

Read the following essay. In the blanks, write a sentence that would provide a smooth transition from the idea in one paragraph to the next. You may add your transitional sentence either at the end of a paragraph or at the beginning of the next. There is no one correct answer.

The tradition of the Snake Dance is one that would rattle many people. It is a practice of the Hopi tribe of Northern California, one of the oldest North American tribes. The Snake Dance, performed in August each year, asked the plumed serpent god to give rain for the crops.

Answers will vary.

_____

_____

The Snake Dance is an impressive ritual. Participants' faces and bodies are adorned with bright paint in bold designs and images. The prayers are offered as chants, performed in voices and tones that range from hushed and low to echoing and high.

_____

_____

The Snake Dancers hang live rattlesnakes from their mouths as they chant the prayers. These huge poisonous snakes twist and wind themselves around the dancers' painted bodies. The snakes' hisses and writhing coils become a part of the prayer dance.

_____

_____

This ancient tradition is still celebrated each year. August is, in fact, a rainy period in northern California, confirming for the Hopis the success of the ritual prayers. Despite the obvious danger of dancing with a poisonous snake, participants have very rarely been bitten. Nonetheless, the Snake Dance is unlikely to become wildly popular.

2. REPEAT KEY WORDS

DEFINITION: **Key words** are terms that are closely related to your topic and main point.

By repeating key words at various points throughout your essay, you help the reader stay focused on the main point. To add variety, your key words can be different words with the same basic meaning. Be careful, however, not to overuse key words and not to stick them in at random, or your writing may seem repetitious. In the following paragraph, the key words are underlined.

KEY WORDS REPEATED AND UNDERLINED

The SAT, the test many colleges require applicants to take, is at the center of controversy once again—some people claim that the time restrictions are unfair. A group representing the rights of specially challenged test takers claim that the SAT's time limits are unfair to people who, due to physical or mental challenges, cannot complete the test items within the time allotted. For example, someone with multiple sclerosis may simply need more time on the SAT than someone without a physical challenge. Another group disagrees strongly, arguing that the time restrictions are an important part of the test. All students would do better if they had more time. This group maintains that if time limits are eased for anyone, they should be eased for everyone; otherwise the results would be unfair. This new controversy, like past ones, will undoubtedly be settled, and the SAT will remain a key factor in college admissions, fair or unfair.

PRACTICE 5   IDENTIFY REPEATED KEY WORDS

Reread the first essay in Practice 1 (p. 89), and circle the key words. Then write those key words in the spaces that follow.

Answers will vary but should include some of these words: successful,

superstar, criticized, money, wealthy, negativity, fame, critics.

For Gene Boroski's draft, see pages 80–81.

In his draft essay presented in Chapter 6, student writer Gene Boroski argued that college students who take courses online rather than on-site should not have to pay activities fees. Look back at that draft, and then read the revised version below, which indicates Gene's changes based on the three revision goals (unity, additional support and detail, and coherence).

GENE'S REVISED DRAFT WITH HIS CHANGES IN BOLD

Added to thesis statement.

Added explanation.

Added sentence that emphasizes thesis.

Added sentence that emphasizes thesis.

Added information that makes the sentence seem smoother.

As a distance education student, I should not have to pay student activities fees **which mainly benefit traditional, on-site students. Distance education is just that: It takes place with a distance between the student and the college classroom.** Distance education via computer is relatively new, and I think that college administrators have not adequately thought about what this means for student activities fees, for one thing. **In some ways we are like on-site students and should be charged as they are, but I draw the line at student activities fees that benefit only the on-site students. I don't mind paying my fair share, but paying for services I will never use is not part of that share.**

Although I am a registered student at Carson, all of my courses are offered online, so I never come to the campus. The courses don't even exist in real time, so I may log on to the course at 11:00 at night if that's the time that's most convenient for me. I do not interact face-to-face with my professor, but we communicate well, and often, by email. I can also interact with other distance education students that way. It is a very different way of taking classes, but it works well for people like me who can't get to campus during regularly scheduled classes.

Even though I do not go to the campus, my tuition is the same as for on-site students. This seems reasonable to me because I am getting the same kind of instruction and knowledge. For example, my tuition helps pay professors' salaries, which I believe is fair whether I'm taking their class in the classroom or at a distance. In that way, on-site and distance education students are equal and should be charged equally. Unfortunately, though, because the courses are online, I am not eligible for academic assistance as on-site students are. **In that way, on-site students have an advantage that I don't have, and no one says that is unfair.**

Added sentence that makes a smooth transition between supporting details.

There are differences between on-site education and distance education, at least in some people's minds, probably because distance education is so new.

One other difference is that distance education students do not use campus facilities, so why should we pay for them? For example, I don't use expensive facilities such as the cafeteria, campus health, campus security, or parking. **I don't benefit from landscaping and building maintenance because I'm never there to see either. I don't use lights or restrooms, and I don't care how prompt snow removal is.** Yes, I use the computer network, but that's already in place; it doesn't cost more to run a course online.

It is time to realize that there are differences in the college experience of on-site and distance education students. I don't ask the college to support my online service provider fees or the electricity I use because I am taking the course online, so why should I be asked to pay for services that I don't use?

> Added transition that helps reader follow Gene's essay.

> Added detail.

> Added detail.

For another example of a student's draft and revision, see pages 18–21.

THINKING CRITICALLY TO REVISE AN ESSAY

FOCUS   After a break, reread your draft with a fresh perspective.

ASK
- What's my point or position? Does my thesis statement clearly state my main point?

- Does my essay have the following?
  - —An introductory paragraph
  - —Three or more body paragraphs
  - —A topic sentence for each paragraph that supports the main point
  - —A forceful concluding paragraph that reminds my readers of my main point and makes an observation

- Does my essay have unity?
  - —Do all of the major support points relate directly to my main point?
  - —Do all the supporting details in each body paragraph relate to the paragraph's topic sentence?

TEAMWORK
Have students break into small groups and use the questions in this guide as prompts for peer review.

TEACHING TIP
Make revision concrete by challenging students to find at least one place in their drafts where detail can be added and at least one place where a transition can be added.

(continued)

—Have I avoided drifting away from my main point?

• Do I have enough support?

—Do the topic sentences together give enough support or evidence for the main point?

—Does each topic sentence have enough support within its paragraph?

—Would more detail strengthen my support?

• Is my essay coherent?

—Have I used transitional words to link ideas?

—Have I used transitional sentences to link paragraphs?

—Have I repeated key words?

—Do both the sentences and the paragraphs flow smoothly?

WRITE   Revise your draft, making any improvements you can.

Use a Computer to Revise Your Draft

Open your draft file and use Save As (in the File menu) to begin a new file for your revision work (these instructions apply to Microsoft Word). Work through the list of questions from the Thinking Critically guide. As you revise your essay, use the highlighting tool to help you concentrate on specific areas, such as your thesis statement, introductory paragraph, and main support points. (To activate highlighting, select from the formatting toolbar. If this toolbar is not visible, select Customize from the Tools menu, and then select Formatting from the Toolbar options.) Highlighting will help you focus on particular parts of your essay, but remember to deselect highlighting before you begin to make specific changes.

When you have revised as much of your essay as you possibly can, your word processor's Insert and Format menus will help you make certain that your pages are numbered, your margins are correct (usually teachers expect one-inch margins), and that your spacing (usually single or double spacing) is uniform. If your teacher has assigned a certain word length, you can quickly check your essay with Word Count in the Tools menu.

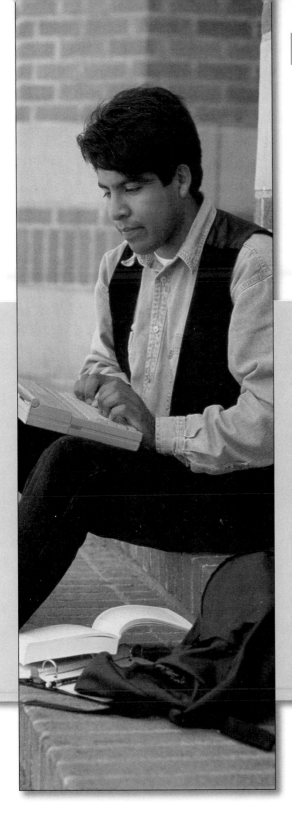

PART TWO

Writing Different Kinds of Essays

8

Narration

Writing That Tells Stories

You Know This
You often use narration.
- You tell a friend about an odd experience you had.
- You tell your boss why you were late.
- You explain what a movie was about.

Understand What Narration Is

DEFINITION: **Narration** is writing that tells a story of an event or experience.

IDEA JOURNAL
Write about the most important thing that happened to you this week.

⬛ Four Basics of Good Narration

1. It reveals something of importance to you (your main point).
2. It includes all of the major events of the story.
3. It uses details to bring the story to life for your audience.
4. It presents the events in a clear order, usually according to when they happened.

Sharing stories is one important way in which we communicate with one another. Whether they are serious or humorous, stories provide information and examples that can show, explain, or prove a point. To show that a story is funny, you present events that make this point clear; to explain that you were late for a good reason, you give details; to prove that you have experience, you recall notable moments during that experience.

DISCUSSION
After students have thought of a good story, ask them what's important about it. Emphasize that a good narration, even a humorous one, must reveal something of importance.

POINT OF VIEW IN NARRATION

In a narration, the events you include and the way you describe them create a story that is based on your point of view. For example, two people

Patty Maloney

CLINICAL NURSE SPECIALIST

Patty Maloney

BACKGROUND: Patty says that she was "always a terrible student who was very shy and lacking in confidence." She hated to read, hated to write, and hated school. After graduating from high school, she took one course at a community college, but she quit because she didn't think she could do it.

She worked as a typist for an insurance company but soon realized she wanted to work with young children. She got a job as a nursing assistant at Shriner's Burn Center in Boston, working with children in the intensive care unit. She loved the children and was impressed by how much the nurses helped them.

Patty completed a one-year program and became a licensed practical nurse (LPN). She continued to work at Shriner's as an LPN for another six years, but she wanted to go beyond this level of nursing. While continuing to work, she became certified as a registered nurse (RN) and got a job in the newborn intensive care unit at Children's Hospital in Boston. As she worked, she took more courses and earned bachelor's and master's degrees in nursing.

In the various nursing degree programs she completed, Patty had to do lots of writing: long papers, summaries of articles, analyses of diseases and of case studies. Because she still felt that she was not a strong writer (particularly when it came to grammar), she always had a couple of other people read her papers before she turned them in.

EMPLOYER: Children's Hospital, Boston

COLLEGE(S)/DEGREES: Massachusetts Bay Community College, Labouré Junior College, Massachusetts College of Pharmacy (B.S.N.), Northeastern University (M.S.N.)

TYPES OF WRITING ON THE JOB: Observations of patients, notes about patients, memos to colleagues, instructions for junior staff, lots of email

HOW PATTY USES NARRATION: Notes on patients are usually narratives. They need to be concise, precise, and clear, as both Patty and others will need to refer to them for patients' treatment. For an example of how Patty uses narration, see Narration in the Workplace, page 112.

COMPUTER SKILLS: Word processing and spreadsheet programs

TEAMWORK ON THE JOB: Most of the nursing work at Children's Hospital is teamwork, with primary teams of four nurses assigned to children. Team members have regular conferences, write weekly summaries of patient care and patients' conditions, and write reports that they share with each other. They must work together well and communicate well, both in speech and in writing; children's lives depend on their effective cooperation.

FUTURE GOAL: Patty has held her current position only for a short time, and her goal is to be successful in her many new roles: consultant, direct patient care provider, researcher, and new staff educator.

who witness or participate in the same series of events may give very different accounts because they focus on different aspects of the events or perceive the whole series differently. The stories that Gloria and Mason tell in the following two paragraphs reflect their different points of view regarding the same experience.

ESL
Ask students to describe any events they see differently than their classmates or coworkers because of language or cultural differences.

GLORIA'S STORY

This morning Mason and I set out for a day at the beach. It was supposed to be great, but Mason's stubborn behavior ruined everything. First, he took the longest route, so we hit traffic that we would have avoided by going the short route. Then we got lost. I suggested that we stop and ask directions, but Mason said he could get us there. After another hour of driving, we passed an intersection that we'd crossed earlier. I again suggested that we stop and ask directions, but Mason wasn't buying it. So we drove some more. Finally, we were about to run out of gas, so we pulled into a gas station. While Mason was filling the tank, I asked the attendant for directions. I swear if we hadn't needed gas, we'd still be driving around looking for that beach!

MASON'S STORY

This morning Gloria and I set out for a day at the beach. It would have been a great day if Gloria hadn't wanted to pick a fight. First she insisted I was going the wrong way, it was going to take us longer, and we'd hit more traffic. Then she decided we were lost. I knew about where we were going and knew I could figure it out. Gloria kept on nagging me to stop and ask directions. When we were almost there, I decided to get gas, and she had to ask the attendant for directions. I don't know what was going on with her, but she was really on my case.

As you can see, the events are the same, but the stories aren't; they are told from two very different points of view. When you write a narration, be careful to describe events in a way that will tell the story you want to tell.

MAJOR EVENTS AND DETAILS IN NARRATION

The support for the main point of your narration is the presentation and explanation of the major events in the story. These major events are your support points and will become the topic sentences for the body paragraphs in your essay. Ask yourself what the major events are and what was so important about them.

For more on supporting a point, see Chapter 4.

If you give only the major events, your readers will not be able to experience those events as you did. You must also supply **supporting details** that bring the experience to life for the readers.

For example, one student stated the main point of an event in the following thesis: *Skydiving is the most thrilling experience I have ever had.* Then that student presented major events and supporting details about those events.

MAJOR EVENTS	SUPPORTING DETAILS
opening door	rush of cold air
	flapping of suit
jumping	lump in throat
	goosebumps
parachute	drifting to ground

CHRONOLOGICAL (TIME) ORDER IN NARRATION

DISCUSSION
As a class, outline Gloria's and Mason's stories, from page 107. Discuss the differences and similarities in the outlines' use of chronological order.

Because narration tells a story, it uses chronological (time) order. Start at the beginning of the story, and describe the events in the sequence in which they occurred.

Introduction (including thesis)

First major event

    Details about the first event

Second major event

    Details about the second event

For more on chronological order, see page 59.

Third major event

    Details about the third event

Conclusion

DISCUSSION
Choose a general topic and have the class generate sample sentences for intro- duction, body, and conclusion para- graphs using the list of common time transitions.

Time transitions (see p. 109) are important in narration because they make the order of events clear to readers. Writers of narration use these common transitions not only within a paragraph to move from one detail about the event to the next but also between paragraphs to move from one major event to the next.

When you are writing narration, particularly for college or work, make sure that your essay has a main point that readers can recognize. Your readers should not come to the end of your narration and think, "So what?" Here are some ways you might use narration:

COLLEGE

• In a marketing course, you recount the history of Coca-Cola's advertising strategies.

Common Time Transitions

after	eventually	meanwhile	soon
as	finally	next	then
at last	first	now	when
before	last	second	while
during	later	since	

WORK

• You write up what took place in a staff meeting.

EVERYDAY LIFE

• You write an accident report for your insurance company.

For more on transitions, see pages 94–99.

DISCUSSION
As a class, generate other possible uses of narration in each of these three areas.

Read and Analyze Narration

Read the following examples of narration—one each from college, the workplace, and everyday life—and answer the questions that accompany each. Reading and analyzing the examples will help you understand how to write a good narration essay.

1. NARRATION IN COLLEGE

The following essay was part of Giovanni Bohorquez's application to business schools. (Bohorquez is featured in the Profile of Success in Chapter 12.) Read the essay and complete the questions that follow it.

From the time I was very young, I saw challenge in difficult situations and always tried my best to meet that challenge. If lemonade stands made millions, I would be rich. I have made lemonade out of the many lemons that life has tossed me, and that experience has served me well.

My teenage parents divorced after a year of marriage, and virtually all of my relatives took their turns raising me. At the age of eleven, I left Colombia to come to the United States. I arrived in the poor town of Elizabeth, New Jersey, to find that my dad was not excited to have me living with him. Those days opened my eyes to poverty. I didn't know it at the time, but hardship was just what I needed. I became a hard worker and helped my family greatly by becoming monetarily self-sufficient at age twelve.

I learned the value of work, knowledge, time, and money. With my work money, I managed to send my mother school money and to get cool clothes, two cars, three guitars, and lots of records. I became responsible, but I was just making the best out of a bad situation.

At fourteen, I got a job in a bicycle shop and came up with the idea of forming a cycling team sponsored by the shop. It was a great success, and the shop owner loved having us advertise to the local aficionados. We never won awards, but we had great fun and got in great shape during the two years I was there. I understood then that I could help other people like me who were trying to find a positive escape from their problems.

When I was fifteen, I came to California and started a guitar club in my high school. I got support from music companies and the school, and in just a month we had a budget, facilities, and twenty members. To culminate the year, we had two concerts. We had a sound engineer, lighting, the school theater, photographers, and videographers—and we even appeared in the local newspaper.

When I got to junior college, I was working sixty hours a week. I managed to become a Business Senator, though, and the vice president of a chapter of the Society of Hispanic Professional Engineers (SHPE). In student government we decided how to use the student funds and helped a lot of school initiatives get started. At SHPE I headed events to help at-risk high school students and organized trips to events at universities. These were some of my hardest times in terms of work and school, but the school activities kept me going. Out of my groups, a good 80 percent of us went to top universities.

When I transferred to UCLA, I wanted to take the hardest, most marketable classes. So I minored in computer programming, specialized in econometrics (data analysis), and even took half a year of Mandarin Chinese. It all paid off. A year before finishing school I already had an offer from the consulting group at Ernst & Young. In order to help other (students,) I started the UCLA Student Consulting Society. We guided students into the world of consulting through workshops and a course roadmap. A good ten members (50 percent of the group) went into Big Five accounting firms and *Fortune* 100 companies.

✓ I am still the same person today. I still like to help my community and the programs that got me where I am. At Ernst & Young, I got the company to participate in SHPE's national yearly event in which more than seven thousand young professionals from all over the world meet top firms. I led EY's participation at the Stanford Career Day for two years. I often participate in Habitat for Humanity events, and I have been an active mentor for the Puente Program (an outreach program for college students at risk of dropping out) for many years. Through programs such as UCLA's Riordan Fellows, I have helped put together community events for needy children and the homeless. I get great joy out of contributing and helping out. I hope to contribute to my business school the same things I have contributed to other programs. I have a great deal of positive experience in the challenge of excelling in difficult situations and have learned to welcome these challenges.

1. Who is Giovanni's **audience** for this essay? _admissions representative,_ _business school_

For more on audience and purpose, see pages 7–9.

2. What is Giovanni's **purpose** in telling this story? _to show how he has_ _met life's challenges and to make a good impression so that he will be_ _accepted into the M.B.A. program_

TEAMWORK
Have students work on this activity in pairs.

3. Fill in the blanks with the topic and the main point of Giovanni's essay

TOPIC: _Giovanni's life_

MAIN POINT: _meeting difficult challenges has had positive effects_

4. Double-underline the **thesis statement**.

5. Put a check mark (✓) at the beginning of each **topic sentence**.

6. Underline the **supporting details** that Giovanni uses, and indicate which you think are the most effective by starring them. Be prepared to discuss your choices. *Answers may vary.*

TEACHING TIP
Ask students what they would write about on an application such as Giovanni's.

7. Circle the (transitions) that Giovanni used in his essay.

For a list of the four basics of good narration, see page 105.

8. Does Giovanni's essay have the **four basics of good narration**? Why or why not?   *Answers may vary.* _____

2. NARRATION IN THE WORKPLACE

As a neonatal clinical nurse specialist, Patty Maloney cares for at-risk infants. The following is a narrative that describes her experience with a patient, the patient's parents, and her staff. Nurses need to write accounts of their patients regularly, and those accounts must be clear, descriptive, and accurate. The narration that follows was part of a seminar for nurses interested in becoming managers.

In the neonatal intensive care unit, we work with high-risk infants. Because we are health care professionals, we must maintain objectivity and clinical distance, a tall order when patients are tiny humans just beginning life. As a clinical nurse specialist who manages other staff, I am responsible for helping others see the complete picture when they may be too involved with a patient to do so. Late one recent Christmas Eve, my management skills were put to a painful test.

The patient was a premature infant who weighed only 700 grams and who had been in critical condition since birth. (On Christmas Eve,) the patient went into shock and experienced respiratory failure. ✓Because of the holiday, the complete medical team wasn't on-site, but the physician and nurse who were caring for this child were unsure about how much longer the child would live. They were faced with a difficult question: Will maximum invasive medical therapy help this child?

✓The attending physician and nurse concluded that they had exhausted all treatment options. They (then) decided to call the family in to spend time with the infant and to discuss redirection of support (which means, in essence, acknowledging that most avenues have been exhausted). Redirection of support would avoid any treatment that would be both radical and unlikely to save the patient.

✓ Before contacting the parents, however, the nurse sought my advice. She asked me if I felt there was anything more that she and the doctor could offer the infant. Based on the information I had received, I believed that further treatment was unlikely to change the child's condition. I offered that opinion.

The situation was particularly painful for the team: They did not want to unnecessarily prolong the inevitable death of the infant, so they were inclined to call the parents right away to discuss redirection of support. At this point, I realized that the caregivers' discomfort was preventing them from considering all aspects of the situation. ✓ It was my responsibility to fill in the whole picture.

✓ I wanted to ease the pain of my colleagues, which I well understood, but I did not believe that calling the family on Christmas Eve was the best course of action. I explained that I fully appreciated why the team wanted to act quickly, but I also called upon my experience in working with bereaved families, which taught me that the most intense bereavement comes when a loved one dies on a holiday. In this particular case, I reasoned, the child was not going to die in the next few days, so the only reason to call the parents was to ease the medical team's pain. Then I suggested that we wait until after Christmas to meet with the parents, which would also mean that the rest of the medical team could be present and involved in the decision-making process. My colleagues agreed, and they planned a care conference for the day after Christmas.

Personally, I wanted to ease my colleagues' discomfort. ✓ Professionally, I couldn't do that. I had to give advice based on a range of circumstances that included my responsibilities to the patient, the patient's family, and my staff. Certainly I won't forget that Christmas Eve, but I know we made the right decisions.

1. What is Patty's **purpose** for writing? *to tell a story that shows how she managed a difficult situation*

For more on purpose, see pages 7–9.

2. Double-underline the **thesis statement**.

3. Put a check mark (✓) at the beginning of each **topic sentence**.

4. Underline the **supporting details** that Patty uses, and place a star by those you think are the most effective. Be prepared to discuss your choices. *Answers may vary.*

5. Circle the (time transitions) that Patty uses.

6. What key words does she repeat? *Answers might include: infant, objectivity, see complete picture, patient, parents, family, responsibility, decision, manager.*

7. Underline the sentence in the concluding paragraph that relates back to the introduction.

3. NARRATION IN EVERYDAY LIFE

The following is a report to an insurance company following a car accident.

The details of my accident involving a truck on the afternoon of June 1, 2002, will indicate that the truck driver was at fault. I hope this account will help clarify the matter for insurance purposes. I do not want to have my rates raised when another person was at fault.

I was driving north on Route 16 and was following a large truck with the license plate 3819KG. I had followed the truck for about one mile when its left turn indicator started blinking. The truck slowed, and I slowed behind it.

Then the truck pulled into the left lane. I thought the driver was getting ready to make the left turn that he had indicated by turning on his left blinker. The truck then stopped.

Because the truck was mostly in the left lane, I had plenty of room in my lane to continue on, which I did at a very slow pace. All of a sudden the truck turned right and slammed into my car. Fortunately, the truck was going very slowly, but my small Ford Escort was left with significant damage on the left side.

The driver and I then exchanged licenses. He claimed that, during this whole time, it was his intention to turn right and that he had moved left in order to allow clearance for his truck. When I said that he had signaled a left turn, he denied it and refused further discussion.

I would not have pulled to the side of a huge truck just as it was turn-ing in my direction. But all indications were that the driver was making a left turn, not a right one. As I explained to the police officer who came to the accident scene, the truck driver's actions clearly caused this accident. Please consider my letter carefully because I do not want to be charged higher insurance rates for an accident that I did not cause. Thank you for your consideration.

DISCUSSION
Ask students to reread the letter to the insurance company through the eyes of the insurance inspector. Would he or she be convinced?

1. What is the writer's **purpose** in preparing this report?

   to report the events of the accident and show the insurance agent that

   the driver of the car was not at fault

For more on purpose and audience, see pages 7–9.

2. Who is the **audience**? *an insurance agent*

3. Double-underline the **thesis statement**.

4. Identify each of the **major events** with a check mark.

5. Underline the **supporting details**.

6. Circle the (**transitions**,) including transitional sentences.

7. Underline the sentence in the concluding paragraph that relates back to the introduction.

Write a Narration Essay

In this section, you will write your own narration essay. To do so, follow this sequence:

REVIEW the four basics of good narration (p. 105).

CHOOSE your writing assignment (p. 116).

WRITE your narration using the step-by-step Writing Guide (p. 118).

CHECK your final essay (p. 122).

■ **WRITING ASSIGNMENT 1   COLLEGE, WORK, EVERYDAY LIFE**

TEACHING TIP
Assign these writing prompts as journal entries. Then invite students to expand on one for their narration essay. Have students use the Thinking Critically questions on page 118 to help them select which entry to revise.

Write a narration essay on *one* of the following topics, or on a topic of your own choice.

COLLEGE

• Tell a story about one of your professors that shows something significant about this person.
• Explain the most important or interesting event that has happened to you in college.
• Recount the events of one historic day.

WORK

• Tell the story of something positive you did at work (some achievement).
• Explain what you learned from getting or doing your first job.
• Describe an incident that shows your boss as _____ (supportive, fair, unfair, clueless, sharp, unrealistic, honest, dishonest).

EVERYDAY LIFE

• Tell the story of your first love (or your most recent one), showing how it changed or influenced you.
• Write about an event when you were proud of someone in your family.
• Write about an event when you were proud or ashamed of your behavior.

■ **WRITING ASSIGNMENT 2   USE THE INTERNET**

For advice about how to cite a source, see Chapter 20.

WRITE A COMPLAINT: The Web site Complaints.com (**<www.complaints. com>**) contains complaints about all kinds of products and services. Select either "Read Complaints by Date Posted" or "List of Most Recent Complaints," and read some examples of complaints. As you read, think of similar complaints that you have had, and then write an essay that traces your experience with a particular product or service.

WRITING ASSIGNMENT 3   YOUR JOB INTERVIEW

Read the situation that follows, and then choose *one* of the assignment options (3A or 3B) that appear after it.

> SITUATION: You have an interview at a company where you really want to work. You are determined to get this job, so you search the library and the Web for information on interviewing, and you find a source that includes sample preparation questions. You can easily answer the first few sample questions (about job history, for example), but then you come to some questions that require you to talk about yourself. You realize that you are less prepared for these, and you decide to write out some answers to help you prepare for your interview.

ASSIGNMENT OPTION 3A: RESPONSE TO THE SITUATION

Write a narration essay in response to the following interview question: What is your greatest personal or professional strength? Your essay should include a chain of specific events that shows this strength in action. Remember that you want to present yourself as a strong candidate for the job. To do so, you must not only present your strengths as an employee but also support your claims with concrete details and examples.

ASSIGNMENT OPTION 3B: ANOTHER PERSPECTIVE

Addressing a possible future employer, write a letter that traces a chain of specific events that demonstrate one of your personal or professional strengths. Begin your letter with this opening sentence:

I believe that I am ideally suited for the position at _____

(fill in the name of the company or organization) and look forward to

meeting the challenges of the _____ job (include

position for which you would like to interview).

Writing Guide

Narration

Follow the steps in this Writing Guide to help you prewrite, draft, revise, and edit your narration. Check off each step as you complete it.

THINKING CRITICALLY ABOUT NARRATION

FOCUS   Think about who will read your narration and what point you want your readers to understand from your story.

ASK   • What experience or series of events do I want to write about?
          • What is important about the story from my point of view?
          • What main point do I want to make with this story?
          • To make that point, what major events do I need to include?
          • What details, examples, and facts will bring these events to life and show my readers what the point is and why it is important?
          • Should I include conversation (something that was said)?

TEACHING TIP
Explain to students that the Thinking Critically guide will help them understand how to approach the writing assignment.

PREWRITE TO EXPLORE YOUR TOPIC

Prewriting for narration involves considering several possible experiences or stories to retell and deciding on the one that you can bring to life for your readers. Your topic should also reveal something important.

For more on purpose and audience, see pages 7–9.

_____   Determine your purpose for writing.

_____   Identify the audience for your essay.

_____   Decide what story you want to tell.

_____   Use a prewriting technique (freewriting, listing/brainstorming, questioning, discussing, clustering) to explore your impressions and thoughts about what happened; how it affected you or others; and what the story shows, explains, or proves.

WRITE A THESIS STATEMENT

The thesis statement in narration includes the topic and the main point you want to make about it.

| Topic | + | Main point | = | Thesis statement |

Skydiving   is the most thrilling experience I have ever had.

The details of my accident   will indicate that the truck driver was at fault.

_____ Decide what is important about the story you will tell from your point of view. Imagine telling your story and hearing someone say, "So what?" How would you respond?

_____ Specify the point you want your readers to understand from your narrative.

_____ Write a working thesis statement that includes your topic and main point.

SUPPORT YOUR POINT

Your support in narration includes the major events in your story and the supporting details that explain the events for readers.

_____ List all of the major events in the story.

_____ Review your working thesis statement, and drop any events that do not help you explain, show, or prove your main point. Make your thesis more specific.

_____ Choose at least three major events that will help your readers understand your main point.

_____ Add supporting details about each event that will help your reader experience it as you did. It might help to think about how familiar your readers are with your topic and what details would bring your major events to life for them.

MAKE A PLAN

Making a written plan—an outline—helps you decide how to order your narration. Narration usually tells a story in chronological (time) order, presenting events in the order in which they happened.

TEAMWORK
In pairs or small groups, have students share the plans for their narrative with their peers. Classmates can make suggestions about the logical order of the plan, as well as suggest other supporting details that might be helpful for understanding the narrative.

_____ Arrange your major events according to when they occurred (in chronological order, first to last).

_____ Write a plan or an outline for your narration that includes your main support points (the major events) and supporting details for each event.

DRAFT

Drafting a narration means writing in complete sentences and including the following:

- An introduction
- A thesis statement that communicates your topic and main point
- The major events in the story, supported by concrete, specific details
- A conclusion that reminds your readers of the main point and makes an observation about the importance of the story

_____ Think about how you can show your readers what's important about the story you are telling.

_____ Write an introduction that hooks your readers' interest and presents your thesis statement.

_____ Using your plan or outline, write a topic sentence for each of the main events. Be sure that each topic sentence is directly related to your thesis statement.

_____ Write body paragraphs that include concrete, specific details that further explain your support points and bring the major events of your story to life. Your readers should be able to experience the events of the story as you did through the supporting details.

_____ Write a concluding paragraph that reminds your readers of your main point and makes a final observation about the importance of the story.

_____ Title your essay.

REVISE

TEAMWORK
Have students use these prompts in small groups, taking turns reviewing each group member's draft.

Revising means changing whole sentences or paragraphs to make your writing clearer or stronger. To revise a narration, imagine that you do not know the events in the story or their importance. Read your draft, looking for the following:

- Places where the ideas are off the main point (revising for unity)
- Gaps in information or detail (revising for support and detail)
- Areas in need of "glue" to move readers smoothly from one point to the next (revising for coherence)

_____ Ask another person to read your draft and give you feedback.

For more on peer review, see pages 87–88.

_____ Begin revising by considering how you can make the main point of the story clearer or more convincing to your readers.

_____ Reread your thesis statement. Revise to make it clearer, more concrete, and more forceful.

_____ Reread the body of your narration to see if the events and details support your thesis. If you have left out key events that would show, explain, or prove your thesis, add them now. Add any additional supporting details that would help your readers experience the events as you did or as you want them to.

_____ Reread your introduction. Make changes if the opening is dull or lacks force.

_____ Reread your conclusion to make sure that it is energetic and convincing, reminds readers of your main point, and makes an observation on the importance of the story you have told. Your purpose in telling the story should be clear to your readers.

_____ Add transition words and sentences to connect your ideas smoothly.

_____ Make at least five changes to your draft to improve the unity, support, or coherence of your narration or to make the introduction, thesis statement, or conclusion stronger or more convincing.

EDIT

Some grammar, spelling, word use, or punctuation errors may confuse your readers and make it difficult for them to understand a point you are trying to make. Even if they do not confuse your readers, errors detract from the effectiveness and overall quality of your writing. Edit your narration carefully, correcting any errors you find.

_____ Ask a classmate or a friend to read your narration and highlight any errors.

_____ Use the spell checker or grammar checker on your computer, but do not rely on those programs to catch all errors.

_____ Read your narration carefully, looking for errors in grammar, spelling, word use, or punctuation. Focus first on sentence fragments, run-on sentences, problems with subject–verb agreement, problems with verbs, and other areas where you know you often make errors.

_____ Print a clean, final copy.

_____ Ask yourself: Is this the best I can do?

A FINAL CHECK BEFORE HANDING IN YOUR NARRATION ESSAY

If you've followed the Writing Guide for narration, your essay will already include the four basics of good narration. Use this list to double-check each basic.

_____ My thesis statement reveals what is important about the story.

_____ Each of my paragraphs has a topic sentence that presents a major event in the story.

_____ Each paragraph in the body of my essay has supporting details to show or explain the major event. (I have found at least three supporting details.)

_____ My narration presents the major events in chronological order and uses transitions to connect ideas. (I have found at least three transitions.)

9

Illustration

Writing That Shows Examples

> **You Know This**
> Anytime you give examples to explain what you mean, you are using illustration.
> • You tell a friend why you like or dislike your job.
> • You answer the question "Like what?"
> • You select incidents from your experience to show that you are qualified for a different job or new responsibilities.

Understand What Illustration Is

DEFINITION: **Illustration** is writing that uses examples to show, explain, or prove a point. Giving examples is the basis of all good writing and speaking. You make a statement, and then you give an example that shows what you mean.

> IDEA JOURNAL
> Write about the things that keep your life busy.

■■ Four Basics of Good Illustration

1. It makes a point.
2. It gives specific and detailed examples to show, explain, or prove the point.
3. It uses examples that the readers will understand.
4. It uses enough examples to get the writer's point across.

Illustrations make explanations clear and general statements powerful. They draw readers into essays by providing specifics that make the point.

EXAMPLES FOR ILLUSTRATION

For effective illustration, focus on finding examples that show, explain, or prove your thesis. Listing/brainstorming and clustering are particularly useful prewriting techniques for exploring an illustration topic.

> For more on prewriting techniques, see pages 27–31.

123

Pamela O'Berry Evans

DEPUTY COMMONWEALTH ATTORNEY

Pamela O'Berry Evans

BACKGROUND: Pam grew up in a low-income housing project in Philadelphia, one of five children raised by a working mother. Early in school, she was a gifted student but was ridiculed by her friends for doing well and for speaking standard English. In high school, she wanted to be popular, so she turned away from academics and took business prep classes. She had fun, but three months before graduating Pam realized that she wanted to go to college. She had not taken the SAT and did not have good grades. Fortunately, her high school counselor pointed her in the direction of the ACT 101 program. She entered Shippensburg University through this special program and had to work hard on her study skills in order to pass courses.

EMPLOYER: Virginia Commonwealth Attorney's Office

COLLEGE(S)/DEGREES: Shippensburg University (B.A.), American University (J.D.L.)

TYPES OF WRITING ON THE JOB: Letters to crime victims, letters and email among many state and city agencies, legal briefs, correspondence with judges, indictments (summary of the crime), reports tracking crimes and court dates

HOW PAM USES ILLUSTRATION: Legal briefs must include examples of behaviors, actions to be taken, or restrictions. For an example of how Pam uses illustration, see Illustration in the Workplace, page 128.

COMPUTER SKILLS: Word processing, Excel, PowerPoint

TEAMWORK ON THE JOB: Pam leads several teams of attorneys who share information and experience with each other while building prosecution cases against defendants.

FUTURE GOAL: Pam says her goal is to always keep learning. She is also planning to move from the public sector into a private firm that handles civil, rather than criminal, cases.

For example, the writer of the thesis *Homeschooling is beneficial to both the child and the parent* would focus her prewriting on finding examples of benefits of homeschooling. Here are some examples from her brainstorming:

individualized to child	*parent and child have control*
parent and child together	*more flexibility*
at child's own pace	*considers child's learning style*
one-on-one	*education as part of regular life*

SUPPORT FOR ILLUSTRATION

For more on support, see Chapter 4.

An illustration essay may use several examples as support points. The writer of the prewriting on the previous page selected "individualized to child" as one support point and asked herself, "What do I mean? How? In what ways?" to find supporting details.

She also chose "parent and child have control" as another major example that would support the thesis. She then asked herself, "How do they have more control?" and listed potential supporting details:

control over materials used (what books, what computer programs,

what approach)

control over time of instruction (what hours of the day, based on

child's natural rhythms, vacations—not tied to a school's calendar)

ORDER OF IMPORTANCE FOR ILLUSTRATION

For more on order of importance, see page 60.

An illustration often uses order of importance to organize several examples, saving the most vivid, convincing one for last. Keep your readers in mind as you arrange your examples. A typical plan for an illustration essay might look like this:

Introduction (including thesis)

First example

    Supporting details that explain the first example

Second example

    Supporting details that explain the second example

Third (and most important) example

    Supporting details that explain the third example

Conclusion (refers back to your main point and makes an observation)

Illustrations often use transitions such as the following to lead from one major example to the next or from one supporting detail to the next.

For more on transitions, see pages 94–97.

Common Illustration Transitions

also	finally	for instance	in addition
another	for example	for one thing	one example

Whenever we explain something, we use examples to show what we mean. Here are some ways that you might use illustration:

COLLEGE

- In a criminal justice course, you are asked to discuss and give examples of the most common criminal violations.

WORK

- Your written self-evaluation includes specific and measurable examples of how well (or poorly) you performed your job and achieved your goals.

EVERYDAY LIFE

- You take your car to a mechanic, and you give the mechanic examples that show how the car is not running properly.

Read and Analyze Illustration

Read the following examples of illustration—one each from college, the workplace, and everyday life—and answer the questions that accompany each. Reading and analyzing the examples will help you understand how to write good illustration.

1. ILLUSTRATION IN COLLEGE

Read the essay by Lindsey Ducharme, a student in a first-year writing course, and answer the questions that follow it.

Italy: My Dream Destination

Lindsey Ducharme

Where would you go if you had the opportunity to travel anywhere in the world? If I could visit any location, I would go somewhere filled with fascinating sights. I would visit a place I have seen often in movies and magazines. I would visit Italy, an enchanting country of diverse landscapes, historic landmarks, and inspiring art masterpieces.

✓ Italy's first allure is its diverse landscapes, with cosmopolitan cities, small villages, and silent countrysides all within its boundaries. One day I could be exploring an ancient, walled hill town, and the next day I could be purchasing jewelry from a vendor on a crowded street in front of a small restaurant in Florence. (Later) in my visit, I could be having lunch on the rocky cliff of a very quiet and peaceful fishing village that overlooks the Mediterranean Sea.

✓ (In addition to its many diverse cities and villages,) Italy is filled with historic landmarks. In Rome alone, there are many places I would visit, such as the remnants of the ancient Roman Forum. There I would observe the meeting place where noblemen gathered in the times of Julius Caesar and Cleopatra. (Across from) the ruins of the Forum is the great Colosseum, a stadium where gladiators fought to the death to entertain the upper class. The living quarters of former Italian leader Benito Mussolini would be a quick stop on my way to the home of the Catholic Church's living authority: the Vatican. While visiting places important in Italy's history would be a large part of my agenda, (I would also like to view some of the world's greatest works of art.)

✓ (Not only is Italy a land of assorted landscapes and historical sites, it is also an art connoisseur's dream.) Italy is home to Michelangelo's extraordinary sculpture of David, which resides in the Academy, an art museum in Florence. Another famous work of Michelangelo's that I would love to see, the *Pietà,* is in St. Peter's Church in Rome. It is a moving and incredibly lifelike sculpture of Christ dying. (My last stop) would be the Sistine Chapel, which houses hundreds of great works of art that depict biblical stories.

Where would I go if I could travel anywhere? I would set out for Italy, land of diverse scenery, historical landmarks, and majestic artwork. It is filled with places to go and sights to see, all of which are different from what I have known. But Italy would just be my first choice: I hope to travel widely to experience the world's rich wonders and diverse cultures.

1. Who is Lindsey's **audience** for this essay? *her instructor and other students*

2. What is Lindsey's **purpose** for writing? *to explain why Italy would be her favorite place to visit*

For more on audience and purpose, see pages 7–9.

TEAMWORK
This activity works
well in pairs or small
groups.

3. Fill in the blanks with the **topic** and **main point** of Lindsey's essay.

   TOPIC: _Italy_

   MAIN POINT: _an enchanting country_

4. Double-underline the **thesis statement**.

5. Put a check mark (✓) next to the **topic sentences** that present the major examples supporting Lindsey's thesis.

DISCUSSION
Ask students how the
essay would be
different if Lindsey
were writing a
description rather than
an illustration.

6. Underline the **supporting details** that Lindsey uses to describe her examples.

7. What **introductory technique** does Lindsey use?

   asks a question

8. Circle the (transitions) and (transitional sentences) in Lindsey's essay.

9. How does Lindsey relate the **conclusion** back to the introduction?

   She repeats the question she asked in her introduction.

For a list of the four
basics of good illus-
tration, see page 123.

10. Does Lindsey's essay have the **four basics of good illustration**?

    Why or why not? _Answers will vary._

2. ILLUSTRATION IN THE WORKPLACE

The following is an example of a legal brief of the type that attorney Pamela O'Berry Evans writes nearly every day. (The names have been changed.) Although this document is not written in essay form, it is an example of illustration in the workplace. Read the brief, and answer the questions that follow it.

1
2
3
4
5
6
7
8
9
10
11
12
13
14
15
16
17
18
19

VIRGINIA:
IN THE CIRCUIT COURT FOR
THE CITY OF RICHMOND

JANE PARSONS, **Petitioner,**
versus
HECTOR RAZO, **Respondent.**

Preliminary Protective Order
     This day pursuant to Virginia Code sections 19.2-152.9-10, Petitioner's affidavit, and good cause having been shown, it is ordered that a preliminary protective order be issued against the Respondent, Hector Razo, commanding that any acts of stalking cease immediately.

     a. That the Respondent (Razo) shall have no contact whatsoever with the Petitioner (Parsons). This includes, but is not limited to contact by letter, telephone, in person or through agents or confederates of the Respondent.

     b. That the Respondent (Razo) shall not follow, contact, telephone, or harass family, friends or co-workers of the Petitioner (Parsons) for the purpose of discussing or making contact, with the Petitioner.

     c. That the Respondent (Razo) shall not come within 100 feet of the Petitioner (Parsons).

     It is further ordered that a full hearing on the protective order shall be held within fifteen (15) days of the issuance of this order on _____.

_____   _____
Date   Judge

1. Who is the **audience** for this document? *the respondent, Hector Razo*

_____

2. What is the **purpose** of this document? *to give examples of "stalking"*

_____

For more on audience and purpose, see pages 7–9.

3. How do Pamela O'Berry Evans's audience and purpose make the tone of this document different from the tone used by student writer Lindsey Ducharme in her illustration essay? (See p. 126.)

Pam's tone is official while Lindsey's is familiar.

4. What is the **main point** of the document? *that all acts of stalking*

must stop

5. The document gives **examples** of *contact that is considered stalking*

6. Underline each **specific example**.

7. Which example gives the most **details**? *b.*

8. If you were to add one more detail to an example of "contact," what would you add?

Answers will vary but could include fax or email.

3. ILLUSTRATION IN EVERYDAY LIFE

The following is an example of a letter written by a town resident and father of a high school student to the editor of the local newspaper. It shows how you might use illustration in your everyday life to explain your point of view. Read it, and answer the questions that follow.

TO THE EDITOR:

Last week this paper reported in great detail the episode of drug dealing at the high school. An entire page was devoted to a description of what happened, interviews with the principal and the arresting police officer, and a disturbing picture of two handcuffed students being led out of school. While I know that this is news, I wonder why this paper doesn't give equal coverage to some of the many positive activities at the high school.

✓ Earlier this year, a group of high school students organized a fundraiser to help families who were left homeless after a fire. They worked nights and weekends planning the event, a flea market. They solicited donations from residents and local businesses, and they baked items to sell. They placed notices in the paper, the school newsletter, and buildings around town. They worked the night before setting up, all the next day, and the next night cleaning up. The paper reported the event in a single paragraph on page 10.

✓ Another example of positive behavior is the students' ongoing relationship with the senior center. Several times this year, students have organized events to entertain the seniors, including a performance by the jazz band, a humor night, and three dinners. In addition, the students organized a book drive for the senior center's library and collected hundreds of books and videos. Also, a group of students regularly visits the senior center to read to its residents. These activities weren't covered at all by this newspaper.

✓ One last example of positive behavior is the tribute to a young teacher who suddenly passed away this year. The students put together a memorial for Ms. Sessions, with written stories and testimonials. For this event, they organized a class donation to a memorial scholarship fund and student speeches. They invited the teacher's family to the memorial, and the family was very moved.

Yes, we have problem students and, yes, they make sensational news. I don't suggest that this paper ignore the problems or gloss them over, but in the interest of balanced reporting, I ask that you give the good news equal time.

1. Who is the **audience** for this essay?   *the editor of the newspaper*

2. What is the writer's **purpose** for writing?   *to suggest that the newspaper give equal coverage to positive actions and negative ones*

For more on audience and purpose, see pages 7–9.

3. Double-underline the **thesis statement**.

4. Put a check mark (✓) next to each of the major **examples**.

5. Underline the **details** that support the examples.

6. Circle the **transitions**.

Write an Illustration Essay

In this section, you will write your own illustration. To do so, follow this sequence:

REVIEW the four basics of good illustration (p. 123).

CHOOSE your writing assignment (below).

WRITE your illustration using the step-by-step Writing Guide (p. 134).

CHECK your final essay (p. 138).

WRITING ASSIGNMENT 1   COLLEGE, WORK, EVERYDAY LIFE

TEACHING TIP
Assign students to
spend one or two days
listening for how
people use illustration
in conversation,
keeping notes in their
journals. Also ask them
to note how illustration
in speech compares to
illustration in writing.

Write an illustration essay on *one* of the following topics or on a topic of your own choice.

COLLEGE

• Make a point about your college to a prospective student and back it up with examples.

• Assess the value of a course you have taken, giving specific examples.

• Explain how _____ (someone you learned about in a college course) made a meaningful contribution to society.

WORK

• Tell a job applicant what the typical responsibilities might be in your job.

• Explain to your supervisor your claim that there is too much work to be done in the time allotted.

• Demonstrate the following statement: "I am a very _____ person." Your audience is a potential employer.

EVERYDAY LIFE

• Write a letter to your landlord about how your apartment needs more regular maintenance.

• Write a letter to a friend in which you explain that your _____ _____ (mother, father, sibling, sweetheart) is the most _____ (selfish, generous, irresponsible, capable) person you know.

• Write a report explaining your living costs and expenses in order to show how well (or how poorly) you are managing your money.

WRITING ASSIGNMENT 2   **USE THE INTERNET**

Write an illustration essay in which you complete the following sentence and use it as your thesis statement:

For advice about how to cite a source, see Chapter 20.

If you are interested in finding information about _____,

the Internet _____.

Use examples to show a reader why you hold the view expressed in this thesis.

WRITING ASSIGNMENT 3   **HARASSMENT ON THE JOB**

Read the problem and the situation that follow, and then choose *one* of the assignment options (3A or 3B) that appear after it.

PROBLEM: Although most companies have written policies designed to prevent sexual harassment, problems still occur frequently in the workplace. Sexual harassment situations are always uncomfortable, and often the person being harassed doesn't know what to do. Victims want to stop the unwanted advances, but they may fear that making a formal complaint will hurt their chances for success at work—or worse, will lead to their getting fired.

SITUATION: Kim Alleya, a young woman with whom you work, asks for your advice one day during lunch. She is an administrative assistant, and she started with the company just two months ago. She tells you the following:

> Jerry Churney is bothering me. He asked me out a month or so ago, and I said no. I think he was mad, and since then he's been harassing me. Recently he's been coming up to me and saying or doing stuff that makes me uncomfortable; I dread coming to work.
>
> You know, he's good friends with my boss, and I'm afraid if I say anything that I'll get in trouble. I'm still technically in the probation period, and I really need this job. What would you do if you were me?

You advise Kim to write a report for your company's human resources department that illustrates (gives detailed examples of) the harassing behavior, and you offer to help her write it. This is a very sensitive subject, but the writing should be professional and objective in tone. The conclusion should emphasize both the victim's concern about the inappropriate behavior and her willingness to work cooperatively to solve the problem.

ASSIGNMENT OPTION 3A: DOCUMENTING A COMPLAINT

Using what you know about illustration, assume you are Kim and write a report for the human resources department.

ASSIGNMENT OPTION 3B: ANOTHER PERSPECTIVE

Write an illustration essay from the perspective of Jerry Churney, who has been informed of Kim's complaint of harassment. Again, the audience is the human resources department.

TEACHING TIP
Allow students to complete both options to see how their own writing would change as the viewpoint changes.

Illustration

Follow the steps in this Writing Guide to help you prewrite, draft, revise, and edit your illustration. Check off each step as you complete it.

THINKING CRITICALLY ABOUT ILLUSTRATION	
FOCUS	Think about what you want to explain and who will read your illustration essay.
ASK	• What main point am I trying to illustrate (explain with examples)? • Which examples will most clearly and vividly explain my point? • What examples will my readers most easily understand? • How can I make the examples specific and detailed? • How should I order my examples so that they will be the most effective?

PREWRITE TO EXPLORE YOUR TOPIC

Prewriting for illustration involves considering what aspect of a topic you know well enough to illustrate. Then you need to select good examples and make sure that they demonstrate your main point.

_____ Decide on your purpose for writing.

_____ Identify the audience for your essay.

> For more on purpose and audience, see pages 7–9.

_____ After you select a writing assignment, use a prewriting technique (freewriting, listing/brainstorming, questioning, discussing, clustering) to get some ideas about the topic.

_____ Narrow your ideas to a topic you can write about in a short essay, and then generate examples that would demonstrate your point about the topic.

WRITE A THESIS STATEMENT

The thesis statement in illustration usually includes the topic and the main point you want to make about it.

| Topic | + | Main point | = | Thesis statement |

Homeschooling   is beneficial to both the child and the parent.

I would visit Italy,   an enchanting country of diverse land-scapes, historic landmarks, and inspiring art masterpieces.

_____ Decide what is important to you about your topic.

_____ Write a working thesis statement that presents your point about what is important.

SUPPORT YOUR POINT

The major support points in illustration are the examples you give to demonstrate or prove your thesis. These examples will become the topic sentences for the body paragraphs. To come up with examples, assume someone has read your thesis and asked, "What do you mean?" or "Like what?"

_____ Use a prewriting technique to help you get ideas for examples.

_____ Choose at least three examples that will show your readers what you mean.

_____ Reread your prewriting to find supporting details that you may have already generated.

_____ Find additional supporting details by asking yourself more questions: What do I mean? How? In what ways?

_____ For each of your examples, add supporting details that will help your readers understand how the example demonstrates your main point. Give your readers specific and detailed information about each major example.

MAKE A PLAN

TEAMWORK
Have students share their plans in pairs or small groups. Ask them to focus on the major support examples.

Making a written plan—an outline—helps you decide how to order your illustration. An illustration essay with several examples is often organized by order of importance, building up to the most significant or persuasive example.

_____ Arrange your major support examples in order of importance, leading up to the one that you think will have most impact on your readers.

_____ Make a plan or outline for your illustration essay that includes your main support points (your examples) and supporting details for each example.

DRAFT

Drafting in illustration means writing in complete sentences and including the following:

• An introduction with a thesis statement that communicates your topic and your main point about that topic

• The examples that demonstrate or prove your main point

• Supporting details that explain the examples for your reader

_____ Reread your thesis so that it is fresh in your mind.

_____ Write an introductory paragraph that includes your thesis statement and hooks your readers' interest.

_____ Using your plan or outline, write a topic sentence for each of your major examples.

_____ Fill in the supporting details that explain your major support points, your examples. Add any details that occur to you as you write and think about your thesis. Ask yourself what other specific, concrete details would help your readers understand each example as you would like them to.

_____ Write a strong conclusion that refers back to your main point and makes a final observation or recommendation.

_____ Title your essay.

REVISE

Revising means changing whole sentences or paragraphs to make your writing clearer or stronger. To revise an illustration, imagine that you are a reader with no idea how your topic is what your thesis claims it is. Read your draft, looking for the following:

- Examples and details that don't really demonstrate your thesis (revise for unity)
- Places where you would stop and think, "I don't get it," because there isn't enough concrete information (revise for support and detail).
- Places where the examples need transitions to connect ideas and move a reader smoothly from one idea to the next (revise for coherence).

_____ Get feedback from others through peer review.

_____ Begin by asking, "If a reader didn't know much about this topic, would my examples give that reader enough information to understand my main point?"

_____ Reread your thesis statement. Revise it so that your point is clearer, more concrete, and more forceful.

_____ Reread the body paragraphs of your illustration essay to see if the examples and supporting details demonstrate your thesis to your readers. Suppose that, after reading your thesis, a reader asked, "How? Give me some examples." Would your body paragraphs supply the answer?

_____ Reread your introduction and make changes if it is dull or weak.

_____ Reread your conclusion to make sure it is energetic and drives home your thesis.

TEACHING TIP
Explain to students that revision consists of numerous, but manageable, small steps.

For more on peer review, see pages 87–88.

TEAMWORK
Have students use the checklist items here as prompts for peer review. Ask them to pay special attention to transitional words.

_____ Add transitions, words and sentences that connect your examples and details.

_____ Make at least five changes to your draft, to improve its unity, support, or coherence or to make the introduction, thesis statement, or conclusion stronger or more convincing.

EDIT

Some grammar, spelling, word use, or punctuation errors may confuse your readers and make it difficult for them to understand a point you are trying to make. Even if they do not confuse your readers, errors detract from the effectiveness and overall quality of your writing. Edit your illustration carefully, and correct any errors you find.

_____ Ask a classmate or friend to read your illustration and highlight errors.

_____ Use the spell checker or grammar checker on your computer, but do not rely on them to catch all errors.

_____ Read your illustration carefully, looking for errors in grammar, spelling, word use, or punctuation. Focus first on sentence fragments, run-on sentences, problems with subject–verb agreement, problems with verbs, and other areas where you know you often make errors.

_____ Print a clean, final copy.

_____ Ask yourself: Is this the best I can do?

A FINAL CHECK BEFORE HANDING IN YOUR ILLUSTRATION ESSAY

If you've followed the Writing Guide for illustration, your essay will already include the four basics of good illustration. Use this list to double-check each basic feature.

____ My thesis statement reveals the point of my illustration essay.

____ Each of the paragraphs in the body of my essay presents a detailed example that supports and explains my main point.

____ My examples are clear, detailed, and specific so that my readers can understand them.

____ My illustration essay includes enough examples to get my point across.

10

Description

Writing That Creates Pictures in Words

You Know This
You use description
every day.
- You describe what
  someone looks
  like.
- You describe an
  item you have
  lost.
- You describe a
  place you have
  visited.

Understand What Description Is

DEFINITION: Description is writing that creates a clear and vivid impression of the topic. Description translates your experience of a person, place, or thing into words, often by appealing to the senses: sight, hearing, smell, taste, and touch.

▪▪ Four Basics of Good Description

1. It creates a main impression—an overall effect, feeling, or image—about the topic.
2. It uses specific sensory images to support the main impression.
3. It uses concrete details that appeal to the senses: sight, hearing, smell, taste, and touch.
4. It brings a person, place, or physical object to life for the reader.

In a description, you create an impression for your audience through the sensory images and details you present. These details help your audience share your experience and understand your impression of the topic.

IDEA JOURNAL
Write about the most beautiful, the most interesting, or the ugliest chair, car, T-shirt, or other object you've ever seen.

TEACHING TIP
Ask students to create a profile of someone who has an interesting job that involves writing. With students' permission, send these profiles to the publisher for consideration for the next edition of this textbook.

Daigo Fujiwara
ASSISTANT ART DIRECTOR

Daigo Fujiwara

BACKGROUND: Daigo came to the United States from Japan as an exchange student when he was a senior in high school. After graduation he remained—against the wishes of his parents—to continue his education. Although he wanted to go to college, his English-language test scores were low, so he took writing courses in English as a second language (ESL) at Becker Junior College and then enrolled there. Although he could speak English fairly well, his writing skills were still poor. Through continuing on with ESL writing courses, Daigo improved his skills and graduated first from Becker and then from Northeastern University. In addition to his job as an assistant art director, Daigo is a photographer and plays bass in a band.

EMPLOYER: *Inc.* magazine

COLLEGE(S)/DEGREES: Becker Junior College (A.A.), Northeastern University (B.A.)

TYPES OF WRITING ON THE JOB: Summaries of articles for illustrators, memos to illustrators, follow-up letters to illustrators, notes about layout, directions for interns, forms describing necessary changes in artwork

HOW DAIGO USES DESCRIPTION: Daigo has to write detailed descriptions of what he needs for the magazine's art program. These descriptions, called specifications, are written for freelance artists. For an example of Daigo's use of description, see page 145.

COMPUTER SKILLS: Word processing, photo imaging software (Photoshop), illustration software, Internet

TEAMWORK ON THE JOB: Daigo works with *Inc.*'s art director and editor to develop a concept, to decide whether to use photographs or illustrations for each article, and to make individual selections.

FUTURE GOAL: Daigo hopes, first, to remain interested in whatever he's doing by learning new skills and, second, to continue his bass playing.

For more on prewriting techniques, see pages 27–31.

TEACHING TIP
Have students bring in descriptions of interesting places from books or newspapers. The Travel section of the *New York Times* (available on the Web at <www.nytimes.com/pages/travel/index.html>) often has such descriptions.

SPECIFIC DETAILS FOR DESCRIPTION

Good description uses specific, concrete details to present the sights, sounds, smells, tastes, and touches that contribute to vivid sensory images and a clear overall impression. You can use prewriting techniques to generate or recall effective details that will help readers to understand your experience.

SIGHT	SOUND	SMELL
Colors	Loud/soft	Sweet/sour
Shapes	Piercing/soothing	Sharp/mild
Sizes	Continuous/off-and-on	Good (like what?)

SIGHT	SOUND		SMELL
Patterns	Pleasant/unpleasant (how?)		Bad (rotten?)
Brightness	Does it sound like anything else?		New (like what?)
Does it look like anything else?			Does it smell like anything else?

TASTE	TOUCH
Good (What does good taste like?)	Hard/soft
Bad (What does bad taste like?)	Liquid/solid
Bitter/sugary	Rough/smooth
Metallic	Dry/oily
Burning/spicy	Textures
Does it taste like anything else?	Does it feel like anything else?

TEACHING TIP
Encourage your students to close their eyes while generating sensory details to be used in writing a description.

SUPPORT POINTS FOR DESCRIPTION

As you think about the main impression you want to convey, ask yourself what major sensory images your details might bring to life. Look for clusters or groups of details that describe the major sensory images as you recall them. Add other details to convey each sensory image more accurately or vividly.

For example, one student wrote this thesis statement, *When I take her coat from the closet, it's as if my grandmother is standing beside me.* To support this main impression, the writer might describe sensory images such as the smell of the coat, the feel of the fabric, or the candy left in the pocket. She might give details about the smell of the coat (*sweet like Grandma's perfume, with a faint odor of mothballs and home-baked bread*); the feel of the fabric (*nubby and rough, with some smooth spots where the fabric has worn thin*); and the candy in the pocket (*single pieces of butterscotch that rustle in their wrappings, and a round cylinder that is a roll of wintergreen Life Savers*).

TEAMWORK
Have students, working in small groups, choose an object from one group member's book bag or briefcase and agree on a main impression to use in describing that object.

ORDER OF IDEAS FOR DESCRIPTION

Description may use any of the orders of organization: time, space, or importance, depending on the purpose of the description. If you are describing what someone or something looks like, you might use spatial order. If you are describing a main impression that is more than visual, you might use order of importance.

For more on ordering ideas, see pages 58–64.

For example, the student who is writing about her grandmother's coat might use order of importance, saving for last the sensory image and the details that most vividly bring her grandmother to life. Her plan for her description might be as follows:

Introduction (including thesis)

First sensory image (candy in the pocket)

    details

Second sensory image (feel of fabric)

    details

Most important sensory image (smell of coat)

    details

    why most important

Conclusion

    Remind reader of the main impression (coat reminds me of grandmother)

    Make an observation (to others just an old coat, but the feel and smell of it belong to my grandmother)

For more on transitions, see pages 94–99.

Add transitions to be certain that your reader can move smoothly from sensory image to sensory image and detail to detail.

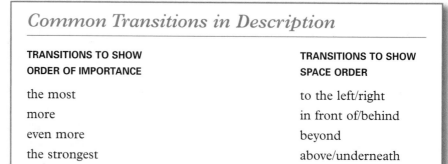

Common Transitions in Description

TRANSITIONS TO SHOW ORDER OF IMPORTANCE	TRANSITIONS TO SHOW SPACE ORDER
the most	to the left/right
more	in front of/behind
even more	beyond
the strongest	above/underneath
the most intense	

Being able to describe something or someone accurately and in detail is important not only in school but also in other settings. Describing something well involves using specific, concrete details. Here are some ways that you might use description:

COLLEGE

- For a science lab report, you have to describe the physical and chemical properties of an element.

WORK

- You write a letter to your office cleaning contractor describing the unacceptable conditions of the office.

EVERYDAY LIFE

- You describe a jacket that you want a friend to buy for a birthday gift for you.

Read and Analyze Description

Read the following examples of description—one each from college, work, and everyday life—and answer the questions that accompany each. Reading and analyzing the examples will help you understand how to write a good description.

1. DESCRIPTION IN COLLEGE

Read the following description essay, written by a student for a course assignment, and complete the questions following it.

Photograph of My Father

Florence Bagley

This old black-and-white photograph of my father fills me with conflicting emotions. He died very young, and this photo is one of the few that my family has of him. The picture seems to show a strong, happy man, young and smiling, but to me it also reveals his weakness.

✓Looking at this picture of my father, I feel how much I have lost. In it, my father is sitting upright in a worn plaid easy chair. It was "his" chair, and when he was at work I'd curl up in it and smell his aftershave lotion and cigarette smoke. His pitch-black hair is so dark that it blends into the background of the photo. His eyes, though indistinct in this photo, were a deep, dark brown. Although the photo is faded around my father's face, I still can make out his strong jaw and the cleft in his chin. In the photo my father is wearing a clean white T-shirt that reveals his thick, muscular arms. Resting in the crook of his left arm is my younger brother, who was about one year old at the time. Both of them are smiling.

✓ However, when I study the photo, my eyes are drawn to the can of beer that sits on the table next to him. Against my will, I begin to feel resentful. I have so many wonderful memories of my father. Whether he was carrying me on his shoulders, picking me up from school, or teaching me to draw, he always made time for me. All of these memories fade when I see that beer. From what I remember, he always made time for that beer as well. The smell of beer was always on him, the cool, sweating can always within reach.

✓ In this photo, my father appears to be a strong man; however, looks are deceiving. My father died at the age of thirty-seven because he was an alcoholic. I was eleven when he died, and I really did not understand that his drinking was the reason for his death. I just knew that he left me without a father and the possibility of more memories. He should have been strong enough to stop drinking.

In spite of the resentment I may feel about his leaving me, this photo holds many loving memories as well. It is of my father—the strong, wonderful man and the alcoholic—and it is the most precious thing I own. Although I would much rather have him here, I stay connected to him when I look at it.

For more on purpose and audience, see pages 7–9.

1. What is Florence's **purpose** for writing this essay?

   to describe a photograph of her father and what it means to her

2. Who is Florence's **audience** for this essay? *her instructor and classmates*

TEAMWORK
Have students do one or more of the activities in this section in pairs.

3. Fill in the blanks with the **topic** and the **main impression** from Florence's essay.

   TOPIC: *the photograph of her father*

   MAIN IMPRESSION: *shows a man who seems to be strong but also reveals his weakness*

4. Double-underline the **thesis statement**.

5. Each major support point should be a topic sentence for a paragraph in the body of the essay. Put a check mark (✓) next to each **topic sentence** in this essay.

6. Underline some of the **details** that create a picture of Florence's father.

7. What, to you, is the strongest image in the essay? Why?

   Answers will vary.

8. What type of **organization** does the writer use? *top to bottom/spatial*

9. Does Florence's essay have the **four basics of good description**? Why or why not? *Answers will vary.*

For a list of the four basics of good description, see page 139.

2. DESCRIPTION IN THE WORKPLACE

The following is an example of the kind of description that Daigo Fujiwara writes in his job as graphic artist and assistant art director. Although the memo to the photo researcher is not in standard essay form, it is a clear example of description in the workplace.

May 8, 2002

TO: Jonathan Kuvicek, Photo Researcher

FR: Daigo Fujiwara, Assistant Art Director

RE: Photographs to accompany article

As we discussed earlier today, we need four photographs to accompany the article on innovative work spaces. Overall, the photos should be colorful, upbeat, and somewhat playful, demonstrating the positive attributes of the spaces.

The photographs should include people working in them. We would like to have a representative group of people: a variety of racial and ethnic groups balanced by gender. Probably most of the people will be younger, in that the companies piloting these innovative spaces tend to attract younger employees. As we discussed, the opening photo might contrast a traditional cubicle arrangement with the newer arrangements.

All photographs should be in full color. The opening photograph will be sized at 3" × 6"; the other three will be 5" × 4". When you submit photos for our consideration, please indicate any cropping suggestions.

As we agreed, you will submit a group of photographs for our consideration by May 20.

For more on audience and purpose, see pages 7–9.

1. Who is Daigo's **audience** for this memo? *the photo researcher*

2. What is his **purpose** for writing? *to describe the types of photographs he needs for the article*

3. Like Florence's essay, Daigo's memo is an example of descriptive writing. How does his purpose for writing make his memo different from Florence's essay? *Daigo's memo is more concise and businesslike than Florence's essay.*

4. Double-underline the **thesis statement**.

5. Circle at least three **specific details**.

For a list of the four basics of good description, see page 139.

6. Does this memo have the **four basics of good description**? Why or why not? *Answers will vary.*

3. DESCRIPTION IN EVERYDAY LIFE

The following essay is a description of water damage to the writer's apartment and possessions. The writer took pictures of the damage but wanted to have a written backup for the photos.

On Wednesday, February 10, I returned to my apartment (275 Marlboro Avenue, #3D) to find significant water damage in my bedroom. I was not completely surprised because the leaky shower in the apartment above me has been a problem for over six months. This time, however, it wasn't a matter of a few spots on the ceiling. Part of the ceiling had caved in, leaving my room and my possessions a soggy mess.

✓The floor was covered with chunks of plaster. Larger pieces of the falling plaster had scratched and chipped my dresser and night table. Plaster dust mixed with water formed a gluey substance that was caked on my floor, the television, the CD player, and my computer. (Not only) did this make a disgusting mess, (but it also) gummed up my computer and keyboard, which now are nonfunctional.

✓(In addition to the plaster,) rancid, rusty brown water filled with who knows what had come through the hole in the ceiling and through the light fixture. It permanently soaked some texts and notebooks lying on the bed, as well as the blankets and sheets—it even soaked through and stained the mattress. Replacing these items will mean significant cost.

✓(The worst, though,) is that my guitar was also ruined, with nicks and scratches from the falling plaster and warped, stained wood and strings. That rusty stinking water ruined my most valuable possession. (The worst) (part) of the soggy mess is not the cost or the time involved in replacing damaged items. It is the permanent loss of that guitar. When I saw my guitar that night, I stood there aching.

1. What is the writer's **purpose** in this essay? *to describe the damage in his* *apartment*

For more on purpose and audience, see pages 7–9.

2. Who is the writer's **audience** for this essay? *a landlord or insurance* *company*

3. What is your strongest reaction to the essay? Why? *Answers will vary.*

4. What is the **main impression** that the thesis statement creates?
   The writer's things were a soggy mess.

5. Double-underline the **thesis statement**.

6. Put a check mark (✓) next to each **topic sentence** that supports the thesis statement.

7. Underline at least four **supporting details**.

8. Circle the (transitional words).

9. How does the concluding paragraph relate back to the main point?

repeats the words "soggy mess"

Write a Description Essay

In this section, you will write your own description essay. To do so, follow this sequence:

REVIEW the basics of good description (p. 139).

CHOOSE your writing assignment (below).

WRITE your description using the step-by-step Writing Guide (p. 150).

CHECK your final essay (p. 154).

WRITING ASSIGNMENT 1   COLLEGE, WORK, EVERYDAY LIFE

ESL
Ask ESL students to describe a significant place in their native country or current neighborhood.

Write a description essay on *one* of the following topics or on a topic of your own choice.

COLLEGE

• Describe the setting of your college to someone who has never seen it but is interested in attending.

• Describe your favorite place on campus so that a reader understands why you like to be there.

• Describe an average student at your college in order to create an impression of your school.

WORK

• Describe an area of your workplace that is not worker-friendly.

• Describe a product or service that your company produces.

• Describe your boss or another person with whom you work.

EVERYDAY LIFE

• Describe a favorite place.

• Describe someone in your family.

• Describe a favorite photograph.

■ **WRITING ASSIGNMENT 2   USE THE INTERNET**

Write a description essay about a place you would like to visit—a geographic area, a resort, a museum, a theme park. To get information about the location, visit its Web site. (For instance, visiting **<www.grandcanyon.com>** will lead you to information about one of America's most traveled sites.) You will need to cite, or acknowledge, any source information that you include in your essay.

For advice about how to cite a source, see Chapter 20.

■ **WRITING ASSIGNMENT 3   WRITE A REPORT**

Read the problem and the situation that follow, and then choose *one* of the assignment options (3A or 3B) that appear after it.

> **PROBLEM**: Increasingly, companies are being urged to provide more attractive workplaces for their employees. This initiative grows out of recent research that indicates that employees' productivity increases and the amount of sick time taken by employees decreases when a workplace is attractive and comfortable.

> **SITUATION**: Your boss has asked you to be part of a task force that will recommend how a specific area of the workplace could be made more attractive and comfortable for employees.

ASSIGNMENT OPTION 3A: RESPONSE TO THE SITUATION

Choose a specific area of your workplace (or your college, if you are not working). Using what you know about description, recommend some ways in which this area could be made more worker-friendly (or student-friendly). Your recommendations should be detailed enough that your boss (or a college official) could visualize what you have in mind.

TEAMWORK
Both assignments 3A and 3B work well as small-group projects.

ASSIGNMENT OPTION 3B: ANOTHER PERSPECTIVE

Read assignment option 3A. Instead of writing from your own perspective, write a description essay from the perspective of the other gender. For example, if you are a man, make recommendations from the perspective of a woman; if you are a woman, make them from a man's perspective. Talk to a member of the opposite sex to understand how he or she may see things differently. Would you focus on the same area? What kinds of changes would make the area more appealing to the other person?

Writing Guide

Description

Follow the steps in this Writing Guide to help you prewrite, draft, revise, and edit your description. Check off each step as you complete it.

THINKING CRITICALLY ABOUT DESCRIPTION

FOCUS   Think about what you want to describe and the overall impression you want to give your readers.

ASK
- What person, place, or thing do I want to write about? Why? What main impression about it do I want to convey?
- Who will be reading this essay, and what do they know or need to know about my topic?
- What thesis statement would introduce my topic and state my main impression?
- To convey my main impression, what aspects of my topic do I need to describe?
- What sensory images will my readers need in order to understand my topic? What details might create those sensory images?

PREWRITE TO EXPLORE YOUR TOPIC

Prewriting for description involves selecting a topic about which you have strong impressions and then getting ideas about those impressions. Description creates strong sensory images in words, allowing your reader to see, feel, or experience your topic as intensely as you have.

For more on purpose and audience, see pages 7–9.

_____   Decide on your purpose for writing.

_____   Identify the audience for your essay.

_____   Jot down some ideas about what you see when you visualize your topic.

_____   Think about what main impression you want to convey to your readers.

_____   Use a prewriting technique (freewriting, listing/brainstorming, questioning, discussing, clustering) to explore your impressions and visual or other sensory images.

WRITE A THESIS STATEMENT

The thesis statement in description includes the topic and the main impression about it that you want to convey to your reader.

| Topic | + | Main impression | = | Thesis statement |

When I take my grandmother's coat from the closet,

it's as if she is standing beside me.

Overall, the photos

should be colorful, upbeat, and somewhat playful.

_____ Review your prewriting and decide what main impression you want to create.

_____ Write a working thesis statement that includes your topic and main impression.

SUPPORT YOUR POINT

The major support points in description are the sensory images that, together, create the main impression. The sensory images will become the topic sentences for the body paragraphs.

The sensory images are supported by concrete details that allow readers to see, hear, or feel the topic as you do.

_____ Review your thesis statement and prewriting, and make other notes. Try to find strong sensory images that will support your main impression and make the topic come alive for your readers.

_____ Choose at least three sensory images that will help to convey your main impression.

_____ Add specific, concrete details that vividly describe each sensory image. Try to appeal to the senses: sight, sound, smell, touch, taste.

MAKE A PLAN

Making a written plan—an outline—helps you decide how to order your description. A description may use time order, space order, or order of importance, depending on the purpose.

For more on ordering ideas in description, see page 141.

_____ Arrange your support points—your sensory images—in a logical order.

_____ Identify vivid details that will describe each sensory image for your readers.

_____ Make a plan or outline for your description essay.

DRAFT

Drafting a description means writing in complete sentences and including the following:

• An introduction with a thesis that states your topic and main impression
• Body paragraphs with topic sentences that identify the major sensory images
• Supporting details that show readers each sensory image
• A conclusion that refers back to the main impression and makes a further observation

_____ Close your eyes and try to experience the topic and main impression you are writing about.

_____ Write an introduction that draws your readers in and makes them want to know about your topic.

_____ Write a topic sentence for each of the major sensory images.

_____ Add specific details in each paragraph to bring the sensory images and main impression to life.

_____ Write a conclusion that reminds your readers of your main impression of your topic and makes an observation based on the sensory images you have presented.

_____ Title your essay.

REVISE

Revising means changing whole sentences or paragraphs to make your writing clearer or stronger. To revise a description, imagine that you are a reader who has never seen or experienced the topic. Read your draft, looking for the following:

• Places where the ideas are off the main point (revise for unity)
• Gaps in information or detail (revise for support and detail)

- Areas in need of transitions to connect ideas and move your readers smoothly from one point to the next (revise for coherence)

_____ Get feedback from others through peer review.

_____ Begin revising by considering how you can make your description more lively or vivid for your readers.

_____ Reread your thesis statement. Revise to convey your main impression more concretely and forcefully.

_____ Reread the body of your essay to see whether the sensory images and details support your thesis. Replace or cut any sensory images that do not support your main impression. Add any supporting details that would help readers understand your main impression of the topic.

_____ Reread your introduction. Make changes if the opening is dull or vague.

_____ Reread your conclusion to make sure that it is energetic and vivid, reminds readers of your main impression, and makes an observation on the topic you have described. Your purpose in describing the topic should be clear to your readers.

_____ Add transition words and sentences to connect your details and lead readers smoothly from one sensory image to another.

_____ Make at least five changes to your draft to improve the unity, support, or coherence of your description or to make the introduction, thesis statement, or conclusion stronger or more interesting.

For more on peer review, see pages 87–88.

EDIT

Some grammar, spelling, word use, or punctuation errors may confuse your readers and make it difficult for them to understand a point you are trying to make. Even if they do not confuse your readers, errors detract from the effectiveness and overall quality of your writing. Edit your description carefully, and correct any errors you find.

_____ Ask a classmate or friend to read your description and highlight any errors.

_____ Use the spell checker or grammar checker on your computer, but do not rely on those programs to catch all errors. Check spelling and grammar yourself as well.

_____ Reread your essay, looking for errors in grammar, spelling, word use, or punctuation. Concentrate especially on finding fragments, run-on sentences, problems with subject–verb agreement, and problems with verb tense.

_____   Print a clean final copy.

_____   Ask yourself: Is this the best I can do?

A FINAL CHECK BEFORE HANDING IN YOUR DESCRIPTION ESSAY

If you've followed the Writing Guide for description, your essay will already include the four basics of good description. Use this list to double-check each basic feature.

____   My essay creates a clear main impression about my topic.

____   Each paragraph in the body of my essay presents a strong sensory image that supports the main impression.

____   The details in my essay create strong sensory images by appealing to several senses—sight, hearing, smell, taste, and touch.

____   My description brings my topic to life.

11

Process Analysis

Writing That Explains How Things Happen

You Know This
You already use
process analysis.
- You learn or teach
  someone how to
  do something
  (drive, operate a
  DVD player, or
  assemble a
  bookcase).
- You give
  directions to your
  home.
- You explain a
  process to a child,
  like leaves turning
  color.

Understand What Process Analysis Is

DEFINITION: **Process analysis** either explains how to do something (so your readers can do it) or explains how something works (so your readers can understand it). Both types of process analysis present the steps involved in the process.

IDEA JOURNAL
Write about a goal you have for yourself and what you will do to accomplish it.

▪▪ Four Basics of Good Process Analysis

1. It helps readers either perform the steps themselves or understand how something works.
2. It presents the essential steps in the process.
3. It explains the steps in detail.
4. It arranges the steps in a logical order (usually in chronological order).

DISCUSSION
Have the class discuss the process of learning how to drive, play a sport, or play a musical instrument. Then list similarities and differences between learning this activity and learning how to write.

Process analysis is an important way to help readers either follow or understand a series of steps. It helps empower others, and it gets things done.

155

Maureen Letendre

DIRECTOR OF HUMAN RESOURCES

Maureen Letendre

BACKGROUND: After graduating from a commercial studies program in high school, Maureen spent several years at a small, family-owned business before taking a clerical position for the court system and putting herself through college. She then got a job at Digital Equipment Corporation in the clerical placement group. She stayed at Digital for more than twenty years, moving into increasingly higher-level positions. In each of those positions, she looked for someone to learn from, and that person became her informal mentor. She took a lot of initiative and found that Digital consistently rewarded her hard work and commitment.

When Digital was bought out by Compaq, Maureen moved to Inforonics, a rapidly growing and fast-paced e-commerce consulting firm, where she is now the director of human resources.

EMPLOYER: Inforonics, Inc.

COLLEGE(S)/DEGREES: Framingham State College

TYPES OF WRITING ON THE JOB: Maureen writes many personnel-related reports and statements about the company for job fairs; explanations to managers of how to implement new plans; letters to prospective employees and outside sources; and, as she says, "tons of email." She is particularly careful in writing her email messages because, although they seem informal and casual, the emails often become part of a permanent record. According to Maureen, something as small as a misplaced comma has actually slowed down projects and caused misunderstandings.

HOW MAUREEN USES PROCESS ANALYSIS: Maureen uses process analysis often in her position when she writes to managers and employees, explaining how to implement a new program or policy or how a new plan (such as a pension or profit-sharing plan) works. For an example of how Maureen uses process analysis, see Process Analysis in the Workplace, page 161.

COMPUTER SKILLS: Word processing, Excel and other spreadsheets, Microsoft Office, and human resource–specific applications

TEAMWORK ON THE JOB: Inforonics uses teams at all levels: It is an essential part of the company's operational philosophy. The company believes that involving people at all levels in decision making makes implementation of any new policy, plan, or procedure much more effective than it would be otherwise.

FUTURE GOAL: Inforonics, like most companies, has very specific performance goals, and Maureen is committed to exceeding them each year. One of her personal goals is to make more time for analyzing a situation before responding or reacting. She wants always to be evaluating what's working and what's not, in every area of her life, rather than coasting along without seeking growth.

COMPLETE STEPS FOR PROCESS ANALYSIS

A clear process analysis presents all the essential steps in the process. Each step is explained by supporting details. For example, the writer of the thesis *Learning how to use the advanced functions on my computer is frustrating*, might identify several essential steps and the details to explain each step.

WHAT ARE THE ESSENTIAL STEPS OF THE PROCESS?

- Using the Help feature or a tutorial
- Consulting a reference book such as *Word 98 for Dummies*
- Trying to undo automatic functions

For more on supporting your thesis, see Chapter 4.

WHAT IS INVOLVED IN EACH OF THOSE STEPS?

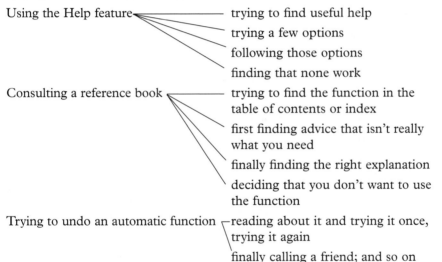

Using the Help feature
— trying to find useful help
trying a few options
following those options
finding that none work

Consulting a reference book
— trying to find the function in the table of contents or index
first finding advice that isn't really what you need
finally finding the right explanation
deciding that you don't want to use the function

Trying to undo an automatic function
— reading about it and trying it once, trying it again
finally calling a friend; and so on

Sometimes you will need to write about a process that you are very familiar with, but your readers are not. Make sure you include all of the essential steps in the process, particularly if you want your readers to be able to do something based on your instructions. Read the following process analysis example. What essential step is missing?

TEAMWORK
Have students, in pairs, discuss whether they agree on which step is missing and whether any other steps are missing.

You shouldn't have any trouble doing a load of laundry before I get home. The clothes are in the baskets next to the machine. One of the baskets has all dark clothes. Put these in the washing machine, with the heaviest, biggest items on the bottom. You can fill the machine to the top, but don't mash the clothes down. If you put in too many clothes, the machine will stall out. As you load the machine, check to make sure that there aren't any white things mixed in by mistake. After all of the clothes are in, set the level on Extra High. Then turn the knob on the left to Warm Wash, Cool Rinse. Press the Start button. After about half an hour the laundry should be done, and you can transfer it to the dryer.

Although these directions cover loading the machine and operating it, they leave out adding the soap.

CHRONOLOGICAL ORDER FOR PROCESS ANALYSIS

For more on chronological order, see page 59.

Because process analysis explains how to do something or how something works, it usually uses chronological order. Start with the first step, and then explain each step in order as it should occur. The plan for a process analysis often looks like this:

Introduction (including thesis)

First step

> details about the first step

Second step

> details about the second step

Third step

> details about the third step

Conclusion

Add transitional words to your essay to help your readers follow your process analysis as you move from step to step.

For more on transitions, see pages 94–99.

Common Transitions in Process Analysis

after	eventually	meanwhile	soon
as	finally	next	then
at last	first	now	when
before	last	second	while
during	later	since	

Whenever you give someone directions about how to do something or explain how something works, you are using process analysis. Here are some ways you might use process analysis:

COLLEGE

- In an information management course, you must write an essay explaining the process for implementing a new data management system.

WORK

- The office has a new security system, and you are asked to write a memo explaining to employees how to access their work areas during and after normal business hours.

EVERYDAY LIFE

- You write directions telling your child how to operate the microwave oven.

Read and Analyze Process Analysis

Before writing your own process analysis essay, read the following examples — one each from college, the workplace, and everyday life — and answer the questions that accompany each. Reading the examples and answering the questions will help you understand how to write a good process analysis.

1. PROCESS ANALYSIS IN COLLEGE

The following is an essay that student Jessica Foote wrote for her first-year composition class.

How to Fall Out of Love

Jessica Foote

Falling in love is easy; people do it every day. Most "love" doesn't last though, and after the initial period of passion, many romances fall apart. Unfortunately, in most cases one person falls out of love before the other, and that can result in a very painful breakup. If you learn how to fall out of love, you will minimize the pain of a breakup.

✓ First of all, don't blame yourself. You will probably ask yourself what you did or what you said or what's wrong with you to cause the breakup. Analyzing the situation isn't bad, but assuming that it's your fault is. Don't assume you are to blame: It happens all the time. So don't beat yourself up, because that won't change a thing. Take some time for yourself to do things that will help you heal. Go out for a walk, write down your feelings, watch a movie, eat a pint of rocky road ice cream. Whatever you do, just remember that the hurt will lessen with time. Give yourself that time to put things in perspective.

✓ Next, accept what happened. It's not the end of the world, even though at first it may seem that way. To love and lose is part of the relationship cycle. We learn from each experience. Remember the old saying "It is better to have loved and lost than never to have loved at all." You will be wiser because of your experience, and you are better prepared to face life's future challenges.

✓ Finally, see friends and have fun; don't isolate yourself and sulk. Have people over to watch a movie; or go to a movie, a restaurant, a party; or go on a blind date. Give yourself the opportunity to meet new people.

Falling out of love is much harder than falling in love. But there are ways to help yourself heal. Many people believe that there is someone out there for everybody; perhaps now you are closer to finding that person.

For more on audience and purpose, see pages 7–9.

1. Who is Jessica's **audience** for this essay? *her instructor and classmates*

2. What is her **purpose** for writing? *to explain the process of falling out of love*

3. Fill in the blanks with the **process** and the **main point** of Jessica's essay.

   PROCESS: *learning how to fall out of love*

   MAIN POINT: *will minimize the pain of a breakup*

4. Double-underline the **thesis statement**.

5. Put a check mark (✓) next to each **topic sentence**.

6. Underline the **details** that Jessica gives to help the reader understand each step of the process.

7. Circle the (**transitions**) (words, phrases, and sentences) that Jessica uses to guide readers from one step to the next.

8. What **key words** does Jessica repeat? _love, blame, hurt, fault, heal, time_

9. Describe how Jessica links the concluding paragraph to the introductory paragraph. _restates main idea_

10. Does Jessica's essay have the **four basics of good process analysis**? Why or why not? _Answers will vary._

> For a list of the four basics of good process analysis, see page 155.

2. PROCESS ANALYSIS IN THE WORKPLACE

Maureen Letendre, a human resources director at a high-tech company, often has to write directions for how to implement a new policy or procedure. While this piece of writing is not in essay form, it is a good example of process analysis.

PURPOSE

The Performance Review Program is designed to be a dynamic, ongoing process of open and constructive communication between managers and employees focusing on discussion and documentation of each employee's goals, progress, and performance. Both managers and employees are responsible for the success of this program. Please read, understand, and follow the steps of the Performance Review Program as outlined below.

PROCESS

1. Goal Setting, February

✓ (As a first step,) the employee and manager use the Goals Worksheet to establish and agree upon expectations for the coming year. (When) a new employee starts, the manager needs to initiate the goal-setting process.

> **TEACHING TIP**
> Ask students to bring in documents from their workplace that outline a process (if these documents are not confidential, that is).

The employee and manager each keep a copy of the completed worksheet and use it in their goal review meetings.

Employee Feedback

Employees may use the recommended Employee Feedback Form to track their progress. This form then can be used as a basis for discussion during quarterly manager/employee meetings.

2. Goals Review, March–September

✓ (The next step) is to hold goal review meetings, where the manager and employee meet to discuss progress and accomplishments. The results of these discussions are documented on the Goals Worksheet. This is an opportunity to recognize good performance as well as to address performance problems. It is also an opportunity to adjust goals when necessary.

3. Annual Review, December

✓ (Next,) the manager requests completed **recommended** Employee Feedback Forms and any supporting documentation from the employee. Using this information in addition to the Goals Worksheets, the manager evaluates the employee's performance and completes the Employee Annual Performance Review Form.

✓ (Following the annual review,) the manager and employee meet to discuss the manager's final review and rating. The Annual Performance Review is signed by both employee and manager and forwarded to Human Resources. At this same meeting, the manager and employee discuss and agree upon expectations for the coming year and document their agreements on the Goals Worksheet.

Escalation Process

✓ (When the employee and manager cannot agree on the final evaluation,) the employee may request a review by his or her manager's manager.

When the employee, manager, and manager's manager cannot agree on the final evaluation, the employee may request an objective review of the process and evaluation by contacting HR.

This revised Performance Review Program is the product of your input, and we believe the review process will be fair, satisfying, and productive. As we go through the first year of this new program, we welcome continued input on the various stages of the process.

1. What is the **purpose** of Maureen's memo? *to explain the company's performance review process*

For more on purpose and audience, see pages 7–9.

2. Who is Maureen's **audience**? *employees of the company*

3. Double-underline the **thesis statement**.

4. Put a check mark (✓) next to each **major step** in the process.

5. What order of organization does Maureen use? *chronological*

6. Circle the (transitions) that Maureen uses.

7. Describe how the concluding paragraph relates back to the thesis.
   repeats name of program, stresses input (communication)

3. PROCESS ANALYSIS IN EVERYDAY LIFE

The following essay is an example of a process analysis that provides practical advice on how to do something—in this case, how to avoid a speeding ticket.

How to Avoid a Speeding Ticket

Perry Buffington

The best and safest advice about how to get out of a speeding ticket is simply DON'T SPEED. If, however, you are stopped for speeding and you'd like to avoid the punishment, or you feel the ticket is genuinely unfair, there are several psychological tricks or steps you can use to your advantage.

✓ The best thing you can do is try to reduce the officer's anxiety. *You* are feeling anxiety because you've been caught, and another person now has control of you. The patrol officer is experiencing anxiety because he or she knows nothing about you. The officer may even fear that your behavior is unpredictable. His or her life may be in jeopardy, and in these violent times, that is a very understandable apprehension. As you ease the police officer's anxiety, you will reduce the probability that you will be given a ticket. There are several steps you can follow.

✓ First, stop immediately after seeing the blue lights. Then show both hands as quickly as possible. Put both hands on the steering wheel or even wave out the window. It is not necessary to hold your hands above your head; that makes you look like a criminal. Greet the officer and call him or her by name if identification is visible. This turns the officer into a fellow human being instead of an authority figure.

✓ Don't try to immediately talk your way out of it. Patrol officers are taught to keep conversation to a minimum. For legal reasons, this makes sense (the case may go to court, and the less said now, the better). Officers also are trained to keep their objectivity; if they talk to you they are more likely to identify with you. In other words, trying to talk your way out of a ticket is probably not going to work. Crying can actually *increase* your chances of receiving a ticket; the officer is forced into an uncomfortable and anxious position and may want to remove him- or herself from the scene as soon as possible. It is also easier for officers to view you as a subordinate when you are bathed in tears.

✓ Next, if it looks as if you are going to get a ticket, ask the officer for a warning, and state your reasons for leniency. *Make sure the reasons are plausible.* If you believe you were stopped unfairly, tell the officer courte-ously, but only after you've reduced his or her anxiety. Never argue: If you do, you immediately start a power struggle, and you will lose.

✓ (Finally,) turn the officer into a helper. If the officer gives you a warn-ing instead of a ticket, immediately ask for directions—even if you know where you are. Most patrol officers would prefer to be helpers rather than enforcers. Providing you with directions helps him or her deal with "cav-ing in" to your wish for a warning.

It's best not to speed, but if you are stopped for speeding, think before acting. Try to get the officer to see you as a person rather than a speed demon and scofflaw. Put yourself in his or her shoes, and try a little psychology.

—Perry W. Buffington, *Cheap Psychological Tricks*
(Atlanta, GA: Peachtree, 1996).

1. What **audience** is Perry Buffington writing for? *a general audience of drivers*

2. What is his **purpose**? *to explain a process for avoiding a speeding ticket*

3. Double-underline the **thesis statement**.

4. Which does the essay tell the reader: how to do something or how some-thing works? *how to do something*

5. Put a check mark (✓) next to the **topic sentence** in each paragraph.

6. Circle the (transitions).

7. What **key words** are repeated? *Answers will vary but may include speed, ticket, fear, anxiety, police, officer, uncomfortable.*

8. How does the author's **concluding paragraph** relate back to his main point or thesis statement? *restates main idea*

For more on audience and purpose, see pages 7–9.

Write a Process Analysis Essay

In this section, you will write your own process analysis essay. To do so, follow this sequence:

REVIEW the four basics of good process analysis (p. 155).

CHOOSE your writing assignment (below).

WRITE your process analysis using the step-by-step Writing Guide (p. 168).

CHECK your final essay (p. 172).

WRITING ASSIGNMENT 1   COLLEGE, WORK, EVERYDAY LIFE

Write a process analysis essay on *one* of the following topics or on a topic of your own choice.

COLLEGE

TEACHING TIP
Students also may wish to write about applying for financial aid, finding supplemental scholarships, registering for classes, meeting with an adviser, choosing a major, or another process that affects their education.

• How to use the computers in the computer lab
• How to get an A in a course
• How _____ (a process in your major field of study) works

WORK

• How to do one of your major tasks at work
• How a benefit plan works (a 401k, another retirement plan, a medical plan)
• How the human resources department can help with a problem

EVERYDAY LIFE

• How to calm down or get to sleep
• How to buy or sell a car (or some other item)
• How a checking account works

WRITING ASSIGNMENT 2   USE THE INTERNET

Search the Internet for information on one of the following topics. Then write a process analysis essay on how to find information about the topic.

- Your family tree (Try the National Genealogical Society's Web site at <**www.ngsgenealogy.org**>.)
- Getting a job (Try Career Builder's site at <**www.careerbuilder.com**>.)
- Getting medical information online (Try the U.S. National Library of Medicine's MEDLINEplus site at <**www.nlm.nih.gov/medlineplus**>.)

For advice about how to cite a source, see Chapter 20.

WRITING ASSIGNMENT 3   HOW TO KEEP A JOB

Read the problem and situation that follow, and then choose *one* of the assignment options (3A or 3B) that appear after it.

TEAMWORK
Assignment 3 works well in small groups.

PROBLEM: Many people, even those who have worked for some time, do not understand either the basic rules for keeping a job (things you do in order not to get fired immediately) or the behaviors that employers value. As a result, they get passed over for promotions or salary increases, or they get fired.

SITUATION: Your company has agreed to work with a social services agency in town and to hire former welfare recipients in a welfare-to-work program. Your boss has found that although the individuals have gone through a brief training program, they often jeopardize their continued employment because they don't understand what being a responsible employee means.

Your boss asks you to write a report that helps these new employees understand what is expected of them.

ASSIGNMENT OPTION 3A: RESPONSE TO THE SITUATION

Using what you know about process analysis, write an essay that explains the basics of holding a job. First make a list of basic expectations of any employee. Within the essay, suggest steps an employee can take that go beyond the minimum of keeping a job to becoming a valuable employee.

ASSIGNMENT OPTION 3B: ANOTHER PERSPECTIVE

Assume you are a manager, and write an essay that gives advice about how to get a promotion. If you have never been a manager, this assignment will get you to think about what makes an employee a valuable, promotable asset to a manager. If you can't come up with ideas yourself, do a little

For advice about doing research, see Chapter 20.

research. You can find articles on this subject online, or you could go to a company or store and ask to interview a manager.

Writing Guide

Process Analysis

Follow the steps in this Writing Guide to help you prewrite, draft, revise, and edit your process analysis. Check off each step as you complete it.

ESL
Ask students how differences in language and culture may affect readers' understanding of a process analysis.

THINKING CRITICALLY ABOUT PROCESS ANALYSIS

FOCUS Think about the process you want to explain to your readers, the steps involved in the process, and the main point you want to make.

ASK
- What process do I know well?
- Who will be reading this, and how much are they likely to know about the process?
- What do I want my readers to be able to do? Should they be able to perform the process themselves? Or should they understand how the process happens?
- Can I write a thesis statement that identifies the process and the main point I want to write about it?
- What steps in the process do my readers need to know about? What details, facts, and examples will help them understand each step?
- How should I arrange the steps?

PREWRITE TO EXPLORE YOUR TOPIC

Prewriting in process analysis involves considering all of the steps involved in doing something or in explaining how something works.

For more on purpose and audience, see pages 7–9.

_____ Decide on your purpose for writing.

_____ Identify the audience for your essay. Consider whether your readers will need to follow the steps necessary for the process or want only to understand the process.

_____ Choose a process you understand well. You will need to know all the steps and write about the essential ones in your essay.

_____ Once you know what process you want to explain, use a prewriting technique (freewriting, listing/brainstorming, questioning, discussing, clustering) to jot down some ideas about how to explain that process to a reader who isn't familiar with it.

WRITE A THESIS STATEMENT

The thesis statement in a process analysis usually identifies the process and the main point you want to make about that process.

| Topic | + | Main point | = | Thesis statement |

Learning how to use the advanced functions on my computer   is frustrating.

If you learn how to fall out of love,   you will minimize the pain of a breakup.

_____ Decide on the main point you want to make about the process. What do you want your readers to know or learn about this process?

_____ Once you know your main point, write a thesis statement that contains both the process (your topic) and your main point about that process.

SUPPORT YOUR POINT

The major support points in a process analysis are the essential steps involved in explaining how to do the process or how the process works. These steps should demonstrate the main point about the process that you have stated in your thesis. The supporting details in process analysis explain each of the essential steps to your readers.

_____ List all the essential steps in the process.

_____ Review your thesis statement, and drop any steps that are not essential.

_____ Choose the steps that are necessary for readers to perform this activity or to understand how it works.

_____ Add details that describe the steps and would help your readers do this activity correctly. Imagine that you are not already familiar with the process, and ask yourself whether you could do it or understand how it works after reading the essay.

MAKE A PLAN

Making a written plan—an outline—helps you decide how to order your process analysis. A process analysis generally uses chronological (time) order, presenting each step from first to last as it would take place.

_____ Arrange the steps in the process in chronological order.

_____ Make a plan or an outline for your process analysis essay.

DRAFT

Drafting in process analysis means writing in complete sentences and including the following:

- An introduction with a thesis statement that identifies the process and the point you want to make about the process
- The essential steps in the process, supported by explanations of those steps
- A conclusion that reminds your readers of your main point and makes another observation about the process

_____ Think about how you can show your readers your main point about the process.

_____ Write an introductory paragraph that includes your thesis statement and hooks your readers' interest.

_____ Write a topic sentence for each of the steps.

_____ Write body paragraphs that explain each step in detail to your readers.

_____ Write a concluding paragraph that has energy, refers back to your point about the process, and makes a final observation or recommendation.

_____ Title your essay.

REVISE

Revising means changing whole sentences or paragraphs to make your writing clearer or stronger. To revise a process analysis, imagine that you have no idea how to perform the process or how the process works. Read your draft, looking for the following:

- Places where the essay strays from the essential steps and details about those steps (revise for unity)
- Places where readers might not understand the steps (revise for support and detail)
- Places where transitions are needed to help readers move smoothly from one step to the next (revise for coherence)

_____ Get feedback from others through peer review.

_____ Begin revising by asking yourself how you could make the steps of the process clearer for your readers.

_____ Reread your thesis statement to see whether it clearly identifies the process and your main point about it.

_____ Reread the body of your essay to make sure you haven't left out any essential steps. Add any details that would make the steps clearer.

_____ Reread your introduction, and make changes if it is dull.

_____ Reread your conclusion to be certain that it is energetic and reinforces your opening and your thesis.

_____ Add your transition words and sentences to connect your steps and lead readers smoothly from one to another.

_____ Make at least five changes to your draft to improve the unity, support, or coherence of your process analysis or to make the introduction, thesis statement, or conclusion stronger or more convincing.

> For more on peer review, see pages 87–88.
>
> **TEAMWORK**
> For peer review, ask students to focus especially on correct order, completeness, and transitions.

EDIT

Some grammar, spelling, word use, or punctuation errors may confuse your readers and make it difficult for them to understand a point you are trying to make. Even if they do not confuse your readers, errors detract from the effectiveness and overall quality of your writing. Edit your process analysis carefully, and correct any errors you find.

_____ Ask a classmate or friend to read your process analysis and highlight any errors.

_____ Use the spell checker or grammar checker on your computer.

_____ Look yourself for additional errors in grammar, spelling, word use, or punctuation. Focus first on sentence fragments, run-on sentences, problems with subject–verb agreement, problems with verbs, and other areas where you know you often make errors.

_____ Print a clean, final copy.

_____ Ask yourself: Is this the best I can do?

> For more on editing, see Chapters 22–41.

A FINAL CHECK BEFORE HANDING IN YOUR PROCESS ANALYSIS ESSAY

If you've followed the Writing Guide for process analysis, your essay will already include the four basics of good process analysis. Use this list to double-check each basic feature.

_____ My process analysis helps readers follow the steps in the process themselves or understand how the process works.

_____ The paragraphs in the body of my essay present the essential steps in the process.

_____ Each paragraph that presents a step also includes a detailed explanation of how that step works.

_____ The steps are arranged in chronological order, as they occur, or in some other logical order.

12

Classification

Writing That Puts Things into Groups

You Know This
You already use classification.
- You walk into a video store where movies are classified in categories such as comedy, drama, and horror.
- You use the college bookstore, where books are classified by discipline (English, biology, economics) and by course number.
- You shop at the drugstore where products are classified by use, such as hair, skin, or dental care.

Understand What Classification Is

DEFINITION: **Classification** is writing that organizes, or sorts, people or items into categories.

DEFINITION: The **organizing principle** for a classification is *how* you sort the group of people or items, not the categories themselves. For example, you might sort clean laundry using one of the following organizing principles: by ownership (yours, your roommate's, and so on); by where it goes (the bedroom, the bathroom).

IDEA JOURNAL
Write about the different kinds of friends you have.

▪▪ Four Basics of Good Classification

1. It makes sense of a group of people or items by organizing them into categories.
2. It has useful categories.
3. It uses a single organizing principle.
4. It gives examples of the people or items that fit into each category.

Profile of Success

Giovanni Bohorquez

TECHNICAL CONSULTANT

Giovanni Bohorquez

BACKGROUND: At the age of eleven, Giovanni left Colombia, where he was born and lived with his mother, and came to the United States to live with his father in New Jersey. His father was poor and wasn't particularly happy to have responsibility for taking care of anyone else, so Giovanni worked several jobs and was earning significant wages by the age of twelve.

After high school, Giovanni went to a community college and then transferred to the University of California–Los Angeles (UCLA), where he finished his bachelor's degree. He then went to work for Ernst & Young, a financial consulting company, and is now pursuing a master's degree in business administration (M.B.A.) at UCLA's Anderson School while continuing to work.

EMPLOYER: Hewlett-Packard Consulting

COLLEGE(S)/DEGREES: El Camino College (A.A.), UCLA (B.S.)

TYPES OF WRITING ON THE JOB: Proposals, project plan reports, contracts, sales letters, documentation of business processes, change order reports, email

HOW GIOVANNI USES CLASSIFICATION: As a consultant, Giovanni must perform a good deal of analysis for clients. For example, he recently completed a detailed analysis of the types of emerging technologies. For an example of how Giovanni uses classification, see Classification in the Workplace, page 179.

COMPUTER SKILLS: Word processing, UNIX, BroadVision, Advanced PL/SQL, Java, HTML, statistical analysis software

TEAMWORK ON THE JOB: Giovanni's analytical work often involves both Ernst & Young employees and employees from the client's company. Teamwork is essential in compiling all of the technical information necessary to generate a thorough analysis. As the team leader, Giovanni is responsible for pulling together varied bits of data gathered from across the office and across the country.

FUTURE GOAL: Giovanni hopes to complete his M.B.A. program and to successfully manage a high-tech product.

ORGANIZING PRINCIPLE FOR CLASSIFICATION

A classification applies an organizing principle—a method of sorting—to a group. Imagine the following situation, in which the classification system does not arrange things in useful categories following a single organizing principle.

You go into your local video store to find that it has been rearranged. The signs indicating the location of different types of videos—comedy, horror, drama—are gone. You take a look around, but you can't figure out how the videos are now classified, so you don't know where to look for what you want.

When you ask the clerk at the desk how to find a video, she says, "The videos over on this side are arranged by length of the film, starting with the shortest. The videos on the other side are arranged alphabetically by the leading actor's last name."

This new arrangement is confusing for two reasons:

- It doesn't have useful categories. (Who's likely to select a video based on its exact length?)
- It doesn't have a single organizing principle. (Even if you know the length of the video and the actor's last name, you still don't know on which side of the store to start looking.)

The following diagram shows how videos at most stores are classified, following a single organizing principle.

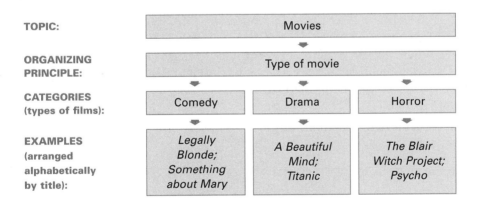

TOPIC:	Movies		
ORGANIZING PRINCIPLE:	Type of movie		
CATEGORIES (types of films):	Comedy	Drama	Horror
EXAMPLES (arranged alphabetically by title):	*Legally Blonde; Something about Mary*	*A Beautiful Mind; Titanic*	*The Blair Witch Project; Psycho*

SUPPORT POINTS FOR CLASSIFICATION

Once you decide on a group to classify and select an organizing principle, your categories provide support points for your essay. Examples of the things or people in each category provide the supporting details that help explain your categories to readers. The following plan is often used to organize a classification essay. Arrange your categories and examples logically, according to your purpose and your readers' expectations.

Topic

Organizing principle

Category

examples

Category

examples

Category

examples

As you write your essay, the following transitions may be helpful in leading from one category to the next or from one example to another.

For more on transitions, see pages 94–99.

Common Transitions in Classification

another	first, second, third, and so on
another kind	for example
for instance	

Whenever you organize or sort things to make sense of them, you are classifying them. Here are some ways you might use classification:

COLLEGE

- In a nursing course, you are asked to discuss three types of antibiotics used to treat infections.

WORK

- For an inventory report, you have to list the types of software the store carries and report how many of each type you have in stock.

EVERYDAY LIFE

- You look at the types of payment plans that are available with your car loan.

Read and Analyze Classification

Before writing your own classification essay, read the following examples — one each from college, the workplace, and everyday life — and answer the questions that accompany each. Reading the examples and answering the questions will help you understand how to write a good classification.

1. CLASSIFICATION IN COLLEGE

The following is an essay that a student, Danny Fitzgerald, wrote for his English composition class.

Blood Type and Personality

Danny Fitzgerald

In Japan, the question "What's your blood type?" is as common as "What's your sign?" in the United States. Some Japanese researchers claim that people's personalities can be classified by their blood types. You may be skeptical about this method of classification, but don't judge its validity before you read the descriptions the researchers have put together. Do you see yourself?

✓ If you have blood type O, you are a leader. When you see something you want, you strive to achieve your goal. You are passionate, loyal, and self-confident, and you are often a trendsetter. Your enthusiasm for projects and goals spreads to others who happily follow your lead. When you want something, you may be ruthless about getting it or blind to how your actions affect others.

✓ Another blood type, A, is a social, people person. You like people and work well with them. You are sensitive, patient, compassionate, and affectionate. You are a good peacekeeper because you want everyone to be happy. In a team situation, you resolve conflicts and keep things on a smooth course. Sometimes type A's are stubborn and find it difficult to relax. They may find it uncomfortable to do things alone.

✓ People with type B blood are usually individualists who like to do things on their own. You may be creative and adaptable, and you usually say

TEACHING TIP
Read this essay aloud, give students a few minutes to respond to the questions in writing, and discuss the responses as a group. Ask students what other organizing principles they might use to classify personalities (for example, birth order).

exactly what you mean. Although you can adapt to situations, you may choose not to do so because of your strong independent streak. You may prefer working on your own to being part of a team.

✓ The final blood type is AB. If you have AB blood, you are a natural entertainer. You draw people to you because of your charm and easygoing nature. ABs are usually calm and controlled, tactful and fair. On the downside, though, they may take too long to make decisions. And they may procrastinate, putting off tasks until the last minute.

Classifying people's personalities by blood type seems very unusual until you examine what researchers have found. Most people find the descriptions fairly accurate. When you think about it, classification by blood type isn't any more far-fetched than classification by horoscope sign. What will they think of next? Classification by hair color?

For more on audience and purpose, see pages 7–9.

1. What type of **audience** is Danny writing for? *his instructor and classmates*

2. What is the **purpose** of his classification of blood types? *to explain what the Japanese believe about the relationship between blood type and personality*

3. Fill in the blanks with the **topic** and the **method of classifying** (the organizing principle) for Danny's essay.

   TOPIC: *people's personalities*

   HOW CLASSIFIED: *blood type*

4. Double-underline the **thesis statement**.

5. What **introduction techniques** does Danny use to get the reader's attention? *opens with a surprising fact and a question*

6. What **categories** does Danny present? *blood types O, A, B, and AB*

7. Put a check mark next to each **topic sentence** identifying a category.

8. Underline the **examples** of each category that Danny gives.

9. What **key words** are repeated? *Answers may include blood type, personalities, people, classifying.*

10. Does Danny's essay have the **four basics of good classification**? Why

   or why not? *Answers will vary.* _____

For a list of the four basics, see page 173.

2. CLASSIFICATION IN THE WORKPLACE

The following essay was part of Giovanni Bohorquez's application for the Anderson School, the graduate business school at UCLA. Notice how Giovanni presents the types of key skills he has learned.

One day I would like to manage a high-tech product, so over the last ten years I have learned the types of skills that product managers must have: production management, system design, and entrepreneurism.

✓ I learned the first type of skill—production management—when I worked as a plant controller for three years with control over production of modem components and responsibility for more than one hundred employees. As a plant controller, I managed the raw materials, created production schedules, and oversaw inventory.

✓ I learned the second type of skill—system design—by designing and implementing Enterprise Resource Planning (ERP) systems, which are integrated information-sharing software programs that serve the needs of all departments within a single company. Companies such as ConAgra, SUN, Genentech, and Hewlett-Packard are currently benefiting from systems that I have designed.

✓ The third type of skill—entrepreneurism—I learned by consulting with start-up and middle-market projects. Though entrepreneurial environments need to cultivate creativity and vision, they also need to recognize and meet the realities of a business environment. Many good entrepreneurial ventures fail because, though they have a wealth of good ideas, they do not understand accounting, production, and the need for good systems. As a consultant, I have been able to help entrepreneurs recognize business necessities.

With these types of key skills, I am closer to being able to attain my goal of managing a product. I have worked steadily and purposefully to acquire these types of skills, and now I am ready to learn the other skills that will allow me to successfully manage a product. It is for this reason that I am applying to the Anderson School, where I believe I can develop the expertise I need to become a well-rounded, responsible member of the business community.

For more on purpose and audience, see pages 7–9.

1. What is Giovanni's **purpose** for writing? *to demonstrate that he would be a good candidate for admission to the Anderson School M.B.A. program*

2. Who is Giovanni's **audience**? *an admissions officer*

3. Double-underline the **thesis statement**.

4. Put a check mark (✓) next to the topic sentences that present the **categories** in Giovanni's essay.

5. Underline the **supporting details** that give examples of items in each category.

6. What observation does the concluding paragraph make? *Answers will vary but should relate to the idea that the writer believes he is closer to being a good product manager because of the skills he has learned.*

3. CLASSIFICATION IN EVERYDAY LIFE

The following essay was written by a student who considers herself an expert in yard sale bargain hunting.

Yard Sale Treasures

Susan Robinson

When I started attending yard sales several years ago, I bought a lot of items that were inexpensive but turned out to be low-quality junk. Now I search only for the treasures that I know are real deals. As part of my education as a bargain hunter, I have learned to look for three kinds of items.

✓ The (first) kind of yard sale treasure is kid stuff. You can find lots of nearly new equipment, furniture, toys, and clothing at yard sales. Often there's nothing wrong with the merchandise; owners just want to sell items that take up room in the house or the basement once their children have outgrown them. Last year one of my friends found a nearly new name-brand baby stroller at a yard sale and paid $15 for it. Others have found good cribs, swings, and baby clothing that has never been worn— all at bargain prices.

✓ (Another) treasure I've come to respect is costume jewelry. People tend to collect tons of inexpensive jewelry over the years, and jewelry doesn't wear out. In the $1 box at a recent yard sale, I bought a "pearl" necklace and matching earrings for $2. They weren't real pearls, but they looked so real that no one but an expert would know the difference. In the same box, my friend found a "ruby" ring that looked authentic, with a small, well-shaped stone and an antique-like setting.

✓ (A third kind) of treasure is kitchen stuff, especially sets of plates, sets of glasses, serving pieces, and vases. When you are setting up an apartment, there is no better place than a yard sale to find dishes and glasses. Maybe a set of dishes that originally had twelve pieces is down to ten, but who really needs twelve of the same dish?

When people have yard sales, they put out all kinds of things, and shoppers should beware of junk. Instead, look for the things that you know are good values, and avoid the odd knickknacks or old Christmas decorations or worn-down shoes. You can get great bargains at yard sales if you choose carefully. A word of caution to the buyer of junk: You will soon have to have your own yard sale.

1. What type of **audience** is Susan writing for? _a general audience_

2. What is Susan's **purpose** for writing? _to explain what types of items are_ _good yard sale bargains_

For more on audience and purpose, see pages 7–9.

3. Fill in the diagram using the elements of Susan's essay.

   TOPIC: _yard sales_

   ORGANIZING PRINCIPLE: sorted by _good buys_

   CATEGORIES: _kid stuff_   _costume jewelry_   _kitchen stuff_

EXAMPLES: equipment/stroller   "pearl" necklace/earrings   sets of glasses

swings   "ruby" ring   serving pieces

furniture/cribs   vases

toys

clothing

4. Double-underline the **thesis statement**.

5. Circle the (transitions) in the essay.

6. Put a check mark (✓) next to the **topic sentences** that present the categories.

Write a Classification Essay

In this section, you will write your own classification essay. To do so, follow this sequence:

REVIEW the four basics of good classification (p. 173).

CHOOSE your writing assignment (below).

WRITE your classification using the step-by-step Writing Guide (p. 184).

CHECK your final essay (p. 188).

WRITING ASSIGNMENT 1   COLLEGE, WORK, EVERYDAY LIFE

DISCUSSION
On the board, write the four basics as separate headings. Then have students provide examples from the essay "Yard Sale Treasures" (p. 180) that illustrate each basic.

Write a classification essay on *one* of the following topics or on a topic of your own choice.

COLLEGE

Types of
- Degree programs
- Student services
- Choose a classifiable subject from another course

WORK

Types of
- Work spaces
- Customers or clients
- Skills needed for a particular job

EVERYDAY LIFE

Types of
- Drivers
- Restaurants in your town
- Wireless phone calling plans

■ WRITING ASSIGNMENT 2   **USE THE INTERNET**

Visit Amazon.com (**<www.amazon.com>**), or the Web site of another major retailer, and write a classification essay in which you explain how the site is organized.

For advice about how to cite a source, see Chapter 20.

■ WRITING ASSIGNMENT 3   **MAKE A BUDGET**

Read the problem and situation that follow, and then choose *one* of the assignment options (3A or 3B) that appear after it.

> PROBLEM: Many people, even those with a good salary, have trouble managing their money. Because they have no idea how to organize their expenses, at the end of the week or month they wonder where their money has gone. They know only that they seem to be spending lots of money, have trouble making ends meet, and can't ever seem to save.

> SITUATION: You finally decide that you need to create a budget for yourself. The first thing you need to do is to figure out how you spend your money.

ASSIGNMENT OPTION 3A: RESPONSE TO THE SITUATION

Using what you know about classification, write an essay that sorts your monthly expenses. (Hint: You might begin by making a list of all the monthly expenses you have. The idea is to account for as much of what you spend in a month as possible and then to give examples of or details about those expenses.)

ASSIGNMENT OPTION 3B: ANOTHER PERSPECTIVE

Using what you know about classification, discuss the kinds of expenses that are associated with going to college.

Writing Guide

Classification

Follow the steps in this Writing Guide to help you prewrite, draft, revise, and edit your classification essay. Check off each step as you complete it.

TEACHING TIP
After students choose an essay topic, ask them to respond to the Thinking Critically prompts in their journals.

THINKING CRITICALLY ABOUT CLASSIFICATION

FOCUS | Think about what you want to classify (sort) for your readers and the main point you want to make about that topic.

ASK |
- Who will be reading this piece of writing, and what do they know or need to know about my topic?
- What is my purpose—my reason for sorting or classifying? What is my main point about the topic?
- To accomplish my purpose, how should I sort things? What should my organizing principle be?
- What categories will help my readers make sense of my topic?
- What people or items fit into each category? What examples, facts, and details will my readers need to understand how I have classified things?

PREWRITE TO EXPLORE YOUR TOPIC

Prewriting in classification involves considering how to sort your topic into useful categories and thinking about how to give good examples of or details about those categories.

For more on purpose and audience, see pages 7–9.

_____ Decide on your purpose for writing.

_____ Identify the audience for your essay.

_____ Select the topic or group that you want to classify.

_____ Once you have decided on a narrowed topic, use a prewriting technique (freewriting, listing/brainstorming, questioning, discussing, clustering) to generate useful categories for sorting your topic. In classification, a variation on the technique of clustering is often useful: filling in a diagram like the one shown at the top of the next page.

TEACHING TIP
Try to help students
match prewriting
options to their
learning preferences.

WRITE A THESIS STATEMENT

The thesis statement in a classification essay can take one of several forms:

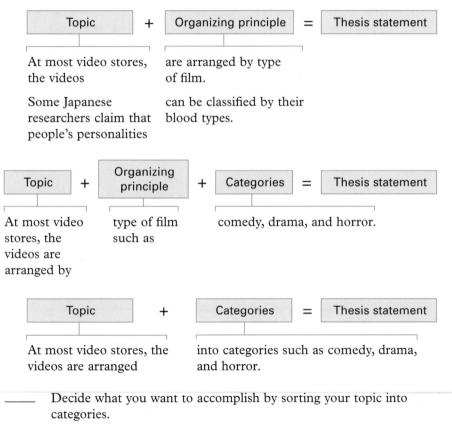

_____ Decide what you want to accomplish by sorting your topic into categories.

_____ Write a thesis statement that follows one of the suggested formats above.

SUPPORT YOUR POINT

The support points in classification are the categories into which you choose to sort your topic. These will become the topic sentences for the body paragraphs in your essay. The supporting details will be specific examples of people or items that fit into the categories. Fill in below categories you want to use and examples of each category.

Topic _____

Organizing principle _____

Category _____

     examples _____

Category _____

     examples _____

Category _____

     examples _____

_____ Choose at least three useful categories into which you can sort your topic.

_____ Add facts and details for each example you want to use under the categories.

MAKE A PLAN

Making a written plan—an outline—helps you decide how to order your classification. If you filled in the list above, you already have a written plan. Now you need to decide on a logical sequence of categories that accomplishes your purpose and will make sense to your readers. (Writers of classification essays may or may not use standard organizational patterns such as chronological order, spatial order, and order of importance.)

_____ Arrange the categories in a logical order.

_____ Make a new outline that shows the order you have chosen.

DRAFT

In classification, drafting involves writing in complete sentences and including the following:

- An introduction with your thesis statement
- The categories you have chosen with examples and details of items that fit into those categories

- A conclusion that reminds your readers of your main point and makes an observation about your classification

_____   Write an introductory paragraph that includes your thesis statement and hooks your readers' interest.

_____   Write a topic sentence for each of the categories.

_____   Write body paragraphs that include the topic sentence and the specific examples and details.

_____   Write a concluding paragraph that reminds your readers of the purpose of classifying your topic into these categories and makes a further observation.

_____   Title your essay.

REVISE

Revising means changing whole sentences or paragraphs to make your writing clearer or stronger. To revise a classification essay, imagine that you have no idea how or why one might sort your topic. Read your draft, looking for the following:

- Places where the ideas are off the main point (revising for unity)
- Gaps in information or detail (revising for support)
- Areas in need of transitions that will help readers move smoothly from one point to the next (revising for coherence)

_____   Get feedback from others through peer review.

_____   Begin revising by considering how to make your classification clearer or more interesting for your readers.

_____   Reread your thesis statement. See whether it is clear about what the single organizing principle is, the categories into which you will sort your topic, or both.

_____   Reread the body paragraphs of your classification essay. Replace or cut any categories that do not follow your organizing principle.

_____   Look at the examples you have used in each category. Add details or replace examples to make sure that they will help your readers understand the kinds of things that fit into the category.

_____   Reread your introduction, and make changes if it is dull. Even when you're just introducing categories, be enthusiastic about what you're classifying.

> **TEAMWORK**
> Tell students to use these revision prompts in small groups for peer review of their drafts.

> For more on peer review, see pages 87–88.

_____   Reread your conclusion with the same goal: to make it energetic and memorable to your readers. Make your final observation a personal comment about the classification system.

_____   Add transitions and transitional sentences to help your readers move smoothly from one category to another.

_____   Make at least five changes to your draft, to improve the unity, support, and coherence of your classification or to strengthen your introduction, thesis statement, or conclusion.

EDIT

Some grammar, spelling, word use, or punctuation errors may confuse your readers and make it difficult for them to understand a point you are trying to make. Even if they do not confuse your readers, errors detract from the effectiveness and overall quality of your writing. Edit your classification carefully, and correct any errors you find.

For more on editing, see Chapters 22–41.

_____   Ask a classmate or friend to read your classification and highlight any errors.

_____   Use the spell checker and grammar checker on your computer, but do not rely on those programs to catch all the errors.

_____   Look yourself for errors that the spell checker or grammar checker didn't catch. Focus first on sentence fragments, run-on sentences, problems with subject–verb agreement, problems with verbs, and other areas where you know you often make errors.

_____   Print a clean final copy.

_____   Ask yourself: Is this the best I can do?

A FINAL CHECK BEFORE HANDING IN YOUR CLASSIFICATION ESSAY

If you've followed the Writing Guide for classification, your essay will already include the four basics of classification. Use this list to double-check each basic feature.

_____   My thesis statement explains how I organize a group into categories.

_____   My categories are useful and make sense.

_____   My categories follow only one organizing principle.

_____   The body of my essay gives examples, members of the group that fit into each category.

13

Definition

Writing That Tells What Something Means

Understand What Definition Is

DEFINITION: **Definition** is writing that explains what a term means. Having a clear understanding of what a term means can help you avoid confusion and mistakes.

IDEA JOURNAL
Write about what
success means.

▪▪ Four Basics of Good Definition

1. It tells readers what term is being defined.
2. It presents a clear and precise basic definition.
3. It includes examples to show what the writer means.
4. It uses words and examples that readers will understand.

Definition helps you convey what you mean so that you are under-stood. It also helps you understand what other people mean. Before you define a term for a reader, you need to understand the meaning yourself. Start by reading the dictionary definition; then try to explain the meaning in your own words. Your definition essay needs to include a good basic def-inition of the term as you are using it for your reader.

Gary Knoblock

BUSINESS OWNER

Gary Knoblock

BACKGROUND: Gary grew up in New Orleans, and while neither of his parents had much formal education themselves, they valued education. After high school, Gary tried college for a year but was told by a professor that he wasn't college material and should try manual labor. Gary left college and moved to Fort Worth, Texas, where he took law enforcement exams. He passed the exams and joined the Fort Worth Police Department. During his ten years with the force, he attended a junior college at night, earning an associate's degree. He also had numerous promotions at work and became a member of the force's SWAT team.

"Believe it or not," said Gary, "police work can be boring [because] you're not always involved in a case." In 1999, Gary decided to start his own business. He moved to Mississippi, where his parents now live, and started a sign company, Lightning Quick (LQ) Signs. Since then the company has grown steadily into a successful business.

EMPLOYER: Self

COLLEGE(S)/DEGREES: Tarrant County Junior College (A.A.)

TYPES OF WRITING ON THE JOB: Proposals to get jobs, advertising copy, follow-up reports and letters, loan applications, correspondence with clients and prospective clients, precise and descriptive specifications for govern-ment jobs

HOW GARY USES DEFINITION: Gary often needs to define terms for clients. In addition, his letter about the company that he uses in sales situations defines how LQ Signs is "customer-oriented." For an example of Gary's use of definition, see Definition in the Workplace, page 194.

COMPUTER SKILLS: WordPerfect, Quicken, and Adobe Photoshop and Illustrator, two types of design software

TEAMWORK ON THE JOB: Teamwork saved Gary's life a number of times when he was a police officer and SWAT team member. He brings the value of teamwork to his own small business. He and his employees work as a team to prioritize and schedule activities, assign responsibilities, prepare job sites, secure any necessary permits, and plan graphics. Even as company president, Gary feels his role is to be part of the team.

FUTURE GOAL: Gary says, "Never to feel *too* comfortable, because that can lead to stagnation and boredom. I am constantly reevaluating things, because I never want to coast or get stale."

POINT OF VIEW IN DEFINITION

You can depend on a dictionary to discover the definitions of words like *desk, chair,* and *paper*—which have definite, concrete meanings. The meanings of other words—like *love, success,* or *freedom*—depend on a person's point of view. These words need to be carefully explained, or they could be misunderstood.

For example, if a friend says, "Summer in New York City is awful," you don't know what she means by *awful.* Is it the weather? The people? The transportation? Until you ask, you won't know whether you would think New York City in the summer is awful or not.

DISCUSSION
Say aloud, "This class is boring." Then quickly call on students to give a word or term that means *boring class.* List the words on the board to illustrate subjectivity.

SUPPORT IN DEFINITION

When you write a definition essay, your thesis statement may present your basic definition. It may also tell what larger class or category the word belongs to and what details distinguish it from other words in that class. Just as a terrier is one member of the class of dogs, so Jo-Jo, your dog, is one member of the class of terriers.

DISCUSSION
Have students modify a dictionary definition for a variety of audiences.

Your major support points in a definition are your examples. You develop your examples by adding details and explanations that will show your readers what you mean by a term. The examples in a definition are often organized by importance, or the impact you think the examples will have on your readers. Save the most important example for last.

For more on order of importance, see page 60.

The plan for a definition essay might look like this:

Introduction (including thesis)

First Example of Your Meaning

> specific details that show how that example demonstrates your definition

Second Example of Your Meaning

> specific details that show how that example demonstrates your definition

Third Example of Your Meaning

> specific details that show how that example demonstrates your definition

As you write, add transitions to connect one example to the next.

For more on
transitions, see pages
94–99.

Common Transitions for Definition

another	for example
another kind	for instance
first, second, third, and so on	

Many situations—in college, at work, or in everyday life—require you to explain the meaning of a term, particularly how you are using it. Here are some ways you might use definition.

COLLEGE

- On a U.S. history exam you are asked to define the term *carpetbagger*.

WORK

- In a conversation with a benefits customer, you have to define *reasonable and customary charges*.

EVERYDAY LIFE

- You explain the term *fair* to your child in the context of games or sports.

Read and Analyze Definition

Before writing your own definition essay, read the following examples—one each from college, the workplace, and everyday life—and answer the questions that accompany each. Reading the examples and answering the questions will help you understand how to write a good definition essay.

TEACHING TIP
Have several
dictionaries in your
classroom. Advise
students to have their
own dictionary as well.

ESL
Encourage ESL
students to buy both
an English dictionary
and a bilingual
dictionary.

1. DEFINITION IN COLLEGE

The following is an essay that a student wrote in an introductory psychology course. This was the assignment:

> Define a term from Part One of the textbook, and give examples of that term in a well-organized essay that demonstrates your understanding of the term.

Two Intelligences

Emma Brennan

Until this semester, I thought that intelligence was just being smart academically. Over the course of the semester, I learned that while intelligence means "acquired or applied knowledge," there are different types of intelligence, two of which I will discuss here.

✓ The first type, crystallized intelligence, is the knowledge an individual has built up and stored in memory. This intelligence includes information, skills, and experiences that a person can draw on to operate in this world. The basic math skills that we learn and use in a variety of ways — to add a tip to a restaurant bill, to add the prices of items we want to purchase, to calculate whether we have enough gas to get home — are examples of crystallized intelligence. Another is the ability to read. Once we know how to read, we don't have to relearn that skill every time we need to do it. We also store information such as what dates are holidays or important events in history, what substances are poisonous, what our social security number is. We have learned how to handle situations such as being hurt (emotionally or physically), being in danger, and being hungry. We walk around with a whole universe of facts, information, skills, and strategies that we can call up at any time. These things are just with us, part of our past experiences.

✓ Fluid intelligence, on the other hand, is the ability to deal with new problems and situations. Although fluid intelligence may draw upon information and experience that is actually crystallized intelligence, it is an individual's ability to meet completely new challenges and contexts and learn how to work within them. For example, if at work you have a problem that you've never experienced before, the amount of fluid intelligence you have will determine whether you try to solve the problem or just give up. If you have a new computer program and something goes wrong, for example, fluid intelligence would prompt you to try to figure out a solution and move forward. If your fluid intelligence is not highly developed, you will likely either call the help line or sit there frustrated.

(Both types) of intelligence are important as one, crystallized intelligence allows us to incorporate the sum of what we have learned into our supply of skills and behaviors while the other, fluid intelligence, allows us to continue to learn and rise to new challenges. Though an individual may have natural abilities (and natural weaknesses) in a variety of areas, it is the preservation and balance of these two basic types of intelligence that allow him or her to be successful in the world.

For more on audience and purpose, see pages 7–9.

1. Who is Emma's likely **audience**? *her instructor*

2. What is Emma's **purpose** in this essay? *to demonstrate understanding of two terms presented in her textbook*

3. Double-underline the **thesis statement**.

4. Put a check mark (✓) next to each **topic sentence** in the body paragraphs.

5. Underline the **examples** that Emma provides.

6. Circle any (transitions) that Emma has used.

7. What **key words** are repeated? *intelligence, knowledge, skills, learn, ability*

For a list of the four basics of good definition, see page 189.

8. Does Emma's essay have the **four basics of good definition**? Why or why not? *Answers will vary.*

2. DEFINITION IN THE WORKPLACE

The following is a piece of writing that Gary Knoblock has incorporated into a variety of situations: when trying to get a contract for his sign company, as part of advertising copy, and as part of his company's mission statement.

TEACHING TIP
Assign each student (in alphabetical order) to present a new word at the end of each class and challenge students to use the word during the next class.

The fundamental principle of Lightning Quick (LQ) Signs is customer orientation. While most companies claim that they are customer-oriented, most have no idea what that really means. I tell my employees that I would like to have a customer giggle at the completion of the job, delighting in the product and service we have delivered, his every expectation met and exceeded. For all of us at LQ Signs, *customer-oriented* means that from start to finish to follow-up, the customer comes first.

✓ Our customer orientation begins before the job begins. Before doing anything, we interview the customer to learn what his or her needs are and to determine the most cost-effective route to meet those needs. No job for us is "standard." Each is unique.

✓ Our customer orientation means that we produce high-quality products quickly. We keep signs simple, because our customers want their prospective customers to be able to read the sign in a glance. We use the most current digital printing processes to produce sharp, readable signs quickly. Because we have previously determined, with the customer, the most cost-effective method of producing the signs, the high quality and rapid return do not come at extra cost.

✓ Our customer orientation means that our products are thoroughly checked for flaws and installed at the customer's convenience. Our signs leave our workshop in perfect condition, as the customer has ordered. Our well-trained team of installers works with the customer to determine the installation schedule.

✓ Finally, our customer orientation means that the job is not complete when the sign is in place. We follow up every sale to make sure that the product is in top shape and that the customer is pleased.

LQ Signs is truly customer-oriented, from start to finish to follow-up. Our customers are our partners.

TEAMWORK
Have students read this essay aloud and respond to the questions in pairs.

1. Who is the **audience** for this piece of writing? *potential customers*

2. What is Gary's **purpose**? *to persuade potential customers to use his company's services*

For more on audience and purpose, see pages 7–9.

3. Double-underline the **thesis statement**.

4. Put a check mark (✓) next to each **topic sentence** that supports Gary's thesis statement.

5. Were you familiar with the term that Gary defined? Restate the meaning of *customer-oriented* in your own words.
Answers will vary.

3. DEFINITION IN EVERYDAY LIFE

With the rapid growth of residential development, some new homes are poorly built, even those situated in very affluent communities. The following example is a letter written by a woman who had recently moved into a new home. She sent this letter both to her lawyer and to the local newspaper.

To Whom It May Concern:

I am writing to protest the careless workmanship that has resulted in my new home being substandard. According to the *American Heritage Dictionary, substandard* means failing to meet a standard or falling below standard, and my home meets that definition in many areas. I write not only in hopes of some correction of the problems, but also to warn potential buyers of things to watch for.

✓ The siding on my home is substandard. I was told that the siding would be actual stucco, but in reality the siding is an artificial stucco that falls off and allows water damage. After six months, the siding on my house hangs off in some places, and the structure underneath is severely water damaged. This is substandard, to be sure.

✓ In addition to the exterior siding, the roof is also substandard. The tiles, of the lowest quality, were not affixed properly, and, like the siding, are falling off and allowing water to damage the structure. Not only do I have a leaky roof, but a roofing specialist whom I consulted says the entire roof must be replaced immediately. This roof is substandard.

✓ Finally, the landscaping is not only substandard, it's just plain missing. The contract promises a seeded, thriving lawn. Instead, I have lived with churned up dirt and mud. Not only is there no seeding or evidence of grass, but the entire area is littered with nails and razor blades left on the site by the builders. I discovered the razor blades after my five-year-old daughter was injured by one of them. As I investigated the yard, I found these were all around. Surely, this meets the definition of substandard.

These are just three examples of the many substandard areas in my new home, which was to be the fulfillment of my American dream. As a single parent, I have put my entire savings into this house that I wanted for my family. My dream, like those of others in this development, has become a nightmare, and an extremely expensive one. The builders are wholly unresponsive. Their work defines the word *substandard*. I write in hopes that they will live up to basic standards and remedy their substandard practices.

Sincerely,

Elena Fetzer

1. What is Elena's **purpose** for writing this letter? *to demonstrate how the building practices used to build her home resulted in a substandard product*

For more on purpose and audience, see pages 7–9.

2. Who is Elena's **audience**? *her lawyer and readers of the newspaper*

3. Double-underline the **thesis statement**.

4. Put a check mark (✓) next to the **topic sentences** for the support paragraphs.

5. From Elena's description, can you visualize the areas she cites as substandard? Using what you know about description, add another detail to each body paragraph to make the image stronger.
   Answers will vary.

6. Circle the (transitions) in the letter.

7. What **key word** does Elena repeat? *substandard*

8. Reread the **concluding paragraph**. Imagine this has happened to you: that you spent everything you had on something that turns out to be junk. Rewrite the conclusion, making it stronger.
   Answers will vary.

Write a Definition Essay

In this section, you will write your own definition essay. To do so, follow this sequence:

REVIEW the four basics of good definition (p. 189).

CHOOSE your writing assignment (p. 198).

WRITE your definition using the step-by-step Writing Guide (p. 199).

CHECK your final essay (p. 204).

WRITING ASSIGNMENT 1   COLLEGE, WORK, EVERYDAY LIFE

Write a definition essay on *one* of the following topics or on a topic of your own choice.

COLLEGE

Define

- A term or concept from another course you have taken
- A good teacher
- Cheating

WORK

Define

- Any term you use at work
- Probationary period
- A model employee

EVERYDAY LIFE

Define

- An attitude or behavior (such as assertiveness, generosity, negativity, optimism, and so on)
- Scam
- Road rage

WRITING ASSIGNMENT 2   USE THE INTERNET

For advice about how to cite a source, see Chapter 20.

Basic computer skills are necessary for most jobs today. Many job descriptions, whether in the newspaper or on the Web, list *computer literacy* among the requirements for a position. Go to the Web to find out more about computer literacy, and then write a definition of the term in your own words. You might start by entering the key words "information literacy" or "computer literacy" into search engines such as Google (**<www.google .com>**) or AltaVista (**<www.altavista.com>**). In your essay, define and give examples of the term. Assume your audience is someone who is seeking a job in your company.

WRITING ASSIGNMENT 3   WRITE A SECTION IN A MANUAL

Read the problem and situation that follow, and then choose *one* of the assignment options (3A or 3B) that appear after it.

PROBLEM: Most people are aware that communication skills are ranked among the top skill sets that employers seek and value. But what exactly are communication skills? While most people have a good general idea of what the term *communication skills* means, they don't have a clear idea of what those skills are, specifically, and how they should be applied.

SITUATION: Your company is putting together a new employee handbook. To make the handbook both realistic and relevant, the company has decided that the contents will come directly from the employees. Your department has been assigned the section on communication.

ASSIGNMENT OPTION 3A: RESPONSE TO THE SITUATION

Using what you know about definition, write an essay that defines *communication skills* and gives specific examples of how you apply those skills in your job. Of course, you'll also want your essay to demonstrate the use of good communication skills. Think of the various people with whom you need to communicate at work and what defines good communication with those people.

First look up the meaning of *communication* in a dictionary. Then list the various types of communication skills. (Remember, communication is not just the ability to speak well.) Next, make a list of communication skills you need in your job. Give specific examples from your workplace of how a communication skill is used or needed.

ASSIGNMENT OPTION 3B: ANOTHER PERSPECTIVE

Instead of writing about your own communication skills on the job, write an essay about what skills a new employee will need. Use the same process that is outlined in assignment option 3A.

Definition

Writing Guide

Follow the steps in this Writing Guide to help you prewrite, draft, revise, and edit your definition. Check off each step as you complete it.

THINKING CRITICALLY ABOUT DEFINITION	
FOCUS	Think about what the term you are defining means to you and what it is likely to mean to your readers.
ASK	• Who am I writing this for, and how familiar are my readers likely to be with the term I'm defining? • What is my purpose in defining this term? Do I want to give a formal definition, or do I want to explain what I mean when I use the word? • What basic definition should I use? • What examples or other information about the term will make the meaning clear to my readers?

PREWRITE TO EXPLORE YOUR TOPIC

Prewriting for definition involves coming up with various meanings of the term or concept you are going to define. Most words have more than one meaning, and you want to decide how you want to present your topic.

For more on purpose and audience, see pages 7–9.

_____ Decide on your purpose for writing.

_____ Identify the audience for your essay.

_____ Look up the dictionary meaning of the word you might define.

_____ Use a prewriting technique (freewriting, listing/brainstorming, questioning, discussing, clustering) to come up with the different uses of the word. Decide on the meaning you will develop in your essay.

WRITE A THESIS STATEMENT

The thesis statement in a definition essay often follows one of three basic patterns. You do not have to follow these patterns exactly, but they provide a simple guide to what a thesis statement in a definition essay might include.

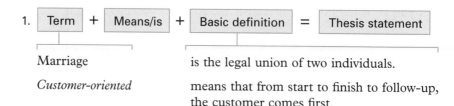

1. Term + Means/is + Basic definition = Thesis statement

Marriage   is the legal union of two individuals.

Customer-oriented   means that from start to finish to follow-up, the customer comes first.

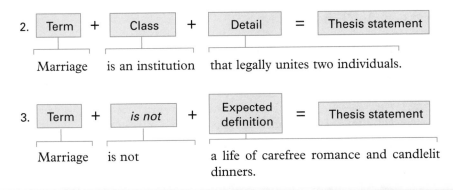

2. Term + Class + Detail = Thesis statement

Marriage   is an institution   that legally unites two individuals.

3. Term + *is not* + Expected definition = Thesis statement

Marriage   is not   a life of carefree romance and candlelit dinners.

This last pattern is a little tricky, but if used correctly, it can grab your readers' attention.

_____ Review your ideas about the term, and decide what basic definition you will give or whether you want to give several different meanings.

_____ Do not just copy the dictionary definition. Write the definition in your own words, and think about what wording will make sense to your readers.

_____ Write a thesis statement that includes both the term and your basic definition.

SUPPORT YOUR POINT

The major support points in definition are the examples that show what you mean by your use of the term or concept you are defining. The supporting details are the explanations and specific details that you give about each of your examples. These examples and explanations show your readers what you mean by the term. Think about what kinds of examples will make sense to them.

_____ Use a prewriting technique to find examples and details that explain what you mean by the term.

_____ Choose at least three good examples that demonstrate your use of the term being defined.

_____ Explain each example with details that clearly show how the example demonstrates your definition.

MAKE A PLAN

Making a written plan—an outline—helps you decide how to order your definition. A definition generally uses order of importance, arranging the examples to build up to the one with the most impact on readers.

_____ Arrange your examples (your support points) according to which you think best demonstrates the meaning of your term.

_____ Make a plan or outline for your definition essay.

DRAFT

Drafting a definition means writing in complete sentences and including the following:

- An introduction with a thesis statement
- Examples of the term with specific details that demonstrate your definition of the term
- A conclusion that reminds your readers about your definition

_____ Write an introductory paragraph that includes your thesis statement and gets your readers' interest.

_____ Write a topic sentence for each of the examples.

_____ Write body paragraphs with topic sentences and specific, concrete details about each example.

_____ Write a concluding paragraph that reminds your readers of the term and its meaning and that makes a final observation.

_____ Title your essay.

REVISE

Revising means changing whole sentences or paragraphs to make your writing clearer or stronger. To revise a definition essay, remember that most words can mean different things, depending on how they are being used. Remind yourself of other possible meanings so that you can make sure that your examples clearly explain your particular definition. Read your draft, looking for the following:

- Places where the ideas are off the main point (revising for unity)
- Gaps in information or detail (revising for support and detail)

- Areas in need of transitions to help readers move smoothly from one point to the next (revising for coherence)

_____ Get feedback from others through peer review.

For more on peer review, see pages 87–88.

_____ Begin revising by considering how you can make your definition clearer and more precise for your readers.

_____ Reread your thesis statement. Revise it so that both the term and your definition are clear.

_____ Reread the body of your essay to make sure the examples support your definition and the details about the examples demonstrate what you mean. Add other examples and details that would help explain what you mean by the term.

_____ Reread your introduction to make sure that it has energy and uses concrete words to define your topic.

_____ Reread your conclusion, again judging its energy and interest level. Make a further comment or observation about the topic or definition.

_____ Add transitions and transitional sentences to connect your examples.

_____ Make at least five changes to your draft to improve the unity, support, or coherence of your definition, or to make the introduction, thesis statement, or conclusion clearer or more interesting.

EDIT

Some grammar, spelling, word use, or punctuation errors may confuse your readers and make it difficult for them to understand a point you are trying to make. Even if they do not confuse your readers, errors detract from the effectiveness and overall quality of your writing. Edit your definition carefully, and correct any errors you find.

_____ Ask a classmate or friend to read your definition essay and highlight any errors.

_____ Use the spell checker and grammar checker on your computer.

_____ Look yourself for errors that the spell checker or grammar checker didn't catch. Focus first on sentence fragments, run-on sentences, problems with subject–verb agreement, problems with verbs, and other areas where you know you often make errors.

_____ Print a clean final copy.

_____ Ask yourself: Is this the best I can do?

TEACHING TIP
Have students write a self-assessment cover letter for their essay that includes their responses to this final check.

A FINAL CHECK BEFORE HANDING IN YOUR DEFINITION ESSAY

If you've followed the Writing Guide for definition, your essay will already include the four basics of good definition. Use this list to double-check each basic feature.

____ My definition essay tells readers what term I am defining.

____ My thesis statement presents a clear, precise definition.

____ Each paragraph in the body of my essay presents an example with supporting details to help show what the term means.

____ My definition uses examples and words that my readers can easily understand.

14

Comparison and Contrast

Writing That Shows Similarities and Differences

You Know This
You already use comparison and contrast to help make decisions.
- You compare and contrast features of several DVD players.
- You compare and contrast two job offers.
- You compare and contrast two courses you might want to take.

Understand What Comparison and Contrast Are

DEFINITION: **Comparison** is writing that shows the similarities among subjects—people, ideas, situation, or items; **contrast** shows the differences. In conversation, we often use the word *compare* to mean either compare or contrast, but as you work through this chapter, the terms will be separated.

IDEA JOURNAL
Write about some differences you see between men and women when it comes to movies they like.

■■ Four Basics of Good Comparison and Contrast

1. It uses subjects that have enough in common to be usefully compared and contrasted.

2. It serves a purpose—either to help readers make a decision or understand the subjects.

3. It presents several important, parallel points of comparison and contrast.

4. It arranges points in a logical organization.

Salvador Torres

FINANCIAL CONSULTANT

Salvador Torres

BACKGROUND: Salvador is the son of farm-workers who moved to California from rural Mexico. He spoke only Spanish at home and did not learn English until he was in the fourth grade. He worked with his parents at times, which taught him that the life of a manual laborer is extremely difficult. His parents always insisted he should try to do better for himself. A high school teacher and counselor encouraged Salvador academically and introduced him to several people who, like Salvador, had started with poor grades and English skills but had attended community college and were successful working professionals. Salvador was part of and later worked with the Puenté Project, a program for Hispanic students who are at risk of not completing college. He is now a mentor who helps others like him to stay—and succeed—in college.

EMPLOYER: Public Financial Management, Inc.

COLLEGE(S)/DEGREES: Gavilan College (A.A.), Stanford University (B.A.), Princeton University (M.P.A.)

TYPES OF WRITING ON THE JOB: Memos to clients on a variety of financial topics, financial reports and analyses, email

HOW SALVADOR USES COMPARISON/CONTRAST: Because Salvador is a financial consultant, he has to compare and contrast investment options for clients. For an example of the type of comparison/contrast writing Salvador does on the job, see page 212.

COMPUTER SKILLS: Microsoft Office (Word, Excel, PowerPoint, Front Page, Outlook, Access); DBC Finance, Groupwise; Lexis-Nexis; STATA statistical software; Visual Basic programming

TEAMWORK ON THE JOB: Being able to work in a team is vital to success as a financial consultant because on any given project, a consultant works with various other advisers—experts in investment banking, law, insurance, and credit. All of these individuals must pool their knowledge to advise a client who has hired Public Financial Management, Inc.

FUTURE GOAL: Salvador says, "[My goal is] to reach my full personal potential and to help other Chicanos and Latinos meet theirs. I also want to help preserve existing institutions and create new institutions that will aid in the success of members of our community."

A comparison/contrast essay shows how things are alike or different, helping readers understand or choose between alternatives. For example, you might want to compare and contrast two restaurants so that readers can choose between them. Or you might want to compare and contrast two friends or two of your children; your purpose then is not to help your readers choose between them but to give them an understanding of both people.

POINTS FOR COMPARISON AND CONTRAST

You may have heard people say, "That's comparing apples and oranges," meaning that two things aren't alike enough to result in any meaningful comparison. For example, comparing a DVD player and a toaster would not help explain either. Although they are both electronic appliances, they are so different that showing similarities or differences makes no sense. When you write comparison/contrast, choose subjects that are similar enough to be compared or contrasted.

Once you have selected comparable subjects, you need to find **points of comparison**—parallel or matched points that will show how the subjects are similar or different. Supporting details then explain these support points for each subject. For example, the student who wrote the thesis *The ages of twenty and forty are both enjoyable, but they represent very different stages in life,* might go on to list several points of contrast between twenty and forty:

> For more on supporting your thesis, see Chapter 4.

> appearance
>
> place in life
>
> perspective

For each point of comparison, the writer would then come up with details to explain the differences:

AGE TWENTY	AGE FORTY
appearance	
smooth skin	some wrinkles
trendy haircut	classic hairstyle
rounded features	well-defined features
place in life	
just starting out	established
single, no children	married with children
living at home	own home
perspective	
self-centered	more thoughtful
choices to make	many choices made
uncertainty	wisdom

ORGANIZATION IN COMPARISON AND CONTRAST

DEFINITIONS: A **point-by-point organization** first presents one point of comparison or contrast between the two subjects with examples of each and then moves to the next point of comparison or contrast. A **whole-to-whole organization** first presents all the points of comparison or contrast for one subject and then all the points for the second subject.

After you have developed points of comparison and supporting details, you need to decide how to present them in your essay. There are two ways to organize a comparison/contrast essay: point-by-point or whole-to-whole. You have to decide which of the two organizations will best serve your purpose. Choose one and stick with it throughout the essay; otherwise you will confuse your readers.

The two organizations look like this:

POINT-BY-POINT	WHOLE-TO-WHOLE
Thesis statement	Thesis statement
Topic sentence, point 1	Topic sentence, subject 1
subject 1	point 1
subject 2	point 2
Topic sentence, point 2	point 3
subject 1	Topic sentence, subject 2
subject 2	point 1
Topic sentence, point 3	point 2
subject 1	point 3
subject 2	Concluding statement
Concluding statement	

Although the whole-to-whole organization looks as if it might be shorter, the organization has little effect on the length. Select the organization that will be clearest and easiest for readers to follow. Arrange the points and details in a sequence that suits what you have to say—chronological order, space order, order of importance, or any logical order.

For more on transitions, see pages 94–99.

As you write your essay, add transitions to lead from point to point and subject to subject.

> ## Common Transitions in Comparison/Contrast
>
> | COMMON COMPARISON TRANSITIONS | COMMON CONTRAST TRANSITIONS |
> |---|---|
> | one similarity | one difference |
> | another similarity | another difference |
> | similarly | in contrast |
> | like | now/then |
> | both | unlike |
> | | while |

Many situations require you to understand similarities and differences. Here are some examples of how you might use comparison and contrast.

COLLEGE

- In a business course, you compare and contrast practices in e-commerce and traditional commerce.

WORK

- You compare and contrast two health insurance options offered by your company in order to select the one that is best for you.

EVERYDAY LIFE

- Before choosing an Internet service provider, you compare and contrast the fees, services, and options each offers.

Read and Analyze Comparison/Contrast

Before writing your own comparison/contrast essay, read the following examples—one each from college, the workplace, and everyday life—and answer the questions that accompany each. Reading the examples and answering the questions will help you understand how to write a good comparison/contrast essay.

ESL
Ask both ESL and non-ESL students to compare and contrast written and spoken language in their native culture.

1. COMPARISON AND CONTRAST IN COLLEGE

The following essay was written for this assignment in a sociology class:

> Compare some aspect of two different cultures, using your own experience, the video that was shown in class, or the material from Chapter 4 of your textbook.

My Observations on Mexican and American Children

Anna Griffith

In the past few years I have been privileged to go on several mission trips to the Yucatan Peninsula. There our group worked with some Mexican children who live in poverty in the city of Merida. In observing and getting to know the children, I was struck by several diferences in the situations, behaviors, and attitudes of the Mexican children compared to children I know here in Hattiesburg, Mississippi.

✓ The most obvious difference was in the living situations. The children here in Hattiesburg live in sturdy houses or apartments. The houses are of different sizes, and not all are in great shape, but they have multiple rooms, and they are made of wood, brick, or stucco. None of the children I know here share a bedroom with their parents. In contrast, as I arrived with my group to organize a basketball camp and Bible school in one of the neighborhoods of Merida, I was shocked by the homes I saw. Children of all ages peeped out from the doors of their homes: small tin shacks that were roughly the size of my bedroom at home. Many people lived together in these wobbly structures, where one room served for eating, sleeping, bathing, and anything else that takes place inside.

✓ Another difference is in the amount of parental supervision the Meridan children get versus the children in Hattiesburg. Like the children I know here in the States, at our first event the Mexican children were shy, reserved, and a little cautious with us because we were strangers. But that didn't last more than a few minutes, after which they were eager to find out everything about us. Most parents here in the States would accompany their small children to an event such as ours, but these children were rarely seen with adults. Every night I watched a little girl of about five walk down the road holding her little sister's hand. It was common to see several battered strollers with babies around the open-air basketball courts we set up. We realized soon that no one had been at home when the children left, and they were given no time to return — they were on their own. This lack of supervision simply doesn't happen at home, where parents want to keep a close eye on their children's whereabouts. Interestingly, the

Mexican children knew very early that it was their responsibility to take care of their younger siblings, and they did so willingly and with a sense of duty. In contrast, this seems to be a behavior that children here have lost.

✓ The difference that had the most impact on me, though, was the appreciation the Mexican children had for very simple things. They do not have the elaborate, high-tech toys that American children take for granted. Items that are ordinary to American children, such as flashlights, disposable cameras, and marker pens, fascinated Mexican children. One little boy picked up one of our flashlights and ran around clicking it on and off. He had never seen anything like it. When we said he could have it, he stared at us open-mouthed, amazed at his luck. He was giddy with delight and appreciation. Cameras with flashes produced similar responses. But we were most surprised at the children's reactions to Crayola marker pens. One night after a child had been fascinated with a marker, we gave it to her. After thanking us, she ran into the night to show off her new treasure. Within moments, we were surrounded by a crowd of eager faces and reaching hands. Like children anywhere, they were impatient and greedy to have what another child has, but this was just a marker, something American children would not get excited about or appreciate. The Mexican children were grateful for and appreciated simple things.

Through my experiences with children here in America and in Mexico, I have come to realize how much different economic situations affect the children. Although the most obvious difference between American children I know and Mexican children was in their poorer living conditions, the thing that most affected me was how much more thankful and appreciative the Mexican children were. There is much to be said in favor of simplicity, something most American children do not experience.

TEACHING TIP
Ask students to write a journal entry measuring something unfamiliar against something familiar.

1. What is Anna's **purpose** for writing? *to contrast two different cultures*

2. Who is Anna's **audience**? *her instructor and classmates*

3. Fill in the blanks with the **subjects** and the **main point** of Anna's essay.

For more on purpose and audience, see pages 7–9.

SUBJECT 1: *Mexican children*

SUBJECT 2: *American children*

MAIN POINT: *they are different in many ways*

DISCUSSION
How could Anna's essay have been arranged using a whole-to-whole pattern? Would this make it more effective or less?

4. Double-underline the **thesis statement**.

5. Does Anna use **point-to-point** or **whole-to-whole** organization?

   point-to-point

6. What **order** (time, space, or importance) does Anna use to arrange her points? *importance*

7. Put a check mark (✓) next to each **topic sentence** Anna uses to introduce a similarity or a difference.

8. Underline the **details** that Anna gives to help the reader understand each difference.

9. Circle the (**transitions**) (words, phrases, and sentences) that Anna uses.

10. What **key words** does Anna repeat? *Mexican, Merida, children, differences, Hattiesburg, States, American, appreciate, grateful*

11. Double-underline the **sentence in the concluding paragraph** that ties the concluding paragraph to the introductory paragraph.

For a list of the four basics of good comparison and contrast, see page 205.

12. Does Anna's essay have the **four basics of good comparison and contrast**? Why or why not? *Answers will vary.*

2. COMPARISON AND CONTRAST IN THE WORKPLACE

The following memo is similar to those that Salvador Torres, a financial consultant at Public Financial Management, Inc., prepares for clients. Although it is not in essay form, it is an example of how comparison/contrast is used in the workplace.

TO: Investment Client

Based on our discussion of your investment needs, I would recommend that you invest in Stock Mutual Funds rather than Bond Mutual Funds. Your three expressed preferences were 1) to hold on to the stock for more than ten years, 2) that the funds you invest in be professionally managed, and 3) that you wanted a high potential for gain and were not overly concerned with risk and the daily fluctuations of funds. You have no need for present annual income from your investments. We determined, after reviewing numerous options, that either Bond Mutual Funds or Stock Mutual Funds would meet your criteria.

✓ There are several similarities between Bond Mutual Funds and Stock Mutual Funds. One is that they both offer investment horizons greater than ten years. Another is that both are professionally managed. A third is that either fund may pay annual income. Based on these factors, either fund fulfills your investment needs.

✓ However, there are differences worth noting. One is that Stock Mutual Funds have higher potential gains over a ten-year period, though they have more risk and fluctuation in the shorter term. Additionally, though both funds may pay annual income, the Bond Mutual Fund is more likely to do so, at the expense of greater long-term appreciation.

✓ Both funds meet some of your criteria, but the Stock Mutual Funds are more tailored to your expressed preferences than the Bond Mutual Funds. The Stock Mutual Funds are likely to have a greater return on investment over a ten-year period. Since this is a high priority for you, I suggest that you invest in Stock Mutual Funds. I can monitor this investment and inform you of its status at any time.

If you have questions or need further clarification, please do not hesitate to ask. I will look forward to meeting with you again to determine the precise funds in which to invest. Thank you.

---

1. Who is the **audience** for this memo? _the client, who is an investor_

2. What is the **purpose** of the memo? _to explain the similarities and differences between two investment products_

For more on audience and purpose, see pages 7–9.

3. Double-underline the **thesis statement**.

4. Does the writer use **point-by-point** or **whole-to-whole** organization?
   point-by-point

5. Put a check mark next to the **topic sentences**.

3. COMPARISON AND CONTRAST IN EVERYDAY LIFE

The following comparison and contrast was done by Karron Tempesta to help her decide which of two job offers to accept. When comparing things in order to make a decision, it is often helpful to list the points of comparison next to each other so that the differences are easy to see. First look at Karron's list (which is like prewriting), and then read the essay she wrote, which is more casual than a formal essay.

DISCUSSION
Ask students to suggest other situations in which it would help to list points of comparison and contrast. How does putting it all on paper help?

COMPANY A	COMPANY B
• higher salary	• lower salary, but a good bonus plan
• big company	• small company
• farther away but on bus line	• near home
• more jobs at the company because it's big	• fewer jobs because it's small, but maybe more chance to do more and be rewarded
• nice people	• nice people
• entry-level job	• more responsibilities and challenge
• good benefit plan	• okay benefit plan

The job offers I received from Company A and Company B are both good, but they differ on a number of points. I'm writing this because sometimes I think better when I can see things in print, and this is an important decision that I want to think about seriously.

✓ The first difference is the location of the companies. Company A is way across town. It's on a bus line, and that's good, but it would still take me anywhere from thirty to forty-five minutes to get there. It makes for a longer day. Company B, on the other hand, is very close by. I could ride my bicycle and be there in ten minutes. I'd also save the bus fare. But what about when it's raining or really hot?

✓ (Another difference) is in the salaries. The actual salary at Company A is higher than that at Company B. However, Company B is experiencing rapid growth, and it has a good bonus plan. Although I can't count on it, I have the opportunity with Company B to actually make more than at Company A. But then again, maybe I wouldn't get a good bonus.

✓ (Probably the most important difference) is really the size of the two companies: Company A is a big company, and Company B is small. Size is probably the reason that Company A has a better benefit plan — there are more people to enroll, so it gets a good rate. In contrast, Company B has fewer people and probably pays a higher rate because there are fewer people.

✓ Size also affects the type of job and where it will lead. At Company A, the job is an entry-level position with clearly defined responsibilities that aren't that interesting. But the company has lots of jobs, so I'd have more opportunities once I was there. At Company B, the job has more responsibility, and I'd learn more and be more interested. Because it's small, people are more likely to let me try new things — and to notice when I've done well. So there are good opportunities there, too.

So there are the differences. Which of those differences are most important to me, and where will I be the happiest? The location isn't really very important. I need money, so a higher salary is attractive, but I like the idea of being rewarded with a bonus if I do well. I might make more at Company B that way, and it's good motivation. Also, I like smaller companies better; I just felt better there, and I like that I get to do more on the job and be noticed. The benefit difference isn't good for Company B, but I think, overall, Company B is best. I'll go with it.

1. What is Karron's **purpose** for this comparison? _to help her decide which_
   job offer to accept

   For more on purpose and audience, see pages 7–9.

2. Who is Karron's **audience**? _herself_

3. Double-underline the **thesis statement**.

4. Does Karron use **point-by-point** or **whole-to-whole** organization?
   point-by-point

5. What order of **organization** (chronological, spatial, or importance) does Karron use? *importance*

6. Put a check mark (✓) next to each **topic sentence**.

7. Circle the (transitions) that Karron uses.

8. What **key words** does she repeat? *job, differ, difference, Company A, Company B, salary, size*

Write a Comparison/Contrast Essay

In this section, you will write your own comparison/contrast essay. To do so, follow this sequence:

REVIEW the basics of good comparison/contrast writing (p. 205).

CHOOSE your writing assignment (below).

WRITE your comparison/contrast essay using the step-by-step Writing Guide (p. 219).

CHECK your final essay (p. 223).

WRITING ASSIGNMENT 1   COLLEGE, WORK, EVERYDAY LIFE

Write a comparison/contrast essay on *one* of the following topics or on a topic of your own choice.

COLLEGE

• Being a working student/Being a nonworking student

• Two topics from another course

• Being an older, returning student/Coming right from high school

WORK

• Two jobs you have had

• Two companies you have worked for

• A job and a career

EVERYDAY LIFE

- Two different kinds of families

- Good customer service and bad customer service

- Your feeling about commitment in a relationship now versus ten years ago

WRITING ASSIGNMENT 2   USE THE INTERNET

Choose two Internet search engines from the following list of popular search engines or your list of personal favorites. Write an essay in which you compare and contrast the two.

For advice about how to cite a source, see Chapter 20.

AltaVista: **<www.altavista.com>**   Google: **<www.google.com>**

Excite: **<www.excite.com>**   Lycos: **<www.lycos.com>**

Fast Search: **<www.alltheweb.com>**   Yahoo: **<www.yahoo.com>**

Compare or contrast them on these three points: (1) ease of use, (2) types of search help offered, and (3) quality of results.

WRITING ASSIGNMENT 3   COMPARING OFFERS

Read the problem and situation that follow, and then choose *one* of the assignment options (3A or 3B) that appear after it.

PROBLEM: These days there are many laptop computers available. But there are significant differences among them that you should consider before buying. What facts and features should you compare?

SITUATION: You decide that you need a laptop computer that you can bring to class and use at home. You check a recent issue of *Consumer Reports* that rates laptops and you find the chart on page 218.

TEAMWORK
Have students bring in advertisements from magazines, newspapers, or the Web that use comparison or contrast. Working in small groups, students can identify the subjects being compared or contrasted, the points of comparison or contrast, and the purpose.

KEY NO.	BRAND & MODEL	PRICE	OVERALL SCORE	APPLICATION SPEED	DISPLAY QUALITY	MULTIMEDIA	FEATURES AND USABILITY	EXPANSION AND UPGRADES	BATTERY LIFE (HR.)	POWER CONSERVATION	MANUALS	WARRANTY AND SUPPORT
WINDOWS LAPTOPS												
1	**Compaq** Presidio 1800T	$2,300		●	●	◗	◗	◗	4	●	●	○
2	**Toshiba** Satellite 2805-S401	2,200		●	●	◗	◗	◗	3	◗	●	○
3	**HP** Pavilion n5270	2,000		●	◗	◗	●	◗	2 3/4	◗	◗	○
4	**Sony** Vaio PCG-FX170	3,000		●	●	◗	●	◗	3	○	◗	○
5	**Dell** Inspiron 8000	2,460		◗	●	◗	◗	●	2 3/4	○	○	◖
6	**Sony** Vaio PCG-Z505LS	2,550		●	●	◗	◗	◗	2 1/4	○	●	○
7	**Dell** Inspiron 4000	1,725		◗	◗	◗	◗	◗	3 1/2	◗	○	◖
8	**Gateway** Solo 5300	2,230		◗	◗	◗	○	◗	3 1/4	◗	●	◖
9	**IBM** ThinkPad i1200	1,850		◗	◗	○	○	○	4 1/4	●	●	◖
10	**Toshiba** Satellite 1735	1,200		◗	○	○	◗	○	2 1/2	○	●	◖
11	**Compaq** Presario 1200 12XL400	1,400		◗	○	◗	◗	○	2	○	◗	◖
12	**Toshiba** Portegé 3480CT	2,000		◗	◗	○	○	◗	2 1/4	○	●	○
MACINTOSH LAPTOPS												
13	**Apple** PowerBook G4 Titanium	3,200		●	◗	●	○	○	3	●	◗	○
14	**Apple** iBook 466 Special Edition	1,950		◗	●	◗	○	◖	3 1/4	◗	◗	○

Overall Ratings — Within types, in performance order

Legend: ● Excellent ◗ Very good ○ Good ◖ Fair ● Poor

Overall score scale: 0 — P F G VG E — 100

ASSIGNMENT OPTION 3A: RESPOND TO THE SITUATION

Read the rating chart about laptop computers, and contrast two of the models. Identify three important points of difference, and look at what the chart says about each model for each point. Explain why these points are important to you. After analyzing the points, choose the laptop you would buy. In the concluding paragraph, review what you have learned about the two models of laptop, state which you would select, and tell why.

ASSIGNMENT OPTION 3B: ANOTHER PERSPECTIVE

Read the rating chart about laptop computers. Instead of comparing models for yourself, imagine that you are recommending a model that would be good for your company. Consider what functions you would need most for work, and then choose points to contrast. Explain why each point is important, and in the last paragraph make a recommendation to your boss about what model to purchase and why.

Comparison and Contrast

Follow the steps in this Writing Guide to help you prewrite, draft, revise, and edit your comparison and contrast. Check off each step as you complete it.

Writing Guide

THINKING CRITICALLY ABOUT COMPARISON AND CONTRAST

FOCUS   Think about what you want to compare or contrast and the main point you want to make about your subjects.

ASK
- What are my readers likely to know about these subjects?
- What do I want my readers to be able to do: make a decision or understand my subjects?
- What are some parallel points of comparison or contrast between my two subjects? Which points will best help me to achieve my purpose?
- Which of the two organizations would best help me get my point across: point-by-point or whole-to-whole?

PREWRITE TO EXPLORE YOUR SUBJECTS

Prewriting for comparison and contrast involves considering what subjects to compare or contrast and then coming up with some points of comparison or contrast for them.

_____ Decide on your purpose for writing.

_____ Identify the audience for your essay.

_____ Select two subjects with similarities and differences you want to explore.

_____ Decide whether you want readers to choose between or to understand your two subjects.

_____ Consider whether the subjects have enough in common to allow a valid comparison or contrast between them.

_____ Once you decide what subjects to compare or contrast, use a prewriting technique (freewriting, listing/brainstorming, questioning, discussing, clustering) to explore in what ways the subjects are alike or different.

For more on purpose and audience, see pages 7–9.

WRITE A THESIS STATEMENT

The thesis statement in a comparison/contrast essay includes the two subjects you are comparing or contrasting and the main point you want to make about them.

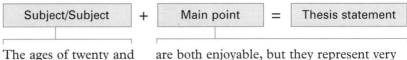

| Subject/Subject | + | Main point | = | Thesis statement |

The ages of twenty and forty   are both enjoyable, but they represent very different stages in life.

The job offers I received from Company A and Company B   are both good, but they differ on a number of points.

_____ Decide why you are comparing and contrasting the subjects and what's important about the comparison and contrast.

_____ Write a thesis statement that includes your subjects and the main point you want to make about them.

SUPPORT YOUR POINT

The major support points in comparison and contrast are the points of comparison that you use. The supporting details are the specific details and explanations you give about the points of comparison or contrast.

_____ Review your ideas about the subjects.

_____ List some differences or similarities, depending on whether you are comparing, contrasting, or doing both.

_____ Select from your list the points of comparison that you will use in the essay, choosing points that your readers will understand and that serve your purpose. These points of comparison are the major support points for your thesis statement.

_____ Add supporting details and examples to explain the points of comparison.

MAKE A PLAN

Making a written plan — an outline — helps you decide how to order your comparison and contrast. A plan for a comparison/contrast essay must use either point-by-point organization or whole-to-whole organization. Your plan should follow one of the structures shown here:

POINT-BY-POINT	**WHOLE-TO-WHOLE**
Thesis statement	Thesis statement
Topic sentence, point 1	Topic sentence, subject 1
subject 1	point 1
subject 2	point 2
Topic sentence, point 2	point 3
subject 1	Topic sentence, subject 2
subject 2	point 1
Topic sentence, point 3	point 2
subject 1	point 3
subject 2	Concluding statement
Concluding statement	

> **DISCUSSION**
> To emphasize the differences between the two patterns of organization, have students state their topics and ask the class whether these topics lend themselves to point-by-point or whole-to-whole organization.

_____ Decide whether you will use a point-by-point or whole-to-whole organization.

_____ Make a plan or outline that follows the point-by-point or whole-to-whole structure as shown here.

DRAFT

Drafting a comparison/contrast essay means writing in complete sentences and including the following:

- An introductory paragraph that includes your thesis statement about your two subjects
- Body paragraphs that explain your points of comparison
- A concluding paragraph that reinforces your thesis

_____ Think about what is interesting about the comparison you are about to make.

_____ Write an introductory paragraph that introduces your two subjects and the main point you will make about them. Try to spark your readers' attention.

_____ Write a topic sentence for each of the points of comparison or contrast.

_____ Write body paragraphs that provide specific details about the points of comparison so that your readers can understand the similarities or differences between your two subjects.

_____ Write a concluding paragraph that refers back to your main point and makes a further comment or observation based on your points of comparison or contrast.

_____ Title your essay.

REVISE

TEAMWORK
Have students use the revision checklist in small groups.

Revising means changing whole sentences or paragraphs to make your writing clearer or stronger. To revise your comparison/contrast essay, imagine that you know little about the subjects. Read your draft from that perspective, looking for ways to make the similarities or differences clearer. Read your draft, looking for the following:

- Places where the ideas are off the main point (revising for unity)
- Gaps in information or detail (revising for support and detail)
- Areas in need of transitions to help readers move smoothly from one point to the next (revising for coherence)

For more on peer review, see pages 87–88.

_____ Get feedback from others through peer review.

_____ Reread your thesis. Make sure it presents the two subjects forcefully and clearly, and states the point you want to make in your essay.

_____ Reread the body paragraphs. Add other points of comparison and contrast or details that would clearly demonstrate your main point. Add details that would show the similarities or differences between the subjects.

_____ Make sure that you have followed either point-by-point or whole-to-whole organization all the way through your essay.

_____ Reread your introduction. If it lacks energy or clarity, rewrite it to give it some life.

_____ Reread your conclusion to make sure that it sounds energetic, confirms your main point about the two subjects, and makes a further observation.

_____ Add transitions that move your readers from one point of comparison to another, and decide whether you want to repeat key words.

_____   Make at least five changes to your draft to improve the unity, support, or coherence of your comparison and contrast or to make the introduction, thesis statement, or conclusion stronger or more convincing.

EDIT

Some grammar, spelling, word use, or punctuation errors may confuse your readers and make it difficult for them to understand a point you are trying to make. Even if they do not confuse your readers, errors detract from the effectiveness and overall quality of your writing. Edit your comparison and contrast carefully, and correct any errors you find.

_____   Ask a classmate or friend to read your essay and highlight any errors.

_____   Use the spell checker and grammar checker on your computer.

_____   Look yourself for errors that the spell checker or grammar checker didn't catch. Focus first on sentence fragments, run-on sentences, problems with subject–verb agreement, problems with verbs, and other areas where you know you often make errors.

_____   Print a clean final copy.

_____   Ask yourself: Is this the best I can do?

A FINAL CHECK BEFORE HANDING IN YOUR COMPARISON/CONTRAST ESSAY

If you've followed the Writing Guide for comparison and contrast, your essay will already include the four basics of good comparison and contrast. Use this list to double-check each basic feature.

_____ My thesis statement identifies two subjects that can be usefully compared and contrasted.

_____ The purpose of my essay is to help readers make a decision or understand the subjects.

_____ The body of my essay presents several major points of comparison, supported by details about both subjects.

_____ My essay arranges the points of comparison in a logical order.

You Know This
You already use cause and effect to understand things.
- You try to figure out what caused your partner to get angry.
- You explain to a child why she shouldn't eat too fast.
- You think about what will happen if you change jobs.

15

Cause and Effect

Writing That Explains Reasons or Results

Understand What Cause and Effect Are

IDEA JOURNAL
Write about a time when you should have thought before you spoke or acted.

DEFINITION: A **cause** is what makes an event happen. An **effect** is what happens as a result of an event.

■■ Four Basics of Good Cause and Effect

1. It clearly distinguishes between a cause and an effect.
2. It discusses real causes, not just something that happened before another event.
3. It discusses real effects, not just something that happened after another event.
4. It gives clear and detailed examples of causes, effects, or both.

Analyzing causes and effects goes beyond asking "What happened?" to also ask "Why?" and "How?"

SITUATION: On a hot summer day, you leave a video you need to return on the front seat of your car while you are at work. When you come out of work, you find the video has melted.

224

Profile of Success

Jolanda Jones

ATTORNEY AND CONSULTANT

Jolanda Jones

BACKGROUND: Jolanda grew up in a low-income housing project in Houston, Texas. Her father committed suicide, her uncles spent time in prison, and she lost several family members to street violence. Jolanda's life was a tough one. Her mother and grand-mother gave her the confidence to try hard and believe in herself, however. A good student, she became an athlete as a teenager and is a three-time NCAA hep-tathalon champion, two-time Academic All-American, and a 1989 U.S. heptathalon champion. She participated in the 1996 U.S. Olympic Team Trials and won the high jump, beating Jackie Joyner-Kersee, an elite track and field athlete and gold medalist.

Jolanda went to college and to law school, and then went on to practice law. In 2000, she received the NAACP's Award for Legal Excellence for dedication to community service. She still practices law, and recently she has started her own consulting business.

EMPLOYER: Self

COLLEGE(S)/DEGREES: University of Houston, Central Campus (B.A.), University of Houston—Bates School of Law (J.D.L.)

TYPES OF WRITING ON THE JOB: Legal briefs, proposals, letters, evaluations, emails, Web site content, speeches

HOW JOLANDA USES CAUSE/EFFECT: As part of her consulting business, Jolanda is in great demand as a speaker, particularly to inner-city youth. When she addresses students, she emphasizes the importance of under-standing that for every action they take there is a consequence that they should consider. For an example of how Jolanda uses cause and effect, see Cause and Effect in the Workplace, on pages 230–32.

COMPUTER SKILLS: WordPerfect, Microsoft Word, Excel, Internet

TEAMWORK ON THE JOB: Jolanda says, "In my legal practice, my clients and I must work together as a team to be the most effective. I also consult with schools and school districts, where it is important for adminis-trators, teachers, parents, and students to work together to achieve common goals."

FUTURE GOAL: Jolanda hopes to set up a nonprofit organization to teach young people how to empower themselves to accomplish all their goals and to be the best and most positive people they can be.

CAUSE: The **cause** of the video melting was **leaving it all day in a hot car**.

EFFECT: The **effect** of leaving the video in a hot car all day was that **it melted**.

Jim Rice of Quinsigamond Community College helps his students visualize the cause/effect relationship by suggesting that they think of three linked rings:

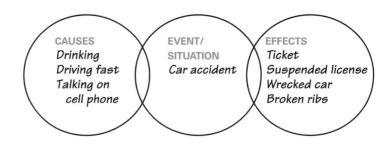

CLEAR CAUSES AND EFFECTS

When you are writing about causes, be careful that you don't say something caused an event or situation just because it happened beforehand. For example, one summer night when I was a child, my family went out for ice cream, and I got a chocolate cone. Later that night I was sick to my stomach. It turned out that I had the flu, but it was many years before I would again eat chocolate ice cream, despite my mother's assurance that the cone I'd eaten did not cause my sickness. I had confused something that happened before a situation with its cause. In fact, one thing just happened before another. I would have been sick from the flu whether I had eaten chocolate ice cream or not.

When you are writing about effects, do not confuse something that happens after something else with the effect. Just as the chocolate ice cream did not cause me to get the flu, getting the flu was not the effect of eating the ice cream.

SUPPORT FOR CAUSE AND EFFECT

In a cause/effect essay, the causes and effects that you explain are the support points. They demonstrate the main point stated in your thesis. For example, the student who wrote the thesis *Irresponsible behavior caused my car accident* goes on to write about the following causes and explanations:

CAUSE: Driving too fast	CAUSE: Talking on my cell phone
It was rainy and slippery	Not paying close attention
Going too fast to control car	Hit a curve while laughing
Couldn't stop	Didn't react fast enough

CAUSE: Drinking

Not focused

Slowed reaction time

Each cause (or effect) is developed by supporting details that explain exactly how the situation happened.

ORDER OF IDEAS FOR CAUSE AND EFFECT

Cause/effect essays are often organized by **order of importance**, saving the most important or intense cause or effect for last in order to create a strong impression on the readers. The plan for a cause/effect essay generally looks like this:

For more on order of importance, see page 60.

Introduction (including thesis)

First cause or effect

    explanation of cause or effect

Second cause or effect

    explanation of cause or effect

Most important cause or effect

    explanation of cause or effect

Conclusion

As you write your essay, add transitions to show how each cause or effect relates to your main point. Here are some common transitions that are used in cause/effect writing.

For more on transitions, see pages 94–96.

Common Transitions for Cause and Effect

one cause, reason, effect, result	first, second, third, and so on
also	as a result
another	because

Many situations require you to determine causes or effects. Here are some examples showing how you might find yourself considering causes and effects:

COLLEGE

- In an information technology course, you must discuss the effects of a virus on a local-area computer network.

WORK

- You analyze the likely effects of laying off 15 percent of your department's employees.

EVERYDAY LIFE

- You try to figure out what is causing your computer to freeze.

Read and Analyze Cause/Effect

Before writing your own cause/effect essay, read the following examples — one each from college, the workplace, and everyday life — and answer the questions that accompany each. Reading the examples and answering the questions will help you understand how to write a good cause/effect essay.

1. CAUSE AND EFFECT IN COLLEGE

A student wrote the following cause/effect essay for a political science course. The assignment, given in January 2002, asked students to write about the effects of the September 11, 2001, terrorist attacks on the World Trade Center in New York City and the Pentagon in Washington, D.C.

Life after the World Trade Center and Pentagon Attacks

James Freeman

DISCUSSION
Read this essay aloud and answer the questions as a class. Measure the essay against the four basics of good cause and effect.

As Americans watched the attacks on the World Trade Center and the Pentagon, many were heard to say, "The world as we know it will never be the same." Several months later, that statement is perhaps a little strong, but the terrorist attacks have produced significant changes in Americans' attitudes and behaviors.

✓ One immediate effect of the attacks was felt by the airlines, as people shied away from flying. Airports were like ghost towns, even over the Thanksgiving holiday, which is traditionally the busiest air travel weekend of the year. Instead of flying, <u>people drove to their destinations, took buses or trains, or simply stayed home</u>. The bottom line for many commercial airlines, already in financial distress, <u>plummeted even further</u>. Some airlines consolidated, some went bankrupt, but all were significantly affected by the events of September 11.

✓ (The attacks also resulted in) a recession much worse than what was already on the horizon. <u>People stayed at home rather than going out for entertainment or to make unnecessary purchases</u>. As people became more conservative and cautious, <u>less money was flowing into an already unstable economy</u>. <u>Businesses closed up, and many people lost their jobs through the fall and into the winter</u>. As a result, people's fiscal conservatism increased even more. More businesses have gone bankrupt in the new year, and we seem to be caught in a vicious cycle of decline as one bankruptcy stems from another.

✓ (The most significant, and perhaps the longest-lasting effect of) September 11, however, is the loss of the naively secure attitude that most Americans—especially younger Americans—felt when they believed, "Nothing like that can happen here." It has happened, and it has forever changed the way we perceive our personal safety and security. <u>As a student, I am now uncertain about what my major will be and what the future will, should, or could bring</u>. For the first time, <u>I feel that terrorist acts could occur at any time and to anyone</u>. <u>I'm more cautious</u>, as if I'm always looking over my shoulder. I don't feel as certain about the future—even if there will be one. <u>I go about my life, but I will never feel the same level of personal safety</u> that I did before September 11, and that influences everything I do.

The world that most Americans knew never will be the same. Some of the effects of September 11, particularly on the economy or the airlines or the postal service, will lessen as time passes. But the belief that we are living at risk because we are within the reach of terrorism is here to stay. My world is still a very good one, but make no mistake, it is forever changed.

> **DISCUSSION**
> Ask students whether their reactions to the events of September 11, 2001, have changed since January 2002, when James wrote this essay.

1. What is James's **purpose** for writing? *to explain some of the effects of the September 11, 2001, terrorist attacks*

> For more on purpose and audience, see pages 7–9.

2. Who is James's **audience**? *his instructor and classmates*

3. Fill in the blanks with the **topic** and the **main point** of James's essay.

   TOPIC: *September 11 terrorist attacks*

   MAIN POINT: *produced significant effects*

4. Double-underline the **thesis statement**.

5. Put a check mark (✓) next to each **topic sentence**. The topic sentences should be the causes or effects that the writer presents.

6. Underline the **details** that James gives to help the reader understand each effect.

7. What kind of **organization** (chronological, spatial, or importance) does James use? *importance*

8. Circle the (transitions) (words, phrases, and sentences) that James uses.

9. What **key words** does James repeat? *bankrupt, terrorist, effect, change*

10. Double-underline the **sentence in the concluding paragraph** that ties the concluding paragraph to the introductory paragraph.

For a list of the four basics of good cause and effect, see page 224.

11. Does James's essay have the **four basics of good cause and effect**? Why or why not?

   Answers will vary.

2. CAUSE AND EFFECT IN THE WORKPLACE

The following piece of writing is representative of the kinds of inspirational presentations that Jolanda Jones makes to students. She wants students to learn to think through their decisions and choices, so she talks about the causes and effects of certain actions, giving examples from her own experience. The piece is a speech—meant to be spoken and heard.

Some of the worst life situations I've seen were caused simply by people failing to consider the effects of their actions. Each of you in this room must learn for yourselves that every single decision you make has consequences, whether you think much about it or not. It is super important that you think about the decisions you make **before** you make them because if you don't, then you will end up somewhere you didn't plan for. Take charge of your life by making informed and well-thought-out decisions.

✓ For me it seems like my best decisions are the ones I make when I think my grandmother might find out about them. If I would be proud for her to know the decision I've made, then it's probably a good decision. If I have to sneak or would be ashamed for her to know my decision, then it is probably a bad decision. In any case, here are some examples of the thought process in good decision making. They show what happens when you don't consider consequences.

✓ Some of you girls might be getting pressured by your boyfriends to have sex. What should you think about? Well, you're probably wondering what he'll say if you don't sleep with him. Will he break up with you or call you "Prude"? Well, don't let him define you. What if you get pregnant? What if you get a sexually transmitted disease? What if you get AIDS? What if you break up after you have sex with him? Will he tell everyone how good you were in bed? Will everyone know your business?

✓ Single parenthood is hard. I know from personal experience. I had graduated from college, was working as a minority recruiter and admissions counselor and was training for the Olympics. I also planned to go to law school at Stanford. Then I got pregnant without planning for it. All of a sudden I was expecting a child with a man who was both abusive and unsupportive. I was not married. I was disappointed in myself. I was ashamed of the shame I brought on my grandmother. I was a coward. I fled the United States and hid my pregnancy in Spain. I absolutely love my son, but I gave up my Olympic aspirations and Stanford Law School.

✓ Some of you might be thinking about using drugs. Think long and hard. I have crackheads in my family whose lives have been destroyed. Some are homeless. Some are dying of AIDS. My aunt was murdered in a drug house. My brother was murdered buying marijuana. I have an alcoholic cousin who does not take care of her children, and she is on welfare. People who do drugs come to love drugs more than they love anyone or anything else. Then the drugs control you. You lose control of your life.

✓ What about crime, just little stuff, like shoplifting that little pair of earrings at the neighborhood Target. When I was sixteen, I'd worked to earn money to buy stuff I wanted. I wanted a pair of jeans. Instead my mother took my check for herself. I still thought I was entitled to the jeans, so I went to Target and took a pair. I got caught. I was arrested, handcuffed, put in the back of a patrol car and detained. I ducked my head down in the back of the patrol car. I just knew the whole world was looking at me. I was humiliated. I should have thought about the consequences. It wasn't right to steal from Target even if my mother took my check. You best believe I've thought about that ever since that date because I've never shoplifted again. I even told my son about it. I don't want him to make the same mistake that I did.

TEACHING TIP
Ask students to think about some effects in their own lives brought about by thoughtlessness. This might be a good writing topic for them.

You have choices in life, and it's up to you to make the decisions that will most positively benefit your life. We are all capable of thinking through stuff and making the right decision. The question is: Are you gonna do it or are you gonna just take the easy road through life? My grandmother said, "If you make a bad decision, learn from it and move on, that way it's not your fault. If, however, you make the same mistake twice, you're stupid and it is your fault." I don't know about you, but I'm not stupid.

I've made good and bad decisions in my life. Thankfully, I've made more good ones than bad. I hope to continue to make good decisions by considering consequence and learning from my mistakes. I hope that's your philosophy too.

For more on audience and purpose, see pages 7–9.

1. Who is Jolanda's **audience**? _a group of students_

2. What is Jolanda's **purpose**? _to show the importance of considering consequences_

TEAMWORK
These questions, and the ones on page 234, can be answered in teams.

3. Double-underline the **thesis statement**.

4. Put a check mark (✓) next to each **topic sentence** for the body paragraphs of the essay.

5. Use the ring diagrams to show one of the situations Jolanda presents, along with the causes or effects.

Answers will vary. One possibility:

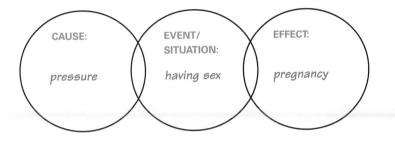

3. CAUSE AND EFFECT IN EVERYDAY LIFE

The following is an example of cause/effect writing in everyday life. In this case, a man has consulted his physician about several health problems that he believes might be caused by the new carpeting and cubicles at his workplace. The doctor writes a letter to the man's employer.

July 2, 2002

To Whom It May Concern:

The health of one of my patients, George Hanson, is being seriously affected by conditions in the offices of Kirkland Brothers. I am recommending that Mr. Hanson apply immediately for short-term disability to separate himself from the unhealthful environment that allegedly includes harmful chemicals and poor ventilation. Over the course of the next few weeks, I will closely monitor his symptoms, all of which have appeared since Mr. Hanson began work at Kirkland Brothers.

✓ One of the symptoms is a dull but constant headache that Mr. Hanson develops each day within an hour of arriving at work. The pain is centered in the sinus passages above the eyes and is a growing annoyance, making it difficult for Mr. Hanson to concentrate on his work.

✓ A more severe symptom is a chronic watering and stinging of Mr. Hanson's eyes. This condition is not merely unpleasant; it has advanced to a burning sensation and has affected Mr. Hanson's eyesight. The condition disappears a few hours after his shift ends every night.

✓ The most serious medical effect is the impact on Mr. Hanson's lungs. His breathing is labored, and he has become asthmatic, although he has no previous history of lung or breathing problems. Unlike his sight, Mr. Hanson's asthma is progressively worsening, and he now <u>depends on the frequent use of inhalers.</u>

Given the range and intensity of Mr. Hanson's symptoms and the appearance that they are connected to the interior of Kirkland Brothers, I recommend that he remain away from the building until further medical testing can be completed. If you have further questions, please do not hesitate to contact me.

Sincerely,

Althea Sedoris, M.D.

For more on purpose and audience, see pages 7–9.

1. What is the **purpose** of the doctor's letter? <u>*to inform the employer of*</u>
   <u>*the employee's medical condition*</u>

2. Who is the **audience**? <u>*the employer of the patient*</u>

3. Which does the doctor discuss: causes or effects? <u>*effects*</u>

4. Put a check mark (✓) next to the **topic sentences** that are the major causes or effects.

5. Underline the **details** that support the causes or effects.

6. Circle the (transitions).

7. What **key words** are repeated? <u>*health, symptoms, Mr. Hanson*</u>

Write a Cause/Effect Essay

In this section, you will write your own cause/effect essay. To do so, follow this sequence:

REVIEW the four basics of good cause/effect writing (p. 224).

CHOOSE your writing assignment (p. 235).

WRITE your cause/effect essay using the step-by-step Writing Guide (p. 237).

CHECK your final essay (p. 241).

WRITING ASSIGNMENT 1   COLLEGE, WORK, EVERYDAY LIFE

Write a cause/effect essay on *one* of the following topics or on a topic of your own choice.

COLLEGE

- Immediate effects of being in college, or the desired long-term effects of going to college
- Causes of a legitimate absence that resulted in your missing a test (directed to your professor)
- Probable causes of a poor grade or a good grade

WORK

- Causes of low employee morale
- Causes, effects, or both of a situation at work
- Causes and effects of stress at work

EVERYDAY LIFE

- Causes of an argument with a friend or a member of your family
- Effects of a bad decision you or someone you know made (refer to the idea journal assignment at the start of this chapter)
- Effects of a particular drug

> **ESL**
> Invite ESL students to write about the causes or effects of a cultural or linguistic misunderstanding. Native English-speaking students might focus on causes/effects of a misunderstanding based on race, social class, gender, or age.

WRITING ASSIGNMENT 2   USE THE INTERNET

Choose an illness or disorder that has affected you or someone you know. Use the Internet to find out about why it occurs and what happens because of it. Then, in your own words, write an essay in which you discuss the causes, effects, or both of the illness or disorder you have chosen to investigate.

As you search, be as specific as possible about the topic. For example, if you want to find out what causes abuse in families, try entering a term such as *spouse abuse, domestic abuse,* or *child abuse* in the search field of a search engine such as Google or Lycos. Keep narrowing your search until you find information that you want, and bookmark useful sites you may want to return to later.

> For advice about how to cite a source, see Chapter 20.

WRITING ASSIGNMENT 3   AN ACTION PLAN

Read the problem and situation that follow, and then choose *one* of the assignment options (3A or 3B) that appear after it.

PROBLEM: Some of us are so busy just trying to cope with our present lives that we don't have time to think about or plan for the future. As a result, we don't always act in ways that will get us where we want to be.

SITUATION: You have finally decided to make planning your future a priority. You know you need to think carefully about where you want to be or what you want to do and how you might get there. Start by identifying a particular goal you have for yourself. Consider the actions or behaviors that will result in (cause) that goal to happen or the benefits that will come from (be effects of) achieving that goal. Use a ring diagram like the one on page 226 to help you do this.

ASSIGNMENT OPTION 3A: RESPOND TO THE SITUATION

First think hard about something concrete that you would like to achieve, something that will be a challenge but that you believe will be worth the time and effort it takes. Choosing a topic may be the most difficult part of the assignment because it involves thinking about a future goal instead of living only in the present. The goal should be something that really matters to you. It doesn't have to be unique or earth shattering: Maybe you want to lose weight, stop smoking, get some regular exercise, or spend more time with your family. Maybe you want to make more money, spend less on useless things, or get a new car or new job. Spend some time thinking about a goal that is important to you.

Then write an essay that identifies and gives details about what actions you could take to make this goal happen.

ASSIGNMENT OPTION 3B: ANOTHER PERSPECTIVE

TEAMWORK
Assignment option 3B would work well as a collaborative project for students who wish to work on a college or community problem.

Rather than making an action plan for yourself, consider instead another person whom you care about (pick a real friend or family member with a real problem). One way in which friends can help each other is to suggest alternatives to destructive behaviors. In this essay, identify a problem that a friend or family member has, and then suggest positive effects of addressing the problem or changing the behavior.

Cause and Effect

Follow the steps in this Writing Guide to help you prewrite, draft, revise, and edit your cause and effect essay. Check off each step as you complete it.

Writing Guide

THINKING CRITICALLY ABOUT CAUSE AND EFFECT

FOCUS   Think about a topic that matters to you and whether you want to describe its causes, its effects, or both.

ASK
- Who are my readers? Who are the people I am writing for?
- Are my causes *real* causes, not just events that happened before? Are my effects *real* effects, not just events that follow?
- What examples and details do I need to give in order to make the causes and effects stand out?
- How should I organize the essay? Should I arrange the causes and effects by order of importance, chronologically, or in some other way?

TEACHING TIP
Clearly state whether you want students to write about causes, effects, or both.

PREWRITE TO EXPLORE YOUR TOPIC

Prewriting for cause and effect involves thinking about the actual causes of an event or the actual results of it, as opposed to an event that came before another event but didn't really cause it or came after it but was not an effect of it.

_____   Decide on your purpose for writing.

_____   Identify the audience for your essay.

_____   Jot down some ideas about a situation that affects you. Using the ring diagram as a prewriting technique works well for cause and effect.

_____   Consider how the situation occurred and what will happen because of it.

For more on purpose and audience, see pages 7–9.

WRITE A THESIS STATEMENT

The thesis statement in a cause/effect essay usually includes the topic and your main point about it. To state your main point clearly in a cause/effect essay, you might use a word such as *because, cause, reason, result,* or *effect* in your thesis statement.

| Topic | + | Main point | = | Thesis statement |

Irresponsible behavior   caused my car accident.

Note that the above writer groups the items in the "causes" ring in the ring diagram (see page 226) for this topic into the more general term *irresponsible behavior.*

| The health of one of my patients, George Hanson, | is being seriously affected by conditions in the offices of Kirkland Brothers. |

_____ Determine whether you are writing about causes, effects, or both.

_____ Decide what point you want to convey about the situation's causes or effects.

_____ Write a thesis statement that presents the situation or event and the main point you want to make about the causes or effects.

SUPPORT YOUR POINT

The major support points in a cause/effect essay are the causes, effects, or both that you present to demonstrate your main point.

The supporting details explain how the cause or effect you have identified directly caused the situation or resulted from it. The explanations are important because they tell your readers *how* the causes or effects relate to the situation.

_____ List the most important causes or effects of a situation.

_____ For each cause or effect, give an example and details about how it caused or resulted from the event or situation. Think about what information and explanation your reader needs to know.

MAKE A PLAN

Making a written plan—an outline—helps you decide how to order your cause and effect. A cause/effect essay often uses order of importance to arrange causes or effects. By building up to the most important point, the essay creates a strong final impression on readers.

_____ Make a plan or outline for your essay that arranges the causes and effects in order of importance, from least to most significant, or in some other logical order.

_____ Include explanations of each cause and effect in your plan.

DRAFT

Drafting a cause/effect essay means writing in complete sentences and including the following:

- An introduction with a thesis statement that communicates your topic and main point about it
- The causes, effects, or both for the situation, with detailed explanations
- A conclusion

_____ Think about how you can present the causes or effects so that your readers clearly understand your main point.

_____ Write an introductory paragraph that includes your thesis statement and interests your readers in finding out more about the causes or effects of a particular situation or event.

_____ Write a topic sentence for each of the causes or effects.

_____ Write body paragraphs that present and carefully explain each cause or effect.

_____ Write a strong conclusion that refers back to your main point and makes a final observation.

_____ Title your essay.

REVISE

Revising means changing whole sentences or paragraphs to make your writing clearer or stronger. To revise a cause and effect essay, imagine that you have no idea what caused or resulted from the situation. Read your draft, looking for the following:

- Places where the ideas are off the main point (revising for unity)
- Gaps in information or detail (revising for support and detail)

    • Areas in need of transitions to move readers smoothly from one point to the next (revising for coherence)

For more on peer review, see pages 87–88.

_____ Get feedback from others through peer review.

_____ Begin revising by asking yourself how you could make your causes and effects clearer for your readers.

TEACHING TIP
In a newspaper article with cause/effect organization, have students circle the transitions and make a list of any not included in this section of the textbook.

_____ Reread your thesis statement, and make changes so that it has more impact on your readers.

_____ Reread the body of your cause and effect essay to see whether the causes or effects are directly related to the situation or event. Be sure that each is clearly explained, based on what you know about your readers. Add other details that would help explain the causes or effects.

_____ Reread your introduction to make sure that it is as effective as possible.

_____ Reread your conclusion to make sure that it is energetic and convincing, that it reminds your readers of your main point, and makes a final observation.

_____ Add transition words and sentences to connect your ideas and lead readers smoothly from one to another.

_____ Decide whether repeating key words would increase your emphasis.

_____ Make at least five changes to your draft to improve the unity, support, or coherence or to make the introduction, thesis statement, or conclusion stronger or more convincing.

EDIT

Some grammar, spelling, word use, or punctuation errors may confuse your readers and make it difficult for them to understand a point you are trying to make. Even if they do not confuse your readers, errors detract from the effectiveness and overall quality of your writing. Edit your cause/effect essay carefully, and correct any errors you find.

_____ Ask a classmate or friend to read your cause/effect essay and highlight any errors.

_____ Use the spell checker and grammar checker on your computer.

_____ Look yourself for errors that the spell checker or grammar checker didn't catch. Focus first on sentence fragments, run-on sentences, problems with subject–verb agreement, problems with verbs, and other areas where you know you often make errors.

_____ Print a clean, final copy.

_____ Ask yourself: Is this the best I can do?

A FINAL CHECK BEFORE HANDING IN YOUR CAUSE/EFFECT ESSAY

If you've followed the Writing Guide for cause and effect, your essay will already include the four basics of good cause and effect. Use this list to double-check each basic feature.

____ My thesis clearly distinguishes causes and effects.

____ The causes in my essay are real causes, not just events that happened before another event.

____ The effects in my essay are real effects, not just events that happened after another event.

____ The body of my essay includes clear and detailed examples of the causes, effects, or both that I have considered.

16

Argument

Writing That Persuades

Understand What Argument Is

DEFINITION: **Argument** is writing that takes a position on an issue and offers reasons and supporting evidence to persuade someone else to accept, or at least consider, the position. Argument is also used to convince someone to take an action (or not to take an action).

■■ Four Basics of Good Argument

1. It takes a strong and definite position on an issue or advises a particular action.
2. It gives good reasons and supporting evidence to defend the position or recommended action.
3. It considers opposing views.
4. It has enthusiasm and energy from start to finish.

Knowing how to argue is critical. We use argument every day as a way to persuade someone to lend us something or to do something for us. We present an argument to persuade someone to give us a job, or not to give us a parking ticket, to buy something we're selling, or to give us more time. And we argue when something important is at stake, like keeping a job or

Wayne Whitaker

Wayne Whitaker
ASSISTANT DIRECTOR OF ADMISSIONS

BACKGROUND: Wayne grew up in New York City's South Bronx and Brooklyn. School was difficult for him, and most of his classes were in the vocational/technical program. At the end of his senior year, Wayne told his guidance counselor that he wanted to go to college. Although his grades weren't good, he was admitted to Bloomsburg University through a special admissions program, ACT 101. Wayne, now a recruiter for the school he attended, helps others also gain admission to Bloomsburg University.

EMPLOYER: Bloomsburg University

COLLEGE(S)/DEGREES: Bloomsburg University (B.A. and M.S.)

TYPES OF WRITING ON THE JOB: Letters to students telling them about Bloomsburg and encouraging them to apply; federal and state grant proposals for recruitment programs; reports to administration and granting agencies; frequent emails; presentations to prospective students

HOW WAYNE USES ARGUMENT: It is part of Wayne's job to convince students to apply to and attend Bloomsburg. He does this through persuasive letters, presentations, and personal conversations. For an example of how Wayne uses argument, see Argument in the Workplace, on page 254.

COMPUTER SKILLS: Word processing, PowerPoint, Web design

TEAMWORK ON THE JOB: Wayne says, "Recruitment can't be done by a single person: It requires a unified team effort." As a recruiter, he works with high school guidance counselors, colleagues, the athletic department, and other offices. To ensure successful campus visits, he works with everyone from maintenance and cafeteria staff to faculty and administration.

FUTURE GOAL: Wayne says, "[My goal is] to be director of admissions and then to broaden my role and become a dean of student life."

---

protecting our rights. To argue effectively, we need to do more than just say what we want or believe; we need to give solid reasons and evidence.

Argument is the method you use to persuade people to see things your way, or at least to understand your position. Argument helps you to take action in problem situations, rather than standing by, silent and frustrated. Although knowing how to argue won't eliminate all such situations, it will help you to defend your position.

DISCUSSION
Ask students to give examples of situations in which they needed to defend a position.

ENERGY AND ENTHUSIASM FOR A STRONG POSITION

ESL
Ask students how differences in languages and cultures help shape the presentation of an argument.

The topic of an argument is the issue you are writing about. In order for something to be an issue, it has to be something that people have different opinions about. A good argument starts with a strong and definite position on an issue. As a writer, you need to be very clear about what your position is so that you can take a stand and defend that position with energy.

When you are free to choose an issue to write about, choose something you care about or are interested in. But even when you are assigned an issue, you still need to defend it powerfully by finding some aspect of it that you care about.

Take a few minutes to either think about the issue, talk it over with a partner, or jot down ideas related to it. Here are some tips to get you started.

DISCUSSION
Ask students to identify a good argument or speech they have heard and explain what made it effective.

Tips for Building Energy and Enthusiasm

- Imagine yourself arguing your position with someone who holds the opposite position.
- Imagine that your whole grade rests on persuading your teacher of your position.
- Imagine how this issue could affect you or your family personally.
- Imagine that you are representing a large group of people who very much care about the issue and whose lives will be forever changed by it. It's up to you to win their case.

A THESIS STATEMENT OF YOUR POSITION

Your thesis statement in an argument presents your position on the issue. It should include the topic (the issue you are writing about) and your position.

| Topic (Issue) | + | Position | = | Thesis statement |

Students should be required to take   at least one public speaking course before graduating.

Many thesis statements for arguments use words such as the following because they clearly express a position:

For more on writing a thesis statement, see Chapter 3.

could (not)	ought (not)
must (not)	requires
must have	should (not)
needs	would

■ **PRACTICE 1   WRITING A STATEMENT OF YOUR POSITION**

Write your position on the following issues.

Lowering the drinking age to eighteen   *Answers will vary.* _____

_____

Mandatory drug testing as a requirement for employment _____

_____

Bilingual education at every grade level _____

_____

_____

TEACHING TIP
Have students write at least three different versions of a position statement and then evaluate which they think is the most effective, and why.

Now take one of the position statements that you just wrote and put more energy into it. *Answers will vary.* _____

_____

When you start to write your argument, you need to be clear about your position—and make your readers clear about it too.

SUPPORT FOR YOUR POSITION

TEACHING TIP
Explain to students that *reasons* are the major support points and *evidence* is the supporting details.

For more on supporting a thesis, see Chapter 4.

DEFINITION: **Reasons** are the points that support your position, points that must be backed up with evidence.

DEFINITION: **Evidence** consists of the **facts and statistics, examples,** and **expert opinions** that support your reasons.

The strength of your argument depends on the quality of the reasons and evidence that you present to support your position.

Facts: Accurate information that can be verified. Statistics—numerical facts based on research—can be persuasive evidence to back up your position.

POSITION: It pays to stay in college.

REASON: College graduates earn more than high school graduates.

EVIDENCE/FACT: College graduates earn 58 percent more than high school graduates and 320 percent more than high school dropouts.

Examples: Stories and experiences that directly support your position.

POSITION: It pays to stay in college.

REASON: Students learn up-to-date skills that they will need to find a job.

EVIDENCE/EXAMPLE: Understanding how to use technology in your field may make the difference between getting a job and coming in second.

Expert Opinion: The testimony of someone who is considered knowledgeable in the field. The person must be known for his or her expertise in the area you are writing about. For example, a doctor's opinion on the effects of a certain drug is more convincing support than a movie star's. *Note:* Just because a person's opinion appears on a Web site does not mean that he or she has any expertise. Find out about the person's credentials before using his or her words as expert opinion.

POSITION: It pays to stay in college.

REASON: An increasing number of jobs require college degrees.

EVIDENCE/EXPERT OPINION: John Sterling, president of one of the largest recruiting agencies, said recently, "Ten years ago, a college degree was perceived as an advantage. Today, the college degree is the basic ticket of entry for the majority of jobs." *Note:* When you use expert opinion, you need to identify the source of the quote.

As you choose reasons and evidence to support your position, consider what your audience is likely to think about your stand on the issue. Are they likely to agree with you, to be uncommitted, or to be hostile? Think about what kinds of reasons and evidence would be most convincing to a typical member of your audience.

OPPOSING POSITIONS

When you write your thesis, you state your position on the issue. The rest of your essay should be devoted to supporting that position. Part of supporting your own position, however, is acknowledging the opposing position and presenting some evidence against it.

TEACHING TIP
Remind students that arguments are often ineffective because they either lack evidence entirely or include evidence that is inappropriate for the particular audience and purpose.

TEACHING TIP
Have the class choose an issue, bring in evidence (facts, examples, expert opinions), and compare and contrast what they find.

For more on using quotations and citing sources, see Chapters 20 and 21.

For more on finding sources, see Chapter 20.

TEACHING TIP
Critique a misleading ad that uses weak evidence (such as a diet ad that promises instant weight loss). Ask students to bring in other examples.

If, for example, you are arguing in favor of lowering the drinking age in your state to eighteen, you should not ignore the position that it should be kept at age twenty-one. If you don't say anything about the other position, you are leaving your argument unprotected. To defend your own position, you need to acknowledge the opposing view and address it by showing some weakness in it or another way of looking at it.

POSITION: The drinking age should be lowered to eighteen.

OPPOSING POSITION: The drinking age should not be lowered because people begin drinking before the legal age. If the age were lowered to eighteen, more sixteen-year-olds would drink.

RESPONSE TO THE OPPOSING POSITION: Laws should not be based on the extent to which they are abused or broken. Enforcement (or lack of enforcement) should not influence the law itself.

STATEMENTS THAT ACKNOWLEDGE AND ADDRESS OPPOSING POSITION:

Some people feel strongly that the drinking age should not be lowered because, if drinking is legal at eighteen, teenagers will start drinking at sixteen. While many teenagers do in fact drink before it is legal to do so, there is no evidence to show that the higher legal age has anything to do with the age at which teenagers start to drink. Other factors involved, such as peer pressure and the availability of fake ID's, have more impact on whether teenagers drink. Laws should not be based on ease of enforcement. Otherwise, our legal system would be a joke.

While some people believe that lowering the legal drinking age will lower the age that teenagers start drinking, there is no evidence to show that the legal age is a major influence on teenaged drinking. (Writer then gives other evidence such as in the above paragraph.)

> **DISCUSSION**
> Ask students to suggest a topic, a position, and some evidence. Then ask for ideas about how the opposition would try to knock down the evidence.

> Acknowledge opposing position

> Address the opposing position

PRACTICE 2   ACKNOWLEDGING AND ADDRESSING THE OPPOSING VIEW

For each of the following positions, in the spaces indicated, state the opposing position and at least one point someone holding the opposing view might make against your position.

> **TEAMWORK**
> Practice 2 works well in pairs.

Answers will vary. Suggested answers follow.

ISSUE: The "Three Strikes and You're Out" rule in some high schools that says students are expelled after three serious offenses

POSITION: Against it

OPPOSING POSITION: *in favor of the rule*

POINT THAT SOMEONE HOLDING THE OPPOSING POSITION WOULD MAKE: _____

The rule serves as a deterrent.

ISSUE: Mandatory retirement at age sixty-five
POSITION: In favor of it

OPPOSING POSITION: *opposed to mandatory retirement at age sixty-five*

POINT THAT SOMEONE HOLDING THE OPPOSING POSITION WOULD MAKE: _____

People live longer these days than they used to.

ISSUE: Stricter gun control laws
POSITION: Against it

OPPOSING POSITION: *in favor of stricter gun control laws*

POINT THAT SOMEONE HOLDING THE OPPOSING POSITION WOULD MAKE: _____

Stricter laws would decrease the number of accidental shootings.

Writing a good argument is like arguing a case in court. A lawyer representing one side not only builds his or her own case but also tries to anticipate what the opposing lawyer will say and how to weaken the opposing lawyer's case. In a short essay, you may not be able to address all the points of the opposing view, but you should know what they are and address at least the most important point.

As you gather support for your position, keep the opposing position in mind and follow the tips given in the box.

Tips for Supporting Your Position by Addressing the Opposing Position

- Visualize someone who holds the opposing position and what that person would say to defend it.
- In part of the body of your essay, acknowledge the opposing position. Do so politely; if you try to ridicule the opposing view, you will alienate people and immediately weaken your argument.
- Poke some holes in the opposing position by addressing it head-on and showing what's wrong, or misguided, about the position. Again, do this politely; don't make your opposition look foolish.
- Return to the reasons and the evidence that support your position.

ORDER OF IDEAS FOR ARGUMENT

Argument most often uses order of importance to organize reasons for the writer's position on the issue. Consider what you think your readers will find your most convincing reason. Think about how you can arrange the reasons and evidence so that they build the strongest case for your position. Save the most convincing reason for last.

For more on order of importance, see page 60.

Do not forget to acknowledge and address the opposing position. Where you do that within the body of your essay depends on where it will have the most impact on your readers. Some writers acknowledge and address the opposing position for each reason they give; others may choose to do so in a separate paragraph. You have to be the judge of where and how, but you must acknowledge and address the opposing position or your argument is not adequately supported.

The plan for an argument often looks like this:

Introduction (including thesis)

First reason

    evidence and information to back up reason

Second reason

    evidence and information to back up reason

Most important reason

    evidence and information to back up reason

Conclusion

    reminds readers of your position on the issue and makes a final pitch for that position

    may also make a further recommendation or issue a warning about what will happen if your position is ignored or defeated

As you write your argument, use transitions to connect your reasons to your thesis and your evidence to your reasons.

For more on transitions, see pages 94–97.

Here are some transitions often used for argument.

Common Transitions in Argument

TRANSITIONS FROM ONE POINT TO ANOTHER	TRANSITIONS TO ADD EMPHASIS
also	above all
another fact to consider	best of all
another reason	especially

(continued)

Common Transitions in Argument

TRANSITIONS FROM ONE POINT TO ANOTHER	TRANSITIONS TO ADD EMPHASIS
another thing	in fact
consider that	in particular
for example	more important
in addition	most important
in the first place	remember
	the last point to consider
	worst of all

Putting together a good argument is one of the most useful skills you can learn. Knowing how to argue well will equip you to defend effectively what you believe and to convince others to support your opinion. Many situations require good argument skills:

COLLEGE

- An essay exam question in a human services course asks you to agree or disagree, using information from the course, with the following statement: "Government agencies should not have the authority to separate families."
- You present reasons why you should be able to make up a test that you missed.
- An exit essay from a writing course contains the following instruction: "Develop a well-balanced argument on the subject of free speech on the Internet."

WORK

- You present reasons why you should get a raise.
- You negotiate a better benefits package than the one that was offered.
- You give a customer or client reasons why he or she should invest in your company's product or services.

EVERYDAY LIFE

- You convince a large company that it has made a mistake on your bill.
- You persuade a child to share a favorite toy with a friend.
- You take a stand on a local issue or policy that you believe is unfair.

Read and Analyze Argument

Before writing your own argument essay, read the following examples — one each from college, the workplace, and everyday life — and answer the questions that accompany each. Reading the examples and answering the questions will help you understand how to write a good argument essay.

1. ARGUMENT IN COLLEGE

The following is an essay written by a student for her English composition course. Since the writer, Edna Crespo, consulted several sources as she wrote, her essay includes a list of works cited.

For more on writing from sources, see Chapter 21.

How Violence on TV Affects Children and Adolescents

Edna Crespo

"Children who watch the violent shows, even 'just funny cartoons,' are more likely to hit out at their playmates, argue, disobey class rules, leave tasks unfinished, and be less willing to wait for things than those who watch nonviolent programs," says Aletha Huston, Ph.D., now at the University of Kansas. Nearly five violent scenes are displayed during one hour of prime time shows. There is violence even in many cartoons. Several studies in North America of children who watch violent television programs consistently reveal that they are directly affected by televised violence. Violent programming negatively affects youth, changing children's interests, making them less sensitive to the pain of others, and teaching them to be aggressive toward others.

✓ The impact of aggressive television programs upon children may be so strong that it can cause them to lose interest in many other activities. The passive activity of watching violence on television often becomes more attractive to children than socializing or participating in outdoor activities. Specifically, community programs, such as various sports or outdoor excursions, appear less interesting to them. They also spend less time playing with friends, reading, and doing homework. Because of their lack of activity, they have the tendency to become idle and overweight. Furthermore, "many adolescents admit that they just find it very difficult to turn off the TV. . . . They recognize the seductive power of the medium" (Ledingham).

✓ (In addition,) several studies have shown that most children who are exposed to violent scenes become less sensitive to the suffering of people and more tolerant of aggressiveness. For example, studies of some children who watched heavy violence on television found them "slower to intervene or to call for help when they saw younger children fighting or playing destructively" (Huston). They seem not to be bothered by violent acts. Actually, they tolerate aggressive behavior as if it were common and acceptable.

✓ (Worst of all) is that too much exposure to television violence induces aggressiveness in children. By watching violent television shows, children's aggressiveness is increased, sometimes to dangerous levels. It seems that they think this is the normal pattern of behavior in everyday life, and they copy this hostile conduct at home with family members and friends. There are cases in which children have harmed classmates in an attempt to mimic a fight or a particular maneuver shown on a television program. For example, Aaron Auffhammer, an eight-year-old boy, was victimized by his own classmates when they tried to imitate some violent actions they had seen in a television show. Aaron's mother, Mykie Auffhammer, explained, "After being tripped by a kid, Aaron was trying to get up when a third kid picked up his legs so that he was upside down, and then slammed his head on the ground" (Brossett). Aaron was harmed and could have been seriously injured by children of his own age who were simply trying out something they had seen.

✓ While some people argue that any monitoring of violent behavior in television goes against the principle of free speech, I wonder what those people say about the impact on children. Is free speech more important than helping children to become good, responsible, healthy adults? Is the violent content of so many television programs necessary to ensure free expression?

For eighteen years, I have worked in the marketing and advertising business, and I know how powerful television can be in influencing and teaching values and shaping behaviors in children and adolescents. The television broadcasts in the intimacy of our homes can help to establish close relationships between parents and children. Unfortunately, this power is not frequently used to build positive qualities and feelings.

Instead, violent scenes predominate in a culture where billions of dollars are made by this industry. What is violent television doing to us? It is making lots of money while destructively shaping the values of children.

Works Cited

Brossett, Tonja. "Does Violence on Television Affect Our Kids?" 23 Apr. 2001 <www.parenthoodweb.com>.

Huston, Aletha, Ph.D. "Violence on Television." 23 Apr. 2001 <www.apa.org/pubinfo/violence.html>.

Ledingham, Jane, Dr. "The Effect of Media Violence on Children." The National Clearinghouse on Family Violence. 23 Apr. 2001 <www.media.awareness.ca/eng/med>.

1. What is Edna's **purpose**? *to argue that violent television programming*

   negatively affects youth

For more on purpose and audience, see pages 7–9.

2. Who is Edna's **audience**? *her instructor and classmates*

3. Fill in the blanks with the **issue** and Edna's **position** on the issue.

   ISSUE: *violence on television*

   POSITION: *negatively affects child and adolescent viewers*

4. Double-underline the **thesis statement**.

5. What kind of **introductory technique** does Edna use to get the reader's attention? *uses expert opinion*

6. Put a check mark (✓) next to each **topic sentence**.

7. What kinds of **support** (facts, examples, expert opinion) does Edna use to demonstrate her thesis statement? *expert opinion and examples*

8. In what paragraph does Edna acknowledge the **opposing position**? *paragraph 5*

9. What **order of organization** does Edna use? *importance*

10. Circle the (transitions) in the essay.

11. Edna does not have a sentence in her concluding paragraph that relates back to her introduction. Write one that would do so, and indicate where you would place it in the concluding paragraph.

For a list of the four basics of good argument, see page 242.

Answers will vary.

_____

_____

DISCUSSION
Ask students if they agree or disagree with Edna Crespo's argument. This might be a good writing topic for those who disagree. Do the same with the letter on pages 255–56.

12. Does Edna's essay have the **four basics of good argument**? Why or why not?

Answers will vary.

_____

_____

2. ARGUMENT IN THE WORKPLACE

Some of the argument writing you do in college will involve issues that you are passionate about and that directly affect you. In the workplace, you may be less passionate about the topic, but you still use the principles of good argument regularly, perhaps even more than you do in college. When you work with others and your success depends on what they do, hardly a day will go by when you don't use argument strategies to persuade someone of something.

The following letter to a student is similar to ones that Wayne Whitaker writes when he is trying to convince a student to apply to Bloomsburg University. One measure of Wayne's success at his job is how many students enroll for each new class, so it is important that he convince people to apply. Note how Wayne uses what he knows about his audience, the student Ms. Petrona, to present reasons that will be important to her.

Dear Ms. Petrona:

I'm glad that we had an opportunity to talk during your recent visit to Bloomsburg University. Based on our conversation, I am convinced that Bloomsburg is the ideal college for you. I hope to convince you of that, too.

✓ Bloomsburg University will offer you unparalleled support that will help you adjust to and succeed in college. We discussed the fact that you feel a little intimidated by the whole idea of college. Well, Ms. Petrona, you certainly aren't alone in that feeling, and I can assure you that we have the resources you need to set you on the strong course. Our ACT 101 summer program will ensure that you have the basic skills you need for your first-year courses. Your ACT 101 counselor will be your mentor and adviser throughout college, a wise and savvy guide who is there to help you with any issue. As one of our ACT 101 graduates, Roberta Connoni, said, "I wouldn't have made it in college without ACT 101. The people there gave me the information and confidence I needed to believe I could get a college degree."

✓ Bloomsburg University also has a very strong business program that should be attractive to you since you are interested in majoring in business. Our courses are small, so you receive individual attention. Many of our faculty members are also working professionals who have real-life experience to bring to the classroom. And the university has strong relationships with local and state businesses. Last year, 85 percent of our business majors had received job offers prior to graduation.

✓ Bloomsburg University is a community, not just an institution. Our rural location helps us focus on our shared purpose: to learn and develop as citizens. We are a community of learners rather than some buildings set among other city buildings. This setting reinforces our mission and joins us all in the mission of learning.

Ms. Petrona, you will thrive here. Based on your background and the needs you cited, Bloomsburg is a perfect match. We are eager to welcome you to our community and will look forward to helping you achieve your best.

1. What is Wayne's **purpose**? _to convince a student to apply to_ _Bloomsburg_

For more on purpose and audience, see pages 7–9.

2. What do you learn about Wayne's **audience** from his letter? _____
   The student feels intimidated by school and wants to major in business.

3. What issue is Wayne writing about? What is his position on that issue?
   appropriateness of Bloomsburg to student's needs; the school is ideal for _the audience_

4. Double-underline his **thesis statement**.

5. Put a check mark (✓) next to his **topic sentences.**

6. Underline the **evidence** that supports his reasons.

7. Is there any obvious organization to the argument? *parallels the*

   student's needs

3. ARGUMENT IN EVERYDAY LIFE

The following is the body of a letter that one Philadelphia-area resident
wrote to the chair of the school committee in her town.

I am painfully aware that violence in schools is a clear and present
danger, in our town as everywhere. I realize that schools must take
precautions to ensure the safety of their students. However, recent events
in our schools make me wonder whether we have overreacted to the threat
of violence and have lost our common sense. With the enactment of new
rules, we must make sure that common sense still prevails as the judge of
what is punishable behavior.

✓ Common sense dictates that there are legitimate exceptions to every
rule. Many items are banned from school for good reason: guns, knives,
and so on. The penalty for having any contraband item is immediate suspension. These rules make sense. But what of the young woman, a dia-
betic, at the high school who was suspended for having a needle? It was
part of her medical kit—she gives herself daily injections of insulin. Does
it make sense to suspend her without consideration of the circumstances?

✓ Common sense also dictates that a student should not be punished
for fulfilling an assignment. What about the student whose teacher made
an assignment to write an imaginative short story, a horror story, with
details that made it lifelike and truly scary. When the student wrote a powerful short story about a student who stalks and then murders an English
teacher, the student was suspended because of the threat to the teacher.
Maybe the student didn't use the best judgment, but was there a punishable act?

In both of the above cases, the students were eventually reinstated,
but not without a good deal of trauma and embarrassment for everyone
involved. What message does that send to our students? I believe that

common sense is a key element to good judgment, something I want my children to learn. What are they learning when common sense goes out the window? As adults, we need to apply common sense, particularly in the schools, our institutions of learning.

1. What is the writer's **purpose** in this letter? *to argue that the community*

   overreacts in certain situations

For more on purpose and audience, see pages 7–9.

2. What does the letter suggest about the writer's **audience**? *that they are*

   anxious about the very real threat of violence

3. What is the issue that the writer discusses? *how schools react to the*

   threat of violence

4. What is the writer's position on the issue? *At times her community*

   overreacts.

5. Double-underline the **thesis statement**.

6. Put a check mark (✓) next to each **topic sentence**.

7. Does the writer offer convincing evidence? Why or why not? _____

   Answers will vary.

Write an Argument Essay

In this section you will write your own argument essay. To do so, follow this sequence:

>**REVIEW** the basics of good argument (p. 242).
>
>**CHOOSE** your writing assignment (below).
>
>**WRITE** your argument using the step-by-step Writing Guide (p. 261).
>
>**CHECK** your final essay (p. 265).

▊ WRITING ASSIGNMENT 1   COLLEGE, WORK, EVERYDAY LIFE

Write an argument essay on *one* of the following topics or on a topic of your own choice. Select an issue that you care about so that you can argue powerfully.

COLLEGE

- Persuade the college president to make a change that would help students.
- Persuade one of your teachers to raise the grade on your last assignment (in a course you are currently taking).
- Defend the following statement: "A college degree means something."

WORK

- Argue against a company policy that you believe is unfair.
- Laws in many states prohibit an employer from sharing information with another employer about a former employee—even if the individual was dangerous. Agree or disagree with that policy.
- Argue that you should get a promotion.

EVERYDAY LIFE

- Argue for or against a 7:00 A.M. starting time at the local high school.
- Argue against a rent increase.
- Argue for or against tobacco companies being sued by cancer patients.

WRITING ASSIGNMENT 2   USE THE INTERNET

For advice about how to cite a source, see Chapter 20.

Visit a Web site devoted to taking action on some controversial issue. Spend time reading through the site's home page, mission statement, action plan, and headlines. Then write an essay in which you take a position on the issue. You can agree or disagree with the sponsors of the site you have investigated. Here is a brief list of Web sites that tackle controversial issues:

People for the Ethical Treatment of Animals **<www.peta.org>** (Click on "Action alerts" or "Campaigns" from the home page.)

The American Civil Liberties Union's Freedom Network page on racial profiling **<www.aclu.org/profiling>**

Freedom From Religion Foundation page on school prayer **<www.ffrf.org/issues>**

Physicians for Compassionate Care, an organization of health professionals against assisted suicide **<www.pccef.org>**

WRITING ASSIGNMENT 3   ARGUMENT WRITING TESTS

Many states and colleges require students to take a timed writing test. Often the test calls for an argument essay on an assigned topic, and students must argue pro (for) or con (against), as directed. Many people believe that a good writer should be able to argue either side of an issue regardless of his or her personal feelings. Choose one of the following questions, come up with evidence to support both sides of the issue, and write an essay defending one side or another. *Note:* Part of the requirement of the essay is to be able to support each side, so you will need to turn in the support you develop for each side of the position.

- Should students be penalized for poor attendance?
- Should the government make it more difficult for couples to divorce?
- Should personal email messages written on a company's computer be company property or personal property?

WRITING ASSIGNMENT 4   THE COLLEGE COUNCIL

Read the problem and situation that follow, as well as "David's Problem," and "The President's Instructions." Then choose *one* of the assignment options to write about.

TEAMWORK
Assignment 4 works well as a small-group project.

PROBLEM: At some point, we all find ourselves in ethical dilemmas, where we are presented with a situation that pulls us in different directions, but about which we need to make a decision one way or the other. Understanding argument helps us make thoughtful choices as we weigh evidence to reach a conclusion. Although in difficult situations we may not feel completely easy with our decision, we know that that decision is based on careful consideration of everything involved and that we've done our best.

SITUATION: You are a student representative to the College Council, which reviews requests and issues that affect the college as a whole. The college president opens today's session by saying, "We have before us a difficult question to consider that affects not only the student involved but others as well." The president then describes the situation.

Professor McNamara teaches English 100A, the basic writing course in the English department. All students must pass the course before they can be accepted into a degree program. A student in Professor McNamara's course, David K., has made a request that the professor does not feel she can grant without advisement by the College Council.

DAVID'S PROBLEM: David is a mechanic at a large automotive repair center. He has a wife and four children, one of whom has a chronic illness that requires expensive medical treatments. In order to pay for the treatments, David must either make more money or sign up for welfare assistance. David recently applied for a supervisor position at the center where he works. The position includes a substantial pay raise, but the company requires its management to have a degree in automotive engineering. Because David is a good worker, the boss will make an exception to the rule *if* David enrolls in a degree program.

David is failing English 100A, a prerequisite for enrolling in the automotive engineering degree program. He attends every class, does all the homework, and completes all the writing assignments, but his writing is so poor that he receives F's. He has finally approached Professor McNamara, hoping that she will give him a passing grade if she knows how important it is. Professor McNamara is caught between the very real needs of this student and her responsibility both to the college and to other students.

THE PRESIDENT'S INSTRUCTIONS: "I would like your recommendation about what should be done. But first, here are some of the angles of the situation that I would like you to consider. I'm sure there are others; please raise them in your written opinion."

- The college recognizes that the student's reasons for wanting to enter the program are very serious.
- If the student fails English 100A, he will not get a much-needed promotion.
- Other students in the basic writing course also have good reasons for needing a passing grade.
- The college made a passing grade in English 100A necessary for good reasons. For the college degree to mean anything, certain basic skills must be guaranteed.
- As a supervisor at the automotive center, David has to write weekly production reports.

ASSIGNMENT OPTION 4A: RESPONSE TO THE SITUATION

Consider the facts of the case, and then write an argument essay either in favor or against giving David a passing grade.

ASSIGNMENT OPTION 4B: ANOTHER PERSPECTIVE

Imagine that you are a local businessperson who sits on the College Council. From this perspective, write an argument essay either in favor or against giving David a passing grade.

Argument

Follow the steps in this Writing Guide to help you prewrite, draft, revise, and edit your argument. Check off each step as you complete it.

Writing Guide

THINKING CRITICALLY ABOUT ARGUMENT

FOCUS	Before and as you write, think about your position on the issue and how you can persuade your readers.
ASK	• Who will be reading this essay, and what are they likely to know about the issue? • Why is this issue important to me? What do I have at stake? • What is my position on the issue? • What are my reasons for taking this position? • What are some reasons for the opposing position? • What is my readers' position? • How can I build and maintain enthusiasm for my position? • What facts, statistics, examples, and expert opinions can I include to convince readers of my position?

PREWRITE TO EXPLORE YOUR ISSUE

Prewriting for argument involves exploring an issue you care about and deciding what your position on that issue is. As you prewrite, also think about the reasons you hold a particular view.

_____ Decide on your purpose for writing.

_____ Identify the audience for your argument.

For more on purpose and audience, see pages 7–9.

_____ Jot down some ideas about an issue that is important to you, focusing on what your position is and why. Various prewriting techniques work well for argument, so you should choose the one that you are most comfortable with. Freewriting, listing/brainstorming, and clustering work well for many writers.

_____ Take a few minutes to build some energy about the issue. How does this issue affect you personally? Why does it matter to you?

WRITE A THESIS STATEMENT

The thesis statement of an argument essay usually includes the issue and the writer's position on that issue. Writers may also use a thesis statement to preview the reasons they will offer to support their position.

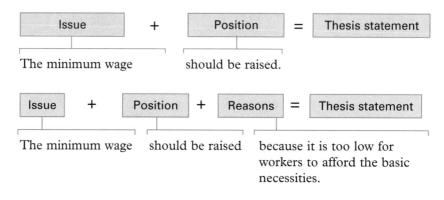

The minimum wage   should be raised.

The minimum wage   should be raised   because it is too low for workers to afford the basic necessities.

As you develop and revise your argument, you will also need to revise your thesis statement, right up to the very end, making it clearer and more forceful each time.

SUPPORT YOUR POINT

The major support points in an argument are the reasons you give for your position on the issue. These reasons will become the topic sentences for the body paragraphs of your essay. The supporting details in argument are the evidence and information you provide for each of your reasons. To come up with convincing support, keep a specific audience in mind, particularly readers who may not care about the issue or (if they do care) may not share your position on the issue.

_____   Use a prewriting technique to come up with support (convincing reasons and evidence) for your position. Look for persuasive facts, statistics, examples, and expert opinions to support your position.

_____   Clearly state each reason and give specific evidence and details to back it up.

_____   Acknowledge the opposing position and show weaknesses in it by addressing points an opponent might raise.

_____   Consider whether you will need to use outside sources.

_____   Test your reasons and evidence.

_____   Reread your reasons and evidence from your opponent's point of view, looking for their weaknesses. Anticipate your opponent's objections, and include evidence to answer those objections.

_____   Consider every important angle of the issue.

_____   Make sure that your reasons support your position and that your evidence supports your reasons.

MAKE A PLAN

Making a written plan—or outline—helps you decide how to order your argument. An argument generally uses order of importance to arrange the reasons it discusses. As you organize, think about what your audience will find most convincing. Be sure to acknowledge and address opposing positions, too.

_____   Arrange your reasons according to their importance to your position. End with the most important reason.

_____   Make a plan or outline with your reasons and evidence in order.

DRAFT

Drafting an argument essay means writing in complete sentences and including the following:

• An introduction, including a thesis statement that presents your position on an issue
• Major reasons for your position
• Evidence and information that support your reasons
• An acknowledgment of the opposing view with responses to it
• A conclusion

_____   Think about how your readers might react to each point you make.

_____   Write an introductory paragraph that includes your thesis statement and interests your readers in the issue.

_____   Using your outline or plan, write a topic sentence for each of the reasons that will support your position on the issue.

_____ Write body paragraphs that give facts, examples, and expert opinion that support your reasons.

_____ End on a strong note. Before writing your conclusion, build up your energy and enthusiasm again (see p. 244). Save your best reason for last, and write a conclusion that refers back to your issue and position, reviews the support you give, and makes a final strong statement urging your readers to see it your way and act accordingly.

_____ Title your essay.

REVISE

Revising means changing whole sentences or paragraphs to make your writing clearer or stronger. To revise an argument, assume that you are someone who holds the opposing view but is willing to listen to the other side. Think about how to make your reasons and evidence more convincing to that kind of a reader. Read your draft, looking for the following:

- Places where the ideas are off the main point (revise for unity)
- Gaps in information or detail (revise for support and detail)
- Areas in need of transitions to help the reader move smoothly from one reason to the next (revise for coherence)

For more on peer review, see pages 87–88.

_____ Get feedback from others through peer review. Ask one or more readers to listen carefully to your reasons and to challenge any that they find weak or don't understand. Find new reasons and evidence if needed.

_____ Begin revising by asking yourself how you could make your argument clearer and more persuasive for your readers.

_____ Reread your thesis to make sure that you clearly state your position on the issue.

_____ Reread your topic sentences to make sure that they clearly support your position and are written in strong, concrete language. Focus on whether you could provide additional reasons that would convincingly support your position.

_____ Reread each body paragraph to see if the evidence you give clearly explains and backs up your reasons. Add other evidence and information that might further persuade your reader that your reasons are valid.

_____ Reread your introduction to make sure that it states a definite opinion, with confidence, and hooks your readers' interest.

_____ Reread your conclusion to make sure that it sounds energetic and convincing, reminds your readers of your position, and makes a final attempt to persuade your readers.

_____ Add transitions to help your readers move smoothly from one reason to the next and to connect the backup evidence you provide.

_____ Decide whether repeating key words would increase your emphasis.

_____ Make at least five changes to your draft to improve the unity, support, or coherence of your argument or to make the introduction, thesis statement, or conclusion stronger or more convincing.

EDIT

Some grammar, spelling, word use, or punctuation errors may confuse your readers and make it difficult for them to understand a point you are trying to make. Even if they do not confuse your readers, errors detract from the effectiveness and overall quality of your writing. Edit your argument carefully, and correct any errors you find.

_____ Ask a classmate or friend to read your argument and highlight any errors.

_____ Use the spell checker and grammar checker on your computer.

_____ Look yourself for errors that the spell checker or grammar checker didn't catch. Focus first on sentence fragments, run-on sentences, problems with subject–verb agreement, problems with verbs, and other areas where you know you often make errors.

_____ Print a clean final copy.

_____ Ask yourself: Is this the best I can do?

TEAMWORK
Have students use these prompts as they review each other's drafts.

A FINAL CHECK BEFORE HANDING IN YOUR ARGUMENT ESSAY

If you've followed the Writing Guide for argument, your essay will already include the four basics of good argument. Use this list to double-check each basic feature.

_____ My argument has a thesis statement that takes a definite position or advises a particular action on a clear issue.

_____ The body paragraphs in my argument present good reasons and evidence to support my position.

_____ My essay acknowledges and addresses opposing views.

_____ My argument is enthusiastic and energetic.

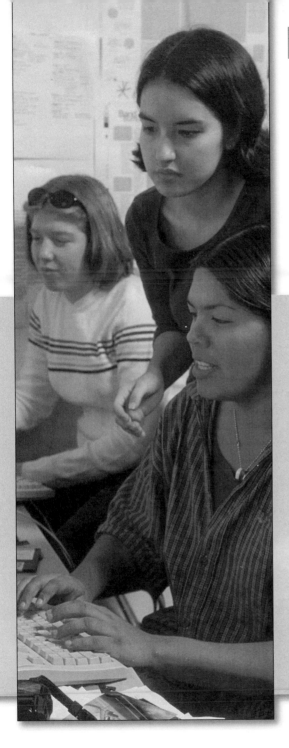

PART THREE

Writing in College and at Work

17

Solving Problems

Case Studies for Writing and Teamwork

You Know This
You've probably solved all kinds of problems.
- There's a traffic jam on your way to work, and you determine what alternative route to use.
- You figure out how to pay your bills when you're a little short on cash.
- You work with a friend to get a big job done on a tight schedule.
- You and a brother or sister decide how to get your parents to agree to something.

Understand What Problem Solving Is

IDEA JOURNAL
Write about a problem that you have encountered at work or in your everyday life.

ESL
Invite your ESL students to write about a problem they have encountered due to cultural differences, language differences, or immigration status.

DEFINITION: **Problem solving** is the process of identifying the problem and figuring out a good solution.

Think of the situations in your life that you might classify as problems. Perhaps you're falling behind in one of your courses. Or maybe you are managing a sales staff that hasn't met its quota for the third straight month. It could be that your child's day care center is having trouble retaining quality staff. While they often disrupt our lives, problems give us opportunities to tackle difficult situations with confidence. Being able to find reasonable solutions to problems is critical to success in every arena of life.

Sometimes you may be paralyzed by a problem. You may freeze because you don't have strategies for attacking it. Backing away from a problem is rarely a good solution; you simply become a victim, often feeling helpless and angry. When you know how to approach a challenging situation, you are better able to take charge of your life. Problem-solving skills are life skills that you'll use in college, at work, and in everyday life. Here are some ways in which you might use problem solving:

DISCUSSION
As a class, discuss additional problems that could be posed in each category. Write the most interesting or complicated problems on the board.

COLLEGE

- You have been working on a major assignment, and your computer breaks down the night before it is due.
- You lose your notebook near the end of the semester.
- Your college is eliminating its career services center when you need its services most.

WORK

- Your work schedule changes three weeks before the end of the semester and conflicts with class time.
- When several coworkers are laid off, you are assigned more work than you can handle.
- You have to work on a project with a colleague whom you don't like.

EVERYDAY LIFE

- You know you need major dental work, but you don't have insurance.
- Your child is afraid to go to school because two other children are making fun of him and taking his things during recess.
- You rely on public transportation, and you've just discovered that bus service in your town is being suspended indefinitely.

Problem solving, the process of identifying a problem and figuring out a reasonable solution to it, includes several basic steps.

THE PROBLEM-SOLVING PROCESS

1. Identify the problem. You should be able to describe it, orally or in writing, in a few sentences.

2. List people, information, and other resources that can help you solve the problem.

3. Identify possible solutions.

4. Evaluate each possible solution.
   - Identify the steps the solution would require.
   - List possible obstacles to the solution (e.g., money or time constraints).
   - List the advantages and disadvantages of the solution.

5. Choose the most reasonable solution, one that seems realistic and sensible. Keep in mind that problems seldom have right and wrong

solutions—just better and worse ones. Be able to explain and support your choice.

The problem-solving process can be used effectively by either an individual or a group. Increasingly in college, and particularly in the workplace, the task of solving a problem is assigned to a team, so it's important that you learn how to work with others toward a common goal of solving a problem.

TEACHING TIP
Have students read their idea journal entry and write another entry that follows the problem-solving process.

Understand What Teamwork Is

DEFINITION: **Teamwork** is the combined effort of two or more individuals to solve a problem and achieve a common goal.

Working with others has many benefits: more ideas and perspectives, more possible solutions, more people to share the work. But being part of an effective team requires more than simply meeting with people: You need to understand how a team functions well. In order to achieve a common goal, members of a team need to work *as* a team rather than trying to showcase their individual efforts and talents.

Sports teams don't win just because the individual players are talented; they win because the players pool their talents into a coordinated whole. Each player on the team works hard and supports the other players.

The same is true of teamwork in other arenas as well: To benefit from teamwork in college, work, and everyday life, individuals must not only understand and perform their own responsibilities well but also mesh those responsibilities with the work of the team. Take a moment to look back at a few of the Profiles of Success in Chapters 8–16. Notice that each of the people in the profiles emphasizes the importance of teamwork and gives examples of how he or she uses team skills on the job.

FIVE BASICS OF EFFECTIVE TEAMWORK

1. The team establishes ground rules to ensure that each person on the team can contribute.

2. Members listen to each other and respect different points of view.

3. Although one person may function as team leader, all individuals participate and are equally appreciated.

4. Members recognize that they must depend on one another.

5. All members contribute and feel responsible for their own work as it affects the outcomes of the team's effort.

DISCUSSION
Ask students how they have used teamwork in their own lives. First give an example from your own experience.

You will work in a team to complete the problem-solving assignments in this chapter. After your instructor forms the teams, you and your team-mates should work together to decide who will play which team roles. If the members of your group do not know each other, your instructor may plan some activities to help you get acquainted before the team determines roles. Each team member will play an active role as a **contributor**, but teams should also select people to fulfill the following additional roles:

Team leader: The leader keeps the group focused on the task. He or she leads the team as a facilitator, or one who helps move the process along, not as a bully. For example, the leader might help the group stay focused on listing possible solutions to a problem, like this:

> Rob and Shawna think we should write a letter to the college president, and Paolo says we should collect students' signatures on a petition instead. What other ideas can we come up with?

not like this:

> I think we need to have a fund-raiser. Does anyone have a problem with that?

The team leader's opinions carry no more weight than those of other team members, and it's the team leader's responsibility to make sure that every team member has an opportunity to participate.

Recorder: The recorder takes notes on the group's work, keeping track of the agreed-on outcomes of each step. He or she does not write down everything that is said—just the ideas that the group agrees are the best and most helpful. If each group member is required to write an essay or report, the recorder's notes can be photocopied or typed and printed so that everyone has a copy to use.

Timekeeper: Sometimes teams find that they are spending more time on a task than they had planned. When this happens, it is the time-keeper's responsibility to interrupt the group and report the time spent and the time remaining in the meeting. The team can then decide, collectively, to either continue the task or move on to the next step.

If your assignment stretches over a number of days or weeks, your team may need to meet several times. If this is the case, try rotating roles.

Solve Problems from Real-World Case Studies

Using the problem-solving process and working as part of a team, you will suggest a reasonable solution to a real-life problem presented in one of the following case studies. Once you have chosen or been assigned a case, read the case carefully. Then the team can meet to start working through the process of problem solving.

CASE STUDIES

1. *Network Administrator*

You are a network administrator for a large corporation and have the ability, though not the authority, to read all messages sent to and from employees using company email. Your company has a strict policy that safeguards the privacy of personal email, and the last network administrator was fired for reading other employees' mail. During one of your routine monitoring sessions, you notice an unusually large number of messages being sent from one internal email address to another. Out of curiosity, you open and read some of these email messages. The messages are from the boss's son to his girlfriend (both of whom are employees of the company), but they are not love letters. In his email, the young man talks about hurting his girlfriend, and each message is more threatening than the one before it. What do you do?

2. *College Ice Hockey Coach*

It is two nights before the conference game that will decide whether or not your ice hockey team advances to the championship playoffs. You learn that four key players have violated their curfew. Curfews are an important part of the discipline program created by the coaching staff. Both the rules of the curfew and the school's zero-tolerance policy for rule breaking are clearly established during preseason training. The punishment for breaking curfew is a one-game suspension. The group of players facing punishment includes the team's leading scorers. The team, which includes fourteen other players, has worked hard all season to achieve the school's best record in more than two decades. What do you do?

3. *High School Principal*

You are the principal of a high school. One of your best English teachers comes to you, very upset, and tells you that she fears for her safety. Around Halloween, she had assigned students in her creative writing class to write a story that was truly frightening and descriptive. One of her students had turned in a story that was indeed bloodcurdling—a detailed, graphic, gory account of a student who had executed his English teacher. The teacher has taken this story as a real threat and demands that the student be reported to the authorities and expelled. You read the story and agree that it is threatening. However, the student who wrote it has good grades, positive

RESOURCES
For advice on setting up groups, coaching them through the problem-solving process, monitoring the teamwork, and assessing individual members' contributions to the team effort, see Chapter 6 in *Practical Suggestions for Teaching REAL ESSAYS*.

TEAMWORK
Invite students to identify a pressing problem in their school or home community. Have small groups write a case study (similar to the ones listed in this section) that focuses on a practical concern or ethical dilemma related to the problem they identified.

relationships with teachers and other students, and no history of violence. The school has a written policy that informs students that any threats to the school community will result in suspension, expulsion, or possible legal action. What do you do?

4. Warehouse Floor Supervisor

You are the floor supervisor at a warehouse. One day a coworker you supervise tells you that he has tested HIV-positive. The man, John, tells you that he has already informed the Human Resources Department of his diagnosis, and its administrators are following the company's policy of nondiscrimination and privacy that requires the diagnosis to be kept confidential. You confirm this fact with the Human Resources Department and assure the employee that you will maintain his privacy.

A few months later, there is an accident in the warehouse. A person on one of the high ladders is loading heavy boxes onto a vehicle when two boxes drop from a height of 25 feet. One lands on John. He collapses onto the concrete floor, unconscious and bleeding. While one worker goes to call for help, several others rush to help John, wiping the blood from his cuts with their hands or shirttails. You know John is HIV-positive; you are also bound to confidentiality. What do you do?

▌ WRITING ASSIGNMENT   SOLVE A PROBLEM

TEACHING TIP
At the end of each class, give students time to take notes on how their team meetings went.

Using the problem-solving process (p. 270) and the basics of good teamwork (p. 271), propose a reasonable solution to the case study you have chosen or been assigned. As your team works through the problem-solving process, make sure that you keep good records of the ideas you agree on during every step. Though each team member will write his or her own essay, each essay should present what the team agrees is the most reasonable solution. Each essay should also explain the reasons for your team's choice of that solution. Before turning in your essays, you may want to read one another's drafts to suggest revisions and point out errors.

THINKING CRITICALLY ABOUT SOLVING A PROBLEM	
FOCUS	Read the case study carefully. Make a genuine effort to take on the team role you have chosen or been assigned.
ASK	• What is the core of the problem? • What factors make the situation a problem? • What people or information might help the team identify a solution to the problem?

- What are all the possible solutions?
- What are the advantages and disadvantages of each possible solution?
- What does the team see as the most reasonable and realistic solution? Why?
- What is the best way to explain the solution so that readers will understand what the problem is, what the proposed solution is, and why it is a reasonable solution?

WRITE   Write an essay that summarizes the problem, explains the possible solution, and supports your choice of this solution.

Tips for the Assignment

1. Try to be as specific as possible in identifying the problem.

2. When listing possible solutions, avoid censoring yourself. Be bold, daring, and imaginative. List as many possible solutions as your team can think of before you begin to discuss the advantages and disadvantages of any single possibility.

3. Once you've identified the most promising solution, work together to come up with the strongest reasons why the chosen solution is the best one. You might take turns defending that solution from readers who might say, "Your solution isn't fair," or "That would just cause more problems," or even "It's a good idea, but it's not practical." As a team, you should generate at least three strong reasons to support your choice.

4. Your introductory paragraph should state the problem and your proposed solution. It should also state why the situation is a problem.

5. The body paragraphs should serve two basic purposes: explain your proposed solution and give reasons that support your choice of this solution. Your instructor may specify which method of development to use in writing your proposal essay. If not, you may find it helpful to review the following chapters: Chapter 9, Illustration; Chapter 11, Process Analysis; Chapter 15, Cause and Effect; and Chapter 16, Argument.

6. Your conclusion should restate your solution and confirm that it is the most reasonable course of action.

You Know This
You've taken tests
under pressure.
• You study for the
  test for your driver's
  license.
• You practice and try
  out for a team.
• You respond to
  questions during a
  job interview.

18

Writing under Pressure

Tests, Essay Exams, and Timed Writing

Studying for Tests

Everyone, no matter how well prepared, gets nervous about taking tests. The trick is to turn that nervousness into positive energy by learning test-taking strategies. This chapter will give you tips on studying for different kinds of tests as well as specific advice about essay exams and other timed writing assignments.

Here are five reliable tips to help you study for any exam:

FIVE TIPS FOR STUDYING

1. Ask about the test.
2. Study with a partner or group.
3. Predict what will be on the exam.
4. Use study aids.
5. Review actively.

1. ASK ABOUT THE TEST

When you know you are having a test, ask your instructor about it. Just make sure you ask reasonable questions.

DISCUSSION
Ask students why the questions in the "Not" column are inappropriate. Use humor to describe how you as an instructor might react to such questions.

ASK	NOT
• What part of the course or text will it cover?	• What's on the test?
• Will the format be multiple choice, short answer, or essay?	• You're not going to give us an essay question, are you?
• Will we be allowed to use notes or books?	• We can just look up the answers, right?
• What percentage of my course grade will this count for?	• Is this test important?
• Can you recommend what to review?	• Do I need to read the book? Is the stuff you said in class important?
• Will we have the whole period to complete the test?	• How long is it?
• I know I have to miss class that day (give your reason). Can I arrange to take the test at another time?	• Is there a makeup test?

Write down your instructor's answers to your questions. Don't rely on your memory; you will be busy enough remembering the material for the exam without having to remember what your instructor said.

2. STUDY WITH A PARTNER OR GROUP

Although everyone is busy, forming a study group is well worth the time and effort it takes. Setting a time to study with others guarantees that you'll study, and pooling ideas improves everyone's ability to predict what will be on the test. List the names of three people in the class you might like to study with. Contact them by phone, by email, or in person to ask if they would be interested in joining a study group.

Do some preparation before group meetings so that you make the most of the study time. The following are some tips on how study group members can prepare for a meeting:

TEACHING TIP
If students are willing, create a contact list for the class with everyone's telephone number and email address. Students can then use the list to arrange study groups.

For more on teamwork, see Chapter 17.

- Each person could take responsibility for a particular section of the material, preparing a list of five to ten questions that might be on the test. Questions and possible responses could then be discussed in the group.
- Each person could copy his or her notes on a particular chapter, section, or topic and distribute them to the members of the group.
- Each person could come up with a list of "the five most important things we learned during the course."
- Each person could come up with a list of "things I don't understand."

3. PREDICT WHAT WILL BE ON THE EXAM

Whether you are studying with other people or by yourself, it's a good idea to make a list of what you think will be covered on the exam. Look over your notes, assignments, and any previous tests or quizzes. What has your instructor stressed? Try writing questions for that material, and then try answering your own questions.

If you are confused about any material, ask about it either in class, after class, or during your instructor's office hours. Your instructor will probably welcome questions by email as well. Do not go into an exam knowing that you don't understand a major concept.

PRACTICE 1 PREDICTING THE CONTENT OF A TEST

Imagine that you are having a quiz in this class next week. With a partner or in a small group, identify three topics that might be on that quiz, and write one question for each.

TOPIC: Process for solving a problem

QUESTION: List the steps involved in the problem-solving process.

TOPIC: _Answers will vary._ _____

QUESTION: _____

TOPIC: _____

QUESTION: _____

TOPIC: _____

QUESTION: _____

4. USE STUDY AIDS

Use one or more of the following study aids — or any other that is available to you — to ensure your success:

- Reread your notes, looking especially for anything you've underlined or marked in some other way.
- If you are being tested on material from your textbook, reread any chapter reviews, summaries, or boxes containing key concepts.
- Review any handouts from your instructor.
- Consider other available ways to review material — audiotapes, videos, computer exercises, study guides, the course or textbook Web site, and so on.

TEACHING TIP
Show students the study aids in a chapter: the major headings, the Thinking Critically boxes, definitions, and so forth.

5. REVIEW ACTIVELY

The following are some suggestions for reviewing material actively:

- If you're reviewing material from a book, take notes. Improve your memory by putting information in your own words, writing it down, and seeing it on the page of your notebook, on the screen of your computer, or in the margin of a book.
- If you're reviewing handouts, use a colored pen or highlighter to mark the most important ideas, most useful facts, or any other key information.
- Say important material aloud. Many people learn well by hearing something in addition to seeing it.
- If you are studying from notes, rewrite your notes. For example, if you've written an outline, transform it into a concept map.

What I will do to study more actively: _____

_____

Doubling Your Chances of Passing Exams

Some students fail exams or get low grades because they don't understand the material. Others know the material but still score low because they don't have any useful strategies for taking exams.

FIVE STRATEGIES FOR TAKING EXAMS

1. Be prepared.
2. Manage your nerves.
3. Understand the directions.
4. Survey the whole exam before starting.
5. Develop a plan.

1. BE PREPARED

If you have found out all the particulars about the exam and have studied for it using the five tips listed on page 276, you've already done the most important preparation. But don't arrive at the exam and discover that you've left something essential at home. Take some time the night before to think about what you need. Make a list of what to bring (pen? books? calculator? notebook? textbook? computer disk? watch?), and assemble everything so that it's ready to go.

2. MANAGE YOUR NERVES

Get as much rest as possible the night before the exam, and allow extra time to get to class. Arrive early enough to settle in. Sit up straight, take a deep breath, and remind yourself that you know the material. You're prepared; you're ready; you will pass. When your instructor starts to talk, look up and listen.

3. UNDERSTAND THE DIRECTIONS

First, listen to the spoken directions your instructor gives. It's tempting to start flipping through the exam as soon as you get it rather than listening to what your instructor is saying. Resist the temptation. Your instructor may be giving you key advice or information that's not written elsewhere, and you may miss it if you're not paying attention.

Second, when you begin the test, carefully read the written directions for each part. Sometimes students answer all of the questions in a section only to find out afterward that the directions said to answer only one or two. If you don't understand any part of the directions, be sure to ask your instructor for clarification.

4. SURVEY THE WHOLE EXAM BEFORE STARTING

To survey means to examine something as a whole before approaching any single part. Surveying an exam before starting to answer questions is a crucial step that will help you budget your time. Often the toughest questions (and the ones worth the most points) are at the end. You don't want to answer all the two-point questions and leave the thirty-point ones unanswered. Ask yourself the following questions:

- *How many parts does the test have?* Be sure to look on both sides of all exam pages.

- *How many points is each part worth?* This information will help you decide how much time to spend on each part.

- *What questions can I answer quickly and easily?* Start with these. Answering them will assure you of some good points and build your confidence and momentum.

DISCUSSION
Ask students to discuss their experiences with taking tests that have multiple parts (including standardized tests). What strategies not listed here did they find especially effective?

5. DEVELOP A PLAN

First, **budget your time**. After surveying the whole test, write down how much time you will allow for each part. You might even find it helpful to calculate what time you want to start each section: Part 1 at 9:40, Part 2 at 9:55, and so on. Make sure you leave enough time for the parts with the highest point values. Also leave enough time to answer essay questions: They can take longer than you think they will. As you plan your time, keep in mind how much time you *really* have for the exam: A "two-hour" exam may be only one hour and fifty minutes once your instructor finishes giving directions and so on. Remember also to leave a few minutes to check your work.

Second, **decide on an order**: where you should start, what you should do second, third, and so on. Start with the questions you can answer quickly and easily.

Finally, **monitor your time** during the exam. If you find you're really stuck on a question and you're going way over your time budget, move on. If you have time at the end of the exam period, you can always go back to it.

TEACHING TIP
Assure students that neither surveying nor developing a plan takes much time away from the test-taking process. Planning should take only three to five minutes.

Answering an Essay Question or a Timed Writing Assignment

DEFINITION: An **essay question** is an examination item that asks you to write one or several paragraphs explaining and illustrating your answer.

DEFINITION: A **timed writing** is an assignment that requires writing one or several paragraphs in response to a question or prompt within a set amount of time.

Essay questions on an exam are usually worth more points than short-answer or multiple-choice questions, so they deserve special strategies. The following strategies apply also to timed writing.

FIVE STRATEGIES FOR ANSWERING AN ESSAY QUESTION OR TIMED WRITING ASSIGNMENT

1. Read the question carefully.
2. Write a thesis statement.
3. Make an outline.
4. Write your answer.
5. Reread and revise your answer.

1. READ THE QUESTION CAREFULLY

Be sure to read an essay question carefully so that you know exactly what to write. Look for three kinds of key words in an essay question:

- Words that tell you *what subject* to write on.
- Words that tell you *how to write about it.*
- Words that tell you *how many parts* your answer should have.

Discuss two major causes of personal bankruptcy in this country.

Tells how to write the response   Tells how many parts the answer should have   Tells what subject to write about

Define and give examples of the phenomenon of global warming.

Tells how to write the response   Tells what subject to write about

Once you understand the type of answer expected, you can both follow the directions and draw on your experience writing similar essays.

Common Key Words in Essay Exam Questions

KEY WORD	WHAT IT MEANS
Analyze	Break into parts (classify) and discuss
Define	State the meaning and give examples
Describe the **stages** of	List and explain steps in a process
Discuss the **causes** of	List and explain the causes
Discuss the **concept** of	Define and give examples
Discuss the **differences between**	Contrast and give examples
Discuss the **effects/results** of	List and explain the effects
Discuss the **meaning** of	Define and give examples
Discuss the **similarities between**	Compare and give examples
Discuss the **stages/steps** of	Explain a process
Explain the **term**	Define and give examples
Follow/Trace the **development** of	Give the history; narrate the story
Follow/Trace the **process** of	Explain the sequence of steps or stages in the process
Identify	Define and give examples
Should	Argue for or against
Summarize	Give a brief overview of narrative

TEACHING TIP
Ask students to bring in exams with essay questions from other classes. Look for the key words used on these exams—whether from this list or in addition to it—and discuss what they mean.

TEACHING TIP
Give students practice essay exams on topics that will allow them to determine how to focus their ideas.

■ **PRACTICE 2   IDENTIFYING KEY WORDS**

Read the following samples from essay tests. Circle the key words that tell what subject to write about, how to write about it, and how many parts to write. In the space below each item, explain what the question asks a writer to do. Example:

TEAMWORK
This practice works well in pairs. Have students discuss the reasons for their responses.

(Define) and (illustrate) (dependency.)

Give the meaning of the term dependency and give examples of it.

1. (Identify)(three)(causes) of the (Persian Gulf War.)

   List and explain three causes of the Persian Gulf War.

2. (Trace) the stages of (grieving.)

   Explain the steps in the grieving process.

3. (Discuss) the problem of the current (energy crisis.)

   Identify and explain the problem of the current energy crisis.

4. (Should) drivers be banned from (using handheld cell phones while driving?) Why or why not?

   Argue for or against banning drivers from using handheld cell phones.

2. WRITE A THESIS STATEMENT

A thesis statement lets the reader know what your topic is and what your position or main point about that topic is. Your response should include a thesis statement that is simple and clear. You may want to preview what you plan to cover in your answer, as in some exams you may get partial credit for information contained in the thesis statement even if you run out of time to explain fully.

For more on writing a thesis statement, see Chapter 3.

The best way to stay on track in an essay exam is to write a thesis statement that contains the key words in the essay question and restates its main idea. It also helps to reread your thesis statement several times as you write your exam response.

    ■   **PRACTICE 3**   **WRITING THESIS STATEMENTS**

TEAMWORK
This practice works well in pairs. Have students create at least two different thesis statements for each prompt.

Write possible thesis statements in response to the following sample essay exam questions. Even if you do not know the answer to the question, write a thesis statement that responds to the question and lets the reader know what you will cover.

ESSAY EXAM QUESTION: Discuss the concept of First Amendment (free speech) protection related to pornography on the Internet.

POSSIBLE THESIS STATEMENT: The protection of First Amendment rights is often cited as a reason not to ban pornography on the Internet.

1. Discuss the causes of the decline of the traditional "nuclear family" (two married parents and their children living under the same roof, without others).

   Answers will vary.
   _____

2. Explain the effects of binge drinking.

   _____

3. Trace the development of the Industrial Revolution in Lowell, Massachusetts.

   _____

4. Describe the atmospheric conditions that precede a thunderstorm.

   _____

5. Discuss three advantages and/or disadvantages of reliance on email.

   _____

3. MAKE AN OUTLINE

Before you answer an essay question, jot down some notes on how you will answer it. Write down any important names, dates, or facts that occur to you. Make a short informal outline that you can use as a basic map for laying out the parts of your answer. These notes will help you stick to your main points and remember essential details as you write.

For more on outlining, see Chapter 5.

4. WRITE YOUR ANSWER

Your answer to an essay question should always be in essay form, with an introductory paragraph, several support points, and a concluding paragraph.

    Here is an essay written by Brenda White of Quinsigamond Community College, in response to the essay prompt "Discuss your role model."

For more on the parts of an essay, see page 4 and Chapters 5 and 6.

> My role model is my best friend, Tanya, a single mother. Although young unmarried parents are often looked down upon in our society, Tanya has overcome many obstacles and is doing an excellent job raising her son. I admire her patience, independence, and willingness to work hard. With these qualities, she defies the stereotype of the teen parent.

Introduction states thesis and previews support points

Support point 1

Tanya could have made the choice to terminate her pregnancy, but she decided not to because she knew that she had the patience to raise a child, even under difficult circumstances. She has incredible patience with her son, Quentin. For example, when he's crying—even for a long time—she'll just rock him until he sleeps. Tanya also has patience with her friends. She understands that they have other things to do and can't always be counted on to watch Quentin. Tanya never gets mad if we can't help her out. She is also patient with her mother, who is very critical. Tanya's steady patience has gotten her through many difficult situations.

Support point 2

Independence is another trait that makes Tanya a good role model. She is raising her son without the help of her parents and mostly without Quentin's father. Tanya does not rely on others to care for her son or make decisions about his care; she does what needs to be done. She is also financially independent. She spends the money she earns wisely, only on things that are necessary. She pays her own tuition, rent, and, of course, the expenses of bringing up Quentin. Tanya has earned her independence and is wise about the actions she takes.

Support point 3

Tanya is a very hard worker, pushing herself to the maximum. She works two jobs so she can provide for her growing son. Tanya also maintains an A average in her college courses. She has always gone beyond the normal, everyday achievements. For example, she graduated from high school on the honor roll while living on her own and supporting her son. She works hard and sticks to her belief that education is valuable. Tanya has gone beyond the traditional definition of hardworking.

Conclusion sums up and strengthens response to essay prompt

In some people's eyes, Tanya is just a single, teenage mother, a burden on society. But to me, Tanya is a wonderful role model. She has accomplished a lot in her young life. She has also gained control of her life and her surroundings by being patient, independent, and hardworking. Tanya is a single, teenage parent, but she is also a worthy role model.

5. READ AND REVISE YOUR ANSWER

After you have finished writing your answer to an essay question, reread it carefully. Make corrections or changes so that your response is clearer, more precise, and more detailed.

Teachers sometimes use a *scoring rubric*, which consists of the criteria—or standards—they use to judge the quality of an essay. Although scoring rubrics vary from one teacher to the next, most rubrics used to evaluate writing include some basic elements:

TEACHING TIP
If your department, university, or state has a rubric for grading standardized essay exams, distribute it to the students and explain each point so that students will have a better sense of their audience's expectations.

- Adherence to the assignment. (Has the writer followed the assignment and answered the question? Does the essay stay focused on the topic?)

- Thesis statement. (Does the essay clearly state the topic and the writer's main point about it?)
- Accuracy. (Does the essay include correct answers or reliable information?)
- Development. (Are explanations clear and supported with examples?)
- Language and expression. (Is the essay free of major errors in grammar, mechanics, and usage?)

Scoring rubrics often have points or percentages attached to each element. A typical scoring rubric might look like this:

ELEMENT	TOTAL POINTS POSSIBLE	STUDENT SCORE
Adherence to assignment	20	18
Thesis statement	15	15
Accuracy	30	25
Development	25	20
Language and expression	10	10
TOTAL POSSIBLE POINTS	**100**	**88**

RESOURCES
For advice on creating and using scoring rubrics, see Chapter 10 in *Practical Suggestions for Teaching* REAL ESSAYS.

If your teacher provides you with a rubric, use it to set priorities as you review and revise your essay. Otherwise, consider the elements in the sample rubric above as you revise your essay exam.

If on a test you are writing by hand (rather than using a computer), you can revise your essay by neatly crossing out mistakes and adding extra words or sentences between the lines or in the margin, like this:

Groups of people living together have expectations about how the

group should function and how to keep order within the group.

~~Societies need to have rules and laws.~~ This semester, we learned about

social deviance, which is any behavior that does not conform to

expectations of the group and which violates the group's sense of order. For
, those who break society's rules,
example, criminals are social deviants. Rather than thinking that we can
^
or should eliminate deviant behavior altogether, I agree with sociologist
a necessary element of any healthy social group.
Emile Durkheim that deviance is ~~necessary.~~
^

TEACHING TIP
If your department (or university or state testing board) has examples of questions from standardized essay exams from previous semesters, get permission to distribute these questions to students for practice.

WRITING ASSIGNMENTS

Choose one of the following topics and write an essay on it, using the five strategies for answering an essay question or timed writing assignment introduced on page 282. To practice with timed writing, give yourself a one-hour time limit.

1. Write an essay agreeing or disagreeing with one of the following statements:

   Schoolchildren have too many vacations.

   Most students cheat.

   People should be required to retire at age sixty-five.

   People should live together before they get married.

   There are no valuable lessons to be learned from studying history.

2. Define *responsibility*.

3. Propose a solution to a major problem in your town or city.

4. Discuss a person who has had great influence on you.

5. Discuss an event that changed your life.

19

Writing Summaries and Reports

Important College Writing Tasks

Writing a Summary

DEFINITION: A **summary** is a condensed version of a piece of writing, a conversation, or an event. A summary presents main ideas and key support points, stripping down the information to its essential elements. A summary is stated in your own words, generally without opinion or judgment.

To summarize something — an event, an article, a chapter in a book, a movie plot, or a conversation — you have to understand it thoroughly so that you can explain its important parts in your own words. Think of a summary as making a long story short, as when you tell a friend about the plot of a television program or a movie, or about something that happened to you. There are many uses for summarizing.

COLLEGE

- You answer exam questions that ask you to summarize information.
- You may summarize recent findings on a topic for a research project.
- You summarize readings in your notes and written assignments.

TEACHING TIP
Have students write at least three more examples of summaries for each category as journal entries.

WORK

- You summarize events or situations for a manager who needs to know what's going on but doesn't have the time to hear every small detail.
- You write a memo that summarizes the issues discussed and decisions made at a meeting.
- You prepare monthly or quarterly reports that summarize achievements, trends, and goals.

EVERYDAY LIFE

- You summarize for a partner your conversation with a plumber who was at your home to fix a pipe.
- You write a résumé and a job application letter summarizing your work experience and educational accomplishments.
- You summarize a novel that you recommend to your book group.

FIVE BASICS OF A GOOD SUMMARY

1. It includes a thesis statement that identifies what is being summarized and the main idea of the original piece of writing, event, or conversation.
2. It concisely identifies the key support points presented in the original.
3. It includes any final observations or recommendations made in the original.
4. It is objective in tone, presenting information without opinions.
5. It is written (or stated) in your own words.

READ AND ANALYZE A SUMMARY

TEAMWORK
This activity works well in pairs. Ask a student to read the essay aloud to the class; then have pairs work together to respond to the questions.

A typical assignment in college is to summarize something you have read. Here is a summary of the student essay in Chapter 16 (p. 251). Reread the original essay ("How Violence on TV Affects Children and Adolescents"), read the summary here, and answer the questions that follow the summary.

In her essay, "How Violence on TV Affects Children and Adolescents," Edna Crespo argues that violence has definite negative effects on children and adolescents. She identifies three significant effects and presents evidence of them.

Crespo reports that frequent viewing of violent television causes children to become passive and to lose interest in more healthy activities such as playing with friends, getting physical exercise, and enjoying outdoor activities. She bases her statement on evidence from a physician who says that children themselves admit they are addicted to television. Crespo also discusses how <u>TV leads children to become insensitive to violence and more tolerant of aggressiveness.</u> She cites a study showing that students who watched a lot of violent television were less likely to help other students who were the victims of aggressive behavior. The worst effect of television violence, according to Crespo, is that <u>children themselves become more aggressive.</u> She points out that children often try out behaviors they have seen on television, without seeming to realize they might hurt other children.

The author concludes by drawing upon her eighteen years of work experience in the marketing and advertising industry, where, she says, she has learned exactly how powerful—and destructive—television can be. She makes the powerful statement that we are spending millions of dollars to destroy our children's values.

1. Double-underline the **thesis statement**.

2. Underline the **key points** of the summary. Do they match the key points in Crespo's essay? _yes_____ Does the summary leave out any of the essay's key points? _no_____

3. Do you think that this summary gives you a good understanding of the original piece? Why or why not? _Answers will vary._____

   _____

4. Is the summary written in the writer's words or in Crespo's? _____
   _in the writer's words_____

5. Does this piece have the five basics of a good summary? _____
   _Answers will vary._____

Writing a summary is not a mysterious process: It just requires that you understand the key points of a piece of writing, a conversation, or an event and communicate them simply and accurately. Follow the five steps here to write a good summary.

FIVE STEPS FOR WRITING A GOOD SUMMARY

1. Preview the original piece of writing, looking for visual clues to what is important, such as the title, headings, words in bold or italics, quotations, or boxed information.

2. Read the entire original piece carefully, first for overall meaning. Then reread to note key points. If you are summarizing an event or conversation, recall and review the entire happening.

3. Make an outline of the writer's or speaker's key points.

4. Write your summary.

5. Revise your summary.

PRACTICE 1 **WRITE A SUMMARY**

Apply the five steps for writing a good summary as you read the following article and respond to the questions about it.

1. Preview the Writing

Before reading, skim over the article, looking for visual clues to what is important (title, headings, words in bold or italics, quotations, and so forth). What visual clues in the article below suggest items of importance?

title, callout

2. Read and Reread the Article

First read the article to understand its overall meaning. As you read, you might want to make check marks next to points you think might be important. But your purpose in reading right now is to understand the overall content, not to figure out the specific points.

Survey Finds Many Firms Monitor Staff

Your employer could be watching you. Such are the findings of a new study released last week by the American Management Association (AMA) in New York. The survey of 1,626 large and midsize companies found that nearly 80 percent of major US firms routinely check their employees' email, Internet, or telephone connections, and some regularly videotape them at work.

"It's not just a matter of corporate curiosity," said Eric R. Greenberg, director of management studies at the American Management Association. "Personal email can clog a company's telecommunications system, and sexually explicit or other inappropriate material downloaded from the Internet can lead to claims of a hostile work environment."

Researchers have found that companies are more likely to conduct random checks versus 24-hour surveillance of messages, phone conversations, or Internet usage. Even so, the AMA advises that employees use discretion at work.

According to the survey, 63 percent of US companies check employees' Internet connections, up 54 percent since last year. Forty-seven percent read workers' email, up from 38 percent in the year 2000. Forty percent have installed firewalls to prevent employees from using the Internet inappropriately, up from 29 percent last year.

When asked whether they had fired workers because of inappropriate use of electronic equipment, 27 percent of the employers said they had dismissed staff for misuse of office email or Internet connections. Sixty-five percent of the companies had disciplined offenders.

Ellen Bayer, the AMA's practice leader on human rights issues, said the findings indicate that privacy in the modern-day workplace is "largely illusory."

"In this era of open space cubicles, shared desk space, networked computers, and teleworkers, it is hard to realistically hold onto the belief in private space," said Bayer. She added that some employees do not understand that their employers have a legal right to monitor equipment that workers use on the job.

Employers also reported other forms of surveillance, such as monitoring telephone numbers called (43 percent), logged computer time (19 percent), and video surveillance for security purposes (38 percent).

> "In this era of open space cubicles, shared desk space, networked computers, and teleworkers, it is hard to realistically hold onto the belief in private space," said Bayer.

"In previous years, the growth in monitoring went hand in hand with increases in the share of employees gaining access to email and the Internet," added AMA's Greenberg. "This year, the average share of employees with office connections barely grew at all, while monitoring of those activities rose by nearly 10 percent. It is important to note, however, that 90 percent of the companies engaging in any of these practices inform their employees that they are doing so."

But companies don't have to inform employees of any monitoring practice. In fact, most US courts have ruled in favor of employers who routinely monitor telephones, computers, or other electronic equipment used on the job. It is best not to misuse company media: Your employer may be watching you.

> —Staff reporter, "Survey Finds Many Firms Monitor Staff," *Boston Sunday Globe,* April 29, 2001.

What is the subject of the article? *routine monitoring of employees' activities by employers*

What is the main point of the article? *Since companies routinely monitor employees' activities, employees should practice discretion.*

Reread the Article.   Now go back and reread the article, placing a check mark by each major point that your summary should include and making notes to yourself about how to present the information.

3. Make an Outline of Key Points

TEAMWORK
Have students compare their responses to steps 1–3 in pairs and discuss their responses.

TEAMWORK
Have students bring in a newspaper article. Divide students into small groups, and have them work through steps 1–3 as listed here.

Now review your notes, and make an outline for the summary you will write. Note both the writer's key points and any examples that you might include.

Key points/examples: *Answers will vary.*

_____

_____

_____

_____

_____

Final observation or recommendation that article makes: *You may be under close watch by your employer.*

4. Write Your Summary

Using your outline as a guide, write a summary of the article in your own words. This is a draft, so just try to capture the key points of the article. Reread parts of the original article as necessary.

5. Revise Your Summary

Read over your summary carefully to see if it has the five basics of a good summary (p. 290). If not, add necessary information or modify what you have written so that your summary accurately and clearly represents the original. Because a summary is a shortened version of a longer piece, using transitions (such as "first," "second," "next," and "finally") to help your reader move smoothly from one key point to another is especially important.

While your summary should focus on the main points, make sure you provide enough detail (examples) so that your reader, who has not read the piece, will understand each point.

Finally, read your answer to make sure that it is free of errors in grammar, spelling, and punctuation.

WRITING ASSIGNMENTS

1. Summarize the cover story of a recent issue of a magazine (print or online).
2. Summarize the plot of a movie you have seen recently.
3. Summarize an article from today's newspaper.
4. Summarize an essay or article, either from this book (if you are using the version with readings; see pp. 615–717) or from another book you use in a course.
5. Summarize Giovanni Bohorquez's narration essay from Chapter 12 (p. 174).

Writing a Report

DEFINITION: A **report** usually begins with a summary that condenses a piece of writing, a conversation, or an event and then goes on to give some type of analysis. Recall that a summary is objective: You present a brief version without stating your opinions. In contrast, a report summarizes key points and also includes reactions to, opinions about, or recommendations based on the piece, conversation, or event. A **review** is a type of report in which the writer evaluates a film, performance, product, or piece of writing.

COLLEGE

- Your theater class reviews a play opening on campus.
- An instructor in a business class assigns you to write a report based on a campus event, such as a presentation on marketing trends by a local professional.
- You review a film for the student paper.

DISCUSSION
Ask students to discuss other occasions in college, work, and everyday life where they might be asked to write a report. List students' responses on the board.

WORK

- Your manager asks you to review software from different suppliers who want your company's business. Your review must recommend which supplier to use.
- Your committee reviews last year's employee awards program and recommends changes.
- You write a report on your company's insurance options, reviewing each plan.

EVERYDAY LIFE

- You informally review a new restaurant for your friends.
- You report on a nonfiction book for your book club.
- You review a performance for your local newspaper.

In order to write a good report, you must thoroughly understand the original event, conversation, or piece of writing. Because you will also include your opinions, think carefully about what your reactions were and why you had those particular reactions.

TEACHING TIP
Give students a list of campus or local events and suggest that they attend the same event but write separate reports. Students can compare and contrast their responses to the same event.

FOUR BASICS OF A GOOD REPORT

1. It includes a thesis statement that identifies the subject and the main idea of the original piece of writing, event, or conversation.

2. It includes the key support points.

3. It includes your opinion of or recommendations concerning the piece of writing, event, or conversation, along with your specific support for that opinion. Reviews of books or films often include specific passages or quotations in supporting statements.

4. It is written or stated primarily in your own words. Specific quotations may be used to support your opinions.

For example, in an English class, you may be asked to write a book report or a film review. You would need to summarize the work, but your instructor would also expect you to include your opinions about the piece and provide reasons or examples for those opinions.

Read the following example of a film review.

Delay Gives "Damage" a Fighting Chance

Wesley Morris

What a difference six months makes. Nixed from the fall 2001 schedule in the haze of Sept. 11, *Collateral Damage* reemerges — jaw clenched — ready to take terrorism down. And who but Arnold Schwarzenegger is a more apt action figure for the "new patriotism" conducted on a global scale?

Playing a Los Angeles firefighter who treks to the Colombian jungles to punish the terrorist who killed his wife and child in a bombing, Schwarzenegger bounds out of obsolescence like a figure from the cover of a Marvel comic book. Accordingly, *Collateral Damage* is an SUV of a movie driven by a one-man National Guard.

The film is directed by Andrew Davis ("The Fugitive"), a man who never met a bus under siege, a death-defying leap down a waterfall, or a quest for a spouse's murderer that didn't turn him on. The story itself is recyclable, right down to Elias Koteas — Tommy Lee Jones to Schwarzenegger's Harrison Ford — playing a seemingly crooked CIA operative trying to catch Schwarzenegger before he nabs his prey.

Despite its action-in-a-can mentality, the movie's generic roots gain a new post-terror specificity that lends it an almost bombastic level of relevance it was never meant to have. Initially, Warner Bros.'s postponement had a glum take-one-for-the-team dimension: It was the right thing to do when the wrong thing happens. It was a gesture that seemed designed to save the movie from terrible timing by releasing it later the following year, and there may have been something to it.

Six months ago, *Collateral Damage* was another dated attempt to relaunch Schwarzenegger out of the moribund-action-star silo as another heat-seeking missile. Now the movie, incidentally but not insignificantly, taps into its audience's own revenge fantasies — not unlike the domestic drama *In the Bedroom* — only with a cartoonish blur around its moral edges.

Sensing the necessity to represent the alternative side to Schwarzenegger's unrelenting need for personal justice, the movie deigns to give a human face to its terrorist, an embittered guerrilla bomb-maker who calls himself El Lobo. The face belongs to Cliff Curtis, the alluring New Zealand changeling whose American career has oscillated between troubled ethnicities (Saudi, Iraqi, Nicaraguan) in such movies as *Three Kings* and *Blow*.

Here, he's playing not a monster so much as a revolutionary with money to burn and a political ax to grind against America. But you can tell El Lobo is a gentleman caught in the gears of a formula flick when he barely bats an eyelash at his wife's bond with the man trying to kill him.

Curtis lets the mask slip on his villain long enough for it to be jarring when El Lobo reverts to his bomb-planting self and heads back to America for more mayhem — in time, of course, for our hero to try to stop him.

This brings us back to Schwarzenegger, finally making good on his decade-old "I'll be back" promise. There had been some concern that we'd lost him. After an on-set accident and heart problems, Arnold had recently taken a back seat to the subject of his mortality. His plunge into millennial outlandishness, once battling not simply the Bad Guy but Satan himself in "End of Days," was as desperate as Michael Jackson naming his first new album in five years "Invincible."

In *Collateral Damage,* the metaphysical lunacy is gone, and so are the shades, leather tunics, and heavy artillery. In fact, Schwarzenegger at 55 — in a shirt and khakis, and serving homemade knuckle-sandwiches — is decidedly dress-casual for the proceedings. Vengeance, the movie seems to say, is the new normal.

His physique, still mighty, but only discreetly alluded to, is secondary to his extended emotional capacity. He's still a rock, but it seems you can squeeze blood and tears from this stone. If this film is a hit — and judging from the fact that it strikes all the right populist notes, even the sour ones, it will be — that will be because Schwarzenegger's mortality for the first time suits him.

Not only does he feel your pain, he's living through it — the erstwhile last action hero, born again.

To write a report on a piece of writing, an event, or a conversation, you need to understand its key points and to communicate them simply and accurately. You also need to include your own opinions or recommendations based on the original work or happening and to provide support for those opinions or recommendations. Use the seven steps here to write a report.

SEVEN STEPS FOR WRITING A REPORT

1. Preview the original, looking for visual clues to what is important, such as headings, words in bold or italics, boxed quotations, or other elements.

2. Read the original piece carefully, making note of key points as you read. If you are reporting on an event, conversation, performance, or something that isn't a written work, recall and review the entire happening.

3. Make an outline of the writer's or speaker's key points.

4. Make notes on your outline about your reactions to the work. Note your opinions about both the main idea and the key points. Include the main point you want to make about it and examples that support your point.

5. Write a thesis statement that includes the title of the work, its purpose, and the main point you want to make about the piece.

6. Write your report.

7. Revise your report.

WRITING ASSIGNMENTS

1. Write a review of a book that you have read for either this class or another one.

2. Write a review of a movie or live performance that you either very much liked or very much disliked.

3. Write a report that includes a summary of and reaction to a recent or proposed change in your town or on your campus.

4. Write a report of a class that you have taken recently.

5. Attend a public event and report on it.

20

Finding, Evaluating, and Documenting Sources

Key Research Skills

DEFINITION: Conducting **research** means finding information that will help you or others understand a subject. Knowing how to find information that you need is an important skill, not just for college but for all areas of your life. Here are a few examples of the kinds of research you might need to do.

COLLEGE

• For your history class, you need to investigate different accounts of an event.

• In your psychology course, you are required to write a paper using outside sources, such as books, periodicals, or the Internet.

• For a business course, you need to interview an entrepreneur and learn about his or her product or industry.

WORK

• You need to plan a customer survey, asking people for their opinions of a new product.

• You have been asked to research the sales history of a competitor's product.

• You need to gather demographic data to support your company's plans to expand into a new region.

EVERYDAY LIFE

- You want to trace your family history and start a family tree.
- A doctor diagnoses a family member's illness and recommends a certain method of treatment. You want to find out more about both the illness and the possible treatments.
- You need to buy a new television and want to find a reliable but inexpensive model.

As you find information, you'll need to take two additional steps. First, you must evaluate your sources to determine if the information within them is reliable. Second, to avoid plagiarism, you must give credit to your sources by documenting them.

Find Sources

Finding reliable information about your research topic may seem like an overwhelming job, but keeping in mind a process for conducting research can help guide your work. As you start your search, try the strategies described in the following sections.

For more on finding and narrowing a topic for a research essay, see page 325.

CONSULT A REFERENCE LIBRARIAN

Although much information is available on the Internet, you will still need to use the library for books and some other materials. If you are not familiar with finding materials in the library, you will save yourself time and possible frustration by talking with the reference librarian. If your library allows, schedule an appointment with the librarian. Before your appointment, jot down some questions you want to ask, such as those listed below. Begin your conversation by telling the librarian your research topic.

QUESTIONS FOR THE LIBRARIAN

- How do I use an online catalog or a card catalog? What information will the library's catalog give me?
- What other reference tools would you recommend as a good starting place for research on my topic?
- Once I identify a source that might be useful, how do I find it?
- Can I get onto the Internet from a library computer? If so, how?
- Can you recommend an Internet search engine that will help me find information on my topic? Can you also recommend some useful key words?

- I've already found some articles related to my topic. Can you suggest some other places to look for sources?

USE THE ONLINE CATALOG OR CARD CATALOG

TEACHING TIP
Schedule a tour of the library to show students areas such as the reference room, the online catalog, the periodical room, and so on.

Most libraries now list their holdings on a computer rather than in a card catalog, but both systems give the same information: titles, authors, subjects, publication data, and call numbers. If you are working with a librarian, he or she may offer step-by-step instructions for using the online catalog. If you are working on your own, the online catalog help is usually easy to find (generally on the screen or in a Help menu) and easy to follow. Catalogs allow you to search by author, title, subject, or key word. If you are just beginning your research, you will probably use the subject heading or a key word because you may not know specific authors or titles.

For more on conducting key word searches, see page 305.

Florence Bagley, a student whose research process and completed essay appear in Chapter 21, searched her library's online catalog using the name *Aretha Franklin* as a key word. Here is one source she found.

```
Record 6 of 11


         Author:        Sheafer, Silvia A.

         Title:         Aretha Franklin: Motown superstar / Silvia
                        A. Sheafer.

         Publisher:     Detroit : Enslow, 1996.

         Subject:       Franklin, Aretha.

                        Motown music.

                        Rhythm and blues -- Soul music -- United
                            States -- 20th century.

                        Women singers.

                        Women musicians -- United States -- 20th
                            century.

         Location:      Worcester Greendale

         Call Number:   899.304b

         Status:        Available
```

A call number is a book's identification number. Knowing the call number will help you to locate a source in the library. Once you do locate the source, browse the nearby shelves. Since a library's holdings are organized by subject, you may find other sources related to your topic.

USE OTHER REFERENCE MATERIALS

The reference section of the library has many resources that will help you find information on your topic. Here is a sampling of common databases and other reference sources. Most are available online or on CD-ROM.

Periodical Indexes

Periodical indexes help you locate information published in magazines, journals, and newspapers. If your topic is a current one, periodicals may be more useful than books. The following are some of the most popular periodical indexes:

- *InfoTrac*
- *LexisNexis*
- *NewsBank*
- *New York Times Index*
- *Readers' Guide to Periodical Literature*

General Encyclopedias

Encyclopedias can offer information when you are seeking an overview of a subject. Some encyclopedias, like the *Encyclopædia Britannica,* are available in print, online, and on CD-ROM. An encyclopedia entry is generally followed by a bibliography of other useful sources. In addition to general encyclopedias, your library may have specialized encyclopedias that give more detailed information on your topic. An example would be the *Encyclopedia of Psychology* for a research paper in a social sciences course.

TEAMWORK Send groups of students on a collaborative research trip to the library, asking each group to find and report to the rest of the class on one of the reference sources listed here. Students should be able to explain how the source they reported on could be relevant to their classmates' research process.

Specialized Indexes

Specialized indexes—either in book form, online, or on CD-ROM—direct you to resources in various broad subject areas. A few of the many indexes are the following:

- *America: History and Life*
- *Biological Abstracts*
- *Educational Resources Information Center (ERIC)*
- *MLA International Bibliography of Books and Articles on the Modern Languages and Literatures*
- *PsycLIT*

Visit <**www.census .gov**>, the official Web site of the U.S. Census Bureau, for current state and national statistical data related to population, economics, and geography.

Statistical Sources

Some research essays use statistical data, or facts and figures, as excellent support. As one example, the *Statistical Abstract of the United States* (published annually by the U.S. Census Bureau) can help you locate useful statistics related to social issues, population, economics, and other topics.

USE THE INTERNET

The Internet, a vast global computer network, now provides access to all kinds of information. The biggest part of the Internet is called the World Wide Web, which allows users to jump from site to site using links. If you are new to using the Internet and the World Wide Web to search for sources, this section will offer some basics. You may also want to work with a librarian, a writing-center tutor, or a knowledgeable friend as you continue to search.

When you discover a Web site that you might want to return to, bookmark it or add it to your list of favorites. Doing so ensures that you don't have to remember the URL each time you want to go to the site. Different browsers have different ways of bookmarking; choose "Bookmarks" in Netscape or "Favorites" in Microsoft Internet Explorer.

Uniform Resource Locator (URL)

Every site on the World Wide Web has an address, called a uniform resource locator (URL). You may already be familiar with some frequently advertised URLs, such as <**www.amazon.com**> (the Internet address for bookseller Amazon.com) or the URL for your college's Web site. If you know the URL of a Web site that you think would be helpful for your research, enter it into the Address field of your Web browser. (Web browsers, like Microsoft Internet Explorer and Netscape Navigator, are software programs that allow a computer to read Web pages.) If you do not know the URL of a particular site you want to visit, you will need to use a search engine.

TEACHING TIP
Ask students to test three different search engines by typing in key words related to their research paper. Which search engine seemed most effective for their research needs? Why?

Search Engines

Search engines function very much like the electronic catalogs and databases in your college or local library. You can conduct searches for information by subject, title, or author, or by key words. It's important to know that all search engines have a Help feature that offers guidance in using the engine, selecting key words, and refining your search.

POPULAR SEARCH ENGINES AND THEIR URLS

- AltaVista <**www.altavista.com**>
- Ask Jeeves <**www.askjeeves.com**>
- Excite <**www.excite.com**>
- Google <**www.google.com**>
- HotBot <**www.hotbot.com**>
- Lycos <**www.lycos.com**>
- Yahoo! <**www.yahoo.com**>

Searching with Key Words

One drawback of typing key words into a search engine is having to sift through the number of matches, or "hits," that often result from a search. For example, when student writer Florence Bagley used *Aretha Franklin* as a key word on Yahoo, her search returned 54,728 hits. As she scrolled through those hits, she quickly realized that many were not related to her topic — the role that music has played in Aretha's life. For example, her results included sites that auctioned celebrity items, a site for the church where her father was the minister, and a site for the history of rhythm and blues.

Although she would certainly have found some useful sites, Florence didn't want to scroll through 54,728 possibilities. Instead, she made her keyword search more specific: *Aretha Franklin's life.* This search produced 1,070 hits, which was still more than enough. However, Florence found some promising sources: the Aretha Franklin home page, fan-club sites, and a link to Amazon.com's list of books on Aretha Franklin's life.

RESOURCES
Direct students to the English Research Room (at <**www.bedfordstmartins.com/english_research**>) for interactive tutorials on searching with key words and conducting Boolean searches.

RESULTS FROM A KEYWORD SEARCH ON YAHOO USING *ARETHA FRANKLIN'S LIFE* **IN THE SEARCH BOX**

If you find too much information or, worse, too little, try making your key words more specific or using different combinations of key words. Consult the search engine's built-in Help feature for tips on conducting successful searches.

Use a Computer to Build Research Skills

For help with research, visit the *English Research Room* at **<www.bedford stmartins.com/english_research>**. The site is organized into three main areas designed to help you to develop stronger research writing skills. The "reference units" offer concise information to help you understand your research process and conduct research online. The "interactive tutorials" guide you through the most important parts of online research as if you had a librarian and teacher sitting next to you. The "research links" connect you to many of the basic tools research writers are likely to use, such as online writing labs and popular search engines. Use Bookmarks in Netscape or Favorites in Internet Explorer to keep this important Web site handy.

INTERVIEW PEOPLE

Personal interviews can be excellent sources of information. Before interviewing anyone, however, plan carefully. First consider what kind of person to interview. Do you want information from an expert on the subject or from a person directly affected by the issue? How would the experience or comments of each person help support your points? The person should be knowledgeable about the subject and have firsthand experience. When you have decided whom to interview, schedule an appointment.

Next, to get ready for the interview, prepare a list of five to ten questions. Ask more open-ended questions (What is your position on regulating cell-phone use by drivers?) than closed ones that require only a simple "yes" or "no" response (Do you favor regulating cell-phone use by drivers?). Leave space for notes about the person's responses and for additional questions that may occur to you during the interview. Include the person's full name and qualifications and the date of the interview in your research notes.

TEAMWORK
Have students interview each other on their research topics. Students can write a short summary of the interview using both direct quotations and paraphrases.

As you conduct the interview, listen carefully and write down any important ideas. If you plan to use any of the interviewee's exact words (i.e., direct quotations), make sure to put them in quotation marks in your notes. Doing so will help you figure out if your notes are the exact words of the person you interviewed, your own interpretation of something he or she said, or a thought you had during the interview.

For more on using quotation marks correctly, see Chapter 39.

NOTE: Recording what a person says without notifying him or her first is unethical and, in some states, is against the law. If you plan to record an interview on videotape or audiotape, get your subject's permission first.

Evaluate Sources

Evaluating sources means judging them to determine how reliable they are—a critical skill in college, on the job, and in everyday life. Reliable sources are those that present accurate, up-to-date information written by authors with appropriate credentials for the subject matter. Reliable sources support claims with evidence and use objective, reasonable language. Research materials found in a college library (books, journals, and newspapers, for example), are generally considered reliable sources.

When you are using the Internet, don't assume that a source is reliable just because it exists there. Just about anyone can create a Web site and put whatever he or she wants on it. If you are searching the Web for information about the psychological benefits of weight loss, for example, you may find a range of sources—reliable ones such as an article published by the *Journal of the American Medical Association* or a report by faculty at Johns Hopkins University and questionable ones such as an individual's personal weight-loss story or an advertisement for a product that claims to "eliminate pounds while you sleep." Whether you are doing research for a college course, a work assignment, or personal use, you need to make sure that the source is reliable and legitimate for your purpose. Otherwise, you may receive a failing grade on a paper, make a big mistake at work, or foul up something in your personal life.

When you're viewing a Web site, try to determine its purpose. A Web site set up solely to provide information may be more reliable than an online product advertisement. A keyword search for attention-deficit/hyperactivity disorder (ADHD), for example, would point a researcher to thousands of sites; the two shown here are just samples. Which do you think contains more reliable information?

1. Site sponsored by the Centers for Disease Control, a U.S. government agency dedicated to protecting the health of American citizens by providing information.

2. Objective presentation of information.

3. Link to current research.

4. Date of last update, showing that information is current.

5. Clear contact information.

6. Mission statement for the subagency, the National Center on Birth Defects and Developmental Disabilities.

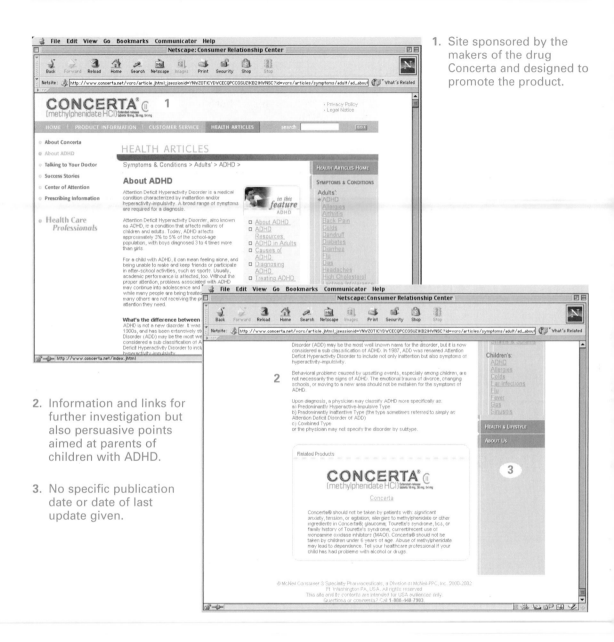

1. Site sponsored by the makers of the drug Concerta and designed to promote the product.

2. Information and links for further investigation but also persuasive points aimed at parents of children with ADHD.

3. No specific publication date or date of last update given.

Here are some questions you can ask to evaluate a source. If you answer "no" to any of these questions, think twice about using the source.

TEN QUESTIONS FOR EVALUATING A PRINT OR ELECTRONIC SOURCE

1. Is the source up-to-date?

2. Is the source one that you know is reliable (such as a well-known magazine or a reputable Web site)?

TEACHING TIP
Have students apply these questions to an article or Web site printout that you (or they) bring to class. Decide as a class whether or not the source is reliable.

3. Has the author published other material on this subject?

4. Does the author offer other sources to support his or her ideas?

5. Does the author present only information that will support his or her point, ignoring other perspectives? (If the author presents all sides of the topic but lets the reader know his or her own views, the source may still provide good information.)

6. Does the author have a balanced, objective tone? (An objective author does not make other points of view seem wrong or dangerous.)

7. Does the author provide adequate support for his or her thesis?

8. If the source is a Web site, is the site's sponsoring organization well known and generally well respected?

9. Will using this source actually strengthen the point you want to make?

10. Can the information in the source be verified by checking other sources?

One way to evaluate a source is to consider the URL extension, the part of the URL that follows the "dot."

Guide to URL Extensions

EXTENSION	TYPE OF SITE	HOW RELIABLE?
.com	A commercial, or business, organization	Varies. Consider whether you have heard of the organization, and be sure to read its home page carefully.
.edu	An educational institution	Reliable, but may include many varied course materials.
.gov	A government agency	Reliable.
.net	A commercial, or business organization, or a personal site	Varies. This extension indicates just the provider, not anything about the source. Go to the source's home page to find out what you can about the author or the sponsor.

EXTENSION	TYPE OF SITE	HOW RELIABLE?
.org	A nonprofit organization	Generally reliable, although each volunteer or professional group promotes its own view or interests.

PRACTICE 1   EVALUATING WEB SITES

To practice analyzing two sites that address the same subject, visit <**www.whitehouse.gov/nsc**> and <**www.edreport.com**>. Which site is more likely to offer valid information about the National Security Council? How can you tell which site is legitimate and which one is phony?

The official White House Web site offers more valid information. The Ed Report

site's home page offers no clues about authorship, sponsorship, currency, or

evidence.

Avoid Plagiarism

DEFINITION: Plagiarism means passing off ideas and information you gather from another source as your own. Writers who plagiarize, either deliberately or by accident, risk failing a course, being expelled from school, losing their jobs, or damaging their reputations. You must be careful to avoid plagiarism when you are writing a research essay.

ESL
In some cultures, copying someone else's work is a gesture of respect. Be very clear with students about what constitutes plagiarism.

DELIBERATE PLAGIARISM

When you copy someone's work with no intention of crediting your source, you make a deliberate choice to plagiarize. Here are several examples of deliberate plagiarism:

1. A friend has a paper that fits your assignment, and you turn it in as your own work.

2. You find a paper on the Internet that fits your assignment, and you print it out and turn it in as your own work.

3. You see a great article in a newspaper or magazine, and you copy it word for word and turn it in as your own work.

As described, these three cases are plagiarism, plain and simple—you have intentionally put your name to someone else's work. Even crediting the source would not solve the problem: Your instructor would not want you to use someone else's paper. Plagiarism can be avoided, however, by quoting parts of the sources in your own essay and crediting them properly.

ACCIDENTAL PLAGIARISM

Too often, plagiarism results from taking sloppy notes, as illustrated in the following scenarios:

1. When it is time to write your paper, you find that you have forgotten to note the exact source of a useful fact or detail.
2. You can't remember whether a statement in your notes is a direct quotation or a paraphrase (a statement putting another person's ideas into your own words).
3. You can't remember whether an idea is yours or another person's, and you can't tell from your notes.

Accidental plagiarism that results from a poor note-taking process is still considered unethical or, in some cases, illegal. It often takes several weeks to write a research paper, and during this time many other events are going on in your life. Don't rely on your memory; use a trustworthy system for taking notes. Some such systems are described in the following section.

USE A SYSTEM FOR TAKING NOTES

Some writers take notes by hand on notecards (or index cards). These writers may enjoy the ease with which they can shuffle their notes as they organize and draft their essay. Others prefer to take notes in a word processing program. Doing so enables writers to cut and paste directly from notes to a draft. Use whatever method you find most comfortable, but be systematic about it. In other words, use a consistent format for all of your notes. Doing so will ensure that you have the information you need to avoid plagiarism.

Florence Bagley, a student writer, took notes on index cards. On one side of the card she noted the author and title of the source, the page numbers on which she found key information, and the parts of the source she wanted to use in her essay. She also clearly indicated what each note contained: a summary, a paraphrase, or a direct quotation. (She recorded full details about each source in her running bibliography, illustrated on p. 314.)

SAMPLE NOTE CARD—FRONT SIDE

Page number

Name of source

Type of information

> *Sheafer, Aretha Franklin: Motown Superstar*   *pp. 95–110*
>
> *Summary*
>
> *Aretha's career flourished, but her personal life was a mess.*
>
> *Marriage to Ted White (controlling and abusive).*
>
> *Divorce, 1969, shortly after birth of 3rd child.*
>
> *1969 — father arrested and charged with drug possession.*
>
> *Meanwhile, she won Grammy awards 1969–1975.*
>
> *Had 4th child (not married).*
>
> *Father died (from gunshot wound he'd gotten earlier).*

Florence used the back side of each note card to record her own comment about the source or a plan for using the information in her paper.

SAMPLE NOTE CARD—BACK SIDE

> *— What songs came out during those years?*
> *— How did her father get shot?*
> *— What happened to these kids?*

KEEP A RUNNING BIBLIOGRAPHY

If you are using a computer, you can alphabetize sources as you list them or use the Sort option in the Table menu in Microsoft Word. If you are not using a computer, add each source to your list as you use it, and don't worry about alphabetizing until you have finished.

DEFINITION: A **bibliography** is a complete list, alphabetized by author, of the sources you consulted as you investigated your topic. A **list of works cited** is a complete list, alphabetized by author, of the sources that you actually mention within your essay. Most instructors require a list of works cited at the end of a research essay. Some may require a bibliography as well.

To help you manage your sources, keep a running bibliography and add to it as you examine each source. Make sure that you include all of the information you will need to correctly identify the source in your bibliography or list of works cited.

BOOKS	ARTICLES	WEB SITES
Author name(s)	Author name(s)	Author name(s)
Title and subtitle	Title and page numbers	Title of page or site
Year of publication	Title of magazine, journal, or newspaper	Date of publication or latest update
Publisher and location of publisher	Year, month, day of publication (1999, December 9)	Name of sponsoring organization
		Date on which you accessed the source
		The URL (online address) in angle brackets (</>)

Here is a sample entry from Florence Bagley's running bibliography:

```
Sheafer, Silvia A. Aretha Franklin: Motown Superstar. Detroit:
    Enslow, 1996.
```

Using a Computer to Avoid Plagiarism

Avoiding plagiarism is necessary in college, work, and everyday writing tasks. In the age of computers and the Internet, it is easy to cut and paste chunks of writing from sources. This mechanical ease of moving text may seem to make it easier for students to plagiarize, but computer resources also make it easier than ever before for teachers to detect plagiarism. Many teachers discover that a student has copied material from a Web source simply by using a search engine like Google and typing in a sentence or two from the student's paper. Search engines are now so powerful that they often find the source of a sentence in a fraction of a second.

In some cases though, teachers may suspect plagiarism when all that really happened was revision. In addition to learning to be careful about noting your sources, you should also be careful about saving each draft of your research essay and maintaining control of your research notes. By doing so, you can prove to your teacher that you aren't plagiarizing by showing how your writing has improved draft by draft.

CITE SOURCES AS YOU TAKE NOTES

Your running bibliography will help you keep track of the sources of all the facts, details, and examples you may want to use in your essay. If you are writing a paper in Modern Language Association (MLA) style (the style most commonly used in English courses), you will use parentheses to identify the author (or title) and page number for each source within your paper—immediately following the fact, detail, or example you borrow. At the end of your paper, you will list full information about each source.

TEACHING TIP
Have students practice citing sources throughout the semester. For example, if they write summaries of readings from this textbook, articles, or Web sites, ask them to use in-text citations and to include a list of works cited at the end of each summary.

TEACHING TIP
Ask students to bring in a draft bibliography after they have gathered and read their sources, but before they finish writing the research paper. This will allow you to make sure they are compiling one.

EXCERPT FROM A RESEARCH ESSAY

```
Many American college stu-
dents today go to a computer
rather than to campus for a
lecture, exam, or class dis-
cussion. A recent survey
revealed that "more than
half of the nation's col-
leges and universities
deliver some courses over
the Internet" (Press and
Washburn 34).
```

ENTRY IN THE LIST OF WORKS CITED

```
Press, Eyal, and Jennifer
Washburn. "Digital
Diplomas." Mother Jones
Jan.-Feb. 2001: 34+.
```

Besides identifying sources accurately, think about how each source can best help you explain or prove your thesis. Would using exact words from a source lend strength to your argument? Perhaps your essay needs technical evidence written in everyday language. Or maybe a source contains key information that you would be better off condensing. For each source you read, take notes in the form you think will be most useful in your research essay—direct quotation, paraphrase, or summary.

For an example of notes with proper source publication information, see page 332.

Direct Quotation

DEFINITION: When you use a person's exact words, you are using a **direct quotation**. Use these guidelines when you write direct quotations:

- Record the exact words of the source.

- Record the name of the writer or speaker so that you can use it later to introduce the quotation in your paper. If there is more than one author or speaker, record all names.

- Enclose the writer or speaker's words in quotation marks.

- For written sources, include the page number on which the quote appeared in the original source in parentheses after the end quotation mark but before the period. If the person quoted is not the author of the book or the article (that is, if you're quoting a quotation), give the author's name in parentheses along with the page number.

Identifying phrase   Quotation marks

DIRECT QUOTATION: According to Dr. Min Xiao, "The psychological benefits of a well-lit workspace are significant" (28).

Parenthetical citation

Paraphrase

TEACHING TIP
Remind students that they must cite source information even when they summarize and paraphrase. Students often think they need to cite only when quoting directly.

TEACHING TIP
If you use the version of the text with readings, Marie Winn's whole essay, "Cookies or Heroin?," appears on page 673.

DEFINITION: **Paraphrasing** is putting someone else's idea into your own words and restating it. Be careful if you choose to paraphrase. It is easy to think you are using your own words while you are actually using only some of your own and some of the author's or speaker's. When you paraphrase, follow these guidelines:

- Don't look at the source while you are writing the paraphrase.

- Check your paraphrase against the original source to make sure you have not used the author's words or copied the author's sentence structure.

- Cite your source in parentheses after your paraphrase.

Read the examples that follow to see acceptable and unacceptable paraphrases.

ORIGINAL SOURCE

Not unlike drugs or alcohol, the television experience allows the participant to blot out the real world and enter into a pleasurable and passive mental state. To be sure, other experiences, notably reading, also provide a temporary respite from reality. But it's much easier to stop reading and return to reality than to stop watching television. The entry into another world offered by reading includes an easily accessible return ticket. The entry via television does not. In this way television viewing, for those vulnerable to addiction, is more like drinking or taking drugs — once you start it's hard to stop.

—Marie Winn, "Cookies or Heroin?"

UNACCEPTABLE PARAPHRASE, TOO CLOSE TO ORIGINAL

Marie Winn says that like drugs or alcohol, television allows people to blot out reality and escape into the passive world of television. Reading also provides a break from the real world, but it's easier to put down a book than to turn off the television. Therefore, in people susceptible to addiction, television viewing is more like drinking or taking drugs than reading: It's much harder to stop once you've started.

This paraphrase is unacceptable for several reasons:

- The first sentence uses the same structure and some of the same words as the first sentence of the original.
- The paraphrase too closely follows the sentences and ideas of the original source.
- The writer hasn't cited the source.

The writer has obviously written the paraphrase while looking at the original source rather than expressing the ideas in his or her own words.

ACCEPTABLE PARAPHRASE

Marie Winn says that although television and reading both offer a break from reality, television watching is harder to stop and can therefore be considered "addictive," in a way that reading cannot (32).

The acceptable paraphrase presents Winn's basic ideas, but in the writer's own words and structures. It also includes a parenthetical citation. The writer carefully read Winn's paragraph but then wrote the paraphrase without looking at the original. Then the writer checked the original again to make sure she hadn't missed any ideas or repeated words or sentence structures.

Summary

DEFINITION: A **summary** presents only the main points of a source in your own words.

Let's say you read a three-page article on rhythm and blues singers. Although it supports your thesis and contains useful background information, the article doesn't contain any one person's words or ideas you want to include in your paper. Overall, though, the article does offer support because it appears in a reputable source and is current. If you decide to summarize and cite the source, you will need to do the following:

- State the source's main points briefly, in your own words.
- Note author's name so that you can use it in your paper to introduce your summary.
- Include in parentheses the page numbers of the entire section you have summarized.

For more on writing summaries, see Chapter 19.

SUMMARY OF AN ARTICLE: As reported in a recent issue of *Psychology Today,* people often listen to music when they are feeling depressed or are trying to work out a problem or move on from a difficult situation (Rayne 16–18).

Document Sources

The model entries in this section are presented in four groups: books, periodicals, electronic sources, and other nonprint sources. If you cannot find a model for a type of source you are using in your essay, consult the MLA Handbook for Writers of Research Papers, fifth edition, or Research and Documentation online at <www .bedfordstmartins .com/hacker/resdoc>.

DEFINITION: Responsible researchers **document**, or give credit to, their sources. Each source cited or mentioned in a research essay should also be fully credited in a list of works cited, bibliography, or reference list at the end of the paper. When you write research papers in college courses, you will be required to document your sources using a particular documentation style. Ask your instructor which one to use for your assignment. Most English instructors prefer the MLA (Modern Language Association) system. The last few pages of this chapter present the MLA system of documenting twenty common types of sources.

Use the following section as you add sources to your running bibliography. Look for the type of source (book, journal, Web site, and so on), and then format your source as shown, paying attention to the information required, the order of information, and the punctuation. Few people can remember the specifics of how to document sources; the key is to refer to this section as you gather your running bibliography and prepare your list of works cited.

BOOKS

1. BOOK WITH ONE AUTHOR

Author   Title

Anker, Susan. *Real Essays: Writing Projects for College, Work, and Everyday Life.* Boston: Bedford/St. Martin's, 2003.

Publisher   Publication date

2. BOOK WITH TWO OR THREE AUTHORS

> Piccioto, Richard, and Daniel Paisner. Last Man Down: A New York
> City Fire Chief and the Collapse of the World Trade Center.
> New York: Berkley, 2002.

> Quigley, Sharon, Gloria Florez, and Thomas McCann. You Can Clean
> Almost Anything. New York: Sutton, 1999.

3. BOOK WITH FOUR OR MORE AUTHORS

(Note: *et al.* means "and others.")

> Roark, James L., et al. The American Promise: A History of the
> United States. Boston: Bedford/St. Martin's, 1998.

4. BOOK WITH AN EDITOR

> Tate, Parson, ed. Most Romantic Vacation Spots. Cheyenne:
> Chandler, 2000.

5. WORK IN AN ANTHOLOGY

> Cisneros, Sandra. "Barbie Q." Literature. Ed. Robert DiYanni.
> 5th ed. New York: McGraw Hill, 2002. 235-36.

6. ENCYCLOPEDIA ARTICLE

> "Kosovo." Encyclopædia Britannica. 16th ed. 1999.

PERIODICALS

7. MAGAZINE ARTICLE   Author   Title of article   Name of periodical

> Kluger, Jeffrey. "Hunting Made Easy." Time 11 Mar. 2002: 62-63.

Date   Inclusive pages

8. NEWSPAPER ARTICLE

> Fox, Maggie. "Scientists Report Experiment Creating Immune
> Cells." Boston Globe 1 May 2002: A20.

9. SIGNED EDITORIAL IN A MAGAZINE OR NEWSPAPER

> Udall, Don. "When Someone Is Alive but Not Living." Editorial.
> Newsweek 14 June 1999: 12.

10.   UNSIGNED EDITORIAL IN A MAGAZINE OR NEWSPAPER

> "The Fall of a Telecom Gunslinger." Editorial. New York Times
>   1 May 2002: A22.

ELECTRONIC SOURCES

Electronic sources include Web sites; reference databases (online or on CD-ROM); works from subscription services such as LexisNexis, Electric Library, or PsycLIT; and electronic communications such as email. Because many electronic sources change often, always note the date you accessed or read the source as well as the date on which the source was posted or updated online. To make sure your records are accurate, you may want to bookmark, download, or print out hard copies of the pages you have used.

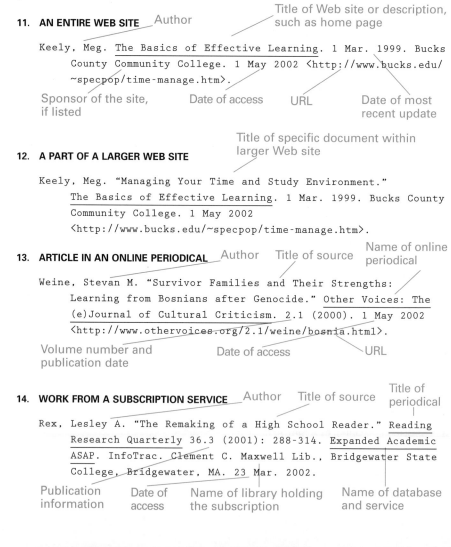

11.   AN ENTIRE WEB SITE   Author   Title of Web site or description, such as home page

> Keely, Meg. The Basics of Effective Learning. 1 Mar. 1999. Bucks
>   County Community College. 1 May 2002 <http://www.bucks.edu/
>   ~specpop/time-manage.htm>.

Sponsor of the site, if listed   Date of access   URL   Date of most recent update

12.   A PART OF A LARGER WEB SITE   Title of specific document within larger Web site

> Keely, Meg. "Managing Your Time and Study Environment."
>   The Basics of Effective Learning. 1 Mar. 1999. Bucks County
>   Community College. 1 May 2002
>   <http://www.bucks.edu/~specpop/time-manage.htm>.

13.   ARTICLE IN AN ONLINE PERIODICAL   Author   Title of source   Name of online periodical

> Weine, Stevan M. "Survivor Families and Their Strengths:
>   Learning from Bosnians after Genocide." Other Voices: The
>   (e)Journal of Cultural Criticism. 2.1 (2000). 1 May 2002
>   <http://www.othervoices.org/2.1/weine/bosnia.html>.

Volume number and publication date   Date of access   URL

14.   WORK FROM A SUBSCRIPTION SERVICE   Author   Title of source   Title of periodical

> Rex, Lesley A. "The Remaking of a High School Reader." Reading
>   Research Quarterly 36.3 (2001): 288-314. Expanded Academic
>   ASAP. InfoTrac. Clement C. Maxwell Lib., Bridgewater State
>   College, Bridgewater, MA. 23 Mar. 2002.

Publication information   Date of access   Name of library holding the subscription   Name of database and service

15. **ELECTRONIC MAIL (EMAIL) OR ONLINE POSTING**

Eisenhauer, Karen. "Learning Styles." Email to Susan Anker. 24
    Apr. 2002.

Collins, Terence. "Effective Grammar Activities." Online posting.
    14 Dec. 2001. CBW Listserv. 3 May 2002 <cbw-l@tc.umn.edu>.

OTHER SOURCES

16. **PERSONAL INTERVIEW**

Okayo, Margaret. Personal interview. 16 Apr. 2002.

17. **SPEECH**

Glenn, Cheryl. "Toward an Understanding of Silence and
    Silencing." Conf. on Coll. Composition and Communication
    Convention. Minneapolis Convention Center, Minneapolis.
    13 Apr. 2000.

18. **FILM OR VIDEO**

To the Limit. Dir. Nandana Krishna. Perf. Kristin Peri, Sarah
    Saltrick, and Jason Willey. Universal, 2000.

19. **TELEVISION OR RADIO PROGRAM**

"Playing Cards." Ally McBeal. Fox. KTTV, Rancho Cucamonga. 30
    Nov. 2001.

20. **RECORDING**

Keys, Alicia. "A Woman's Worth." Songs in A Minor. J-Records,
    2001.

21

Writing the Research Essay

Working with Sources

This chapter will guide you through the process of writing a research essay. Many stages are demonstrated by the work of student writer Florence Bagley, who wrote her essay, "The Queen of Soul," on the influence of music in Aretha Franklin's life.

For Florence Bagley's
completed essay, "The
Queen of Soul," see
pages 338–42.

THE RESEARCH WRITING PROCESS

1. Get organized.
2. Find and narrow your topic.
3. Explore your topic, and write a thesis statement.
4. Take careful notes to build support.
5. Organize your notes, and plan your draft.
6. Draft and revise your essay.
7. Edit your essay.

Get Organized

Writing a good research essay requires organization from the very beginning. Two ways to get—and stay—organized are (*a*) to make a schedule and (*b*) to keep all of your research material in one place.

MAKE A SCHEDULE

After you receive your assignment, create a schedule that divides your research assignment into small, manageable tasks. Keep the schedule handy; you will need to refer to it often.

You can use the following schedule as a model for making your own:

TEACHING TIP
Walk students through the process of creating a schedule, starting with the date the essay is due and working backward. Suggest and discuss the amount of time they should allow for each key step.

SAMPLE RESEARCH ESSAY SCHEDULE

Assignment: _____

_____
(Write out what your instructor has assigned.)

Length: _____

Draft due date: _____

Final due date: _____

My general topic: _____

My narrowed topic: _____

TASK	DO BY
Review some of the information available about my general topic.	_____
Narrow my general topic, and write a research question.	_____
Find sources.	_____
Evaluate my sources; decide which ones to use.	_____
Take notes, and record publication information for each source.	_____
Review all notes; choose the best support for my working thesis.	_____

(continued)

For an electronic version of this schedule, visit the *Real Essays* Web site at <**www .bedfordstmartins .com/realessays**>.

Organize notes; make an outline.   _____

Write a draft.   _____

Review the draft; get feedback; add more support if needed.   _____

Revise the draft.   _____

Prepare a list of works cited using correct documentation form.   _____

Edit the revised draft.   _____

Print out and submit the final copy.   _____

KEEP ALL OF YOUR RESEARCH MATERIAL IN ONE PLACE

As you do your research, you will accumulate numerous items: a schedule, print material, electronic material, index cards or notes, an outline, and so on. Keeping everything together will help you manage your project successfully.

Managing Print Material

Some research writers prefer to keep hard copies, or paper copies, of sources, notes, schedules, and other project materials. If this system appeals to you, keep everything together in a file folder or large envelope. Label it "Research" or, more specifically, label it with your topic—such as "The Effects of Workspace on Workplace Productivity." Within the folder or envelope, use binder clips to hold together groups of materials.

Managing Electronic Material

Some research writers prefer to save sources, notes, schedules, and other project materials to a disk, a hard drive, or a list of bookmarks on their computer. If this system appeals to you, be sure to name your files as descriptively as possible (for example, "Notes on Turner article Feb-03" is better than "res. notes"). Then organize individual files within folders in your word processor. The following example shows a well-organized system for managing research materials:

Main research folder ("Workspace and Productivity") with subfolders

Dated contents of open "Essay" folder

Find and Narrow Your Topic

In college, your instructor may want you to think of your own topic for a research paper assignment. If you are free to choose your topic, find a subject that you are personally interested in or curious about. If your instructor assigns a topic, you can skip ahead to the next main section, "Explore Your Topic, and Write a Thesis Statement," on page 330.

FIND YOUR TOPIC

If your instructor has not assigned a general topic but has said something like "Write about something that interests or affects you," consider it an opportunity. The best research essays often start with a personal connection. Ask and answer questions like the following to find a topic connected to your life:

1. What is going on in my own life that I want to know more about?
2. What have I heard about lately that I'd like to know more about?
3. What possible careers am I interested in?
4. What famous person—living or deceased—most interests me?

5. What do I daydream about? What frightens me? What do I see as a threat to me or my family? What inspires or encourages me?

6. Is there something I do in my spare time (sports, music, computer games) that I'd like to know more about?

Also look back at the writing you have done so far in this class. Are you personally interested in any of the topics you have already written about? What topics could you explore further by using research sources? Try rereading the paper you most liked to see if it includes a topic you can research.

For more on prewriting techniques, see page 27.

If you can't think of anything right away, take a little break and flip through a magazine or newspaper, watch the news, think about things that have mattered to you and made you react. Try a prewriting technique such as freewriting or brainstorming to find a general topic.

See the box below for some current topics and issues that you might want to explore.

Possible Topics for a Research Essay

TEACHING TIP
Have students select three of these topics to write about in their journals. Their journal entries should answer the following questions: Why does this topic interest me? What would be my purpose in writing about this topic? What audience would be interested in reading about this topic? Why?

A contemporary or historical figure	Free speech and the Internet
ADHD	Gang membership
Advertising	Gay marriage
An illness	Homeschooling
Assisted suicide	Mandatory drug testing
Cell phones	Road rage
Competitive sports in schools	Sexual harassment
Dating services	Standardized testing/placement testing
Dieting/eating disorders	Uniforms in school
Discrimination	Violence in the media
The draft for military service	Women in military combat
Executive salaries	Working parents
The family in America	

Write before You Research

When you have a general topic, write answers to these questions:

1. Why is this topic important to me or of interest to me? How does it affect me? What do I hope to gain by exploring it?
2. What do I know about the topic? What do I want to find out?

Florence Bagley, a second-year college student, was assigned a research paper on the general topic "A contemporary figure who has influenced your life." As she listened to CDs late one night, she thought about how much she loved Aretha Franklin's music and always had. She didn't know much about the singer and wondered if writing about her life would be a good topic for a research essay. She knew it couldn't just be a biography, like an encyclopedia entry, but thought she might be able to think of some part of Aretha's life she could write about.

After writing some notes to herself about Aretha's songs and how they really meant something to her, she then answered the two sets of questions listed above, applying them to her general topic.

1. Why is this topic important to me or of interest to me? How does it affect me? What do I hope to gain by exploring it?

FLORENCE'S RESPONSE (FREEWRITING)

> *Ever since I can remember, I loved Aretha Franklin's music. It's more than just the music, though. It's the words and the way Aretha puts her heart into her music. It's like she knows about how life can be tough, and she's able to get that across in her music. A bunch of times when I'm going through something bad, I just put on her music and listen, and it really helps me. I feel like I know her, but I don't. I just know I love her music.*

2. What do I know about the topic? What do I want to find out?

FLORENCE'S RESPONSE (FREEWRITING)

> *I really don't know anything about her which is funny because we usually know a lot about most famous people. I know she started singing in a church, but that's all I know. Since her songs have been so important to me, I'd like to know a bit more about her.*

██ **PRACTICE 1   FINDING YOUR TOPIC**

Write your general topic here: _____

With your general topic in mind, write your answers to these two questions about your general topic.

1. Why is this topic important to me or of interest to me? How does it affect me? What do I hope to gain by exploring it?

   Answers will vary. _____

   _____

2. What do I know about this topic? What do I want to find out?

   Answers will vary. _____

   _____

NARROW YOUR TOPIC

For more narrowing and exploring a topic, see Chapter 2.

The general topic you choose is likely to be too big to cover in a short research paper. It would be impossible, for example, to write a good five-page essay on the general topic "Crime." A more specific topic—something like "Neighborhood watch programs as crime deterrents"—is more manageable. To narrow your general topic to one that is more specific, you need to get an overview of the topic and find out what kinds of sources are available.

Ask and Answer Questions

TEACHING TIP
Have students narrow topics by focusing on how the topic affects their school or home community.

You probably know more than you think you do about your general topic. One way to narrow your topic is to determine what you already know. Ask and answer the following questions to narrow your general topic.

1. What do I know or what have I heard about this topic?

2. What can I write about in a short research essay?

Now read Florence's answers to the questions about her general topic, "A contemporary figure who has influenced your life."

1. What do I know or what have I heard about this topic?

FLORENCE'S RESPONSE

> *I only know that Aretha Franklin started singing in church. I don't know anything else about her life. I'd like to find out more about it because her singing has been so important to me. I wonder how she put so much into her music and whether what she sang about was related to her life. Maybe she had a whole other life apart from her music, but I bet music was a key part of her life. Otherwise, I don't know how it could be so powerful.*

2. What can I write about in a short research essay?

FLORENCE'S RESPONSE

> *I can write about the basic facts of her life and music's role in it, maybe what it meant to her.*

■   **PRACTICE 2   NARROWING YOUR TOPIC**

Write your answers to these two questions to narrow your topic:

1. What do I know or what have I heard about this topic?

   Answers will vary. _____

2. What can I write about in a short research essay?

   Answers will vary. _____

Review Possible Sources

As you narrow your topic, spend a little time in the library, on the Internet, or with someone who is an authority on the subject to find out what information is available. With some help from a reference librarian, Florence found several articles and a book about Aretha Franklin, as well as a few promising Web sites. She discovered a good deal of information on Franklin's life and her music. After skimming and thinking about the information, Florence was able to narrow her topic.

FLORENCE'S NARROWED TOPIC: How music helped Aretha Franklin throughout her life, including some bad times.

THINKING CRITICALLY TO NARROW YOUR TOPIC	
FOCUS	Think about the general topic you have chosen; then use the following questions to narrow your general topic.
ASK	• What part of my topic do I find interesting? What was I really thinking about when I chose it? • On what aspects (or parts) of the topic could I find sources? • Which of these aspects am I most interested in?
WRITE	Write your narrowed topic.

Explore Your Topic, and Write a Thesis Statement

Once you have a narrowed topic, you need to write a working thesis state-ment—a sentence that identifies your narrowed topic and the main point you want to make in your essay. If you have trouble deciding on your main point, try exploring your narrowed topic by asking a guiding research question.

ASK A GUIDING RESEARCH QUESTION

TEAMWORK
Have students work in groups to help each other come up with research questions about their topics. This activity would work especially well with students who have similar topics. These "focus groups" could work together through-out the project, compar-ing notes and sources and serving as peer reviewers for rough drafts.

When you ask a guiding research question, your goal is to arrive at a single question about your narrowed topic that you will address in your paper. Write as many possible questions as you can think of before you decide on one.

FLORENCE'S NARROWED TOPIC: How singing helped Aretha Franklin throughout her life, including some bad times

POSSIBLE GUIDING RESEARCH QUESTIONS

How did Aretha's singing affect her life?

Was singing always a part of her life?

How important a part was it?

What role did singing play in Aretha's life?

How did Aretha become famous?

What was Aretha's childhood like?

What is Aretha's place in musical history?

FLORENCE'S GUIDING RESEARCH QUESTION: What role has singing played in Aretha Franklin's life?

PRACTICE 3   WRITING A RESEARCH QUESTION

Write at least three possible guiding research questions for your narrowed topic, and choose the most promising one.

Answers will vary.

WRITE A THESIS STATEMENT

Although your thesis statement may change as you find out more about your topic, it is important to start with a good working thesis statement. Before writing your thesis, remind yourself of what your purpose (or reason) for writing is and who your readers are. Your thesis statement should contain your narrowed topic and your main point. To find a good working thesis statement, try answering your guiding research question.

For more on writing a thesis statement, see Chapter 3.

FLORENCE'S THESIS STATEMENT: Aretha Franklin's life wasn't easy, but music helped her at every stage.

PRACTICE 4   WRITING A THESIS STATEMENT

Think about your narrowed topic and research question, and come up with a good working thesis statement.

1. What is the single main point about my narrowed topic that I want to show, explain, or prove?

   Answers will vary.

2. Write a working thesis statement.

   Answers will vary.

TEACHING TIP
To help students stay focused on their research question, have them write it on a Post-it note and then stick the note directly onto their source as they read.

For more on supporting your thesis, see Chapter 4.

Take Careful Notes to Build Support

As in any other kind of writing, the quality of your research essay depends on the support you present to explain or prove your thesis. As you read possible sources, take notes that might help you answer your guiding research question. If you find later that you don't want to use some of the information, you can discard it. But start with a good supply of potential support.

As Florence read her sources, she noted examples and details that she could use to support her thesis. The following notecard includes a paraphrase of source information that Florence used to support her point that music helped Aretha Franklin through difficult periods in her life.

Author and title of source ————

Date of access and URL

Type of note ————

Source information in the student's own words

Layne, "Aretha Franklin Biography."   March 16, 2001
<www.rollingstone.com/artists/bio.asp?oid=457&cf=457>
Paraphrase
Aretha Franklin recorded "Bridge over Troubled Water" during some of her most difficult times. Her father was arrested on drug charges, and Franklin herself was abusing alcohol.

For more on paraphrasing, summarizing, and using direct quotations, see pages 316–18.

As you work with sources, think about how source information can help you explain or prove your thesis. Writers generally support their points by using exact words, or direct quotations, from a source or by paraphrasing or summarizing source material.

Organize Your Notes, and Plan Your Draft

For more on making a plan, see Chapter 5.

When you think you have enough support for the thesis of your research essay, you need to make a plan, just as you would for any other essay. First, review your notes to decide what your major support points will be. Then make an outline that includes your thesis statement and the major support points.

Once you've completed this much of your outline, group your research notes under the major support points. Then review the notes for each major support point and arrange them in the most logical order (chronological, spatial, or importance). If you have taken notes using a word processor, cut and paste to place your notes within each section. If you are using index cards, arrange them in sequence and then number them according to the order in which you will use them in each paragraph. You may find that it helps to indicate source information within your outline. Student writer Florence Bagley carried her citations over from her notes to her outline (see below).

After you have arranged your notes, fill in the rest of the outline. If you haven't already done so, write a topic sentence for each of the major support points. During this step, you may notice gaps in your support. If you find that you need more information or support, return to your sources or seek out additional sources.

FLORENCE'S OUTLINE

I. Introduction

    Song lyric sung to Aretha by her father (quoted in Sheafer 9)

    Thesis: Aretha Franklin's life hasn't been easy, but music has helped her at every stage.

II. How song and soul music became important: the early years

    A. Music at New Bethel Baptist Church

        1. Father was a Baptist minister whose sermons drew people from all around, very soulful

        2. Famous gospel singers came to the church (Bego 14)

        3. Singing at church

    B. Music at home

        1. Famous musicians would visit and play

        2. Mother's desertion; music was solace (Bego 12)

    C. Singing at church revivals

        1. Traveled around the country

        2. Met founders of Motown Music and recorded for them (Bego 30)

III. How music helped Aretha Franklin through hard times

    A. Pregnant at 15

        1. Dropped out of school

        2. Music career on hold

        3. At 17, single mother of two children

      B. Her grandmother encouraged her singing

        1. Got her to make tapes

        2. Scraped together money for Aretha to go to NYC

        3. Met Jerry Wexler, rhythm and blues (Franklin and Ritz 90)

      C. Problems with her father (Sheafer 85–110)

        1. Arrested for possession of marijuana

        2. Died from a gunshot wound

  IV. How she became known as the "Queen of Soul"

      A. Fame

        1. Wexler, "mysterious lady of sorrow" (Bego 8)

        2. First woman inducted into Rock and Roll Hall of Fame

        3. Cover of *Time*

        4. Lifetime achievement award

      B. "Respect," her most famous song

        1. Women and African Americans

        2. Two Grammy awards

      C. "A Bridge over Troubled Water"

        1. Drinking heavily

        2. Quote from *Rolling Stone* (Layne)

  V. Conclusion

      A. Relate back to introduction, maybe the opening song lyric

      B. Her special ability to reach us and help all of us

Draft and Revise Your Essay

For more on writing a draft, see Chapter 6.

Use your outline to help you draft your research essay from your notes, writing in complete sentences and paragraphs. As you draft your essay, you will need to work the source material into your writing smoothly. If you just drop a quotation, paraphrase, or summary into a paragraph with no explanation or context, you risk confusing your readers. Instead, you should add an identifying phrase at either the beginning or the end of the source material to distinguish your ideas from those of your source.

SAMPLE IDENTIFYING PHRASES

Sheafer reports . . .

As Sheafer writes . . .

According to a recent article in *Psychology Today,*

A recent survey in *Psychology Today* shows that...

"She was the mysterious lady of sorrow," said...

You may be able to work a fact or detail into your paragraph without an identifying phrase. In either case, though, you need to cite the source immediately afterward by giving the last name of the author and the page number in parentheses. (If a source does not have an author, use a short title instead.)

Tips for Writing an Essay Based on One Source

You may have been assigned to write an essay on a single source, such as one of the selections in "Readings for Writers" at the end of this book. If so, keep these guidelines handy.

- Read the source carefully. Identify the main idea and supporting ideas presented in the source.
- Take careful notes.
  - Record your own ideas about the topic. Note the ideas with which you agree and those with which you disagree.
  - Identify direct quotations that may help you to show or prove your own point. Place quotation marks around the passage in your notes, and write down the page number.
  - Write paraphrase notes or summary notes when you need to borrow ideas but not exact language from the source. Note the page number on which you find the material.
- Write a thesis statement that includes your narrowed topic and the point you want to make about it.
- As you draft, be certain that you are using the ideas in the source to support your own idea. Unless you have been asked simply to summarize a source (see Chapter 19), avoid stringing together ideas from the source without any indication of the point you are making.
- As you draft, use identifying phrases to distinguish your ideas from those of your source.
- Unless required by your instructor, do not include a list of works cited in a paper that uses only one source. Instead, cite the title of the source and the author's name early in your essay, and then use exact page numbers in parentheses for quotations, paraphrases, and summaries.

For more on revising a draft, see Chapter 7.

As you revise your research essay, ask yourself many of the same questions you ask when revising other types of essays.

THINKING CRITICALLY TO REVISE A RESEARCH ESSAY	
FOCUS	After a break, reread your draft with a fresh perspective.
ASK	What's my point or position? Does my thesis statement clearly state my main point?

Does my essay have the necessary parts?
- Do I have an introductory paragraph that presents my research topic and states my main point about it?
- Do I have three or more body paragraphs, each with a topic sentence that supports the main point?
- Do I have a forceful concluding paragraph that reminds my readers of my main point and makes an observation?
- Do I use information and ideas from reliable sources?

Does my essay have unity?
- Do all of the major support points in my essay relate directly to the main point in my thesis?
- Do all the supporting details in each body paragraph relate to the paragraph's topic sentence?
- Have I avoided drifting away from my main point?

Do I have enough support?
- Do the quotations, summaries, and paraphrases drawn from source material provide ample support for my thesis?
- Does each paragraph have enough support for its topic sentence?
- Would more information or information from different types of sources strengthen my support?

Is my essay coherent?
- Have I used appropriate identifying phrases to integrate quotations, paraphrases, and summaries into my text?
- Have I used transitional words to link ideas within paragraphs and transitional sentences to link paragraphs?
- Do both the sentences and the paragraphs flow smoothly?

WRITE	Revise your draft, making any improvements you can.

Edit Your Essay

After you have carefully revised your research essay, take the time to edit and proofread it thoroughly. After all of your hard work, you don't want to be marked down for errors in grammar, spelling, punctuation, word use, or documentation format. Keep in mind that errors are unacceptable in research writing at work as well.

For more on editing, see Chapters 22–41.

Be sure to follow the documentation system required by your instructor. In your English classes, you will probably use the Modern Language Association (MLA) format for documentation. As you edit, be sure that you have correctly identified in parentheses the source for every quotation, paraphrase, summary, or other detail from a source. At the end of your research essay, also be sure that you have included a page headed "Works Cited," listing all the sources you have used in your essay.

For more on MLA style, see pages 318–21.

Sample Student Research Essay

Here is Florence Bagley's final research essay, "The Queen of Soul: The Influence of Music in Aretha Franklin's Life." You may notice that she has added some sections that did not appear in her outline. Before getting to this stage—the final paper—Florence wrote two drafts. She carefully reread each draft and got feedback before revising the essay thoroughly.

TEAMWORK
Have students work together in groups of two or three to evaluate Florence Bagley's use of sources. Ask students to consider the following questions:
• How effectively does the writer integrate the sources she has used?
• What other types of sources might the writer have used?

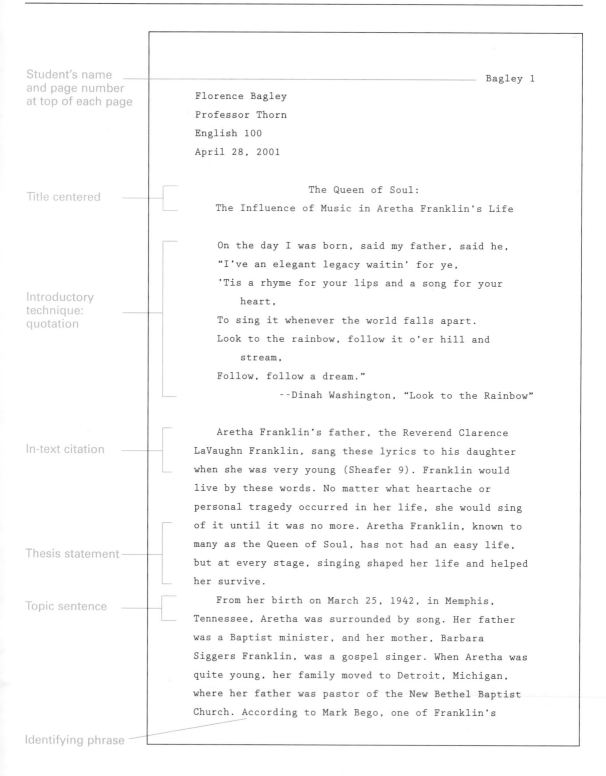

Student's name and page number at top of each page

Bagley 1

Florence Bagley

Professor Thorn

English 100

April 28, 2001

Title centered

The Queen of Soul:

The Influence of Music in Aretha Franklin's Life

Introductory technique: quotation

On the day I was born, said my father, said he,

"I've an elegant legacy waitin' for ye,

'Tis a rhyme for your lips and a song for your

    heart,

To sing it whenever the world falls apart.

Look to the rainbow, follow it o'er hill and

    stream,

Follow, follow a dream."

        --Dinah Washington, "Look to the Rainbow"

In-text citation

Aretha Franklin's father, the Reverend Clarence LaVaughn Franklin, sang these lyrics to his daughter when she was very young (Sheafer 9). Franklin would live by these words. No matter what heartache or personal tragedy occurred in her life, she would sing of it until it was no more. Aretha Franklin, known to many as the Queen of Soul, has not had an easy life,

Thesis statement

but at every stage, singing shaped her life and helped her survive.

Topic sentence

From her birth on March 25, 1942, in Memphis, Tennessee, Aretha was surrounded by song. Her father was a Baptist minister, and her mother, Barbara Siggers Franklin, was a gospel singer. When Aretha was quite young, her family moved to Detroit, Michigan, where her father was pastor of the New Bethel Baptist Church. According to Mark Bego, one of Franklin's

Identifying phrase

Bagley 2

biographers, this is where her lifelong passion for singing began. People from all over came to this church to hear the Reverend Franklin's sermons and to sing in the choir (Bego 14). Famous gospel singers, such as Mahalia Jackson and Clara Ward, sang in the church and were among Aretha's early inspirations. The Franklins' home, too, was full of music. Song artists Sam Cooke, Dinah Washington, and Lionel Hampton were among the many who came to the Franklin home to eat, play the piano, and sing. Into this life of song came Aretha's first heartache: her mother left her family when Aretha was six (Bego 18). Song carried her through the pain of an early disappointment.

Paraphrase of source information

Singing became Aretha's passion. Standing on a chair, she would belt out gospel songs and, at the age of twelve, she sang her first solo. People would flock around her father, praising his daughter's talent. She expanded her world to church revivals, traveling around the country to sing. All the while, she remained friends with Sam Cooke, who introduced her to Berry Gordy and Billy Davis, the founders of Motown Music. On hearing Aretha sing, the two men invited her to record with them, though she was only fifteen. This she did, over the objections of her father, who protested that she was too young (Bego 20-30).

Topic sentence

Summary of source information

Singing would see Aretha through the toughest times of her life. At fifteen, she became pregnant and dropped out of school. By the age of seventeen, Aretha was a single parent of two children. Although she had to put her musical career on hold, she continued to sing for her life. With the encouragement of her grandmother, Aretha went to New York to jump-start her career while her children stayed in her grandmother's

Topic sentence

Bagley 3

care. In 1960, she began recording tapes that brought her many contract offers; she signed a contract withColumbia Records as a pop singer. Still, however, pop was not the music that she sang from her soul. In 1966, Aretha met Jerry Wexler, a famous record producer, who repackaged her as a rhythm and blues singer. From then on, there was no turning back. Over the next three years, she would sell millions of albums (Franklin and Ritz 90).

Topic sentence — While Aretha's career flourished, her personal life was once again in turmoil, as another biographer, *Identifying phrase* — Silvia Sheafer, tells us. Her brief marriage to Ted White, a controlling and abusive man, ended in 1969, shortly after the birth of her third child. In that same year, her father was arrested and charged with drug possession. Aretha's album sales soared, her songs became deeper and more powerful, and she won Grammy awards for six successive years, 1969 to 1975. In the meantime, however, she had a fourth child out of wedlock, and her father died from an earlier gunshot wound (Sheafer 95-110).

It seems that Aretha's many personal tragedies fueled the passion of her singing and were key to her *Identifying phrase* — success. Her producer, Jerry Wexler, would refer to her as "the mysterious lady of sorrow" (Bego 8), singing *Direct quotation* — through the most dire personal traumas, as if compelled to do so. Her accomplishments are unmatched: She was the first woman inducted into the Rock and Roll Hall of Fame, the first African American woman to appear on the cover of *Time* magazine, and the recipient in 1996 of the Lifetime Achievement Award (Fanclub.com 1-3). Her greatest success sprang from her hardship.

Bagley 4

Aretha's songs and powerful lyrics help us deal with serious issues in our lives and culture. One of her greatest, "Respect," is a song of equality for African Americans and women. It earned Aretha two of her fifteen Grammy awards. She recorded "Bridge over Troubled Water" during some of her most difficult times, when she was rumored to have been drinking heavily. Of the words "Like a bridge over troubled water, I will lay me down," Aretha says, "What it says to me is even though you may want to give up, just be strong and things will get better. The storm will pass" (qtd. in Layne).

The way each of us interprets music and song lyrics is very similar to how we interpret other language: It may mean different things to different people. What I hear in a song may not be what you hear. Whatever our individual interpretations, however, the vibrating soul in Aretha's voice has touched many lives. Her natural ability to reach into our hearts and minds to create a feeling of wellness and hope is a special gift. Her deep expression of language and feeling through her soul music is, for many of us, the most expressive language of our time.

Aretha Franklin has followed her father's message, singing "whenever the world falls apart," following it as a dream. Song has made her a strong person who will be remembered long after her time. The Queen of Soul's music not only helped her through but has also touched many of our lives. Her ability to reach into our hearts and minds to create a feeling of well-being and connectedness is a special gift. Her soul reaches into ours and brings us together in times of joy and sorrow. She is truly the Queen of Soul.

Topic sentence

Franklin's words quoted in another source—in this case, a Web source

Topic sentence

Refers back to introduction

Refers to introduction and makes an observation

Another observation

Reference to title, also tying conclusion back to introduction

Bagley 5

Works Cited

<u>Aretha Franklin: The Life Story</u>. 2001. VH1. 16 Mar.
     2001 <http://www.vh1.com/fanclubs/
     bio.jhtml?id=7622>.

Bego, Mark. <u>Aretha Franklin: The Queen of Soul</u>. New
     York: St. Martin's, 1989.

Franklin, Aretha, and David Ritz. <u>From These Roots</u>.
     New York: Crown, 1989.

Layne, Anni. <u>Aretha Franklin: Biography</u>. 2000.
     Rollingstone.com. 16 Mar. 2001. <http://www
     .rollingstone.com/artists/bio.asp?oid=457&cf=457>.

Sheafer, Silvia Anne. <u>Aretha Franklin: Motown Super-
     star</u>. Detroit: Enslow, 1996.

Web site with
unknown author

For all entries,
indent after first
line

Book by two
authors

Titles of books are
either underlined
or italicized

PART FOUR

The Four Most Serious Errors

22

The Basic Sentence

An Editing Overview

The Four Most Serious Errors

This book puts special emphasis on the four grammar errors that people most often notice. These four errors may make your meaning harder to understand, but even if they don't, they give a bad impression of you.

THE FOUR MOST SERIOUS ERRORS

1. Fragments (see Chapter 23).
2. Run-ons (see Chapter 24).
3. Problems with subject–verb agreement (see Chapter 25).
4. Problems with verb form and tense (see Chapter 26).

If you can edit your writing to correct the four most serious errors, your sentences will be clearer and your grades will improve. Learning how to correct these errors will make a big difference in your writing.

This chapter will review the basic element of the sentence; the next four chapters cover the four most serious errors.

Understand What a Sentence Is

DEFINITION: A **sentence** is the basic unit of written communication. A complete sentence written in standard English must have three elements:

ESL
Give ESL students the opportunity to discuss this statement in terms of their own struggles with written English. Have students share editing processes that have worked for them, and write the best suggestions on the board.

DISCUSSION
Ask students how much time they leave for editing before turning in a paper or assignment. Remind students that even the most experienced writers must leave time for editing and proofreading.

1. It must have a **subject**.
2. It must have a **verb**.
3. It must express a **complete thought**.

To edit your writing, you need a clear understanding of what *is* a sentence and what *is not* a sentence. You can find out if a group of words is a complete sentence by checking to see if it has a subject, if it has a verb, and if it expresses a complete thought.

SUBJECTS

DEFINITION: The **subject** of a sentence is the person, place, or thing that the sentence is about. The subject of the sentence can be a noun (a word that names the person, place, or thing) or a pronoun (a word that replaces the noun, such as *I, you, she,* or *they*).

For a list of pronoun types, see page 440.

To find the subject, ask yourself, *Who or what is the sentence about?*

In this section on subjects, only the subject is underlined.

PERSON AS SUBJECT   <u>Vivian</u> works for the police department.

[*Who* is the sentence about? *Vivian*]

THING AS SUBJECT   The <u>tickets</u> cost $65 apiece.

[*What* is the sentence about? The *tickets*]

A compound subject consists of two (or more) subjects joined by *and, or,* or *nor.*

TWO SUBJECTS   <u>Marty</u> and <u>Kim</u> have a new baby girl.

SEVERAL SUBJECTS   The <u>jacket</u>, <u>pants</u>, and <u>sweater</u> match perfectly.

For a list of common prepositions, see page 347.

DEFINITIONS: A **prepositional phrase** is a word group that begins with a preposition and ends with a noun or pronoun. A **preposition** is a word that connects a noun, pronoun, or verb with some other information about it.

The subject of a sentence is *never* in a prepositional phrase.

preposition

The <u>check</u> is in the mail.

prepositional phrase

The subject of the sentence is *check*. The subject can't be the word *mail*, which is in the prepositional phrase *in the mail*.

Common Prepositions

about	beneath	like	to
above	beside	near	toward
across	between	next to	under
after	by	of	until
against	down	off	up
along	during	on	upon
among	except	out	with
around	for	outside	within
at	from	over	without
before	in	past	
behind	inside	since	
below	into	through	

preposition

One of my best friends is a circus clown.

prepositional phrase

Although the word *friends* may seem to be the subject of the sentence, it isn't. *One* is the subject. The word *friends* can't be the subject because it is in the prepositional phrase *of my best friends*.

When you are looking for the subject of a sentence in your writing, it may help you to cross out any prepositional phrases, as in the following sentences.

The rules ~~about smoking~~ are posted everywhere.

The sound ~~of lightning striking a tree~~ is like gunfire.

Many ~~of the students~~ work part-time.

PRACTICE 1   IDENTIFYING SUBJECTS AND PREPOSITIONAL PHRASES

In each of the following sentences, cross out any prepositional phrases and underline the subject of the sentence.

For more practice, visit Exercise Central at <www.bedfordstmartins.com/realessays>.

EXAMPLE: ~~For many,~~ a first <u>apartment</u> is a welcome taste ~~of independence.~~

1. Every year, <u>thousands</u> ~~of young people from all over the country~~ move ~~to New York City.~~

2. <u>Each</u> ~~of them~~ hopes to become successful ~~in the big city.~~

3. These young <u>artists</u> ~~with big talent and very little money~~ soon discover the difficulty ~~of finding an apartment in New York.~~

4. Every apartment <u>listing</u> ~~in the newspaper~~ will be seen ~~by hundreds of other apartment-seekers.~~

5. The <u>advice</u> ~~of a real estate broker~~ can be helpful.

6. Naturally, the <u>apartment</u> ~~of a young person's dreams~~ is likely to be out ~~of his or her price range.~~

7. Unfortunately, even a tiny <u>apartment</u> ~~with no closets and no view~~ can be unaffordable ~~on the island of Manhattan.~~

8. The <u>salary</u> ~~for an entry-level position~~ is unlikely to be enough to rent even a small, shabby apartment.

9. Many young <u>people</u> ~~without money~~ share their apartments ~~with roommates.~~

10. Sadly, <u>living</u> ~~among total strangers~~ is usually more fun ~~in movies~~ and ~~on television~~ than ~~in real life.~~

VERBS

DEFINITION: Every sentence has a **main verb**, the word or words that tell what the subject does or that link the subject to another word that describes it. Verbs do not always immediately follow the subject: Other words may come between the subject and the verb.

There are three kinds of verbs: action verbs, linking verbs, and helping verbs.

In the examples throughout this chapter, the subject is underlined once, and the verb is underlined twice.

Action Verbs

DEFINITION: An **action verb** tells what action the subject performs.

To find the main action verb in a sentence, ask yourself, *What action does the subject perform?*

ACTION VERBS	The <u>puppy</u> <u>cried</u> all night.
	The <u>building</u> <u>collapsed</u> around midnight.
	After work, <u>we</u> often <u>go</u> to Tallie's.
	My <u>aunt and uncle</u> <u>train</u> service dogs.

Linking Verbs

DEFINITION: A **linking verb** connects (links) the subject to a word or group of words that describe the subject. Linking verbs show no action. The most common linking verb is *be,* along with all its forms (*am, is, are,* and so on). Other linking verbs such as *seem* and *become* can usually be replaced by the corresponding form of *be,* and the sentence will still make sense.

LINKING VERBS	The <u>dinner</u> <u>is</u> delicious.
	<u>I</u> <u>felt</u> great this morning.
	This <u>lasagna</u> <u>tastes</u> just like my mother's.
	The <u>doctor</u> <u>looks</u> extremely tired.

Some words can be either action verbs or linking verbs, depending on how they are used in a particular sentence.

ACTION VERB	The <u>dog</u> <u>smelled</u> Jake's shoes.
LINKING VERB	The <u>dog</u> <u>smelled</u> terrible.

Common Linking Verbs

FORMS OF *BE*	FORMS OF *BECOME* AND *SEEM*	FORMS OF SENSE VERBS
am	become, becomes	appear, appears
are	became	appeared
is	seem, seems	feel, feels, felt
was	seemed	look, looks
were		looked
		smell, smells
		smelled
		taste, tastes, tasted

Helping Verbs

DEFINITION: A **helping verb** joins with the main verb in the sentence to form the **complete verb.** The helping verb is often a form of the verb *be, have,* or *do.* A sentence may have more than one helping verb along with the main verb.

| Helping verb | + | Main verb | = | Complete verb |

Sunil was talking on his cell phone.

[The helping verb is *was;* the complete verb is *was talking.*]

Charisse is taking three courses this semester.

Tomas has missed the last four meetings.

My brother might have passed the test.

Common Helping Verbs

FORMS OF *BE*	FORMS OF *HAVE*	FORMS OF *DO*	OTHER
am	have	do	can
are	has	does	could
been	had	did	may
being			might
is			must
was			should
were			will
			would

▉ **PRACTICE 2 IDENTIFYING THE VERB (ACTION, LINKING, OR HELPING + MAIN)**

In the following sentences, underline each subject and double-underline each verb. Then identify each verb as an action verb, a linking verb, or a helping verb + a main verb.

EXAMPLE: At first, Miguel did not want to attend his high school

reunion.   *helping verb + main verb*

1. Miguel's family moved to Ohio from Guatemala ten years ago.
   action verb

2. He was the new kid at his high school that fall.   *linking verb*

3. Miguel was learning English at that time.   *helping verb + main verb*

4. The football players teased small, quiet boys like him.   *action verb*

5. After graduation, he was delighted to leave that part of his life

   behind.   *linking verb*

6. Recently, the planning committee sent Miguel an invitation to his high

   school reunion.   *action verb*

7. His original plan had been to throw the invitation in the trash.
   helping verb + main verb

8. Instead, he is going to the party to satisfy his curiosity.   *helping verb +*
   main verb

9. His family is proud of Miguel's college degree and his new career as a

   graphic artist.   *linking verb*

10. Perhaps some of the other students at the reunion will finally get to

    know the real Miguel.   *helping verb + main verb*

COMPLETE THOUGHTS

DEFINITION: A **complete thought** is an idea, expressed in a sentence, that makes sense by itself without other sentences. An incomplete thought leaves readers wondering what's going on.

INCOMPLETE THOUGHT	as I was leaving	[*What's going on?*]
COMPLETE THOUGHT	The phone rang as I was leaving.	
INCOMPLETE THOUGHT	the people selling the car	[*What's going on?*]
COMPLETE THOUGHT	The people selling the car placed the ad.	

DISCUSSION
Have students discuss the differences between a complete thought in speaking and one in writing. Remind students that the context for speaking can be quite different from that for a written text—and that in writing a complete thought always needs a subject and a verb in order to be considered a complete sentence.

To identify a complete thought, ask yourself: *Do I know what's going on, or do I have to ask a question to understand?*

INCOMPLETE THOUGHT   in the apartment next door

[Do I know what's going on, or do I have to ask a question to understand? *You would have to ask a question, so this is not a complete thought.*]

COMPLETE THOUGHT   Carlos lives in the apartment next door.

PRACTICE 3   IDENTIFYING COMPLETE THOUGHTS

Some of the following items contain complete thoughts, and others do not. In the space to the left of each item, write either "C" for complete thought or "I" for incomplete thought. If you write "I," add words to make a sentence.

I cleaned the bathroom

EXAMPLE: __I__ Because my mother asked me to do it.
Answers will vary. Possible edits shown.

He walked down the red carpet, smiling
__I__ 1. Smiling broadly as the cameras flashed all around him.

__C__ 2. Nobody spoke.

__I__ 3. The man who lives in the big brick house on Valley Street is my new boss.

__C__ 4. Her shoes were tight.

__C__ 5. It's raining.

__I__ 6. After the last customer had gone home, Mary cleaned the coffee machine.

Sandra had her appendix removed, which
__I__ 7. Which explains why she missed class last week.

__I__ 8. Although you could have gotten away with cheating, you made the right decision.

__C__ 9. Leave them alone.

She usually comes home on
__I__ 10. On the five o'clock train.

23

Fragments

Incomplete Sentences

Understand What Sentence Fragments Are

DEFINITIONS: A **sentence** is a group of words that has a subject and a verb and expresses a complete thought, independent of other sentences. A **sentence fragment** is a group of words that is missing a subject or a verb or that does not express a complete thought.

SENTENCE	I'm going to a concert on Friday at Memorial Arena.
FRAGMENT	I'm going to a concert on Friday. *At Memorial Arena.*
	[*At Memorial Arena* does not have a subject or a verb.]

IN THE REAL WORLD, WHY IS IT IMPORTANT TO CORRECT FRAGMENTS?

A sentence fragment is one of the grammatical errors that most people notice. When people outside of the English classroom notice errors such as fragments, they don't assign you a course grade, but they do judge you by your communication skills. Prospective employers sometimes rule out candidates who make certain kinds of errors. For this reason, make sure you know how to edit your writing for fragments and how to correct them before you turn in any piece of writing, either in college or in the work-place.

SITUATION: James is responding to an ad he has seen for a job at a consulting firm. He sends the following cover letter, along with his résumé.

Dear Ms. Letendre:

I am interested in the computer technician position I saw. In the *Low-ell Sun*. I have held two similar positions that I have described. In my attached résumé. I believe I have the skills you are looking for. I would like an opportunity to meet with you. To discuss possible employment opportunities.

Thank you for your consideration.

Sincerely,

James Cosentini

RESPONSE: Maureen Letendre, the human resource director who is profiled in Chapter 11, had the following response to James's letter.

This letter and résumé go right into the "reject" pile.

Find and Correct Fragments

To find fragments in your own writing, look for the five fragment trouble spots listed below. If you find a potential trouble spot, read the sentence carefully to make sure it has a subject, has a verb, and expresses a complete thought.

FIVE FRAGMENT TROUBLE SPOTS

1. A word group that **starts with a preposition**, such as *in, at, with* (for a list, see p. 355).

2. A word group that **starts with a dependent word** such as *although, because, who, that.*

3. A word group that **starts with an -*ing* verb form**.

4. A word group that **starts with *to* and a verb**.

5. A word group that **starts with an example or explanation**.

When you are editing your own writing and find a fragment, you can usually correct it in one of two ways.

TWO WAYS TO CORRECT FRAGMENTS

1. Add what is missing (a subject, a verb, or both).
2. Attach the fragment to the sentence before or after it.

1. FRAGMENTS THAT START WITH A PREPOSITION

Finding Fragments

Whenever a preposition starts what you think is a sentence, check for a subject, a verb, and a complete thought. If any one of those is missing, you have a fragment.

Remember, the subject of a sentence is *never* in a prepositional phrase (see p. 346).

FRAGMENT   The plane crashed into the house. *With a deafening roar.*

[*With a deafening roar* is a prepositional phrase starting with the preposition *with* and ending with the noun *roar*. The phrase has neither a subject nor a verb. It is a fragment.]

FRAGMENT   Take the second left and head west. *Toward the highway.*

[*Toward the highway* is a prepositional phrase starting with the preposition *toward* and ending with the noun *highway*. The phrase has neither a subject nor a verb. It is a fragment.]

Common Prepositions

about	beneath	like	to
above	beside	near	toward
across	between	next to	under
after	by	of	until
against	down	off	up
along	during	on	upon
among	except	out	with
around	for	outside	within
at	from	over	without
before	in	past	
behind	inside	since	
below	into	through	

Correcting Fragments

Correct a fragment that starts with a preposition by connecting it to the sentence either before or after it. If you connect a fragment to the sentence after it, put a comma after the fragment to join it to the sentence.

FRAGMENT	The plane crashed into the house. *From a height of eight hundred feet.*
CORRECTED	The plane crashed into the house./ ᶠF̶rom a height of eight hundred feet.
CORRECTED	From a height of eight hundred feet, the plane crashed into the house.

PRACTICE 1   CORRECTING FRAGMENTS THAT START WITH PREPOSITIONS

In the following items, circle any preposition that appears at the beginning of a word group. Then correct any fragment by connecting it to the previous or the next sentence.

EXAMPLE: (Since) the discovery of fingerprint e̶v̶i̶d̶e̶n̶c̶e̶.̶ ᵉᵛⁱᵈᵉⁿᶜᵉ, ᵖᵒˡⁱᶜᵉ P̶o̶l̶i̶c̶e̶ departments all over the world have used it to convict wrongdoers.

1. Fingerprinting must have seemed like magic./ (ᵀₒTo) the public a hundred years ago.

2. (On) most surfaces, such as the handle of a weapon./, ᶠF̲ingerprints are nearly invisible.

3. (With) the development of techniques for finding and preserving fingerprints./, ᵈD̲etectives gained an advantage over criminals who did not wear gloves.

4. (For) most juries./, ᶠF̲ingerprint evidence was absolute proof.

5. (Until) recently./, ᶠF̲ew people realized that identifying fingerprints was not an exact science.

6. Fingerprint experts can sometimes disagree. *On* whether two prints match.

7. When two prints were very similar, there have even been a few cases. *Of* mistaken fingerprint identification.

8. *To* most investigators, Fingerprint evidence is no longer the most reliable tool for identifying criminals.

9. DNA evidence has become the new industry standard. *In* the past decade.

10. DNA identification is much more exact than fingerprinting, and it is very difficult. *For* a criminal to avoid leaving his or her DNA at a crime scene.

2. FRAGMENTS THAT START WITH A DEPENDENT WORD

DEFINITIONS: A **dependent word** is the first word in a dependent clause. A **dependent clause** has a subject and a verb but does not express a complete thought.

DEPENDENT CLAUSE	because the apartment was already rented

[*because* is the dependent word that begins the clause]

FRAGMENT THAT STARTS WITH A DEPENDENT WORD	I didn't fill out an application. *Because the apartment was already rented.*
DEPENDENT CLAUSE IN A SENTENCE	I didn't fill out an application *because the apartment was already rented.*
DEPENDENT CLAUSE	who came into the restaurant last week

[*who* is the dependent word that begins the clause]

FRAGMENT THAT STARTS WITH A DEPENDENT WORD	The server remembered the two sets of twins. *Who came into the restaurant last week.*

DISCUSSION
Have students look up the meaning of *dependent* in the dictionary and give an example in their own words. After hearing some responses, ask how *dependent* in *dependent clause* is similar to *dependent* as used in everyday life.

DEPENDENT CLAUSE IN A SENTENCE	The server remembered the two sets of twins *who came into the restaurant last week.*

Finding Fragments

A word group that starts with a dependent word (see list below) is a dependent clause, not a complete sentence. Although a dependent clause has a subject and a verb, it does not express a complete thought. It is a fragment unless it is connected to a complete sentence.

FRAGMENT   Last night we went to a movie. *After we had dinner at Luigi's.*

[Does the word group have a subject? Yes, *we.* A verb? Yes, *had.* Then why isn't it a sentence? Because it isn't a complete thought: After we had dinner at Luigi's, what happened?]

FRAGMENT   I'll go pick up the pizza and soda. *While you put the baby to bed.*

[Does the word group have a subject? Yes, *you.* A verb? Yes, *put.* Then why isn't it a sentence? Because it isn't a complete thought: While you put the baby to bed, what will happen?]

Common Dependent Words

after	if	what(ever)
although	since	when(ever)
as	so that	where
because	that	whether
before	though	which(ever)
even though	unless	while
how	until	who/whose

Correcting Fragments

Correct a fragment that starts with a dependent word by connecting it to the sentence before or after it. If the dependent clause is connected to the sentence before it, you usually do not need to put a comma in front of it. If the dependent clause is joined to the sentence after it, put a comma after the dependent clause.

FRAGMENT   Chris looked for a job for a whole year. *Before he found the right one.*

CORRECTED	Chris looked for a job for a whole year*/* ~~B~~efore he found the right one. *(b)*
CORRECTED	Before he found the right ~~job.~~ ~~Chris~~ looked for a whole year. *(one,)* *(a job for)*
FRAGMENT	My boss docked my pay for the half hour I was late. *Even though I worked through my lunch hour.*
CORRECTED	My boss docked my pay for the half hour I was late*/* ~~E~~ven though I worked through my lunch hour. *(e)*

PRACTICE 2   FINDING AND CORRECTING FRAGMENTS THAT START WITH A DEPENDENT WORD

In the following items, circle any dependent word that appears at the beginning of a word group. Then correct any fragment by connecting it to the previous or the next sentence.

EXAMPLE: (Since) many jobs involve working on a computer all ~~day.~~ ~~Some~~ *day, some*

employees can work wherever a computer is available.

1. (If) a company mainly sells information*/,* ~~I~~ts workers are more likely *(i)*

than employees of other businesses to be allowed to do their jobs at

home.

2. (Before) a worker begins telecommuting*/,* ~~H~~e or she must often convince *(h)*

the company that there is a good reason for the change.

3. Some companies are reluctant to approve telecommuting*/,* (Unless) their *(u)*

workers already have the necessary computer equipment at home.

4. Telecommuting sounds like a wonderful idea to many employees*/,* (Who) *(w)*

do not look forward to getting dressed for work and commuting to the

office.

5. (While) going to work in a bathrobe may be appealing, *t*elecommuters sometimes discover that working at home also has drawbacks.

6. Some telecommuters discover that they are not as productive at home, *a*s they are at the office.

7. A telecommuter needs motivation and discipline, *s*o that he or she can concentrate on the job while surrounded by all the distractions of home.

8. Telecommuters sometimes feel isolated, *w*hen they are not in daily contact with other employees.

9. Finally, telecommuters may find the pace of their work slowed down by their home Internet connection, *w*hich may not be as fast as an office's high-speed line.

10. (Even though) telecommuting is not for everyone, *a* growing percentage of workers are on the job at home one or two days a week.

3. FRAGMENTS THAT START WITH *-ING* VERB FORMS

DEFINITION: An *-ing* **verb form** is the form of a verb that ends in *-ing: walking, writing, swimming.* When this verb form is part of a complete verb, it must be used with a helping verb (*am, is, was*—for a complete list see p. 350). By itself, it can act as a subject but not as a verb. An *-ing* verb form acting as a subject or other noun is also known as a *gerund*.

-ING FORM USED WITH A HELPING VERB AS A VERB

I am swimming every day this summer.

[In this sentence, *am* is the helping verb; *am swimming* is the complete verb.]

Tom *was running* when he saw the accident.

[In this sentence, *was* is the helping verb; *was running* is the complete verb.]

-*ING* FORM USED ALONE AS A SUBJECT

Swimming is a wonderful form of exercise.

[In this sentence, *swimming* is the subject, not the verb; *is* is the verb.]

Running strains the knees.

[In this sentence, *running* is the subject, not the verb; *strains* is the verb.]

Finding Fragments

Whenever a word group begins with a word in *-ing* form, look carefully to see if the word group contains a subject and a verb and if it expresses a complete thought.

FRAGMENT   Snoring so loud I couldn't sleep.

[If *snoring* is the main verb, what is the subject? There isn't one. Is there a helping verb used with *snoring*? No. It is a fragment.]

FRAGMENT   *Hoping to make up for lost time.* I took a back road to school.

[If *hoping* is the main verb, what is the subject? There isn't one. Is there a helping verb used with *hoping*? No. It is a fragment.]

Correcting Fragments

Correct a fragment that starts with an *-ing* verb form either by adding whatever sentence elements are missing (usually a subject and a helping verb) or by connecting the fragment to the sentence before or after it. Usually, you will need to put a comma before or after the fragment to join it to the complete sentence.

-ING FRAGMENT   The audience applauded for ten minutes. *Whistling and cheering wildly.*

CORRECTED   The audience applauded for ten minutes., *W̷histling and cheering wildly.*

CORRECTED   The audience applauded for ten minutes. ~~Whistling and~~ cheering wildly.
They were whistling and

-ING FRAGMENT   *Working two jobs and going to school.* I am tired all the time.

CORRECTED   Working two jobs and going to school., I am tired all the time.

CORRECTED   *I am working*
~~Working~~ two jobs and going to school. I am tired all the time.

PRACTICE 3   CORRECTING FRAGMENTS THAT START WITH A DEPENDENT WORD

In the following items, circle any *-ing* verb that appears at the beginning of a word group. Then correct any fragment either by adding the missing sentence elements or by connecting it to the sentence before or after it.

EXAMPLE: (Quilting) with a group of other ~~women. My~~ *women, my* grandmother found a social life and a creative outlet.

Answers will vary. Possible edits shown.

1. My grandmother spent her entire life/ (Living) on a farm in eastern Wyoming.

2. (Growing) up during World War II/, $\overset{s}{S}$he learned from her mother how to sew her own clothes.

3. She was a natural seamstress. (Creating) shirts and dresses more beautiful *My grandmother created* than anything available in a store.

4. (Joining) a quilting circle at the age of twenty/, $\overset{m}{M}$y grandmother learned how to make quilts.

5. The quilting circle made quilts for special occasions/ ($\overset{u}{U}$sing) scraps of cloth left over from other sewing projects.

6. (Laying) the scraps out in an interesting pattern. The women then chose *The quilters laid* a traditional design for the stitching that joined the top and bottom parts of the quilt.

7. (Celebrating) the birth of her first child, my father/ $\overset{t}{T}$he quilting circle gave my grandmother a baby quilt that is now a treasured heirloom.

8. She told me that the quilt was made of memories. ~~Incorporating~~ *It incorporated* fabric

    from her wedding dress, her maternity outfits, and all of the baby

    clothes she had stitched.

9. ~~Looking~~ at each bit of cloth in that quilt~~,~~ ~~My~~ *m*y grandmother could still

    describe, years later, the garment she had made it from.

10. ~~Trying~~ to ensure that those memories would survive~~,~~ I asked her to

    write down everything she recalled about my father's baby quilt.

4. FRAGMENTS THAT START WITH *TO* AND A VERB

DEFINITION: An **infinitive** is the word *to* plus a verb: *to hire, to eat, to study.*
If a word group begins with *to* and a verb, it must have another verb or it
is not a complete sentence.

> **FRAGMENT**   I will go to the store later. *To buy a card.*

[The first word group is a sentence, with *I* as the subject and *will go* as the verb.
There is no subject or verb in the word group *to buy a card.*]

> **FRAGMENT**   I ate nothing but popcorn for a week. *To lose ten pounds,*
> *my goal.*

[The word group that begins with *to lose* has no subject and no verb.]

Finding Fragments

When you have written what you think is a sentence, and it begins with the
word *to* and a verb, check to see if there is another verb. If there is not
another verb in the word group, it is a fragment.

> **FRAGMENT**   Last week a couple in New York fulfilled their wedding fan-
> tasy. *To get married on the top of the Empire State Building.*

[Is there another verb in addition to *to get married* in the word group that starts
with *to* and a verb? No; the word group is a fragment.]

> **FRAGMENT**   David brought a magazine to the post office. *To read in the*
> *long line of customers.*

[Is there another verb in addition to *to read* in the word group that starts with *to*
and a verb? No; the word group is a fragment.]

Correcting Fragments

To correct a fragment that starts with *to* and a verb, connect it to the sentence before or after it, or add the missing sentence elements (a subject and a verb.)

FRAGMENT	Geri climbed up on the roof. *To watch the fireworks.*
CORRECTED	Geri climbed up on the roof./, To watch the fireworks.
CORRECTED	Geri climbed up on the roof. ~~To~~ *She wanted to* watch the fireworks.
FRAGMENT	*To save on her monthly gas bills.* Tammy sold her SUV and got a Honda Civic.
CORRECTED	To save on her monthly gas bills./, Tammy sold her SUV and got a Honda Civic.
CORRECTED	*Tammy wanted to* ~~To~~ save on her monthly gas bills. *She* ~~Tammy~~ sold her SUV and got a Honda Civic.

PRACTICE 4   FINDING AND CORRECTING FRAGMENTS THAT START WITH *TO* AND A VERB

In the following items, circle any examples of *to* and a verb that begin a word group. Then correct each fragment either by adding the missing sentence elements or by connecting it to the previous or the next sentence.

EXAMPLE: Convincing Americans to use less energy is one way./ To ensure that there is enough for everyone.
Answers may vary. Possible edits shown.

1. In 1976, several oil-producing countries in the Middle East made an agreement./ To refuse to sell oil to the United States.

2. During the energy crisis that followed, drivers could not always buy enough gasoline./ To fill the tanks of their cars.

3. American automakers increased the fuel efficiency of their cars./ To meet consumers' demands for vehicles with better gas mileage.

4. ~~To use~~ less fuel, / Ḥomeowners in the mid-1970s kept their homes cooler in the winter and warmer in the summer.

5. Oil and gasoline soon became widely available again, so many Americans made a decision, / ~~To stop~~ worrying about conserving energy.

6. ~~To drive~~ a giant sport utility vehicle. / ~~This~~ was a goal of large numbers of middle-class Americans at the end of the twentieth century.

7. *The nation had to* ~~To deal~~ with energy shortages in California and rising gas prices across the country in 2001. Some people suggested that Americans needed to consume less energy.

8. Others argued that the United States needed to invest in new technology, / ~~To develop~~ renewable sources of energy, such as wind and solar power.

9. Perhaps the booming economy of the 1990s convinced too many Americans that there would never be a need for them, / ~~To consider~~ a less wasteful lifestyle.

10. ~~To combat~~ rising energy prices in the winter of 2001–2002, / American politicians wanted to tap into the country's emergency fuel reserves, not to urge citizens to use less.

5. FRAGMENTS THAT START WITH EXAMPLES OR EXPLANATIONS

As you edit your writing, pay special attention in each sentence to groups of words that are examples or explanations of information you have given in the previous sentences. These word groups may be fragments.

FRAGMENT   Shoppers find many ways to save money on food bills. *For example, using double coupons.*

[The second word group has no subject and no verb. The word *using* is an *-ing* verb form that needs either to be the subject of a sentence or to have a helping verb with it.]

FRAGMENT   Parking on this campus is a real nightmare. *Especially between 8:00 and 8:30 A.M.*

[The second word group has no subject and no verb.]

Finding Fragments

Finding fragments that start with examples or explanations can be difficult because there is no single kind of word to look for. The following are a few starting words that may signal an example or explanation, but fragments that are examples or explanations do not always start with these words:

especially   for example   like   such as

When a group of words that you think is a sentence gives an example of information in the previous sentence, stop to see if it has a subject and a verb and if it expresses a complete thought. If it is missing any of these elements, it is a fragment.

FRAGMENT   The Web has many job search sites. *Such as Monster.com.*

[Does the second word group have a subject? No. A verb? No. It is a fragment.]

FRAGMENT   I wish I had something to eat from Chipotle's right now. *A giant burrito, for example.*

[Does the second word group have a subject? Yes, *burrito.* A verb? No. It is a fragment.]

FRAGMENT   I had to push seven different voice-mail buttons before I spoke to a real person. *Not a helpful one, though.*

[Does the second word group have a subject? Yes, *one.* A verb? No. It is a fragment.]

Correcting Fragments

To correct a fragment that starts with an example or an explanation, connect it either to the previous or to the next one. Sometimes you can add the missing sentence elements (a subject, a verb, or both) instead. When you connect the fragment to a sentence, you may need to reword or to change some punctuation. Many fragments that are examples are set off by commas.

FRAGMENT   The Web has many job search sites. *Such as Monster.com.*

CORRECTED   The Web has many job search sites*, s*uch as Monster.com.

FRAGMENT   I had to push seven different voice-mail buttons before I spoke to a real person. *Not a helpful one, though.*

CORRECTED   I had to push seven different voice-mail buttons before I

He was not

spoke to a real person. ~~Not a~~ helpful ~~one~~, though.

▪ PRACTICE 5 CORRECTING FRAGMENTS THAT ARE EXAMPLES OR EXPLANATIONS

In the following items, circle any word groups that are examples or explanations. Correct each fragment either by connecting it to the previous sentence or by adding the missing sentence elements.

EXAMPLE: Some studies estimate that the number of teenage girls

suffering dating abuse is very high. (Perhaps as many as one

experiences some type of abuse from her boyfriend.

out of three girls.)

Answers may vary. Possible edits shown.

1. Many parents believe that they would know if their daughters were

e

being abused./ (Either physically or emotionally.)

2. Most parents would certainly be concerned to see signs of violence on

s

their children./ (Such as bruises or scratches.)

3. A young man can be abusive without laying a finger on his girlfriend.

He might

(A guy who monitors her actions and keeps her from spending time

with other friends.)

They may want to make

4. Abusive boyfriends often want to control their partners. (Make sure that

a certain way,

their girlfriends dress ~~conservatively~~ for example.)

5. Around her parents, a teenager's boyfriend may act like a perfect

He may be polite,

gentleman. (Polite, attentive, and kind to the young woman.)

abusing her verbally,

6. When the couple is alone, however, he may be ~~subjecting her to verbal~~

~~abuse.~~ (Like telling her that she is fat, stupid, and ugly.)

7. A young woman with an abusive boyfriend may develop psychological problems that will be difficult to treat. *s*/(Such as low self-esteem.)

8. Parents should look for signs that their daughter needs help. *like slipping*/(Slipping) (grades, loss of interest in her friends, and unwillingness to confide in) (parents.)

9. Friends who think that a young woman is involved in an abusive relationship should try to be supportive of her. *n*/(Not turn away even if) (she will not leave her boyfriend.)

10. Young women need to know that help is available. *f*/(From parents,) (guidance counselors, women's support services, and even the police, if) (necessary.)

Edit Paragraphs and Your Own Writing

As you complete the practices and edit your own writing, use the Thinking Critically guide that follows. You may also want to refer to the Quick Review Chart on page 372.

THINKING CRITICALLY TO EDIT FRAGMENTS	
FOCUS	Whenever you see one of the five trouble spots in your writing, stop to check for a possible fragment.
ASK	• Does it have a subject? • Does it have a verb? • Does it express a complete thought?
EDIT	If your answer to any of these questions is "no," you have a fragment that you must correct.

■ PRACTICE 6   **EDITING PARAGRAPHS FOR FRAGMENTS**

Find and correct any fragments in the following paragraphs.

Answers will vary. Possible edits shown.

1. (1) Genetically modified foods are being marketed. (2) As the foods of the future. (3) For the past decade, gene technology has been advancing dramatically. (4) Inserting a gene from one species into the DNA of another species is easily possible. (5) A gene from a fish may be found. (6) To make tomatoes more resistant to disease. (7) Of course, this genetic modification may have unintended effects. (8) As in the case of genetically modified corn. (9) Which may harm monarch butterfly caterpillars. (10) Arguing that the long-term effects of genetic modification may not be known for years to come. (11) Some scientists urge caution before marketing genetically modified foods.

2. (1) The year 2001 brought more bad news. (2) For beef eaters and for British cattle farmers struggling to overcome the bad publicity brought on by mad cow disease. (3) Cattle in England and Scotland suffered an epidemic of an extremely contagious illness. (4) Hoof-and-mouth disease. (5) Many people were frightened of eating British beef even though the disease does not harm humans. (6) To contain the outbreak. (7) Hiking trails were closed. (8) Because the disease could travel on the shoes or clothing of people walking from one region to another. (9) Before the epidemic was contained, thousands of infected cattle were slaughtered. (10) In the end, many farmers wondered how they would be able to survive. (11) After losing so many of their livestock.

3. (1) The term *organic* means different things. (2) To different people. (3) Organic foods are supposed to be grown without pesticides. (4) A

TEAMWORK
Divide the class into small groups and have each group present a corrected paragraph. Compare the different ways in which the groups correct the fragments.

method that reduces a farm's impact on the environment. (5) But is organic food a healthier choice for the person eating it? (6) Most people who buy organic food think so. (7) They pay premium prices for organic products because they think the food is good for their own well-being, (8) Not just that of the environment. (9) Surprisingly, however, some foods labeled *organic* today are highly processed. (10) The label merely means that the ingredients meet a certain government standard, (11) While guaranteeing nothing about the nutritional content or health benefits of the food.

4.   (1) For several years, (2) The U.S. Department of Agriculture has permitted the irradiation of certain foods sold in American supermarkets. (3) Irradiating produce kills bacteria on the food, (4) Increasing its shelf life. (5) Without irradiation, a strawberry may last only a day or two after being purchased. (6) An irradiated strawberry, on the other hand, can last a week or more, (7) Because the bacteria that would cause it to spoil are killed by radiation. (8) While some consumers worry about buying irradiated food, (9) Others dismiss these concerns as the effect of too many science-fiction movies. (10) In stores where irradiated fruits and vegetables are sold under banners announcing the radiation treatment, (11) The owners report a booming market.

5.   (1) Bacteria that resist antibiotics could be a real health threat in the next century. (2) Doctors have begun to explain to their patients, (3) That antibiotics are useful only for certain kinds of infections and that patients must finish every course of antibiotics they start. (4) Antibiotic use in agriculture, however, has continued, (5) To increase. (6) The government does not even keep records, (7) Of antibiotic use in farm animals. (8) Many

cattle, pigs, and chickens get antibiotics for economic reasons, (9) Such as
to keep them healthy and to make them grow faster. (10) Many scientists
fear that antibiotic residue in the meat Americans eat may contribute to
antibiotic resistance. (11) If so, agricultural antibiotics could eventually
endanger human health.

PRACTICE 7 EDITING YOUR OWN WRITING FOR FRAGMENTS

As a final practice, carefully read a piece of your own writing—a paper
you are working on for this class, a paper you've already finished, a paper
for another course, or a recent piece of writing from your work or everyday life. Use the Thinking Critically guide on page 368 and the Quick
Review Chart that follows as you edit for fragments.

Quick Review Chart

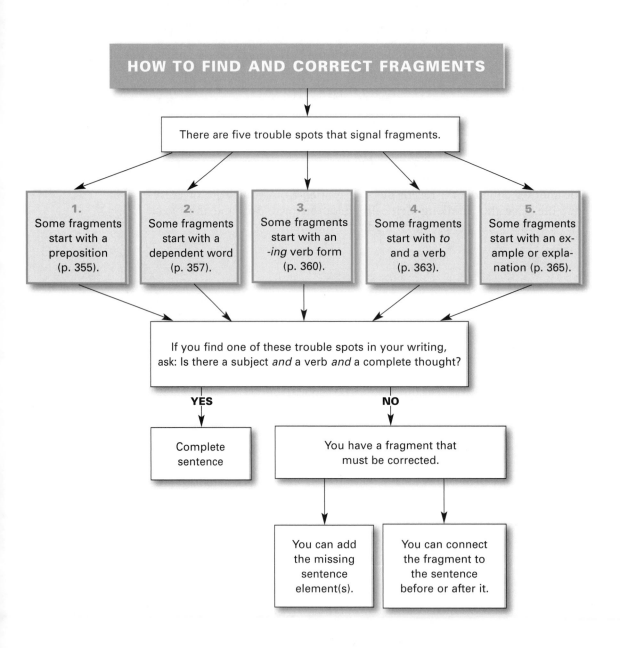

HOW TO FIND AND CORRECT FRAGMENTS

There are five trouble spots that signal fragments.

1. Some fragments start with a preposition (p. 355).

2. Some fragments start with a dependent word (p. 357).

3. Some fragments start with an *-ing* verb form (p. 360).

4. Some fragments start with *to* and a verb (p. 363).

5. Some fragments start with an example or explanation (p. 365).

If you find one of these trouble spots in your writing, ask: Is there a subject *and* a verb *and* a complete thought?

YES

NO

Complete sentence

You have a fragment that must be corrected.

You can add the missing sentence element(s).

You can connect the fragment to the sentence before or after it.

24

Run-Ons

Two Sentences Joined Incorrectly

Ever Thought This?
"I tried putting in commas instead of periods so I wouldn't have fragments. Now I have run-ons instead."
—Jimmy Lester, student

This chapter:
- explains what run-ons are.
- shows you how to find them.
- gives you practice finding run-ons and shows four ways to correct them.

Understand What Run-Ons Are

DEFINITION: A sentence is also called an **independent clause,** a group of words with a subject and a verb that expresses a complete thought. Sometimes two independent clauses can be joined in one sentence.

SENTENCE WITH TWO INDEPENDENT CLAUSES

independent clause   independent clause

The fog was very thick, so the airport closed.

DEFINITIONS: A **run-on** is two sentences (each containing a subject and a verb and expressing a complete thought) that are joined incorrectly and written as one sentence. There are two kinds of run-ons: **fused sentences** and **comma splices**.

A **fused sentence** is two complete sentences joined without any punctuation.

In the examples throughout this chapter, the subject is underlined once and the verb is underlined twice.

independent clause   independent clause

FUSED SENTENCE   Anger is a dangerous emotion it has many bad effects.

↑
no punctuation

373

A **comma splice** is two complete sentences joined by only a comma instead of a comma and one of the following words: *and, but, for, nor, or, so, yet.*

COMMA SPLICE   Anger is a dangerous emotion, it has many bad effects.

comma

IN THE REAL WORLD, WHY IS IT IMPORTANT TO CORRECT RUN-ONS?

Run-ons, like fragments, are errors that people notice. Their presence in your writing can result in a bad grade on a paper or, worse, a rejection from a potential employer. Because a run-on is one of the four most serious errors you can make, an important editing task is to find and correct both fused sentences and comma splices.

SITUATION: Marion is new to her position as a licensed practical nurse at a large hospital. Each day she updates patients' records and writes brief summaries of their progress for other nurses. The following is a report that Marion wrote in her first week on the job.

Trudari Kami is a premature infant she was born with a birth weight of 1.7 pounds her lungs were not fully developed and she was not able to breathe on her own. As of 2:15 A.M. on Thurday, April 6, she remains in stable condition her condition is still critical though she is being carefully monitored.

RESPONSE: Patty Maloney, the clinical nurse specialist profiled in Chapter 8, had the following response to Marion's report.

I had to meet with Marion, who is obviously not sure how to communicate clearly in medical documents. I explained to her that what she had written was very difficult to understand, and I worked with her on revising the report so that the next person would understand what Marion was trying to say. I had to do this because the reports must be clear; otherwise, the next person might not be sure how to treat the baby.

Find and Correct Run-Ons

FINDING RUN-ONS

There is only one good way to find run-ons in your writing: Read each sentence carefully, checking specifically to make sure that you have not fused two sentences or created a comma splice. As you get used to correcting run-ons in your writing, you won't have to spend as much time looking for them because you will write fewer of them with each new assignment or project.

Read the following paragraph. Does it include any run-ons? _____

If so, how many? _____

The concert to benefit AIDS research included fabulous musicians and songs. One of the guitarists had six different guitars they were all acoustic. One had a shiny, engraved silver shield on it, it flashed in the lights. The riffs the group played were fantastic. All of the songs were original, and many had to do with the loss of loved ones. At the end of some songs, the audience was hushed, too moved with emotion to begin the applause right away. When the concert was over, the listeners, many of them in tears, gave the performers a standing ovation.

TEACHING TIP
Suggest to students that they review the definitions of *subject* and *verb* on pages 346 and 348 before completing the following activity. They can underline the subjects and circle or double-underline the verbs in order to identify the difference between dependent and independent clauses—and to identify and correct run-ons.

CORRECTING RUN-ONS

When you are editing your writing and find a run-on, you can correct it in one of four ways.

FOUR WAYS TO CORRECT A RUN-ON
1. Add a period.
2. Add a semicolon.
3. Add a comma and a coordinating conjunction.
4. Add a dependent word.

1. Add a Period

You can correct a run-on by adding a period to make two separate sentences.

independent clause   independent clause

FUSED SENTENCE   I tried to call about my bill I got four useless recorded
messages.

COMMA SPLICE   I finally hung up, my question remained unanswered.

2. Add a Semicolon

TEACHING TIP
Remind students that
a semicolon balances
two independent
clauses; what is on
either side of the
semicolon must be
able to stand alone as
a complete sentence
with a subject and a
verb.

You can correct a run-on by adding a semicolon (;) to join the two independent clauses into one sentence. Use a semicolon only when the two independent clauses express closely related ideas that make sense in a single combined sentence.

independent clause   independent clause

FUSED SENTENCE   My father had a heart attack he is in the hospital.

COMMA SPLICE   My mother called 911, the ambulance was there in
four minutes.

A semicolon is sometimes used before a transition from one independent clause to another, and the transition word is followed by a comma.

transition

I tried to visit my father; however, I couldn't get a ride.

semicolon   comma

■   **PRACTICE 1   CORRECTING A RUN-ON BY ADDING A PERIOD
OR A SEMICOLON**

For more practice,
visit Exercise
Central at <**www
.bedfordstmartins
.com/realessays**>.

For each of the following run-ons, indicate in the space to the left whether it is a fused sentence (FS) or a comma splice (CS). Then correct the run-on by adding a period or a semicolon.

EXAMPLE: _CS_   A cellular phone in the car can be a lifesaver in an

emergency; a cell phone may also contribute to

an accident.

Answers may vary. Possible edits shown.

_FS_ 1. The invention of cell phones made telephoning from a car

possible. People could telephone for help if they were stranded on

the highway.

_CS_ 2. Almost as soon as cell phones became common, people began to

use them in traffic. Some drivers were undoubtedly distracted by

their telephones, creating a danger.

_CS_ 3. Some communities in the United States have banned drivers from

talking on handheld cell phones; a driver must stop the car to

place a call legally in those areas.

_FS_ 4. Cell-phone makers have come up with hands-free phones. Even in

places with cell-phone restrictions, these phones can be used by

the driver of a moving car.

_FS_ 5. No one debates that drivers can be distracted by cell phones.

Some people wonder, however, whether the problem is really the

fact that a driver is holding the phone.

_CS_ 6. If lawmakers simply want to make sure that drivers have their

hands free, they should ban eating while driving as well; they

could also stop people from shaving or putting on makeup behind

the wheel.

_FS_ 7. Some people worry that drivers are distracted not by holding the

telephone, but by having a conversation. A tense discussion with the boss or good news from a relative can take the driver's attention from traffic.

_CS_ 8. Cell-phone supporters argue that the same kinds of distractions can come from elsewhere in the car; music and talk radio, for example, can suddenly make a driver lose concentration.

_CS_ 9. There are differences, however, between talking on a cell phone and listening to music in the car; the telephone requires interaction from the driver, but the radio calls for passive listening.

_FS_ 10. Drivers who love making calls on the road will resist cell-phone restrictions; many other people will feel safer in communities that do not allow driving while telephoning.

3. Add a Comma and a Coordinating Conjunction

DEFINITION: Coordinating conjunctions are the words used to combine two independent clauses of equal importance into one sentence. There are only seven coordinating conjunctions: *and, but, for, nor, or, so, yet.*

To correct a comma splice, keep the comma but add a coordinating conjunction. If the run-on is a fused sentence, add both a comma and a coordinating conjunction. Before adding just any coordinating conjunction, read the independent clauses to see which of the seven makes the most sense.

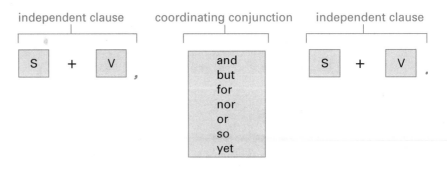

FUSED SENTENCE	We warned Tim to wear a seat belt ^*, but* he never did.
COMMA SPLICE	He got into an accident, ^*and* he went through the windshield.

PRACTICE 2   CORRECTING A RUN-ON BY ADDING A COMMA AND A COORDINATING CONJUNCTION

Correct each of the following run-ons. First underline the subjects and double-underline the verbs to find the separate sentences. Then add a comma (unless the run-on already includes one) and a coordinating conjunction.

EXAMPLE: Tasmania, an island off the coast of Australia, is the home of many unusual kinds of wildlife, *but* it also has been the site of several oil spills.

Answers will vary. Possible edits shown.

1. Fairy penguins, a small breed of penguin, live in Tasmania *,and* these birds have often been the victims of oil spills.

2. The birds clean their feathers with their beaks *,and* they swallow the oil on their feathers.

3. Unfortunately, the penguins' attempts to clean off their feathers can be *,for* fatal crude oil is poisonous to penguins.

4. Wildlife conservationists in Tasmania expected future spills, *,so* they created a plan to save the penguins.

5. One of the conservationists created a pattern for a sweater for the penguins, *,and* volunteers from around the world knitted these unusual sweaters.

6. The sweaters cover everything but the penguins' heads and feet, *,so* they can't lick the oil-poisoned feathers.

DISCUSSION
The following practice can be completed together as a class. Have students suggest appropriate conjunctions for each pair of dependent clauses. Discuss how the choice of conjunction can change the meaning of a sentence.

7. Most of the sweaters <u>were made</u> by elderly nursing-home residents in
   but
   Tasmania,ˌ some <u>were sent</u> from as far away as Japan.

8. After future spills, a fairy <u>penguin</u> <u>may wear</u> a sweaterˌ *, or* it also <u>might</u>
   <u>wear</u> a tiny football jersey.

9. <u>Some</u> creative knitters <u>made</u> tuxedo-patterned sweatersˌ *, and* a <u>few</u> of these
   penguin suits even <u>have</u> bow ties.

10. The <u>penguins</u> <u>have</u> a variety of protective outfitsˌ *, but* they don't like any of
    the garments.

4. Add a Dependent Word

The fourth way to correct a run-on is to make one of the independent clauses a dependent clause.

Common dependent words are listed below.

DEFINITION: A **dependent clause** is a group of words with a subject and a verb. However, it is not a complete sentence because it begins with a dependent word and does not express a complete thought. It is dependent on a sentence or independent clause to do that.

dependent clause

The ice cream melted fast because it was really hot out.

dependent word

Common Dependent Words

after	if	what(ever)
although	since	when(ever)
as	so that	where
because	that	whether
before	though	which(ever)
even though	unless	while
how	until	who/whose

When you add a dependent clause to an independent clause, place the addition where it makes more sense. If the dependent clause starts off the sentence, you need to add a comma after it. If the dependent clause is added to the second part of the sentence, you don't need a comma. Always begin a dependent clause with a dependent word.

until

COMMA SPLICE   I took deep breaths,/ I was calmer.

In this case, the sentence would not make much sense if the word *until* was added to the first independent clause: Until I took deep breaths, I was calmer.

In other cases, though, the dependent word can be added to either independent clause. The writer can choose where to place the word according to what part of the sentence he or she wants to emphasize.

Although

FUSED SENTENCE   I ordered a salad I wanted the fried clam plate with fries.

In this example, the dependent word *although* would also make sense before the second independent clause:

I ordered a salad although I wanted the fried clam plate with fries.

▗ **PRACTICE 3   CORRECTING A RUN-ON BY MAKING A DEPENDENT CLAUSE**

Correct each of the following run-ons. First underline the subjects and double-underline the verbs to find the separate sentences. Then make one of the clauses a dependent clause by adding a dependent word. Add a comma after the dependent clause if it comes first in the sentence.

before

EXAMPLE: Mr. Johnson was a sheet-metal worker,/ he retired.

Answers will vary. Possible edits shown.

because

1. My neighbor, Mr. Johnson, began his hobby his children were worried

    about his ability to keep busy after retirement.

that

2. In his basement, he built small replicas of local buildings,/ ~~the buildings~~

    were familiar to him and his family.

because

3. He made the models out of sheet metal, he was used to working with

    that material.

    When he
4. ~~He~~ made a copy of his own house, he used wire mesh for the porch

    railing.

    After he
5. ~~He~~ finished the metal work, Mr. Johnson painted the house white with

    a green roof, just like the original.

    Until
6. Mr. Johnson drove by our town's century-old sandstone courthouse, he

    had planned to make just one model house.

    While he
7. ~~He~~ was working on the model courthouse, he found photographs of his

    childhood home.

                   so that
8. He found enough photographs, he had a view of every part of the old

    farmhouse.

    When he
9. ~~He~~ finished his model of the old house, his family began to show the

    models to other people.

10. Mr. Johnson's retirement suddenly became busier than his working
      because
    life,/everyone in town seemed to want a model house.

5. *A Word That Can Cause Run-Ons:* Then

Many run-ons are caused by the word *then*. You can use *then* to join two sentences, but if you add it without the correct punctuation, your sentence will be a run-on. Often writers mistakenly use just a comma before *then*, but that makes a comma splice.

To correct a run-on caused by the word *then*, you can use any of the four methods presented in this chapter.

    COMMA SPLICE   I grabbed the remote, then I ate my pizza.

    CORRECTED   I grabbed the remote. Then I ate my pizza.   [added period]

    CORRECTED   I grabbed the remote; then I ate my pizza.   [semicolon added] *and*

CORRECTED   I grabbed the remote, then I ate my pizza.   [coordinating
conjunction *and* added]

before

CORRECTED   I grabbed the remote, then I ate my pizza.   [dependent
word *before* added to make a dependent clause]

Edit Paragraphs and Your Own Writing

As you complete the practices and edit your own writing, use the Thinking Critically guide that follows. You may also want to refer to the Quick
Review Chart on page 386.

THINKING CRITICALLY TO EDIT RUN-ONS

FOCUS   Read each sentence aloud, and listen carefully as you read.

ASK
- Am I pausing in the middle of the sentence?
- If so, are there two subjects and two verbs?
- If so, are there two complete sentences in this sentence?
- If there are two sentences (independent clauses), are they
  separated by punctuation? If the answer is "no," the
  sentence is a **fused sentence**.
- If there is punctuation between the two independent
  clauses, is it a comma only, with no coordinating
  conjunction? If the answer is "yes," the sentence is a
  comma splice.

EDIT   If the sentence is a run-on, correct it using one of the four
methods for editing run-ons.

PRACTICE 4   EDITING PARAGRAPHS FOR RUN-ONS

Find and correct any run-ons in the following paragraphs. Make the corrections using whichever of the four methods seems best to you. You may
want to refer to the preceding Thinking Critically guide or the Quick
Review Chart on page 386.

Answers will vary. Possible edits shown.

1.　(1) Your memory can play tricks on you. (2) It's often easy to forget

things ~when~ you want desperately to remember them. (3) You have probably

had the experience of forgetting an acquaintance's name ~, which~ ~the name~ comes

to your mind only when it's too late. (4) You have also probably been

unable to find your keys once in a while ~because~ you put them down somewhere

without thinking. (5) At other times, however, you may find it difficult to

forget some things ~even though~ you wish you could never think of them again. (6) If

you have an annoying song in your mind, you may spend hours wishing

desperately to forget it. (7) Sometimes you may find yourself forced to

relive your most embarrassing moment over and over again in your mind ~;~

your memory won't let you leave that part of your past behind. (8) Some

scholars believe that these annoying habits of memory evolved for a rea-

son ~. It's~ ~it's~ hard to imagine, though, any good reason for developing the abil-

ity to forget where you left your keys.

2.　(1) Most scientists now agree that human beings are changing the cli-

mate ~. I~ industrial activities release gases into the air that trap heat in the

earth's atmosphere. (2) The number one problem gas is carbon dioxide ~because~

factories and gasoline engines release tons of it into the air. (3) In inter-

national discussions of global warming, industrial countries like the

United States have argued that planting forests might reduce the amount

of carbon dioxide in the air. (4) Trees absorb carbon dioxide, ~and~ then they

release oxygen. (5) A recent study tested trees in North Carolina ~;~ it

exposed them to high levels of carbon dioxide. (6) At first, the trees grew

rapidly, ~but~ after a while, their growth returned to normal. (7) Dead trees did

not release their accumulated carbon into the soil ~;~ instead, the carbon

went back into the air as carbon dioxide. (8) The study will continue for years, this is not the last word on the subject. (9) However, perhaps reducing carbon dioxide in the atmosphere will be difficult the United States may yet have to come up with a way to reduce the amount of the gas getting into the air in the first place.

PRACTICE 5   EDITING YOUR OWN WRITING FOR RUN-ONS

As a final practice, carefully read a piece of your own writing—a paper you are working on for this class, a paper you've already finished, a paper for another course, or a recent piece of writing from your work or everyday life. For extra help in editing for run-ons, use the Thinking Critically guide on page 383 and the Quick Review Chart that follows.

Quick Review Chart

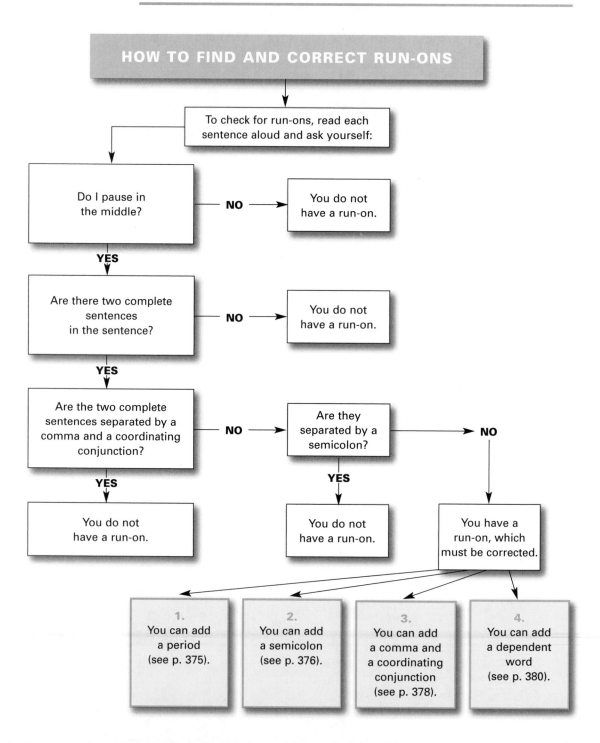

HOW TO FIND AND CORRECT RUN-ONS

To check for run-ons, read each sentence aloud and ask yourself:

Do I pause in the middle? —**NO**→ You do not have a run-on.

YES

Are there two complete sentences in the sentence? —**NO**→ You do not have a run-on.

YES

Are the two complete sentences separated by a comma and a coordinating conjunction? —**NO**→ Are they separated by a semicolon? —**NO**→ You have a run-on, which must be corrected.

YES (from comma/conjunction) → You do not have a run-on.

YES (from semicolon) → You do not have a run-on.

1.
You can add a period (see p. 375).

2.
You can add a semicolon (see p. 376).

3.
You can add a comma and a coordinating conjunction (see p. 378).

4.
You can add a dependent word (see p. 380).

25

Problems with Subject-Verb Agreement

When Subjects and Verbs Don't Match

Ever Thought This?
"I get confused about when a verb ends in -*s*. The singular and plural rules mix me up."
—Mayerlin Fana, student

This chapter:
- explains what *agreement* between subjects and verbs is.
- explains the simple rules for *regular verbs*.
- identifies five trouble spots that can cause confusion.
- gives you practice finding and fixing errors in subject-verb agreement.

Understand What Subject-Verb Agreement Is

DEFINITION: In any sentence, the subject and the verb must agree or match in number. If the subject is singular (one person, place, or thing), then the verb must also be singular in form. If the subject is plural (more than one), the verb must also be plural in form.

SINGULAR   The <u>phone</u> <u><u>rings</u></u> constantly at work.

[The subject, *phone,* is singular — just one phone — so the verb must take the singular form: *rings.*]

PLURAL   The <u>phones</u> <u><u>ring</u></u> constantly at work.

[The subject, *phones,* is plural — more than one phone — so the verb must take the plural form: *ring.*]

DEFINITION: **Regular verbs** are verbs with forms that follow standard English patterns. They have two forms in the present tense: one that does not add an ending and one that ends in -*s*.

In the examples throughout this chapter, the <u>subject</u> is underlined once and the <u><u>verb</u></u> is underlined twice.

387

Regular Verbs, Present Tense

	SINGULAR FORM	PLURAL FORM
First person	I walk.	We walk.
Second person	You walk.	You walk.
Third person	He/she/it walks.	They walk.
	Percy walks.	Percy and Don walk.
	The dog walks.	The dogs walk.

First-person (*I, we*) subjects, second-person (*you*) subjects, and plural (more than one person, place, or thing) subjects have verbs with no *-s* ending. Third person singular subjects (*he, she, it,* and singular nouns) always have a verb that ends in *-s*.

IN THE REAL WORLD, WHY IS IT IMPORTANT TO CORRECT SUBJECT-VERB AGREEMENT PROBLEMS?

Like fragments and run-ons, errors in subject-verb agreement are widely considered to be one of the four most serious grammar errors. When people notice them, they form a negative impression of your writing ability. It is important that you learn to edit your writing for problems with subject-verb agreement.

SITUATION: Daigo Fujiwara, the assistant art director profiled in Chapter 10, communicates frequently with freelance artists and designers. The following email message from one designer caught his attention.

Today we talk about specs for the photographs. I has several possibilities that I be sending you by the end of the week.

RESPONSE: I had to reread this message a few times to make sure I understood. These kinds of mistakes make me stop, so it takes longer for me to process the message. On the one hand, I sympathize with the person because I also had to learn to write correct English. On the other hand, when my writing was really bad, I reread anything I wrote very carefully to make sure that it was right, and I think this person should have taken the time to do that.

Find and Correct Errors in Subject-Verb Agreement

To find problems with subject-verb agreement in your own writing, learn to look for five trouble spots that often signal errors in subject-verb agreement. The best way to find these errors is to read your writing carefully, looking specifically for these trouble spots.

TROUBLE SPOTS IN SUBJECT-VERB AGREEMENT

1. The verb is a form of *be, have,* or *do.*
2. Words or phrases come between the subject and the verb.
3. The sentence has a compound subject.
4. The subject is an indefinite pronoun.
5. The verb comes before the subject.

1. THE VERB IS A FORM OF *BE, HAVE,* OR *DO*

The verbs *be, have,* and *do* do not follow the regular patterns for forming singular and plural forms; they are **irregular verbs** (irregular because they do not conform to the regular patterns).

Forms of the Verb Be

PRESENT TENSE	SINGULAR	PLURAL
First person	I am	we are
Second person	you are	you are
Third person	she/he/it is	they are
	the student/Joe is	the students are
PAST TENSE		
First person	I was	we were
Second person	you were	you were
Third person	she/he/it was	they were
	the student/Joe was	the students were

TEACHING TIP
Remind students that correcting each of the four major grammar errors depends on being able to identify the subject and the verb in a sentence. As students work through each practice in this chapter, ask them to slow down a bit in order to find the subject and the verb first.

ESL
Have ESL students check their writing for examples of each of these trouble spots and ask them for their solutions. It may help to ask ESL students in conference the rules about subject-verb agreement in their native language.

Forms of the Verb Have, *Present Tense*

	SINGULAR	PLURAL
First person	I have	we have
Second person	you have	you have
Third person	she/he/it has	they have
	the student/Joe has	the students have

Forms of the Verb Do, *Present Tense*

	SINGULAR	PLURAL
First person	I do	we do
Second person	you do	you do
Third person	she/he/it does	they do
	the student/Joe does	the students do

These verbs are difficult for many writers because in casual conversation people sometimes use the same form of the verb, no matter what *person* the subject is in and no matter whether the subject is singular or plural. For example, in conversation, one friend might say to another:

He be the craziest person I've ever known.

Johnson have the best car in the lot.

Valery do the bill paying on the first of every month.

In college or professional situations, you need to use the correct form of the verbs *be, have,* and *do.* The verb must agree with the subject.

       is
He be the craziest person I've ever known.
   ^

         has
Johnson have the best car in the lot.
       ^

        does
Valery do the bill paying on the first of every month.
     ^

PRACTICE 1   CHOOSING THE CORRECT FORM OF *BE, HAVE,* OR *DO*

In each sentence, underline the subject of the verb *be, have,* or *do,* and circle the correct form of the verb.

> **EXAMPLE:** A <u>sport</u> (*has* / have) an important role in many children's lives.

1. <u>I</u> (*was* / were) involved in Little League during fifth and sixth grades.

2. My <u>parents</u> (was / *were*) happy to cheer at most of the games.

3. Now <u>I</u> (has / *have*) a Little Leaguer of my own, my daughter Tina.

4. <u>She</u> (am / *is* / are) not a natural athlete.

5. Still, the <u>games</u> (am / is / *are*) usually a lot of fun for her.

6. <u>She</u> (*does* / do) not see too many parents who can't control their tempers.

7. Once in a while, <u>incidents</u> (does / *do*) happen because of angry parents.

8. The local Little League <u>organization</u> (*has* / have) very strict rules about parents' interference.

9. <u>Children</u> (does / *do*) not need to see parents cursing at the opposing team or threatening the coaches.

10. Sports <u>teams</u> (am / is / *are*) supposed to be a way to learn about good sportsmanship, not an opportunity for parents to be terrible role models.

TEACHING TIP
Complete the following practices aloud together as a group. Have students discuss the differences they find in formal written and oral communication and informal conversational speech. How do students account for those differences?

For more practice, visit Exercise Central at <www.bedfordstmartins.com/realessays>.

PRACTICE 2   USING THE CORRECT FORM OF *BE, HAVE,* OR *DO*

In each sentence, underline the subject and fill in the correct form of the verb (*be, have,* or *do*) indicated in parentheses.

> **EXAMPLE:** Our <u>professor</u> *has* (*have*) forty papers to grade this weekend.

1. Most students ___are___ (be) used to the idea that computers sometimes grade tests.

2. You ___have___ (have) probably taken standardized tests and filled in small ovals with a pencil.

3. A computer ___does___ (do) not have to be sophisticated to read the results of a test like the SAT or ACT.

4. Surprisingly, a new software program ___is___ (be) designed to grade student essays.

5. The program ___has___ (have) the ability to sort words in an essay and compare the essay to others in its database.

6. The software ___does___ (do) not check grammar or spelling.

7. Teachers ___are___ (be) still needed to supplement the computer grade, according to the software manufacturer.

8. If a computer grades your essay, you ___have___ (have) to write about one of five hundred specified topics.

9. How ___does___ (do) a computer check the organization, clarity, and style of your writing?

10. Some teachers ___are___ (be) excited about their new computerized assistant, but I ___do___ (do) not like the idea of a computer grading my essays.

2. WORDS COME BETWEEN THE SUBJECT AND THE VERB

When the subject and the verb aren't right next to each other, it can be difficult to make sure that they agree. Most often, what comes between the subject and the verb is either a prepositional phrase or a dependent clause.

Prepositional Phrase between the Subject and Verb

DEFINITION: A **prepositional phrase** starts with a preposition and ends with a noun or pronoun: The line *for the movie* went *around the corner*.

For a list of common prepositions, see page 347.

Remember, the subject of a sentence is never in a prepositional phrase. When you are looking for the subject of a sentence, you can cross out any prepositional phrases. This strategy should help you find the real subject and decide whether it agrees with the verb.

PRACTICE 3   **MAKING SUBJECTS AND VERBS AGREE WHEN THEY ARE SEPARATED BY A PREPOSITIONAL PHRASE**

In each of the following sentences, first cross out the prepositional phrase between the subject and the verb, and then circle the correct form of the verb. Remember, the subject of a sentence is never in a prepositional phrase.

EXAMPLE: Twenty-eight million people ~~in the United States~~ (am / is / (are)) deaf or hard of hearing.

1. Ninety percent of parents ~~with hearing loss~~ (has / (have)) children who can hear.

2. Many ~~of these children~~ (learns / (learn)) sign language as a first language.

3. Communication ~~with words~~ ((comes) / come) later.

4. Few people ~~in the hearing world~~ (understands / (understand)) the lives of deaf people completely.

5. Many deaf people ~~in this country~~ (feels / (feel)) closer to deaf people from other parts of the world than to hearing Americans.

6. The hearing children ~~of deaf parents~~ (comes / (come)) closer to understanding deaf culture than most hearing people.

7. A hearing child ~~in a deaf household~~ ((resembles) / resemble) a child of immigrant parents in many ways.

8. Adapting ~~to two different cultures~~ ((makes) / make) fitting in difficult for some young people.

9. Sometimes ties ~~to the hearing world and the deaf world~~ (pulls / (pull)) in opposite directions.

10. Bridges ~~between cultures~~ (am / is / (are)) more easily built by people who understand both sides.

Dependent Clause between the Subject and the Verb

DEFINITION: A **dependent clause** has a subject and a verb, but it does not express a complete thought. When a dependent clause comes between the subject and the verb, it usually starts with the word *who, whose, whom, that,* or *which.*

The subject of a sentence is never in the dependent clause. When you are looking for the subject of a sentence, you can cross out any dependent clauses.

The FBI agent ~~who conducted the investigation~~ interviewed Rosa Martin.
subject   verb

The house ~~that slid off the cliff~~ was designed by a local architect.
subject   verb

PRACTICE 4 MAKING SUBJECTS AND VERBS AGREE WHEN THEY ARE SEPARATED BY A DEPENDENT CLAUSE

In each of the following sentences, cross out any dependent clauses. Then correct any problems with subject-verb agreement. If a sentence has no problem, write "OK" next to it.

                        is

    EXAMPLE: A person ~~who lies in job applications~~ **are** likely to get caught.

1. A résumé, ~~which is a job applicant's first contact with many prospective~~
   contains
   ~~employers,~~ ~~contain~~ details about past work experience and education.

2. Many people ~~who write résumés~~ are tempted to exaggerate. *OK*

                                               claims
3. Perhaps an applicant ~~who held a previous job for two months~~ ~~claim~~ to
   have spent a year there.

                         looks
4. A job title ~~that sounds impressive~~ ~~look~~ good on a résumé, whether or
   not it is accurate.

5. Often, a person ~~who never completed a college degree~~ wants to add it to
   a résumé anyway. *OK*

                                     needs
6. A person ~~who is considering untrue résumé additions~~ ~~need~~ to think
   twice.

                       check
7. Employers ~~who like a résumé~~ ~~checks~~ the information provided by the
   applicant.

8. A résumé ~~that contains false information~~ goes in the reject pile. *OK*

                             forget
9. In addition, many people ~~who invent material on a résumé~~ ~~forgets~~ the
   inventions when they face a prospective employer in an interview.

10. Even a company ~~that does not check all of the information on résumés~~
    pays attention when interviewees seem to forget some of their quali-
    fications. *OK*

3. THE SENTENCE HAS A COMPOUND SUBJECT

DEFINITION: A **compound subject** consists of two (or more) subjects joined by *and, or,* or *nor.*

If two subjects are joined by *and,* they combine to become a plural subject, and the verb must take a plural form as well.

subject *and* subject plural form of verb

The director and the producer decide how the film will be made.

If two subjects are separated by the word *or* or *nor,* they are not combined, and the verb should agree with whatever subject is closer to it.

subject *or* singular subject singular form of verb

The director or the producer decides how the film will be made.

subject *or* plural subject plural form of verb

The director or his assistants decide how the film will be made.

PRACTICE 5 CHOOSING THE CORRECT VERB IN A SENTENCE WITH A COMPOUND SUBJECT

In each of the following sentences, underline the word (*and, or,* or *nor*) that joins the parts of the compound subject. Then circle the correct form of the verb.

EXAMPLE: A child and an adult (has / have) different nutritional needs.

1. Fruits and vegetables (does / do) not make up enough of most Americans' diets.

2. The U.S. Food and Drug Administration and other government organizations (recommends / recommend) that people eat at least five servings of fruits and vegetables a day.

3. Whole-grain cereal or bread (is / are) another important part of a healthy diet.

4. Neither vitamins nor fiber (is / are) found in many popular snack foods.

5. Potato chips and candy (contains / contain) few useful nutrients.

6. Neither fat nor sugar (helps / help) build a healthy body.

7. However, in small amounts, fat and sugar (contributes / contribute) beneficially by making food taste good.

8. Only motivated dieters and certain health fanatics (eats / eat) nutritious food that tastes terrible.

9. Neither dieters nor health fanatics (is / are) likely to keep eating the unappetizing food for a lifetime.

10. Choosing nutritious food and preparing it well (allows / allow) a person to feel healthy and satisfied.

4. THE SUBJECT IS AN INDEFINITE PRONOUN

DEFINITION: An **indefinite pronoun** does not replace the name of a specific person, place, or thing. It is a general word. Most indefinite pronouns are either always singular or always plural.

Indefinite Pronouns

ALWAYS SINGULAR			ALWAYS PLURAL
another	everyone	nothing	both
anybody	everything	one (of)	few
anything	much	somebody	many
each (of)*	neither (of)*	someone	several
either (of)*	nobody	something	
everybody	no one		

*When one of these words is the subject, mentally replace it with the word *one*. *One* is singular and must have the singular form of the verb to agree with it.

SINGULAR	Everyone loves vacations.
PLURAL	Many prefer beach vacations.
SINGULAR	Either of the vacation locations is fine with me.

Often an indefinite pronoun is followed by a prepositional phrase or a dependent clause; remember that the subject of a sentence is never found in either of these. To choose the correct verb, you can cross out the prepositional phrase or dependent clause to focus on the indefinite pronoun.

Much ~~of a mechanic's work~~ requires precision.

Few ~~of the people in the building~~ favor the rent increase.

Several ~~who are longtime~~ residents recommend a rent strike.

PRACTICE 6   CHOOSING THE CORRECT VERB WHEN THE SUBJECT IS AN INDEFINITE PRONOUN

In each of the following sentences, cross out any prepositional phrases or dependent clauses that come between the subject and the verb. Then underline the subject, and circle the correct verb.

EXAMPLE: One ~~of the best things about the Internet~~ (is / are) the way people can use it to get information from around the world.

1. Anyone ~~who wants to take college courses~~ (needs / need) access to a college campus.

2. Today, nobody ~~with a computer and Internet access~~ (lives / live) too far from a college to get a degree.

3. Several ~~of the hundreds of accredited colleges in the United States~~ (offers / offer) online degree programs.

4. Everything ~~that students need to pass the course~~ (is / are) available online.

5. Everyone ~~who takes online courses~~ (has / have) to participate in email discussions and write papers.

6. No one ~~in an online class~~ (gets / get) to sit silently in the back of the room.

7. Someone ~~who learns best by listening~~ (is / are) probably not a good candidate for an online college course.

8. Some students learn well by reading or by working independently; either ~~of these types~~ (has / have) a good chance to pass an online course.

9. Anybody ~~who is considering an online class~~ (needs / need) to work well without supervision.

10. Some ~~of the people in online college classes~~ (expects / expect) to earn a degree without ever visiting the campus.

5. THE VERB COMES BEFORE THE SUBJECT

In most sentences, the subject comes before the verb. Two kinds of sentences reverse that order: questions, and sentences that begin with *here* or *there*. In these two types of sentences, you need to check carefully for errors in subject-verb agreement.

Questions

In questions, the verb or part of the verb comes before the subject. To find the subject and verb, you can turn the question around as if you were going to answer it.

Where is the nearest gas station? The nearest gas station is . . .

Are the keys in the car? The keys are in the car.

Sentences That Begin with Here or There

When a sentence begins with *here* or *there,* the subject always follows the verb. Turn the sentence around to find the subject and verb.

Here are the hot dog rolls. The hot dog rolls are here.

There is a fly in my soup. The fly is in my soup.

■ PRACTICE 7 **CORRECTING A SENTENCE WHEN THE VERB COMES BEFORE THE SUBJECT**

Correct any problems with subject-verb agreement in the following sentences. If a sentence is already correct, write "OK" next to it.

         are
EXAMPLE: There is several openings for bilingual applicants.

    are
1. Where is the corporation's main offices located?

    are
2. There is branch offices in Paris, Singapore, and Tokyo.

     does
3. How well do the average employee abroad speak English?

    does
4. What do the company manufacture?

       is
5. How many languages are the manual written in?

6. Does the company employ college graduates as translators?   *OK*

    are
7. There is some machines that can do translation.

8. Does learning a second language give an applicant a special advantage?
OK

9. There is never a disadvantage in knowing another language.   *OK*

     are
10. Here is the names of several qualified people.

Edit Paragraphs and Your Own Writing

As you edit paragraphs and your own writing, use the Thinking Critically guide that follows. You may also want to refer to the Quick Review Chart on page 404.

> **THINKING CRITICALLY TO EDIT FOR SUBJECT-VERB AGREEMENT**
>
> FOCUS   Whenever you see one of the five trouble spots in your writing, stop to check that the subject and the verb agree.
>
> ASK   • Where is the subject in this sentence? Where is the verb?
>   • Do the subject and verb agree in number? (Are they both singular or both plural?)
>
> EDIT   If you answer "no" to the agreement question, you need to correct the sentence.

PRACTICE 8   EDITING PARAGRAPHS FOR SUBJECT-VERB AGREEMENT

Find and correct any problems with subject-verb agreement in the following paragraphs. You may want to refer to the preceding Thinking Critically Guide or the Quick Review Chart on page 404.

1. (1) School systems around the country ~~is~~ *are* embracing educational standards. (2) The idea of standards ~~sound~~ *sounds* reasonable. (3) Does anyone want to argue that students should not have to meet certain requirements to graduate? (4) A national standard for all American students ~~have~~ *has* many supporters, too. (5) If the requirements for graduation in Oregon and Tennessee ~~is~~ *are* the same, everyone with a high school diploma gets a similar education. (6) There is a catch, of course. (7) Not everyone with a professional or personal interest in school quality is able to agree on these requirements. (8) Mathematics and writing ~~is~~ *are* important, but so ~~is~~ *are* music and physical education. (9) How ~~is~~ *are* parents, teachers, and administrators ever going to find standards that everyone accepts?

2. (1) Agreeing on school standards ~~are~~ *is* only part of the battle over education. (2) How ~~is~~ *are* students going to prove that they have met the

standards before graduation? (3) The answer, in many cases, ~~are~~ *is* testing.
(4) School tests that are required by state law ~~is~~ *are* becoming more and more
common. (5) These tests are standardized, so all of the students taking an
eighth-grade test in a particular state ~~is~~ *are* given the same test. (6) Both the
individual student and his or her school district ~~is~~ *are* evaluated by the scores.
(7) The parents of a student ~~learns~~ *learn* not only what their child's score is but
also how the school compares to others around the state. (8) Then children who need extra help ~~is~~ *are* supposed to receive it, and schools with very
low scores year after year ~~becomes~~ *become* eligible for additional resources.

3.   (1) In reality, standardized tests for schools have many problems.
(2) Most school districts that have a testing program ~~uses~~ *use* tests that can
be scored by a computer. (3) Computers cannot read, so the tests that
they grade usually ~~offers~~ *offer* multiple-choice questions. (4) A multiple-choice
test in science or mathematics ~~do~~ *does* not allow students to demonstrate critical thinking. (5) How ~~does~~ *do* students show their writing ability on such a
test? (6) There ~~is~~ *are* tricks to answering multiple-choice questions that many
students learn. (7) Frequently, a high score on such a test says more about
the student's test-taking ability than about his or her knowledge of a subject. (8) Nevertheless, the quick results and low cost of a multiple-choice
computer-graded test ~~means~~ *mean* that this imperfect testing system is used in
many school systems.

4.   (1) Another problem with standardized tests ~~are~~ *is* that test material can
begin to change the curriculum. (2) Everyone who teaches wants his or
her students to get high scores on the tests. (3) For one thing, a teacher
of underperforming students ~~are~~ *is* likely to be criticized for not preparing
them better. (4) One result of teachers' fears ~~are~~ *is* that they spend most of

the class time preparing students for the test. (5) In some cases, the

phenomenon of "teaching to the test" ~~become~~ *becomes* school policy. (6) A creative

teacher or one who has been teaching for years ~~are~~ *is* no longer trusted to

engage students with a subject. (7) School officials, who also want high

scores for their districts, encourage teachers to focus on material that the

test will cover. (8) Other material, which may be fascinating to students,

~~are~~ *is* ignored because the test does not require it.

5. (1) Many parents who send their children to public school ~~fears~~ *fear* that

the schools are not teaching the students adequately. (2) As these fears

increase, the number of states that require tests ~~rise~~ *rises* as well. (3) But there

~~has~~ *have* been some teachers and parents willing to resist standardized testing.

(4) A few parents ~~has~~ *have* kept their children home on test days. (5) In rare

cases, teachers who oppose testing ~~has~~ *have* refused to administer standardized

tests to their students. (6) In the places that require students to pass tests

in order to graduate, rebellion against tests ~~have~~ *has* serious consequences for

the student. (7) Elsewhere, however, a parent or student has the option to

refuse. (8) People who believe that standardized testing is not the answer

~~is~~ *are* still trying to change this growing national trend.

    **PRACTICE 9   EDITING YOUR OWN WRITING FOR
SUBJECT-VERB AGREEMENT**

As a final practice, carefully read a piece of your own writing—a paper
you are working on for this class, a paper you've already finished, a paper
for another course, or a recent piece of writing from your work or everyday life. For extra help in making your subjects and verbs agree, use the
Thinking Critically guide on page 401 and the Quick Review Chart that
follows.

TEAMWORK
Invite students to make
several copies of one
page from a rough
draft. Then divide
the class into small
groups, and have
each small group
work together on
sentence structure,
focusing on subject-
verb agreement.

Quick Review Chart

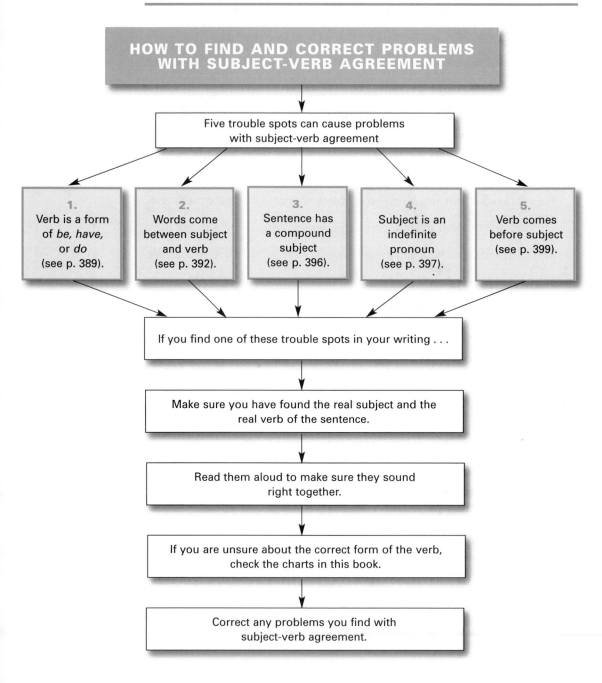

HOW TO FIND AND CORRECT PROBLEMS WITH SUBJECT-VERB AGREEMENT

Five trouble spots can cause problems with subject-verb agreement

1.
Verb is a form of *be, have,* or *do*
(see p. 389).

2.
Words come between subject and verb
(see p. 392).

3.
Sentence has a compound subject
(see p. 396).

4.
Subject is an indefinite pronoun
(see p. 397).

5.
Verb comes before subject
(see p. 399).

If you find one of these trouble spots in your writing . . .

Make sure you have found the real subject and the real verb of the sentence.

Read them aloud to make sure they sound right together.

If you are unsure about the correct form of the verb, check the charts in this book.

Correct any problems you find with subject-verb agreement.

26

Verb Problems

Mistakes in Verb Form and Verb Tense

Ever Thought This?
"The word 'tense' makes me tense. I don't understand all the terms."
—Ken Hargreaves, student

This chapter:
* explains what *verb forms* and *verb tenses* are.
* explains the present and past tenses of verbs.
* gives you a list of irregular verbs.
* gives you practice finding and correcting errors in verb form and tense.

Understand What Verb Form and Verb Tense Are

DEFINITION: **Verb forms** are the different ways a verb can be spelled and pronounced. For example, here are three different forms of the same verb:

> talk   talks   talked

DEFINITION: **Verb tense** indicates *when* the action of a sentence occurred: in the present, in the past, or in the future. Verbs change their form and use helping verbs to indicate different tenses.

> **PRESENT TENSE**   I worry about my mother's health.
>
> **PAST TENSE**   She worried about me when I was a child.
>
> **FUTURE TENSE**   We will worry about each other forever, I guess.

To choose the correct form when you are writing, you need to use the singular or plural form of the verb that agrees with the subject of the sentence. You also need to select the form that shows the time of the action—past, present, and so on.

> I talk to my mother every day.
>
> She talks about the past a lot.
>
> I talked to her this morning and will talk to her tomorrow.

ESL
Many nonnative speakers will use the present tense only, avoiding any other verb forms. Discuss this tendency with students.

For more on subject-verb agreement, see Chapter 25.

In the examples throughout this chapter, the subject is underlined and the verb is underlined twice.

405

IN THE REAL WORLD, WHY IS IT IMPORTANT TO USE CORRECT VERBS?

Using the wrong form of the verb is a mistake that people notice and tend to take seriously. Using incorrect forms may create a negative impression of you as a student or prospective employee. Learning to find and correct errors with verb forms or, better, learning to avoid them in your own writing is worth the effort.

SITUATION: A college student submits an essay to a contest hoping the piece will be published in the school's literary magazine and that she will win the $100 prize. Here is the beginning of the student's essay:

> I had just beginned to work when I heared a loud explosion that came from inside the building. That was the start of a night that I will not forgot.

RESPONSE: One of the judges, a professional journalist, said this to his fellow judges: "I read exactly two lines, not even enough to really get an idea of what the essay was about. Clearly, the person is a poor writer, and I just couldn't bear the idea of having to read the whole piece: It isn't worth my time."

Find and Correct Verb Problems

English verbs can be complicated. You can learn some general rules about them, but some verb forms must simply be practiced until they are memorized and you don't even have to think about them. The best way to learn the correct forms is to read, write, and speak them as often as possible.

1. REGULAR VERBS

DEFINITION: Most verbs in English are **regular verbs**—they follow a few basic, standard patterns.

Two Present-Tense Forms for Regular Verbs: -s *Ending and No Added Ending*

DEFINITION: The **present tense** is used for actions that are ongoing or that are happening at the same time that you are writing about them.

There are two forms for the present tense of regular verbs: -*s* ending or no added ending. Use the -*s* ending when the subject is *he, she,* or *it,* or the name of one person or thing. Do not add any ending for other subjects.

In the chart on page 407, note that only *she, he, it,* and *baby* (the name of one person or thing) have verbs with an -*s* ending. All the rest (*I, we, you, they,* and *babies*) have verbs with no added ending.

Regular Verb Forms in the Present Tense

	SINGULAR	PLURAL
First person	I laugh.	We laugh.
Second person	You laugh.	You laugh.
Third person	She/he/it laugh**s**.	They laugh.
	The baby laugh**s**.	The babies laugh.

PRACTICE 1   **USING THE CORRECT FORM FOR REGULAR VERBS IN THE PRESENT TENSE**

In each of the following sentences, first underline the subject, and then circle the correct verb form.

For more practice, visit Exercise Central at <www.bedfordstmartins.com/realessays>.

EXAMPLE: My son (attends / attend) day care while I am at work.

1. I (enjoys / enjoy) both working and spending time with my four-year-old.

2. My mother (watches / watch) my little boy when I go to school at night.

3. During the day, I (works / work) in the billing department of our local hospital.

4. My son (passes / pass) the time at the hospital's day-care center.

5. He (loves / love) the activities and the other children there.

6. The children (plays / play) games every morning.

7. They (uses / use) crayons, chalk, and paint during their art period.

8. I (misses / miss) him when I'm working.

9. However, the hospital (allows / allow) me to eat lunch in the day-care center with him.

10. The arrangement (enables / enable) my son and me to enjoy some family time during the day.

One Past-Tense Form for Regular Verbs: -ed *Ending*

DEFINITION: The **past tense** is used for actions that have already happened. An *-ed* ending is needed for all regular verbs in the past tense.

	PRESENT TENSE	PAST TENSE
First person	I rush to work.	I rush**ed** to work.
Second person	You lock the door.	You lock**ed** the door.
Third person	Rufus seems strange.	Rufus seem**ed** strange.

ESL
Ask ESL students to think about whether there are standard rules for forming the past tense in their first language. List some of the rules on the board. Then have students make a chart with the past-tense rules from their first language and the past-tense rules in English. This might help them as they edit their essays in English.

PRACTICE 2   **USING THE CORRECT FORM FOR REGULAR VERBS IN THE PAST TENSE**

In each of the following sentences, fill in the correct past-tense form of the verb in parentheses.

EXAMPLE: Between 1830 and 1860, about fifty thousand people
     escaped (*escape*) from slavery in the United States.

(1) Before the Civil War, many African Americans _faced_ (*face*) lives as unwilling, unpaid slaves on American farms and plantations. (2) When northern states _abolished_ (*abolish*) slavery, many southern slaves _tried_ (*try*) to escape to freedom in the North. (3) The journey _covered_ (*cover*) hundreds of miles, and anyone who _wanted_ (*want*) to make the trip _realized_ (*realize*) that it _involved_ (*involve*) terrible danger. (4) Both enslaved and free Americans _worked_ (*work*) to find safe hiding places for escaping slaves along a path leading to the free states of the North. (5) The people aware of this path _called_ (*call*) it the Underground Railroad.

TEACHING TIP
Have students write a paragraph about something annoying they experienced in the past week. Ask each student to write one sentence from their paragraph on the board. As a class, edit for correct past-tense verb forms.

(6) Many slaves in the South _helped_ (*help*) others to escape; they _provided_ (*provide*) fugitive slaves with shelter, food, and clothing whenever they could. (7) Escaping slaves also _needed_ (*need*) information about the route and guides to lead the way. (8) One fugitive, Harriet Tubman, repeatedly _returned_ (*return*) to the South to lead more than three hundred slaves to freedom. (9) Slaveholders _offered_ (*offer*) a

reward of $40,000 for her capture, but they ___*failed*___ (*fail*) to find her.
(10) In addition to Tubman and other African Americans, some white
Americans, especially Quakers, who ___*believed*___ (*believe*) that slavery was
evil, ___*assisted*___ (*assist*) the fugitives. (11) Before the Civil War finally
___*freed*___ (*free*) the slaves, the Underground Railroad ___*carried*___
(*carry*) thousands of them north to freedom.

One Regular Past Participle: -ed Ending

DEFINITION: The **past participle** is a verb form that can be used with helping verbs, such as *have*. For all regular verbs, the past-participle form is the
same as the past-tense form: It needs an *-ed* ending.

PAST-TENSE FORM	PAST-PARTICIPLE FORM
My brother and I argu**ed**.	We have argued before.
Karen help**ed** me.	She has helped often.

■   **PRACTICE 3   USING THE CORRECT FORM FOR THE PAST
PARTICIPLES OF REGULAR VERBS**

In each of the following sentences, underline the helping verb (a form of
have), and fill in the correct form of the verb in parentheses.

EXAMPLE: My father has *served* (*serve*) in the army for twenty years.

1. My father's military career has ___*forced*___ (*force*) our family to move
   many times.

2. We have ___*lived*___ (*live*) in seven towns that I remember.

3. I had ___*attended*___ (*attend*) three different high schools before I turned
   seventeen.

4. None of the towns have ever really ___*seemed*___ (*seem*) like home.

5. I have never ___*objected*___ (*object*) to my family's traveling life.

6. None of us has ever ___*expected*___ (*expect*) to stay in one place for long.

7. My closest friends have all ___traveled___ (*travel*) a lot, too.

8. One of them has ___visited___ (*visit*) Egypt, Australia, Turkey, Pakistan, and seventeen other countries.

9. She had once ___hoped___ (*hope*) for a career as a travel agent.

10. Now, however, she has ___decided___ (*decide*) to accept a position with a large international corporation that will allow her to travel.

2. IRREGULAR VERBS

DEFINITION: Irregular verbs do not follow the regular patterns for verb endings (the ones that you have just practiced in this chapter). Instead, they may change spelling as the chart on pages 410–12 shows.

Irregular Verb Forms

PRESENT-TENSE FORM	PAST-TENSE FORM	PAST PARTICIPLE
am/are/is	was/were	been
become	became	become
begin	began	begun
bite	bit	bitten
blow	blew	blown
break	broke	broken
bring	brought	brought
build	built	built
buy	bought	bought
catch	caught	caught
choose	chose	chosen
come	came	come
cost	cost	cost
do	did	done
draw	drew	drawn
drink	drank	drunk
drive	drove	driven

PRESENT-TENSE FORM	PAST-TENSE FORM	PAST PARTICIPLE
eat	ate	eaten
fall	fell	fallen
feed	fed	fed
feel	felt	felt
fight	fought	fought
find	found	found
forget	forgot	forgotten
get	got	gotten
give	gave	given
go	went	gone
grow	grew	grown
have/has	had	had
hide	hid	hidden
hit	hit	hit
hold	held	held
hurt	hurt	hurt
keep	kept	kept
know	knew	known
lay	laid	laid
leave	left	left
let	let	let
lie	lay	lain
light	lit	lit
lose	lost	lost
make	made	made
mean	meant	meant
meet	met	met
pay	paid	paid
put	put	put
quit	quit	quit
read	read	read
ride	rode	ridden

(continued)

Irregular Verb Forms (continued)

PRESENT-TENSE FORM	PAST-TENSE FORM	PAST PARTICIPLE
run	ran	run
say	said	said
see	saw	seen
sell	sold	sold
send	sent	sent
show	showed	shown
shut	shut	shut
sing	sang	sung
sink	sank	sunk
sit	sat	sat
sleep	slept	slept
speak	spoke	spoken
spend	spent	spent
stand	stood	stood
steal	stole	stolen
stick	stuck	stuck
sting	stung	stung
swim	swam	swum
take	took	taken
teach	taught	taught
tear	tore	torn
tell	told	told
think	thought	thought
throw	threw	thrown
understand	understood	understood
wake	woke	woken
wear	wore	worn
win	won	won
write	wrote	written

Irregular Present-Tense Forms

Only a few verbs are irregular in the present tense. The ones most commonly used are the verbs *be* and *have*.

Present-Tense Forms for Two Irregular Verbs

	BE		HAVE	
First person	I am	we are	I have	we have
Second person	you are	you are	you have	you have
Third person	he/she/it is	they are	he/she/ it has	they have
	the dog is	the dogs are	the dog has	the dogs have
	Chris is	Chris and Dan are	Chris has	Chris and Dan have

> **PRACTICE 4   USING THE CORRECT FORMS FOR *BE* AND *HAVE* IN THE PRESENT TENSE**

In each of the following sentences, fill in the correct form of the verb indicated in parentheses.

EXAMPLE: Disc golf __*is*__ (*be*) a game played with Frisbees.

1. I __*am*__ (*be*) a fanatical disc golfer.

2. The game __*has*__ (*have*) eighteen holes, like regular golf, but uses a Frisbee instead of a ball.

3. A disc golf course __*has*__ (*have*) fairways and holes.

4. A tee __*is*__ (*be*) at the beginning of each fairway.

5. Players __*are*__ (*be*) eager to get the Frisbee from the tee into a metal basket in the fewest possible throws.

6. Some disc golfers __*have*__ (*have*) special Frisbees for teeing off and putting.

7. My brother, who also plays disc golf, __*has*__ (*have*) thirty different Frisbees for the game.

8. His wife _____*is*_____ (*be*) surprisingly patient with his enthusiasm for the sport.

9. "You _____*are*_____ (*be*) in the middle of a second adolescence," she tells him.

10. However, she, too, _____*has*_____ (*have*) formidable Frisbee technique.

Irregular Past-Tense Forms

Irregular verbs do not use the *-ed* ending for the past tense.

PRESENT-TENSE FORM	PAST-TENSE FORM
Tony makes hats.	Tony made hats.
You write well.	You wrote well.
I ride a bike.	I rode a bike.

The verb *be* is tricky because it has two different forms for the past tense: *was* and *were*.

There is no simple rule for forming irregular verbs in the past tense. Until you know them well, you will need to consult the chart on pages 410–12.

The Verb Be, *Past Tense*

	SINGULAR	PLURAL
First person	I was	we were
Second person	you were	you were
Third person	she/he/it was	they were
	the car was	the cars were
	Jolanda was	Jolanda and Ti were

PRACTICE 5   **USING THE CORRECT PAST-TENSE FORM OF THE VERB *BE***

In the paragraph that follows, fill in each blank with the correct past-tense form of the verb *be*.

EXAMPLE: Your father and I __were__ struggling to make ends meet.

(1) Before you ___were___ born, your father and I ___were___ very worried. (2) He ___was___ still in school at the time. (3) I ___was___ a part-time waitress, so we ___were___ not exactly rich in those days. (4) Having a baby ___was___ a big step for us. (5) My mother ___was___ thrilled that she would be a grandmother, but she ___was___ not even in the same state. (6) Your other grandparents ___were___ no longer living. (7) I ___was___ terrified that we would not be able to take good care of you. (8) But when you ___were___ born, your father's friends and my coworkers ___were___ an amazing support system. (9) They ___were___ all as much in love with you as we ___were___ . (10) You ___were___ the most beautiful thing that any of us had ever seen.

PRACTICE 6   **USING THE CORRECT FORM FOR IRREGULAR VERBS IN THE PAST TENSE**

In each of the following sentences, fill in the correct past-tense form of the irregular verb in parentheses. If you do not know the answer, find the word in the chart of irregular verb forms on pages 410–12.

EXAMPLE: The *Titanic* __set__ (*set*) out from England in 1912.

1. The White Star Line ___built___ (*build*) the *Titanic,* which was the biggest moving object in the world at that time.

2. The huge ship ___held___ (*hold*) over 2,200 passengers on its maiden voyage.

3. Twenty lifeboats, which could hold 1,178 people altogether, ___hung___ (*hang*) from the upper deck of the *Titanic*.

4. The shipbuilders ___felt___ (*feel*) that the giant liner was the safest ship in the world and that more lifeboats were simply unnecessary.

5. On April 14, 1912, during its first trip across the Atlantic, the *Titanic*

   ___*struck*___ (*strike*) an iceberg.

6. The sharp ice ___*tore*___ (*tear*) a gaping hole in the bottom of the ship.

7. Icy ocean water ___*began*___ (*begin*) to pour into the hold, dragging the

   Titanic down in the water.

8. Few passengers ___*understood*___ (*understand*) the danger at first.

9. Half-empty lifeboats ___*left*___ (*leave*) the sinking ship while other

   passengers ___*stood*___ (*stand*) on deck, refusing to depart.

10. Hundreds of people ___*froze*___ (*freeze*) to death in the ocean before the

    nearest ship ___*came*___ (*come*) to rescue the *Titanic*'s 705 survivors.

PRACTICE 7   USING THE CORRECT FORM FOR PAST-TENSE IRREGULAR VERBS

In the following paragraph, replace any incorrect present-tense verb forms with the correct past-tense form of the verb. If you do not know the answer, look up the verbs in the chart of irregular verb forms on pages 410–12.

> **EXAMPLE:** Dewayne faced a judge and jury of his fellow high school
>   *hit*
> students after he ~~hits~~ a boy in the classroom.
>   ^

                                  set
(1) Two years ago, my high school ~~sets~~ up a student court to give students
                  ^

a voice in disciplining rule breakers. (2) Before the court opened its doors,
       taught
adults ~~teach~~ students about decision making and about courtroom pro-
    ^
                                        became
cedures. (3) Some of us served as members of juries, and others ~~become~~
                                sat   ^
advocates or even judges. (4) I ~~sit~~ on a jury twice when I was a junior.
                       ^

(5) Then, last spring, my friend Dewayne appeared before the student
         lost   *struck*
court after he ~~loses~~ his temper and ~~strikes~~ a fellow student. (6) I agreed to
        ^   ^

thought
be his advocate because I ~~think~~ he truly regretted his behavior. (7) I
told
~~tell~~ the jury that he knew his violent reaction was a mistake. (8) The jury
sent
~~sends~~ Dewayne for counseling to learn to manage his anger and made him

write an apology to the other student. (9) After hearing the verdict,
shook
Dewayne ~~shakes~~ hands with all the jurors and thanked them for their fair-
made
ness. (10) The experience ~~makes~~ me eager to learn more about America's

system of justice.

Irregular Past Participles

DEFINITION: For regular verbs, the **past-participle form** (used with helping verbs such as *have*) is the same as the past-tense form; they both use
the *-ed* ending. For irregular verbs, the past-participle form may be different from the past-tense form.

	PAST-TENSE FORM	PAST-PARTICIPLE FORM
REGULAR VERB	Danielle smiled.	Danielle has smiled.
IRREGULAR VERB	Lara drove fast.	Lara has driven fast.

Until you know the right form for a verb, check the chart of irregular
verb forms on pages 410–12.

PRACTICE 8   USING CORRECT PAST-PARTICIPLE FORMS FOR IRREGULAR VERBS

In each of the following sentences, underline the helping verb (a form of
have) and fill in the correct past-participle form of the verb in parentheses. If you do not know the correct form, find the word in the chart on
pages 410–12.

> **EXAMPLE**: Hector has ___*found*___ (*find*) that a dot-com career has ups
> and downs.

1. By the time Hector graduated from college in 1998, he had ___*taken*___

   (*take*) dozens of hours of computer courses.

2. He had ___chosen___ (*choose*) a career in programming.

3. Before getting his diploma, Hector had ___begun___ (*begin*) to work for an Internet service provider.

4. By the end of the summer, a rival online service had ___stolen___ (*steal*) Hector away from his employer.

5. His new bosses had ___been___ (*be*) in business for only a few months.

6. After a year, the company still had never ___made___ (*make*) a profit.

7. However, hundreds of investors had ___bought___ (*buy*) shares of the company's stock.

8. By early 2000, the stock's prices had ___grown___ (*grow*) to more than fifty times their original worth.

9. Hector often wishes that he had ___sold___ (*sell*) his shares then and retired a rich man.

10. Instead, the company went bankrupt, and Hector has ___gone___ (*go*) to work for an old-fashioned but secure banking firm.

3. USING PAST PARTICIPLES

A **past participle**, by itself, cannot be the main verb of a sentence. But when it is combined with another verb, called a **helping verb**, it can be used to make the **present perfect tense**, the **past perfect tense**, and the **passive voice**.

Have/Has + Past Participle = Present Perfect Tense

DEFINITION: The **present perfect tense** of a verb is used for an action begun in the past that is ongoing into the present or that was completed at some unspecified time in the past.

PAST TENSE   My car stalled .

[The car stalled at some point in the past but does not stall now, in the present.]

helping verb   past participle

PRESENT PERFECT TENSE   My car has stalled often.

[The car began to stall in the past but may continue to do so into the present.]

PRACTICE 9   USING THE PRESENT PERFECT TENSE

In each of the following sentences, circle the correct verb form.

EXAMPLE: Dishonest people (found / have found) new ways to cheat since the Internet became widely available.

1. As long as there have been grades, some students (were / have been) willing to cheat.

2. For the past ten years, the Internet (made / has made) all kinds of resources available to students.

3. By now, many students (found / have found) that term papers are available online.

4. Some of the sites that help students cheat (operated / have operated) for years.

5. Cheating is so easy now that teachers are at a disadvantage, but some (began / have begun) to fight back.

6. Two years ago, a professor at the University of Virginia (created / has created) a program to check student papers for plagiarism.

7. In the spring of 2001, he (discovered / has discovered) dozens of plagiarized papers.

8. Since it was founded in the eighteenth century, the University of Virginia (made / has made) students agree to obey a strict honor code.

9. For more than two hundred years, University of Virginia students caught cheating (faced / have faced) expulsion; in the case of graduates, diplomas (were / have been) revoked.

10. Cheating (got / (has gotten)) easier with Internet availability, but students

who believe that cheating is risk-free are fooling themselves.

Had + *Past Participle* = *Past Perfect Tense*

DEFINITION: The **past perfect tense** is used for an action that was begun in the past but completed before some other past action took place. Use *had* (the past-tense form of *have*) plus the past participle to make the past perfect tense.

past tense of helping verb   past participle

PAST PERFECT TENSE   My head had ached for a week before I called a doctor.

[Both of the actions (head ached and I called) happened in the past, but the ache happened before the calling.]

Neither the past tense nor the present perfect tense uses *had*.

PAST TENSE   My head ached.

PRESENT PERFECT TENSE   My head has ached often.

PRACTICE 10   USING THE PAST PERFECT TENSE

In each of the following sentences, circle the correct verb form.

EXAMPLE: By the time I reached home, rolling blackouts (darkened / (had darkened)) the city.

1. The temperature was unseasonably hot when I ((got) / had gotten) out of

bed that morning.

2. By noon, the air conditioners at the office (were running /

(had been running)) at high power for three hours.

3. My boss told me that she (heard / (had heard)) that energy use that day

was skyrocketing.

4. I ((asked) / had asked) how we could conserve energy.

5. I mentioned that I (just learned / (had just learned)) that some household

and office machines use power even when they are turned off.

6. My boss (read /(had read) the same information, so we unplugged

   computers in the office that were not in use.

7. We also (raised)/ had raised) the office temperature from sixty-eight

   degrees to seventy-two, and then we turned off some of the lights.

8. We (did /(had done)) everything we could think of to save energy, but it

   was not enough.

9. We knew that the city (warned /(had warned)) residents that rolling

   blackouts were possible.

10. However, when the office ((suddenly darkened)/ had suddenly darkened),

    everyone was stunned.

Be + *Past Participle* = *Passive Voice*

DEFINITION: A sentence that is written in the **passive voice** has a subject that performs no action. Instead, the subject is acted upon. To create the passive voice, combine a form of the verb *be* with a past participle.

helping verb   past participle

PASSIVE   The memo was written by an employee.

[The subject, *memo*, did not write itself. An employee wrote the memo, but the subject in the sentence, *memo*, performs no action.]

DEFINITION: In sentences that use the **active voice**, the subject performs the action.

ACTIVE   An employee wrote the memo.

Use the passive voice when no one person performed the action, when you don't know who performed the action, or when you want to emphasize the receiver of the action. Use active voice whenever possible, and use passive voice sparingly.

PASSIVE   The dog was hit by a passing car.

[If the writer wants to focus on the dog as the receiver of the action, the passive voice is acceptable.]

ACTIVE   A passing car hit the dog.

TEACHING TIP
Encourage students to identify the nouns in a passive-voice sentence. Remind them that they usually can revise the sentence by exchanging the noun that comes before the verb and the noun that comes after the verb. They will also need to change the form of the verb when they change passive voice to active.

■ **PRACTICE 11   CHANGING FROM PASSIVE VOICE TO ACTIVE VOICE**

Rewrite the following sentences in the active voice.

Answers may vary. Possible edits shown.

EXAMPLE: *Someone stole my*
My umbrella was stolen.

The Senate denied
1. Robert Bork's nomination to the Supreme Court was denied by the Senate.

Someone was playing annoyingly
2. Annoyingly loud music was being played in the apartment downstairs.

Genzyme, Inc., is laying off eighty
3. Eighty employees are being laid off by Genzyme, Inc.

Your joke hurt my
4. My feelings were hurt by your joke.

I mailed the
5. The check was mailed by me last Tuesday.

4.   CONSISTENCY OF VERB TENSE

DEFINITION: **Consistency of tense** means that all the verbs in your sentence that are happening (or happened) at the same time are in the same tense. If all of the actions happen in the present, use the present tense for all verbs in the sentence. If all of the actions happened in the past, use the past tense for all verbs in the sentence.

	past tense present tense
INCONSISTENT TENSE	The bell chimed just as I am running up the stairs.
CONSISTENT PRESENT TENSE	The bell chimes just as I am running up the stairs.
CONSISTENT PAST TENSE	The bell chimed just as I was running up the stairs.

■ PRACTICE 12   **USING CONSISTENT TENSE**

In each of the following items, double-underline the verbs in the sentence, and correct any unnecessary shift in verb tense. Write the correct form of any incorrect verb in the blank space provided.

EXAMPLE: __become__ As suburban sprawl increases, downtown areas and urban centers ~~became~~ emptier.

1. __want__ Americans love their cars because they ~~wanted~~ independence and convenience.

2. __buy__ As people ~~bought~~ more and more cars, the traffic in cities and downtown areas seems to get worse every day.

3. __counts__ A strip mall on the edge of town is rarely beautiful, but convenience ~~counted~~ for a lot.

4. __offer__ Big stores with big parking lots usually ~~offered~~ low prices, and they also allow customers to do most of their shopping in one place.

5. __have__ These discount stores appear everywhere; most communities ~~had~~ one close by.

6. __worry__ Some Americans ~~worried~~ that these chain stores are changing the country's landscape for the worse.

7. __went__ Once, small towns had unique stores owned by local people, and the residents ~~go~~ downtown to shop.

8. __got__ A small local business in those days probably provided only a limited selection of products at standard prices, but the customers ~~get~~ personalized service for their money.

9. ___*have*___ Today, discount superstores had the ability to sell products

for a lower price than their small local competitors can offer.

10. ___*will be*___ Convenience and low prices win customers, but the

atmosphere in American towns and cities would never be the same.

Edit Paragraphs and Your Own Writing

As you edit paragraphs and your own writing, use the following Thinking Critically guide and the Quick Review Chart on page 427.

THINKING CRITICALLY TO EDIT FOR VERB PROBLEMS	
FOCUS	Read all of your sentences carefully, looking for verb problems.
ASK	• Is my sentence about the present? About the past? About something that happened before something else? • Is each verb a regular verb or an irregular verb? • Have I used the tense that tells the reader when the action happened? • Have I used the correct form of the verb? • If the verbs in the sentence are not all in the same tense, is it because the actions actually happened at different times?
EDIT	Edit to correct any problems with verb form or verb tense.

PRACTICE 13 EDITING PARAGRAPHS FOR CORRECT VERB USE

Find and correct any problems with verb form or tense in the following paragraphs.

1. (1) Since 1835, trapeze artists consider *have considered* the triple somersault the most dangerous maneuver. (2) That year, a performer tried to do a triple somersault on a trapeze for the first time and dies *died* in the attempt.

(3) Only one person ~~has~~ managed to do the trick successfully for the next sixty-three years. (4) That man, a trapeze artist named Armor, did a triple somersault in 1860 and ~~is~~ *was* afraid to try it again. (5) According to circus legend, the second person to survive the triple, Ernie Clarke, once ~~done~~ *did* a quadruple somersault in private. (6) Ernie Lane, the third person to complete a triple somersault, was later killed by the maneuver when his catcher missed. (7) Circus historians now ~~believed~~ *believe* that Alfredo Codona, a performer in the 1920s and 1930s, was the greatest master of the triple somersault. (8) He has ~~went~~ *gone* down in history as the King of Trapeze.

2. (1) Many people go through life without even knowing that there is a record for peeling an apple or hopping on a pogo stick. (2) However, some people are very aware of such records, and ordinary folks around the world have ~~did~~ *done* some peculiar things to qualify for the *Guinness Book of World Records*. (3) For example, a New Jersey disc jockey, Glen Jones, recently ~~setted~~ *set* a new record for the longest continuous radio broadcast. (4) In the spring of 2001, he ~~has~~ stayed on the air for one hundred hours with only a few fifteen-minute breaks. (5) Another world record, for hopping up steps on a bicycle, is ~~hold~~ *held* by Javier Zapata of Colombia. (6) He climbed 943 steps without letting his feet touch the ground, breaking a record that he ~~has~~ *had* previously set. (7) Ashrita Furman of New York also ~~be~~ *is* a record breaker. (8) She balanced a milk bottle on her head and then ~~walks~~ *walked* almost eighty-one miles around a track. (9) These strange endurance contests may not make Jones, Zapata, and Furman famous, but their names ~~had~~ *have* entered the record book.

3. (1) The Olympic Games first let women compete in swimming events in 1912, and with that, the swimsuit revolution ~~begun~~ *began*. (2) In 1913, the

first mass-produced women's swimsuit hit the market. (3) Before that

year, women ~~have~~ *had* only been able to wade at the beach in bathing cos-

tumes with long, baggy legs. (4) The 1913 suits, designed by Carl Jantzen,

~~was~~ *were* ribbed one-piece outfits that allowed actual swimming. (5) An engi-

neer, Louis Réard, ~~comed~~ *came* up with the next major development in

swimwear in 1946 while working in the lingerie business. (6) He ~~has~~ called

it the "bikini," after a Pacific island used for testing the atomic bomb.

(7) In the 1950s, few Americans ~~had~~ dared to wear bikinis, which ~~was~~ *were*

considered scandalous. (8) Two-piece swimsuits ~~catch~~ *caught* on in the 1960s

and 1970s. (9) The bikini ~~losted~~ *lost* some popularity in the last decades of the

twentieth century, but it has made a triumphant return in the new

millennium.

PRACTICE 14   EDIT YOUR OWN WRITING FOR CORRECT VERB TENSE AND FORM

Use a piece of your own writing—a paper you are working on for this class
or another class, a paper you've already finished, or a recent piece of writing from work or everyday life. For extra help, use the Thinking Critically
guide on page 424 and the following Quick Review Chart.

Quick Review Chart

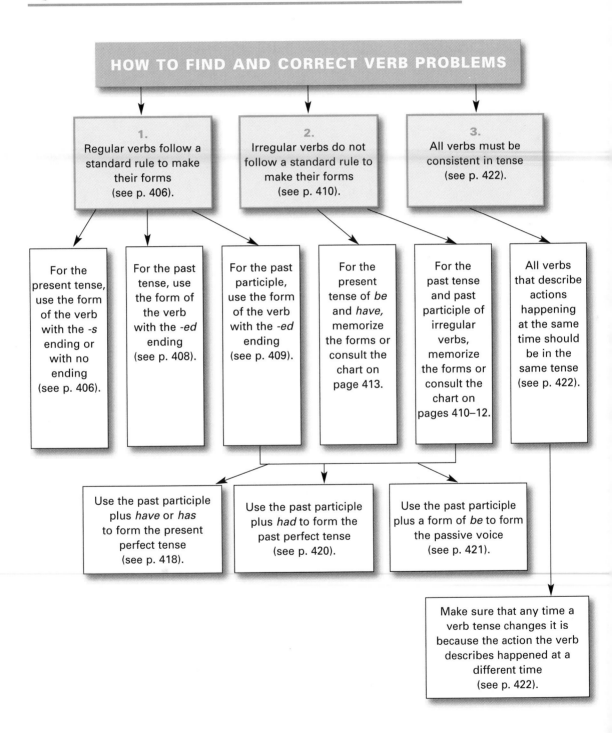

HOW TO FIND AND CORRECT VERB PROBLEMS

1.
Regular verbs follow a standard rule to make their forms (see p. 406).

2.
Irregular verbs do not follow a standard rule to make their forms (see p. 410).

3.
All verbs must be consistent in tense (see p. 422).

For the present tense, use the form of the verb with the -s ending or with no ending (see p. 406).

For the past tense, use the form of the verb with the -ed ending (see p. 408).

For the past participle, use the form of the verb with the -ed ending (see p. 409).

For the present tense of *be* and *have,* memorize the forms or consult the chart on page 413.

For the past tense and past participle of irregular verbs, memorize the forms or consult the chart on pages 410–12.

All verbs that describe actions happening at the same time should be in the same tense (see p. 422).

Use the past participle plus *have* or *has* to form the present perfect tense (see p. 418).

Use the past participle plus *had* to form the past perfect tense (see p. 420).

Use the past participle plus a form of *be* to form the passive voice (see p. 421).

Make sure that any time a verb tense changes it is because the action the verb describes happened at a different time (see p. 422).

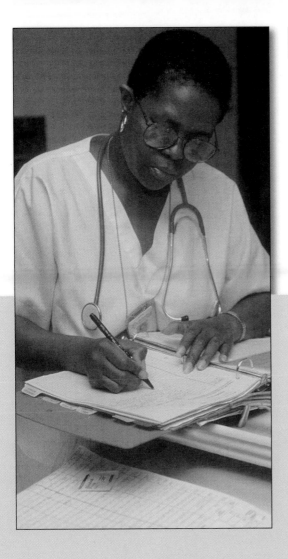

PART FIVE

Other Grammar Concerns

27

Pronouns

Using Substitutes for Nouns

Understand What Pronouns Are

DEFINITION: Nouns are words that name people, places, or things. **Pronouns** replace nouns or other pronouns in a sentence so that you do not have to repeat them.

> *her*
> Tessa let me borrow ~~Tessa's~~ jacket.

> *He*
> You have met Carl. ~~Carl~~ is my cousin.

DEFINITION: The noun or pronoun that a pronoun replaces is called the **antecedent**, which means "something that comes before." In most cases, a pronoun refers to a specific antecedent nearby.

> I filled out the (health form.) It was complicated.
>
> antecedent   pronoun replacing antecedent

ESL
ESL students may have particular trouble with pronouns and would benefit from extra practice. Encourage students to work with pronoun usage as they revise their own writing.

PRACTICE 1   IDENTIFYING PRONOUNS

In each of the following sentences, circle the pronoun, underline the antecedent (the noun to which the pronoun refers), and draw an arrow from the pronoun to the antecedent.

EXAMPLE: My uncle is a hard-working entrepreneur who knew he could succeed with a business loan.

1. Many poor people don't feel as if they can depend on big banks.

2. A bank in an underdeveloped area, however, needs to find customers wherever it can.

3. Microlending has become a popular banking trend. It has helped people in impoverished neighborhoods all over the world.

4. Microlending has succeeded because it involves lending very small amounts of money.

5. For many poor owners of a small business, microlending helps them to get a jump start.

6. For example, street vendors sell small quantities and earn small profits, so they may never save up enough to expand.

7. Yet a woman selling tacos from a cart may have enough experience to manage her own business successfully.

8. If the taco vendor gets a microloan, she may be able to open a storefront restaurant and earn larger profits.

LEARNING JOURNAL
Use your learning journal as a place to record sentences with pronoun problems that you find in your writing. Also write down edited versions of the sentences, with the problems corrected.

9. After receiving a small loan, a young entrepreneur can make his or her business more successful.

10. According to my uncle, getting a microloan allowed him to pursue a childhood dream.

Practice Using Pronouns Correctly

CHECK FOR PRONOUN AGREEMENT

DEFINITION: A pronoun must agree with (match) the noun or pronoun it refers to in number. **Number** tells how many of something, either one (singular) or more than one (plural).

If a pronoun is singular, it must also match its noun or pronoun in gender (*he, she,* or *it*).

CONSISTENT   Sherry talked to *her* aunt.

[*Her* agrees with *Sherry* because both are singular and feminine.]

CONSISTENT   The Romanos sold *their* restaurant.

[*Their* agrees with the *Romanos* because both are plural.]

Watch out for singular nouns that are not specific. If a noun is singular, the pronoun must be as well.

INCONSISTENT   Any cook has had *their* disasters.

[*Cook* is singular, but the pronoun *their* is plural.]

CONSISTENT   Any cook has had *his* or *her* disasters.

[*Cook* is singular, and so are the pronouns *his* and *her.*]

As an alternative to using the phrase *his or her,* make the subject plural if you can. (For more on this, see the note on p. 434.)

CONSISTENT   All cooks have had *their* disasters.

Two types of words often cause errors in pronoun agreement: indefinite pronouns and collective nouns.

Indefinite Pronouns

DEFINITION: An **indefinite pronoun** does not refer to a specific person, place, or thing; it is general. Most indefinite pronouns are either always singular or always plural. Whenever a pronoun refers to an indefinite person, place, or thing, check for agreement.

Someone forgot ~~their~~ *his* coat.

Everybody practiced ~~their~~ *his or her* lines.

TEACHING TIP
Have students focus on the "significant seven" indefinite pronouns: *any, each, either, neither,* and words ending in *-one, -thing,* or *-body.*

Indefinite Pronouns

ALWAYS SINGULAR			ALWAYS PLURAL
anybody	everyone	nothing	both
anyone	everything	one (of)	few
anything	much	somebody	many
each (of)	neither (of)	someone	several
either (of)	nobody	something	
everybody	no one		

NOTE: Although still grammatically correct, using a masculine pronoun (*he, his,* or *him*) alone to refer to a singular indefinite pronoun such as *everyone* is now considered sexist. Here are two ways to avoid this problem:

1. Use *his or her.*

    Someone forgot his or her coat.

2. Change the sentence so that the pronoun refers to a plural noun or pronoun.

    The children forgot their coats.

PRACTICE 2   USING INDEFINITE PRONOUNS

Circle the correct pronoun or group of words in parentheses.

(1) Everyone who has battled an addiction to alcohol has (his or her /
their) own views of the best ways to stop drinking. (2) Millions of former
problem drinkers have quit, and many have made (his or her / their) way
through recovery programs. (3) Few begin the road to recovery without
attending (his or her / their) first Alcoholics Anonymous (AA) meeting.
(4) With its famous twelve-step program, AA has helped countless alcoholics, but someone who is not religious may have (his or her / their) dif-
ficulties with one of the twelve steps. (5) No one can complete the whole

AA recovery program without turning (himself or herself)/ themselves)
over to a "higher power." (6) In addition, everybody who joins AA is asked
to admit that (he or she is) / they are) powerless over alcohol. (7) Many
object that (he or she needs /(they need) to feel empowered rather than
powerless in order to recover. (8) Anyone who does not feel that (he or she)
/ they) can believe in a higher power might participate instead in a group
like Secular Organizations for Sobriety. (9) Some can take responsibility
for (his or her /(their) drinking and stop more easily with groups such as
Smart Recovery. (10) Different approaches work for different people, but
former problem drinkers offer this sober advice to others with alcohol
problems: Anyone can quit drinking if (he or she wants) / they want) to
stop badly enough.

Collective Nouns

DEFINITION: A **collective noun** names a group that acts as a single unit.

TEACHING TIP
Have students work
in small groups to
expand the list of
collective nouns. See
which group adds
the most, and have
all students write the
added words next
to the box.

Common Collective Nouns

audience	company	group
class	crowd	jury
college	family	society
committee	government	team

Collective nouns are usually singular, so when you use a pronoun to
refer to a collective noun, it too must usually be singular.

             its
The class had ~~their~~ final exam at 8:00 A.M.

                   its
The group turned in ~~their~~ report.

If the people in a group are acting as individuals, however, the noun is plural and should be used with a plural pronoun.

The audience took *their* seats.

PRACTICE 3   USING COLLECTIVE NOUNS AND PRONOUNS

Fill in the correct pronoun (*their* or *its*) in each of the following sentences.

EXAMPLE: The basketball team was playing all of _____*its*_____ games in a damp, dark gymnasium.

1. The downtown branch of the university needed to overhaul several buildings on _____*its*_____ campus.

2. The theater department wanted to enlarge the auditorium used for _____*its*_____ productions.

3. In the present theater, the audience had to wait in _____*its*_____ seats until the performance was over and then exit through the stage door.

4. A sorority also needed more space to house _____*its*_____ members.

5. In addition, the football team could not go to any out-of-town games because _____*its*_____ bus had broken down.

6. The science teachers had to hold _____*their*_____ office hours in the student cafeteria.

7. The university president appointed a commission to study renovations and agreed to abide by _____*its*_____ findings.

8. The graduating class agreed to ask _____*its*_____ parents to make contributions.

9. One wealthy family donated _____*its*_____ slightly used luxury car to a fund-raising auction.

10. A record homecoming crowd shouted _____*their*_____ approval as the

renovation plans were announced.

MAKE PRONOUN REFERENCE CLEAR

If the reader isn't sure what a pronoun refers to, the meaning of a sentence may be confusing. You should edit any sentence that has an ambiguous, vague, or repetitious pronoun reference.

Avoid Ambiguous or Vague Pronoun References

DEFINITION: An **ambiguous pronoun reference** is one in which the pronoun could refer to more than one noun.

AMBIGUOUS   Michelle told Carla that she should get a better hourly wage.

[Did Michelle tell Carla that Michelle herself should get a better hourly wage? Or did Michelle tell Carla that Carla should get a better hourly wage?]

EDITED   Michelle told Carla that she wanted to get a better hourly wage.

AMBIGUOUS   I threw my bag on the table and it broke.

[Was it the bag or the table that broke?]

EDITED   My bag broke when I threw it on the table.

DEFINITION: A **vague pronoun reference** is one in which the pronoun does not refer clearly to any particular person or thing. (To correct a vague pronoun reference, substitute a noun for the pronoun.)

VAGUE   After an accident at the intersection, they installed a traffic light.

[Who installed the traffic light?]

EDITED   After an accident at the intersection, the highway department installed a traffic light.

VAGUE   When I heard it, I laughed.

[Heard what?]

EDITED   When I heard the message, I laughed.

PRACTICE 4 AVOIDING AMBIGUOUS OR VAGUE PRONOUN REFERENCES

Edit each of the following sentences to eliminate any ambiguous or vague pronoun references. Some sentences may be revised correctly in more than one way. *Possible edits shown.*

scientists
EXAMPLE: In a recent study, ~~they~~ found that people do not always
see objects that are in unexpected places.

who
1. In a psychology study, volunteers watched a video of two basketball

   teams,/ ~~and they~~ had to count the number of passes.

Focusing   *the volunteers*
2. ~~As the volunteers focused~~ on the players, some of ~~them~~ did not notice a

   person in a gorilla suit walking onto the basketball court.

meeting   *the volunteers*
3. Later, when ~~the volunteers met~~ with the researchers, many of ~~them~~

   asked, "What gorilla?"

an object
4. At the end of the study, the researchers had learned that if ~~it~~ was

   unexpected, many people simply could not see it.

5. The way the human brain processes visual information may keep people
   that information
   from using ~~it~~ wisely.

the danger
6. For example, if a car crosses into the lane facing oncoming traffic, ~~it~~

   may not register in the mind of a driver who expects a routine trip.

7. A stop sign appearing at an intersection cannot prevent an accident if
   the sign
   drivers do not see ~~it~~.

most people
8. Before the psychology study, ~~they~~ thought that drivers who missed signs

   of danger were simply not paying attention.

9. However, the study indicates that drivers make mistakes because they
   problems
   may not see ~~them~~ ahead.

10. Traffic safety regulations cannot make people's brains and eyes work
    laws   *people*
    differently, but ~~they~~ can make ~~them~~ wear seat belts.

Avoid Repetitious Pronoun References

DEFINITION: In a **repetitious pronoun reference**, the pronoun repeats a reference to a noun rather than replacing the noun. Such pronouns should be removed.

ESL
With ESL students, read aloud some sentences from the students' own writing, and ask students to raise their hands when they hear a repetitious reference. Then ask students to edit the sentence for clarity.

The police officer ~~he~~ told me I had not stopped at the sign.

The sign ~~it~~ was hidden by a tree.

PRACTICE 5   AVOIDING REPETITIOUS PRONOUN REFERENCES

Correct any repetitious pronoun references in the following sentences.

EXAMPLE: The science of robotics ~~it~~ already has practical applications.

1. Robots ~~they~~ have been part of many science-fiction classics, from *The Jetsons* to *Star Wars*.

2. Is there any child who ~~he~~ hasn't wished for a robot friend, a robot tutor, or a robot maid?

3. In some industries, robots ~~they~~ are already part of the workforce.

4. Robots ~~they~~ make sushi for some Japanese fast-food restaurant chains.

5. A factory might use robots to handle substances that ~~they~~ are dangerous for humans to touch.

6. But business ~~it~~ is not the only area in which the robot population is increasing.

7. Some children who ~~they~~ wanted a robot friend have already gotten their wish.

8. Toy manufacturers have created a robot dog that ~~it~~ can respond to human commands.

9. The robot dog ~~it~~ was first on many holiday and birthday gift lists for children in the past few years.

10. The day ~~it~~ may still arrive when people can have friendly robot

assistants around the house.

USE THE RIGHT TYPE OF PRONOUN

There are three types of pronouns: subject pronouns, object pronouns, and possessive pronouns. These different types show the way pronouns can be used in a sentence. Note that the pronouns in the following sentence are all different types.

her (possessive)

When Mariah sang at the Super Bowl, ~~Mariah's~~ voice sounded beautiful,

her (object)   *she (subject)*

the crowd loved ~~Mariah~~, and ~~Mariah~~ looked thrilled.

Pronoun Types

	SUBJECT	OBJECT	POSSESSIVE
First person	I/we	me/us	my, mine/ our, ours
Second person	you/you	you/you	your, yours/ your, yours
Third person singular	he, she, it	him, her, it	his, her, hers, its
Third person plural	they who/who	them whom/whom	their, theirs its, whose

Subject Pronouns

DEFINITION: A **subject pronoun** refers to the person, place, or thing that is the subject of a verb.

She took my parking space.

I honked my horn.

Object Pronouns

If a pronoun in a sentence is not a subject pronoun or a possessive pronoun, it is probably an object pronoun.

DEFINITION: **Object pronouns** either receive the action of a verb (the object of the verb) or are part of a prepositional phrase (the object of the preposition).

OBJECT OF THE VERB	Carolyn asked *me* to drive.
	Carolyn gave *me* the keys.
OBJECT OF THE PREPOSITION	Carolyn gave the keys to *me*.

Possessive Pronouns

DEFINITION: **Possessive pronouns** show ownership.

Giselle is *my* best friend.

Don't forget to bring *your* book.

Three trouble spots make it difficult to know what type of pronoun to use.

Never put an apostrophe in a possessive pronoun.

THREE PRONOUN TROUBLE SPOTS

1. Compound subjects and objects.
2. Comparisons.
3. Sentences that need *who* or *whom*.

Pronouns Used with Compound Subjects and Objects

DEFINITION: A **compound subject** has more than one subject joined by a conjunction such as *and* or *or*.
   DEFINITION: A **compound object** has more than one object joined by a conjunction.

In grammar, the word *compound* means containing two or more equal elements.

COMPOUND SUBJECT	Tim and *I* work together.
COMPOUND OBJECT	Joan baked the cookies for Jim and *me*.

To decide what type of pronoun to use in a compound construction, try leaving out the other part of the compound and the conjunction. Then say the sentence aloud to yourself.

When you are writing about yourself and someone else, always put yourself after everyone else. *My friends and I went to a club*, not *I and my friends went to a club.*

~~Jerome and~~ (me/I) like chili dogs.   [Think: *I* like chili dogs.]

The package was for ~~Karen and~~ (she/her).   [Think: The package was for *her*.]

If a pronoun is part of a compound object in a prepositional phrase, use an object pronoun.

Many people make the mistake of using *I* in the phrase *between you and (me/I)*. The correct pronoun with *between* is the object *me*. If *between me* sounds odd to you, try thinking *with me*.

I will keep that information just between you and (I/me).

[*Between you and me* is a prepositional phrase, so an object pronoun, *me*, is required.]

■ PRACTICE 6   **EDITING PRONOUNS IN COMPOUND CONSTRUCTIONS**

Edit each sentence using the proper type of pronoun. If a sentence is already correct, write "C" next to it.

EXAMPLE: Getting an MBA was one choice ~~him~~ *he* and ~~me~~ *I* had.

1. I met Jun when we were students in an engineering program, and ~~him~~ *he* and ~~me~~ *I* both decided that we were interested in business careers.

2. It seemed to Jun and ~~I~~ *me* that we should finish our engineering degrees first.

3. The day they handed diplomas to Jun and me, we started looking into corporate consulting.   *C*

4. Some people told Jun and ~~I~~ *me* that we needed master's degrees in business administration.

5. ~~Him~~ *He* and I were convinced that smart people with degrees in engineering would be useful in the business world, with or without an MBA.

6. In just a few weeks, Jun and ~~me~~ *I* were accepted as management consultant trainees.

7. He and I were not the only trainees who did not have MBA degrees.   *C*

8. Nancy had a degree in philosophy, and Andrew was a lawyer; both ~~him~~ *he* and ~~her~~ *she* had decided to look for jobs in business.

9. Nancy said that ~~her~~ *she* and Andrew had learned that people without MBAs perform just as well in corporate America as people who have business degrees.

10. Our new employer told her and him that intelligence was a better predictor of success in business than an MBA was.   *C*

Pronouns Used in Comparisons

Using the right type of pronoun in comparisons is particularly important because using the wrong type can change the meaning of the sentence. Editing comparisons can be tricky because they often imply words that aren't actually included in the sentence.

> To find comparisons, look for the words *than* or *as.*

Bill likes Chinese food more than *I.*

[This sentence means Bill likes Chinese food more than I like it. The implied words after *I* are *like Chinese food.*]

Bill likes Chinese food more than *me.*

[This sentence means Bill likes Chinese food more than he likes me. The implied words after *than* are *he likes.*]

To decide whether to use a subject or object pronoun in a comparison, try adding the implied words and saying the sentence aloud.

> Add the implied words to the comparison when you speak and write. Then your meaning will be clear.

The professor knows more than (us/we).

[Think: The professor knows more than *we know.*]

Jen likes other professors more than (he/him).

[Think: Jen likes other professors more than *she likes him.*]

PRACTICE 7   EDITING PRONOUNS IN COMPARISONS

Edit each sentence using the correct pronoun type. If a sentence is correct, put a "C" next to it.

EXAMPLE: Gardening was a competitive sport for my mother, and I
take it almost as seriously as ~~her~~. *she*

1. My mother and father had a garden in their backyard, but she spent
   much more time there than ~~him~~. *he*

2. My father always said that my mother had a greener thumb than he.   *C*

3. The garden was filled with tomatoes because my mother loved no other
   vegetable as much as ~~they~~. *them*

4. No one I have ever known has had as many tomato recipes as ~~her~~. *she*

5. She won many blue ribbons at the county fair with her garden produce,

and nothing in our house was displayed more proudly than they.   *C*

6. My brother, who is two years older than ~~me,~~ began helping her when he
   ^ *I*

was a little boy.

7. He made sure that the leaf of each plant was free of slugs, for few other
   they

garden pests are as destructive as ~~them.~~
   ^

8. To this day, he is a better gardener than ~~me.~~
   ^ *I*

9. I spend just as much time as ~~him~~ working in the garden, however.
   he ^

10. Every summer, we compare notes to see if I have grown as many
    he

tomatoes as ~~him.~~
   ^

Choosing between Who *and* Whom

Who is always a subject; use this form if the pronoun performs an action.
Whom is always an object; use this form if the pronoun does not perform
an action.

> **WHO = SUBJECT**   I don't know *who* rang the alarm.

> **WHOM = OBJECT**   Billy is the person to *whom* I report.

Whoever is a subject
pronoun; *whomever* is
an object pronoun.

In sentences other than questions, when the pronoun (*who* or *whom*)
is followed by a verb, use *who*. When the pronoun (*who* or *whom*) is followed by a noun or pronoun, use *whom*.

> The person (who/whom) spoke was boring.

> [The pronoun is followed by the verb *spoke*. Use *who*.]

> The person (who/whom) I met was boring.

> [The pronoun is followed by another pronoun: *I*. Use *whom*.]

 PRACTICE 8   **CHOOSING BETWEEN *WHO* AND *WHOM***

In each sentence, circle the correct word, *who* or *whom*. Remember, if the
pronoun is followed by a verb, use *who*. If it is followed by a noun or pronoun, use *whom*.

EXAMPLE: Chester Himes was the writer ((who)/ whom) created the

characters Coffin Ed Johnson and Grave Digger Jones.

1. Chester Himes, (who /(whom)) readers know best as a detective novelist,

    wrote several novels in the 1940s and 1950s analyzing race relations in

    the United States.

2. Himes, ((who)/ whom) was the youngest son of a middle-class family,

    spent many years living in Los Angeles.

3. Like many African American writers (who /(whom)) he knew, Himes

    moved to Paris in the 1950s.

4. One of his novels about two African American detectives ((who)/ whom)

    work in Harlem, *Cotton Comes to Harlem,* was made into a successful

    movie.

5. Himes, ((who)/ whom) died in Spain in 1984, actually knew other parts of

    the United States and of Europe much better than he knew Harlem.

MAKE PRONOUNS CONSISTENT IN PERSON

DEFINITION: **Person** is the point of view a writer uses—the perspective from which he or she writes. Pronouns may be in first person *(I, we);* second person *(you);* or third person *(he, she, it,* or *they).* (See the chart on p. 440.)

INCONSISTENT PERSON   *I* wanted to use the copy machine, but the attendant said *you* had to have an access code.

[The sentence starts in the first person *(I)* but shifts to the second person *(you).*]

CONSISTENT PERSON   *I* wanted to use the copy machine, but the attendant said *I* had to have an access code.

[The sentence stays with the first person, *I.*]

INCONSISTENT PERSON   After *a caller* presses 1, *you* get a recording.

[The sentence starts with the third person *(a caller)* but shifts to the second person *(you).*]

CONSISTENT PERSON	After *a caller* presses 1, *he* or *she* gets a recording.
CONSISTENT PERSON, PLURAL	After *callers* press 1, *they* get a recording.

PRACTICE 9 MAKING PRONOUNS CONSISTENT IN PERSON

In the following items, correct the shifts in person. There may be more than one way to correct some sentences. *Answers may vary. Possible edits shown.*

EXAMPLE: I have a younger brother with an allergy to peanuts, and

I
~~you~~ have to be very careful with his food.

1. Experts agree that the percentage of people with allergies to foods is
they
rising, but ~~we~~ don't know why.

2. Someone who has a mild allergic reaction the first time ~~you eat~~ a food
he or she eats

may develop more severe allergies from future contacts with the food.

3. If a person has a severe allergy to a food and unknowingly eats even a
he or she
small amount of that food, ~~you~~ could die.

4. However, if people with allergies are protected from any contact with
their
the food for several years, ~~his or her~~ allergies may disappear or become

milder.

children have
5. When ~~a~~ young ~~child has~~ severe allergies, their parents can be extremely

cautious.

I am
6. My little brother is severely allergic to peanuts, so ~~you are~~ not allowed

to eat anything containing peanuts while he is nearby.

his   *he goes*
7. He carries an adrenaline pen that can save ~~your~~ life if ~~you go~~ into shock

from a food allergy.

I
8. I love peanut butter, but ~~you~~ can't eat a peanut butter sandwich in my

house.

she

9. My mother will not take my brother to any public place where ~~you~~ can

   even smell peanuts.

10. Some people think that her precautions are extreme, but she knows that
    she   *her*
    ~~you~~ can't be too careful when ~~your~~ child's life is at stake.

Edit Paragraphs and Your Own Writing

PRACTICE 10   EDITING PARAGRAPHS FOR PRONOUN USE

Find and correct any problems with pronoun use in the following paragraphs. You may want to use the Quick Review chart on page 450.

1. (1) The picture phone never caught on with consumers, but video-
                                         who
    conferencing ~~it~~ uses the same idea. (2) Anyone ~~whom~~ has a video camera

    hooked up to a home computer can connect to someone else with a sim-

    ilar setup. (3) A person simply sits in front of the camera and talks; a per-
                                                        him or her
    son or group of people on the other end is able to see and hear ~~them~~.
    Videoconferencing
    (4) ~~It~~ has been wonderful for both businesses and families.
                                                          its
        (5) In the new global economy, a company often has ~~their~~ offices all

    over the world. (6) Once, a businessperson might have had to travel a great
                                  his or her
    deal to keep in touch with ~~their~~ clients, suppliers, and fellow employees
                                          business
    around the globe. (7) Today, much ~~of it~~ can be done with videoconfer-
                        People
    encing. (8) ~~Anyone~~ can attend a meeting and see their clients face to face

    while remaining on a different continent. (9) The technology has improved
              anyone
    so that ~~you~~ can transmit high-quality images and sound, and the cost of

    videoconferencing continues to drop. (10) And of course, a videoconfer-

    encing businessperson with competitors who travel the world will save
                                they
    much more money than ~~them~~ on airfare and accommodations.

(11) Businesses are not the only ones to benefit from videoconferencing technology. (12) A family today may find that ~~it~~ *they* often must spend time apart. (13) A parent traveling for business may not see ~~their~~ *his or her* spouse or children for days at a time. (14) People move across the country from where ~~you~~ *they* grew up, leaving parents and siblings behind. (15) Parents ~~they~~ sometimes divorce, and sometimes one starts a new job far away from the children. (16) Today, however, ~~someone~~ *people* who cannot be present to kiss their children goodnight or wish their sister a happy birthday can see family members across the miles through videoconferencing. (17) Divorced parents ~~who~~ *whom* judges have allowed to move to another state have actually been required by law to buy videoconferencing technology to keep in touch with their children.

(18) Most people do not feel that videoconferencing can replace being physically present with family members and clients, but ~~it costs~~ *videoconferences cost* less than regular visits while offering more intimacy than a telephone call. (19) ~~They say that~~ *If* the eyes are the windows of the soul, ~~and~~ videoconferencing helps people look into those windows and stay connected.

2. (1) Some people travel the world without ever leaving ~~his or her~~ *their* house by reading books about exotic locations. (2) ~~A person~~ *People* who ~~is~~ *are* afraid to fly can nevertheless immerse themselves in a far-off place. (3) Someone ~~whom~~ *who* does not speak a word of any foreign language can pretend to fit in like a native while reading travel literature. (4) At the end of a good travel book, ~~you~~ *readers* can feel as if ~~you~~ *they* know a place ~~you've~~ *they've* never visited — even if ~~you~~ *they* never want to go there. (5) Armchair travel is, in fact, less dangerous and more comfortable than much actual tourism. (6) Unfamiliar customs and food that might make a traveler feel out of place often seem very

they are
amusing when ~~it is~~ described in a good book. (7) And many people who

read avidly about a traveler getting food poisoning in a strange place or

sitting on a plane that nearly crashes say to themselves, "I am glad that

me
happened to him rather than ~~I~~!" (8) Armchair travel books are one genre

that ~~it~~ often turns up on best-seller lists. (9) A growing audience will con-

their
tinue to demand such books from ~~its~~ local bookstores and libraries.

▊ PRACTICE 11   EDITING YOUR OWN WRITING FOR PRONOUN USE

As a final practice, edit a piece of your own writing for pronoun use. It can be a paper you are working on for this course, a paper you've already finished, a paper for another course, or a recent piece of writing from your work or everyday life. Record in your learning journal any problem sentences you find, along with their corrections. You may want to use the following Quick Review Chart.

LEARNING JOURNAL
Do you understand the terms *pronoun agreement* and *pronoun reference*? How would you explain them to someone else?

TEACHING TIP
Have students underline every pronoun in their paragraphs and draw an arrow to the word or words to which it refers.

Quick Review Chart

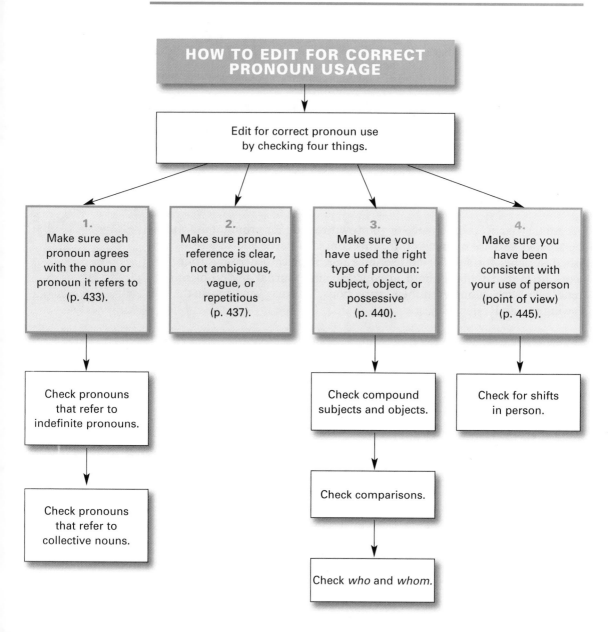

HOW TO EDIT FOR CORRECT PRONOUN USAGE

Edit for correct pronoun use by checking four things.

1.
Make sure each pronoun agrees with the noun or pronoun it refers to (p. 433).

2.
Make sure pronoun reference is clear, not ambiguous, vague, or repetitious (p. 437).

3.
Make sure you have used the right type of pronoun: subject, object, or possessive (p. 440).

4.
Make sure you have been consistent with your use of person (point of view) (p. 445).

Check pronouns that refer to indefinite pronouns.

Check compound subjects and objects.

Check for shifts in person.

Check pronouns that refer to collective nouns.

Check comparisons.

Check *who* and *whom*.

28

Adjectives and Adverbs

Describing *Which One?* or *How?*

Understand What Adjectives and Adverbs Are

DEFINITION: Adjectives describe or modify nouns (words that name people, places, or things) and pronouns (words that replace nouns). They add information about what kind, which one, or how many.

City traffic was *terrible* last night.

The highway was *congested* for *three* miles.

Two huge old tractor trailers had collided.

DEFINITION: Adverbs describe or modify verbs (words that tell what happens in a sentence), adjectives, or other adverbs. They add information about how, how much, when, where, why, or to what extent. Adverbs often end with -*ly*.

MODIFYING VERB	Dave drives *aggressively.*
MODIFYING ADJECTIVE	The *extremely* old woman swims every day.
MODIFYING ANOTHER ADVERB	Dave drives *very* aggressively.

DISCUSSION
Make two columns on the board, one for adjectives and one for adverbs. In each column, have students list words related to a common subject such as a description of your classroom or the weather outside.

451

Note that both adjectives and adverbs can come before or after the words they modify, and that you can use more than one adjective or adverb to modify a word.

Practice Using Adjectives and Adverbs Correctly

CHOOSING BETWEEN ADJECTIVE AND ADVERB FORMS

Many adverbs are formed by adding *-ly* to the end of an adjective.

ADJECTIVE	ADVERB
The *new* student introduced himself.	The couple is *newly* married.
That is an *honest* answer.	Please answer *honestly*.

It can be difficult to decide whether to use the adjective form or the adverb form of a word. To decide which form to use, find the word you want to describe or modify. If that word is a noun or pronoun, use the adjective form. If it is a verb, adjective, or another adverb, use the adverb form.

PRACTICE 1 CHOOSING BETWEEN ADJECTIVE AND ADVERB FORMS

In each sentence, underline the word in the sentence that is being described or modified, and then circle the correct word in parentheses.

EXAMPLE: Teenagers who want a summer job (usual / usually) can find work.

1. Even in a slowing economy, many summer jobs for unskilled workers are (easy / easily) to find.

2. Of course, teenaged workers without much experience should not have (extreme / extremely) rigid requirements for a summer job.

3. Fast-food restaurants are a (frequent / frequently) employer of teenagers.

4. The <u>wages</u> at a fast-food restaurant will not be (high)/ highly) for a starting position, however.

5. In addition, the <u>work</u> may not be very (interesting)/ interestingly).

6. However, teenagers can learn (valuable)/ valuably) <u>lessons</u> from going to almost any job.

7. Arriving on time and <u>behaving</u> (responsible /(responsibly)) will impress any supervisor.

8. <u>Working</u> (close /(closely)) with other employees also may teach a teenage worker to get along with people who are not friends or family.

9. Earning money can make a high school student feel more (financial / (financially)) independent.

10. Saving for college tuition is one way in which a teenager can <u>use</u> money from a summer job (wise /(wisely)).

USING COMPARATIVE AND SUPERLATIVE FORMS

ESL
Point out that comparative constructions often use the word *than*.

DEFINITION: To compare two persons, places, or things, use the **comparative** form of adjectives or adverbs.

Sheehan drives *faster* than I do.

Francis is *more gullible* than Tara is.

DEFINITION: To compare three or more persons, places, or things, use the **superlative** form of adjectives or adverbs.

Sheehan drives the *fastest* of all our friends.

Francis is the *most gullible* of the children.

Comparatives and superlatives can be formed either by adding an ending to an adjective or adverb or by adding a word. If an adjective or adverb is short (one syllable), add *-er* to form the comparative and *-est* to form the superlative. Also use this pattern for adjectives that end in -*y* (but change the -*y* to -*i* before adding -*er* or -*est*). If an adjective or adverb is longer than one syllable, add the word *more* to make the comparative and the word *most* to make the superlative.

Comparative and Superlative Forms

ADJECTIVE OR ADVERB	COMPARATIVE	SUPERLATIVE
ADVERBS AND ADJECTIVES OF ONE SYLLABLE		
tall	taller	tallest
fast	faster	fastest
ADJECTIVES ENDING IN -Y		
happy	happier	happiest
silly	sillier	silliest
ADVERBS AND ADJECTIVES OF MORE THAN ONE SYLLABLE		
graceful	more graceful	most graceful
gracefully	more gracefully	most gracefully
intelligent	more intelligent	most intelligent
intelligently	more intelligently	most intelligently

For more on changing a final -*y* to -*i* when adding endings, and on other spelling changes involving endings, see Chapter 36.

Use either an ending (-*er* or -*est*) or an extra word (*more* or *most*) to form a comparative or superlative—not both at once.

One of the ~~most~~ easiest ways to beat stress is to exercise regularly.

TEACHING TIP
Go over this practice together as a class. Then have students proofread a piece of their own writing to make sure that they have used comparatives and superlatives correctly.

PRACTICE 2 USING COMPARATIVES AND SUPERLATIVES

In the space provided in each sentence, write the correct form of the adjective or adverb in parentheses. You may need to add *more* or *most* to some adjectives and adverbs.

EXAMPLE: One of the _most beautiful_ (*beautiful*) sights in the West is a herd of wild horses.

1. Mustangs live in several western states, but Nevada is the place where

   they are _most commonly_ (*commonly*) found.

2. Thousands of wild horses live on public lands in the West, but cattle are

   seen ____*more frequently*____ *(frequently)* than horses are.

3. Horses have lived in the Nevada mountains for a ____*longer*____ *(long)* time

   than cattle have; some may be descendants of Spanish conquistadors'

   horses.

4. Soon, the Bureau of Land Management expects to conduct one of the

   ____*biggest*____ *(big)* roundups of wild mustangs in recent decades.

5. Government officials believe that the land should have a ____*smaller*____

   (small) population of horses than it now supports.

6. Many people find a mustang roundup, which often involves helicopters

   and horseback riders, one of the ____*most exciting*____ *(exciting)* events

   they have ever witnessed.

7. After government roundups, mustangs are sold at auction to the

   ____*highest*____ *(high)* bidder.

8. Experienced horse trainers find that they can get horses ____*more*____

   ____*cheaply*____ *(cheaply)* at government auctions than at many other sales.

9. Wild mustangs may be ____*more difficult*____ *(difficult)* to train than

   domestic horses, but some mustangs have gone on to become champions.

10. Horse lovers may view the mustangs ____*more romantically*____ *(romanti-*

    cally) than cattle ranchers do; cattle ranchers see the horses as

    competition for scarce food.

GOOD, WELL, BAD, AND BADLY

Four common adjectives and adverbs have irregular forms: *good, well, bad,*
and *badly.*

> *Irregular* means not following a standard rule.

Forms of Good, Well, Bad, *and* Badly

	COMPARATIVE	SUPERLATIVE
ADJECTIVE		
good	better	best
bad	worse	worst
ADVERB		
well	better	best
badly	worse	worst

TEAMWORK
Using an article from the newspaper, a Web site, or some other source, have students draw arrows from the adjectives and adverbs to the words they modify. This activity can be done in small groups or assigned as homework and reviewed in teams the next day.

People often get confused about whether to use *good* or *well*. *Good* is an adjective, so use it to describe a noun or pronoun. *Well* is an adverb, so use it to describe a verb or an adjective.

ADJECTIVE   She is a *good* friend.

ADVERB   He works *well* with his colleagues.

Well can also be an adjective to describe someone's health:

I am not *well* today.

■ PRACTICE 3   USING *GOOD* AND *WELL*

Complete each sentence by circling the correct word in parentheses. Underline the word that *good* or *well* modifies.

EXAMPLE: A (good)/ well) storyteller can hold an audience's attention.

1. Mark Twain's ability to tell an amusing story is (good / well) known.

2. Twain's famous story "The Notorious Jumping Frog of Calaveras County" is a (good)/ well) example of traditional American tale-telling.

3. The story is narrated by an Easterner whose proper speech contrasts (good / well) with the country dialect of Simon Wheeler, a storyteller he meets.

4. Wheeler may not be (good / well) educated, but he is a master of the tall tale.

5. The narrator claims that Wheeler has told him a "monotonous" story, but the tale is apparently (good / well) enough for the narrator to repeat.

6. The frog in the story is famous for being a (good / well) jumper.

7. Wheeler explains that the frog's owner lives (good / well) by gambling on the frog's jumping ability.

8. The frog's owner, Jim Smiley, makes the mistake of leaving the frog with a man whom Smiley does not know (good / well).

9. The stranger makes the frog swallow heavy shot so that he can no longer jump (good / well).

10. In Twain's story, Simon Wheeler has such a (good / well) time telling stories that the narrator has to escape from him at the end.

PRACTICE 4   USING COMPARATIVE AND SUPERLATIVE FORMS OF *GOOD* AND *BAD*

Complete each sentence by circling the correct comparative or superlative form of *good* or *bad* in parentheses.

EXAMPLE: The (better / best) way my family found to learn about another culture was to allow an exchange student to live in our home.

1. Simone, a French high school student, spent last summer getting to know the United States (better / best) by living with my family.

2. She had studied English since the age of five, and her understanding of grammar was (better / best) than mine.

3. She told me that she had the (worse / worst) accent of any student in her English classes, but I liked the way she spoke.

4. Her accent was certainly no (worse / worst) than mine would be if I tried to speak French.

5. My (worse / worst) fear was that she would find our lives boring.

6. However, the exchange program's administrator explained that the (better / best) way for Simone to learn about our country was for us to do ordinary things.

7. For me, the (better / best) part of Simone's visit was the chance to see my world through fresh eyes.

8. I felt (better / best) about my summer job, trips to the supermarket, and afternoon swims at the pool because Simone found all of these things exotic and fascinating.

9. Simone even liked summer reruns on television; she claimed that French television was much (worse / worst).

10. The (worse / worst) part of the visit was having to say goodbye to Simone at the end of the summer.

Edit Paragraphs and Your Own Writing

PRACTICE 5   EDITING PARAGRAPHS FOR CORRECT ADJECTIVES AND ADVERBS

Find and correct any problems with adjectives and adverbs in the following paragraphs. You may want to use the Quick Review Chart on page 461.

1.   (1) For an average European in the Middle Ages, wearing stripes was
         simply
not ~~simple~~ a fashion mistake. (2) According to Michel Pastoureau, a
                                                                          worst
scholar of the medieval period, wearing stripes was one of the ~~worse~~

things a European Christian could do in the thirteenth and fourteenth

centuries. (3) Stripes might be taken as a sign that the wearer was ~~more~~

sillier than other people; jesters, for example, often wore them. (4) Pros-

titutes also wore striped clothes, so stripes might be seen as an indica-

more sinful
tion that the person was ~~sinfuller~~ than others. (5) Wearing stripes was

most dangerous
~~dangerousest~~ for clergymen. (6) At least one clergyman in fourteenth-
^

foolish
century France was executed because he had been ~~foolishly~~ enough to
^

wear striped clothes. (7) Carmelite monks who wore striped cloaks were

frequently
~~frequent~~ attacked, and several popes insisted that the monks change to a

simpler
~~more simple~~ costume. (8) People in medieval Europe certainly took their
^

seriously
clothing ~~serious~~. (9) The only reason some people don't wear stripes
^   ^

today is that they are afraid of looking fat.

embarrassing
2. (1) Many people no longer find it ~~embarrassingly~~ to admit that
^
better
they have seen a psychotherapist. (2) Some patients argue that it is ~~gooder~~
^

to seek mental help than to suffer silently. (3) Others seem to feel that

more interesting
needing a therapist is a sign that their lives are ~~interestinger~~ than other
^

people's. (4) At any rate, the stigma that some people once attached to

quickly
psychotherapy is disappearing ~~quick~~. (5) Therapists have lately become
^
more visible
~~visibler~~ in popular culture, and this visibility may result in even wider
^

acceptance of psychotherapy. (6) For example, when a mobster on the

cable television show *The Sopranos* asks a therapist to treat his panic

toughest
attacks, viewers see that the ~~most tough~~ of men is still able to discuss his
^

relationships and feelings with a mental health specialist. (7) If Tony

bad
Soprano can do it, what ordinary person is going to feel ~~badly~~ about seek-
^

ing help for ordinary problems?

(8) However, people considering seeing a therapist are not the only ones who love to watch Tony Soprano trying to work through his problems. (9) Indeed, *The Sopranos*, which is one of the ~~bigger~~ *biggest* hits ever on cable television, includes many psychologists in its audience. (10) One online magazine ~~regular~~ *regularly* publishes a therapist's analysis of each episode. (11) Other therapists chat online about whether or not the psychologist on the television show is practicing psychology. (12) The audiences of psychological professionals seem to agree that therapy is portrayed ~~accurater~~ *more accurately* on the show than in many popular films. (13) As they point out, at least the therapist is not in love with her patient, unlike several psychiatrists in ~~recently~~ *recent* movies. (14) Although Mr. Soprano, like many actual therapy patients, does things that are not good for his mental health, his therapist thinks that he is functioning ~~best~~ *better* now than before. (15) Perhaps someday he will ~~honest~~ *honestly* discuss his criminal day job with her—and if he does, even the therapists tuning in might have trouble figuring out the ~~bestest~~ *best* possible response.

■ **PRACTICE 6 EDITING YOUR OWN WRITING FOR CORRECT ADJECTIVES AND ADVERBS**

LEARNING JOURNAL
What kind of mistake in using adjectives or adverbs do you make most often in your writing? What are some ways to avoid or correct this mistake?

As a final practice, edit a piece of your own writing for correct use of adjectives and adverbs. It can be a paper you are working on for this course, a paper you've already finished, a paper for another course, or a recent piece of writing from your work or everyday life. Record in your learning journal any problem sentences you find, along with their corrections. You may want to use the following Quick Review Chart.

Quick Review Chart

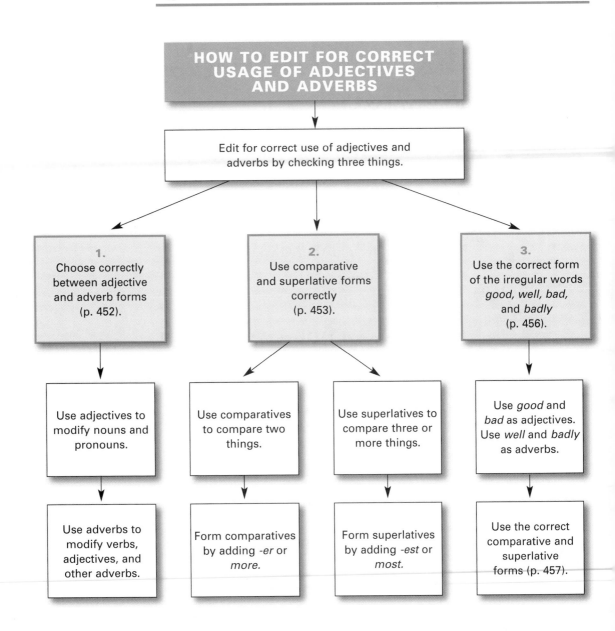

HOW TO EDIT FOR CORRECT USAGE OF ADJECTIVES AND ADVERBS

Edit for correct use of adjectives and adverbs by checking three things.

1.
Choose correctly between adjective and adverb forms (p. 452).

2.
Use comparative and superlative forms correctly (p. 453).

3.
Use the correct form of the irregular words *good, well, bad,* and *badly* (p. 456).

Use adjectives to modify nouns and pronouns.

Use comparatives to compare two things.

Use superlatives to compare three or more things.

Use *good* and *bad* as adjectives. Use *well* and *badly* as adverbs.

Use adverbs to modify verbs, adjectives, and other adverbs.

Form comparatives by adding -*er* or *more.*

Form superlatives by adding -*est* or *most.*

Use the correct comparative and superlative forms (p. 457).

29

Misplaced and Dangling Modifiers

Avoiding Confusing Descriptions

Understand What Misplaced and Dangling Modifiers Are

DEFINITION: **Modifiers** are words or word groups that describe or give more information about other words in a sentence. So that this information is clear, the modifier must be near the words it modifies and must modify only one sentence element. In most cases, the modifier should be right before or right after that sentence element.

DEFINITION: A **misplaced modifier** ends up describing the wrong sentence element because it is incorrectly placed within the sentence.

MISPLACED   Lorene saw my dog *driving her car on the highway.*

[Was my dog driving her car?]

CLEAR   *Driving her car on the highway,* Lorene saw my dog.

DEFINITION: A **dangling modifier** is said to "dangle" because it has nothing to attach itself to; the sentence element it is supposed to modify may be implied, but it is not actually stated in the sentence. A dangling modifier usually appears at the beginning of a sentence and seems to modify the noun or pronoun that immediately follows it.

DANGLING   *Talking on my cell phone,* my car drove into a ditch.

[Was the car talking on the cell phone?]

CLEAR   *Talking on my cell phone,* I drove my car into a ditch.

Even if readers can guess what you are trying to say, misplaced and dangling modifiers are awkward. Be sure to look for and correct misplaced and dangling modifiers in your writing.

Practice Correcting Misplaced and Dangling Modifiers

MISPLACED MODIFIERS

To correct a misplaced modifier, move the modifier as close as possible to the sentence element it modifies. The safest choice is often to put the modifier directly before the sentence element it modifies.

Using her computer, Suzy illustrated the story.
~~Suzy illustrated the story using her computer.~~

Three constructions in particular often lead to misplaced modifiers. Be sure to check your writing for these three trouble spots.

Trouble Spots: Misplaced Modifiers

1. Limiting modifiers such as *only, almost, hardly, nearly,* and *just.* These words need to be right before—not just close to—the words or phrases they modify.

ordered only
I ~~only~~ ordered half a pound.

collected nearly
Griffin ~~nearly collected~~ 100 cans.

TEAMWORK
Ask students, in pairs, to write two or three sentences that seem funny or confusing because of misplaced or dangling modifiers. Read the best ones aloud, asking the class to make corrections.

2. Phrases

PREPOSITIONAL PHRASES

to the house for his sister.
Jim was carrying the bags ~~for his sister to the house.~~
                                          ^

for ice cream in her glove compartment.
Julie found money ~~in her glove compartment for ice cream.~~
                                          ^

PHRASES BEGINNING WITH *-ING* VERB FORMS

Using cash,   .
Timothy bought the car ~~using cash.~~
^   ^

Wearing an oven mitt,   .
Elena took out the hot pizza ~~wearing an oven mitt.~~
^   ^

3. Clauses beginning with *who, whose, that,* or *which*

that was missing   .
I finally found the sock stuck to a T-shirt ~~that was missing.~~
                             ^   ^

PRACTICE 1   CORRECTING MISPLACED MODIFIERS

Find and correct any misplaced modifiers in the following sentences. If a sentence is correct, write a "C" next to it.

who work in U.S. hospitals
EXAMPLE: Many nurses are being trained to perform therapeutic
                         ^

touch ~~who work in U.S. hospitals.~~
      ^

in a human body   ?
1. Are there energy fields that can be touched by trained professionals
                         ^   ^

~~in a human body?~~

who practice therapeutic touch
2. People claim to be able to feel and move invisible energy fields ~~who~~   .
         ^   ^

~~practice therapeutic touch.~~

3. According to believers in therapeutic touch, an energy field can cause *that is out of alignment*

   pain and illness ~~that is out of alignment.~~

4. A practitioner treating a patient does not touch the sick person.   *C*

5. After a session of therapeutic touch, many patients ~~just~~ report that they *just*
   felt better without knowing why.

6. Emily Rosa, the twelve-year-old daughter of a nurse, made news when
   to test practitioners of therapeutic touch
   her experiment appeared in an important medical journal ~~to test prac-~~

   ~~titioners of therapeutic touch.~~

7. In her experiment, practitioners *who could not see Emily* were supposed to use the invisible

   energy field to determine when her hands were near theirs ~~who could~~

   ~~not see Emily.~~

8. Even though guessing should have allowed a 50 percent accuracy rating,

   the practitioners Emily tested were correct only 44 percent of the time.   *C*

9. Anyone who can demonstrate the ability to detect a human energy field *in a similar experiment*

   can claim a million-dollar prize ~~in a similar experiment.~~

10. The prize has not been awarded yet, *, which is offered by a foundation that investigates supernatural claims,* ~~which is offered by a foundation~~

    ~~that investigates supernatural claims.~~

DANGLING MODIFIERS

DEFINITION: When an opening modifier does not modify any word in the sentence, it is a **dangling modifier.** Writers often fail to include the word being modified because they think the meaning is clear. To be certain that your sentence says what you intend it to say, be sure to include the word being modified.

I was
While watching the movie, my purse was stolen.

TEACHING TIP
Students some-
times try to correct
a dangling modifier
by adding a subordi-
nating conjunction
(such as *while*) without
sufficiently reworking
the sentence itself.
Point out that adding
while alone does not
correct the problem
with this sentence:
*Trying to eat an
orange, the juice
streamed down my
chin.*

There are two basic ways to correct dangling modifiers. Use the one that makes the most sense.

1. You can add the word being modified right after the opening modifier so that the connection between the two is clear.

        I twisted   .
Running to catch up, my ankle ~~twisted.~~
          ^   ^

2. You can add the word being modified in the opening modifier itself.

    As I was running
~~Running~~ to catch up, my ankle twisted.
  ^

PRACTICE 2   CORRECTING DANGLING MODIFIERS

TEACHING TIP
Have students try this
practice on their own
and then discuss the
results with a class-
mate. Go over the
practice as a whole
class so that the
students can demon-
strate their corrections.

Find and correct any dangling modifiers in the following sentences. If a sentence is correct, write "C" next to it. It may be necessary to add new words or ideas to some sentences. *Answers will vary. Possible edits shown.*

              the owner will get a better price for
     EXAMPLE: Selling a used car, a resale ~~will bring a better price~~ than a
                     ^

     trade-in.

                  seller will get
1. Trading in a used car, a ~~buyer will offer~~ a better price if the car is clean.
                        ^

   If the owner hires
2. ~~Hiring~~ a professional detailer, a used car can still impress potential
  ^

   buyers.

   With the used car
3. ~~Looking~~ like new, the owner can get the best price for a trade-in or a
  ^

   resale.

4. With essential repairs completed, a used car should be in good working

   order to be sold.   *C*

                              a used car may still have
5. Approved as safe and drivable by a reputable mechanic, minor
                   that do   ^
   mechanical problems ~~may~~ not have to be fixed.
                 sellers should tell prospective buyers
6. Winning points for honesty, ~~prospective buyers should know~~ about a
                              ^

   used car's minor problems.

7. ~~Deducted~~ *By deducting the cost of repairing minor problems* from the asking price, the owner can be fair with a buyer.

8. No matter how expensive, decorative lighting and other details usually do not add to the value of a car.   *C*

9. With higher than usual mileage, ~~the owner may have to reduce the~~ *a used car might need a reduced* asking price.

10. Advertising in a local newspaper, a used car is likely to reach ~~its~~ *his or her* target market.
    the owner of

Edit Paragraphs and Your Own Writing

PRACTICE 3   EDITING PARAGRAPHS FOR MISPLACED AND DANGLING MODIFIERS

Find and correct any misplaced or dangling modifiers in the following paragraphs. You may want to refer to the Quick Review Chart on page 470.
Answers will vary. Possible edits shown.

1. (1) ~~When ordering items online,~~ *S*hipping and handling costs can make or break a business. (2) By charging too much, ~~customers may~~ *a site may force customers to* abandon their order. (3) A customer may never return to the site ~~who feels that shipping and handling charges are too high.~~ *who feels that shipping and handling charges are too high* (4) Most people have shipped packages, *at least occasionally,* so they know how much shipping costs ~~at least occasionally.~~ (5) Going too far in the other direction, some online ~~customers get~~ *sites offer their customers* free shipping and handling. (6) The sites lose money, *that offer free shipping* ~~that offer free shipping,~~ and may have to either close down for good or start charging shipping fees. (7) Most shipping companies charge by weight. (8) ~~Buying from the~~ *Using* ~~sites that use~~ these shippers, the online sites must either charge a flat fee, which may be too much or too little, or make the customer wait until the order is complete to find out the shipping fee. (9) Neither option is per-

TEAMWORK
Have students complete Practice 3 in pairs, comparing notes to see the different possibilities for revising the paragraphs.

that wants to keep expanding its customer base .

fect, so a business ~~must~~ choose the least unattractive solution ~~that wants~~

~~to keep expanding its customer base online.~~

2.   MEMO

To: All staff

From: Sara Hollister

Re: Dress code

employees were encouraged

(1) After ~~encouraging employees~~ to wear casual clothing on Fridays,

the casual dress code was soon in force all week long. (2) With some

employees received a memo

uncertainty about what was appropriate casual wear, ~~a memo was circu-~~

When all of the staff members began

~~lated~~ last year with guidelines for dress. (3) Wearing khakis and polo

shirts, suits and ties became very rare in the halls of Wilson and Hollister.

(4) Some younger staff members almost never wore anything but jeans.

When Mr. Wilson arrived

(5) ~~Arriving~~ in the office in a Hawaiian shirt, some employees hardly

him

recognized ~~Mr. Wilson~~ without his trademark pinstriped suit. (6) Believ-

the company felt that

ing that informality improved productivity and morale, the casual dress

code was well liked.

The company must recommend

(7) ~~Recommending~~ changes in the dress policy now, for several rea-

sons. (8) The human resources department feels that the relaxed attitude

toward dress may have contributed to the recent increases in absenteeism

and lateness at Wilson and Hollister. (9) Other problems have also sur-

who have dropped in unexpectedly .

faced. (10) Clients have sometimes expressed surprise ~~who have dropped~~

we have observed that

~~in unexpectedly.~~ (11) Hoping to keep their respect and their business, the

clients appear to feel more comfortable with employees in suits. (12) Finally,

Wilson and Hollister will no longer permit

fearing an increase in sexual harassment, sleeveless shirts, shorts, miniskirts,

and halter tops ~~will no longer be permitted.~~ (13) Human resources ~~almost~~

recommends *an almost* a complete change in the casual-dress policy. (14) While *employees may continue* ~~continuing~~ to wear casual clothing on Friday, *they must wear* business attire on Monday

through Thursday, effective immediately. (15) As an employee who prefers casual clothing, *I find* this news ~~is~~ rather sad, but the decision is for the best.

(16) Certain that you will understand the necessity for these changes, necessity for these changes, I appreciate your cooperation.

PRACTICE 4   EDITING YOUR OWN WRITING FOR MISPLACED AND DANGLING MODIFIERS

As a final practice, edit a piece of your own writing for misplaced and dangling modifiers. It can be a paper you are working on for this course, a paper you've already finished, a paper for another course, or a recent piece of writing from your work or everyday life. Record in your learning journal any problem sentences you find, along with their corrections. You may want to use the following Quick Review Chart.

LEARNING JOURNAL
Which is more difficult for you, finding misplaced and dangling modifiers or correcting them? What can you do to help yourself find or correct them more easily?

Quick Review Chart

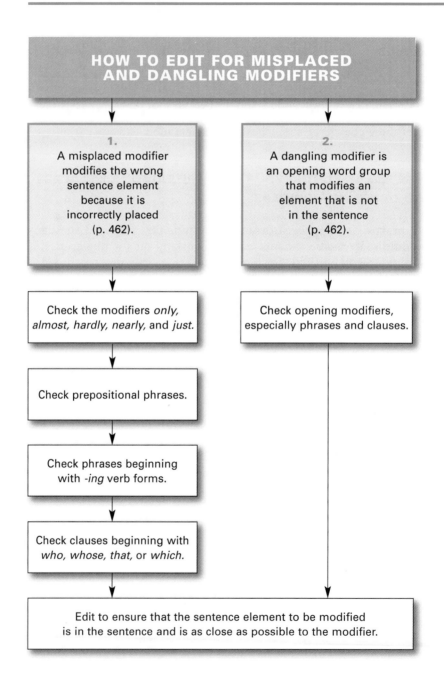

HOW TO EDIT FOR MISPLACED AND DANGLING MODIFIERS

1.
A misplaced modifier modifies the wrong sentence element because it is incorrectly placed (p. 462).

2.
A dangling modifier is an opening word group that modifies an element that is not in the sentence (p. 462).

Check the modifiers *only, almost, hardly, nearly,* and *just.*

Check opening modifiers, especially phrases and clauses.

Check prepositional phrases.

Check phrases beginning with *-ing* verb forms.

Check clauses beginning with *who, whose, that,* or *which.*

Edit to ensure that the sentence element to be modified is in the sentence and is as close as possible to the modifier.

30

Coordination and Subordination

Joining Ideas

Understand Coordination and Subordination

DEFINITION: **Coordination** can be used to join two sentences when the ideas in them are equally important.

TWO SENTENCES	The internship at the magazine is very prestigious. Many interns have gone on to get good jobs.
JOINED THROUGH COORDINATION	The internship at the magazine is very prestigious, *and* many interns have gone on to get good jobs.

DEFINITION: **Subordination** can be used to join two sentences when one idea is less important than the other. Adding a dependent word (such as *although*, *because*, *if*, or *that*) to one sentence shows that it is subordinate to, or less important than, the other.

TWO SENTENCES	The internship was advertised last week. The magazine received many calls about it.

> The word *subordinate* means "lower in rank" or "secondary." In the workplace, for example, you are subordinate to your boss. In the army, a private is subordinate to an officer.

| JOINED THROUGH SUBORDINATION | *When* the internship was advertised last week, the magazine received many calls about it. |

[The word *when* makes the first sentence dependent, or subordinate, and puts more emphasis on the second part, the idea that the magazine received many calls.]

If all of your sentences are short, they will seem choppy and hard to read. To vary the rhythm and flow of your writing and to clarify the relationship between ideas, use coordination or subordination to join sentences with related ideas.

Practice Using Coordination and Subordination

COORDINATION USING COORDINATING CONJUNCTIONS

DEFINITIONS: A **conjunction** is a word that joins words, phrases, or clauses. **Coordinating conjunctions** are the words *and, but, for, nor, or, so,* and *yet.* (You can remember them by thinking of FANBOYS—*for, and, nor, but, or, yet, so.*) They join ideas of equal importance. To join two sentences with ideas that are equally important, put a comma and one of these conjunctions between the sentences.

Choose the conjunction that makes the most sense for the meaning of the two sentences.

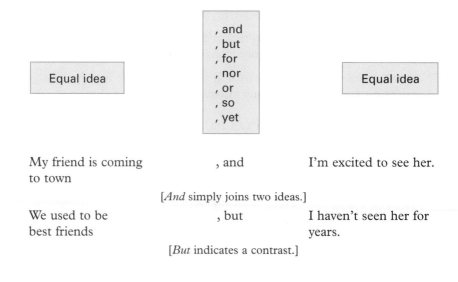

| Equal idea | , and
, but
, for
, nor
, or
, so
, yet | Equal idea |

| My friend is coming to town | , and | I'm excited to see her. |

[*And* simply joins two ideas.]

| We used to be best friends | , but | I haven't seen her for years. |

[*But* indicates a contrast.]

| I'm a little nervous | , for | we may not have anything in common anymore. |

[*For* indicates a reason or cause.]

| We haven't talked much | , nor | have we written. |

[*Nor* indicates a negative.]

| Maybe we will pick up our friendship | , or | we may be like strangers. |

[*Or* indicates alternatives.]

| We are having dinner tonight | , so | we will know soon. |

[*So* indicates a result.]

| It's hard to keep old friends | , yet | they are very important. |

[*Yet* indicates a reason.]

PRACTICE 1   JOINING IDEAS WITH COORDINATING CONJUNCTIONS

In each of the following sentences, fill in the blank with an appropriate coordinating conjunction. There may be more than one correct answer for some sentences. *Possible edits shown.*

> EXAMPLE: Some students may not be ready for promotion at the end of the school year, _*but*_ teachers, principals, and parents are often reluctant to keep them back.

1. Is social promotion in American schools a problem, ___*or*___ is it better for students to remain with classmates their own age than for them to repeat a grade?

2. In almost every school, some children will not be able to keep up with the required work, ___*nor*___ will they have the skills to move on to the next grade when the school year ends.

3. Many schools promote such children to the next grade anyway, ___*and*___ they continue to advance with the rest of their classmates.

4. Social promotion may be harmful, ___*for*___ the student may never learn the material without repeating a grade.

5. Socially promoted students may graduate from high school without

basic skills, ___*so*___ they may never be able to function well in society.

6. Other students earn the right to graduate, ___*but*___ their diplomas may

even be less valuable because unprepared students have the same

certificates.

7. On the other hand, holding students back can cause terrible harm,

___*for*___ the students lose friends and respect when their classmates go

on without them.

8. People need self-respect to accomplish their goals, ___*and*___ students

who are left back may feel worthless or stupid.

9. Students who are left back are likely to be bigger and stronger than their

younger classmates, ___*and*___ some people have suggested that holding

students back can endanger younger children.

10. Perhaps summer school can help some underprepared students catch up

with classmates, ___*or*___ perhaps schools should provide students with

additional help throughout the school year.

**PRACTICE 2   COMBINING SENTENCES WITH COORDINATING
CONJUNCTIONS**

Combine each pair of sentences into a single sentence by using a comma
and a coordinating conjunction. As you choose a coordinating conjunction, consider how the ideas in the two sentences are related to each other.
In some cases, there may be more than one correct answer. *Possible edits
shown.*

EXAMPLE: Americans have recently experienced unpleasant shocks at

, but people

the gas station./People in the United States still pay lower

gas prices than much of the world.

1. Gasoline prices are lower in the United States than in many other
   , but most
   industrialized countries./ ~~Most~~ Americans do not find this news
   ^
   comforting.

2. People in the United States are used to low gas prices./ ~~Many~~ drivers feel
   , so many
                                                        ^
   cheated when prices increase.

3. In 2000, Hong Kong drivers paid over three times as much as Americans
   , and
   paid for gasoline./ Italians and Japanese were buying gas at more than
   ^
   four dollars a gallon.

4. Canadians also pay higher gas prices than Americans pay./ ~~The~~ taxes on
   , for the
                                                        ^
   gasoline are higher in Canada than they are in this country.

5. Few people would argue that gasoline prices in the United States are too
   , but the
   low./ ~~The~~ reason for these relatively cheap prices is that gasoline is not
   ^
   heavily taxed.

6. In many countries, taxes on gasoline support social services./ ~~The~~ money
   , and the
                                                        ^
   may also pay for research on reducing air pollution.

7. Gasoline taxes can help to pay for roads./ ~~They~~ can raise money for
   , or they
                                          ^
   research into fuel efficiency.

8. However, taxes on gasoline are very unpopular with most drivers./
   , so politicians
   ~~Politicians~~ are not eager to vote for gasoline taxes.
   ^

9. Many Americans do not want to pay gas taxes of even two or three cents
   , nor do most
   per gallon./ ~~Most also do not~~ want to spend tax money on mass transit
   ^
   systems.

10. Gasoline prices will probably never be as high in the United States as
    , yet a
    they are in Asia./ ~~A~~ few Americans are not sure that this is a good thing.
    ^

COORDINATION USING SEMICOLONS

TEACHING TIP
Remind students that a semicolon balances two independent clauses; what's on either side must be able to stand alone as a complete sentence.

DEFINITION: A **semicolon** is a punctuation mark that can join two sentences through coordination. When you use a semicolon, make sure that the ideas in the two sentences are not only of equal importance but also very closely related.

EQUAL IDEA	;	EQUAL IDEA
My computer crashed	;	I lost all of my files.
I had just finished my research paper	;	I will have to redo the whole thing.

DEFINITION: A semicolon alone does not tell readers much about the relationship between the two ideas. To give more information about the relationship, use a semicolon followed by a word that indicates the relationship; such words are known as **conjunctive adverbs**. They must be followed by a comma.

Here are some of the most common conjunctive adverbs, along with some examples of how they are used.

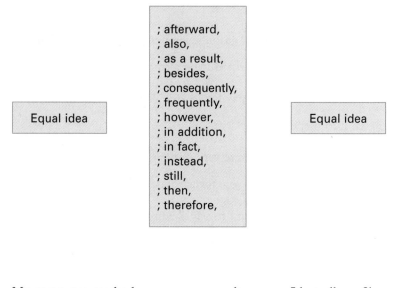

Equal idea	; afterward, ; also, ; as a result, ; besides, ; consequently, ; frequently, ; however, ; in addition, ; in fact, ; instead, ; still, ; then, ; therefore,	Equal idea

My computer crashed	; as a result,	I lost all my files.
I should have made backup files	; however,	I did not.
The information is lost	; therefore,	I will have to try to rebuild the files.

■ **PRACTICE 3 JOINING IDEAS WITH SEMICOLONS**

Join each pair of sentences by using a semicolon alone.

EXAMPLE: Different countries have different laws. *; a* A law school usually

teaches students about the laws of a particular country.

1. Legal differences can cause problems in the global marketplace. *; businesses* ~~Businesses~~

from two different countries working together will probably not use the

laws of either country when they draw up a contract.

2. Businesspeople need to decide which laws to follow in creating interna-

tional contracts and deals. *;* U.S. law is often the one they choose.

3. The American legal system is set up to deal with corporations and business

interests. *; it* ~~It~~ is not surprising that many international businesses choose to

follow U.S. laws.

4. Lawyers with experience in the U.S. system are now in demand. *; bright* ~~Bright~~

people from all over the world are applying to law schools in the United

States.

5. International students can often find good jobs after finishing law school. *;*

they
~~They~~ usually know more than one language and understand more than

one culture.

■ **PRACTICE 4 COMBINING SENTENCES WITH SEMICOLONS
AND CONNECTING WORDS (CONJUNCTIVE ADVERBS)**

Combine each pair of sentences by using a semicolon and a connecting
word. Choose a conjunctive adverb that makes sense for the relationship
between the two ideas. In some cases, there may be more than one correct
answer. *Possible edits shown.*

EXAMPLE: High school graduation is the unofficial end of adoles-
; afterward, graduates
cence. *;* ~~Graduates~~ choose different paths.

1. Some high school graduates want to grow up as quickly as possible. *; however, others* ~~Others~~ want to enjoy a period with limited responsibilities.

2. Many high school students intend to go directly to college. *; consequently, they* ~~They~~ must spend their junior and senior years reading brochures, filling out applications, and taking standardized tests.

3. Some students are not ready to think about college yet. *; therefore, they* ~~They~~ should choose another option.

4. Working attracts many high school graduates. *; frequently, a* ~~A~~ job can help a young person to feel independent and adult.

5. Many high school graduates have minimal living expenses. *; as a result, they* ~~They~~ can experiment with careers and find out what they enjoy doing.

6. Young graduates may not be committed yet to a family or a particular place. *; instead, they* ~~They~~ can travel and seek interesting opportunities.

7. Volunteer work allows many high school graduates to help causes they believe in. *; in addition, they* ~~They~~ may get to visit other parts of the world.

8. Many young Americans choose to serve their country by joining the military. *; besides, such* ~~Such~~ service can teach them skills and help them earn money.

9. Some high school graduates work, volunteer, or join the military as an intermediate step. *; in fact, they* ~~They~~ may plan to go to college after spending some time away from school.

10. Some young graduates want more education from an academic institution. *; however, others* ~~Others~~ prefer to learn from life's experiences.

SUBORDINATION USING SUBORDINATING CONJUNCTIONS

DEFINITIONS: A **conjunction** is a word that joins words, phrases, or clauses. **Subordinating conjunctions** are dependent words that can join two sentences when one is more important than the other. The sentence with the subordinating conjunction in front of it becomes a subordinate or dependent clause; because of the subordinating conjunction, it no longer expresses a complete thought and cannot stand by itself as a sentence.

Choose the conjunction that makes the most sense with the two sentences. Here are some of the most common subordinating conjunctions.

TEACHING TIP
Write two sentences on the board, and have students suggest how they would have to edit to accommodate different subordinating conjunctions.

Main idea	after although as as if because before even though if	since so that unless until when where while	Subordinate idea

I decided to go to work	although	I had a terrible cold.
I hate to miss a day	unless	I absolutely can't get there.

When a subordinate idea ends a sentence, it usually does not need to be preceded by a comma unless it is showing a contrast. When a subordinate idea begins a new sentence, use a comma to separate it from the rest of the sentence.

ESL
Point out that, unlike conjunctive adverbs, most subordinating conjunctions are never used with a semicolon in front of them or a comma after.

Subordinating conjunction	Subordinate idea	,	Main idea

Although	I had a terrible cold	,	I decided to go to work.
Unless	I absolutely can't get there	,	I hate to miss a day.

PRACTICE 5   JOINING IDEAS THROUGH SUBORDINATION

In the following sentences, fill in the blank with an appropriate subordinating conjunction. In some cases, there may be more than one correct answer. *Possible edits shown.*

EXAMPLE: Smokey Bear spent most of his life in the National Zoo in Washington, D.C., _where_ he received so much mail that he had his own zip code.

1. Smokey Bear began reminding people that "Only you can prevent forest fires" in 1944 _because_ government officials during World War II were concerned about preserving valuable resources like trees.

2. However, Smokey Bear existed only as a cartoon _until_ a tragedy occurred six years later.

3. _After_ a fire destroyed part of Lincoln National Forest near Capitan, New Mexico, in 1950, forest rangers found a badly burned bear cub clinging to a tree.

4. The "real" Smokey Bear became a celebrity _when_ the public heard his story.

5. After his death, Smokey Bear's body was returned to New Mexico _so that_ he could be buried near his former home.

6. The character of Smokey Bear has been used continuously in U.S. and Canadian fire safety campaigns _since_ it first appeared more than fifty years ago.

7. Smokey has also appeared in public service announcements in Mexico, _where_ he is known as Simon.

8. Recently, Smokey's famous line was changed to "Only you can prevent wildfires" _because_ research indicated that most adults did not believe they could cause a wildfire.

9. However, humans can easily set fires _if_ they discard cigarettes carelessly, burn trash on windy days, or even park a car with a catalytic converter in a dry field.

10. ___As___ the Smokey Bear campaign heads for its sixtieth anniversary,

Smokey is as recognizable to most Americans as Mickey Mouse and

Santa Claus.

PRACTICE 6   COMBINING SENTENCES THROUGH SUBORDINATION

Combine each pair of sentences into a single sentence by using an appropriate subordinating conjunction either at the beginning or between the two sentences. Use a conjunction that makes sense with the two sentences.
Answers will vary. Possible edits shown.

                                when they
EXAMPLE: **Children like to assert themselves./They are between one**

              and four years old.

  Although toddlers   *, they*
1. ~~Toddlers~~ do not get to make many decisions./~~They~~ want to have some

power over their own lives.

                            when parents
2. Young children often become frustrated./~~Parents~~ do not let them have

their own way.

  If parents   *, the*
3. ~~Parents~~ want to avoid power struggles with their toddlers./~~The~~ parents

should learn to pick their battles.

                            so that the
4. Experts recommend letting even young children make some choices./~~The~~

children will feel that they have some control.

                            even though the
5. Parents should not let a child do anything dangerous./~~The~~ child may

want to.

  While toddlers   *, most*
6. ~~Toddlers~~ can be difficult to handle./~~Most~~ parents worry more about

power struggles with their teenagers.

  Although adolescents   *, they*
7. ~~Adolescents~~ need to establish their independence from their parents./~~They~~

also want their parents to set some limits.

  Because teenagers   *, parents*
8. ~~Teenagers~~ can be skilled at arguments./~~Parents~~ should learn not to

argue about or renegotiate rules that the household has established.

9. Food, sleep, clothes, and grooming are often battlefields for children and

        unless parents

parents./ Parents- remember their own rebellious phases and try to

understand what their children are feeling.

                                        if they

10. Parents and children can work through power struggles./ They have

respect for each other.

Edit Paragraphs and Your Own Writing

PRACTICE 7   EDITING PARAGRAPHS FOR COORDINATION AND SUBORDINATION

In the following paragraphs, join the underlined sentences by using either coordination or subordination. Be sure to punctuate correctly. You may want to use the Quick Review Chart on page 484 to help you. *Answers will vary. Possible edits shown.*

               , which

1. (1) Lyme disease is carried by deer ticks./ (2) The disease appears

most frequently in the northeastern United States. (3) Hikers, gardeners,

and other lovers of the outdoors in that area often become victims of the

         After people

illness. (4) People venture into tall grass or brush against other foliage./

    they

(5) They should inspect any exposed skin carefully for the minuscule ticks.

(6) Researchers now know that the disease is more widespread than was

once thought. (7) Limiting exposed skin by wearing socks, long pants, and

                                                  ; so

long sleeves gives ticks fewer chances to attach themselves./ (8) So does

washing exposed skin within about ninety minutes of being outdoors.

(9) These simple precautions can prevent most cases of potentially dan-

gerous Lyme disease.

2. (1) Al-Qurain is a community in the small Middle Eastern country of

Kuwait. (2) Thirty years ago, Kuwait City officials began to use an abandoned

                                          because none

quarry in al-Qurain as a garbage dump./ (3) None of them thought the area would ever be populated. (4) Fifteen years ago, the government

began to build subsidized housing in al-Qurain. (5) The dump was

supposed to be closed./ (6) Kuwaitis continued to use the al-Qurain *, but*

landfill. (7) People soon lived all around the foul-smelling garbage pit.

(8) Residents of the area were teased and insulted for living in the neigh-

borhood./ (9) Al-Qurain now houses sixty thousand people. *, which*

(10) For years, the dump sickened people around it./ (11) Sometimes *; sometimes*

the garbage caught fire and sent fumes into the homes nearby. (12) Finally,

the Kuwaiti Environmental Protection Agency decided to try to help.

(13) The agency gets little government funding./ (14) It needed to rely *, so it*

on donations for the cleanup effort.

(15) Soon, a mountain of garbage had been removed./ (16) The *, and the*

leveled site was covered with pebbles from the desert. (17) Engineers

found a way to siphon methane gas from the seventy-five-foot-deep

garbage pit. (18) Kuwait is famous for oil production./ (19) A methane- *, yet a*

powered generator may soon provide electricity for al-Qurain residents.

(20) The air in the neighborhood now ranks among the country's clean-

est. (21) For many environmentalists and residents of this neighborhood,

the cleanup of al-Qurain is almost a miracle.

██ **PRACTICE 8 EDITING YOUR OWN WRITING FOR
COORDINATION AND SUBORDINATION**

As a final practice, edit a piece of your own writing for coordination and
subordination. It can be a paper you are working on for this course, a
paper you've already finished, a paper for another course, or a recent piece
of writing from your work or everyday life. Record in your learning journal any choppy problem sentences you find, along with the edited versions. You may want to use the following Quick Review Chart.

LEARNING JOURNAL
How would you
explain coordination
and subordination to
someone who had
never heard of them?

Quick Review Chart

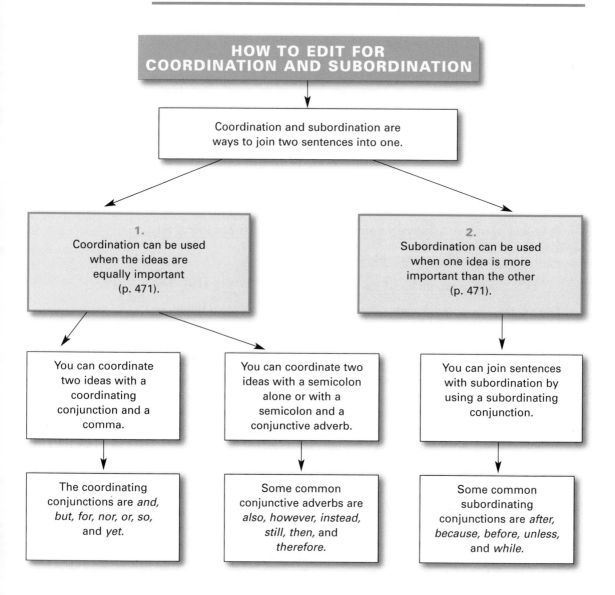

HOW TO EDIT FOR COORDINATION AND SUBORDINATION

Coordination and subordination are ways to join two sentences into one.

1.
Coordination can be used when the ideas are equally important (p. 471).

2.
Subordination can be used when one idea is more important than the other (p. 471).

You can coordinate two ideas with a coordinating conjunction and a comma.

You can coordinate two ideas with a semicolon alone or with a semicolon and a conjunctive adverb.

You can join sentences with subordination by using a subordinating conjunction.

The coordinating conjunctions are *and, but, for, nor, or, so,* and *yet.*

Some common conjunctive adverbs are *also, however, instead, still, then,* and *therefore.*

Some common subordinating conjunctions are *after, because, before, unless,* and *while.*

31
Parallelism
Balancing Ideas

Understand What Parallelism Is

DEFINITION: **Parallel** means having evenly matched parts. If you have ever watched a gymnastics meet, you might have seen parallel bars. The bars match in height, and the gymnasts' performances depend on the bars being correctly lined up and evenly balanced.

DEFINITION: **Parallelism** in writing means that similar parts in a sentence have the same structure: Their parts are comparable and balanced. Parallelism makes your writing flow smoothly and helps your readers understand your meaning. To create parallelism, use similar structures to express similar ideas. Put nouns with nouns, verbs with verbs, and phrases with phrases.

TEACHING TIP
When explaining parallelism, ask students to visualize an old-fashioned scale; it won't balance unless the contents of both trays are equal.

NOT PARALLEL	I like <u>math</u> more than <u>studying English</u>.

[*Math* is a noun, but *studying English* is a phrase.]

PARALLEL	I like <u>math</u> more than <u>English</u>.
NOT PARALLEL	On vacation, we <u>swam</u>, <u>snorkled</u>, and <u>were eating</u> at great restaurants.

[Verbs must be in the same tense to be parallel.]

PARALLEL	On vacation, we <u>swam</u>, <u>snorkled</u>, and <u>ate</u> at great restaurants.

LEARNING JOURNAL
Use your learning journal as a place to record sentences with problems in parallelism that you find in your writing. Also record edited versions of these sentences, with the problems corrected.

485

ESL
Tell students that
parallel constructions
often depend on using
infinitives and idioms
correctly. See Chapter
33 for details.

NOT PARALLEL   Last night we went to a movie and dancing at a club after.

[*To a movie* and *dancing at a club* are both phrases, but they have different forms. *To a movie* should be paired with another prepositional phrase: *to a dance club.*]

PARALLEL   Last night we went to a movie and to a dance club.

Practice Writing Parallel Sentences

PARALLELISM IN PAIRS AND LISTS

TEACHING TIP
Review these examples
with students, and ask
them to explain why
each of the nonparallel
sentences needs
correction.

When you present two or more items in a series joined by the word *and* or *or*, use a similar form for each item.

NOT PARALLEL   The fund-raiser included a bake sale and also holding an auction.

PARALLEL   The fund-raiser included a bake sale and an auction.

NOT PARALLEL   Students got items for the auction from local businesses, from their own families, and ran an advertisement in the newspaper.

PARALLEL   Students got items for the auction from local businesses, from their own families, and from their advertisement in the newspaper.

PRACTICE 1   USING PARALLELISM IN PAIRS AND LISTS

In each sentence, underline the parts of the sentence that should be parallel. Then edit the sentence to make it parallel. *Answers may vary. Possible edits shown.*

EXAMPLE: Sometimes even a well-maintained car can break down or
~~you might forget to fill up the gas tank.~~
                              ^ run out of gas.

1. When your car breaks down on the road, you should follow simple rules
   to remain safe and ~~so that assistance will come quickly.~~
                        ^ get assistance quickly.

2. When contacting a garage for help, you should give your location

   accurately by identifying the street or highway, the nearest cross street
                              nearby
   or exit, and ~~which~~ landmarks or stores ~~are nearby.~~
                  ^   ^

3. All of the cars in a parking lot look similar, so a mechanic may have trouble finding your car unless you <u>open the hood</u>, <u>put on emergency flashers</u>, or <s>you could</s> <u>tie a handkerchief to the antenna</u>.

4. If you decide to <u>read a book</u> or _∧ <u>a nap</u> take <s>sounds good</s> while you wait for the mechanic, you may not see the tow truck.

5. A mechanic who sees <u>no obviously broken-down car</u> and <s>he or she</s> <u>has other calls to deal with</u> may simply go on to the next customer.

6. You should leave a <u>cell-phone number</u> or a <u>nearby</u> <s>business</s> business's number _∧ with the garage so the mechanic can call you back.

7. Most pay phones nowadays do not receive incoming calls, so the garage may not be able to call you back on a pay phone to let you know <u>about problems</u> or <s>if there are</s> <u>delays</u>.

8. The garage will not be able to reach you on your cell phone if you <u>make a lot of calls</u> or <s>it is time for</s> have <u>a long talk with your best friend</u>.

9. <u>Sitting in a car</u> or <s>if you stand</s> standing _∧ <u>behind it</u> can be very dangerous when a breakdown occurs on the side of the highway.

10. Relying on <u>common sense</u>, <u>patience</u>, and <s>remembering</s> <u>basic safety guidelines</u> will help you get through your car's breakdown.

PARALLELISM IN COMPARISONS

In comparisons, the items being compared should have parallel structures. Comparisons often use the word *than* or *as*. When you edit for parallelism, check to make sure that the items on either side of the comparison word are parallel.

NOT PARALLEL	<u>Driving downtown</u> is as fast as <u>the bus</u>.
PARALLEL	<u>Driving downtown</u> is as fast as <u>taking the bus</u>.
NOT PARALLEL	Reasonable <u>dieting</u> is better than <u>fasts</u>.

| **PARALLEL** | Reasonable <u>dieting</u> is better than <u>fasting</u>. |
| **OR** | A reasonable <u>diet</u> is better than a <u>fast</u>. |

In order to make the parts of a sentence parallel, you may need to add or drop a word or two.

NOT PARALLEL	<u>A multiple-choice test</u> is easier than <u>answering an essay question.</u>
PARALLEL, WORD ADDED	<u>*Taking* a multiple-choice test</u> is easier than <u>answering an essay question.</u>
NOT PARALLEL	<u>The cost of a train ticket</u> is less than <u>to pay the cost of a plane ticket.</u>
PARALLEL, WORDS DROPPED	<u>The cost of a train ticket</u> is less than <u>the cost of a plane ticket.</u>

PRACTICE 2   USING PARALLELISM IN COMPARISONS

In each sentence, underline the parts of the sentence that should be parallel. Then edit the sentence to make it parallel. *Answers may vary. Possible edits shown.*

EXAMPLE: <u>New appliances</u> are usually much more energy-efficient than ~~running~~ old ones.

1. For many people, <u>getting the household electric bill</u> is more worrisome
   than ~~to pay~~ ^paying^ the rent each month.

2. <u>The amount of the rent bill</u> usually changes much less from month to
   month than <u>~~what an energy company charges.~~</u> ^the amount of the energy bill.^

3. <u>Saving money</u> appeals to many consumers more than ~~to use~~ ^using^ less electricity.

4. Compact fluorescent light bulbs use less energy than ~~continuing to use~~
   regular incandescent bulbs.

5. In most households, <u>running the refrigerator</u> uses more energy than
   ~~the use of~~ ^using^ all other appliances.

6. Many people worry that buying a new refrigerator is more expensive
   keeping
   than ~~if they~~ simply ~~keep~~ the old one.
   running ^
7. However, an energy-efficient new refrigerator uses much less electricity
   ^
   than running an inefficient older model.

8. Some new refrigerators use only as much energy as ~~keeping~~ a 75-watt

   light bulb ~~burning~~.
   ^
9. Householders might spend less money to buy an efficient new refrigerator

   than ~~it would take~~ to run the old one for another five years.

10. Researching information about energy efficiency can save consumers as
    remembering
    much money as ~~when they remember~~ to turn off lights and air conditioners.
    ^

PARALLELISM WITH CERTAIN PAIRED WORDS

DEFINITION: When a sentence uses certain paired words, called **correlative conjunctions**, the items joined by them must be parallel. These words link two equal elements and show the relationship between them. Here are the paired words:

both . . . and	neither . . . nor	rather . . . than
either . . . or	not only . . . but also	

NOT PARALLEL	Brianna dislikes *both* fruit *and* eating vegetables.
PARALLEL	Brianna dislikes *both* fruit *and* vegetables.
NOT PARALLEL	She would *rather* eat popcorn every night *than* to cook.
PARALLEL	She would *rather* eat popcorn every night *than* cook.

▪ **PRACTICE 3   USING PARALLELISM WITH CERTAIN PAIRED WORDS**

In each sentence, circle the paired words and underline the parts of the sentence that should be parallel. Then edit the sentence to make it parallel. You may need to change the second part of the correlative conjunction.
Answers may vary. Possible edits shown.

EXAMPLE: A recent survey of young women reported that a majority of them would (rather) lose twenty pounds permanently (than) to live to be ninety.

1. People in the United States are (both) pressed for time (and) have gotten used to convenient but fattening foods.

2. Many Americans are (neither) willing to exercise regularly (nor) do they have *required* to do anything physical during a normal day.

3. Being overweight can be unhealthy, but many Americans would (rather) look thinner (than) to stay the same size and get in better shape.

4. In fact, some Americans are (not only) out of shape (but) are dangerously obsessed with being thin.

5. The idea that thinner is better affects (both) overweight people (and) it even influences people of normal weight.

6. In their quest to lose weight, many Americans have tried (either) fad diets (or) have taken prescription drugs.

7. Dozens of healthy, average-sized Americans in the past ten years have died from (either) surgical procedures to remove fat (or) they have died from dangerous diet drugs.

8. A thin person is (neither) guaranteed to be attractive (nor) is he or she necessarily healthy.

9. Some people who are larger than average are (not only) in good health (but also) can be physically fit.

10. Americans who would (rather) pay for risky drugs and surgery (and prefer) *than* (not) to eat moderately and exercise may have hazardous priorities.

PRACTICE 4   COMPLETING SENTENCES WITH PAIRED WORDS

The following practice items contain only the first part of a correlative conjunction. Complete the correlative conjunction and add more information to form a whole sentence. Make sure that the structures on both sides of the correlative conjunction are parallel. *Answers will vary. Possible edits shown.*

> EXAMPLE: I am both enthusiastic about your company *and eager to work for you* .

1. I could bring to this job not only youthful enthusiasm *but also leadership experience.*

2. I am willing to work either in your Chicago office *or in your San Francisco office.*

3. My current job neither encourages creativity *nor allows flexibility.*

4. I would rather work in a difficult job *than work in an unchallenging one.*

5. In college I learned a lot both from my classes *and from other students.*

Edit Paragraphs and Your Own Writing

PRACTICE 5   EDITING PARAGRAPHS FOR PARALLELISM

Find and correct any problems with parallelism in the following paragraphs. You may want to refer to the Quick Review Chart on page 494.

TEAMWORK
Practice 5 can be completed in pairs or small groups. Have the whole class compare results.

1. (1) Some employees who want to advance their careers would rather
    look
    transfer within their company than ~~looking~~ for a new job elsewhere. (2)
    In-house job changes are possible, but employees should be sure that they
    both meet the criteria of the job and ~~to~~ avoid making their present boss
    angry. (3) Because businesses invest money in each person they hire,

many companies would rather hire from within ~~and not~~ *than* bring an outsider

into a position. (4) By hiring an employee from another department, a

company neither needs to make an investment in a new employee ~~but~~ *nor loses a*

~~may also prevent the~~ current employee ~~from leaving.~~ (5) Transfers usu-

ally go more smoothly now than in the past; however, an in-house job

move can still require diplomacy and ~~being honest.~~ *honesty.* (6) Experts caution

employees who are considering an in-house transfer to tell their current

manager the truth and ~~that they should~~ *to* discuss their wish to transfer with

the potential new manager. (7) Employees should neither threaten to quit

if they do not get the new job nor ~~is it a good idea to~~ spread the word

around the department that they are anxious to leave their present job.

(8) Employees' goals for in-house transfers should be ~~career advancement~~ *advancing their careers*

and making sure that they create no bad feelings with the move.

2.   (1) Black motorists frequently arouse police suspicion either when

driving in neighborhoods that are mainly white or when ~~they are~~ driving

an expensive car. (2) A higher percentage of African Americans than

~~among people who are white~~ *whites* are pulled over by the police. (3) Many

African Americans feel insulted, endangered, and ~~react with anger~~ *angry* when

they are ~~accused of "driving while black."~~ *stopped seemingly randomly.* (4) African Americans are

liable to be singled out by police who suspect they are criminals not only

while in a car but ~~African Americans~~ *while* also ~~report being wrongly stopped~~

on foot. (5) Racial profiling is illegal yet ~~a~~ fairly common ~~phenomenon.~~

(6) According to a 2001 poll, ~~among black women the figure is~~ 25 per-

cent, *of black women* and 52 percent of black men have been singled out by police. (7)

Victims of racial profiling have done nothing wrong, yet they are made to

feel that others are either afraid *of them* or do not trust them. (8) Law-abiding

African Americans should neither expect such treatment nor ~~should they~~

put up with it from public officials who are supposed to protect citizens.

(9) Police departments around the country must make their employees
aware that automatically stopping, ~~asking them questions,~~ *questioning,* and searching
African Americans will not be tolerated. (10) ~~Treating all citizens fairly~~ *Fair treatment of all citizens* is
a more important American value than ~~that there is~~ a high arrest rate for
the police.

PRACTICE 6   EDITING YOUR OWN WRITING FOR PARALLELISM

As a final practice, edit a piece of your own writing for parallelism. It can
be a paper you are working on for this course, a paper you've already finished, a paper for another course, or a recent piece of writing from your
work or everyday life. Record in your learning journal any problem sentences you find, along with their corrections. You may want to use the following Quick Review Chart.

LEARNING JOURNAL
How would you
explain parallelism to
someone who had
never heard of it? How
would you explain how
to edit for it?

Quick Review Chart

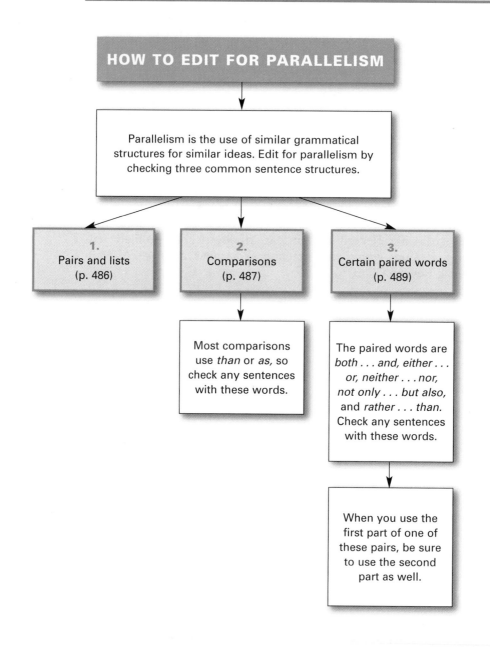

HOW TO EDIT FOR PARALLELISM

Parallelism is the use of similar grammatical structures for similar ideas. Edit for parallelism by checking three common sentence structures.

1.
Pairs and lists
(p. 486)

2.
Comparisons
(p. 487)

3.
Certain paired words
(p. 489)

Most comparisons use *than* or *as,* so check any sentences with these words.

The paired words are *both . . . and, either . . . or, neither . . . nor, not only . . . but also,* and *rather . . . than.* Check any sentences with these words.

When you use the first part of one of these pairs, be sure to use the second part as well.

32

Sentence Variety

Putting Rhythm in Your Writing

Understand What Sentence Variety Is

DEFINITION: Having **sentence variety** in your writing means using assorted sentence patterns, lengths, and rhythms. Most of us like variety: We don't want to eat the same dinner every night, own ten shirts of the same style and color, or listen to the same song ten times in a row.

If your sentences all have the same pattern and are the same length, your readers will quickly tire of them and may not keep reading long enough to understand your point. Many writers use too many short, simple sentences, mistakenly thinking that short is always easier to understand than long. In fact, that is not true, as the following examples show.

LEARNING JOURNAL
Use your learning journal as a place to record an example of a brief passage with short, similar-sounding sentences. Also record an edited version after you have introduced sentence variety.

WITH SHORT, SIMPLE SENTENCES

Age discrimination can exist even in unpaid jobs. The newspaper today reported that a magazine has been accused of age discrimination. The magazine is *The Atlantic Monthly*. A woman was told she was too old to be an unpaid intern. The woman was forty-one. The position was for a senior in college. The woman was a senior. She had raised three children before going to college. She is suing the magazine. The next day another woman, age fifty-one, reported that the same thing had happened to her a year earlier. She had filed a discrimination suit. The suit was brought to

TEAMWORK
After completing the chapter, students can work in small groups to reexamine this small paragraph. Have them try to identify which kinds of sentence variety the writer has used.

495

court by the Council on Age Discrimination. The magazine never showed up. The court never took any follow-up action against the magazine. Apparently the matter was not of great importance to either the magazine or the justice system.

WITH SENTENCE VARIETY

Age discrimination can exist even in unpaid jobs. The newspaper today reported that a magazine, *The Atlantic Monthly,* has been accused of age discrimination by a forty-one-year-old woman. This woman, who raised three children before going to college and is now in her senior year, was told she was too old to be an unpaid intern, even though the position was for a college senior. She is suing the magazine. The next day another woman, age fifty-one, reported that the same thing had happened to her a year earlier and she, too, had filed an age discrimination suit. The suit was brought to court by the Council on Age Discrimination, but the magazine didn't appear for the court date, and the court never took any follow-up action. Apparently the matter was not of great importance to either the magazine or the justice system.

Good writing results when you mix long and short sentences and use a variety of sentence patterns. Sentence variety is what gives your writing good rhythm and flow.

Practice Creating Sentence Variety

For two additional techniques used to achieve sentence variety—coordination and subordination— see Chapter 30.

To create sentence variety, you need to edit your writing so that it has sentences of different types and lengths. Because many writers tend to write short sentences that start with the subject, this chapter will focus on techniques for starting with something other than the subject and for writing a variety of longer sentences.

Remember that the goal is to use variety to achieve a good rhythm. Do not simply change all your sentences from one pattern to another, or you still won't have variety: You'll have just another set of similar-sounding sentences. When you are changing the patterns of your sentences, make sure that your revised sentences are correct.

START SOME SENTENCES WITH ADVERBS

ESL
Remind students that an adverb answers the question *how, when, where, why,* or *how often.*

DEFINITION: Adverbs are words that modify or describe verbs, adjectives, or other adverbs; they often end with -*ly*. As long as the meaning is clear, an adverb can be placed at the beginning of a sentence instead of in the middle. An adverb at the beginning is usually followed by a comma. If an adverb indicates time, such as *often* or *always*, a comma may not be needed. However, always use a comma if the reader should pause slightly after reading the adverb.

For more about adverbs, see Chapter 28.

ADVERB IN MIDDLE	Stories about haunted houses *frequently* surface at Halloween.
STARTS WITH ADVERB	*Frequently,* stories about haunted houses surface at Halloween.
ADVERB IN MIDDLE	These tales *often* reveal the life stories of former inhabitants.
STARTS WITH ADVERB	*Often* these tales reveal the life stories of former inhabitants.

PRACTICE 1 STARTING SENTENCES WITH AN ADVERB

Edit each sentence so that it begins with an adverb.

EXAMPLE: *Frequently, hurricanes*
~~Hurricanes frequently~~ strike barrier islands.

1. *Annually, harsh*
~~Harsh~~ weather takes a toll ~~annually~~ on sandy beaches.

2. *Once that*
~~That~~ island house ~~once~~ stood on solid ground.

3. *Eventually, the*
~~The~~ ocean ~~eventually~~ washed the ground out from under it.

4. *Finally, the*
~~The~~ house was ~~finally~~ condemned as unsafe.

5. *Now it*
~~It~~ is ~~now~~ going to be demolished.

PRACTICE 2 STARTING SENTENCES WITH AN ADVERB

In each sentence, fill in the blank with an adverb that makes sense. Add a comma when necessary. There may be several good choices for each item. In the example sentence, *luckily, thankfully,* or any of several other adverbs also would have been a good choice. *Answers will vary. Possible edits shown.*

EXAMPLE: _*Fortunately,*_ no one was living in the house at the time.

1. _*Once*_ a row of houses stood on the east side of the channel.

2. _*Suddenly,*_ a hurricane washed away most of the land nearby.

3. _*Overnight,*_ most of the houses vanished.

4. _____*Finally,*_____ the house stood alone on a sandy peninsula.

5 _____*Later,*_____ maps of the island were redrawn.

▮ PRACTICE 3   WRITING SENTENCES THAT START WITH AN ADVERB

Write three more sentences that start with an adverb. Use commas as necessary. Choose from the following adverbs: *often, sadly, amazingly, luckily, lovingly, gently, frequently, stupidly, quietly.* *Answers will vary.*

EXAMPLE: _*Luckily, I remembered to save my file on a disk.*_

1. _____

2. _____

3. _____

TEACHING TIP
Explain to students that in their own writing they will need to consider the context when deciding which sentence contains the more important idea.

JOIN IDEAS USING AN -*ING* VERB FORM

One way to combine sentences is to turn one of them into a phrase using an ***-ing* verb form** (such as *walking* or *racing*). The *-ing* verb form indicates that the two parts of the sentence are happening at the same time. The more important idea (the one you want to emphasize) should be in the main clause, not in the phrase you make by adding the *-ing* verb form.

ESL
Remind students that an *-ing* verb form that modifies the subject cannot be the main verb in the sentence.

TWO SENTENCES   Jonah did well in the high jump. He came in second.

JOINED WITH -*ING*   Jonah did well in the high jump, *coming* in second.
VERB FORM

To combine sentences this way, add *-ing* to the verb in one of the sentences and delete the subject. You now have a modifier phrase that can be added to the beginning or the end of the other sentence, depending on what makes sense.

He also won the long jump/ ~~He broke~~ *, breaking* the record.

If you add the phrase to the end of a sentence, you will usually need to put a comma before it, as in the preceding example, unless the phrase is essential to the meaning of the sentence. If you add a phrase starting with an *-ing* verb form to the beginning of a sentence, put a comma after it. Be sure that the word being modified follows immediately after the phrase. Otherwise, you will create a dangling modifier.

For more on finding and correcting dangling modifiers, see Chapter 29.

TWO SENTENCES	I dropped my bag. My groceries spilled.
DANGLING MODIFIER	Dropping my bag, my groceries spilled.
EDITED	Dropping my bag, I spilled my groceries.

PRACTICE 4   JOINING IDEAS USING AN *-ING* VERB FORM

Combine each pair of sentences into a single sentence by using an *-ing* verb form. Add or delete words if necessary. *Answers may vary. Possible edits shown.*

Wanting the guests at his fourth birthday party to stay away from his toys, he
EXAMPLE: ̭He hit the other children. ~~He wanted the guests at his fourth~~

   ~~birthday party to stay away from his toys.~~

Paying   *, some*
1. ~~Children pay~~ attention to role models.⁄ ~~Some~~ children learn aggression
                                              ̭
   from people at home, at school, or on television.

Reacting
2. ~~I react~~ to some frustrating situations with fury.⁄I forget that my son
   ̭   ̭
   Sean watches and learns from me.

Acting violently under stress, his
3. ~~His~~ favorite television characters do not model good behavior, either.
   ̭
   ~~They act violently under stress.~~

Fearing that Sean would not learn to control his temper,
4. I wanted expert advice on anger management. ~~I feared that Sean would~~
   ̭
   ~~not learn to control his temper.~~

Punishing
5. ~~I punished~~ my son for his angry outbursts.⁄I used to take away his toys
   ̭   ̭
   and privileges.

Saying that punishing Sean for losing his temper was ineffective, an
6. ~~An~~ expert told me that angry children need positive lessons in how to
   ̭
   cope. ~~She said that punishing Sean for losing his temper was ineffective.~~

Giving him something to focus on before lashing out,
7. I taught my son concrete ways to react to his anger. ~~I gave him some-~~
   ̭
   ~~thing to focus on before lashing out.~~

Saving the lessons for his calm moods,
8. I did not try to reason with my son when he was furious. ~~I saved the~~
   ^

   ~~lessons for his calm moods.~~

   Counting   *, Sean*
9. ~~Sean counts~~ to ten when he gets angry./ ~~He~~ now gives himself time to
   ^   ^

   cool off.

                    Learning   *, preschoolers*
10. ~~Preschoolers can learn~~ ways to handle their anger./ ~~They~~ can modify
    ^   ^

    their reactions before they understand why they should.

■ **PRACTICE 5** **JOINING IDEAS USING AN -*ING* VERB FORM**

Fill in the blank in each sentence with an appropriate -*ing* verb form.
There are many possible ways to complete each sentence. *Answers will vary.*
Possible edits shown.

> **EXAMPLE:** ___*Lounging*___ in his cubicle, Franklin tossed pencils
> aimlessly at the ceiling.

1. ___*Staring*___ at the computer screen, Franklin tried to concentrate.

2. In the next cubicle sat Martina, ___*annoying*___ Franklin with a loud
   telephone conversation.

3. ___*Pounding*___ on the wall between them, he tried to get her attention.

4. A stapler flew over the wall into Franklin's cubicle, ___*landing*___ on his
   head.

5. ___*Returning*___ the stapler, Franklin thanked Martina for waking him up.

■ **PRACTICE 6** **JOINING IDEAS USING AN -*ING* VERB FORM**

Write two sets of sentences, and join each set using an -*ing* verb form.

> **EXAMPLE:** a. *Teresa signed onto eBay.com.*
>
> b. *She used her password.*

COMBINED: *Using her password, Teresa signed onto eBay.com.*

Teresa signed onto eBay.com using her password.

1. a. _____

    b. _____

    COMBINED: _____

    _____

2. a. _____

    b. _____

    COMBINED: _____

    _____

JOIN IDEAS USING AN -*ED* VERB FORM

For more on helping verbs, see Chapters 25 and 26.

DEFINITION: Another way to combine sentences is to turn one of them into a phrase using an **-*ed* verb form** (such as *waited* or *walked*). You can join sentences this way if one of them has a form of *be* as a helping verb along with the -*ed* verb form.

TWO SENTENCES   Leonardo da Vinci was a man of many talents. He was noted most often for his painting.

JOINED WITH -*ED* VERB FORM   Noted most often for his painting, Leonardo da Vinci was a man of many talents.

To combine sentences this way, drop the subject and the helping verb from a sentence that has an -*ed* verb form. You now have a modifier phrase that can be added to the beginning or the end of the other sentence, depending on what makes the most sense.

Interested

~~Leonardo was interested~~ in many areas./ He investigated problems of geology, botany, mechanics, and hydraulics. *, Leonardo*

If you add a phrase that begins with an -*ed* verb form to the beginning of a sentence, put a comma after it. Be sure the word that the phrase

For more on finding and correcting dangling modifiers, see Chapter 29.

modifies follows immediately. Otherwise, you will create a dangling modifier. Sometimes, as in the preceding example, you will need to change the word that the phrase modifies from a pronoun to a noun. If you add the phrase to the end of the sentence, you will need to put a comma before it unless the meaning of the sentence would change without the phrase.

PRACTICE 7 JOINING IDEAS USING AN -*ED* VERB FORM

Combine each pair of sentences into a single sentence by using an -*ed* verb form.

EXAMPLE: ~~Alligators are hatched~~ *Hatched* from eggs when they are only a few inches long. ~~Alligators~~ *, alligators* can reach a length of ten feet or more as adults.

1. ~~An alligator was spotted in a pond in Central Park in New York in June of 2001.~~ Many New Yorkers refused to believe in the existence of the alligator/ *spotted in a pond in Central Park in New York City in June of 2001.*

2. ~~Alligators were released~~ *Released* by their owners for growing too large to be pets/ ~~These~~ alligators were sometimes said to be living in New York City sewers.

3. ~~Rumors were believed~~ *Believed* by some gullible people/ ~~The~~ *, the* rumors about giant sewer alligators were untrue.

4. ~~The story of the alligator in Central Park was denied~~ *Denied* by city officials/ ~~The~~ *, the* story *of the alligator in Central Park* sounded like another wild rumor.

5. ~~Central Park alligator sightings were reported~~ *Reported* by several New Yorkers/ ~~The~~ *, the Central Park alligator* sightings were confirmed when a television news crew filmed a reptile in the pond.

6. ~~A professional alligator wrestler was hired~~ *Hired* to catch the reptile/ ~~He~~ *, a professional alligator wrestler* came to New York from Florida.

7. ~~The pond in Central Park was surrounded~~ by news cameras and
Surrounded
, the pond in Central Park^
curious onlookers./ It was brightly lit just before 11:00 P.M. on June 22.

8. ~~The creature was captured~~ in just a few minutes by the alligator
Captured
, the
wrestler's wife./ The so-called alligator turned out to be a spectacled
caiman, a species native to Central and South America.

9. ~~Some New Yorkers were surprised~~ to find that the caiman was only two
Surprised
, some New Yorkers^
feet long./ They may have felt a bit foolish for expecting to see a giant
alligator in the park.

10. ~~The caiman was removed~~ from Central Park./ It soon found a home in
Removed *the caiman*
a warmer climate.

PRACTICE 8 JOINING IDEAS USING AN *-ED* VERB FORM

Fill in the blank in each sentence with an appropriate *-ed* verb form. There
are several possible ways to complete each sentence. *Answers will vary. Possible edits shown.*

EXAMPLE: ___*Decorated*___ in unusual colors and textures, fingernails
are sometimes as stylish as clothing.

1. ___*Trained*___ to perform manicures, nail stylists are setting up shop
all over the United States.

2. Style-conscious women today are seldom satisfied with old-fashioned
fingernails ___*painted*___ with a simple solid color.

3. ___*Treated*___ as an art form, manicures have become a new fashion
trend.

4. Some expensive manicures turn fingernails into exotic little sculptures
___*designed*___ to last only a few days.

5. _____*Asked*_____ to create fingernail designs to match the latest fashions,

a manicurist with an artistic touch can make a good living today.

> ### PRACTICE 9   JOINING IDEAS USING AN *-ED* VERB FORM

Write two sets of sentences and join them using an *-ed* verb form.

EXAMPLE: a. *Lee is training for the Boston Marathon.*

b. *It is believed to have the most difficult hill to run.*

COMBINED: *Lee is training for the Boston Marathon, believed to have the most*

difficult hill to run.

1. a. _____

   b. _____

   COMBINED: _____

   _____

2. a. _____

   b. _____

   COMBINED: _____

   _____

JOIN IDEAS USING AN APPOSITIVE

DEFINITION: An **appositive** is a phrase that renames a noun. Appositives can be used to combine two sentences into one.

TWO SENTENCES   Elvis Presley continues to be popular many years after his death. He is "the King."

JOINED WITH AN   Elvis Presley, "the King," continues to be popular many
APPOSITIVE   years after his death.

[The phrase *"the King"* renames the noun *Elvis Presley.*]

To combine two sentences this way, turn the sentence that renames the noun into a phrase by dropping its subject and verb. The appositive phrase can appear anywhere in the sentence, but it should be placed before or after the noun it renames. Use a comma or commas to set off the appositive.

Elvis's home is visited by millions of people each year. ~~It is~~
          , Graceland,

~~called Graceland.~~

PRACTICE 10   **JOINING IDEAS USING AN APPOSITIVE**

Combine each pair of sentences into a single sentence by using an appositive. Be sure to use a comma or commas to set off the appositive.

> **EXAMPLE**: A decade ago, a majority of college students wanted one
> thing from their ~~education. They wanted~~ a high-paying job.
>   *education,*

1. In the late 1980s, political activists ~~were~~ a rare breed. ~~They~~ were almost unknown on many college campuses.

2. Political demonstrations ~~had~~ once ~~been~~ a common sight. ~~They~~ seemed as outdated as the hippie lifestyle by 1990.

3. Protests made the news again in 1999. ~~That was~~ the year activists targeted the Seattle meeting of the World Trade Organization.

4. The destruction of property did not win many supporters to the Seattle protesters' cause. ~~It was an unpopular tactic.~~
      , an unpopular tactic,

5. But the Seattle protests publicized the idea of social activism. ~~It was~~ a concept that was out of fashion at the time.

6. Young Americans today are not united by a single political cause. ~~They are a diverse group with diverse interests.~~
                          , a diverse group with diverse interests,

7. Most social activists share a common goal. ~~That goal is~~ to have a positive effect on others' lives.

8. Many young people interested in making a difference nationally or globally turn to their college campuses. ~~These are~~ the traditional training grounds for social activism.

9. College courses can provide young activists with a knowledge of history, This is an essential subject for anyone who hopes to improve society.

10. Some college students are motivated and idealistic, They dream of a fairer and more tolerant world.

PRACTICE 11   JOINING IDEAS USING AN APPOSITIVE

Fill in the blank in each sentence with an appropriate appositive. There are many possible ways to complete each sentence. *Answers will vary. Possible edits shown.*

> **EXAMPLE:** My sister Clara, _a busy mother of three_, loves to watch soap operas.

1. Clara's favorite show, _Love and Desire_, comes on at three o'clock in the afternoon.

2. Clara, _a hardworking seamstress_, rarely has the time to sit down in front of the television for the broadcast.

3. Instead, she programs her VCR, _an aging but reliable machine_, and tapes the show for later.

4. Clara's husband, _her childhood sweetheart_, used to tease her for watching the soaps.

5. But while he was recovering from the flu recently, he found her stack of tapes, _a pile over two feet high_, and Clara insists that he watched every show of the previous season.

Use *who* to refer to a person, *which* to refer to places or things (but not to people), and *that* for people, places, or things. When referring to a person, *who* is preferable to *that*.

JOIN IDEAS USING AN ADJECTIVE CLAUSE

DEFINITION: An **adjective clause** is a group of words with a subject and a verb that modifies or describes a noun. Adjective clauses often begin with the word *who, which,* or *that* and can be used to combine two sentences into one.

TWO SENTENCES	Lorene owns an art and framing store. She is a good friend of mine.
JOINED WITH AN ADJECTIVE CLAUSE	Lorene, who is a good friend, owns an art and framing store.

> An adjective clause is sometimes called a relative clause. The word it begins with is called a relative adjective because it *relates* the word group to a specific word in the sentence.

To join sentences this way, use *who, which,* or *that* to replace the subject of a sentence that describes a noun in another sentence. Once you have made this change, you have an adjective clause that you can move so that it follows the noun it describes. The sentence with the more important idea (the one you want to emphasize) should become the main clause. The less important idea should be in the adjective clause.

TWO SENTENCES	Rosalind is director of human services for the town of Marlborough. Marlborough is her hometown.

[The more important idea here is that Rosalind is director of human services. The less important idea is that the town is her hometown.]

JOINED WITH AN ADJECTIVE CLAUSE	Rosalind is director of human services for the town of Marlborough, her hometown.

NOTE: Punctuating adjective clauses can be tricky. If an adjective clause can be taken out of a sentence without completely changing the meaning of the sentence, put commas around the clause.

Lorene, who is a good friend, owns an art and framing store.

[The phrase *who is a good friend* adds information about Lorene, but it is not essential; the sentence *Lorene owns an art and framing store* means almost the same thing as the sentence in the example.]

If an adjective clause is an essential part of the meaning of a sentence, do not put commas around it.

Lorene is a good friend who saved my life.

[*Who saved my life* is an essential part of this sentence. The sentence *Lorene is a good friend* is very different in meaning from the whole sentence in the example.]

PRACTICE 12   JOINING IDEAS USING AN ADJECTIVE CLAUSE

Combine each pair of sentences into a single sentence by using an adjective clause beginning with *who, which,* or *that.*

Allergies that

EXAMPLE: ~~Some allergies~~ ^ cause sneezing, itching, and watery eyes. ~~They~~

can make people very uncomfortable.

that

1. Cats produce a protein./ ~~It~~ ^ keeps their skin soft.

, which   ,

2. This protein ^ makes some people itch and sneeze./ ~~The protein~~ ^ is the

   reason for most allergic reactions to cats.

who

3. Some cat lovers ^ are allergic to cats./ ~~They~~ can control their allergies with

   medication.

that

4. Allergic cat lovers may get another option from a new company./ ~~The company~~ ^

   wants to create a genetically engineered cat.

that

5. Scientists have successfully cloned mice./ ~~Some mice~~ ^ have been

   genetically engineered for scientific study.

, which

6. Researchers may soon have the technology to clone cats./ ~~Cats~~ could be

   genetically engineered to remove the allergen.

7. ~~Many people have allergic reactions to cats.~~ According to cat experts,

   who have allergic reactions to cats

   more than 10 percent of those people are allergic to something other ^

   than the skin-softening protein.

8. ~~A single gene produces a cat's skin-softening protein.~~ Scientists are not

   that produces a cat's skin-softening protein

   sure whether the gene ^ is necessary for the cat's good health.

9. However, owning a genetically engineered cat would allow an allergic

   , which

   person to avoid taking allergy medications./ ~~The medications~~ ^ can

   sometimes cause dangerous side effects.

that

10. Cloning and genetic engineering raise ethical questions./ ~~These~~ ^ are

    difficult to answer.

PRACTICE 13   JOINING IDEAS USING AN ADJECTIVE CLAUSE

Fill in the blank in each of the following sentences with an appropriate adjective clause. Add commas, if necessary. There are many possible ways to complete each sentence. *Answers will vary. Possible edits shown.*

EXAMPLE: Interactive television ___*, which may soon be available to consumers,*___ is a potential threat to viewers' privacy.

1. Many Web sites ___*that receive hundreds or thousands of hits each day*___ try to make a profit by selling information about visitors to the site.

2. Consumers ___*who buy products online*___ must provide information to retail Web sites before being allowed to complete a purchase.

3. Consumer privacy ___*, which is becoming rarer every day,*___ may suffer further when interactive television stations begin to operate.

4. A viewer ___*who tunes in to an interactive television program*___ may not realize that the television station is collecting information about him or her.

5. The sale of personal information ___*, which companies use to target potential customers,*___ can bring huge profits.

Edit Paragraphs and Your Own Writing

PRACTICE 14   EDITING PARAGRAPHS FOR SENTENCE VARIETY

Create sentence variety in the following paragraphs. Join at least two sentences in each of the paragraphs. Try to use several of the techniques discussed in this chapter. There are many possible ways to edit each paragraph. You may want to refer to the Quick Review Chart on page 512. *Answers will vary. Possible edits shown.*

(1) Lotteries *, which* were illegal until recently in most U.S. states./(2) ~~They~~ have now been legalized in most parts of this country. (3) ~~The lotteries~~ *Run* ~~are run~~ by state governments in many places./ (4) ~~Lotteries~~ *, lotteries* allow the

governments to raise money without raising taxes. (5) The money can

help fund education and other projects./ (6) ~~These projects~~ *that* are necessary

and expensive. (7) Many citizens *who* consider lotteries an ideal way to raise

funds./ (8) ~~These people~~ reason that no one is forced to buy a lottery

ticket. (9) However, lotteries have a dark side that should be discussed

more often.

(10) Many experts on gambling worry about the increasing numbers

of state lotteries./ (11) ~~Lotteries~~ *, which* are difficult for many people to resist.

(12) ~~The games offer~~ *Offering* prizes of millions of dollars./ (13) ~~They~~ *, lotteries* make

people fantasize about easy wealth. (14) ~~Lottery~~ *Costing very little, lottery* tickets ~~cost very~~

~~little.~~ (15) ~~They~~ are sold in grocery stores and shops in every neighbor-

hood. (16) Unfortunately, the people least able to afford lottery tickets

spend the most money on them./(17) ~~They are~~ convinced that they will

strike it rich someday. (18) In many impoverished areas, large numbers of

people regularly buy several lottery tickets each week./ (19) ~~They hope~~ *, hoping* to

escape boring, low-paying jobs.

(20) Nor are the poor the only victims of lottery fever. (21) Many

people ~~are~~ addicted to gambling./ (22) ~~They~~ do not consider the nearly

impossible odds of winning a lottery jackpot. (23) ~~They are hooked~~ *Hooked* by

occasional small payoffs of two or three dollars./ (24) ~~Addicted~~ *, addicted* gamblers

will keep buying tickets until they have no money left.

(25) ~~Lotteries promise~~ *Promising* a big payoff for a little investment./ (26) ~~They~~ *, lotteries*

bring vast amounts of money into state treasuries. (27) ~~Many people believe~~ *But lottery supporters, believing*

that lotteries save everyone money./(28) ~~But lottery supporters~~ seldom

think about the victims of lotteries. (29) When taxes fund state programs,

wealthier people must contribute more than poorer people. (30) But gambling addicts and people desperate to escape poverty pay more heavily than anyone else into state lottery funds. (31) Governments should not rely on the poor and addicted to come up with money to run essential state programs.

PRACTICE 15   EDITING YOUR OWN WRITING FOR SENTENCE VARIETY

As a final practice, edit a piece of your own writing for sentence variety. It can be a paper you are working on for this course, a paper you've already finished, a paper for another course, or a recent piece of writing from your work or everyday life. Record in your learning journal any examples of short, choppy sentences you find, along with the edited versions. You may want to use the following Quick Review Chart.

LEARNING JOURNAL
Do you tend to write short, similar-sounding sentences? Which sentence patterns covered in this chapter do you think you will use most often when you are editing for sentence variety?

Quick Review Chart

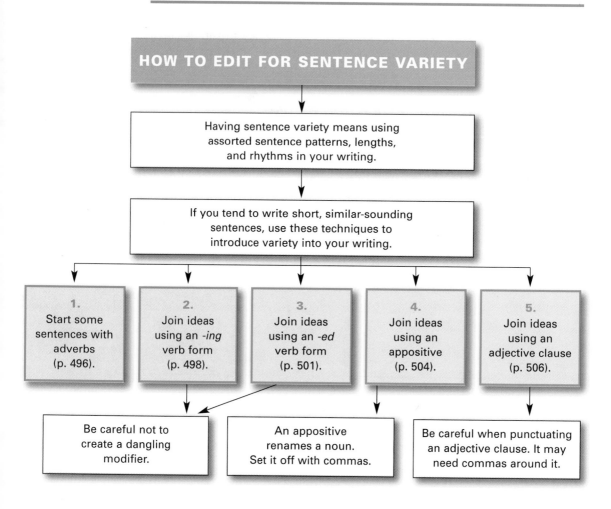

HOW TO EDIT FOR SENTENCE VARIETY

Having sentence variety means using assorted sentence patterns, lengths, and rhythms in your writing.

If you tend to write short, similar-sounding sentences, use these techniques to introduce variety into your writing.

1. Start some sentences with adverbs (p. 496).

2. Join ideas using an *-ing* verb form (p. 498).

3. Join ideas using an *-ed* verb form (p. 501).

4. Join ideas using an appositive (p. 504).

5. Join ideas using an adjective clause (p. 506).

Be careful not to create a dangling modifier.

An appositive renames a noun. Set it off with commas.

Be careful when punctuating an adjective clause. It may need commas around it.

33

ESL Concerns

Areas of Special Interest to Nonnative Speakers and Speakers of Nonstandard English

If English is not your first language or if you grew up speaking a different version of English than what is expected in college papers, you may need some help with certain aspects of English that may be very different from your own first or your current spoken language. This chapter will focus on those areas.

Nouns and Articles

SUBJECTS

DEFINITION: The **subject** of a sentence is the person, place, or thing the sentence is about. It is either a noun, a pronoun (a word that substitutes for a noun), or a word or phrase that functions like a noun. Be sure to include a subject in every sentence and every dependent clause.

> It is
> ~~Is~~ hot outside.

>   she does
> My teacher makes us write a lot, although not grade us.

This chapter focuses on problems that many nonnative speakers of English have when they write papers for college, but native speakers may find it useful as well.

RESOURCES
For more advice and recommendations on teaching ESL students, see *Practical Suggestions.*

COUNT AND NONCOUNT NOUNS

DEFINITION: A **noun** is a word that names a person, place, or thing. English nouns fall into two categories: those naming things that can be counted, and those naming things that cannot be counted.

Singular means one; plural means more than one.

COUNT NOUN	I sold ten of my old *CD*s at the yard sale.
NONCOUNT NOUN	I sold lots of *music* at the yard sale.

DEFINITION: A **count noun** names a distinct individual item that can be counted. The noun *CD* is a count noun.

DEFINITION: A **noncount noun** names a general category or group that cannot be divided easily into distinct, countable items. The noun *music* is a noncount noun. In English, it would not make sense to say *I bought ten new musics.* Here are some more examples.

LEARNING JOURNAL
Use your learning journal as a place to record sentences with the types of problems covered in this chapter or other problems that you think may be related to the fact that you speak English as a second language or that your spoken English differs from the English expected in college writing. Also record edited versions of these sentences, with the problems corrected.

COUNT	NONCOUNT
apple/apples	fruit
tree/trees	grass
dollar/dollars	money
beach/beaches	sand
fact/facts	information

Count nouns can be made plural. Noncount nouns usually cannot be plural; they are usually singular.

TEAMWORK
Have students, in small groups, create two separate lists: one of count nouns and the other of noncount nouns. Then ask students to write two brief, silly stories, each using all the words from one of the lists.

COUNT/SINGLE	I got a *ticket* for the concert.
COUNT/PLURAL	I got two *tickets* for the concert.
NONCOUNT	The Internet has all kinds of *information.*

NOTE: Some noncount nouns, such as *fruit, money,* and *sand,* are occasionally treated as count nouns *(the sands of time).*

ARTICLES

DEFINITION: The words *a, an,* and *the* are called **articles**; they are used with nouns. You can choose *a, an, the,* or no article at all. Use *a* before words that start with a consonant sound; use *an* before words that start with a vowel sound: *a* dog, *an* elevator. The box that follows shows how to use articles and when to use no article at all.

Never use *a* or *an* with noncount nouns.

Articles with Count and Noncount Nouns

COUNT NOUNS	ARTICLE
SINGULAR	
Identity known	*the*
	I want to read *the book* on taxes that you recommended.
	[The sentence refers to one particular book: the one that was recommended.]
	I can't stay in *the sun* very long.
	[There is only one sun.]
Identity not known	*a* or *an*
	I want to read *a book* on taxes.
	[It could be any book on taxes.]
PLURAL	
Identity known	*the*
	I enjoyed *the books* we read.
	[The sentence refers to a particular group of books: the ones we read.]
Identity not known or a general category	**(no article at all or another kind of word such as *this, these, that, some*)**
	I usually enjoy *books*.
	[The sentence refers to books in general.]
	She found *some books*.
	[I don't know which books she found.]

NONCOUNT NOUNS	ARTICLE
SINGULAR	
Identity known	*the*
	I put away *the food* we bought.
	[The sentence refers to particular food: the food we bought.]
Identity not known or a general category	**(no article at all or another kind of word such as *this, these, that, some*)**
	There is *food* all over the kitchen.
	[The reader doesn't know what food the sentence refers to.]
	Give *some food* to the neighbors.
	[The sentence refers to food in general.]

TEAMWORK
Practice 1 works well in pairs. Afterward, students can discuss the corrections as a whole class.

■ **PRACTICE 1**   **EDITING NOUNS AND ARTICLES**

Edit the following paragraph, adding and changing articles and nouns as necessary. Also, add a subject to any sentence that is missing one.

EXAMPLE: Restaurant work is not an easy way to earn ~~the~~ money.

(1) I am *a* waitress at ~~the~~ *a* restaurant four days a week. (2) My shift is at lunchtime*s*, and *it* is usually very busy then. (3) *There is a* ~~Is an~~ university close by, so ~~the~~ many college students eat at my restaurant because it serves cheap food*s*. (4) I am *a* college student too; however, some of my student cus- tomers do not treat me as ~~a~~ *an* equal. (5) They seem to think that *it* is okay to be rude to *the* person serving them. (6) Many of them do not tip me well even though I am *a* very good waitress and take good care*s* of my customers. (7) I do not make *a* high ~~salaries~~ *salary*, so I need the tips from my customers to make *a* good living. (8) I understand that college students are often pinch- ing ~~penny.~~ *pennies.* (9) However, I think that people*s* who cannot afford to leave *a* tip should not eat in a restaurant.

Verbs

DEFINITION: **Verbs** tell what action the subject in a sentence performs or link the subject to a word that describes it.

USING THE *-ING* FORM OR THE *TO* FORM AFTER CERTAIN VERBS

To improve your ability to write and speak standard English, read magazines and your local newspaper, and listen to television and radio news programs. Also read magazines and newspaper articles aloud; it will help your pronunciation.

DEFINITIONS: A **gerund** (or *-ing* form of the verb) is a verb form that ends in *-ing* and acts as a noun. An **infinitive** is a verb form that is preceded by the word *to* but has no ending added. These verb forms (gerunds and infinitives) cannot be the main verbs in sentences; each sentence must have another word that is the main verb.

In the sentences that follow, the gerund and the infinitive are objects — they receive the action of the verbs.

| GERUND | I enjoy *skating*. |
| INFINITIVE | I like *to skate*. |

For advice on verbs with prepositions, see page 520. For more on the position of verbs in questions, see page 523. For other problems with verbs, see Chapter 26.

How do you decide whether to use a gerund or an infinitive as the object of a verb? The decision often depends on the main verb in a sentence. Some verbs can be followed by either a gerund or an infinitive, some can be followed only by a gerund, and some can be followed only by an infinitive. Knowing which to use can be tricky because the correct form is based on common practice, not logic. Practice using the correct structures for the verbs you use most often.

In the examples in this section, the verbs in the sentences are double-underlined.

Verbs That Are Followed by Either an Infinitive or a Gerund

begin	hate	remember	try
continue	like	start	
forget	love	stop	

These verbs can be followed by either an infinitive or a gerund. Sometimes the meaning is about the same.

He loves to drive. = He loves driving.

Sometimes the meaning changes depending on whether you use an infinitive or a gerund.

Mario stopped to smoke.

[This sentence means that Mario stopped what he was doing and smoked a cigarette.]

Mario stopped smoking.

[This sentence means that Mario no longer smokes cigarettes.]

Verbs That Are Followed by an Infinitive

agree	decide	need	refuse
ask	expect	offer	want
beg	fail	plan	
choose	hope	pretend	
claim	manage	promise	

Aunt Sally <u>wants</u> to help.

Cal <u>hopes</u> to become a millionaire.

Verbs That Are Followed by a Gerund

admit	discuss	keep	risk
avoid	enjoy	miss	suggest
consider	finish	practice	
deny	imagine	quit	

The representative <u>risks</u> losing the election.

Sophia <u>considered</u> quitting her job.

PROGRESSIVE TENSE

DEFINITION: The **progressive tense** consists of a form of the verb *be* plus the *-ing* form of a verb. It is used to indicate a continuing activity. Use the present progressive tense to indicate that an action is in progress now.

Lottie <u>is learning</u> to paint.

Our instructor <u>is posting</u> grades today.

Not all verbs can form the progressive tense. Certain verbs that indicate sensing or a state of being are not generally used this way.

> ## *Verbs That Cannot Form the Progressive Tense*
>
> | | | | |
> |---|---|---|---|
> | appear | have | mean | taste |
> | believe | hear | need | understand |
> | belong | know | see | want |
> | cost | like | seem | weigh |

appears
The dog is ~~appearing~~ angry.

costs
That bag is ~~costing~~ too much.

PRACTICE 2   EDITING VERBS

Edit the following paragraph to make sure that the verbs are used correctly.

(1) Marlene and Agnetha wanted ~~seeing~~ *to see* a certain movie after they saw the advertisement for it in the newspaper. (2) David Manning, the reviewer who was quoted in the ad, ~~was liking~~ *liked* the film a lot. (3) The two women did not want to miss ~~to see~~ *seeing* the film at their neighborhood theater, so they arranged their schedules carefully. (4) They managed ~~attending~~ *to attend* the first show on Saturday afternoon. (5) After they ~~were seeing~~ *saw* the movie, they were very angry that they had wasted their time and money. (6) They ~~were not understanding~~ *did not understand* how the reviewer could have enjoyed ~~to watch~~ *watching* such a stupid film. (7) Then Marlene read in a different newspaper that the movie studio had admitted to ~~invent~~ *inventing* David Manning. (8) Every well-known film critic ~~was hating~~ *had hated* the movie. (9) Therefore, the studio executives had decided ~~publishing~~ *to publish* advertisements that contained a made-up quotation saying that the film was wonderful. (10) Marlene and Agnetha were so disgusted by this deception that they planned to write to the head of the movie studio and ask ~~getting~~ *to get* their money back.

TEACHING TIP
Have students submit (anonymously, if they prefer) paragraphs from one of their rough drafts. Then, as a whole class, edit the paragraphs with attention to verb forms.

Prepositions

For more on prepositions, see Chapter 22. For a list of prepositions, see page 347.

DEFINITION: A **preposition** is a word (such as *of, above, between, about*) that connects a noun, pronoun, or verb with some other information about it. Knowing which preposition to use can be difficult because the correct preposition is often determined by idiom or common practice rather than by its actual meaning.

DEFINITION: An **idiom** is any combination of words that is always used the same way, even though there is no logical or grammatical explanation for it. The best way to learn English idioms is to listen and read as much as possible and then to practice writing and speaking the correct forms.

PREPOSITIONS WITH ADJECTIVES

Adjectives are often followed by prepositions. Here are some common examples.

afraid of	full of	scared of
ashamed of	happy about	sorry for
aware of	interested in	tired of
confused by	proud of	
excited about	responsible for	

Tanya is excited ~~of~~ *about* going to Mexico.

However, she is afraid ~~by~~ *of* taking time off.

PREPOSITIONS WITH VERBS

Many verbs consist of a verb plus a preposition (or adverb). The meaning of these verbs usually has nothing to do with the literal meanings of the verb and the preposition. Taken together, however, the verb and the preposition have a particular meaning in English. Often, the meaning of the verb changes completely depending on which preposition is used with it.

You must *take out* the trash. [*take out* = bring to a different location]

You must *take in* the exciting sights of New York City. [*take in* = observe]

Here are a few common examples.

call off (cancel)	They *called off* the pool party.
call on (choose)	The teacher always *calls on* me.
drop in (visit)	*Drop in* when you are in the area.

fill in (refill)	Please *fill in* the holes in the ground.
fill out (complete)	Please *fill out* this application form.
fill up (make something full)	Don't *fill up* with junk food.
go over (review)	He wants to *go over* our speeches.
grow up (age)	All children *grow up*.
hand in (submit)	You may *hand in* your homework now.
look up (check)	I *looked up* the word in the dictionary.
pick out (choose)	Sandy *picked out* a puppy.
pick up (take or collect)	When do you *pick up* the keys?
put off (postpone)	I often *put off* doing dishes.

PRACTICE 3   EDITING PREPOSITIONS

Edit the following sentences to make sure that the correct prepositions are used.

> **EXAMPLE:** Several U.S. presidents have said that they were sorry of^*for* the mistreatment of Japanese Americans during World War II.

1. During World War II, more than 120,000 Japanese Americans were shut ~~down~~^*up* in internment camps.

2. Many young Japanese Americans still chose to sign ~~away~~^*up* for the U.S. military.

3. These soldiers often had to fight ~~for~~^*against* prejudice as well as the enemy.

4. About eight hundred Japanese American soldiers gave ~~in~~^*up* their lives during the fighting.

5. After the war, many Japanese Americans who had been interned were ashamed ~~for~~^*of* their experience.

6. More than fifty years after the war, some Americans of Japanese descent became interested ~~on~~^*in* creating a memorial to the Japanese Americans of the war years.

7. They wanted to make other Americans aware ~~on~~ *of* the sacrifices of

   Japanese Americans during World War II.

8. A city full ~~with~~ *of* memorials to the country's past, Washington, D.C., was

   chosen to be the site of the National Japanese American Memorial.

9. For the center of the memorial park, the designers picked ~~on~~ *out* a sculpture

   by a Japanese American artist, Nina Akamu, featuring two cranes

   tangled in barbed wire.

10. Visitors to the park will be reminded ~~on~~ *of* Japanese Americans' struggle

    for acceptance in the United States.

PRACTICE 4 EDITING PREPOSITIONS

Edit the following paragraph to make sure that the correct prepositions are
used.

(1) Students who are anxious ~~on~~ *about* mathematics take fewer math classes

and perform worse in them than students who do not have math anxiety.

(2) Scientists used to believe that students were afraid ~~about~~ *of* math

because they were not good at it, but that belief was incorrect. (3) It turns

~~up~~ *out* that worry prevents students from understanding mathematics as well

as they could. (4) Fear interferes ~~in~~ *with* the working memory that is necessary

for math, making students less able to think about math problems. (5)

Starting ~~on~~ *at* about the age of twelve, students with math anxiety become

less able to compensate for the loss of working memory. (6) The good news

is that effective treatment is available for math anxiety. (7) Students who

once thought they would never be able to understand math may someday

find ~~up~~ *out* that they can conquer their anxiety and cope with numbers.

Negatives and Questions

NEGATIVES

To form a negative statement, you can usually use one of these words:

never	nobody	no one	nowhere
no	none	not	

DEFINITION: The word *not* is often combined with a verb in a shortened form called a **contraction**. Contractions are common in spoken English and in informal written English, but they may not be appropriate in all papers.

They aren't finished. = They are not finished.

In standard English, there can be only one negative word in each clause.

Johnetta will ~~not~~ call no one.

anyone
Johnetta will not call ~~no one~~.

When you write a negative statement using the word *not*, the *not* must come after the first helping verb in the sentence. If there is no helping verb, you must add a form of *do* as well as *not* to make a negative statement.

A clause is a group of words with a subject and a verb. It may or may not be able to stand on its own as a sentence. For more on clauses, see Chapter 22.

Common Helping Verbs

FORMS OF *BE*	FORMS OF *HAVE*	FORMS OF *DO*	OTHER VERBS
am	have	do	can
are	has	does	could
been	had	did	may
being			might
is			must
was			should
were			will

POSITIVE	Candace *will go* with us.
NEGATIVE	Candace *will not go* with us.
POSITIVE	I *enjoyed* the party.
NEGATIVE	I *did not enjoy* the party.

[Notice that the verb *enjoyed* changed to *enjoy* once the verb *did* was added.]

QUESTIONS

To turn a statement into a question, move the helping verb in the statement so that it comes before the subject. If the only verb is a form of *be*, it should also be moved before the subject. If there is no helping verb or form of *be* in the statement, you must add a form of *do* and put it before the subject. Be sure to end the question with a question mark.

STATEMENT	Tory *can work* late.
QUESTION	*Can* Tory *work* late?
STATEMENT	Cia *is* smart.
QUESTION	*Is* Cia smart?
STATEMENT	You *helped* my sister.
QUESTION	*Did* you *help* my sister?

[Notice that the verb *helped* changed to *help* once the verb *did* was added.]

PRACTICE 5   WRITING NEGATIVE STATEMENTS AND QUESTIONS

For each positive statement, write one negative statement and one question.

EXAMPLE:

Positive statement: *The weather forecast calls for rain tomorrow.*

Negative statement: *The weather forecast does not call for rain tomorrow.*

Question: *Does the weather forecast call for rain tomorrow?*

1. **Positive statement:** We will have to cancel the picnic.

   Negative statement: *We will not have to cancel the picnic.*

   Question: *Will we have to cancel the picnic?*

2. **Positive statement:** The forecast on television could be wrong.

   Negative statement: _The forecast on television could not be wrong._

   Question: _Could the forecast on television be wrong?_

3. **Positive statement:** The garden needs water this year.

   Negative statement: _The garden does not need water this year._

   Question: _Does the garden need water this year?_

4. **Positive statement:** The children liked playing in the rain.

   Negative statement: _The children did not like playing in the rain._

   Question: _Did the children like playing in the rain?_

5. **Positive statement:** Carrying an umbrella was a good idea.

   Negative statement: _Carrying an umbrella was not a good idea._

   Question: _Was carrying an umbrella a good idea?_

Adjectives

DEFINITION: Adjectives modify or describe nouns and pronouns. Many sentences have several adjectives that modify the same word.

For more on adjectives, see Chapter 28.

The happy old brown dog slept on the sidewalk.

ORDER OF ADJECTIVES

When you use more than one adjective to modify the same word, you should use the conventional order for adjectives in standard English. The list that follows indicates this order.

1. Judgment or overall opinion: *awful, friendly, intelligent, strange, terrible.*
2. Size: *big, huge, tiny, small, large, short, tall.*
3. Shape: *round, square, fat, thin, circular.*
4. Age: *old, young, new, youthful.*

5. Color: *blue, green, yellow, red.*

6. Nationality or location: *Greek, Italian, California, southern.*

7. Material: *paper, glass, plastic, wooden.*

EXAMPLE, ORDER OF ADJECTIVES

The (1) friendly (4) old (5) black terrier was chasing the squirrel.

I lost a (2) small (3) round (6) Italian (7) leather purse on the subway.

■ PRACTICE 6 **EDITING ADJECTIVES**

LEARNING JOURNAL
Which topic in this
chapter is most difficult
for you? How could
you explain that
problem to someone
else? How can you try
to avoid it in your own
writing?

For each item, write a sentence using the noun listed and the adjectives in parentheses. Be sure to put the adjectives in the correct order: judgment or overall opinion, size, shape, age, color, nationality or location, and material.

EXAMPLE: program (television, silly, black-and-white, old)

We watched a silly old black-and-white television program last night.
Answers will vary.

1. handkerchief (faded, lace)

   We found a faded lace handkerchief lying in the drawer.

2. creature (green, frightening, Martian)

   Smitty was startled by the approach of a frightening green Martian creature.

3. stairway (marble, massive, new)

   During the restoration, builders added a massive new marble stairway to the
   entrance.

4. classroom (cold, downstairs, little)

   We ended up shivering in a cold little downstairs classroom.

5. tomatoes (red, New Jersey, delicious)

   I put several delicious red New Jersey tomatoes in the salad.

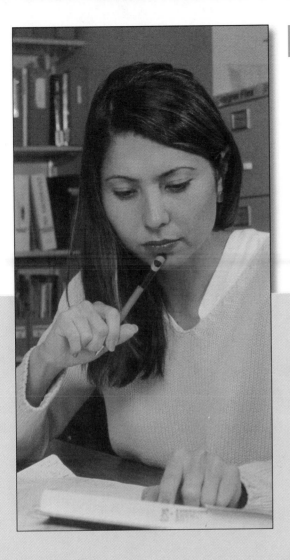

PART SIX

Word Use

34

Word Choice

Avoiding Language Pitfalls

Understand the Importance of Choosing Words Carefully

In conversation, much of your meaning is conveyed by your facial expression, your tone of voice, and your gestures. In writing, you have only the words on the page to make your point, so you must choose them carefully. If you use vague or inappropriate words, your readers may not understand what you have to say. Carefully chosen, precise words tell your readers exactly what you mean.

Two resources will help you find the best words for your meaning: a dictionary and a thesaurus.

LEARNING JOURNAL
Use your learning journal as a place to record sentences with the types of problems covered in this chapter. Also write down edited versions of these sentences, with the problems corrected.

DICTIONARY

You need a dictionary. For a very small investment, you can have a complete word resource for all kinds of useful information about words: spelling, division of words into syllables, pronunciation, parts of speech, other forms of words, definitions, and examples of use. Following is a sample dictionary entry.

ESL
ESL students can use a dictionary written especially for non-native speakers (such as the *Longman Dictionary of American English*) in addition to a standard English dictionary.

529

spelling and
end-of-line division

pronunciation

parts of
speech

other
forms

definition

example

con • crete (kon′kret, kong′-, kon kret′, kong-), *adj., n., v.* **-cret • ed**, **-cret • ing**, *adj.* **1.** constituting an actual thing or instance; real; perceptible; substantial: *concrete proof.* **2.** pertaining to or concerned with realities or actual instances rather than abstractions; particular as opposed to general: *concrete proposals.* **3.** referring to an actual substance or thing, as opposed to an abstract quality: The words *cat, water,* and *teacher* are concrete, whereas the words *truth, excellence,* and *adulthood* are abstract....

—*Random House Webster's College Dictionary*

For online help with words, visit Merriam-Webster Online at <www.m-w.com>. You can look up words in both the dictionary and the thesaurus on this Web site.

THESAURUS

For a map of synonyms for any word, visit the Plumb Design Visual Thesaurus at <**www.plumbdesign.com/thesaurus**>.

A thesaurus gives *synonyms* (words that have the same meaning) for the word you look up. Like a dictionary, it comes in inexpensive and even electronic editions. Use a thesaurus when you can't find the right word for what you mean. Be careful, however, to choose a word that has the precise meaning you intend. If you are not sure how a word should be used, look it up in the dictionary.

Concrete, *adj.* **1.** Particular, specific, single, certain, special, unique, sole, peculiar, individual, separate, isolated, distinct, exact, precise, direct, strict, minute; definite, plain, evident, obvious; pointed, emphasized; restrictive, limiting, limited, well-defined, clear-cut, fixed, finite; determining, conclusive, decided.

—J. I. Rodale, *The Synonym Finder*

DISCUSSION
Say aloud, "Your paper is late," in different tones of voice with different facial expressions. Have students write descriptions of each variation. Compare the results in a whole-group discussion on word choice.

Practice Avoiding Four Common Word-Choice Problems

Four common problems with word choice may make it hard for you to get your point across. You can eliminate them by using specific words that fit your meaning and make your writing clearer.

VAGUE AND ABSTRACT WORDS

Your words need to create a clear picture for your readers. Vague and abstract words are too general. They don't give your readers a clear idea of what you mean. Here are some common vague and abstract words.

Vague and Abstract Words

a lot	dumb	nice	school
awful	good	OK (okay)	small
bad	great	old	thing
beautiful	happy	person	very
big	house	pretty	whatever
car	job	sad	young

TEACHING TIP
Encourage students to look up in a dictionary words that they find in the thesaurus. Remind students that not all thesaurus words are interchangeable. Model specific examples of this problem for the class.

TEAMWORK
Form groups, assign each group a column of words, and have them come up with more specific words to replace the words that you've given them. List the most interesting words on the board for students to copy in their journals.

When you see one of these words or another general word in your writing, try to replace it with a concrete or more specific word. A **concrete word** names something that can be seen, heard, felt, tasted, or smelled. A **specific word** names a particular individual or quality. Compare these two sentences:

> **VAGUE AND ABSTRACT**   It was a beautiful day.
>
> **CONCRETE AND SPECIFIC**   The sky was a bright, cloudless blue; the sun was shimmering; and the temperature was a perfect 78 degrees.

The first version is too general to be interesting. The second version creates a clear, strong image. Some words are so vague that it is best to avoid them altogether.

> **VAGUE AND ABSTRACT**   It's like *whatever.*

[This sentence is neither concrete nor specific.]

PRACTICE 1   AVOIDING VAGUE AND ABSTRACT WORDS

In the following sentences, underline any words that are vague or abstract. Then edit each sentence by replacing any vague or abstract words with concrete, specific ones. You may invent any details you like. *Answers will vary. Possible edits shown.*

cousin Jonathan collects teeth, and my Aunt Farielle has the world's
EXAMPLE: My relatives are weird.   *loudest laugh.*

four-year-old   *cleans up her room, puts away her toys and books, and*
1. My ~~little~~ sister ~~is a good girl.~~   *helps my parents and me with simple chores.*
     ^

spend more than forty hours a week working,   *after school and on weekends for*
2. Both of my parents ~~work a lot,~~ so I babysit ~~pretty often.~~   *five or six hours.*
    ^   ^

enjoy playing board games and reading books
3. My sister and I ~~have fun~~ together.

My mother's parents and her two brothers
4. ~~Our relatives~~ visit ~~very frequently.~~ *at least twice a month.*
 ^   ^

hugs me enthusiastically and has been encouraging me to try to get a
5. My grandmother ~~is the nicest person I know.~~ *dance scholarship.*
              ^

tagines and couscous   *her childhood in Algeria.*
6. She likes to cook ~~things~~ that remind her of ~~home.~~
             ^   ^

My uncle Mahmoud wears loud purple suits and spikes his hair straight up.
7. ~~One of my uncles is a little crazy.~~
  ^

invents songs that have my name in them and sings them at top volume
8. He ~~does dumb things~~ to get my attention.
    ^

pinches my cheeks   *a kindergartner instead of a college student.*
9. He ~~treats me~~ as if I were ~~very young.~~
    ^   ^

trying to show his affection because he is fonder of me than any of his other
10. I guess he is just ~~happy to see me.~~ *nieces or nephews.*
      ^

SLANG

DEFINITION: Slang is informal and casual language, shared by the group that uses it. Slang should be used only in informal and casual situations. Avoid it when you write, especially for college classes or at work. Use language that is appropriate for your audience and purpose.

SLANG	EDITED
The kid in the store was *freakin'*.	The child was screaming and crying.
I'll give you the *411* tonight.	I'll give you the information tonight.
Getting fired really *bites*.	Getting fired is upsetting.

PRACTICE 2   AVOIDING SLANG

In the following sentences, underline any slang words. Then edit the sentences by replacing the slang with language appropriate for a formal audience and purpose. Imagine that you are writing to a supervisor at work. *Answers will vary. Possible edits shown.*

EXAMPLE: The company's offer of paid paternity leave to full-time

generous
employees is ~~way cool~~.
             ^

1. I wanted to express my appreciation for the ~~fab~~ *wonderful* new benefits package.

2. If I didn't have insurance through the company, the premiums would really ~~put the hurt on~~ *cut into* my paycheck.

3. Now that my wife and I are starting a family, insurance is a ~~biggie.~~ *major factor.*

4. I am planning to take two weeks of paternity leave in October when our ~~rug rat~~ *baby* arrives.

5. Without the company paying for this leave, I would ~~no way~~ *not* be able to afford the time off.

6. ~~Doing the quality-time thing~~ *Spending quality time* with my wife and baby is very important to me.

7. I know that adjusting to fatherhood will not be ~~cake.~~ *easy.*

8. We are both ~~mad~~ *terrifically* grateful that the company is rewarding its employees in this way.

9. If I can do anything to make my absence easier on my coworkers, please ~~give me a shout.~~ *let me know.*

10. This new company policy really is ~~all that~~ *wonderful*, and my family and I thank you.

WORDY LANGUAGE

People sometimes use too many words to express their ideas. They may think that using more words will make them sound smart and important. But too many words can get in the way of a writer's point and weaken it.

Wordy language includes phrases that contain too many words, unnecessarily qualify (comment on) a statement, or use slightly different words without adding any new ideas.

WORDY	We have no openings *at this point in time.*
EDITED	We have no openings now.

[The phrase *at this point in time* uses five words to express what could be said in one word: *now.*]

TEACHING TIP
Beginning writers may
mistake wordiness for
sophistication. Empha-
size that wordiness is
just that.

WORDY *In the opinion of this writer,* tuition fees are too high.

EDITED Tuition fees are too high.

[The qualifying phrase *in the opinion of this writer* is not necessary and weakens the statement.]

WORDY The suspect was *evasive* and *avoided answering the questions.*

EDITED The suspect was evasive.

[The words *evasive* and *avoided answering the questions* repeat the same idea without adding anything new.]

Common Wordy Expressions

WORDY	EDITED
As a result of	Because
Due to the fact that	Because
In spite of the fact that	Although
It is my opinion that	I think
In the event that	If
The fact of the matter is that	(Just state the point.)
A great number of	Many
At that time	Then
In this day and age	Now
At this point in time	Now
In this paper I will show that…	(Just make the point; don't announce it.)

PRACTICE 3   AVOIDING WORDY LANGUAGE

In the following sentences, underline the wordy language. Then edit each sentence to make it more concise.

  EXAMPLE: Television shows ~~are things that~~ contribute to our view of the world.

                                                                                        Many
1. ~~The fact of the matter is that~~ many young people get their first ideas

   about interesting jobs from watching television.

2. Some American scientists became interested in science ~~as a result of the~~ *because* ~~fact that~~ they watched *Star Trek* as children.

3. Shows like *L.A. Law* made the legal profession attractive to ~~a great number~~ *many* ~~of~~ future lawyers.

4. For a long ~~period of~~ time, political careers were not portrayed positively on television.

5. ~~There are some~~ *Some* people ~~who~~ believe that declining respect for politicians began with television shows.

6. ~~It is very true that~~ ~~popular~~ *Popular* shows like *The Simpsons* and *Spin City* have portrayed politicians as stupid, corrupt, or both.

7. ~~In this day and age,~~ *Now,* however, more young people are becoming interested in careers in government.

8. Now ~~there are~~ sympathetic people with political careers ~~who~~ appear on *West Wing* each week.

9. Will the United States have a crop of idealistic young politicians in the next decade ~~due to the fact that~~ *because* they watched *West Wing* as impression-able teens?

10. Motivated political workers are an essential part of any democracy, so ~~in actual fact~~ *West Wing* may even be good for our country.

CLICHÉS

DEFINITION: **Clichés** are phrases used so often that people no longer pay attention to them. To get your point across and to get your readers' attention, replace clichés with fresh language that precisely expresses your meaning.

CLICHÉS	EDITED
Passing the state police exam is no *walk in the park*.	Passing the state police exam requires careful preparation.
I was *sweating bullets* until the grades were posted.	I was anxious until the grades were posted.

COMMON CLICHÉS

as big as a house	light as a feather
the best/worst of times	no way on earth
better late than never	110 percent
break the ice	playing with fire
the corporate ladder	spoiled brat
crystal clear	spoiled rotten
a drop in the bucket	starting from scratch
easier said than done	sweating blood/bullets
hard as a rock	work like a dog
hell on earth	worked his/her way up
last but not least	

> **PRACTICE 4   AVOIDING CLICHÉS**

In the following sentences, underline the clichés. Then edit each sentence by replacing the clichés with fresh language that precisely expresses your meaning.

a challenging task.

EXAMPLE: Keeping children safe is ~~easier said than done~~.

to be constantly alert.

1. People with young children need ~~eyes in the back of their heads~~.

incredibly quickly.

2. Children can put themselves in danger ~~faster than lightning~~.

rethink their safety policies

3. Parents of a toddler should ~~have their heads examined~~ if they do not

   lock cabinets containing household chemicals.

rapidly,

4. Toddlers grow ~~by leaps and bounds,~~ and new levels of childproofing

   must be done as children learn to climb gates and open doors.

5. Parents sometimes recognize dangers ~~in the nick of time~~ *moments before a mishap* and stop their

   children from injuring themselves.

6. When their children play at another child's house, some parents may

   worry that the other parents will not ~~keep an eagle eye on~~ *watch* their

   youngsters./ *closely.*

   worry about
7. Parents ~~have mortal fears of~~ their young children running into traffic to

   chase a ball.

8. Swimming pools can be ~~deathtraps~~ *dangerously attractive* unless they are surrounded by a

   high fence with a locked gate.

9. Children must be taught ~~to keep their hands to themselves~~ *not to touch the weapon* and leave *to*

   the area immediately if they find a gun in someone's home.

10. Someday young children will be old enough to be independent, but their

    independence can also ~~drive~~ *worry* parents ~~out of their minds with worry.~~

Edit Paragraphs and Your Own Writing

PRACTICE 5 **EDITING PARAGRAPHS FOR WORD CHOICE**

Find and edit any examples of vague and abstract language, slang, wordy
language, or clichés in the following paragraphs. You may want to refer to
the Quick Review Chart on page 540. *Answers will vary. Possible edits shown.*

(1) Being the ~~big kahuna~~ *chief executive officer* at a major American corporation almost always

pays extremely well. (2) CEOs earn millions of dollars each ~~and every~~

year, and most also get stock options. (3) Even if the company ~~goes off~~ *performs poorly*

~~the rails~~ and the CEO gets fired, he (and it is almost always a ~~guy~~ *man* ~~thing~~)

often gets a severance package that is worth additional millions. (4) A CEO's salary in the United States is usually several hundred times larger than

company worker's salary.
the average ~~that is paid for a company worker's wages.~~ (5) This ratio is

enormous
~~pretty big~~ compared with the ratios in other industrialized countries.

is at most
(6) In Japan, for example, a CEO's salary ~~maxes out at~~ about ten times

exceptional?
that of a worker. (7) Are American CEOs really ~~that great?~~ (8) Are they,

~~in actual fact,~~ worth what they are paid?

In fact,
(9) ~~The fact of the matter is that~~ highly paid CEOs can rarely do

huge
what corporate directors hope. (10) They may have earned ~~sky-high~~

profits at a previous corporation, but every business is different. (11) There

make another business succeed.
is no guarantee that these men will be able to ~~keep up the good work.~~

(12) If a company promoted a worker from within, he or she probably

company thoroughly   *a smaller salary*
would not only know the ~~biz inside and out~~ but also work for ~~fewer bucks~~

successful current CEO.
than a ~~hired gun from outside.~~ (13) Then the corporation would be

able to spend a few million dollars less on its chief officer.
~~ahead of the game to the tune of a few million dollars.~~ (14) Why, then,

millions of dollars
are corporations willing to pay ~~a lot of money~~ to recruit expensive outsiders

as CEOs?

(15) The problem with promoting a CEO from within the company

is ~~the fact~~ that few companies want to take risks. (16) For a decade or

more, hiring a CEO has meant finding the CEO of another company and

leave his current position.
paying him enough to get him to ~~jump ship.~~ (17) Company directors

expect   *to*
think that their stockholders ~~have the expectation that~~ the company ~~will~~

afraid
bring in a highly paid outsider. (18) The directors are ~~freaked out by the~~

~~idea~~ that an insider might fail and disappoint stockholders. (19) Of course,

fail to satisfy the shareholders,
most CEOs brought in from elsewhere also ~~end up in the dumpster,~~ but

the corporate boards can at least reassure themselves that their choice has

a track record when he arrives. (20) Corporations claim to want leaders

who ~~can think outside the box.~~ *are original thinkers.* (21) However, ~~there are~~ few corporate

boards of directors ~~who~~ are willing to look anywhere other than conven-

tional places for their next leaders. (22) This conventional thinking will

eventually ~~be lousy for~~ *hurt* business; perhaps only then will the trend toward

hiring expensive CEOs change.

▓ PRACTICE 6   EDITING YOUR OWN WRITING FOR WORD CHOICE

As a final practice, edit a piece of your own writing for word choice. It can be a paper you are working on for this course, a paper you've already finished, a paper for another course, or a recent piece of writing from your work or everyday life. Record in your learning journal any problem sentences you find, along with their corrections. You may want to use the following Quick Review Chart.

LEARNING JOURNAL
Which language pitfall do you get trapped by most often? Why do you think you have this problem? How can you avoid it in your writing?

Quick Review Chart

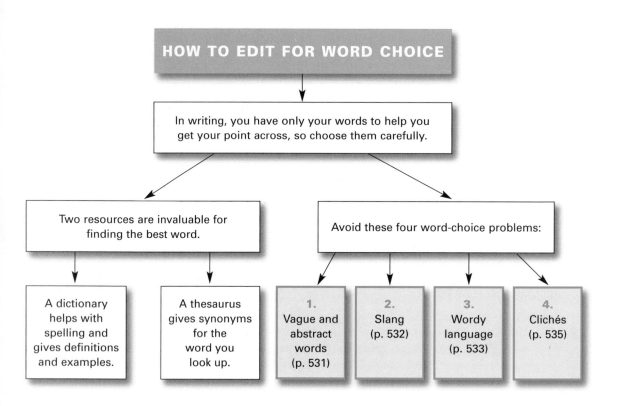

HOW TO EDIT FOR WORD CHOICE

In writing, you have only your words to help you get your point across, so choose them carefully.

Two resources are invaluable for finding the best word.

Avoid these four word-choice problems:

A dictionary helps with spelling and gives definitions and examples.

A thesaurus gives synonyms for the word you look up.

1.
Vague and abstract words
(p. 531)

2.
Slang
(p. 532)

3.
Wordy language
(p. 533)

4.
Clichés
(p. 535)

35

Commonly Confused Words

Avoiding Mistakes with Sound-alikes

Understand Why Certain Words Are Commonly Confused

People often confuse certain words in English because they sound alike and may have similar meanings. In writing, words that sound alike may be spelled differently, and readers rely on the spelling to understand what you mean. When you mean one word but write another that sounds the same, the different spelling and different meaning may confuse your readers. Edit your writing carefully to make sure that you have used the correct words.

> To understand this chapter, you need to know what nouns, verbs, adjectives, and adverbs are. For a review, see Chapters 22, 26, and 28.

STRATEGIES FOR EDITING SOUND-ALIKES

1. Proofread carefully, using the techniques discussed on page 557.

2. Use a dictionary to look up any words you are unsure of.

3. Focus on finding and correcting mistakes you make with the twenty-seven sets of commonly confused words covered in this chapter.

4. Develop a personal list of words you confuse often. In your learning journal or on an index card, record the words that you confuse in your writing, and jot down their meanings. Before you turn in any piece of writing, consult your personal list to make sure you have used the correct words.

Practice Using Commonly Confused Words Correctly

Study the different meanings and spellings of these twenty-seven sets of commonly confused words. Complete the sentence after each set of words, filling in each blank with the correct word.

A/An/And

a: used before a word that begins with a consonant sound
   A bat was living behind the shutter.

an: used before a word that begins with a vowel sound
   An elderly lady sat beside me.

and: used to join two words
   My sister *and* I went to the amusement park.

A friend *and* I got lost in an old maze.

Most classrooms have ____*a*____ worn-out chair ___*and*___ ___*an*___ old desk

for the teacher.

Accept/Except

accept: to agree to receive or admit (verb)
   I plan to *accept* the offer.

except: but, other than (conjunction)
   The whole family was there *except* my brother.

I *accept* all your requests *except* the one to borrow my car.

Do not ____*accept*____ anything from people at airports ____*except*____

from family members.

Advice/Advise

advice: opinion (noun)
   I would like your *advice* on this decision.

advise: to give an opinion (verb)
   My boyfriend *advises* me about car repairs.

Please *advise* me what to do; your *advice* is always helpful.

____*Advise*____ me of your plans, particularly if you don't follow my

____*advice*____.

Affect/Effect

affect: to have an impact on, to change something (verb)
   The whole region was *affected* by the drought.

effect: a result (noun)
   The lack of water will have a tremendous *effect* on many
   businesses.

The sunny weather has had a positive *effect* on people's moods, but it
will negatively *affect* the economy.

Since this year's drought will _____*affect*_____ the cost of food, we'll be

feeling its _____*effect*_____ personally.

Are/Our

are: a form of the verb *be*
   The flowers *are* ready to bloom.

our: a pronoun showing ownership
   I am proud of *our* garden.

Gardens *are* rare in *our* neighborhood.

___*Our*___ bulbs ___*are*___ arriving this week.

TEACHING TIP
Have students read
the sentences in this
section aloud so that
they can focus on
differences in pro-
nunciation. Encourage
them to exaggerate the
pronunciation of words
that do not sound
exactly alike.

By/Buy

by: next to or before
   I'll be standing *by* the door.
   We have to be at the restaurant *by* 8:00.

buy: purchase (verb)
   I would like to *buy* a new car.

By the time I'm ready to leave the dollar store, I have found too
much I want to *buy*.

I have decided to ___*buy*___ the model ___*by*___ the showroom entrance.

Conscience/Conscious

Remember that one
of the words is
con-science; the
other is not.

conscience: a personal sense of right and wrong (noun)
   My *conscience* keeps me from doing bad things.

conscious: awake, aware (adjective)
   The patient is now *conscious*.
   Shelly was *conscious* of Sam's feelings.

Danny made a *conscious* decision to listen to his *conscience*.

The burglar was ___*conscious*___ that someone else was in the house and

for a moment felt a twinge of ___*conscience*___.

Fine/Find

> **fine:** of high quality; feeling well; a penalty for breaking a law
> She works in the *fine* jewelry department.
> After taking some aspirin, Shana felt *fine*.
> The *fine* for exceeding the speed limit is $100.

> **find:** locate, discover (verb)
> Can you help me *find* the key?

> You will *find* a *fine* leather jacket in the coat department.

A ___*fine*___ partner is hard to ___*find*___.

Its/It's

It's is a contraction, short for *it is*. If you are not sure whether to use *its* or *it's* in a sentence, try substituting *it is*. If the sentence doesn't make sense with *it is,* use *its.*

> **its:** a pronoun showing ownership
> The bird went back to *its* nest.

> **it's:** a contraction of the words *it is*
> *It's* important for you to be on time.

> *It's* amazing to see a butterfly come out of *its* cocoon.

___*It's*___ good news for us that the bus changed ___*its*___ route.

Knew/New/Know/No

> **knew:** understood; recognized (past tense of the verb *know*)
> I *knew* we took the wrong turn.

> **new:** unused, recent (adjective)
> Jane has a *new* boyfriend.

> **know:** to understand, to have knowledge of (verb)
> I *know* him from work.

> **no:** used to form a negative
> There are *no* other classes at that time.

> I *knew* that Jason would need *new* shoes.

The ___*new*___ employee already ___*knew*___ some of the other employees.

There is *no* way to *know* what will happen.

Do you __*know*__ what __*no*__ means?

Loose/Lose

loose: baggy, not fixed in place (adjective)
    That button is *loose*.

lose: to misplace, to forfeit possession of (verb)
    I don't want to *lose* my job.

If the muffler is *loose*, you might *lose* it.

You will __*lose*__ that bracelet if it's too __*loose*__.

Mind/Mine

mind: object to; the thinking or feeling part of one's brain
    I don't *mind* loud music.
    Sometimes I think I am losing my *mind*.

mine: belonging to me; a source of ore and minerals
    That parking space is *mine*.
    That store is a gold *mine*.

Keep in *mind* that the sweater is *mine*.

Your __*mind*__ is a lot sharper than __*mine*__.

Of/Have

of: coming from; caused by; part of a group; made from (preposition)
    The president *of* the company pleaded guilty to embezzlement.

have: to possess (verb). Also used as a helping verb.
    Do you *have* a schedule?
    Jeannie should *have* been here by now.

I would *have* helped if you had told me you were out *of* change.

Do not use *of* after *would, should, could,* and *might.* Use *have* after those words.

Joe might __*have*__ been part __*of*__ the band.

Passed/Past

passed: went by or went ahead (past tense of the verb *pass*)
Tim *passed* us a minute ago.

past: time that has gone by (noun); gone by, over, just beyond
The school is just *past* the traffic light.

This past school year, I *passed* all of my exams.

If you go _____*past*_____ the church, you have _____*passed*_____ the

right turn.

Peace/Piece

peace: no disagreement; calm
The sleeping infant is at *peace*.

piece: a part of something larger
May I have a *piece* of paper?

We will have no *peace* until we give the dog a *piece* of that bread.

For the sake of _____*peace*_____, please share that _____*piece*_____ of pie.

Principal/Principle

principal: main (adjective); chief; head of a school (noun)
Making sales calls is your *principal* responsibility.
Darla is a *principal* of the company.
Mr. Tucker is the *principal* of the Sawyer School.

principle: a standard of beliefs or behaviors (noun)
The issue is really a matter of *principle*.

The *principle* at stake is the *principal* issue of the court case.

The _____*principal*_____ problem with many criminals is that they do not

have good _____*principles*_____.

Quiet/Quite/Quit

quiet: soft in sound; not noisy (adjective)
The library was very *quiet*.

quite: completely, very (adverb)
> I have had *quite* enough to eat after that half-pounder and fries.

quit: to stop (verb)
> Will you please *quit* bothering me?

It is not *quite* time to *quit* yet.

The machine _____*quit*_____ running, and the office was _____*quiet*_____.

Right/Write

right: correct; in a direction opposite from left (adjective)
> Are you sure this is the *right* way?
> Take a *right* after the bridge.

write: to put words on paper (verb)
> I will *write* soon.

Please be sure to *write* the *right* address.

_____*Write*_____ your name in the _____*right*_____ column.

Set/Sit

set: a collection of something (noun); to place an object somewhere (verb)
> Junior has a great train *set*.
> Please *set* the package on the table.

sit: to rest with one's rear end supported by a chair or other surface
> You can *sit* right over there.

Set your coat down before you *sit*.

Let's ___*sit*___ and look over my ___*set*___ of travel photos.

Suppose/Supposed

suppose: imagine or assume to be true
> *Suppose* you could go anywhere in the world.
> I *suppose* you want some dinner.

supposed: past tense of *suppose*; intended
> The clerk *supposed* the man was over twenty-one.

You are *supposed* to call when you are going to be late, but I *suppose* that's too much to expect.

I was _____*supposed*_____ to take the ten o'clock train, but I _____*suppose*_____

the eleven o'clock is okay.

Than/Then

than: a word used to compare two or more things or persons
  Joanne makes more money *than* I do.

then: at a certain time
  I will look forward to seeing you *then*.

I weigh a lot more *than* I used to back *then*.

If you want to lose weight, _____*then*_____ you will have to eat less

_____*than*_____ you do.

Their/There/They're

If you aren't sure whether to use *their* or *they're,* substitute *they are* for *they're.* If the sentence doesn't make sense, use *their.*

their: a pronoun showing ownership
  Their new apartment has two bedrooms.

there: a word indicating placement or existence
  Your desk is over *there*.
  There is more work than I can handle.

they're: a contraction of the words *they are*
  They're going to Hawaii.

Their windows are open, and *there* is a breeze, so *they're* not hot.

_____*They're*_____ going to be away, so my friend will be staying

_____*there*_____ and taking care of _____*their*_____ cat.

Though/Through/Threw

though: however; nevertheless; in spite of
  I'll be there, *though* I might be a little late.

through: finished with (adjective); from one side to the other (preposition)
  Jenna is *through* with school in May.
  Go *through* the first set of doors.

threw: hurled, tossed (past tense of the verb *throw*)
 She *threw* away the garbage.

Jimmy *threw* the ball, and it went *through* the window, *though* he had not aimed it there.

_____*Though*_____ she loved him, she _____*threw*_____ him out because she

couldn't go _____*through*_____ the pain he caused.

To/Too/Two

to: a word indicating a direction or movement (preposition); part of the infinitive form of a verb
 I am going *to* the food store.
 Do you want *to* see a movie?

too: also; more than enough; very (adverb)
 Toni was sick, *too*.
 The car was going *too* fast.

two: the number between one and three
 There are *two* tables.

They went *to* a restaurant and ordered *too* much food for *two* people.

The ___*two*___ friends started ___*to*___ dance, but it was ___*too*___ crowded

to move.

Use/Used

use: to employ or put into service (verb)
 I *use* this grill all the time.

used: past tense of the verb *use*. *Used to* can indicate a past fact or state, or it can mean "familiar with."
 I *used* the grill last night to cook chicken.
 I *used to* do yoga.
 I am *used* to juggling school and work.

Paolo *used* to be a farmer, so he knows how to *use* all the equipment.

When you last ___*used*___ the oven, what did you ___*use*___ it for?

Who's/Whose

who's: a contraction of the words *who is* or *who has*
Who's hungry?
Who's been here the longest?

whose: a pronoun showing ownership
Whose bag is this?

The person *whose* name is first on the list is the one *who's* going next.

_____*Who's*_____ the man _____*whose*_____ shoes are on the table?

Your/You're

If you aren't sure of whether to use *your* or *you're,* substitute *you are.* If the sentence doesn't make sense, use *your.*

your: a pronoun showing ownership
I like *your* shirt.

you're: a contraction of the words *you are*
You're going to run out of gas.

You're about to get paint all over *your* hands.

_____*Your*_____ teacher says _____*you're*_____ always late to class.

PRACTICE 1   USING THE RIGHT WORD

In each of the following items, circle the correct word in parentheses.

EXAMPLE: (You're/**Your**) résumé is a critical computer file.

1. I tell all my friends to back up important data on (**their**/ there) computers.

2. Unfortunately, I sometimes forget to take my own (**advice**/ advise).

3. My computer had a serious crash, and now I cannot (**find**/ fine) the most recent copy of my résumé.

4. I should (**have**/ of) made a hard copy and a backup on a floppy disk, but I didn't.

5. Today I have (a / an / and) interview for a job I really want, and I can't locate any résumés (accept / except) one from 1998.

6. (Loosing / Losing) a résumé is not the end of the world, but it will be (quiet / quite) a job reconstructing it.

7. It took me hours to (right / write) and proofread my most recent résumé.

8. This morning I quickly (set / sit) down some information to give to the interviewer, but this version is sloppier (than / then) the résumé I (use / used) to have.

9. (Though / Through) I feel that I am well qualified for this job, I'm afraid that this résumé may have a bad (affect / effect) on my chances of being hired.

10. An interviewer (who's / whose) task is to hire the best person must pay attention (to / too / two) small details.

Edit Paragraphs and Your Own Writing

PRACTICE 2   **EDITING PARAGRAPHS FOR COMMONLY CONFUSED WORDS**

Edit the following paragraphs to correct errors in the use of commonly confused words.

1. (1) Most people no that Americans love to drive there cars. (2) However, many people may not be conscience of how much the government does to support our car culture. (3) For instance, the United States would never of had so many good highways without federal and state assistance

for road construction and maintenance. (4) New highways are usually

paid for mainly ~~buy~~ *by* tax money. (5) It is rare for a new road ~~too~~ *to* be paid

for with tolls, which would come exclusively from the people driving on

it. (6) Americans also expect ~~they're~~ *their* roads to be well maintained, and they

may ~~right~~ *write* to their representatives to complain about potholes and aging

road surfaces. (7) The government is even responsible for keeping gas

prices lower here ~~then~~ *than* in most other industrialized nations.

(8) Few people ~~mine~~ *mind* that the government assists drivers in these

ways. (9) Some would argue that ~~its~~ *it's* a government's job to help pay for

transportation. (10) However, other forms of transportation in this coun-

try are often ~~past~~ *passed* over when Congress hands out funds. (11) Amtrak, the

U.S. railroad, will soon ~~loose~~ *lose* all government funds, even though many

government officials are skeptical of ~~it's~~ *its* ability to keep operating without

government assistance. (12) ~~Accept~~ *Except* for a few places like New York and

San Francisco, most U.S. cities do not have good mass transit systems.

(13) Americans ~~who's~~ *whose* travels have taken them to certain parts of the

world praise the national train systems and city transit systems they find

there. (14) As traffic gets worse in our nation's urban and suburban areas,

some people ~~fine~~ *find* it odd that the United States does not invest more in

transportation that would allow people to leave ~~there~~ *their* cars at home.

2. (1) Hoping to keep ~~are~~ *our* nation's blood supply safe, the U.S. govern-

ment has placed restrictions on donating blood. (2) Anyone ~~whose~~ *who's* spent

more than five years in Europe or more than three months in England

since 1980 is not allowed to give blood. (3) Officials hope that asking

about time in Europe will help them ~~fine~~ *find* people who might ~~of~~ *have* been

exposed to mad cow disease. (4) Men are also asked whether they have had sexual relations with other men in the ~~passed~~ *past* ten years. (5) If they

have, ~~their~~ *they're* asked not to give blood. (6) This is ~~suppose~~ *supposed* to protect the

blood supply from the AIDS virus. (7) Of course, ~~they're~~ *there* are some prob-

lems with these restrictions. (8) First, ~~know~~ *no* one knows how much expo-

sure to infected meat can give a person mad cow disease, and ~~know~~ *no* one

is sure how long the disease can hide in a human body. (9) Second, many

gay men ~~our~~ *are* not infected with HIV, and many women, who are not asked

about sexual activity, are infected. (10) Restricting certain groups of

people from giving blood may not do anything to protect the blood

supply, but it will certainly ~~effect~~ *affect* the amount of blood available. (11) Is it

better to allow the blood supply to become dangerously low ~~then~~ *than* to allow

people ~~who's~~ *whose* blood might carry a disease to donate blood?

PRACTICE 3   EDITING YOUR OWN WRITING FOR COMMONLY CONFUSED WORDS

As a final practice, edit a piece of your own writing for commonly confused words. It can be a paper you are working on for this course, a paper
you've already finished, a paper for another course, or a recent piece of
writing from your work or everyday life. Add any misused words you find
to your personal list of confusing words.

LEARNING JOURNAL
Which of the sets of
commonly confused
words do you mix up
most often? How could
you explain the dif-
ferent words to some-
one else? How could
you try to avoid them
in your own writing?

36

Spelling

Using the Right Letters

DEFINITION: As part of their editing, successful writers **proofread** their writing to find and correct their spelling, punctuation, and capitalization errors before they submit their writing.

Understand the Importance of Spelling Correctly

Some very smart people are very poor spellers. Unfortunately, spelling errors are easy for readers to spot, and they make a bad impression. In fact, spelling errors can be considered the fifth most serious error that writers make.

Read the following paragraph, the body of a follow-up letter one student wrote to a prospective employer after an interview:

Thank you for the oportunity to meet about the summer internship at Margate Associates. I hope you will find that my coursework in graphic design and my excellant communication skills make me a promiseing candidate for the position. I look forward to hearing from you soon. I am happy to provide you with referances if you need them.

Can you find the four spelling mistakes? If you make such mistakes in your writing, your reader may become confused or frustrated—and your message may get lost. In the case of the summer internship at the design firm, another student got the job.

TWO IMPORTANT TOOLS: DICTIONARY AND SPELLING LIST

If you are serious about improving your spelling, you need to have a dictionary and a spelling list—and to use them.

Dictionary

A dictionary contains the correct spellings of words, along with information on how they are pronounced, what they mean, and where they came from. Buy a dictionary; everyone needs one. When proofreading your papers, use a dictionary whenever you are unsure about the spelling of a word. *Checking a dictionary is the single most important thing you can do to improve your spelling.*

> For a sample dictionary entry, see page 530.

Buy a current dictionary rather than an old one because current editions have up-to-date definitions and words that are new to the language, such as *Internet, online, downsizing,* and *Web page.* If you have trouble finding words in a regular dictionary, get a spelling dictionary, which is designed to help you find a word even if you have no idea how to spell it.

Spelling List

Most people misspell the same words over and over. Keeping a spelling list will help you identify your problem words and learn to spell them correctly.

Set aside a section of your course notebook or journal for your spelling list. Every time you edit a paper, write down the words that you have misspelled. Write the correct spelling first, and then in parentheses note the way you actually wrote the word. After you have recorded the spelling errors for three pieces of writing, spend ten minutes analyzing your spelling list. Ask yourself:

> **TEACHING TIP**
> Ask students to turn in a list of at least five words that they often misspell. Compile and distribute the list, and use it to create a spelling quiz.

- What words have I misspelled more than once?
- What do I get wrong about them? Do I always misspell them the same way?
- What are my personal spelling demons? ("Demons" are the five to ten words that you tend to spell wrong over and over.)

Online dictionaries can also help you with spelling. Here are the names and Web addresses of some popular ones.
• Merriam-Webster Online at <**www .m-w.com**>. This dictionary has a feature called the wild card search. If you are fairly sure how the beginning of a word is spelled, you can enter those letters and then an asterisk (*) and get a list of the words that begin with them. From the list, you can choose the word you want.
• Your Dictionary at <**www .yourdictionary .com**>. This site even features specialty dictionaries for business, computers, law, medicine, and other work-related areas.

• What other mistakes do I repeat (leaving the final -s off words, for example)?

Write your personal demons (five to ten words), spelled correctly, on an index card, and keep it somewhere handy so that you can consult the card whenever you write.

Every few weeks, go back to your spelling list to see whether your problem words have changed. Are you misspelling fewer words in each paper? What are your current spelling demons? Using a spelling list will definitely improve your spelling.

Practice Spelling Correctly

You can improve your spelling in several ways. First, learn to find and correct spelling mistakes in your writing. At the same time, work on becoming a better speller so that you make fewer mistakes to begin with.

THREE STEPS FOR FINDING AND CORRECTING MISTAKES

Every time you write a paper, proofread it for spelling errors by focusing only on spelling. Don't try to correct your grammar, improve your message, and check your spelling at the same time. Remember to check the dictionary whenever you are unsure about the spelling of a word and to add all the spelling mistakes you find to your personal spelling list.

Step 1. Use a Spell Checker

ESL
Tell students that many words in English aren't spelled as they sound. Also warn students that some English words may sound like words in their native language but may be spelled slightly differently.

Most word-processing programs have spell checkers. A spell checker finds and highlights a word that may be misspelled, suggests other spellings, and gives you the opportunity to change the spelling of the word. Use this feature after you have completed a piece of writing but before you print it out.

However, since no spell checker can catch every mistake in a piece of writing, never rely on a spell checker to do your editing for you. A spell checker ignores anything it recognizes as a word, so it will not help you find words that are misused or misspellings that are also words. For example, a spell checker would not highlight any of the problems in these phrases:

Just to it.	(Correct: Just do it.)
pain in the nick	(Correct: pain in the neck)
my writing coarse	(Correct: my writing course)

Step 2. Use Proofreading Techniques

Use some of the following proofreading techniques to focus on the spelling of one word at a time. Different techniques work for different people, so try them all and then decide which ones work for you.

Some word-processing programs will automatically highlight words that may be misspelled as you write and suggest alternatives if you click the mouse.

PROOFREADING TECHNIQUES

- Put a piece of paper under the line that you are reading.
- Cut a "window" in an index card that is about the size of a long word (such as *misunderstanding*), and place it over your writing to focus on one word at a time.
- Proofread your paper backward, one word at a time.
- If you are using a computer, print out a version of your paper that looks noticeably different: Make the words larger, make the margins larger, triple-space the lines, or do all of these. Read this version carefully.
- Read your paper aloud. This strategy will help you if you tend to leave words out.
- Exchange papers with a partner for proofreading. Your only task as you proofread your partner's paper should be to identify possible misspellings. The writer of the paper should be responsible for checking the spelling and correcting any spelling errors.

Step 3. Check Your Personal Spelling List

After you proofread each word in your paper, look at your personal spelling list and your list of demon words one more time. Have you used any of these words in your paper? If so, go back and check their spelling again. You may be surprised to find that you missed seeing the same old spelling mistakes.

Most word-processing programs allow you to search for specific words using Find or Search commands from the Edit menu.

PRACTICE 1   USING THE THREE STEPS FOR FINDING AND CORRECTING MISTAKES

Take the last paper you wrote — or one that you are working on now — and use the three steps for finding and correcting spelling mistakes. How many spelling mistakes did you find? Were you surprised? How was the experience different from what you normally do to edit for spelling? How confident are you that your paper now contains no spelling mistakes?

THREE STRATEGIES FOR BECOMING A BETTER SPELLER

Learning to find and correct spelling mistakes that you have already made is only half the battle. You also need to become a better speller so that you do not make so many mistakes in the first place. Here are three strategies.

Strategy 1. Master Your Personal Spelling Demons

Once you know what your spelling demons are, you can start to conquer them. If your list of spelling demons is long, you may want to start by focusing on the top five or the top three. When you have mastered these, you can go on to the next few. Different techniques work for different people. Try them all, and then stick with the ones that work for you.

TECHNIQUES FOR MASTERING YOUR SPELLING DEMONS

TEAMWORK
Have students work in small groups to come up with effective memory aids.

- Create a memory aid, an explanation or saying that will remind you of the correct spelling. For example, "*surprise* is no *prize*" may remind you to spell *surprise* with an *s*, not a *z*.
- Break the word into parts, and try to master each part. You can break it into syllables (*Feb ru ar y*) or separate the prefixes and endings (*dis ap point ment*).
- Write the word correctly ten times.
- Say the letters of the word out loud. See if there's a rhythm or a rhyme you can memorize.
- Write a paragraph in which you use the word at least three times.
- Say the word out loud, emphasizing each letter and syllable even if that's not the way you normally say it. For example, say *prob a bly* instead of *prob ly*. Try to pronounce the word this way in your head each time you spell it.
- Ask a partner to give you a spelling test.

Strategy 2. Master Commonly Confused Words

Chapter 35 covers twenty-seven sets of words that are commonly confused because they sound alike, such as *write/right* and *its/it's*. If you can master these commonly confused words, you will avoid many spelling mistakes.

Strategy 3. Learn Six Spelling Rules

This section of the chapter covers spelling situations in which people often think, "What do I do here?" If you can remember the rules, you can avoid or correct many of the spelling errors in your writing.

Before the six rules, here is a quick review of vowels and consonants.

ⓐ b c d ⓔ f g h ⓘ j k l m n ⓞ p q r s t ⓤ v w x y z

Vowels

Consonants are all the letters that are not vowels.

The letter *y* can be either a vowel or a consonant. It is a vowel when it sounds like the *y* in *fly* or *hungry*. It is a consonant when it sounds like the *y* in *yellow*.

Should I Use *ie* or *ei*?

RULE 1:   *I* before *e*
Except after *c*.
Or when sounded like *a*
As in *neighbor* or *weigh*.

Many people repeat this rhyme to themselves as they decide whether a word is spelled with an *ie* or an *ei*.

piece (*i* before *e*)

receive (except after *c*)

eight (sounds like *a*)

EXCEPTIONS: either, neither, foreign, height, seize, society, their, weird

Should I Drop the Final *e* or Keep It When Adding an Ending to a Word?

RULE 2:   Drop the final *e* when adding an ending that begins with a vowel.

hope + ing = hoping

imagine + ation = imagination

Keep the final *e* when adding an ending that begins with a consonant.

achieve + ment = achievement

definite + ly = definitely

EXCEPTIONS: argument, awful, simply, truly (and others)

Should I Change the *y* to *i* when Adding an Ending?

RULE 3:   When adding an ending to a word that ends in *y*, change the *y* to *i* when a consonant comes before the *y*.

lonely + est = loneliest

happy + er = happier

TEAMWORK
For each rule, have students give three additional examples. Invite groups to share examples with the class.

apology + ize = apologize

likely + hood = likelihood

Do not change the *y* when a vowel comes before the *y*.

boy + ish = boyish

pay + ment = payment

survey + or = surveyor

buy + er = buyer

EXCEPTIONS: 1. When adding *-ing* to a word ending in *y*, always keep the *y*, even if a consonant comes before it: study + ing = studying.
2. Other exceptions include *daily, dryer, said,* and *paid*.

Should I Double the Final Consonant When Adding an Ending?

RULE 4: When adding an ending that starts with a vowel to a one-syllable word, follow these rules.

Double the final consonant only if the word ends with a consonant-vowel-consonant.

strap + ed = strapped

occur + ence = occurrence

prefer + ed = preferred

commit + ed = committed

Do not double the final consonant if the word ends with some other combination.

VOWEL-VOWEL-CONSONANT	VOWEL-CONSONANT-CONSONANT
clean + est = cleanest	slick + er = slicker
poor + er = poorer	teach + er = teacher
clear + ed = cleared	last + ed = lasted

RULE 5: When adding an ending that starts with a vowel to a word with two or more syllables, follow these rules.

Double the final consonant only if the word ends with a consonant-vowel-consonant and the stress is on the last syllable.

admit + ing = admitting

control + er = controller

admit + ed = admitted

Do not double the final consonant in other cases.

problem + atic = problematic

understand + ing = understanding

offer + ed = offered

Should I Add *-s* or *-es*?

The endings *-s* and *-es* are used to make the plural form of most nouns (*two books*) and the he/she/it form of most verbs (*he runs*).

RULE 6:   Add *-s* to most words, including words that end in *o* preceded by a vowel.

MOST WORDS	WORDS THAT END IN VOWEL PLUS *O*
book + s = books	video + s = videos
college + s = colleges	stereo + s = stereos
jump + s = jumps	radio + s = radios

Add *-es* to words that end in words that end in *s, sh, ch,* or *x* and *o* preceded by a consonant.

WORDS THAT END IN *S, SH, CH,* OR *X*	WORDS THAT END IN CONSONANT PLUS *O*
class + es = classes	potato + es = potatoes
push + es = pushes	hero + es = heroes
bench + es = benches	go + es = goes
fax + es = faxes	

EXCEPTIONS: pianos, solos (and others)

One Hundred Commonly Misspelled Words

Use this list as an easy reference to check your spelling.

absence	already	athlete	believe
achieve	analyze	awful	business
across	answer	basically	calendar
aisle	appetite	beautiful	career
a lot	argument	beginning	category

(continued)

chief	exercise	lightning	roommate
column	fascinate	loneliness	schedule
coming	February	marriage	scissors
commitment	finally	meant	secretary
conscious	foreign	muscle	separate
convenient	friend	necessary	sincerely
cruelty	government	ninety	sophomore
daughter	grief	noticeable	succeed
definite	guidance	occasion	successful
describe	harass	occurrence	surprise
dictionary	height	perform	truly
different	humorous	physically	until
disappoint	illegal	prejudice	usually
dollar	immediately	probably	vacuum
eighth	independent	psychology	valuable
embarrass	interest	receive	vegetable
environment	jewelry	recognize	weight
especially	judgment	recommend	weird
exaggerate	knowledge	restaurant	writing
excellent	license	rhythm	written

Edit Paragraphs and Your Own Writing

■ **PRACTICE 2   EDITING PARAGRAPHS FOR SPELLING**

Find and correct any spelling mistakes in the following paragraphs.

1. (1) Anyone ~~intrested~~ in ~~wierd~~ events should visit New York City on
    October 31, when the ~~bigest~~ Halloween parade in the country takes place.
    (2) Everyone in the city, it seems, ~~marchs~~ in the parade, yet ~~they're~~ are

still an estimated two million people watching from the sidewalks. (3) The
parade had its ~~beginings~~ *beginnings* in Greenwich Village, and original parade-goers
walked ~~though~~ *through* ^ the small, winding streets of that old New York ~~nieghborhood.~~ *neighborhood.*
(4) ~~Buy~~ *By* ^ now the parade has ~~goten~~ *gotten* so large that it has to go down one of
the city's broad avenues. (5) The Halloween parade ~~suprises~~ *surprises* ~~alot~~ *a lot* of people
who see it for the first time. (6) The ~~merryment~~ *merriment* ^ begins early in the
evening, as costumed paraders line up. (7) ~~Your~~ *You're* ^ likely to see a huge group
of ~~freinds~~ *friends* dressed as one ~~hunderd~~ *hundred* and one dalmatians or perhaps some
~~comicaly~~ *comically* ~~exagerated~~ *exaggerated* ^ versions of ~~goverment~~ *government* officials. (8) Every kind of
costume is ~~permited~~ *permitted* in the parade, and some people attend ~~skimpyly~~ *skimpily*
dressed, ~~aparently~~ *apparently* without ~~embarassment,~~ *embarrassment* ^ in spite of the October chill.
(9) For a ~~fascinateing~~ *fascinating* look at how ~~strangly~~ *strangely* people can behave on Halloween, the New York City Halloween parade is the place to ~~bee.~~ *be.*

2. (1) During the summer months, people love to head to the
~~beachs.~~ *beaches.* (2) ~~Accept~~ *Except* ^ for those who have recently seen *Jaws,* most people
don't consider going to the ocean a dangerous activity. (3) ~~Usualy,~~ *Usually,* people
can swim ~~safly~~ *safely* at the beach, but ~~its~~ *it's* always wise to be cautious. (4) Shark
attacks are very rare — ~~their~~ *there* were only seventy-nine in the world in
2000 — but a majority of them happen in the waters around the United
States. (5) ~~Shiney~~ *Shiny* ~~jewelery~~ *jewelry* can attract sharks because it resembles fish
scales, and ~~swimers~~ *swimmers* in the early morning or late evening are more likely
to encounter sharks who are ~~hopeing~~ *hoping* to grab a ~~byte~~ *bite* to eat. (6) Of course,
people are much more apt to meet up with jellyfish than with sharks, but
even a jellyfish sting can leave a beachgoer ~~acheing~~ *aching* for hours. (7) ~~Finaly,~~ *Finally,*
everyone ought to be aware that ~~waist~~ *waste* sometimes gets into seawater,
~~specially~~ *especially* near urban areas. (8) Testing is ~~suppose~~ *supposed* to be done ~~periodicaly,~~ *periodically,*
and any beach with unsafe water should be closed; anyone who doesn't

                                              buy
trust government testing can ~~by~~ a kit and do the job at home. (9) People
                           ^
                      too
who think ~~to~~ much about the dangers of going in the ocean may feel safer
              peacefully   *probably*
lying ~~peacfully~~ in the sand. (10) That's ~~probaly~~ fine — as long as they wear
      ^   ^
              sunscreen.
plenty of ~~sonscreen.~~
          ^

PRACTICE 3   EDITING YOUR OWN WRITING FOR SPELLING

LEARNING JOURNAL
Which spelling strategy
is most helpful for
you? What spelling
advice would you give
to someone else?

As a final practice, edit a piece of your own writing for spelling, using the
techniques described in this chapter. It can be a paper you are working on
for this course, a paper you've already finished, a paper for another course,
or a recent piece of writing from work or everyday life. Record in your
learning journal any mistakes you find, along with their corrections.

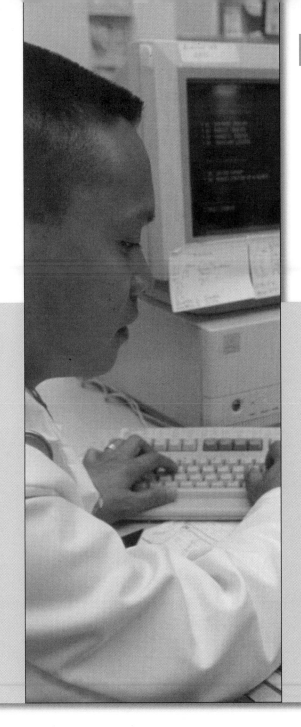

PART SEVEN

Punctuation and Capitalization

37

Commas

,

Understand What Commas Do

To understand this chapter, you need to know what nouns, sentences, phrases, and clauses are. If you need to review, see Chapter 22.

DEFINITION: **Commas (,)** are punctuation marks that separate words and word groups to help readers understand a sentence. Read aloud the following three sentences. How does the use of commas change the meaning?

NO COMMA	After you call Jim I'll leave for the restaurant.
ONE COMMA	After you call Jim, I'll leave for the restaurant.
TWO COMMAS	After you call, Jim, I'll leave for the restaurant.

TEACHING TIP
Have a student read these sentences aloud and ask the class to tell how they differ.

Using commas correctly helps your readers understand what you mean. Commas signal particular meanings to your readers, so it is important that you understand when and how to use them.

TEACHING TIP
Write on the board:
*My daughter is a fast
aggressive, and
competitive soccer
player.* Read the
sentence aloud and
ask students if they
can hear where the
missing comma
should go. Remind
them, however, that
intonation will not help
with comma usage in
every case; give
examples of such
cases.

LEARNING JOURNAL
Use your learning
journal as a place to
record sentences with
comma problems. Also
write down edited
versions of these
sentences, with the
problems corrected.

How does a comma
change the way you
read a sentence aloud?
Most readers pause
when they come to a
comma.

For more practice,
visit Exercise
Central at <www
.bedfordstmartins
.com/realessays>.

Practice Using Commas Correctly

COMMAS BETWEEN ITEMS IN A SERIES

Use commas to separate the items in a series (three or more items). This includes the last item in the series, which usually has *and* before it.

When you go to the store, please pick up *milk, bread, orange juice,* and *bananas.*

Last semester I took *math, reading,* and *composition.*

Students may take the course as a *regular classroom course,* as an *online course,* or as a *distance learning course.*

NOTE: In magazines and newspapers, as well as in some business writing, the comma before the final item is sometimes left out. In college writing it is always best to include it, however, so that your meaning will be clear.

PRACTICE 1   USING COMMAS IN SERIES

Edit the following sentences by underlining the items in the series and adding commas where they are needed. If a sentence is already correct, put a "C" next to it.

> **EXAMPLE:** The money we <u>touch</u>_, <u>carry in our wallets</u> and <u>give to other people</u> may be covered with germs.

1. Money has been called "the root of all evil" and "filthy lucre."   *C*

2. Apparently, money actually is <u>dirty</u>_, <u>tainted</u> and <u>germ-covered.</u>

3. A recent study of sixty-eight dollar bills found <u>five carrying germs that could infect healthy people</u> <u>fifty-nine harboring bacteria that could sicken people with depressed immune systems,</u> and <u>only four that were free of dangerous infectious agents.</u>

4. The bills were <u>selected randomly</u> <u>taken to a laboratory</u> and <u>tested for germs.</u>

5. Of course, this study involved a <u>very small localized and not necessarily</u> <u>representative</u> sample of bills.

6. My mother, a <u>highly trained</u>, <u>experienced</u>, and <u>conscientious</u> nurse, always told me to wash my hands after handling money.   *C*

7. Once, when I was attempting to <u>open my purse accept a receipt from a</u> <u>cashier and hold my change</u> at the same time, I stuck some dollar bills in my mouth for a moment.

8. My mother was <u>astonished concerned and a little angry</u> as she snapped at me to get the money out of my mouth.

9. Although the study of the sixty-eight dollar bills does not reveal whether germs can <u>transfer from bills to people survive for long periods on money</u>, or <u>otherwise contribute to human illness</u>, reading about it made me realize that my mother had been right to be worried.

10. I wonder what would happen if researchers tested <u>random bathroom</u> <u>doors bus seats or any other public and frequently touched objects</u>.

ESL
Because different languages have different intonation patterns, students should not rely on intonation alone to decide where to put commas.

COMMAS IN COMPOUND SENTENCES

DEFINITION: A **compound sentence** contains two independent clauses (sentences) joined by one of these words: *and, but, for, nor, or, so, yet*. Use a comma before the joining word to separate the two clauses.

The words *and, but, for, nor, or, so,* and *yet* are called coordinating conjunctions.

Sentence	**,**	*and, but, for, nor, or, so, yet*	Sentence.

Tom missed class yesterday**,** *and* he called to ask me what he missed.

I would have been happy to help him**,** *but* I was absent, too.

I told him I wasn't there**,** *so* he said he would email the professor.

NOTE: A comma is not needed if the word *and, but, for, nor, or, so,* or *yet* joins two sentence elements that are not independent clauses.

███   **PRACTICE 2**   **USING COMMAS IN COMPOUND SENTENCES**

Edit the following compound sentences by adding commas where they are needed. If a sentence is already correct, put a "C" next to it.

> **EXAMPLE**: The population of the United States is getting older‸ but the number of people trained to care for the elderly is declining.

1. Working in a nursing home is a difficult job‸ for elderly patients can seldom do much for themselves.

2. The labor is sometimes physically difficult‸ but it can also be mentally draining.

3. Few trained nurses and nurse's aides want nursing-home jobs‸ for the pay is also usually lower than that offered by hospitals.

4. Nursing-home workers have high turnover rates‸ and the facilities are constantly in need of new personnel.

5. More workers will be needed as the baby boomers become elderly‸ yet there is already a shortage of people willing to do the tough and often unpleasant work.

6. A director sometimes must hire undertrained workers‸ or the nursing home will face a severe staff shortage.

7. Workers without education and training may have difficulty understand- ing a doctor's orders, so the patients' care may suffer.   *C*

8. Home health aides and hospice workers are also in short supply‸ and the need for such workers is growing every day.

9. Solving these problems will be difficult‸ for long-term care for the elderly is already very expensive.

10. People caring for elderly patients must get better pay, or no one will be available to do the work in a few years.

COMMAS AFTER INTRODUCTORY WORD GROUPS

Use a comma after an introductory word or word group. An introductory word group can be a word, phrase, or clause. The comma lets your readers know when the main part of the sentence is starting.

| Introductory word or word group | , | Main part of sentence. |

INTRODUCTORY WORD: *Happily,* I turned in my final paper.

INTRODUCTORY PHRASE: *According to the paper,* the crime rate went down.

INTRODUCTORY CLAUSE: *As you know,* the store is going out of business.

PRACTICE 3   USING COMMAS AFTER INTRODUCTORY WORD GROUPS

In each item, underline any introductory word or word group. Then add commas after introductory word groups where they are needed.

EXAMPLE: Every year, more than two hundred motorists die in collisions with animals.

1. Along roadsides all across this country, drivers see the bodies of animals hit by cars.

2. Usually, the victims are common species of wildlife, such as deer and raccoons.

3. Of course, hitting a deer is not only disturbing but also potentially harmful or fatal to the occupants of a car.

4. However, the deer population has not suffered much of a decline from traffic accidents.

5. On the other hand‚drivers in wilderness areas may accidentally kill endangered species.

6. For instance‚wildlife experts believe that 65% of the population of endangered Florida panthers has been killed on highways in the past twenty years.

7. Maintaining the world's largest network of roads‚the U.S. Forest Service tries to balance the needs of humans and wildlife.

8. To get access to wilderness areas‚humans, many of whom strongly favor protecting the environment, need roads.

9. Unfortunately‚wilderness roads may isolate populations of animals that will not cross them and kill animals that make the attempt.

10. Although expensive‚underpasses and overpasses have been successful in some areas at reducing human collisions with animals.

COMMAS AROUND APPOSITIVES AND INTERRUPTERS

DEFINITION: An **appositive** comes directly before or after a noun or pronoun and renames it.

For more on appositives, see pages 504–506.

Dick‚ *my neighbor‚* is being sued by a builder.

Apartment prices are high at Riverview‚ *the new complex.*

DEFINITION: An **interrupter** is an aside or transition that interrupts the flow of a sentence and does not affect its meaning.

An interrupter that appears at the beginning of a sentence can be treated the same as an introductory word group.

Campus parking fees‚ *you should know‚* are going up by 30 percent.

A six-month sticker will now be $45‚ *for example.*

Putting commas around appositives and interrupters tells readers that these elements give extra information but are not essential to the meaning of a sentence. If an appositive or interrupter is in the middle of a sentence, set it off with a pair of commas, one before and one after. If an appositive or interrupter comes at the beginning or end of a sentence, separate it from the rest of the sentence with one comma.

Incidentally, your raise has been approved.

Your raise, *incidentally,* has been approved.

Your raise has been approved, *incidentally.*

NOTE: Sometimes an appositive is essential to the meaning of a sentence. When a sentence would not have the same meaning without the appositive, the appositive should not be set off with commas.

The actor *John Travolta* has never won an Academy Award.

[The sentence *The actor has never won an Academy Award* does not have the same meaning.]

The lawyer *Clarence Darrow* was one of history's greatest speakers.

[The sentence *The lawyer was one of history's greatest speakers* does not have the same meaning.]

PRACTICE 4   USING COMMAS TO SET OFF APPOSITIVES AND INTERRUPTERS

Underline any appositives or interrupters in the following sentences. Then use commas to set them off.

EXAMPLE: The reason for the delay, a mechanical problem with the airplane, was not mentioned.

1. Road rage, as most people have heard, occurs when an angry driver overreacts.

2. Another phenomenon, air rage, involves out-of-control and often intoxicated passengers on an airplane.

3. One famous air rage incident, a confrontation between a drunken businessman and a flight attendant, ended with the passenger tied to his seat for the rest of the flight.

4. Ground rage, like air rage, is a term used for incidents between airline passengers and airline employees.

5. Ground rage, however, occurs in the terminal, not in the air.

6. Gate agents, the people who check tickets and allow passengers to board the plane, are frequent victims of ground rage.

7. Oversold seats, a common occurrence in air travel, can mean that some passengers are forced to miss a flight.

8. Passengers, many of whom are on a tight schedule or have a connecting flight to catch, find delayed flights infuriating as well.

9. Some delayed or bumped passengers take out their anger on the gate agent, a convenient target.

10. Although some airline employees may not be helpful or friendly, their attitudes do not excuse passengers who commit assault, a serious crime.

COMMAS AROUND ADJECTIVE CLAUSES

DEFINITION: An **adjective clause** is a group of words that begins with *who,* *which,* or *that,* has a subject and verb, and describes the noun right before it in a sentence. Whether or not an adjective clause should be set off from the rest of the sentence by commas depends on its meaning in the sentence.

If an adjective clause can be taken out of a sentence without completely changing the meaning of the sentence, put commas around the clause.

> Use *who* to refer to a person, *which* to refer to places or things (but not to people), and *that* for people, places, or things. When referring to a person, *who* is preferable to *that.*

The mayor, *who was recently elected,* has no political experience.

SuperShop, *which is the largest supermarket in town,* was recently bought by Big Boy Markets.

I have an appointment with Dr. Kling, *who is the specialist.*

If an adjective clause is essential to the meaning of a sentence, do not put commas around it. You can tell whether a clause is essential by taking it out and seeing if the meaning of the sentence changes significantly, as it would if you took the clauses out of the following examples:

The hair salon *that I liked* recently closed.

Salesclerks *who sell liquor to minors* are breaking the law.

TEACHING TIP
Encourage students to think of the commas on either side of the clause as "handles." If students can "lift" the clause out of the sentence without affecting the meaning of the sentence, they should use commas around the clause.

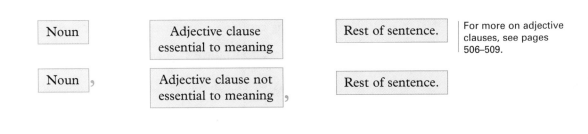

PRACTICE 5   **USING COMMAS TO SET OFF ADJECTIVE CLAUSES**

Edit the following sentences by putting any needed commas around adjective clauses. Remember that if an adjective clause is essential to the meaning of the sentence, you should not use commas. If a sentence is already correct, put a "C" next to it.

EXAMPLE: Stephen King, who understands how to frighten his readers, has depicted evil clowns in his work.

1. The only thing that terrifies Maria is a person dressed as a clown.   *C*

2. The fear of clowns, which is called coulrophobia, is fairly common among children.

3. Some young children who develop this fear are not prepared adequately before seeing a clown for the first time.   *C*

4. Clowns, who usually wear heavy makeup and brightly colored wigs, do not look like ordinary people.

5. Clowns also make sudden and surprising movements that frighten many youngsters.   *C*

6. Most children who fear clowns will get over their phobia as they grow up.   *C*

7. Such people, who may never love clowns, will still be able to tolerate having them around.

8. Many adults have read books and seen movies that show clowns as evil killers.   *C*

9. Few adults admit to having coulrophobia which is most effectively treated when the sufferer confronts the fear.

10. Unlike some other phobias which can trap people in their homes or make them unable to work, coulrophobia has little effect on most sufferers who are not likely to meet clowns frequently in everyday life.

OTHER USES FOR COMMAS

Commas with Quotation Marks

For more on quotation marks, see Chapter 39.

DEFINITION: Quotation marks are used to show that you are using a **direct quotation**, repeating exactly what someone said or wrote. Generally use commas to set off the words inside quotation marks from the rest of the sentence.

"Excuse me, " said the old woman in back of me.

"Did you know, " she asked, "that you just cut in front of me?"

I exclaimed, "Oh, no. I'm so sorry!"

Notice that a comma never comes directly after a quotation mark.

Commas in Addresses

Use commas to separate the elements of an address included in a sentence. However, do not use a comma before a zip code.

My address is 4498 Main Street, Bolton, Massachusetts 01740.

If a sentence continues after the address, put a comma after the address. Also use a comma after individual elements used to name a geographical location such as a city and state.

The house was moved from Cripple Creek, Colorado, to the lot on Forest Street.

Commas in Dates

Separate the day from the year with a comma. If you give the month and year, do not separate them with a comma.

She wrote the letter on April 1, 2003.

The next session is in January 2010.

If a sentence continues after the date, put a comma after the date.

He waited until April 15, 2002, to file his 2001 tax return.

Commas with Names

Put commas around the name of someone you are addressing by name.

Don, I want you to come look at this.

Unfortunately, Marie, you need to finish the report by next week.

Commas with Yes or No

Put a comma after the word *yes* or *no* in response to a question.

No, that isn't what I meant.

PRACTICE 6   USING COMMAS IN OTHER WAYS

Edit the following sentences by adding commas where they are needed. If a sentence is already correct, put a "C" next to it.

EXAMPLE: The new regulations went into effect on April 1, 2001.

1. My sister asked, "James, do you get a lot of telemarketing calls?"

2. "Yes, I do," I replied, "and they always come at dinnertime."

3. She told me that in April 2001, new laws that could help me protect my privacy had taken effect.

4. I wrote to the governor's office in Albany, New York, for information about the telemarketing registry.

5. My address, which is 21 Highland Road, Binghamton, New York, has now been added to the state registry.

6. For a while I still got occasional calls that began with an unfamiliar voice saying "James I have an exciting offer for you."

7. I simply replied "No I have news for you."

8. I pointed out that on August 11 2001 I had added my name and address to a list of people who do not want to receive calls about exciting offers.

9. "As you probably know" I told my unwanted callers "it is illegal for you to contact me in this way."

10. The marketing calls had stopped completely by November 1.   *C*

Edit Paragraphs and Your Own Writing

PRACTICE 7   EDITING PARAGRAPHS FOR COMMAS

TEAMWORK
Put students in small groups and give each group one paragraph to edit. Then have a member of each group read the edited paragraph aloud.

Edit the following paragraphs by adding commas where they are needed. If a sentence is already correct, put a "C" next to it.

1. (1) Everyone who uses cleaning products at home has probably seen warning labels on those products for most household cleaners contain harsh chemicals. (2) The warnings which are required by law are so common that many users probably ignore them. (3) However all cleaning products should be used with care and some of them can seriously injure children or anyone else who misuses them. (4) Drain cleaners toilet bowl cleaners and chlorine bleach can all cause serious damage to skin eyes and other sensitive tissue. (5) Glass cleaners can react with bleach to produce toxic fumes. (6) Alternative cleansers nontoxic products that can be made from items in an average kitchen are cheaper than brand-name cleaning products and usually work just as well. (7) For most cleaning jobs a solution of vinegar and water or baking soda and water is effective. (8) A plunger can often fix a clogged drain as well as a drain cleaner can and club soda cleans windows nicely. (9) As for air fresheners one expert

advises "Open your windows." (10) Economy efficiency and safety are three excellent reasons for choosing homemade cleansers.

2. (1) A few days ago I received an email that told a terrifying story. (2) At a large discount store in Austin Texas a four-year-old girl had disappeared and her mother had asked for the store employees' help in finding the child. (3) Thinking quickly the employees locked all of the doors posted an employee at every exit and systematically searched the store. (4) The child who was found in a bathroom was safe but half of her head had been shaved. (5) In addition someone had changed her clothes so it seemed obvious that an abductor had been trying to slip her out of the store unnoticed. (6) The email message which came from a distant acquaintance ended by advising me "Don't let your children out of your sight!"

(7) Later that day I was talking to my neighbor and I happened to mention the message. (8) She too had seen it and the story had shocked her. (9) Something about the story made me suspicious however so I decided to do some Internet research. (10) I found a site that discussed urban legends Internet hoaxes and chain letters. (11) On the site I discovered an exact copy of the email I had received. (12) I also learned that my neighbor and I were not the first people to fall for this hoax for Ann Landers had even printed a version of it several years earlier. (13) When she learned that she had been fooled she printed a retraction a column explaining that the story was fictional. (14) A reader wrote to her and said "Reminding people to be cautious is one thing. Scaring the pants off of them is another."

(15) After doing the research I felt better about the scary email story but I felt sad that we are so distrustful of one another. (16) Such stories can make us fear that potential abductors are everywhere. (17) Thirty years ago most parents were not usually afraid to let children walk to school alone or play outside but today's parents rarely let children out of their sight until the kids are in their teens. (18) The difference is not in the number of abductions of children a very small number that has remained nearly constant over the decades. (19) No the difference is that people

now hear about these unusual and terrifying instances over and over. (20) Eventually, they reach the conclusion that these stories must be true, and they are convinced that such dreadful things must happen frequently. (21) The email I had received was contributing, I decided, to this climate of irrational fear. (22) "Ann Landers's reader was right," I said to myself. (23) "We should teach our children caution, but we can harm them and ourselves by making them believe that evil strangers are lurking around every corner."

PRACTICE 8   EDITING YOUR OWN WRITING FOR COMMAS

LEARNING JOURNAL
What mistake with commas do you make most often? Why do you think you make this mistake?

As a final practice, edit a piece of your own writing for commas. It can be a paper you are working on for this course, a paper you've already finished, a paper for another course, or a recent piece of writing from your work or everyday life. In your learning journal, record any examples of sentences with comma problems that you find, along with the edited versions.

38
Apostrophes

,

Understand What Apostrophes Do

To understand this chapter, you need to know what nouns and pronouns are. For a review, see Chapters 27 and 33.

DEFINITION: An **apostrophe (')** is a punctuation mark that either shows ownership (*Susan's*) or indicates that a letter has been intentionally left out to form a contraction (*I'm, that's, they're*). Although an apostrophe looks like a comma (**,**), it is not used for the same purpose, and it is written higher on the line than commas are.

apostrophe **'**   comma **,**

Practice Using Apostrophes Correctly

APOSTROPHES TO SHOW OWNERSHIP

- Add -'s to a singular noun to show ownership even if the noun already ends in -s.

Singular means one; plural means more than one.

Darcy's car is being repaired.

Joan got all the information she needed from the hotel's Web site.

Chris's house is only a mile away.

- If a noun is plural and ends in -s, just add an apostrophe to show ownership. If it is plural but does not end in -s, add -'s.

   The actors' outfits were dazzling. [More than one actor]

   Seven boys' coats were left at the school.

   The children's toys were all broken.

- The placement of an apostrophe makes a difference in meaning.

   My neighbor's twelve cats are howling. [One neighbor who has twelve cats]

   My neighbors' twelve cats are howling. [Two or more neighbors who together have twelve cats]

- Do not use an apostrophe to form the plural of a noun.

   Use the stair's or the elevator.

   All of the plant's in the garden are blooming.

- Do not use an apostrophe with a possessive pronoun. These pronouns already show ownership (possession).

   Do you want to take my car or your's?

   That basket is our's.

Possessive Pronouns			
my	his	its	their
mine	her	our	theirs
your	hers	ours	whose
yours			

Its or *It's*

The single most common error with apostrophes and pronouns is confusing *its* (a possessive pronoun) with *it's* (a contraction meaning "it is"). Whenever you write *it's*, test to see if it's correct by reading it aloud as *it is* to hear if it makes sense.

DISCUSSION
Ask students to brainstorm some sentences that include *its* and some that include *it's*. After discussing these sentences, have the students create a tip or two to use when editing their own papers.

PRACTICE 1 **USING APOSTROPHES TO SHOW OWNERSHIP**

For more practice, visit Exercise Central at <www. bedfordstmartins.com/ realessays>.

Edit the following sentences by adding *-'s* or an apostrophe alone to show ownership and by crossing out any incorrect use of an apostrophe or *-'s*.

EXAMPLE: ~~Fever's~~ *Fevers* are an important part of the human ~~bodys~~ *body's* system of defense against infection.

1. A ~~thermometers~~ *thermometer's* indicator mark at 98.6 degrees is supposed to show a ~~persons~~ *person's* normal body temperature.

2. However, normal body temperature can range from 97 degrees to 100.4 degrees, so most ~~doctors~~ *doctors'* view of a temperature lower than 100.5 is that ~~its~~ *it's* not a fever at all.

3. ~~Fever's~~ *Fevers* help the body combat ~~virus's~~ *viruses* and stimulate the immune system.

4. Unless a ~~persons~~ *person's* temperature is raised by an outside source, the ~~bodys~~ *body's* regulatory system will not usually let a fever go higher than 106 degrees.

5. A ~~fevers~~ *fever's* appearance is not necessarily a reason to take fever-reducing ~~medication's~~ *medications,* which can lower a ~~bodys~~ *body's* temperature without doing anything to fight the infection.

6. Taking fever-reducing ~~drug's~~ *drugs* can actually make an illness take longer to run ~~it's~~ *its* course.

7. Many ~~doctors'~~ *doctors* do not recommend using any drugs to treat a fever if ~~its~~ *it's* lower than 102 degrees.

8. Parents should be aware that ~~childrens~~ *children's* fevers can go even higher than ~~their's.~~ *theirs.*

9. Some ~~parents~~ *parents'* fears of fever are so intense that they suffer from "fever phobia" and overreact to their ~~childrens'~~ *children's* symptoms.

10. Fever phobia can cause ~~parent's~~ *parents* to give their child extra medicine, but overdoses of ibuprofen and other fever reducers can impair the ~~livers'~~ *liver's* ability to work properly and can therefore complicate the ~~childs~~ *child's* sickness.

APOSTROPHES IN CONTRACTIONS

ESL
Because contractions are often new to ESL students, you may want to advise them to avoid all contractions in college work that they are submitting for a grade. They should use apostrophes only to show ownership.

DEFINITION: A **contraction** is formed by joining two words and leaving out one or more of the letters. When writing a contraction, put an apostrophe where the letter or letters have been left out, not between the two words.

Carol's studying to be a nurse. = *Carol is* studying to be a nurse.

I'll go when you come back. = *I will* go when you come back.

Be sure to put the apostrophe in the right place.

Don does'n't work here anymore.

Do not use contractions in formal papers or reports for college or work.

Common Contractions

aren't = are not	she'll = she will
can't = cannot	she's = she is, she has
couldn't = could not	there's = there is
didn't = did not	they'd = they would, they had
don't = do not	they'll = they will
he'd = he would, he had	they're = they are
he'll = he will	they've = they have
he's = he is, he has	who'd = who would, who had
I'd = I would, I had	who'll = who will
I'll = I will	who's = who is, who has

I'm = I am

I've = I have

isn't = is not

it's = it is, it has

let's = let us

she'd = she would, she had

won't = will not

wouldn't = would not

you'd = you would, you had

you'll = you will

you're = you are

you've = you have

PRACTICE 2   USING APOSTROPHES IN CONTRACTIONS

Read each sentence carefully, looking for any words that have missing letters. Edit these words by adding apostrophes where needed. Or, if apostrophes are misplaced, cross out and correct the error.

EXAMPLE: ~~Ive~~ *I've* never read a book that I enjoyed more than this one.

1. If ~~youv'e~~ *you've* ever read a book that was so wonderful you wanted all of your

   friends to read it, you may have considered the question "What makes a

   book great?"

2. ~~Thats~~ *That's* the question many students and teachers of literature have been

   asking for several years now, and they still ~~are'nt~~ *aren't* close to coming up

   with a definite answer.

3. ~~Theres~~ *There's* a problem with trying to establish which books are worth

   reading: ~~Whos~~ *Who's* going to decide?

4. Some people argue that a book ~~shouldve~~ *should've* passed the test of time before

   college students should be required to study it.

5. This requirement may mean, however, that a book written a hundred

   years ago is frequently taught and a newer book ~~thats~~ *that's* just as good ~~is'nt~~ *isn't*.

6. ~~Its~~ *It's* also true that books whose authors are women or members of

   minority groups ~~dont~~ *don't* appear as frequently on lists of great books of the

   past as books by white men.

7. In many cases, female and minority writers of the past ~~didnt~~ *didn't* have the
money or connections to get a book published or ~~could'nt~~ *couldn't* find an
audience for a book that was ahead of its time.

8. Some scholars argue that it ~~should'nt~~ *shouldn't* matter what the background of
the author is because great literature is universal.

9. Others think that ~~its~~ *it's* important to introduce college students to books
by female and minority writers because books by dead white men
~~arent~~ *aren't* going to interest a large percentage of today's students.

10. ~~Youre~~ *You're* probably aware that when instructors decide which books to
teach, ~~theyr'e~~ *they're* making political as well as literary choices ~~thatll~~ *that'll* affect
their students.

APOSTROPHES WITH LETTERS, NUMBERS, AND TIME

- Use -'s to make letters and numbers plural. The apostrophe prevents
confusion or misreading.

  Mississippi has four i's.

  In women's shoes, size 8's are more common than size 10's.

- Use an apostrophe or -'s in certain expressions in which time nouns are
treated as if they possess something.

  I get two weeks' vacation next year.

  Last year's prices were very good.

PRACTICE 3   USING APOSTROPHES WITH LETTERS, NUMBERS, AND TIME

Edit the following sentences by adding apostrophes where needed and fixing incorrectly used apostrophes.

EXAMPLE: Changing the marquee was supposed to be just a few
minutes'
~~minute's~~ work.

1. Last year, I turned down a ~~summers~~ *summer's* worth of beachgoing to stay in

   town and work at the local movie theater.

2. When I had two ~~week's~~ *weeks'* experience, the manager handed me a ladder

   and a box of letters to change the marquee outside.

3. I was trying to write *O Brother, Where Art Thou?* and *George Clooney,* but I

   ran out of ~~Es~~ *E's.*

4. The manager gave me a box of numbers and told me to use backward ~~3s~~ *3's.*

5. When I discovered that I didn't have two more ~~os~~ *o's* for *Clooney* and

   turned an 8 on its side instead, the manager told me I would go far in

   the movie business.

Edit Paragraphs and Your Own Writing

PRACTICE 4   **EDITING PARAGRAPHS FOR APOSTROPHES**

Edit the following paragraphs by adding apostrophes where needed and
crossing out incorrectly used apostrophes. If a sentence is already correct,
put a "C" after it.

TEAMWORK
Students can work in
pairs or small groups
to edit the paragraphs.
Discuss the results
with the whole class.

1. (1) Some of the first ~~discussion's~~ *discussions* of global warming focused attention
   on one of the ~~gas's~~ *gases* that contributes to the greenhouse effect: methane.
   (2) Like other greenhouse gases, methane helps to keep the ~~earths²~~ *earth's* heat

   trapped in our atmosphere, and the temperature of the earth goes up as a

   result. (3) Humans ~~are'nt~~ *aren't* the only producers of methane; ~~its~~ *it's* also a

   by-product of ~~cow's~~ *cows'* digestion of their food. (4) For a while, many

   ~~Americans~~ *Americans'* knowledge of global warming ~~didnt~~ *didn't* go much further than

   cow jokes. (5) As ~~scientists²~~ *scientists* have become more convinced that global

   warming is real and a potential threat to ~~human's,~~ *humans,* our knowledge of the

   causes of the greenhouse effect has expanded. (6) Cows ~~arent~~ *aren't* completely

they're
off the hook, but ~~theyre~~ far less guilty of contributing to global warming
than humans and cars are. (7) The amount of methane produced by
cows
~~cows'~~ adds up to about 3 percent of the total amount of greenhouse gases
its   *won't*
produced by people. (8) Getting a cow to change ~~it's~~ diet ~~wo'nt~~ solve the
world's
~~worlds~~ warming problem.

2. (1) Some people are terribly annoyed by misplaced apostrophes,
aren't   *who's*
and some people ~~are'nt~~. (2) In England, John Richards, a man ~~whos~~
annoyed by incorrect apostrophe placement, has founded an organization
called the Apostrophe Protection Society to campaign for the correct use
apostrophes   *dozens*
of ~~apostrophe's~~. (3) He has attracted ~~dozen's~~ of supporters who are infu-
menus
riated by signs, ~~menu's~~, and other notices in public places that contain
apostrophe errors. (4) One woman who joined the society carries small
pieces
apostrophes on sticky ~~piece's~~ of paper so that she can correct signs with
husband's
missing punctuation. (5) She admits that her ~~husbands~~ view of punctua-
hers
tion is not as strict as ~~her's~~, and she says that this sometimes causes arguments between them. (6) An article about the Englishman appeared in a
paper's
major U.S. newspaper, and afterward the ~~papers~~ editors were flooded
with letters related to the subject of apostrophes. (7) Although a few people
Richards's   *shouldn't*
thought ~~Richards~~ crusade ~~shouldnt~~ be taken seriously, the majority of
letter writers supported his view, and one or two couldn't wait to start a
chapter of the society in the United States. (8) It seems that no matter
how relaxed some people get about punctuation, there will always be
others   *i's*   *t's*
some ~~other's~~ who want to make sure that all the *is* are dotted, all the *ts*
apostrophes
are crossed, and all the ~~apostrophe's~~ are in their proper places.

3. (1) In March of 2001, the keyless entry systems of cars in Bremerton,
Washington, suddenly stopped working, and no one knows why. *C*

TEACHING TIP
The URL for Richards's
Web site is <www
.apostrophe.fsnet
.co.uk>.

(2) The ~~cars~~ *cars'* locks were supposed to respond when their ~~owner's~~ *owners* pushed a button, and all at once they ~~wouldnt~~ *wouldn't*. (3) After a few ~~days~~ *days'* wait, the entry systems began functioning again. (4) Many ~~resident's~~ *residents* of Bremerton, the home of a Navy shipyard, were convinced that the ~~militarys~~ *military's* techno-logical activity had affected the cars, but Navy ~~official's~~ *officials* denied it. (5) Other people wondered if radio transmissions might have jammed the frequency and prevented the keyless ~~systems~~ *systems* from functioning. (6) Fortunately, people whose cars have keyless entry systems ~~were'nt~~ *weren't* locked out for those days. (7) These owners simply had to resort to a backup system to open and lock their ~~car's~~ *cars* — ~~its~~ *it's* called a "key."

PRACTICE 5   EDITING YOUR OWN WRITING FOR APOSTROPHES

As a final practice, edit a piece of your own writing for apostrophes. It can be a paper you are working on for this course, a paper you've already fin-ished, a paper for another course, or a recent piece of writing from your work or everyday life. In your learning journal, record any examples of sentences with apostrophe problems that you find, along with the edited versions.

LEARNING JOURNAL
What type of mistake with apostrophes do you make most often? How can you avoid this mistake or be sure to edit for it?

39

Quotation Marks

Understand What Quotation Marks Do

To understand this chapter, you need to know what a sentence is. For a review, see Chapter 22.

DEFINITION: Quotation marks (" ") are punctuation marks with two common uses in college writing: They are used with some quotations, and they are used to set off titles. They always appear in pairs.

DEFINITIONS: A **quotation** is the report of another person's words. There are two types of quotations: **direct quotations** (the exact repetition, word for word, of what someone said or wrote) and **indirect quotations** (a restatement of what someone said or wrote, not word for word). Quotation marks are used only for direct quotations.

DIRECT QUOTATION	George said, "I'm getting a haircut."
INDIRECT QUOTATION	George said that he was getting a haircut.

Practice Using Quotation Marks Correctly

QUOTATION MARKS FOR DIRECT QUOTATIONS

When you write a direct quotation, you need to use quotation marks around the quoted words. These marks tell readers that the words used are exactly what was said or written.

1. "My license expires tomorrow," Gerri told me.
2. I asked, "Are you going to get it renewed?"
3. "Well, I should," Gerri admitted, "but I don't think I have time to get to the Registry of Motor Vehicles. What will happen if I'm late?"
4. "Probably nothing," I replied. "I wouldn't risk it, though."
5. After thinking for a moment, Gerri said, "I think I'll take my chances."

When you are writing a paper in which you use outside sources, use quotation marks to indicate the exact words that you quote from a source. You'll then have to cite, or give credit to, the source.

> The government needs to ensure that when a company fails, employees' pensions are protected. A recent article in the *Boston Globe* reported, "When Polaroid collapsed, pension funds and employee stock programs were suddenly worthless. At the same time, however, the chief financial officer walked away with a package worth more than $2 million." (Richardson B3)

Quoted words are usually combined with words that identify who is speaking, such as *Gerri told me* in the first example. The identifying words can come after the quoted words (example 1), before them (example 2), or in the middle (example 3). Here are some guidelines for capitalization and punctuation:

- Capitalize the first letter in a complete sentence that's being quoted, even if it comes after some identifying words (example 2).
- Do not capitalize the first letter in a quotation if it's not the first word in a complete sentence (*but* in example 3).
- If it is a complete sentence and its source is clear, you can let a quotation stand on its own, without any identifying words (example 4).

LEARNING JOURNAL
Use your learning journal as a place to record sentences with mistakes in the use of quotation marks. Also write down edited versions of these sentences, with the problems corrected.

For information about how to use quotations in research papers, see Chapter 20.

For more on commas with quotation marks, see page 576.

For more on citing sources, see pages 318–321.

TEACHING TIP
As you read each of these guidelines, put a sentence on the board without any quotation marks. Ask students where the quotation marks should go and which letters should be capitalized.

- Attach identifying words to a quotation; these identifying words cannot be a sentence on their own.
- Use commas to separate any identifying words from quoted words in the same sentence.
- Always put quotation marks after commas and periods. Put quotation marks after question marks and exclamation points if they are part of the quoted sentence.

quotation mark   quotation mark

I asked, "Are you going to get it renewed?"

comma   question mark

- If a question mark or exclamation point is part of your own sentence, put it after the quotation mark.

quotation mark   quotation mark

What do you mean by, "I'll take my chances"?

comma   question mark

Setting Off a Quotation within Another Quotation

Sometimes you may directly quote someone who quotes what someone else said or wrote. Put single quotation marks (' ') around the quotation within a quotation so that readers understand who said what.

> The student handbook said, "Students must be given the opportunity to make up work missed for legitimate reasons."

> Terry told his instructor, "I'm sorry I missed the exam, but I would like to take a makeup exam. Our student handbook says, 'Students must be given the opportunity to make up work missed for legitimate reasons,' and I have a good reason."

Terry's entire quotation.

Here, Terry is including a quotation from the student handbook.

PRACTICE 1   PUNCTUATING DIRECT QUOTATIONS

For more practice, visit Exercise Central at <**www .bedfordstmartins.com/ realessays**>.

Edit the following sentences by adding quotation marks and commas where needed.

EXAMPLE: She asked "Did the Supreme Court make the right decision in ending the Florida recount and settling the 2000 presidential election?"

1. Writing about the United States in the nineteenth century, Alexis de Tocqueville noted "If ever the Supreme Court came to be composed of rash or corrupt men, the confederation would be threatened by anarchy or by civil war."

2. After reading us this quote, Professor Patel asked "What do you suppose Tocqueville would have thought of the Supreme Court's decision in *Bush v. Gore?*"

3. "Were the justices 'rash' or 'corrupt'" she continued "or did they do the right thing when they ended the long election?"

4. Natalie announced "I think that more people in Florida intended to vote for Gore than for Bush."

5. "But" Roberto interrupted "we can't ever know people's intentions for certain, so the only important question is how the Florida citizens actually voted."

6. "How are we supposed to know that when the Supreme Court stopped the recount?" Natalie retorted.

7. Professor Patel reminded us "No one has answered my question yet."

8. Roberto said "The country was suffering because no one knew who would be the next president, so the Supreme Court did the right thing."

9. "The justices who stopped the recount were motivated by conservative political views" Natalie fumed. "The decision was obviously corrupt!"

10. Why was Professor Patel smiling when she said "This will be the topic of
your first research paper"?

NO QUOTATION MARKS FOR
INDIRECT QUOTATIONS

TEAMWORK
In pairs, ask students
to interview one
another on a prede-
termined topic and
then write a one-
paragraph report that
includes at least one
direct quotation and
one indirect quotation.
Photocopy several of
these reports to use
for a whole-class
workshop on quota-
tion marks.

When you report what someone said or wrote but do not use the person's
exact words, you are writing an indirect quotation. Do not use quotation
marks for indirect quotations. Indirect quotations often begin with the
word *that*.

INDIRECT QUOTATION	DIRECT QUOTATION
Sophie said that the exam was postponed.	Sophie said, "The exam was postponed."
The boy asked me what time it was.	"What time is it?" asked the boy.
Carolyn told me that she had an accident.	Carolyn told me, "I had an accident."

PRACTICE 2   PUNCTUATING DIRECT AND
INDIRECT QUOTATIONS

TEACHING TIP
Using a reading from
this textbook or an
article from another
text, have students
identify direct and
indirect quotations,
and explain why the
writer may have
chosen one or the
other. Also have them
circle any punctuation
used with the
quotation marks.

Edit the following sentences by adding quotation marks where needed and
crossing out quotation marks that are incorrectly used. If a sentence is
already correct, put a "C" next to it.

EXAMPLE: After being laid off, Sarita told me that "she would never
work for another dot-com."

1. "I loved the informal office at first," she said.

2. Sarita remembered "how much she had enjoyed setting her own hours."

3. She admitted, "I have never been a business-suit kind of person, so I
liked the fact that every day was casual."

4. "But after a while, I wondered how on earth the company was supposed
to earn a profit," she told me.   *C*

5. Sarita had asked the company's founder what his plans for the future
were.   *C*

6. She began to worry when he told her that "he hadn't thought that far ahead yet."

7. "He apparently thought that people would keep giving us money just because the company was cool," she said exasperatedly.   *C*

8. Sarita told a colleague that "she was looking for a new job because she didn't think the dot-com would last."

9. "I was just starting to send out résumés when I got laid off," she recalled, "and fortunately I found something before my severance pay ended."

10. She told me that other people at the company had not been as fortunate as she was, and when the dot-com went bankrupt, the remaining employees were suddenly left without paychecks.   *C*

QUOTATION MARKS FOR CERTAIN TITLES

When you refer to a short work such as a magazine or newspaper article, a chapter in a book, a short story, an essay, a song, or a poem, put quotation marks around the title of the work.

NEWSPAPER ARTICLE	"Mayor Warns of Budget Cuts"
SHORT STORY	"Everyday Use"
ESSAY	"Spice of Life"

Usually titles of longer works, such as novels, books, magazines, newspapers, movies, television programs, and CDs, are underlined or italicized. The titles of sacred books such as the Bible or the Koran are neither underlined, italicized, nor surrounded by quotation marks.

BOOK	The Chocolate War or *The Chocolate War*
NEWSPAPER	Washington Post or *Washington Post*

[Do not underline, italicize, or capitalize the word *the* before the name of a newspaper or magazine, even if it is part of the title: I saw that in the *New York Times*. But do capitalize *The* when it is the first word in titles of books, movies, and other sources.]

If you are writing a paper with many outside sources, your instructor will probably refer you to a particular system of citing sources. Follow that system's guidelines when you use titles in your paper.

NOTE: Do not enclose the title of a paragraph or an essay that you have written in quotation marks when it appears at the beginning of your paper. Do not underline it either.

▨ PRACTICE 3   USING QUOTATION MARKS FOR TITLES

Edit the following sentences by adding quotation marks around titles as needed. Underline any book, magazine, or newspaper titles.

> EXAMPLE: As we rode the elevator to our meeting on the fortieth
>
> floor, we had to listen to a piped-in instrumental version
>
> of "Oops, I Did It Again."

1. At the meeting, an outside consultant tried to motivate us by quoting

   from an article in USA Today called "How to Get the Job Done."

2. Then he gave each of us a copy of a well-known CEO's autobiography

   and asked us to read Chapter 4, "The Road to the Top."

3. Marta looked as if she were taking careful notes, but I knew that she

   was working on the final draft of an essay she was hoping to publish in

   Business Review, her favorite magazine.

4. When she had told me earlier that the essay would be called "Why

   Meetings Are Usually Useless," I had volunteered to provide many

   personal examples to prove her point.

5. When the grueling meeting was over, Marta reminded me that

   Wallace Stevens, the poet who wrote "Sunday Morning," had found

   a way to be creative while he spent his days working at an insurance

   company.

Edit Paragraphs and Your Own Writing

PRACTICE 4   EDITING PARAGRAPHS FOR QUOTATION MARKS

Edit the following paragraphs by adding quotation marks where needed and crossing out any incorrectly used quotation marks. Correct any errors in punctuation.

1. (1) After Michael saw an advertisement in his local newspaper for a concert featuring "The Pink Panther Theme," "Charade," and other songs by Henry Mancini, he immediately bought a ticket. (2) He had just finished reading a book about the film composer, and he told me that "he couldn't wait to hear the music played live." (3) He said that "I should go, too," but I stayed home and watched television. (4) After he went to the show, he told me "I thought that they saved the best for last." (5) He described the final number, when a young woman stepped onto the stage and sang, "Moon river, wider than a mile, I'm crossing you in style someday." (6) He knew "Moon River" from the movie Breakfast at Tiffany's and as a hit song for Andy Williams in the 1960s, but he had never found the song as beautiful as it seemed that night at the concert. (7) "It was an amazing evening," he told me. (8) His description of the concert was so vivid that I went out and bought a CD called "Henry Mancini's Greatest Hits." (9) Now I regret my decision: Why didn't I go to the concert when Michael said, "Come with me; you'll love the music?" (10) As I listen to the CD, I realize that he was right, and next time he tells me about a show that "he thinks I'll love," I'm going to go along.

2. (1) "Did you know that people our age could experience a life crisis?" my twenty-five-year-old friend Beth asked as we browsed at the newsstand. (2) She showed me an article called "The Trouble with Being 25" in a magazine she was looking at.

(3) I told her that "she was crazy." (4) "You wait until midlife for your crisis, silly," I said. (5) I was imagining a middle-aged businessman suddenly buying an expensive sports car and driving around listening to Prince singing "Little Red Corvette."

(6) Beth pointed out that she had plenty of anxiety about being twenty-five. (7) "It's as if people look at me and think I'm still basically a teenager, yet I have a grown-up job and grown-up responsibilities to go with it," she said.

(8) I asked her "what kinds of responsibilities she was talking about." (9) "I have rent and bills to pay," she said, "and I'm trying to decide if I should take a couple of classes at night to get a better job." (10) She thought for a moment and then added, "And sooner or later I'll need to figure out whether I want to get married and have children." (11) She picked up a newspaper and idly turned the pages until she found a headline that said "Confusion Reigns among Young Singles."

(12) "Wow! You're right!" I blurted out. (13) "It's a good thing you read those stupid magazines," I said to Beth. (14) I was only partly kidding when I added that "she and I would never have realized that we were supposed to be having a crisis if we hadn't read about it."

(15) "Let's do something to celebrate," said Beth. (16) That's why we spent the rest of the afternoon sitting around my kitchen table drinking coffee, listening to Beck singing "Loser," and reading out loud to each other from "How to Tell If You're Ready to Settle Down" in the new issue of Cosmopolitan.

■ PRACTICE 5   **EDITING YOUR OWN WRITING FOR QUOTATION MARKS**

As a final practice, edit a piece of your own writing for quotation marks. It can be a paper you are working on for this course, a paper you've already finished, a paper for another course, or a recent piece of writing from your work or everyday life. In your learning journal, record any examples you find of sentences with mistakes in the use of quotation marks. Also write down the edited versions.

LEARNING JOURNAL
In your own words, explain the difference between direct quotations and indirect quotations. Write one example of each.

40

Other Punctuation

; : ( ) — -

Understand What Punctuation Does 600

Practice Using Punctuation Correctly 601

Edit Paragraphs and Your Own Writing 604

Understand What Punctuation Does

To understand this chapter, you need to know what sentences and independent clauses are. For a review, see Chapter 22.

Punctuation helps readers understand your writing. If you use punctuation incorrectly, you send readers a confusing message—or, even worse, a wrong one. This chapter covers five marks of punctuation that people sometimes use incorrectly. Knowing what functions these marks of punctuation serve can help you avoid such mistakes.

TEACHING TIP
Caution students not to use semicolons as a default solution when trying to increase sentence complexity; overuse and misuse are common.

SEMICOLON ;	Joins two independent clauses into one sentence
	Separates complete items in a list that already has commas within individual items
COLON :	Introduces a list
	Announces an explanation
PARENTHESES ( )	Set off extra information that is not essential to the sentence
DASH —	Sets off words for emphasis
	Indicates a pause
HYPHEN -	Joins two or more words that together form a single description
	Shows a word break at the end of a line

Practice Using Punctuation Correctly

SEMICOLON ;

Semicolons to Join Independent Clauses

Use a semicolon to join two very closely related sentences and make them into one sentence.

> In an interview, hold your head up, and don't slouch; it is important to look alert.

> Make good eye contact; looking down is not appropriate in an interview.

For more on using semicolons to join sentences, see Chapter 30.

TEACHING TIP
After each of the explanations and examples in this chapter, ask students to write examples of their own.

Semicolons in Lists Containing Commas

When one or more items in a list contain commas, use semicolons to separate the items. Otherwise, it is difficult for readers to tell where one item ends and another begins.

> Jim's younger sister, Toni, lives in San Francisco; his older sisters, Patti and Lori, live in Denver; and his brother, Marty, lives in Boca Raton.

LEARNING JOURNAL
Use your learning journal as a place to record sentences in your writing that should have semicolons, colons, parentheses, dashes, and hyphens. Try to find one sample sentence for each of these punctuation marks. Write the sentence both before and after you edit it.

COLON :

Colons before Lists

Use a colon after an independent clause to introduce a list.

> In the United States, three ice cream flavors are the most popular: vanilla, chocolate, and strawberry.

> I have three stops to make on the way home: the grocery store, the post office, and the police station.

See Chapter 37, Chapter 38, and Chapter 39 for coverage of commas, apostrophes, and quotation marks, respectively.

Colons before Explanations or Examples

Use a colon after an independent clause to let readers know that you are about to provide an explanation or example of what you just wrote. If the explanation or example is also an independent clause, capitalize the first letter after the colon.

> Sometimes the choice of cereals is overwhelming: My supermarket carries at least five different types of raisin bran.

An independent clause contains a subject and a verb, and it expresses a complete thought. It can stand on its own as a sentence.

TEACHING TIP
It may help students to
think of the colon as a
spotlight, especially in
sentences where an
example follows the
colon (*The plan has
one major problem:
cost*).

I use one criterion to choose a cereal: price.

NOTE: A colon in a sentence must follow an independent clause. A common misuse is to place a colon after a phrase instead of an independent clause. Watch out especially for colons following the phrase *such as* or *for example*.

INCORRECT	The resort offers many activities such as: snorkeling, golf, and windsurfing.
CORRECT	The resort offers many activities: snorkeling, golf, and windsurfing.
CORRECT	The resort offers many activities such as snorkeling, golf, and windsurfing.
INCORRECT	Suzy has many talents. For example: writing, drawing, and painting.
CORRECT	Suzy has many talents: writing, drawing, and painting.

Colons in Business Correspondence

Use a colon after a greeting (called a salutation) in a business letter and after the standard heading lines at the beginning of a memorandum.

Dear Mr. Latimer:

To: Jeffery Siddall

From: Susan Anker

PARENTHESES ( )

Use parentheses to set off information that is not essential to the meaning of a sentence. Parentheses are always used in pairs and should be used sparingly.

TEACHING TIP
Have students find
examples of the
overuse of paren-
theses from news-
papers, magazines,
or Web sites; edit
these as a class.

My grandfather's most successful invention (his first) was the electric blanket.

My worst habit (and also the hardest to break) is interrupting.

When people speak too slowly, I often finish their sentences (at least in my mind).

DASH —

Dashes can be used like parentheses to set off additional information, particularly information that you want to emphasize.

> The essay question—worth 50 percent of the whole exam—will be open book.

> Your answers should be well developed, and points—2 per error—will be deducted for major grammar mistakes.

A dash can also indicate a pause, much as a comma does.

> My son wants to buy a car—more power to him.

Make a dash by typing two hyphens together. Do not leave any extra spaces around a dash.

HYPHEN -

Hyphens to Join Words That Form a Single Description

Writers often join two or more words that together form a single description of a person, place, or thing. To join the words, use a hyphen.

> The eighty-year-old smoker was considered a high-risk patient.

> I followed the company's decision-making procedure.

> I can't wait to see my end-of-the-year grade.

TEACHING TIP
Remind students that a hyphenated compound adjective (the company's *decision-making* procedure) might not be hyphenated as a noun (*Decision making* is one of my strengths). When in doubt, consult a dictionary.

Hyphens to Divide a Word at the End of a Line

Use a hyphen to divide a word when part of the word must continue on the next line.

> If you give me the receipt for your purchase, I will immediately issue a refund.

If you are not sure where to break a word, look it up in a dictionary. The word's main entry will show you where you can break the word: dic • tio • nary. If you still aren't confident that you are putting the hyphen in the right place, don't break the word; write it all on the next line.

Edit Paragraphs and Your Own Writing

▢ PRACTICE 1   EDITING PARAGRAPHS FOR OTHER PUNCTUATION MARKS

For more practice, visit Exercise Central at <www .bedfordstmartins.com /realessays>.

Edit the following paragraphs by adding semicolons, colons, parentheses, dashes, and hyphens where needed. Keep in mind that in some places, more than one type of punctuation may be acceptable. *Answers may vary. Possible edits shown.*

1. (1) The International Olympic Committee met in 2001 to choose the site of the 2008 Olympic Games [;] the winner was Beijing, China's capital. (2) Beijing [(] the loser to Sydney, Australia, for the 2000 Olympics by just two votes [)] had campaigned heavily for the honor of hosting the Olympics. (3) The 2001 vote [—] which had some vocal opponents [—] granted the Olympic Games to China for the first time in history. (4) Those who objected to the Olympic Committee's choice had several strong reasons [:] China has a history of environmental problems, including severe smog in Beijing as a result of coal [-] burning factories, polluting buses, and heavy automobile traffic [;] and, even more important, the country has been scrutinized for human rights abuses. (5) Chinese officials had announced a twelve [-] billion [-] dollar project to cut air pollution in the city before the Olympic Committee made its decision. (6) Human rights abuses are not as easily answered [;] several members of Congress were among those complaining about China's treatment of political and religious dissidents.

(7) Supporters of Beijing's bid to host the Olympics believe that the Games will make China a more open society [: Reporters,] reporters, athletes, and spectators will flood Beijing in 2008. (8) Some members of the Olympic Committee [(] including the outgoing president, said to be a strong supporter of Beijing's bid [)] hope the vote will lead to improved human rights

situations in China. (9) There are many skeptics some argue that Beijing will see the Olympics as a reward, not as an opportunity for change. (10) Some even compare the Beijing Olympics to the 1936 Olympics in Hitler's Berlin one difference, however, is that billions of people will be watching the Games on television in 2008. (11) Whatever happens in China as a result of holding the Games in Beijing, the Chinese people strong supporters of the Beijing Olympics are overjoyed at the chance to show off their capital city. (12) Sports fans and freedom loving people all over the world will be watching China as 2008 approaches.

2. (1) In every state, there are minimum ages for driving these can range from fourteen to eighteen. (2) Eighteen year olds may have to pass a driving test, but sometimes they can renew their licenses by mail. (3) In some states, people can go on renewing drivers' licenses indefinitely or at least until they die or have their licenses revoked. (4) However, as people age, they can become less able to handle an automobile well reflexes get slower, eyesight often becomes less acute, and forgetfulness may increase. (5) Not every driver over seventy is unfit however, some older drivers can pose a danger on the road. (6) Some people argue that drivers no matter what their age should have to prove their physical and mental fitness for keeping a license. (7) Children and friends of the elderly worry about accidents involving older drivers, but they are also concerned about the effects that losing a driver's license may have on an independent minded senior. (8) As the population of the United States ages, the need to balance fairness to older drivers with traffic safety concerns is likely to grow more urgent most of us like it or not will have to face this question whether we are worried about our parents or ourselves.

PRACTICE 2   EDITING YOUR OWN WRITING FOR OTHER PUNCTUATION MARKS

LEARNING JOURNAL
What is one useful piece of information you learned in this chapter?

As a final practice, edit a piece of your own writing for semicolons, colons, parentheses, dashes, and hyphens. It can be a paper you are working on for this course, a paper you've already finished, a paper for another course, or a piece of writing from your work or everyday life. You may want to try more than one way to use these marks of punctuation in your writing. In your learning journal, record any examples of sentences you edited, showing the sentences both before and after you edited them.

41

Capitalization

Using Capital Letters

Understand Three Rules of Capitalization

TEACHING TIP
Remind students that habitually writing or typing in all capital letters will make it difficult for them to recognize and edit errors when they use regular capitalization.

There are three basic rules of capitalization.

THE THREE RULES OF CAPITALIZATION
Capitalize the first letter

1. Of every new sentence
2. Of names of specific people, places, dates, and things
3. Of important words in titles

To understand this chapter, you need to know what a sentence is. For a review, see Chapter 22.

If you can remember these three rules, you will avoid the most common errors in capitalization.

Practice Capitalization

LEARNING JOURNAL
Use your learning journal as a place to record any capitalization problems that you find in your writing. Also write down edited versions of the sentences, with the problems corrected.

CAPITALIZATION OF SENTENCES

Capitalize the first letter in each new sentence, including the first word in a direct quotation.

Mary was surprised when she saw all the people.

She asked, "What's going on here?"

For more practice, visit Exercise Central at <www .bedfordstmartins.com/ realessays>.

PRACTICE 1   CAPITALIZING THE FIRST WORD IN A SENTENCE

Edit the following paragraph, changing lowercase letters to capital letters as needed. If a sentence is already correct, put a "C" next to it.

(1) Many fans of classic films point to 1939 as the greatest year in cinema
history. (2) Moviegoers that year were mesmerized by Rhett Butler telling
Scarlett O'Hara, "frankly, my dear, I don't give a damn." (3) the same
year, audiences thrilled to the story of little Dorothy, who clicked her heels
together and chanted, "there's no place like home." (4) the films of 1939
still make movie buffs shake their heads and mutter, "they don't make
movies like that anymore!"

CAPITALIZATION OF NAMES OF SPECIFIC PEOPLE, PLACES, DATES, AND THINGS

The general rule is to capitalize the first letter in names of specific people, places, dates, and things. Do not capitalize general words such as *college* as opposed to the specific name: *Lincoln College*. Look at the examples for each group.

The word *president* is not capitalized unless it comes directly before a name as part of that person's title: President George W. Bush.

DISCUSSION
Have students come up with their own examples of people, places, and so forth that are "specific" and "not specific."

People

Capitalize the first letter in names of specific people and in titles used with names of specific people.

SPECIFIC	NOT SPECIFIC
Joan Feinberg	my friend
Dr. James	the physician
Professor Clark	your professor
Aunt Jane, Mother	my aunt, my mother

The name of a family member is capitalized when the family member is being addressed directly or when the family title is standing in for a first name.

Do not capitalize directions in a sentence: *Drive south for five blocks.*

Happy Birthday, Sister.

I see Mother is now taking classes.

In other instances, do not capitalize.

It is my sister's birthday.

My mother is taking classes.

Places

Capitalize the first letter in names of specific buildings, streets, cities, states, regions, and countries.

SPECIFIC	NOT SPECIFIC
Bolton Police Department	the police department
Washington Street	our street
Boston, MA	my hometown
Texas	this state
the West	the western part of the country
Italy	that country

ESL
Ask ESL students to identify any English capitalization rules that differ from the rules in the other languages that they speak and write. Invite students to write any examples they want to share on the board.

Dates

Capitalize the first letter in the names of days, months, and holidays. Do not capitalize the names of the seasons (winter, spring, summer, fall).

SPECIFIC	NOT SPECIFIC
Monday	today
January 4	winter
Presidents' Day	my birthday

Organizations, Companies, and Groups

SPECIFIC	NOT SPECIFIC
Bradford College	my college
Toys "R" Us	the toy store
Merrimack Players	the theater group

Languages, Nationalities, and Religions

The names of languages should be capitalized even if you aren't referring to a specific course: I am taking nutrition and Spanish.

SPECIFIC	NOT SPECIFIC
English, Greek, Spanish	my first language
Christianity, Buddhism	your religion

Courses

SPECIFIC	NOT SPECIFIC
English 100	a writing course
Nutrition 100	the basic nutrition course

Commercial Products

SPECIFIC	NOT SPECIFIC
Diet Coke	a diet cola
Hershey bar	a chocolate bar

PRACTICE 2   CAPITALIZING NOUNS

Edit the following sentences by adding capitalization as needed or removing capitalization where it is inappropriate.

EXAMPLE: My High School had a painting by Birger Sandzen on display in an Art classroom.

1. Lindsborg is a small town in McPherson county, Kansas, that calls itself "little sweden, U.S.A."

2. Lindsborg's Restaurant, the Swedish crown, serves Swedish Meatballs at its sunday smorgasbord.

3. The Town's most famous resident was probably a swedish immigrant Artist named Birger Sandzen.

4. He read a book by the founder of Bethany college in lindsborg and came to kansas to teach at the College in 1894.

5. Sandzen intended to stay in *K*ansas for two or three years, but he loved the *g*reat *p*lains and ended up remaining in *L*indsborg for the rest of his life.

6. Sandzen taught *a*Art, but he also taught *l*Languages, and he sang as a *t*Tenor with the Bethany *o*ratorio *s*ociety.

7. Although Sandzen worked mainly in the *M*midwest, the Rocky *M*mountains, and other relatively unpopulated parts of *t*The United States, he exhibited widely.

8. His show at the Babcock *G*galleries in *N*new *Y*york received an enthusiastic *c*Critical response.

9. Sandzen's use of vivid color showed the beauty of the natural landscapes of the *W*west.

10. Sandzen's name may not be familiar to every *a*Art *l*Lover, but his paintings and engravings—which are found in private collections, at *s*Schools in Kansas, and at the Sandzen *M*memorial *G*gallery in Lindsborg— are quite valuable today.

CAPITALIZATION OF TITLES

When you write the title of a book, movie, television program, magazine, newspaper, article, story, song, paper, poem, and so on, capitalize the first word, the last word, and all important words in between. Words that do not need to be capitalized (unless they are the first word) include articles (*the, a, an*); coordinating conjunctions (*and, but, for, nor, or, so, yet*); and prepositions.

For more on punctuating titles, see Chapter 39. For a list of common prepositions, see Chapter 22.

West Wing is a very popular television program.

Newsweek and *Time* often have similar cover stories.

"Once More to the Lake" is one of Chuck's favorite essays.

■ **PRACTICE 3** **CAPITALIZING TITLES**

Edit the following sentences by capitalizing titles as needed.

> **EXAMPLE:** Kermit the Frog sang "it's not easy being green" in *the muppet movie.*

1. The television show *sesame street,* which began in 1969, was an innovator in programming for children.

2. My favorite among the show's friendly puppets, known as the Muppets, was Ernie, who liked to sing "rubber ducky."

3. The popular Muppets Kermit the Frog and Miss Piggy starred in several films, including one based on Charles Dickens's classic *a christmas carol* and one based on Robert Louis Stevenson's *treasure island.*

4. The show contained no advertising, but magazines such as *sesame street parents* and toys based on the characters brought in huge amounts of money.

5. "Elmo's world," a segment added to the show in the 1990s, introduced the small red monster who would become one of the most popular toys in history.

Edit Paragraphs and Your Own Writing

■ **PRACTICE 4** **EDITING PARAGRAPHS FOR CAPITALIZATION**

Edit the following paragraphs by capitalizing as needed and removing any unnecessary capitalization.

(1) Are pennies necessary? (2) In 2001, representative Jim Knowles of arizona introduced legislation, the legal tender modernization act, to

require that prices be rounded up or down to the nearest nickel, eliminating the need for pennies. (3) according to the group Americans For
Common cents, however, "pennies are a part of our culture and our economy." (4) Should the united states keep its least valuable coin?

(5) Opponents of the Copper coin—which has been made of Zinc with
a Copper coating since 1982—say that people don't like to use Pennies.
(6) Although many of us are familiar with the saying, "find a penny, pick
it up; All day long you'll have good luck," a majority of americans do not
think that picking up a dropped penny is worth their time and effort. (7)
many stores place Penny trays on the counter so that Customers can either
leave unwanted pennies or pick a few up for the Cashier to avoid getting
any pennies in change. (8) The U.S. mint says that there are over 130
Billion pennies in circulation, but in 2000 it had to produce fourteen
Billion more—70 Percent of the total number of coins minted—because
people tend to throw loose change in a jar and leave it there.

(9) Yet the penny is undeniably a part of American History. (10) Pennies were the first coins minted in the united states, in 1793. (11) Only
four of these original coins survive, and they are valued at more than a
quarter of a Million dollars each. (12) Pennies were the first U.S. Coins
to carry the image of a historical figure: They have featured the likeness of
president abraham lincoln since 1909, the one hundredth anniversary of
his birth. (13) fifty years later, the lincoln memorial was added to the
reverse side, replacing the stalks of wheat on earlier Pennies.

(14) Pennies are part of the culture, too. (15) Everyone has heard, "a
penny saved is a penny earned," and that saying is not likely to change
even though a penny doesn't buy much today. (16) Music lovers may
know the popular song "pennies from Heaven," which was a hit for frank
sinatra, and film buffs might have seen either the bing crosby or the steve

DISCUSSION
Ask students to submit (anonymously if they choose) a paragraph from a rough draft typed entirely in lowercase letters for a whole-class editing session on capitalization.

        M
martin movie with the same name. (17) finally, unlike the john f. kennedy
   F   *J* *FK*
half-dollar coin, which is no longer minted, people simply expect pennies
to be there.

                   A
(18) Of course, other american coins have disappeared over the years,
              P
and perhaps the Penny has outlived its usefulness. (19) But many U.S.
c
Citizens care about the fate of the penny and don't want it to disappear.

> **PRACTICE 5   EDITING YOUR OWN WRITING
> FOR CAPITALIZATION**

LEARNING JOURNAL
What problem with capitalization do you have most often? How can you edit more effectively for this problem in the future?

As a final practice, edit a piece of your own writing for capitalization. It can be a paper you are working on for this course, a paper you've already finished, a paper for another course, or a recent piece of writing from your work or everyday life. In your learning journal, record any examples of sentences with capitalization problems that you find, along with the edited versions.

PART EIGHT

Readings
for Writers

42

Introduction to the Reading Process

In this part of the book, you will find twenty essays that demonstrate the types of writing you have studied: narration, illustration, description, process analysis, classification, definition, comparison and contrast, cause and effect, and argument. However, these readings are more than just good models of writing. They also tell great stories, argue passionately about controversial issues, and present a wide range of perspectives and information. These essays can also provide you with ideas for your own writing, both in and out of school. Most important, they offer you a chance to become a better reader and writer by examining how others write.

Why Is Reading Important?

Often our lives depend on reading. Before we can do something, we need to understand what it is, how to do it, or how to get information about it. Make no mistake about it: Reading is an essential skill—in college, at work, and in everyday life.

COLLEGE

- You have to do an English assignment: Read the essay and answer the questions.
- You have to do a math assignment: Read pages 49–58 and do Exercises 2.1–2.5.

WORK

- You have to read the procedures manual before starting a new task.
- You have to read the order carefully before filling it.

EVERYDAY LIFE

- You need to read the credit card agreement before applying for a card.
- You need to read the directions before hooking up a DVD player.

In every part of your life, you need to read, and it is important to know how to read carefully rather than just skimming over material without fully understanding it.

How Can These Readings Help You?

This part of the book presents some strategies for reading and then lets you practice those strategies by analyzing essays by professional writers. You can apply these strategies to any piece of writing in any setting.

Reading the essays in this part of the book will help you develop several different abilities.

YOUR ABILITY TO WRITE

The essays in this section are good examples of the types of the writing you are doing in your writing course. By looking at how someone else states main ideas, provides supporting details, organizes ideas, and introduces and concludes an essay, you gain a better sense of how you might write a similar type of essay. The essays can also help you choose writing topics: As you react to an author's ideas, you may discover ideas of your own to explore.

YOUR ABILITY TO READ CRITICALLY

To get the most out of what you read, you need to read closely and critically. **Close reading** means that you pay attention to every word and every point in the essay. **Critical reading** means that you ask yourself why the author has made these points in this way and whether you agree. To help you read closely and critically, the essays in this section contain many notes and questions. Soon you will find that questioning, checking, and probing come naturally to you.

YOUR ABILITY TO UNDERSTAND OTHER EXPERIENCES AND POINTS OF VIEW

The authors of these selections vary in age, gender, race, culture, and experience, and their writing reflects their many differences. In a rapidly changing world, your ability to understand, appreciate, and interact with people whose outlooks and experiences differ from your own is essential.

Increasingly, employers value social skills, communication skills, and the ability to work as part of a team. Being able to understand new and different viewpoints can help you work well in a group. Another benefit may be more personal: As you read more and learn to see things through other people's eyes, you may discover new perspectives on your own life.

YOUR ABILITY TO HELP YOURSELF

Much practical information about living in the modern world is contained in written form, either print or electronic. As a good reader, you will be able to find out whatever you need to know. The list of topics is endless: making money, investing, starting your own business, finding a job, raising a family, treating an illness, protecting yourself from unfairness, buying a car at the best price, and so on. When you read well, you can find help to get what you need, which means you can be independent.

Becoming an Active, Critical Reader

Close, critical reading requires you to be an active reader, one who takes part in the reading experience and doesn't just passively look at the words. Before beginning to read, prepare to engage actively in reading. Find a place where you can be comfortable and where you won't constantly be distracted or interrupted. You need to be mentally alert and ready to concentrate. Be physically alert too: For most people, reading while lying down or slouching results in sleepiness. Instead, try sitting at a table or a desk with a good light source nearby.

When you are ready to begin reading, try some of the following strategies.

BECOMING AN ACTIVE, CRITICAL READER

BEFORE READING	WHILE READING	AFTER READING
• Get an overview. • Ask a guiding question.	• Keep asking questions. • Take notes.	• Answer questions. • Write a summary and/or a response.

BEFORE READING

Get an Overview

RESOURCES
For more information on reading journals, see *Practical Suggestions for Teaching Real Essays*.

Before you begin reading, get an overview. Skim the reading for a general sense of what it contains. Skimming will help you decide what to look for as you read and help keep you on track.

Most written works have one or more aids to understanding. Look these over before you read the piece: They are there to help you.

- *Title.* The title usually indicates the topic and gives an idea of what the piece is about.

- *Author line.* The author's name is generally given at either the beginning or the end of a work. Ask yourself whether you have ever heard of this person and, if so, whether he or she is an expert on the topic of the piece.

- *Headnote.* A headnote is a paragraph (or more) that introduces a written work by giving information about the author, the writing itself, or both. The background information in a headnote can help you understand what an author is trying to say.

- *Headings and words in boldface.* Headings usually appear on a line by themselves within the work. Boldface words look darker than the surrounding text—**like this**. Both are used to indicate important points. Headings also show the major sections within a piece of writing.

- *Definitions and other notes.* Sometimes books define important or difficult words in notes placed in the margins or at the bottom of the page. Other notes about key points may be found there as well. Read the definitions and notes when you skim for a sense of what the writing is about.

- *Asterisks (*).* When you are reading an agreement or an advertisement, make sure you find and carefully read material that is asterisked. An asterisk usually appears at the end of a paragraph or sentence. It means that you need to find the asterisk at the end of the page or piece to get all the information. In ads, such information often makes the offer less inviting. At the very least, the asterisked material gives important extra information that you can't afford to overlook.

Ask a Guiding Question

After you have an overview, you will have some sense of what the reading is about. Now ask yourself a question that you expect the reading to answer. Usually, you can make the title into a question. For example, in Chapter 49 is an essay by Dave Barry titled "The Ugly Truth about Beauty." A guiding question might be "What is ugly about beauty?"

If the reading has been assigned to you, consider what your instructor wants you to learn from it: This might help you form a guiding question. For example, if your algebra instructor tells you to read Chapter 2, "Solving Equations and Inequalities," in your textbook for that course, you might ask, "What are equations and inequalities, and what are the methods of solving them?"

As you read, try to answer your question. A **guiding question** gives you a purpose when you are reading and helps keep you focused. This book supplies a guiding question for each essay in Chapters 43 through 51. Be sure to read the question before you read the essay and keep it in mind while you read.

WHILE READING

Keep Asking Questions

Active readers keep asking questions and try to answer them as they read. You already have a guiding question. As you read, ask yourself, "Have I answered my guiding question yet?" Ask yourself other questions, too: "What does this mean? Do I understand everything so far? Do I agree with it? How is this useful?"

Sometimes it helps to pause in the middle of a reading, just to make sure that you're not turning the pages without absorbing what's on them. When you pause, try to predict what's going to come next. Will the author provide another example? Will the plot take a new twist? Will a new topic be introduced?

Take Notes

Another way to be active while reading is to take notes. Taking notes can help you understand a reading, and the act of writing notes keeps you alert. Your notes can be written in the margin of a book, in a separate reading journal, on notecards, or on your computer. You can also make important parts stand out by underlining, using check marks and other symbols, or highlighting. Find a method that works for you. Here are some ideas about how to take notes:

- Note the **main idea** (double-underline it).
- Note the **supporting points** (underline them).
- Note ideas you agree with (put a check mark (✓) in the margin).
- Note ideas you don't agree with (put an *X* or *!* in the margin).
- Note points or words you don't understand (put a *?* in the margin).
- Note information that answers your guiding question.
- Note thoughts or reactions you have while reading (write them in the margin).

AFTER READING

Answer Questions

After you've read a selection for a college class, you may be asked to answer questions about it. Sometimes you may need to read all or parts of it again to answer the questions fully.

First, try to answer your guiding question.

Second, if you are reading a college textbook, look for questions at the end of each reading or chapter. Try to answer all of them.

Third, always try to answer the following basic questions about what you've read, even if you don't have study questions:

READING QUESTIONS

- What is the author's main point? Why is the author making this point?
- What are the major support points? Which ones are solid?
- Has the author convinced me of his or her point of view? How has the piece changed my feelings about the topic?
- Do I understand what I just read? Do I agree with it?
- What do I think about the author's message? Why?

Each essay in Chapters 43–51 is followed by two kinds of questions: Check Your Comprehension questions check whether you understand the selection, and Read Critically questions help you analyze the reading and your response to it.

Write

Just as the best way to make ideas and information your own is to use them, the best way to be an active reader is to write about what you have read. If you take notes while you read, you have already started to do this. You can also try other kinds of writing.

Summarize: A **summary** is a short account, in your own words, of the main point and the major support points in a reading. Writing an informal summary helps you understand the author's key points. A summary also reminds you of these key points during class discussion, while preparing for a writing assignment, and when studying for a test.

For more on writing a summary, see Chapter 19.

Respond: A **response** is your personal reaction to the reading. We learn new information by connecting it to what we already know. What connections can you make between what you've read and your own life? Have you ever experienced something similar?

Each essay in Chapters 43–51 is followed by a Summarize and Respond suggestion. Writing a response is the best way to make what you've read work for you.

An Active Reader at Work

A sample reading follows below. The notes in the margin and within the text show how one student, Tom, read the essay. You may want to use this sample as a model for the reading you do in the following chapters.

Deborah Tannen
It Begins at the Beginning

read author, title, and headnote

assignment: one-page summary and response

Deborah Tannen is a professor of linguistics at Georgetown University in Washington, D.C. Linguistics—the study of human language—reveals much about people and their culture. Part of Tannen's research in linguistics has focused on differences in the ways women and men use language and the effects of those differences on communication. The following excerpt, taken from her book *You Just Don't Understand,* describes how girls' and boys' language and communication patterns differ from a very early age.

GUIDING QUESTION

How do boys and girls differ in their play and the language they use in their play?

read guiding question

✓ not just different in words!!

Even if they grow up in the same neighborhood, on the same block, or in the same house, girls and boys grow up in different worlds of words. ✓ Others talk to them differently and expect and accept different ways of talking from them. Most important, children learn how to talk, how to have conversations, not only from their parents, but from their peers. [. . .] Although they often play together, boys and girls spend most of their time playing in same-sex groups. And, although some of the activities they play at are similar, their favorite games are different, and their ways of using language in their games are separated by a world of difference. *?*

? does this mean that boys and girls are born with language and play differences?

✓ that's why boys' groups work more efficiently than girls'

Boys tend to play outside, in large groups that are hierarchically[1] structured. Their groups have a leader who tells others what to do and how to do it, and resists doing what other boys propose. ✓ It is by giving orders and making them stick that high status is negotiated. Another way boys achieve status is to take center stage by telling jokes, and by sidetracking[2] or challenging the stories and jokes of others. Boys' games have winners and losers and elaborate systems of rules, and the players frequently boast of their skill and argue about who is best at what.

! what about computer games?

Girls, on the other hand, play in small groups or in pairs; the center of a girl's social life is a best friend. [. . .] In their most frequent games, such as jump rope and hopscotch, everyone gets a turn. *!* Many of their activities (such as playing house) do not have winners or losers. Though some girls are certainly more skilled than others, girls are expected not to boast about it, or show that they think they are better than the others. Girls don't give orders; they express their preferences as suggestions, and suggestions are likely to be accepted. Anything else is put down as bossy. They don't grab center stage—they don't want it—so they don't challenge each other directly. *!* And much of the time, they simply sit together and talk. Girls are not accustomed to jockeying[3] for status in an obvious way; they are more concerned that they be liked.

! maybe girls don't give orders or grab center stage around other girls, but they do around boys

[adapted from *You Just Don't Understand*. Deborah Tannen, William Morrow, 1990. pp. 43–44]

[1]**hierarchically:** by ability or status

[2]**sidetracking:** delaying or blocking the progress

[3]**jockeying:** competing strategically

43
Narration

Each essay in this chapter uses narration to get its main point across to readers. Narration tells a story that reveals something meaningful. Good narration includes all the important events in a story, presents them in a clear order, and brings each to life with details. As you read these essays, note how the writers use vivid stories to convey a message.

Chitra Banerjee Divakaruni
Spice of Life

Chitra Banerjee Divakaruni, born in 1956 in Calcutta, India, is a writer known for her portrayals of immigrant Indian women in the United States. After graduating from Calcutta University, she moved to the United States to continue her education, earning an M.A. from Wright State University and a Ph.D. from the University of California, Berkeley. In 1995, Divakaruni published her first collection of short stories, *Arranged Marriage,* which won an American Book Award. Since then, she has published articles in more than fifty magazines, written several books of poetry and short stories, and authored three novels: *The Mistress of Spices* (1997), *Sister of My Heart* (1999), and *The Vine of Desire* (2002). *The Mistress of Spices* is currently being made into a movie.

In "Spice of Life," Divakaruni shares the story of an abused woman she met while volunteering at an organization that helps victims of domestic violence. A year after the events detailed in this essay, Divakaruni founded a help line for South Asian women in abusive relationships. The essay, originally published by Salon.com, reveals the writer's desire to give readers a fuller view of battered women than the simplistic views often presented in other media.

GUIDING QUESTION
What does Divakaruni want readers to learn from this story?

TEACHING TIP
Encourage students to find the original essay, published online at <www.salon.com/mwt/diva/1997/10/02diva2.html>. Have them look at the links and other features posted on Salon.com to determine the intended audience. What kinds of specific details might appeal to this audience? Why?

DISCUSSION
Discuss the introduction. Does it capture the reader's interest right away? Why or why not? How does it set up the main idea of the narrative? Which details work especially well?

"The writer's story of an abused woman really hit home for me. I enjoyed reading this piece."
—*Roseann Castillo, student*

Seven years ago, soon after I started volunteering with an organization against domestic violence, I was called one morning to come into the office of the Support Network for Women in Mountain View. There was a South Asian woman there, and they needed help talking to her. When I got there, I found, in one of the inner rooms, a young woman with a baby boy. She was a beautiful young woman. Her face, with its strikingly dark, long-lashed eyes and sculpted lips, would not have been out of place on the cover of a fashion magazine. From her designer-label clothes I could see that she, or at least her spouse, was well-to-do. But she was emaciated,[1] as though she hadn't eaten properly in months, and when later, in the course of our conversation, she raised her shirt, I could see that her back was completely lacerated,[2] as though she'd been dragged over a rough surface like a concrete patio. That day, sitting in that tiny room, I learned the smell of fear. It was an odor like rusting metal, rising from her skin. Every breath coming from her was laden with it.

The first thing she said to me was, "I've made a terrible mistake, leaving home like this. My husband will kill me if he finds out, or worse. I've got to get back before he returns from work."

I told her she had been brave and right to leave a home where she was obviously abused. The agency would place her in a safe shelter where her husband wouldn't find her.

She told me of her family back in India, how ashamed they would be that she left her husband's home, that she couldn't make her marriage work. I asked her if they knew about the abuse. She shrugged her shoulders. It didn't matter, she said. What mattered was that she had a younger sister who wouldn't be able to find a good marriage-match if people came to know of her situation. "You have to think about yourself," I said. "You have to take care of yourself and your baby."

She started crying then. That was what was bothering her the most, she said. She'd deprived her son of a good home, all the love and opportunity his father could provide him with—for he was a good father, her husband, and rich also. How could she, who'd never been trained to work, provide for him in America? "There are programs to help you with money and training," I told her. "Your son will be safer and better off in a poorer home, if it is one without abuse." But I could see she wasn't convinced.

---

[1]**emaciated:** extremely thin

[2]**lacerated:** wounded by ripping or tearing

I told her how, in most cases of battering, the abuse gets worse if the   6
woman goes back to the abuser. I told her of women who had died or been
damaged for life. I urged her to report the case to the police and ask for a
restraining order, but from her eyes I could see that the idea of turning her
own husband over to the police was a horrifying one to her. "You have
many other options," I said. "You can start a new life. We've seen hundreds
of women do it."

But not me, her eyes said. It's hard for eyes to say otherwise, when for   7
years they've seen hate and anger and lack of respect on the face of the
man who's supposed to love them more than anyone in the whole world.

"At least think it over carefully before you make any hasty decisions,"   8
I said. "You can always go back, but once you're back, you may not be able
to leave."

Finally she agreed to let us put her in a shelter. She agreed to think   9
about options other than returning to her husband. That was the last time
I saw her. Sometime the next day, she called her husband from a street
phone, and he came and got her. Since she had not given us her name or
an address, we never found out what happened after that.

I think of her often as I last saw her, climbing into the car that is to   10
take her to the shelter. She clutches her baby tightly as she looks over her
shoulder, her beautiful eyes full of fear and guilt and self-doubt and love
and family duty and hopelessness.

Can you blame her for the choice she made, even as you see how   11
wrong it was for her to go back to a violent home? Can you say that in her
situation you could have done better? No matter what your ethnicity or
background, can you say she is that different from you in wanting what she
wanted: security, caring, a chance at happiness? I can't.

It is my hope that more people will think a little more about the place   12
in which the battered woman finds herself: dark and cold and suffocating,
like the bottom of a well. I hope they will look beyond the popular stereotypes of weakness, lack of education, and low self-esteem to see into her
heart. I hope they will feel for themselves the many conflicting and confusing forces pulling her this way and that in the darkness as she tries to
climb out. For some of us, that climbing out takes years, perhaps a lifetime. But it can happen. And it can, perhaps, happen a little sooner if
people around us are a little slower to judge us.

DISCUSSION
Ask students to
consider the point of
view of this essay. How
might the scenes of the
narrative or specific
details change if the
story were told from
the young woman's
point of view? Why
does it make a
difference that the
narrator of the story is
not the victim herself?

▪ SUMMARIZE AND RESPOND

In your reading journal or elsewhere, write a brief summary (three to five
sentences) of "Spice of Life." Next, jot down your initial response to the
reading. Why do you think the woman returned to her abusive husband?

■   **CHECK YOUR COMPREHENSION**

1. Which of the following would be the best alternative title for this essay?

   a. "At the Bottom of the Well"

   b. "A Bad Choice"

   c. "Hasty Decisions"

   d. "Hopeless"

2. The main idea of this essay is that

   a. it is very difficult to counsel women who are victims of abuse.

   b. many victims of domestic abuse return to their abuser because they have low self-esteem or lack the education needed to support themselves.

   c. victims of domestic abuse should consider their children, not themselves, when deciding how to handle their situation.

   d. society needs to look beyond the stereotype of the battered woman to understand the difficult position she is in.

3. According to the author,

   a. the woman's lack of education and low self-esteem contributed to her abusive situation.

   b. the woman was unable to understand the pattern of repeated and escalating violence that could occur if she returned to her husband.

   c. the abuse victim was confused about the types of support that the agency could offer her.

   d. the woman was hesitant to leave her husband because he was a good father and provider.

4. If you are unfamiliar with the following words, use a dictionary to check their meanings: laden (para. 1); deprived (5); ethnicity (11); suffocating (12).

■   **READ CRITICALLY**

1. In paragraph 11, Divakaruni asks a series of questions. How do these questions help her achieve the essay's main purpose?

2. In paragraph 12, to what does Divakaruni compare the abused woman's situation? Why do you think she makes this comparison? Is it effective?

3. Why do you think the abuse victim returned to her husband? Support your answer with examples from the essay.

4. After meeting the woman in the story, how might the author have changed the way she counsels abuse victims?

5. Having read this essay, what suggestions would you make to domestic abuse counselors to help them improve the way they counsel abuse victims? Support your answer with specific examples from the essay.

WRITE AN ESSAY

Write a narration essay about a situation in which you made an important decision. You could write about a decision to attend a particular college, to change your major, to end a relationship, or to confront a serious problem at work. In paragraphs within your essay, explain how you gathered information to make the decision, how you presented the decision to others, and how your life has been affected by that decision.

Pamela J. Transue

A Humbling Experience

Now the president of Tacoma Community College in the state of Washington, Pamela J. Transue earned a B.A. from the University of Washington and an M.A. and Ph.D. in English from Ohio State University. She later continued her studies at the Institute for Educational Management at Harvard University. Transue has given numerous presentations on leadership and trends in higher education, and she devotes much of her time to community service organizations.

Transue's position as college president did not stop her from recently becoming a student in one of her school's Spanish classes. In the following essay, originally published in *Community College Journal* in 2000, Transue shares with readers her experience in the classroom.

DISCUSSION
Have students use the title and Transue's biography to predict her point of view and conclusions in the essay.

GUIDING QUESTION
What did the author learn during her experience?

A little more than a year ago, I had an opportunity to be a community 1 college student for six months. For years, I had wanted to learn Spanish, but couldn't carve out the time to do so. Finally, admitting to myself that there was never going to be a good time, I decided to take the plunge.

After sitting down with a faculty member to find out if she would feel comfortable having the college president in her class, I signed up as an audit. As I shuffled into class on the first day with the other students, I felt elated to be in a classroom again and to have the opportunity to learn something new.

Initially, my fellow students didn't know about my role at the college, and that made it easier to get acquainted. Then, as we struggled together over classroom exercises and homework, we began to bond. It felt great. Our instructor was wonderful as well, and while she might have felt some initial trepidation,[1] she never let it show, and it soon disappeared in the teacher/student relationship we established.

While having the opportunity to learn Spanish was wonderful, I learned so much more in the process. Although I know that many, if not most, of our students struggle to make ends meet, their plight became real to me in a way it never had been before. One of my classmates, who was very capable academically, had nonetheless had his grades slip the previous quarter because he didn't have anyplace to live for a couple of months. His financial aid hadn't come through and he couldn't afford rent, so he lived in his car.

Another student from our Running Start program—I'll call her Sarah—was handling an astonishing level of responsibility. Running Start is our program for high school students, which allows them to earn college credit while fulfilling high school graduation requirements. Sarah was sixteen. She lived out in the countryside and had to drive more than an hour in each direction to attend school. Her mother had been seriously injured in a car accident and was unable to work or to care for herself unaided. Her father was long gone, so Sarah was the sole support for her mother and younger brother. She worked full-time, waiting tables at a restaurant, while attending school full-time and tending to her mother and brother. Despite these responsibilities, she was cheerful, self-disciplined, positive, and determined—truly remarkable.

A young Puerto Rican woman in the class described growing up in abject[2] poverty in New York. As a child, she was subjected to serious physical abuse, and she dropped out of school and ran away at fourteen. Soon after, she became pregnant. Unable to find a job, she survived on public assistance and tolerated further abuse by various boyfriends. Now she was on track, determined to complete a college education and become a role model for her children. Though her financial and other resources were slim indeed, she was extraordinarily generous toward her friends and fellow students.

I have always felt great empathy for our students, especially perhaps, because I come from a similar background myself. However, my experience in this Spanish class pulled me into their reality in a way I could not

---

[1]**trepidation:** fearful uncertainty

[2]**abject:** miserable, hopeless

have otherwise experienced. It was both chastening[3] and inspiring. Of course, I also picked up some valuable information on how well our various student services actually serve students. In most cases, we do a good job, but as you might guess, there is room for improvement.

Most of our colleges have a wide range of support services in place to help our students succeed. Counseling, advising, tutoring, work-study, and job placement continue to be important. Special services available through cohort[4] programs and federal grants can make the critical difference in allowing many students to reach their goals. Targeted services for dislocated workers and people transitioning from public assistance are an important part of the mix. The increasing availability of Web-based services allows students to avoid duplicative[5] trips to campus and long lines. Orientations, information kiosks, computer labs, and responsive learning resources staff provide the necessary tools for learning. Student clubs and other activities offer opportunities for social interaction and community service. Increasingly, internships and service learning options are improving student work skills while instilling good citizenship.

All these services are valuable, and my six months as a community college student have reinforced my commitment to ensuring that our students get the tools they need to move their lives forward.

[3]**chastening:** embarrassing, humbling

[4]**cohort:** partner

[5]**duplicative:** unnecessarily repetitive

DISCUSSION
Why does Transue include shorter narratives of the experiences of several students in the body of a longer narrative essay? Have students find ways to use this technique in their own writing.

▊ SUMMARIZE AND RESPOND

In your reading journal or elsewhere, write a brief summary (three to five sentences) of "A Humbling Experience." Next, jot down your initial response to the reading. Would you be comfortable having the college president in one of your classes? Do you think it is a good idea for school administrators to spend time in the classroom? Why, or why not?

▊ CHECK YOUR COMPREHENSION

1. Which of the following would be the best alternative title for this essay?

    a. "The Trouble with Student Services"

    b. "Why I Wanted to Learn Spanish"

    c. "No More Rose-Colored Glasses"

    (d.) "Learning More Than Spanish"

2. The main idea of this essay is that being in the classroom gave the college president

    a. new ideas for improving the school.

b. a new appreciation for the challenges her students face.

c. the chance to get to know the student population.

d. a feeling of humbleness as she struggled to learn Spanish.

3. According to the author,

   a. many of the college's students were unsuccessful in high school.

   b. most of the students in the classroom were unaware of her role at the college.

   c. she is refocusing her efforts to ensure that student support services address the needs of the students.

   d. she wanted to learn Spanish so that she could communicate with the school's Spanish-speaking students.

4. If you are unfamiliar with the following words, use a dictionary to check their meanings: plunge (para. 1); audit, elated (2); plight (4); empathy (7); dislocated, transitioning, kiosks, instilling (8); reinforced (9).

READ CRITICALLY

1. What is the significance of the essay's title? How does it relate to Transue's main point?

2. Transue describes three students she met in the Spanish class. How are the students similar, and why do you think Transue uses them as examples in her essay?

3. Transue writes that her experience in the classroom "was both chastening and inspiring." What does she mean by this statement?

4. This essay first appeared in *Community College Journal,* an academic publication. What does this tell you about Transue's intended audience? What do you think her purpose was in writing the essay?

5. This essay focuses on what the author learned by sharing the classroom with the students. What do you believe the students might have gained from the experience? How might the instructor have benefited?

WRITE AN ESSAY

Write an essay narrating an experience that changed your life. Did an accident force you to rethink your future? Did losing or finding a job open new opportunities for you? Did the decision to go to college change the direction of your life? Present the events in chronological order, using vivid details to bring your story to life for readers.

44

Illustration

Each essay in this chapter uses illustration to get its main point across to readers. Illustration uses one or more examples to show, explain, or prove a main point. Good illustration contains detailed and specific examples that readers can understand. It also gives enough examples to make the point. Sometimes one extended example is all that's needed, but often writers use a series of briefer examples. As you read these essays, pay attention to how the writers use convincing, interesting examples.

For more on writing an illustration essay, see Chapter 9.

Kerry Pechter
Pet Therapy for Heart and Soul

Since graduating from Kenyon College in 1973, Kerry Pechter has worked as a newspaper reporter, magazine writer, author, and marketing copywriter. Specializing in financial reporting, Pechter has published articles in many periodicals including the *New York Times* and the *Wall Street Journal.* He has also coauthored a book, *A Big Splash in a Small Pond: How to Get a Job in a Small Company* (1994). Pechter, who currently lives in Allentown, Pennsylvania, and works for a financial services company, advises student writers to "always be open to constructive criticism."

In the following essay, Pechter departs from his usual topic of finance. Exploring how animals improve not only our mental but also our physical health, he provides specific examples to illustrate the effects of pet therapy.

GUIDING QUESTION
According to Pechter, how do animals improve people's lives?

It's exercise hour at the Tacoma Lutheran Home in the state of Washington, and P. T., an exotic yellow-crested bird called a cockatiel, is having the time of his life. He's sitting on the foot of 81-year-old Ben Ereth, riding in circles while Ben pedals vigorously on an exercise bicycle. The bird likes it so much that if Mr. Ereth stops too soon, he'll squawk at him.

A bizarre sort of activity to find in a nursing home? Not at Tacoma Lutheran. Three years ago, the nursing home adopted an angora rabbit. Then a puppy. Then tropical birds. The home's elderly residents have taken to these animals with a passion. And, says Virginia Davis, director of resident services, the animals have breathed enthusiasm into what otherwise might have been a listless nursing home atmosphere.

"The animals help in several ways," says Davis. "One of the cockatiels gives a wolf whistle whenever anyone passes its cage. That gives them an unexpected boost in morale. And the birds seem to alleviate[1] the tension associated with exercise. They make exercise more acceptable and relaxing."

What's happening at Tacoma Lutheran is just one example of an increasingly popular phenomenon called pet therapy. Although humans have adopted pets for thousands of years, only recently have social scientists taken a close look at the nature of the relationship that people form with dogs, cats, and other "companion animals."

At places like the Center for the Interaction of Animals and Society in Philadelphia and the Center for the Study of Human Animal Relationships and Environments (CENSHARE) in Minneapolis, they've discovered that there is something mutually therapeutic[2] about these relationships. They say that pets relax us, help us communicate with each other, build our self-esteem, and comfort us when we're feeling down.

In fact, many now believe that pets play a small but very significant role in determining how well, for example, a heart attack survivor recuperates, how a family handles domestic strife, whether a disturbed teenager grows up straight, or even whether a nursing home resident like Mr. Ereth enjoys and sticks to his daily exercycle program.

Pet animals, in short, may affect our health.

Animal Magnetism at Work

Pet therapists have put these capacities to work in a variety of ways. Pet therapy is very often used, for example, to combat the isolation and loneliness so common in nursing homes. At the Tacoma Lutheran Home,

"Pechter does a good job of describing how pets can help people with health problems."
—*Michael Blalock, student*

DISCUSSION
Have students identify the thesis statement and discuss its placement. Have students experiment with the placement of the thesis in their own essay drafts.

[1]**alleviate:** make more bearable

[2]**therapeutic:** beneficial, healing

Davis has found that the pets help many residents break their customary silence.

"Animals are a catalyst[3] for conversation," she says. "Most people can   9
remember a story from their past about a pet animal. And people are more comfortable talking to animals than they are to people. Sometimes a person who hasn't spoken for a long time, or one who has had a stroke and doesn't talk, will talk to an animal."

Animals also seem to draw everyone into the conversation. "Even in a   10
nursing home, there are some people who are more attractive or responsive than others," says Phil Arkow, of the Humane Society of the Pike's Peak Region in Colorado, who drives a "Petmobile" to local nursing homes. "Human visitors try not to do it, but they inevitably focus on those who are most attractive. But animals don't make those distinctions. They focus on everyone equally."

A person doesn't have to live in a nursing home, however, in order   11
to reap the benefits of a pet. Pets typically influence the communication that goes on between family members in a normal household. During a research project a few years ago, University of Maryland professor Ann Cain, Ph.D., discovered that pets help spouses and siblings express highly charged feelings.

"When family members want to say something to each other that they   12
can't say directly," Dr. Cain says, "they might say it to the pet and let the other person overhear it. That also lets the listener off the hook, because he doesn't have to respond directly."

Though it's still in the experimental stage, researchers are discovering   13
that watching or petting friendly animals—not only dogs and cats but almost any pet—can produce the kind of deep relaxation usually associated with meditation, biofeedback,[4] and hypnosis. This kind of relaxing effect is so good that it can actually lower blood pressure.

At the University of Pennsylvania's Center for the Interaction of Animals and Society, for instance, Dr. Katcher and Dr. Friedmann monitored   14
the blood pressure of healthy children while the children were sitting quietly or reading aloud, either with or without a dog in the room. Their blood pressure was always lower when the dog was in the room.

The researchers went on to discover, remarkably, that looking at fish   15
could temporarily reduce the blood pressure of patients with hypertension.[5] In one widely reported study, they found that the systolic and diastolic pressure[6] of people with high blood pressure dipped into the normal

[3]**catalyst:** something that causes or speeds up a result

[4]**biofeedback:** a technique that uses electronic devices to control certain emotional states, such as depression or anxiety

[5]**hypertension:** abnormally high blood pressure

[6]**systolic and diastolic pressure:** two measures of blood pressure, related to the contractions and dilations of the heart

range when they gazed at an aquarium full of colorful tropical fish, green plants, and rocks for 20 minutes.

This calming power of pets has found at least a few noteworthy applications. In Chicago, one volunteer from the Anti-Cruelty Society took an animal to a hospital and arranged for a surgical patient to be greeted by it when he awoke from anesthesia. "It's a comforting way to come back to reality," says one volunteer. "For children, pets can make a hospital seem safer. It's a reminder of home."   16

Animals may also have the power to soften the aggressive tendencies of disturbed adolescents. At Winslow Therapeutic Riding Unlimited, Inc., in Warwick, New York, where horseback riding is used to help handicapped children of all kinds, problem teenagers seem to behave differently when they're put on a horse.   17

"These are kids who fight in school. Some of their fathers are alcoholics," says Mickey Pulis of the nonprofit facility. "But when they come here, they're different. When they groom and tack the horses, they learn about the gentle and caring side of life.   18

"The horse seems to act like an equalizer," she says. "It doesn't care what reading levels these kids are at. It accepts them as they are."   19

Ultimately, researchers like Dr. Friedmann believe that the companionship of pets can reduce a person's risk of dying from stress-related illnesses, such as heart disease.   20

"The leading causes of mortality and morbidity[7] in the United States are stress-related or life-style related," she says. "Pets, by decreasing the level of arousal and moderating the stress response, can help slow the progression of those diseases or even prevent them."   21

Pets Are Comforting

But what is it about pets that make them capable of all this? And why do millions of people go to the trouble and expense of keeping them? Pet therapists offer several answers.   22

For one thing, animals don't talk back to us. Researchers have discovered that a person's blood pressure goes up whenever he talks to another person. But we talk to animals in a different way, often touching them at the same time, which minimizes stress.   23

Another theory holds that pets remind us of our ancestral link with other animals. "By domesticating an animal, man demonstrates his kinship to nature," Dr. Levinson once wrote. "A human being has to remain in contact with all of nature throughout his lifetime if he is to maintain good mental health."   24

Dr. Corson, on the other hand, says that we love pets because they are perpetual[8] infants. Human infants charm us, but they eventually grow up.   25

DISCUSSION
How does Pechter use direct and indirect quotations in this essay? What examples seem particularly effective? Have students practice using direct and indirect quotations in their own writing.

[7]**morbidity:** the rate of disease

[8]**perpetual:** permanent, lasting forever

Pets never do. They never stop being cuddly and dependent. Likewise, pets are faithful. "Pets can offer a relationship that is more constant than relationships with people," says Dr. Cain. "You can count on them."

Some argue that the most important ingredient in our relationships   26
with animals is that we can touch them whenever we want to. "Having access to affectionate touch that is not related to sex is important," says Dr. Katcher. "If you want to touch another person, you can't always do it immediately. But with pets you can."

■ SUMMARIZE AND RESPOND

In your reading journal or elsewhere, write a brief summary (three to five sentences) of "Pet Therapy for Heart and Soul." Next, jot down your initial response to the reading. Do you agree with the author's thesis? Why, or why not? If you agree with Pechter, describe a time that an animal improved your mental or physical health.

■ CHECK YOUR COMPREHENSION

1. Which of the following would be the best alternative title for this essay?
   a. "Animal Magnetism"
   b. "Why Pets Are Good for You"
   c. "Animals: They Don't Talk Back"
   d. "Why Pets Are Affectionate"

2. The main idea of this essay is that
   a. animals can be used to treat depression in hospital and nursing home patients.
   b. pets can improve our health because they help us relax, communicate, and deal with depression.
   c. pet therapy benefits troubled adolescents and patients recovering from operations.
   d. animals often provide a breakthrough in communication for nursing home patients.

3. What does the author say about pet therapy in nursing homes?
   a. Animals often encourage nursing home residents to share stories about former pets.
   b. Certain types of animals should not be placed in nursing homes.

c. Pet therapy is most effective when nursing home residents bring their own pets with them.

d. Very few nursing homes use pet therapy.

4. If you are unfamiliar with the following words, use a dictionary to check their meanings: bizarre, listless (para. 2); ancestral (24).

READ CRITICALLY

1. According to Pechter, what are the major physical and psychological benefits of pet therapy? What are some specific examples he gives to illustrate these benefits?

2. Why do you think Pechter begins this essay with the Tacoma Lutheran Home anecdote?

3. In his essay, Pechter does not provide a dictionary-type definition of pet therapy. Instead, he illustrates the concept with examples. Having read the essay, how would you define the term *pet therapy*?

4. Pechter supports his thesis with two kinds of examples: scientific research and personal observation. Why is it effective to use both kinds of evidence?

5. In paragraph 24, Pechter quotes a researcher who said, "By domesticating an animal, man demonstrates his kinship to nature." What do you think this statement means?

WRITE AN ESSAY

Write an essay that illustrates how a certain activity benefits your emotional or physical health. For example, you could explain how exercise relaxes you or how a hobby takes your mind off stressful situations. Be sure to use enough detailed examples to support your main point.

Bob Greene

Foul Mouths Are Fair Game in Our Coarsening Culture

Bob Greene was born in Columbus, Ohio, in 1947. After graduating with a degree in journalism from Northwestern University, he began his writing career as a reporter for the *Chicago Sun-Times*. Greene quickly shifted from reporting to writing columns, and he joined the *Chicago Tribune* as a columnist in 1978. He resigned from the *Tribune* in 2002. In addition to publishing collections of his columns, Greene has written several full-length works: *Billion Dollar Baby* (1974), an account of his experiences touring with the rock band Alice Cooper; *Good Morning, Merry Sunshine* (1984), a journal about his first year as a father; and *Duty* (2000), a memoir of his own father, a World War II veteran.

In "Foul Mouths Are Fair Game in Our Coarsening Culture," originally published as a column in the *Chicago Tribune,* Greene explores the issue of vulgar language. Note how he presents several specific incidents to illustrate his main point.

GUIDING QUESTION

Why do people use profanity so often, according to Greene?

We claim to want to change the world, but before we attempt anything   1
quite that grandiose,[1] we ought to work on changing how we treat each
other.

Here are two scenes from the lakefront in Chicago, from two recent   2
sunny days:

A fellow who is out with his wife—apparently uncertain of the eti-   3
quette of the lake's bike-and-jogging path—tentatively[2] moves his bicycle
away from the water fountain and horizontally across the path so that he
can get in the proper lane. Another bicyclist is barreling along. He sees the
crossing bicyclist too late, and slams into him. Both men hit the deck.

The man who has been speeding along picks himself up and screams   4
at the top of his voice, "You (bleeping) idiot! You (bleeping) idiot! What is
wrong with you, you (bleeping) idiot?"

[1]**grandiose:** impressive, important

[2]**tentatively:** hesitantly

The man who had been walking the bike across the path is humiliated; 5
he tries to apologize, but the obscenities continue to bellow at him as
people watch. His wife looks as if she is about to cry.

Here is the next scene: 6

Farther north on the trail, a line of six or seven men and women on 7
bicycles is rolling, single file, in a southward direction. It's kind of narrow,
and there isn't much extra room for people on one side or the other.

Walking north, by herself, is a woman considerably older than the bicy- 8
clists. She is not straddling the center line with her feet; she is where she is
supposed to be. The bicyclists, as they speed past her, tell her to "Get
over"—to move out of their way. As she is doing so, a female bicyclist, near
the end of the line, pedals past the woman, whom she knows nothing about
and has never met, and uses a vulgar reference to a female dog.

The expression on the older woman's face is startled, embarrassed, 9
and sad at the same time. She has gone out for a walk—alone, unlike
many people along the lake—and for no apparent reason she has been
gratuitously[3] cursed by some younger woman rolling by.

Now in the first scenario, the man who repeatedly bellowed the 10
obscenity at the crossing bicyclist in front of the crossing bicyclist's wife,
had the right of way; the person he hit was inadvertently[4] in the wrong for
trying to cross. In the second situation the older woman walking by herself was completely in the right. In both cases, though, the aggressors took
control immediately with their foul language.

Why did they do this? They did it because they could. They did it 11
because there is absolutely no value placed, in our current in-your-face
culture, on the concept of restraint. If you don't refer to a man who has
made a regrettable and unintentional mistake as "a (bleeping) idiot," you
are somehow thought to have lost the upper hand. The same applies to the
woman bicyclist's reaction to the elderly woman.

It's everywhere. At the Wimbledon tennis championships, the men's 12
winner, Goran Ivanisevic, was telling reporters about a controversial point
in the match, in which a female official called a foot fault on him.

"My first foot fault all tournament," Ivanisevic said. "That ugly, ugly 13
lady, she was really ugly, very serious, you know. I was kind of scared."

How very, very gentlemanly and compassionate, after you've won the 14
match, to publicly say that about the appearance of a woman whose only
crime was to call a penalty against you that didn't even affect the outcome.
Let the woman think of that in days after the tournament—let her think
about what the new champion has told the world about her.

Of course, it won't make any difference in Ivanisevic's career. He's just 15
doing what comes naturally in our society, in which strength is measured

[3]**gratuitously:** unnecessarily, without reason or cause
[4]**inadvertently:** unintentionally, by mistake

not by what is inside of you, but by the ferocity with which you choose to belittle others.

SUMMARIZE AND RESPOND

In your reading journal or elsewhere, write a brief summary (three to five sentences) of "Foul Mouths Are Fair Game in Our Coarsening Culture." Next, jot down your initial response to the reading. Do you agree with Greene that profanity is becoming increasingly common and accepted in our society? How often and in what situations are you likely to use coarse words or expressions? Why do you think people use profanity?

CHECK YOUR COMPREHENSION

1. Which of the following would be the best alternative title for this essay?
   a. "Dealing with Anger in Everyday Situations"
   b. "Territorial Aggression"
   c. "Poor Sportsmanship"
   d. "Verbal Restraint: A Need in Our Society"

2. The main idea of this essay is that
   a. the increasingly common use of vulgarity is a disturbing trend.
   b. women use vulgar language just as often as men.
   c. vulgarity helps relieve stress and anger.
   d. people should be fined for using vulgar language in public.

3. According to Greene, people are using coarse language more frequently because
   a. they want to demonstrate the depth of their anger.
   b. they have more reasons to be angry.
   c. they don't care about other people's feelings.
   d. it comes naturally in a culture that places little value on politeness.

4. If you are unfamiliar with the following words, use a dictionary to check their meanings: bellow (para. 5); ferocity, belittle (15).

■ **READ CRITICALLY**

1. Greene presents several examples of people using foul language. How do these examples support his main point?

2. How is the example about the tennis player different from Greene's first two examples? What is significant about this difference?

3. Find examples of Greene's use of sarcasm. Is his tone effective? Why, or why not?

4. What does Greene say about the relationship between foul language and the desire to control?

5. According to Greene, how does today's society measure a person's strength?

■ **WRITE AN ESSAY**

Write an essay illustrating one of the following main points:

• People generally treat each other with respect and kindness.
• People generally treat each other with very little respect.

Use examples of incidents you have recently witnessed to support your point.

45

Description

Description uses words to create a main impression—an overall effect, a feeling, or an image. Good descriptions use vivid sensory details to create a picture so realistic that readers can see the person, place, or object being described. These details can appeal to any of the five senses—sight, hearing, smell, touch, or taste.

For more on writing a description essay, see Chapter 10.

The essays in this chapter use description to get their main points across to readers. The writers sometimes simply describe an object or an experience and sometimes use description to make a larger point. Each essay succeeds when the author uses sensory details to bring an experience to life.

Christine Aziz

The Lion of Kabul

Born in 1948, Christine Aziz spent much of her childhood traveling throughout the United Kingdom. She left school at age fifteen and took on a variety of jobs, working as a factory packer, a dental assistant, a television producer, and a radio reporter. While working at a local newspaper, Aziz discovered her interest in journalism. She is now a freelance writer based in London, reporting on international politics for British newspapers. Aziz has also been a regular contributor to the British edition of *Marie Claire* magazine.

First published in 1996 in the magazine *New International*, "The Lion of Kabul" presents an account of Aziz's visit to a zoo in Kabul, the capital of Afghanistan. The essay's descriptive passages create a vivid picture of the war-ravaged city.

GUIDING QUESTION

What sensory images and details does Aziz use to create her impression of Kabul?

"The author paints a vivid picture of devastation in Afghanistan. I felt like I could see the effects of the Soviet Union's [December 1979] invasion."
—Mark E. Skinner, student

Somehow a sightseeing tour of Kabul, the despoiled[1] capital of Afghanistan, seems obscene. Amir Shah, our taxi driver, insists on taking us on what he calls the "scenic route." He refers to everything in the past tense: "This was our university. This was the palace. This was one of our finest hotels." There is a retrospective[2] pride in his voice that I have to respond to. "It must have been lovely," I mumble.

"I'll take you to the zoo," he says in an attempt to cheer me and my companion up. We pull up outside what must have been a pleasant garden, but all that's left now is twisted stumps of trees, their branches torn off for firewood. Cages line the walkways, but the bars are twisted steel and the walls nothing more than rubble. "Most of the animals and birds have been stolen and cooked," Amir Shah explains. "But we do have a lion," he says in an effort to make the visit worthwhile. "I don't remember his name anymore. I just call him Lion."

Lion lies in the only cage that remains intact, his head resting sulkily on his huge front paws. His eyes are missing, and his face is heavily scarred. His mane has been reduced to a few tufts. We stare at the sightless bald lion who is now making a halfhearted attempt to stand up, and as he shuffles forward Amir Shah tells us his story.

"Some mujahideen [guerrillas] came to visit the zoo and they saw Lion. They goaded[3] one of their friends into climbing into the cage and dared him to touch Lion. Lion was sleeping, so the man got out unhurt. Then the mujahideen dared him to go in again, but this time he touched a female and Lion attacked him. The mujahideen's brother threw in a hand grenade that blew up Lion's face, but it was too late. Lion killed him."

It is hard to believe that the mangy specimen now growling weakly in front of us could have managed it. "Lion was taken to the Red Cross hospital," Amir Shah says. "He was in the best hospital in Kabul, and the doctors tried to save his sight. But he was too badly injured. They did the best they could."

The people of Kabul clearly wanted Lion to live. It's as if this proud animal has become a symbol for the city itself and the grisly drama a metaphor[4] for the senseless battles that have been played out in the city's

1

2

3

4

5

6

DISCUSSION
How does the Lion in the reading serve as a symbol and its story as a metaphor? Ask students to find other symbols and metaphors in the essay. How can students add symbols and metaphors to their own writing?

[1]**despoiled:** robbed, deprived of value

[2]**retrospective:** looking back on the past

[3]**goaded:** urged into action

[4]**metaphor:** something that suggests a comparison; a symbol

streets. Both Lion and Kabul are the victims of wanton[5] destruction inspired by a warped belief in "honor" and an obstinate,[6] macho pride. If Lion dies, then the foolishness of men has triumphed.

We settle silently into the back of Amir Shah's taxi. By now we are in respectful awe of this man who can laugh, smile, and joke as he guides us around such utter desolation. Like other Kabul residents, he displays courage and resilience[7] that belie[8] 16 years of a war that began when the Russians arrived to occupy the city in 1979 and then turned into a civil war the moment they left, 10 years later. Whatever destruction the Russians wreaked on Afghanistan, the mujahideen of the various warring factions managed to continue: Schools and universities were looted. Books and equipment were sent to Pakistan to be sold. Water pipes were used as target practice — making the water rehabilitation programs of a number of aid agencies almost impossible. Homes were destroyed in the crossfire as rival groups fought each other from different ends of the city.   7

The sun begins to set, turning the snow on the mountains that surround Kabul a delicate rose pink. Amir Shah starts to sing a song about love and a beautiful woman and then turns off into a side street. He stops the car. "I want to show you where I used to live," he says and ushers us out, warning us not to step off the road because of the land mines that litter the residential areas. He points to a wall standing amid a pile of rubble. "That was my house," he says. We notice that part of the wall has been freshly bricked up. "That was the front door once," he explains, "but I bricked it up to stop people getting into the garden."   8

We can see no sign of a garden until we notice tree branches rising out of the rubble. "I didn't want people coming into my home and tearing down the tree for firewood," he says. "I wanted to protect it for when my family and I return home."   9

In the fading light we notice that the tree is covered in sweet-smelling white blossoms.   10

[5]**wanton:** cruel, excessive

[6]**obstinate:** stubbornly persisting in an opinion or action

[7]**resilience:** ability to recover from misfortune

[8]**belie:** contradict, are inconsistent with

SUMMARIZE AND RESPOND

In your reading journal or elsewhere, write a brief summary (three to five sentences) of "The Lion of Kabul." Next, jot down your initial response to the reading. What did it make you think or feel? Do you think your response to the essay would have been different if you had read it before the events of September 11, 2001? Why, or why not?

CHECK YOUR COMPREHENSION

1. Which of the following would be the best alternative title for this essay?

    a. "Hope among Ruins"

    b. "A Lone Survivor"

    c. "The Scenic Route"

    d. "A City without Hope"

2. The main idea of this essay is that

    a. the lion, though maimed by a hand grenade, managed to survive.

    b. although physically damaged, Kabul and its people, like the lion, will survive.

    c. the people of Kabul need international aid to rebuild their city.

    d. nothing in Kabul was left untouched by war.

3. What does the author say about the citizens of Kabul?

    a. Many of them hope to rebuild their lives in other cities.

    b. They are resigned to the destruction of their city.

    c. They are too focused on their day-to-day survival to worry about the lion.

    d. They are courageous and resilient.

4. If you are unfamiliar with the following words, use your dictionary to check their meanings: intact, sulkily, tufts (para. 3); guerrillas (4); mangy, specimen (5); grisly, warped (6); desolation, looted, rehabilitation (7); ushers (8).

READ CRITICALLY

1. Why do you think the taxi driver, Amir Shah, took Aziz to the zoo? She writes that Amir was attempting "to cheer me and my companion up." How could the demolished zoo cheer them up?

2. What images does Aziz use to bring Kabul to life for readers? What do you think are the essay's strongest images? Explain why these images stand out in your mind.

3. In what ways are Kabul and the lion similar?

4. Why does the author admire Amir? What details does she use to create a picture of him?

5. Reread paragraphs 8–10. How does Aziz's description of the tree in Amir's garden relate to her description of the lion? What do you think the tree symbolizes?

WRITE AN ESSAY

Write an essay that describes a place you have visited. Think about your overall impression of the place, and decide what sensory images will create that impression for readers.

Larry Woiwode

Ode[1] to an Orange

Larry Woiwode was born in 1941 and grew up in rural North Dakota and Illinois. Soon after graduating from the University of Illinois, Woiwode moved to New York City and began publishing stories and poetry in the *New Yorker* magazine. He has published his work in numerous magazines since then, and he has also written several novels, collections of short stories, and books of poetry. One of his novels, *Beyond the Bedroom Wall* (1975), was nominated for a National Book Award. Woiwode has also taught at various universities and is currently the poet laureate of North Dakota, where he lives on a farm with his wife and four children.

Woiwode's writing is often inspired by memories from his childhood. In "Ode to an Orange," first published in the *Paris Review* in 1984, he uses vivid details to recreate the sight, smell, feel, and taste of his favorite childhood treat.

GUIDING QUESTION

In what way does the essay's title indicate how Woiwode feels about oranges?

---

[1]**ode:** a lyric poem with a serious, respectful tone, typically addressed to someone or something

Oh, those oranges arriving in the midst of the North Dakota winters of the forties—the mere color of them, carried through the door in a net bag or a crate from out of the white winter landscape. Their appearance was enough to set my brother and me to thinking that it might be about time to develop an illness, which was the surest way of receiving a steady supply of them.

"Mom, we think we're getting a cold."

"*We?* You mean, you two want an orange?"

This was difficult for us to answer or dispute; the matter seemed moved beyond our mere wanting.

"If you want an orange," she would say, "why don't you ask for one?"

"We want an orange."

"'We' again, *'We want an orange.'*"

"May we have an orange, please."

"That's the way you know I like you to ask for one. Now, why don't each of you ask for one in that same way, but separately?"

"Mom . . ." And so on. There was no depth of degradation² that we wouldn't descend to in order to get one. If the oranges hadn't wended³ their way northward by Thanksgiving, they were sure to arrive before the Christmas season, stacked first in crates at the depot, filling that musty place, where pews sat back to back, with a springtime acidity, as if the building had been rinsed with a renewing elixir⁴ that set it right for yet another year. Then the crates would appear at the local grocery store, often with the top slats pried back on a few of them, so that we were aware of a resinous⁵ smell of fresh wood in addition to the already orangy atmosphere that foretold the season more explicitly than any calendar.

And in the broken-open crates (as if burst by the power of the oranges themselves), one or two of the lovely spheres would lie free of the tissue they came wrapped in—always purple tissue, as if that were the only color that could contain the populations of them in their nestled positions. The crates bore paper labels at one end—of an orange against a blue background, or of a blue goose against an orange background—signifying the colorful otherworld (unlike our wintry one) that these phenomena had arisen from. Each orange, stripped of its protective wrapping, as vivid in your vision as a pebbled sun, encouraged you to picture a whole pyramid of them in a bowl on your dining room table, glowing in the light, as if giving off the warmth that came through the windows from the real winter sun. And all of them came stamped with a blue-purple name as foreign as the otherworld that you might imagine as their place of origin, so that on

²**degradation:** dishonor, disgrace

³**wended:** traveled

⁴**elixir:** a substance believed to cure all ills

⁵**resinous:** like or of resin, a substance exuded by various plants and trees

Christmas day you would find yourself digging past everything else in your Christmas stocking, as if tunneling down to the country of China, in order to reach the rounded bulge at the tip of the toe which meant that you had received a personal reminder of another state of existence, wholly separate from your own.

The packed heft and texture, finally, of an orange in your hand — this   12
is it! — and the eruption of smell and the watery fireworks as a knife, in the hand of someone skilled, like our mother, goes slicing through the skin so perfect for slicing. This gaseous spray can form a mist like smoke, which can then be lit with a match to create actual fireworks if there is a chance to hide alone with a match (matches being forbidden) and the peel from one. Sputtery ignitions can also be produced by squeezing a peel near a candle (at least one candle is generally always going at Christmastime), and the leftover peels are set on the stove top to scent the house.

And the ingenious[6] way in which oranges come packed into their   13
globes! The green nib[7] at the top, like a detonator,[8] can be bitten off, as if disarming the orange, in order to clear a place for you to sink a tooth under the peel. This is the best way to start. If you bite at the peel too much, your front teeth will feel scraped, like dry bone, and your lips will begin to burn from the bitter oil. Better to sink a tooth into this greenish or creamy depression, and then pick at that point with the nail of your thumb, removing a little piece of the peel at a time. Later, you might want to practice to see how large a piece you can remove intact. The peel can also be undone in one continuous ribbon, a feat which maybe your father is able to perform, so that after the orange is freed, looking yellowish, the peel, rewound, will stand in its original shape, although empty.

The yellowish whole of the orange can now be divided into sections,   14
usually about a dozen, by beginning with a division down the middle; after this, each section, enclosed in its papery skin, will be able to be lifted and torn loose more easily. There is a stem up the center of the section like a mushroom stalk, but tougher; this can be eaten. A special variety of orange, without any pits, has an extra growth, or nubbin, like half of a tiny orange, tucked into its bottom. This nubbin is nearly as bitter as the peel, but it can be eaten, too; don't worry. Some of the sections will have miniature sections embedded in them and clinging as if for life, giving the impression that babies are being hatched, and should you happen to find some of these you've found the sweetest morsels of any.

If you prefer to have your orange sliced in half, as some people do, the   15
edges of the peel will abrade[9] the corners of your mouth, making them feel

[6]**ingenious:** imaginative, clever

[7]**nib:** the projecting end of something

[8]**detonator:** fuse for setting off explosives

[9]**abrade:** irritate

TEACHING TIP
Have students highlight descriptive words for each of the five senses and then divide the words into lists for each sense. Ask students to identify places in their own essays where sensory detail might be added to enhance the description.

raw, as you eat down into the white of the rind (which is the only way to do it) until you can see daylight through the orangy bubbles composing its outside. Your eyes might burn; there is no proper way to eat an orange. If there are pits, they can get in the way, and the slower you eat an orange, the more you'll find your fingers sticking together. And no matter how carefully you eat one, or bite into a quarter, juice can always fly or slip from a corner of your mouth; this happens to everyone. Close your eyes to be on the safe side, and for the eruption in your mouth of the slivers of watery meat, which should be broken and rolled fine over your tongue for the essence of orange. And if indeed you have sensed yourself coming down with a cold, there is a chance that you will feel it driven from your head—your nose and sinuses suddenly opening—in the midst of the scent of a peel and eating an orange.

16   And oranges can also be eaten whole—rolled into a spongy mass and punctured with a pencil (if you don't find this offensive) or a knife, and then sucked upon. Then, once the juice is gone, you can disembowel[10] the orange as you wish and eat away its pulpy remains, and eat once more into the whitish interior of the peel, which scours the coating from your teeth and makes your numbing lips and tip of your tongue start to tingle and swell up from behind, until, in the light from the windows (shining through an empty glass bowl), you see orange again from the inside. Oh, oranges, solid *o*'s, light from afar in the midst of the freeze, and not unlike that unspherical fruit which first went from Eve to Adam and from there (to abbreviate matters) to my brother and me.

17   "Mom, we think we're getting a cold."

18   "You mean, you want an orange?"

19   This is difficult to answer or dispute or even to acknowledge, finally, with the fullness that the subject deserves, and that each orange bears, within its own makeup, into this hard-edged yet insubstantial, incomplete, cold, wintry world.

[10]**disembowel:** to remove the insides

■ SUMMARIZE AND RESPOND

In your reading journal or elsewhere, write a brief summary (three to five sentences) of "Ode to an Orange." Next, jot down your initial response to the reading. Did it make you think of a special object from your childhood? Describe the memories and emotions you associate with that object.

■   **CHECK YOUR COMPREHENSION**

1. Which of the following would be the best alternative title for this essay?

    a. "Simple Pleasures"

    b. "How to Eat an Orange"

    c. "The Magic of Oranges"

    d. "North Dakota Winters"

2. The main idea of this essay is that

    a. oranges can help cure the common cold.

    b. a simple childhood treat brought warmth and joy to the cold winters of the author's childhood.

    c. there are many techniques for peeling an orange.

    d. it is impossible to describe an orange.

3. What does the author imply about oranges?

    a. They were very expensive and therefore only eaten during Christmastime.

    b. They were not part of everyday meals, but a special treat.

    c. His family could not afford to buy oranges very often.

    d. They aren't appreciated by people today.

4. If you are unfamiliar with the following words, use a dictionary to check their meanings: pews (para. 10); phenomena (11); heft (12); feat (13).

■   **READ CRITICALLY**

1. Underline some of the images Woiwode uses to describe an orange. What main impression do these images create?

2. Woiwode uses many specific details to bring his description to life. Find examples of details that appeal to each of the five senses.

3. Woiwode begins and ends the essay in the first-person point of view. From what point of view, though, does he write the majority of the essay? Why do you think he chose to do this?

4. In paragraph 16, why does the author compare an orange to "that unspherical fruit which first went from Eve to Adam and from there (to abbreviate matters) to my brother and me"?

5. Woiwode refers to the season several times. Is this a significant detail that contributes to the essay's main impression? Why, or why not?

WRITE AN ESSAY

Write an essay that describes an object from your childhood. Describe the physical characteristics of the object, but also convey the memory of a specific experience that comes to mind when you think of the object. For example, you might write about the sight, smell, and taste of your grandmother's oatmeal raisin cookies. In addition to writing about the cookies' physical characteristics, you might describe the memory of helping her bake them.

46

Process Analysis

Each essay in this chapter uses process analysis to get its main point across to readers. Process analysis explains how something works or how to do something. Good process analysis lists the essential steps in the process, explains each step in detail, and presents the steps in a logical order. Instructions are process analyses that give readers enough information to complete the steps themselves. Other process analyses are intended simply to educate the reader about how something works. As you read these essays, note how the writers present a series of clear, simple steps.

For more on writing a process analysis essay, see Chapter 11.

Andy Rooney

How to Put Off Doing a Job

Andy Rooney was born in Albany, New York, in 1919. Drafted into the army during World War II, Rooney began his career reporting for *Stars and Stripes,* the armed forces' newspaper. After the war he moved to Hollywood and quickly discovered that he preferred writing for television. Rooney has been a writer, producer, and correspondent for various CBS news programs, and he is best known for the humorous short essays he contributes to *60 Minutes*. These commentaries on American life, which Rooney says deliberately focus on "subjects of universal interest," are collected in numerous best-selling books. Rooney also writes a twice-weekly column that appears in more than 200 newspapers across the country.

In "How to Put Off Doing a Job," Rooney humorously outlines a process that many readers are familiar with—procrastination.

GUIDING QUESTION
Why is Rooney analyzing this process?

February is one of the most difficult times of the year to put off doing   1
some of the things you've been meaning to do. There's no vacation coming up, there are no long weekends scheduled in the immediate future; it's
just this long, grim February. Don't tell me it's a short month. February is
the longest by a week.

Because I have so many jobs that I don't like to do, I've been review-   2
ing the notebook I keep with notes in it for how to put off doing a job.
Let's see now, what could I use today?

—Go to the store to get something. This is one of my most depend-   3
able putter-offers. If I start a job and find I need some simple tool or a
piece of hardware, I stop right there. I put on some better clothes, get in
the car and drive to the store. If that store doesn't have what I'm looking
for, I go to another. Often I'm attracted to some item that has nothing
whatsoever to do with the job I was about to start and I buy that instead.
For instance, if I go to the hardware store to buy a new snow shovel so I
can clean out the driveway, but then I see a can of adhesive spray that will
keep rugs in place on the floor, I'm apt to buy the adhesive spray. That
ends the idea I had to shovel out the driveway.

—Tidy up the work area before starting a job. This has been useful to   4
me over the years as a way of not getting started. Things are such a mess
in my workshop, on my desk, in the kitchen, and in the trunk of the car that
I decide I've got to go through some of the junk before starting to work.

—Make those phone calls. There's no sense trying to do a job if you   5
have other things on your mind, so get them out of the way first. This is a
very effective way of not getting down to work. Call friends you've been
meaning to call, or the distant relative you've been out of touch with. Even
if someone is in California, Texas, or Chicago and you're in Florida, call.
Paying for a long-distance call is still easier and less unpleasant than actually getting down to work.

—Study the problem. It's foolish to jump right into a job before you've   6
thought it through. You might be doing the wrong thing. There might be an
easier way to accomplish what you want to do, so think it over carefully from
every angle. Perhaps someone has written a how-to book about the job you
have in front of you. Buy the book and then sit down and read it. Ask friends
who have had the same job for advice about the best way to do it.

Once you've studied the problem from every angle, don't make a   7
quick decision. Sleep on it.

—Take a coffee break. Although the term "coffee break" assumes that   8
you are drinking coffee in an interim period between stretches of solid work,
this is not necessarily so. Don't be bound by old ideas about when it's proper

to take a coffee break. If taking it before you get started is going to help keep you from doing the work, by all means take your coffee break first.

—As a last resort before going to work, think this thing over. Is this   9
really what you want to do with your life? Philosophize. Nothing is better for putting off doing something than philosophizing. Are you a machine, trapped in the same dull, day-after-day routine that everyone else is in? Or are you a person who makes up his or her own mind about things? Are you going to do these jobs because that's what's expected of you, or are you going to break the mold and live the way you feel like living?

Try these as ways for not getting down to work.   10

SUMMARIZE AND RESPOND

In your reading journal or elsewhere, write a brief summary (three to five sentences) of "How to Put Off Doing a Job." Next, jot down your initial response to the reading. Did it make you think of your own procrastination techniques? What kinds of tasks do you often put off doing? Why do you think people procrastinate?

CHECK YOUR COMPREHENSION

1. Which of the following would be the best alternative title for this essay?

   a. "Those Long Winter Months"

   b. "How to Get Ready to Do a Job"

   c. "A Procrastinator's Guide"

   d. "Is This Job Really Necessary?"

2. The main idea of this essay is that

   a. it's human nature to put off doing jobs.

   b. there are many ways to avoid starting a job.

   c. instead of completing all the jobs on your list, you should only do the ones that are very important.

   d. it's important to set priorities when you have a long list of jobs to do.

3. According to the author,

   a. you shouldn't think too hard about a problem.

   b. you need to clear your mind before you can complete tasks efficiently.

   c. you should try not to think about how boring the task you face is.

   d. philosophizing is the best way to put off doing anything.

4. If you are unfamiliar with the following words or phrases, use a dictionary to check their meanings: grim (para. 1); interim (8); philosophize (9).

READ CRITICALLY

1. Although Rooney writes about his own methods of procrastination, does this essay suggest something about human nature? What in the essay makes you think so?

2. Who might be Rooney's intended audience? Although this piece originally appeared as one of Rooney's newspaper columns, could it have been successfully published somewhere else (in a certain magazine, for instance)? Explain why.

3. What is the author's tone? To what extent does he expect readers to follow the process he outlines?

4. In paragraph 1, Rooney writes, "Don't tell me it's a short month. February is the longest by a week." What does he mean by this?

5. According to Rooney, what is the best way to put off doing a job? Why?

WRITE AN ESSAY

Write a humorous essay analyzing a process of your choice. Possible topics include how to avoid being called on in class, how to waste all your money, how to talk your way out of a speeding ticket, how to embarrass or irritate someone you know, how to fail a course, how to explain a car accident, or how to get dumped. Explain each step of the process in detail, and present the steps in a logical order.

Malcolm X

My First Conk[1]

Malcolm X was born Malcolm Little in Omaha, Nebraska, in 1925. When a teacher told Malcolm that he would never fulfill his dream of becoming a lawyer because he was black, Malcolm lost interest in school, dropped out, and spent several years committing drug-related crimes.

[1]**conk:** a method of straightening curly hair

Malcolm turned his life around, though, when he was sentenced to prison on burglary charges, using the time to further his education and to study the teachings of the Nation of Islam, the Black Muslim movement in America. He also changed his surname from Little to X, suggesting that he could never know his true name—the African name of his ancestors who were made slaves. Malcolm became an important leader of the Nation of Islam soon after his release from prison, but he later left the group to form his own, less radical religious and civil rights group. In 1964, Malcolm was assassinated while giving a speech.

"My First Conk" is an excerpt from *The Autobiography of Malcolm X,* which Malcolm cowrote with his friend Alex Haley. Using vivid details to bring the painful process to life, Malcolm takes readers step-by-step through his first "conk"—a process that straightens curly hair.

TEACHING TIP
Copy Chapter 3 ("Homeboy") of *The Autobiography of Malcolm X,* from which this reading is excerpted. Assign this reading for homework and ask students to comment on how the excerpt printed here fits in with the rest of the chapter.

GUIDING QUESTION
What main point does Malcolm X make about the process he analyzes?

Shorty soon decided that my hair was finally long enough to be conked.[2]   1
He had promised to school me in how to beat the barbershop's three- and four-dollar price by making up congolene,[3] and then conking ourselves.

I took the little list of ingredients he had printed out for me, and went   2
to a grocery store, where I got a can of Red Devil lye,[4] two eggs, and two medium-sized white potatoes. Then at a drugstore near the poolroom, I asked for a large jar of vaseline, a large bar of soap, a large-toothed comb and a fine-toothed comb, one of those rubber hoses with a metal spray-head, a rubber apron and a pair of gloves.

"Going to lay on that first conk?" the drugstore man asked me. I   3
proudly told him, grinning, "Right!"

Shorty paid six dollars a week for a room in his cousin's shabby apart-   4
ment. His cousin wasn't at home. "It's like the pad's mine, he spends so much time with his woman," Shorty said, "Now, you watch me—"

He peeled the potatoes and thin-sliced them into a quart-sized Mason   5
fruit jar, then started stirring them with a wooden spoon as he gradually poured in a little over half the can of lye. "Never use a metal spoon; the lye will turn it black," he told me.

A jelly-like, starchy-looking glop resulted from the lye and potatoes,   6
and Shorty broke in the two eggs, stirring real fast—his own conk and dark face bent down close. The congolene turned pale-yellowish. "Feel the jar," Shorty said. I cupped my hand against the outside, and snatched it away. "Damn right, it's hot, that's the lye," he said. "So you know it's going

---

[2]**conked:** straightened

[3]**congolene:** a product used to straighten hair

[4]**lye:** a strong alkaline substance used in soaps and cleaners

TEACHING TIP
Show Spike Lee's film version of *The Autobiography of Malcolm X.* Have students write a process analysis following Malcolm X's steps of self-discovery and transformation.

to burn when I comb it in — it burns *bad*. But the longer you can stand it, the straighter the hair."

He made me sit down, and he tied the string of the new rubber apron   7
tightly around my neck, and combed up my bush of hair. Then, from the big vaseline jar, he took a handful and massaged it hard all through my hair and into the scalp. He also thickly vaselined my neck, ears and forehead. "When I get to washing out your head, be sure to tell me anywhere you feel any little stinging," Shorty warned me, washing his hands, then pulling on the rubber gloves, and tying on his own rubber apron. "You always got to remember that any congolene left in burns a sore into your head."

The congolene just felt warm when Shorty started combing it in. But   8
then my head caught fire.

I gritted my teeth and tried to pull the sides of the kitchen table   9
together. The comb felt as if it was raking my skin off.

My eyes watered, my nose was running. I couldn't stand it any longer;   10
I bolted to the washbasin. I was cursing Shorty with every name I could think of when he got the spray going and started soap-lathering my head.

He lathered and spray-rinsed, lathered and spray-rinsed, maybe ten or   11
twelve times, each time gradually closing the hot-water faucet, until the rinse was cold, and that helped some.

"You feel any stinging spots?"   12

"No," I managed to say. My knees were trembling.   13

"Sit back down, then. I think we got it all out okay."   14

The flame came back as Shorty, with a thick towel, started drying my   15
head, rubbing hard. *"Easy, man, easy,"* I kept shouting.

"The first time's always worst. You get used to it better before long.   16
You took it real good, homeboy. You got a good conk."

When Shorty let me stand up and see in the mirror, my hair hung   17
down in limp, damp strings. My scalp still flamed, but not as badly; I could bear it. He draped the towel around my shoulders, over my rubber apron, and began again vaselining my hair.

I could feel him combing, straight back, first the big comb, then the   18
fine-tooth one.

Then, he was using a razor, very delicately, on the back of my neck.   19
Then, finally, shaping the sideburns.

My first view in the mirror blotted out the hurting. I'd seen some   20
pretty conks, but when it's the first time, on your *own* head, the transformation, after the lifetime of kinks, is staggering.

The mirror reflected Shorty behind me. We both were grinning and   21
sweating. And on top of my head was this thick, smooth sheen of shining red hair — real red — as straight as any white man's.

How ridiculous I was! Stupid enough to stand there simply lost in   22
admiration of my hair now looking "white," reflected in the mirror in Shorty's room. I vowed that I'd never again be without a conk, and I never was for many years.

"I was surprised to find out that Malcolm X once tried doing things to fit in with the crowd. It made me feel like I wasn't the only one."
— *Travis Tennison, student*

This was my first really big step toward self-degradation:[5] When I   23
endured all of that pain, literally burning my flesh to have it look like a white
man's hair. I had joined that multitude of Negro men and women in America who are brainwashed into believing that the black people are "inferior"—
and white people "superior"—that they will even violate and mutilate their
God-created bodies to try to look "pretty" by white standards.

[5]**self-degradation:** loss of moral character or honor

SUMMARIZE AND RESPOND

In your reading journal or elsewhere, write a brief summary (three to five
sentences) of "My First Conk." Next, jot down your initial response to the
reading. Did it surprise you that a well-known black activist leader once
wanted to look more like a white man? What is something you have done
to conform to a particular group?

CHECK YOUR COMPREHENSION

1. Which of the following would be the best alternative title for this essay?
   a. "The Pain of Conformity"
   b. "Why I Hated My First Conk"
   c. "Hairstyles of the Past"
   d. "Does Anyone Remember Congolene?"

2. The main idea of this essay is that
   a. most people regret something they have done to change their appear-
      ance.
   b. making a homemade conking solution is a dangerous process.
   c. when Malcolm X was younger, he wanted to straighten his hair.
   d. conking is a painful and degrading process that Malcolm X later
      regretted having gone through.

3. According to the author,
   a. he was very pleased when he first saw his straightened hair.
   b. Shorty helped him conk his hair the first time because he didn't have
      his family's approval.
   c. conking was such a painful experience that he never did it again.
   d. the conk didn't change the way he saw himself.

4. If you are unfamiliar with the following words, use a dictionary to check their meanings: shabby (para. 4); bolted (10); blotted, staggering (20); sheen (21); endured, brainwashed, inferior, mutilate (23).

READ CRITICALLY

1. What do you think is Malcolm X's purpose in analyzing the process of conking?

2. Reread paragraphs 6 through 11, underlining the details Malcolm X uses that appeal to the senses. How do these details support his main point?

3. Without going into too much detail, list the major steps in the conking process.

4. Describe the author's attitude toward conking when he was a teenager. How and why do you think this attitude changed as he grew older?

5. Are the essay's final two paragraphs a good example of an effective conclusion? Why or why not?

WRITE AN ESSAY

Write an essay about a process you have gone through to change your appearance (dieting, tattooing, body piercing, or bodybuilding, for example). In your essay, explain why you made the decision to change your appearance, and then explain the process. In your conclusion, examine how your perception of the experience has changed over time.

47

Classification

The essays in this chapter use classification to get their main points across to readers. Classification organizes people or items into useful categories, follows a single organizing principle, and gives examples of what belongs in each category. As you read these essays, note how the writers simplify a complex topic by sorting items into clearly defined categories.

For more on writing a classification essay, see Chapter 12.

Franklin E. Zimring

Confessions of a Former Smoker

Born in 1942 in Los Angeles, Franklin E. Zimring earned a B.A. from Wayne State University and a doctorate in law from the University of Chicago. He currently teaches law at the University of California and has written several books about the death penalty, violence, and youth crime. Zimring has also contributed articles to scholarly and popular magazines. Though his father discouraged him from becoming a professional writer, Zimring became one anyway. He felt that writing was "the only way to think with permanent effect."

"Confessions of a Former Smoker" originally appeared in *Newsweek* in 1987. Zimring, an ex-smoker himself, explains that quitters fall into one of four categories: the zealot, the evangelist, the elect, and the serene. The essay provides clear examples to explain this classification.

GUIDING QUESTION
What category of ex-smokers does Zimring suggest is best, and what is the key to becoming this kind of former smoker?

TEACHING TIP
Tell students up front
that this piece
describes a classifi-
cation within a classifi-
cation. Zimring divides
Americans into three
categories and then
further divides one of
those categories, ex-
smokers, into four
types.

TEACHING TIP
Ask students to
underline each
classification of
ex-smoker and then
write a brief defi-
nition. Have them find
another general term
that can be divided
into the same
classifications.

Americans can be divided into three groups — smokers, nonsmokers, and   1
that expanding pack of us who have quit. Those who have never smoked
don't know what they're missing, but former smokers, ex-smokers,
reformed smokers can never forget. We are veterans of a personal war,
linked by that watershed[1] experience of ceasing to smoke and by the temptation to have just one more cigarette. For almost all of us ex-smokers,
smoking continues to play an important part in our lives. And now that it
is being restricted in restaurants around the country and will be banned in
almost all indoor public places in New York state starting next month, it is
vital that everyone understand the different emotional states cessation of
smoking can cause. I have observed four of them; and in the interest of science I have classified them as those of the zealot,[2] the evangelist,[3] the
elect,[4] and the serene.[5] Each day, each category gains new recruits.

Not all antitobacco zealots are former smokers, but a substantial num-   2
ber of fire-and-brimstone[6] opponents do come from the ranks of the
reformed. Zealots believe that those who continue to smoke are degenerates who deserve scorn, not pity, and the penalties that will deter offensive
behavior in public as well. Relations between these people and those who
continue to smoke are strained.

One explanation for the zealot's fervor in seeking to outlaw tobacco   3
consumption is his own tenuous hold on abstaining from smoking. But I
think part of the emotional force arises from sheer envy as he watches and
identifies with each lung-filling puff. By making smoking in public a crime,
the zealot seeks reassurance that he will not revert to bad habits; give him
strong social penalties and he won't become a recidivist.[7]

No systematic survey has been done yet, but anecdotal evidence sug-   4
gests that a disproportionate number of doctors who have quit smoking
can be found among the fanatics. Just as the most enthusiastic revolutionary tends to make the most enthusiastic counterrevolutionary, many of
today's vitriolic[8] zealots include those who had been deeply committed to
tobacco habits.

By contrast, the antismoking evangelist does not condemn smokers.   5
Unlike the zealot, he regards smoking as an easily curable condition, as a
social disease, and not a sin. The evangelist spends an enormous amount of

[1]**watershed:** turning point

[2]**zealot:** someone who is fanatically devoted to a cause

[3]**evangelist:** someone who preaches for a certain cause

[4]**elect:** a privileged, exclusive group

[5]**serene:** calm, peaceful

[6]**fire-and-brimstone:** fiercely judgmental

[7]**recidivist:** a person who returns to a previous bad habit

[8]**vitriolic:** bitter, cutting

time seeking and preaching to the unconverted. He argues that kicking the
habit is not *that* difficult. After all, *he* did it; moreover, as he describes it, the
benefits of quitting are beyond measure and the disadvantages are nil.

The hallmark of the evangelist is his insistence that he never misses   6
tobacco. Though he is less hostile to smokers than the zealot, he is
resented more. Friends and loved ones who have been the targets of his
preachments frequently greet the resumption of smoking by the evangelist
as an occasion for unmitigated glee.

Among former smokers, the distinctions between the evangelist and   7
the elect are much the same as the differences between proselytizing[9] and
nonproselytizing religious sects. While the evangelists preach the ease
and desirability of abstinence, the elect do not attempt to convert their
friends. They think that virtue is its own reward and subscribe to the Puri-
tan theory of predestination.[10] Since they have proved themselves capable
of abstaining from tobacco, they are therefore different from friends and
relatives who continue to smoke. They feel superior, secure that their sal-
vation was foreordained.[11] These ex-smokers rarely give personal testimony on their conversion. They rarely speak about their tobacco habits,
while evangelists talk about little else. Of course, active smokers find such
bluenosed[12] behavior far less offensive than that of the evangelist or the
zealot, yet they resent the elect simply because they are smug. Their air of
self-satisfaction rarely escapes the notice of those lighting up. For active
smokers, life with a member of the ex-smoking elect is less stormy than
with a zealot or evangelist, but it is subtly oppressive nonetheless.

I have labeled my final category of former smokers the serene. This   8
classification is meant to encourage those who find the other psychic styles
of ex-smokers disagreeable. Serenity is quieter than zealotry and evange-
lism, and those who qualify are not as self-righteous[13] as the elect. The
serene ex-smoker accepts himself and also accepts those around him who
continue to smoke. This kind of serenity does not come easily, nor does it
seem to be an immediate option for those who have stopped. Rather it is
a goal, an end stage in a process of development during which some former smokers progress through one or more of the less-than-positive psychological points en route. For former smokers, serenity is thus a positive
possibility that exists at the end of the rainbow. But all former smokers
cannot reach that promised land.

---

[9]**proselytizing:** attempting to convert a person from one belief or faith to another

[10]**theory of predestination:** the belief that God decides everyone's fate before birth

[11]**foreordained:** determined ahead of time

[12]**bluenosed:** moralistic, preachy

[13]**self-righteous:** sure of one's own correctness

What is it that permits some former smokers to become serene? I think 9 the key is self-acceptance and gratitude. The fully mature former smoker knows he has the soul of an addict and is grateful for the knowledge. He may sit up front in an airplane, but he knows he belongs in the smoking section in back. He doesn't regret that he quit smoking, nor any of his previous adventures with tobacco. As a former smoker, he is grateful for the experience and memory of craving a cigarette.

Serenity comes from accepting the lessons of one's life. And ex-smokers 10 who have reached this point in their worldview have much to be grateful for. They have learned about the potential and limits of change. In becoming the right kind of former smoker, they developed a healthy sense of self. This former smoker, for one, believes that it is better to crave (one hopes only occasionally) and not to smoke than never to have craved at all. And by accepting that fact, the reformed smoker does not need to excoriate,[14] envy, or disassociate himself from those who continue to smoke.

[14]**excoriate:** to denounce harshly

◼ SUMMARIZE AND RESPOND

In your reading journal or elsewhere, write a brief summary (three to five sentences) of "Confessions of a Former Smoker." Next, jot down your initial response to the reading. Do you agree with Zimring's classifications? Why or why not? Do you or does anyone you know fit into one of the four categories of quitters?

◼ CHECK YOUR COMPREHENSION

1. Which of the following would be the best alternative title for this essay?
   a. "Reasons to Quit Smoking"
   (b.) "Ex-Smokers Come in Several Types"
   c. "A Personal War"
   d. "Recruiting in the Ex-Smoker Army"

2. The main idea of this essay is that
   a. smoking is quickly becoming socially unacceptable in America.
   b. ex-smokers often judge smokers harshly.
   c. ex-smokers are grateful for the memory of smoking.
   (d.) some former smokers will develop into serene ex-smokers, the best of the four categories of quitters.

3. What does Zimring say about elect ex-smokers?

    a. They all eventually reach the serene stage.

    (b.) They do not actively pressure smokers to quit.

    c. A large number of them are doctors.

    d. They complain about missing smoking.

4. If you are unfamiliar with the following words, use your dictionary to check their meanings: cessation (para. 1); degenerates, deter (2); tenuous, abstaining, revert (3); anecdotal, disproportionate, counterrevolutionary (4); nil (5); hallmark, unmitigated (6); abstinence (7); disassociate (10).

READ CRITICALLY

1. In your own words, describe the attitude of each type of ex-smoker toward people who still smoke. What kind of former smoker do you think Zimring is? Why?

2. Describe the author's tone when he writes that he has classified the types of ex-smokers "in the interest of science." Does he use scientific evidence to support his main point? Explain, using examples from the essay.

3. In paragraph 10, Zimring writes that the serene ex-smoker "believes that it is better to crave (one hopes only occasionally) and not to smoke than never to have craved at all." What does he mean by this statement? What famous quotation is he echoing?

4. Since this essay was first published in 1987, smoking in public has become increasingly regulated. Which type of former smoker would be most supportive of this movement? Explain why.

5. Would this essay be equally effective if it were written by someone who had never smoked? Why or why not?

WRITE AN ESSAY

Write an essay that classifies people based on a personality trait. Choose a characteristic on which you can rate people, such as cleanliness, generosity, or sense of humor. Then create categories of people who exhibit that trait in different degrees. For example, if you decided to write about cleanliness, your categories might be *total slobs, average Joes,* and *neat freaks.* Provide detailed examples of the kinds of people who belong in each category.

Jonathan R. Gould, Jr.
The People Next Door

Born in 1968, Jonathan R. Gould, Jr., grew up on a dairy farm in Fort Plain, New York. He served in the U.S. Army for three years and later attended the State University of New York (SUNY) at Oneonta, earning a B.S. in mathematics. Gould currently lives with his wife and children in Oneonta, where he works for an Internet service provider.

No matter where he lives, Gould always has the same types of neighbors. He identifies these types in "The People Next Door," which he wrote in 1994 for a writing course at SUNY.

GUIDING QUESTION

According to the author, why is it important to classify your neighbors?

"This reading made me laugh. Gould has found the funny side of what can be an annoying life experience."
—*Theresa Dresser, student*

I have moved more often than I care to remember. However, one thing always stays the same no matter where I have been. There is always a house next door, and that house contains neighbors. Over time, I have begun putting my neighbors into one of four categories: too friendly, unsociable, irritable, and just right.

Neighbors who are too friendly can be seen just about anywhere. I mean that both ways. They exist in every neighborhood I have ever lived in and seem to appear everywhere I go. For some strange reason these people become extremely attached to my family and stop in as many as eight to ten times a day. No matter how tired I appear to be, nothing short of opening the door and suggesting they leave will make them go home at night. (I once told an unusually friendly neighbor that his house was on fire, in an attempt to make him leave, and he still took ten minutes to say goodbye.) What is truly interesting about these people is their strong desire to cook for us even though they have developed no culinary skill whatsoever. (This has always proved particularly disconcerting[1] since they stay to watch us eat every bite as they continually ask if the food "tastes good.")

1

2

---

[1]**disconcerting:** upsetting

The unsociable neighbor is a different story altogether. For reasons of   3
his own, he has decided to pretend that we do not exist. I have always
found that one or two neighbors of this type are in my neighborhood. It is
not easy to identify these people, because they seldom leave the shelter of
their own house. To be honest, the only way I know that someone lives in
their building is the presence of a name on the mailbox and the lights shining through the windows at night. My wife often tries to befriend these
unique people, and I have to admire her courage. However, even her
serenity is shaken when she offers our neighbors a fresh-baked apple pie
only to have them look at her as if she intended to poison them.

Probably the most difficult neighbor to deal with is the irritable neigh-   4
bor. This individual probably has several problems, but he has reduced all
those problems down to one cause — the proximity[2] of my family to his
residence. Fortunately, I have only encountered this type of neighbor in a
handful of settings. (He is usually too busy with one group of "trouble-
makers" to pick up a new set.) The times that I have encountered this ras-
cal, however, have proved more than enough for my tastes. He is more
than willing to talk to me. Unfortunately, all he wants to tell me is how
miserable my family is making him. Ignoring this individual has not
worked for me yet. (He just adds my "snobbishness" to his list of faults
that my family displays.) Interestingly, this fellow will eat anything my wife
(bless her soul) might make in an attempt to be sociable. Even though he
never has anything good to say about the food, not a crumb will be left on
the plate when he is finished (which leads me to wonder just how starved
and impoverished[3] he must be).

At the risk of sounding like Goldilocks, there is also a neighbor who is   5
"just right." One of the most wonderful things about this neighbor is that
there has always been at least one everywhere I have gone. We meet often
(though not too often), and our greetings are always sincere. Occasionally,
our families will go out to eat or to shop, or just sit and talk. We tend to
spend as much time at their house as they do at ours (two to three times
a month), and everyone knows just when it is time to say goodnight. For
some reason, this neighbor knows how to cook, and we frequently
exchange baked goods as well as pleasantries. For obvious reasons, this
type of neighbor is my favorite.

As I mentioned before, each type of neighbor I have encountered is a   6
common sight in any neighborhood. I have always felt it was important to
identify the type of neighbors that were around me. Then I am better able
to maintain a clear perspective on our relationship and understand their
needs. After all, people do not really change; we just learn how to live with
both the good and the bad aspects of their behavior.

[2]**proximity:** nearness, closeness

[3]**impoverished:** very poor, reduced to poverty

TEAMWORK
Have students in small
groups identify a place
in Gould's essay where
his classification could
use more supporting
evidence and then
write an additional
paragraph with such
evidence. Ask groups
to share their para-
graphs with the whole
class.

◼ SUMMARIZE AND RESPOND

In your reading journal or elsewhere, write a brief summary (three to five sentences) of "The People Next Door." Next, jot down your initial response to the reading. Do your neighbors fit into Gould's four categories, or would you sort them differently? How do you deal with each type of neighbor?

◼ CHECK YOUR COMPREHENSION

1. Which of the following would be the best alternative title for this essay?

    a. "Friends and Enemies"

    b. "Identifying Types of Neighborhoods"

    c. "Good Neighbors Make Good Friends"

    d. "Not All Neighbors Are 'Just Right'"

2. The main idea of this essay is that

    a. neighbors are often difficult to understand.

    b. the author and his wife have different ways of befriending their neighbors.

    c. with the right approach, neighbors can change.

    d. understanding the types of people who live around us will help us learn to live with their behavior.

3. According to the author,

    a. the most difficult neighbor to deal with is the one who ignores you.

    b. neighbors who are too friendly at first often become your closest friends later on.

    c. the most difficult neighbor to deal with is the one who is overly friendly.

    d. wherever he has lived, he has always found a neighbor who is "just right."

4. If you are unfamiliar with the following words, use your dictionary to check their meanings: serenity (para. 3); pleasantries (5); encountered, perspective (6).

READ CRITICALLY

1. Describe Gould's tone in this essay. Support your response with specific examples from the reading.

2. What organizing principle does Gould use to classify his neighbors? In other words, how does he sort them into categories?

3. Gould writes his essay from the first-person point of view. Would the essay have been equally effective if Gould had written in the third person? Why or why not?

4. Gould and his wife deal with their neighbors differently. How do their approaches differ? Reread the essay's concluding paragraph, and describe Gould's attitude toward neighbors in general.

5. What features of good classification can you find in this essay?

WRITE AN ESSAY

Gould writes about the types of people he lives around. Write an essay that classifies the kinds of people you might live *with*. Whether you write about types of roommates, spouses, family members, or pets, sort them into categories according to their habits.

48

Definition

For more on writing a definition essay, see Chapter 13.

The essays in this chapter use definition to get their main points across to readers. Definition explains what a term means. Good definitions identify the term, give a clear and precise meaning, include examples of the term, and use words and information that the reader will understand. An essay may present and explore a definition of a term, or a definition may be one part of a larger discussion. As you read these essays, note the ways that the writers use easy-to-understand examples and information to explain their terms.

Sydney J. Harris

A Jerk

DISCUSSION
Pointing out that this essay was published in 1961, ask students if the word *jerk* is still frequently used. Discuss its use, as well as that of other such words. You may want to use this occasion to discuss how language changes over time.

TEAMWORK
Assign small groups different paragraphs of Harris's essay. Have them identify the topic sentence and a specific, detailed example. Have the groups compare notes with the entire class.

Newspaper columnist Sydney J. Harris has been called the "perfect master of the short essay form." Harris was born in London, England, in 1917, but at a young age he moved to the United States with his family. He attended Central College in Illinois and the University of Chicago, although he did not graduate from either school. Harris went on to write successfully for various newspapers in Chicago. For nearly forty years, Harris wrote about society and human nature in his column entitled "Strictly Personal." The column, which Harris wrote five times a week for the *Chicago Daily News,* was syndicated to more than two hundred newspapers.

"A Jerk" appears in *Last Things First,* one of Harris's many collections of columns. The essay presents a clear definition of *jerk*—a word we hear often but might not know how to define precisely.

GUIDING QUESTION
Why did Harris decide to think of a suitable definition for *jerk,* and what definition did he come up with?

I don't know whether history repeats itself, but biography certainly does.   1
The other day, Michael came in and asked me what a "jerk" was—the same question Carolyn put to me a dozen years ago.

At that time, I fluffed her off with some inane[1] answer, such as "A jerk   2
isn't a very nice person," but both of us knew it was an unsatisfactory reply. When she went to bed, I began trying to work up a suitable definition.

It is a marvelously apt word, of course. Until it was coined, not more   3
than 25 years ago, there was really no single word in English to describe the kind of person who is a jerk—"boob" and "simp" were too old hat, and besides they really didn't fit, for they could be lovable, and a jerk never is.

Thinking it over, I decided that a jerk is basically a person without   4
insight. He is not necessarily a fool or a dope, because some extremely clever persons can be jerks. In fact, it has little to do with intelligence as we commonly think of it; it is, rather, a kind of subtle but persuasive aroma emanating[2] from the inner part of the personality.

I know a college president who can be described only as a jerk. He is   5
not an unintelligent man, nor unlearned, nor even unschooled in the social amenities.[3] Yet he is a jerk *cum laude*,[4] because of a fatal flaw in his nature— he is totally incapable of looking into the mirror of his soul and shuddering at what he sees there.

A jerk, then, is a man (or woman) who is utterly unable to see himself   6
as he appears to others. He has no grace, he is tactless without meaning to be, he is a bore even to his best friends, he is an egotist without charm. All of us are egotists to some extent, but most of us—unlike the jerk—are perfectly and horribly aware of it when we make asses of ourselves. The jerk never knows.

[1]**inane:** lacking sense or substance

[2]**emanating:** coming out, flowing

[3]**social amenities:** social courtesies, manners

[4]*cum laude:* a Latin phrase meaning "with honors"

"This is a good example of a definition essay. This writing showed me that there are many ways to explain the meaning of a word."
—*Michelle Perez, student*

■ **SUMMARIZE AND RESPOND**

In your reading journal or elsewhere, write a brief summary (three to five sentences) of "A Jerk." Next, jot down your initial response to the reading. Do you agree with Harris's definition? Think of someone whom you or others have called a jerk, and explain why this person does or does not support the essay's definition.

ESL
Ask ESL students to share the words in their native language for people who possess the characteristics Harris describes. Is there an exact translation for *jerk?*

CHECK YOUR COMPREHENSION

1. Which of the following would be the best alternative title for this essay?

    a.   "Jerks: Charming Egotists"

    b.   "Jerks: Fools with Intelligence"

    c.   "Jerks: Egotists without Insight"

    d.   "Jerks: Unlovable Simps"

2. The main idea of this essay is that

    a.   a jerk is different from a boob or a simp.

    b.   *jerk* is a slang term that has been used for many years.

    c.   a jerk is someone who doesn't understand how others view him or her.

    d.   anyone can be a jerk, even a well-educated college president.

3. According to the author, what is the difference between a simp and a jerk?

    a.   Unlike a jerk, a simp can be lovable.

    b.   A jerk is generally more educated than a simp.

    c.   A jerk is smart enough to know how he appears to others, but he doesn't care.

    d.   A simp is usually unaware of making a fool of himself.

4. If you are unfamiliar with the following words, use a dictionary to check their meanings: apt, coined, old hat (para. 3); insight (4); grace, tactless, egotist (6).

READ CRITICALLY

1. In what paragraph does the basic definition of *jerk* appear? Why do you think Harris didn't put it in the first few paragraphs? What purpose does the story about his two children serve?

2. Using only this essay as a guide, write a short definition of *jerk*. Use your own words, but write a definition that you think Harris would agree with.

3. What makes a jerk different from a fool or a dope, according to Harris?

4. What example does Harris use to support his definition of *jerk*? Is it an effective example? Why or why not?

5. Reread paragraphs 5 and 6, underlining phrases that expand on Harris's basic definition ("a jerk is basically a person without insight"). How do these expanded definitions help readers understand Harris's main point?

▇ WRITE AN ESSAY

Write an essay that defines an abstract concept—something that you can't see, smell, taste, touch, or hear. For example, you could write about love, hate, freedom, or courage. Use examples to show readers what you mean. Like Harris, you might want to define the word by showing how it is different from similar words ("Love is not just lust because...").

Marie Winn

Cookies or Heroin?

Marie Winn was born in Czechoslovakia in 1936. As a child she moved with her family to New York City, where she lives today. After studying at Radcliffe College and Columbia University, Winn became a freelance writer, contributing articles to the *New York Times Magazine,* the *New York Times Book Review,* and the *Wall Street Journal.* She is the author of many children's books, as well as several books about child rearing. An avid bird watcher, Winn tells the story of two hawks that nested on a New York high-rise in *Red-Tails in Love: A Wildlife Drama in Central Park* (1998), her latest book.

"Cookies or Heroin?" is an excerpt from Winn's book *The Plug-In Drug* (1977, revised 1985 and 2002), which examines the negative effects of television on children and families. With her definition of *TV addiction,* Winn shows that excessive television watching is a more serious problem than many people might think.

GUIDING QUESTION
Why is TV addiction a serious problem, in Winn's opinion?

The word "addiction" is often used loosely and wryly in conversation.   1
People will refer to themselves as "mystery-book addicts" or "cookie addicts." E. B. White wrote of his annual surge of interest in gardening: "We are hooked and are making an attempt to kick the habit." Yet nobody really believes that reading mysteries or ordering seeds by catalogue is serious enough to be compared with addictions to heroin or alcohol. In these

cases the word "addiction" is used jokingly to denote[1] a tendency to over-indulge in some pleasurable activity.

People often refer to being "hooked on TV." Does this, too, fall into the lighthearted category of cookie eating and other pleasures that people pursue with unusual intensity? Or is there a kind of television viewing that falls into the more serious category of destructive addiction?

Not unlike drugs or alcohol, the television experience allows the participant to blot out the real world and enter into a pleasurable and passive mental state. To be sure, other experiences, notably reading, also provide a temporary respite[2] from reality. But it's much easier to stop reading and return to reality than to stop watching television. The entry into another world offered by reading includes an easily accessible return ticket. The entry via television does not. In this way television viewing, for those vulnerable[3] to addiction, is more like drinking or taking drugs — once you start it's hard to stop.

Just as alcoholics are only vaguely aware of their addiction, feeling that they control their drinking more than they really do ("I can cut it out any time I want — I just like to have three or four drinks before dinner"), many people overestimate their control over television watching. Even as they put off other activities to spend hour after hour watching television, they feel they could easily resume living in a different, less passive style. But somehow or other while the television set is present in their homes, it just stays on. With television's easy gratifications available, those other activities seem to take too much effort.

A heavy viewer (a college English instructor) observes:

> I find television almost irresistible. When the set is on, I cannot ignore it. I can't turn it off. I feel sapped, will-less, enervated.[4] As I reach out to turn off the set, the strength goes out of my arms. So I sit there for hours and hours.

Self-confessed television addicts often feel they "ought" to do other things — but the fact that they don't read and don't plant their garden or sew or crochet or play games or have conversations means that those activities are no longer as desirable as television viewing. In a way, the lives of heavy viewers are as unbalanced by their television "habit" as drug addicts' or alcoholics' lives. They are living in a holding pattern, as it were, passing up the activities that lead to growth or development or a sense of accomplishment. This is one reason people talk about their television

[1]**denote:** mean

[2]**respite:** period of rest

[3]**vulnerable:** more likely to suffer from something

[4]**enervated:** weakened

viewing so ruefully, so apologetically. They are aware that it is an unproductive experience, that by any human measure almost any other endeavor[5] is more worthwhile.

It is the adverse[6] effect of television viewing on the lives of so many 7 people that makes it feel like a serious addiction. The television habit distorts the sense of time. It renders other experiences vague and curiously unreal while taking on a greater reality for itself. It weakens relationships by reducing and sometimes eliminating normal opportunities for talking, for communicating.

And yet television does not satisfy, else why would the viewer continue 8 to watch hour after hour, day after day? "The measure of health," wrote the psychiatrist Lawrence Kubie, "is flexibility . . . and especially the freedom to cease when sated."[7] But heavy television viewers can never be sated with their television experiences. These do not provide the true nourishment that satiation[8] requires, and thus they find that they cannot stop watching.

[5]**endeavor:** undertaking or effort

[6]**adverse:** harmful

[7]**sated:** satisfied

[8]**satiation:** satisfaction

SUMMARIZE AND RESPOND

In your reading journal or elsewhere, write a brief summary (three to five sentences) of "Cookies or Heroin?" Next, jot down your initial response to the reading. Are you or any of your friends addicted to television? Do you agree with Winn that TV addiction is destructive, or do you think that her essay exaggerates the seriousness of the problem?

CHECK YOUR COMPREHENSION

1. Which of the following would be the best alternative title for this essay?

   a. "Hooked on TV"

   b. "The Dehumanizing Effects of Television"

   c. "The Appeal of Television"

   d. "Viewing Habits of Television Watchers"

2. The main idea of this essay is that

   a. television addicts are merely seeking a harmless, pleasurable experience.

b. like an addiction to drugs or alcohol, television addiction can be destructive.

c. watching television distorts viewers' sense of time.

d. addictions are not always destructive.

3. According to the author,

a. television addicts are often disorganized and messy.

b. television addicts often believe that they can control their television watching habits.

c. television viewers are not always passive — they laugh, cheer, criticize, and discuss programs while watching them.

d. television addiction is a bad habit, but it is not a serious problem like drug or alcohol addiction.

4. If you are unfamiliar with the following words, use a dictionary to check their meanings: wryly (para. 1); passive, accessible (3); ruefully (6); renders (7).

READ CRITICALLY

1. Why do you think Winn contrasts the way some people use the term *addiction* before discussing the term *TV addiction*? How does this organization help Winn show readers what she means?

2. How does Winn distinguish between harmless and destructive addictions?

3. According to Winn, how is TV addiction similar to drug or alcohol addiction? What examples does she use to make her point?

4. In paragraph 8, Winn quotes Lawrence Kubie, a psychiatrist, as saying, "The measure of health is flexibility . . . and especially the freedom to cease when sated." What does Kubie mean by this, and how does the quote strengthen Winn's conclusion?

5. Using examples from the essay, discuss the similarities (or differences) between television addiction and computer addiction.

WRITE AN ESSAY

Write an essay that defines a specific type of addict (a "workaholic," "shopaholic," or "chocoholic," for example). Give examples of how the addict's behavior affects his or her life. Your tone can be either lighthearted or serious.

49

Comparison and Contrast

The essays in this chapter use comparison and contrast to get their main points across to readers. Comparison looks at the similarities between two subjects, and contrast looks at their differences. Good comparison/contrast writing uses subjects that have enough in common to be compared or contrasted, and presents several parallel points of comparison or contrast arranged in a logical order—either point-by-point or whole-to-whole. Sometimes writers use comparison and contrast to identify what makes each subject unique; sometimes they use it to choose the better of two possibilities. As you read these essays, note how the writers present similarities and differences between the subjects.

For more on writing a comparison/contrast essay, see Chapter 14.

Dave Barry
The Ugly Truth about Beauty

According to the *New York Times,* humorist Dave Barry is "the funniest man in America." Born in 1947 in Armonk, New York, Barry earned a B.A. from Haverford College. He then worked for several years as a newspaper reporter and a lecturer on business writing before discovering his talent as a humor columnist. The columns he now writes for the *Miami Herald* appear in newspapers nationwide, and his work has been collected in numerous books. Barry's hilarious observations on American life won him the Pulitzer Prize for commentary in 1988.

In "The Ugly Truth about Beauty," first published in the *Philadelphia Inquirer Magazine* in 1998, Barry compares and contrasts men's and women's beauty routines. The essay humorously highlights differences in the ways that men and women view themselves.

GUIDING QUESTION
Why do men and women think of their looks differently?

If you're a man, at some point a woman will ask you how she looks. 1

"How do I look?" she'll ask. 2

You must be careful how you answer this question. The best technique 3 is to form an honest yet sensitive opinion, then collapse on the floor with some kind of fatal seizure. Trust me, this is the easiest way out. Because you will never come up with the right answer.

The problem is that women generally do not think of their looks in the 4 same way that men do. Most men form an opinion of how they look in seventh grade, and they stick to it for the rest of their lives. Some men form the opinion that they are irresistible stud muffins, and they do not change this opinion even when their faces sag and their noses bloat to the size of eggplants and their eyebrows grow together to form what appears to be a giant forehead-dwelling tropical caterpillar.

Most men, I believe, think of themselves as average-looking. Men will 5 think this even if their faces cause heart failure in cattle at a range of 300 yards. Being average does not bother them; average is fine, for men. This is why men never ask anybody how they look. Their primary form of beauty care is to shave themselves, which is essentially the same form of beauty care that they give to their lawns. If, at the end of his four-minute daily beauty regimen,[1] a man has managed to wipe most of the shaving cream out of his hair and is not bleeding too badly, he feels that he has done all he can, so he stops thinking about his appearance and devotes his mind to more critical issues, such as the Super Bowl.

Women do not look at themselves this way. If I had to express, in three 6 words, what I believe most women think about their appearance, those words would be: "not good enough." No matter how attractive a woman may appear to be to others, when she looks at herself in the mirror, she thinks: woof. She thinks that at any moment a municipal animal-control officer is going to throw a net over her and haul her off to the shelter.

Why do women have such low self-esteem? There are many complex 7 psychological and societal reasons, by which I mean Barbie. Girls grow up playing with a doll proportioned such that, if it were a human, it would be seven feet tall and weigh 81 pounds, of which 53 pounds would be bosoms. This is a difficult appearance standard to live up to, especially when you contrast it with the standard set for little boys by their dolls . . . excuse me, by their action figures. Most of the action figures that my son played with when he was little were hideous-looking. For example, he was very fond of an action figure (part of the He-Man series) called "Buzz-Off,"

[1]**regimen:** routine

who was part human, part flying insect. Buzz-Off was not a looker. But he was extremely self-confident. You could not imagine Buzz-Off saying to the other action figures: "Do you think these wings make my hips look big?"

But women grow up thinking they need to look like Barbie, which for most women is impossible, although there is a multibillion-dollar beauty industry devoted to convincing women that they must try. I once saw an Oprah show wherein supermodel Cindy Crawford dispensed makeup tips to the studio audience. Cindy had all these middle-aged women applying beauty products to their faces; she stressed how important it was to apply them in a certain way, using the tips of their fingers. All the women dutifully did this, even though it was obvious to any sane observer that, no matter how carefully they applied these products, they would never look remotely like Cindy Crawford, who is some kind of genetic mutation.

I'm not saying that men are superior. I'm just saying that you're not going to get a group of middle-aged men to sit in a room and apply cosmetics to themselves under the instruction of Brad Pitt, in hopes of looking more like him. Men would realize that this task was pointless and demeaning.[2] They would find some way to bolster their self-esteem that did not require looking like Brad Pitt. They would say to Brad: "Oh YEAH? Well what do you know about LAWN CARE, pretty boy?"

Of course many women will argue that the reason they become obsessed with trying to look like Cindy Crawford is that men, being as shallow as a drop of spit, WANT women to look that way. To which I have two responses:

1. Hey, just because WE'RE idiots, that does not mean YOU have to be; and

2. Men don't even notice 97 percent of the beauty efforts you make anyway. Take fingernails. The average woman spends 5,000 hours per year worrying about her fingernails; I have never once, in more than 40 years of listening to men talk about women, heard a man say, "She has a nice set of fingernails!" Many men would not notice if a woman had upward of four hands.

Anyway, to get back to my original point: If you're a man, and a woman asks you how she looks, you're in big trouble. Obviously, you can't say she looks bad. But you also can't say that she looks great, because she'll think you're lying, because she has spent countless hours, with the help of the multibillion-dollar beauty industry, obsessing about the differences between herself and Cindy Crawford. Also, she suspects that you're not qualified to judge anybody's appearance. This is because you have shaving cream in your hair.

[2]**demeaning:** degrading, lowering one's character

ESL
Ask ESL students to compare and contrast cultural differences in definitions of beauty, including various words for beauty in their native languages.

8

9

10

11

12

13

SUMMARIZE AND RESPOND

In your reading journal or elsewhere, write a brief summary (three to five sentences) of "The Ugly Truth about Beauty." Next, jot down your initial response to the reading. Do you agree with Barry's assessment of why there are differences in the ways men and women view themselves? What examples from your experience do or do not support his points?

CHECK YOUR COMPREHENSION

1. Which of the following would be the best alternative title for this essay?

   a. "Barbie versus He-Man"

   b. "Men and Women: What They See in the Mirror"

   c. "It's Kinder to Lie"

   d. "The Beauty Industry's Dark Secret"

2. The main idea of this essay is that

   a. men don't know how to respond when women ask about their appearance.

   b. men don't care how much effort women put into their looks.

   c. because of society and the media, men and women view their physical appearances differently.

   d. childhood toys influence the way men and women think about their looks.

3. According to Barry,

   a. most men are concerned with how women view their appearance.

   b. women want men to be honest about their looks.

   c. most women are dissatisfied with their appearance.

   d. a woman's perception of her appearance is influenced by her moods and her female friends.

4. If you are unfamiliar with the following words, use a dictionary to check their meanings: societal, proportioned (para. 7); mutation (8); bolster (9).

READ CRITICALLY

1. Who is Barry's intended audience, and what do you think is his purpose in writing this essay?

2. In paragraphs 7 and 8, Barry discusses children's toys. Why did he choose these particular toys, and how do they help him explain his points of contrast?

3. What is Barry's attitude toward Cindy Crawford and Brad Pitt? Explain how he uses these examples to support his main point.

4. Explain the significance of the title. What do you think Barry would say is the ugly truth about beauty?

5. Why do you think the beauty industry is so successful? Support your answer with examples from this essay.

WRITE AN ESSAY

Look through your family photographs, or use the Internet or magazines to view men's and women's fashions over the last fifty years. Think about how fashions have changed, and write an essay that compares and contrasts fashion trends from two different decades. Use concrete examples to show differences and similarities in the two time periods' styles.

Bill Batson
In Africa, Men Hold Hands

Bill Batson is a writer, artist, and political activist. The chief of staff to the New York state senator representing central Harlem, Batson devotes much of his time to community service projects. He has directed the food program for the Coalition for the Homeless, and he cofounded an antiracism project that leads children on a five-thousand-mile trip to historic civil rights sites. Batson is also a contributing writer for publications including *Essence* magazine and the *Amsterdam News.*

When Batson traveled to South Africa, he was surprised to see male friends holding hands. In the following essay, originally published in *Essence* in 1999, Batson compares and contrasts American and African cultural attitudes toward affection.

GUIDING QUESTION

What did Batson learn on his trip to South Africa, and how does he think American society could benefit from that lesson?

It was my first time in a squatter camp[1] in South Africa, so I gladly took the hand of the elder as he led me along narrow unpaved roads. My tour guide was intent on showing me the struggles the poor were facing in the aftermath of apartheid.[2] He led me past improvised villas of corrugated[3] metal and scrap wood, stopping to introduce the young children, covered in dirt from the lack of running water, to their first American visitor.

I had traveled to Africa when I was thirty-three years old, and like many young Black people, I was on a mission of discovery. For two years I would attend classes and work at a museum, while observing the growth of a new democracy. This guided tour was my first exposure to this land.

After about fifteen minutes, as the December heat of the Southern Hemisphere moistened my palms, I realized that my guide had not let go of my hand. I had been walking through an African village holding hands with a man.

In South Africa, it's common for men, young and old, to hold hands. This custom was difficult for me, as an African American from the land of the gangster pose, to comprehend at first. In my world, off the court, on the block, brothers didn't touch, and those who did were usually confined to liberated zones or the closet.

I knew that to have a deeper experience, I would have to put aside the hype and stereotypes that many of us carry in our heads about Africa. And by doing so, I found out that African tradition is a magical thing. Each tradition carries a force through generations that has been responsible for the survival of a people under conditions that are virtually unparalleled in human history. Despite slavery, extermination campaigns, colonialism,[4] and the outright theft of entire countries, the brothers and sisters have survived and even prospered in some places.

Confident of who they are, and caring deeply about the people who are around them, African men use their bodies, nonsexually, to express closeness and joy. I must admit that as I walked through the township with my hand being held by a male elder, surprisingly I did not feel foreign. I felt awkward because of this new attention, but not because of where I was, or for fear that I was out of place. In retrospect, I'd never felt so strong—so male.

A South African intern once tried to describe his relationship with someone to me. Finally, with some difficulty, he used a word foreign to his vocabulary: *cousin.* The closeness among people is like that of family. And I've found that there's an intense intimacy and kinship between families and extended groups who live together. That intimacy produces unflinch-

---

[1]**squatter camp:** place where settlers have no legal claim to the land

[2]**apartheid:** official policy of racial segregation

[3]**corrugated:** ridged or wrinkled

[4]**colonialism:** control by one power over a dependent area or people

ing commitment in times of need or, in good times, the practice of men dancing together in celebration of a political or sporting victory.

Here in the United States, in a community beset with violence, in   8
an environment of court involvement and victimization, intimacy even between blood brothers and sisters is extremely strained. On the male side, fear of intimacy can challenge our closest bonds. In Spike Lee's critically acclaimed *He Got Game,* Lee explores the relationship between a father and son. His characters twist and turn through some of the most obtuse[5] and uptight gestures ever captured on film as they struggle to rekindle familial intimacy—a struggle true to life for too many brothers.

Could the lack of the affectionate hand of an elder man to lead a   9
younger "brother" account for some of the aggression and violence in our communities, or explain our obsession with physical toughness? As a youth worker, I hesitated to encourage a touchy-feely approach, fearing that I might strip away the veneer[6] of roughness that might keep a kid alive in the projects. But after living in Africa, I've begun to wonder if maybe it's that macho posturing that gets our kids killed.

It will be a long time before the sight of two African American men hold-   10
ing hands will do anything other than evoke[7] homophobic slurs or uncomfortable stares. But maybe we can take lessons from overseas. They watch our Spike Lee movies in Africa, all right. And you just might find two brothers, holding hands as they exit, sharing their mixed reviews and wondering why, if we African Americans are so tough, we don't fight back against the "Man" who's coming down so hard on our communities. In Africa, many of those men holding hands were armed revolutionaries who overthrew the apartheid government. Maybe it's time we all tried a little "brotherly" tenderness.

[5]**obtuse:** dull, insensitive

[6]**veneer:** attractive but superficial appearance

[7]**evoke:** elicit, cause to happen

DISCUSSION
What specific comparison and contrast is Batson making here? Do his observations hold true to other groups of men in the United States besides African Americans?

SUMMARIZE AND RESPOND

In your reading journal or elsewhere, write a brief summary (three to five sentences) of "In Africa, Men Hold Hands." Next, jot down your initial response to the reading. What did it make you think or feel? Have you ever met someone from another culture who expresses affection differently?

CHECK YOUR COMPREHENSION

1. Which of the following would be the best alternative title for this essay?

   a.   "Spike Lee's Influence on America"

   b.   "A Dying Tradition"

c.   "Macho Posturing and Violence in America"

(d.) "Africa and America: Attitudes toward Intimacy"

2. The main idea of this essay is that

a.   African men are more affectionate than American men.

b.   it is more acceptable for women to express affection than men.

c.   African American men are afraid to hold hands because they will be stared at.

(d.) Americans could learn a positive lesson from the African attitude toward intimacy in the family and community.

3. According to the author,

(a.) the African tradition of intimacy has contributed to the survival of the culture.

b.   he felt uncomfortable when the guide continued to hold his hand as they walked through the village.

c.   Spike Lee movies contribute to American society's fear of intimacy.

d.   because children must be tough to survive in a violent society, encouraging them to express affection is a bad idea.

4. If you are unfamiliar with the following words or phrases, use a dictionary to check their meanings: intent (para. 1); unparalleled, prospered (5); kinship, unflinching (7); beset, familial (8); posturing (9).

READ CRITICALLY

1. Why does Batson refer to Spike Lee's *He Got Game*? How does this example support his main point?

2. According to Batson, what is the connection in Africa between holding hands and masculinity? How is this connection different in American society?

3. Why does Batson focus on African American males instead of discussing American males of all races?

4. Does Batson use a point-by-point organization, a whole-to-whole organization, or a combination?

5. Reread Batson's concluding paragraph. What specific phrases or sentences show that he has a larger purpose than merely contrasting two cultures? What do you think Batson's purpose is in writing this essay?

WRITE AN ESSAY

Batson writes that "maybe we can take lessons from overseas." Write an essay about a time you learned something positive from someone from a different cultural background. Compare and contrast a specific aspect of that person's culture with your own. You could write about a certain tradition, practice, or attitude. You might even compare and contrast two cultures' foods, and discuss how you learned to enjoy a new cuisine.

50

Cause and Effect

For more on writing a cause/effect essay, see Chapter 15.

The essays in this chapter explain causes and effects to get their main points across to readers. A cause is what makes something happen; an effect is what happens after an event takes place. Often, writers explain both causes and effects in a single essay, providing clear, logical links between them.

Good cause/effect essays distinguish causes and effects without confusing either of them with events that simply happen before or after other events. These essays offer examples and other evidence to support their points. In addition, they arrange their points in a logical order (usually according to time or importance). Sometimes writers use cause and effect to introduce a topic, but other times they want to persuade the reader that their ideas about cause and effect are correct. As you read these essays, note why and how the writers use cause/effect explanations.

Amy L. Beck

Struggling for Perfection

Amy L. Beck was born in 1979 in Greenwich, Connecticut. After graduating from Harvard University in 2000, Beck joined Teach for America, a program that places recent college graduates in inner-city or rural schools. Beck recently finished her second year of teaching first-graders in the Los Angeles area. She has also worked in France as a researcher for the travel guide *Let's Go* and as an intern with the French Public Health Administration.

In "Struggling for Perfection," which she wrote for the *Harvard Crimson* in 1998, Beck explores eating disorders and domestic abuse. How are these two problems linked? According to Beck, they are both partly caused by media images.

GUIDING QUESTION

How does the title of the essay relate to the cause/effect relationship that Beck writes about?

S‌ex sells. This truth is a boon[1] for marketing gurus and the pornography industry but a rather unfortunate situation for women. Every issue of *Playboy,* every lewd poster, and even the Victoria's Secret catalog transform real women into ornaments, valued exclusively for their outward appearance. These publications are responsible for defining what is sexy and reinforce the belief that aesthetic[2] appeal is a woman's highest virtue.   1

Some argue that the proliferation[3] of pornography and other sexually explicit images of women is both harmless for society and inevitable. Just this point was made in a recent *Crimson* column titled "In Defense of Hooters and the St. Pauli Girl." In the tone of an expert, the author boldly claims that the objectification[4] of women in the media does not affect the way men treat the real women in their lives, nor does it give those with pathological[5] tendencies "the decisive nudge into misogyny."[6] Furthermore, the author says, those women who feel pressure to conform to beauty standards set by the media are suffering from a classic psychosis in which they "confuse fiction with reality."   2

My first reaction was to ask how anyone could possibly believe that the pervasiveness[7] of pornography and sexually explicit depictions of women could fail to have any sort of effect on society. Having spent twelve weeks working in a psychiatric hospital last summer, I am writing from a starkly different perspective.   3

During my first eight weeks at the hospital, I worked on an eating disorder unit in constant contact with anorexics and bulimics. Many patients   4

[1]**boon:** a welcome benefit

[2]**aesthetic:** having to do with beauty

[3]**proliferation:** rapid growth

[4]**objectification:** the treatment of a person as an object

[5]**pathological:** abnormal, diseased

[6]**misogyny:** hatred of women

[7]**pervasiveness:** the extension or spread of one thing throughout something else

"The author made me feel the pain she felt while treating her patients. She made it clear how much women suffer just because they think they have to be perfect."
—*Peggy L. Gamble, student*

on the unit were so emaciated[8] that I could never accustom myself to their appearance; every time I saw them I experienced the same shock. Most had been in and out of countless other hospitals and treatment programs, improving slightly each time but always sliding back into eating-disordered behavior when released.

These people were truly at rock bottom, considered by many to be   5
incurable. Their eating disorders had consumed them entirely, leaving no trace of the vibrant, intelligent people that once inhabited their now skeletal bodies. Certainly, these people also had family problems, alcoholic parents, histories of abuse and clinical depression, to name a few, all of which contribute to feelings of worthlessness and extremely low self-esteem — cited by experts as a major cause of eating disorders. What I find significant, however, is not the root of their problems but that these women (there were a few men, but never more than five percent of the patient population) turned to their bodies as a means of expression and self-healing. Profoundly influenced by the depiction of women by the fashion industry, they had been convinced that the only way to attain love, respect, and personal fulfillment was through a relentless pursuit of physical perfection. Most were perfectly aware that they would never look like a super-model, but it was inconceivable not to try to do so. They found that they were good at dieting and that they were praised and rewarded for their success. And by the time things had gone too far, they had lost all sense of perspective.

Convinced by the media and popular culture to believe that, as women,   6
they should look a certain way and that only if they looked that way would they be loved and respected, they turned to dieting as a means of personal fulfillment and self-definition. While cases as extreme as those I saw at the hospital are rare, many women experience milder but still debilitating[9] forms of eating disorders. They may never get sick enough to require hospitalization, but they nonetheless devote excessive mental and physical energy to diet and exercise, often jeopardizing their health in the process.

For my last four weeks at the hospital I transferred from eating disor-   7
ders to a general psychology unit. The diagnoses varied, but the number of patients with histories of abuse was astounding. After listening to and reading countless case histories, I began to recognize the patterns. In many cases, domestic battering was chronic, occurring weekly or daily whenever the victim broke some sort of household rule, such as serving dinner late or dressing "too sexy." The majority of the sexual abuse victims had been raped by people close to them: relatives, ex-boyfriends, or family friends. In one particularly striking case, a patient's boyfriend made her have sex with five of his friends on a frequent basis.

[8]**emaciated:** extremely thin
[9]**debilitating:** weakening

The men who committed these heinous crimes were rarely pathologi-   8
cal rapists or batterers. Few would even be deemed mentally ill or classi-
cally misogynistic. Rather, they are men who view the real women in their
lives in the same manner that they would view a *Playboy* model, a waitress
at Hooters or a prostitute — as objects that exist solely for their pleasure
and convenience. These men are not genetically predisposed[10] to disre-
spect and abuse women. Their attitudes towards women were societally
conditioned.

Some would argue that pornography did not contribute to these men's   9
behavior towards women. I disagree. Rape and battery are not new problems, and objectification of women by the media reinforces historically
entrenched beliefs that a woman's main reason for existence is procreation
and the sexual pleasure of her mate. Pornographic magazines and lewd
posters reduce women to a commodity[11] that can be purchased and
owned, divorcing the physical manifestation[12] from the person within. The
power of popular culture to affect how we eat, how we dress, and how we
behave is enormous. Conceptions of gender are in no way immune to this
phenomenon.

Certainly some of us are more affected by the media than others. Not   10
all teenage girls develop anorexia, nor do all men who read *Playboy* abuse
their wives. Nonetheless, the prevalence of both eating disorders and various forms of domestic and sexual abuse indicate major societal trends.
The American Anorexia/Bulimia Association reports that 5 percent of
women will develop a full-fledged eating disorder, while 15 percent have
"substantially disordered eating." The Family Violence Prevention Program documents that 4 million American women were battered last year.
And, yes, I am absolutely convinced that the objectification of women by
the media is an integral part of both of these problems, presenting women
with unrealistic role models while encouraging men to think of women
solely in terms of their sexuality.

Women are up against a long history of devaluation and oppression,   11
and, unfortunately, the feminist movements have been only partially successful in purging[13] those legacies. Sexually charged images of women in
the media are not the only cause of this continuing problem, but they certainly play a central role.

[10]**predisposed:** susceptible, inclined to something in advance

[11]**commodity:** a thing of use, value, or advantage

[12]**manifestation:** visible presence, outward show

[13]**purging:** removing something unwanted

SUMMARIZE AND RESPOND

In your reading journal or elsewhere, write a brief summary (three to five sentences) of "Struggling for Perfection." Next, jot down your initial response to the reading. Do you agree or disagree with Beck's points? What else do you think causes eating disorders and domestic abuse?

CHECK YOUR COMPREHENSION

1. Which of the following would be the best alternative title for this essay?

    a. "The Alarming Growth of Eating Disorders"

    b. "The Causes and Effects of Eating Disorders"

    c. "The Media's Influence on Eating Disorders and Domestic Abuse"

    d. "Pressure to Conform"

2. The main idea of this essay is that

    a. media images of women are not the only cause of eating disorders.

    b. publications such as *Playboy* and the Victoria's Secret catalog transform women into sexual objects.

    c. low self-esteem is a major cause of eating disorders.

    d. media images of women contribute to eating disorders and violence against females.

3. According to the author,

    a. women who try to look like supermodels are unable to tell the difference between fiction and reality.

    b. many of the women she met while working in the hospital had backgrounds that included abuse, family problems, and depression.

    c. patients with eating disorders are often incurable.

    d. feminist movements have been very successful in their attempts to lessen the prevalence of eating disorders and abuse against women.

4. If you are unfamiliar with the following words, use a dictionary to check their meanings: gurus, lewd (para. 1); inevitable, psychosis (2); anorexics, bulimics (4); depiction (5); chronic (7); heinous, genetically (8); entrenched, procreation (9); integral (10); devaluation, legacies (11).

READ CRITICALLY

1. Why do you think Beck begins her essay by discussing the column "In Defense of Hooters and the St. Pauli Girl"?

2. Media images of women lead to what two major problems, according to Beck? How are these problems linked?

3. Describe Beck's attitude toward men who commit domestic abuse. What examples from the essay support your response?

4. Does Beck provide clear links between media images of women and the effects of those images? Discuss some of the supporting details she uses to show these links.

5. Beck presents some statistics about eating disorders and domestic abuse. How does she use these statistics to make a further observation about her main point?

WRITE AN ESSAY

Beck acknowledges the fact that sexually charged media images of women are not the only cause of eating disorders and abuse. Write an essay about a different possible cause of one of these problems. You could also choose to write about a similar problem (what causes some men to take steroids, for example). If you addressed other causes of eating disorders and abuse for the Summarize and Respond section above, feel free to use those ideas.

TEACHING TIP
Have students research and write an essay on the effects of media culture on women and/or men, using Beck's essay and Barry's essay (in Chapter 49) as outside sources and starting points for examining their own views.

Robert L. Heilbroner

Don't Let Stereotypes Warp Your Judgments

Robert L. Heilbroner, born in New York City in 1919, earned a B.A. from Harvard University and a Ph.D. from the New School for Social Research. He has taught economics at the latter school since 1972. Heilbroner has written numerous books, several of which have become standard introductions to college economics courses. He has also contributed articles to periodicals including the *New Yorker* and the *New York Review of Books*.

TEACHING TIP
Have students write a
cause/effect essay on
racial profiling, using
Heilbroner's essay as
an outside source and
as a starting point to
examine their own
thinking and determine
their own main point.

In the following essay, which first appeared in *Reader's Digest,*
Heilbroner shows how stereotypes, "a kind of gossip about the world,"
cause people to prejudge others before they even get to know them.

GUIDING QUESTION
What are the causes and the effects of stereotypes?

Is a girl called Gloria apt to be better-looking than one called Bertha? Are   1
criminals more likely to be dark than blond? Can you tell a good deal about
someone's personality from hearing his voice briefly over the phone? Can a
person's nationality be pretty accurately guessed from his photograph?
Does the fact that someone wears glasses imply that he is intelligent?

The answer to all these questions is obviously, "No."   2

Yet, from all the evidence at hand, most of us believe these things. Ask   3
any college boy if he'd rather take his chances with a Gloria or a Bertha,
or ask a college girl if she'd rather blind date a Richard or a Cuthbert. In
fact, you don't have to ask: college students in questionnaires have
revealed that names conjure up the same images in their minds as they do
in yours—and for as little reason.

Look into the favorite suspects of persons who report "suspicious   4
characters" and you will find a large percentage of them to be "swarthy"
or "dark and foreign-looking"—despite the testimony of criminologists
that criminals do *not* tend to be dark, foreign or "wild-eyed." Delve into
the main asset of a telephone stock swindler and you will find it to be a
marvelously confidence-inspiring telephone "personality." And whereas
we all think we know what an Italian or a Swede looks like, it is the sad
fact that when a group of Nebraska students sought to match faces and
nationalities of 15 European countries, they were scored wrong in 93 percent of their identifications. Finally, for all the fact that horn-rimmed
glasses have now become the standard television sign of an "intellectual,"
optometrists know that the main thing that distinguishes people with
glasses is just bad eyes.

Stereotypes are a kind of gossip about the world, a gossip that makes   5
us prejudge people before we ever lay eyes on them. Hence it is not surprising that stereotypes have something to do with the dark world of prejudice. Explore most prejudices (note that the word means prejudgment)
and you will find a cruel stereotype at the core of each one.

For it is the extraordinary fact that once we have typecast[1] the world,   6
we tend to see people in terms of our standardized pictures. In another

---

[1]**typecast:** placed people in oversimplified roles; identified people as belonging to a
certain type

demonstration of the power of stereotypes to affect our vision, a number of Columbia and Barnard students were shown 30 photographs of pretty but unidentified girls, and asked to rate each in terms of "general liking," "intelligence," "beauty" and so on. Two months later, the same group were shown the same photographs, this time with fictitious Irish, Italian, Jewish and "American" names attached to the pictures. Right away the ratings changed. Faces which were now seen as representing a national group went down in looks and still farther down in likability, while the "American" girls suddenly looked decidedly prettier and nicer.

Why is it that we stereotype the world in such irrational and harmful   7
fashion? In part, we begin to typecast people in our childhood years. Early in life, as every parent whose child has watched a TV Western knows, we learn to spot the Good Guys from the Bad Guys. Some years ago, a social psychologist showed very clearly how powerful these stereotypes of childhood vision are. He secretly asked the most popular youngsters in an elementary school to make errors in their morning gym exercises. Afterwards, he asked the class if anyone had noticed any mistakes during gym period. Oh, yes, said the children. But it was the *unpopular* members of the class— the "bad guys"—they remembered as being out of step.

We not only grow up with standardized pictures forming inside of us,   8
but as grown-ups we are constantly having them thrust upon us. Some of them, like the half-joking, half-serious stereotypes of mothers-in-law, or country yokels, or psychiatrists, are dinned into us by the stock jokes we hear and repeat. In fact, without such stereotypes, there would be a lot fewer jokes. Still other stereotypes are perpetuated[2] by the advertisements we read, the movies we see, the books we read.

And finally, we tend to stereotype because it helps us make sense out   9
of a highly confusing world, a world which William James once described as "one great, blooming, buzzing confusion." It is a curious fact that if we don't *know* what we're looking at, we are often quite literally unable to *see* what we're looking at. People who recover their sight after a lifetime of blindness actually cannot at first tell a triangle from a square. A visitor to a factory sees only noisy chaos where the superintendent sees a perfectly synchronized[3] flow of work. As Walter Lippmann has said, "For the most part we do not first see, and then define; we define first, and then we see."

Stereotypes are one way in which we "define" the world in order to see   10
it. They classify the infinite variety of human beings into a convenient handful of "types" towards whom we learn to act in stereotyped fashion. Life would be a wearing process if we had to start from scratch with each and every human contact. Stereotypes economize on our mental effort by covering up the blooming, buzzing confusion with big recognizable cut-

[2]**perpetuated:** prolonged, continued

[3]**synchronized:** organized to operate in unison

outs. They save us the "trouble" of finding out what the world is like—they give it its accustomed look.

Thus the trouble is that stereotypes make us mentally lazy. As S. I. 11 Hayakawa, the authority on semantics,[4] has written: "The danger of stereotypes lies not in their existence, but in the fact that they become for all people some of the time, and for some people all the time, *substitutes for observation*." Worse yet, stereotypes get in the way of our judgment, even when we do observe the world. Someone who has formed rigid preconceptions of all Latins as "excitable," or all teenagers as "wild," doesn't alter his point of view when he meets a calm and deliberate Genoese, or a serious-minded high school student. He brushes them aside as "exceptions that prove the rule." And, of course, if he meets someone true to type, he stands triumphantly vindicated.[5] "They're all like that," he proclaims, having encountered an excited Latin, an ill-behaved adolescent.

Hence, quite aside from the injustice which stereotypes do to others, 12 they impoverish ourselves. A person who lumps the world into simple categories, who typecasts all labor leaders as "racketeers," all businessmen as "reactionaries," all Harvard men as "snobs," and all Frenchmen as "sexy," is in danger of becoming a stereotype himself. He loses his capacity to be himself—which is to say, to see the world in his own absolutely unique, inimitable and independent fashion.

Instead, he votes for the man who fits his standardized picture of what 13 a candidate "should" look like or sound like, buys the goods that someone in his "situation" in life "should" own, lives the life that others define for him. The mark of the stereotype person is that he never surprises us, that we do indeed have him "typed." And no one fits this strait-jacket so perfectly as someone whose opinions about *other people* are fixed and inflexible.

Impoverishing as they are, stereotypes are not easy to get rid of. The 14 world we typecast may be no better than a Grade B movie, but at least we know what to expect of our stock characters. When we let them act for themselves in the strangely unpredictable way that people do act, who knows but that many of our fondest convictions will be proved wrong?

Nor do we suddenly drop our standardized pictures for a blinding 15 vision of the Truth. Sharp swings of ideas about people often just substitute one stereotype for another. The true process of change is a slow one that adds bits and pieces of reality to the pictures in our heads, until gradually they take on some of the blurriness of life itself. Little by little, we learn not that Jews and Negroes and Catholics and Puerto Ricans are "just like everybody else"—for that, too, is a stereotype—but that each and every one of them is unique, special, different and individual. Often we do not even know that we have let a stereotype lapse until we hear someone

[4]**semantics:** the study of meaning in language

[5]**vindicated:** justified, proven right

saying, "all so-and-so's are like such-and-such," and we hear ourselves saying, "Well—maybe."

Can we speed the process along? Of course we can.   16

First, we can become *aware* of the standardized pictures in our heads,   17
in other people's heads, in the world around us.

Second, we can become suspicious of all judgments that we allow   18
exceptions to "prove." There is no more chastening[6] thought than that in
the vast intellectual adventure of science, it takes but one tiny exception to
topple a whole edifice[7] of ideas.

Third, we can learn to be chary[8] of generalizations about people. As   19
F. Scott Fitzgerald once wrote: "Begin with an individual, and before you
know it you have created a type; begin with a type, and you find you have
created—nothing."

Most of the time, when we typecast the world, we are not in fact gen-   20
eralizing about people at all. We are only revealing the embarrassing facts
about the pictures that hang in the gallery of stereotypes in our own heads.

[6]**chastening:** humbling

[7]**edifice:** a large building or an elaborate framework

[8]**chary:** very cautious, wary

SUMMARIZE AND RESPOND

In your reading journal or elsewhere, write a brief summary (three to five
sentences) of "Don't Let Stereotypes Warp Your Judgments." Next, jot
down your initial response to the reading. Did it make you think of a time
when a stereotype caused you to make a quick judgment about someone?
Discuss what happened when you stereotyped someone or when other
people made assumptions about you based on your family background or
on where you live, work, or go to school.

CHECK YOUR COMPREHENSION

1. Which of the following would be the best alternative title for this essay?

    a. "It's All in a Name"

    b. "How Television Creates Stereotypes"

    c. "It's Impossible to Eliminate Stereotypes"

    d. "Stereotypes: How and Why They Affect Our Vision"

2. The main idea of this essay is that

   a. it is part of human nature to stereotype people.

   b. we stereotype people based on their names, voices, or physical appearances.

   c. stereotypes are easy to get rid of.

   d. when we stereotype people, we become mentally lazy, we cloud our judgment, and we lose the ability to see the world through our own unique vision.

3. What is one reason Heilbroner gives to explain why we stereotype people?

   a. Our first impression of a person is generally correct.

   b. We learn to stereotype in childhood.

   c. Stereotypes are sometimes accurate.

   d. Once we form stereotypes, it's impossible to get rid of them.

4. If you are unfamiliar with the following words or phrases, use your dictionary to check their meanings: swarthy, delve (para. 4); standardized (6); irrational (7); dinned (8); preconceptions (11); impoverish, inimitable (12).

READ CRITICALLY

1. In his introduction, Heilbroner asks a series of questions. What purpose do these questions serve? How does he address each question in paragraphs 2–4?

2. According to Heilbroner, what are the three major reasons that we view the world in terms of stereotypes?

3. How does Heilbroner say we can eliminate the habit of stereotyping?

4. What effects of stereotyping does Heilbroner discuss? How do the psychological studies that he mentions help show how stereotypes warp our vision?

5. What key phrase does Heilbroner use throughout the essay to describe stereotypes? (Hint: It appears in paragraphs 6, 8, 13, 15, and 17.) How does he refer back to the key phrase in the essay's last paragraph? Why is this an effective technique to use in the conclusion?

WRITE AN ESSAY

Write an essay about stereotypes of college students. Focus on your own situation: Have you been stereotyped because you are a recent high school graduate, a returning student, or an adult learner? Or perhaps people have made assumptions about you based on the college you attend, your major, or your course load (light versus heavy). Discuss a stereotype you've faced in college and use examples from your experiences to explain the stereotype's causes, effects, or both.

51

Argument

For more on writing an argument essay, see Chapter 16.

The essays in this chapter use argument to get their main point across to readers. Argument takes a strong and definite position on an issue. Energetic from start to finish, good arguments give solid reasons and evidence to support the position. They consider opposing views as well. As you read these essays, note how the writers use reasons and evidence to make their point.

This chapter includes a pro and con essay on each topic so that you can compare and contrast the writers' strategies. As you read the essays in each pair, decide which one you find stronger and why.

Suzanne Sievert

It's Not Just How We Play That Matters

Suzanne Sievert, born in 1962, holds a bachelor's degree in English from the University of Pennsylvania and a master's degree in education from Harvard University. She has spent most of her career as an English teacher and has recently discovered that she especially enjoys teaching English as a Second Language (ESL). Sievert teaches a few hours of ESL classes a week, but devotes most of her time now to "enjoying full-time motherhood." She currently lives in Yarrow Point, Washington, with her husband and two sons.

In "It's Not Just How We Play That Matters," Sievert speaks out against eliminating competition from children's games and contests. When everyone wins, she argues, we send children the wrong message.

GUIDING QUESTION

What does the title of Sievert's essay reveal about her views on competition?

The new trend is games and contests where no child loses. But kids need   1
to learn the lessons of defeat. Last Halloween my five-year-old son entered
a pumpkin-decorating contest at his school. He was so proud of his entry—
a wild combination of carvings, paint, and feathers he had constructed all
by himself with his own kindergartner's sense of art. He lugged it proudly
to the school cafeteria, and we placed it among the other entries, a very
creative bunch of witch pumpkins, snowman pumpkins, scary pumpkins,
even a bubble-gum-blowing, freckle-faced pumpkin wearing a baseball
cap. "Wow," I thought to myself, "the judges are going to have a tough
time choosing a winner."

I guess the judges must have thought the same thing because they   2
didn't choose one. When we returned to the school cafeteria for the annual
fall dinner that evening, we saw that all the pumpkins had been awarded
the same black-and-gold ribbon. My son, eagerly searching to see if he'd
won, kept asking me, "Which pumpkin won? Where's the winner?"

What could I say? "Well, it looks like everyone won. Look: You got a   3
ribbon, honey!"

Kids are smart. That didn't satisfy him. "Yeah, but who *won*?" he asked.   4
I could sense his disappointment and my own disappointment as well.
What's the point of having a contest if you're not going to pick a winner?

I understand what the school was trying to do. The judges meant to   5
send the message that all the children had done a great job and deserved
to be recognized. I worry that a different message was sent, one that said
losing is a hardship that no one should have to go through.

I've noticed this trend a lot lately: adults refusing to let children fail   6
at something. It's as if we grown-ups believe that kids are too fragile to
handle defeat. Last year I purchased a game for my son and his four-year-
old brother that I'd found in a catalog. It was touted[1] as teaching kids to
work together to reach an end goal, with lots of fun problem-solving along
the way. "Great!" I thought, and ordered it right away. The game arrived,
and I played it with my boys. The trouble was that everyone won this
game. We all arrived at the end together. This sounds great in theory, but
where's the incentive[2] to keep playing? We played that game twice, and it
has sat gathering dust ever since.

Without a potential winner, a game or contest loses its excitement. If   7
there's nothing to compete for, the drive to do our best is replaced by a

[1]**touted:** praised or advertised in strongly positive terms

[2]**incentive:** reward or motivation

"What's the point?" attitude. Competition is symbiotic[3] with motivation. It's part of human nature to be competitive; after all, survival of the fittest is the basis of evolution. A competitive spirit is key to our success as adults, so why shouldn't we foster[4] it in our children?

I'm not suggesting we pit our children against each other in fierce   8
competitions in all aspects of life. We should be wary of overzealous coaches who lose the spirit of good sportsmanship in the heat of the game. But in the right situations, a healthy rivalry can teach our kids a lot about life. While games and contests illustrate the importance of drive and determination, they also teach our children how to lose. And with that comes other invaluable lessons—about learning from mistakes, searching for ways to improve, and finding the will to try again.

As a parent, I know the easier route is to keep kids from losing at   9
something rather than to face their frustration when it happens. I'm guilty of purposely letting my boys win at Candyland, and when we occasionally have a race to see who can get dressed first, I sometimes declare, "You're both the winners!" rather than listen to them taunt one another, "Ha ha, you lose. I'm the winner!" But when I do hear those taunts, I try to use them to my advantage. I once said to the loser in a game we were playing, "Well, he may be the winner, but *you* are a good sport." This was a new term for my boys at the time, but when I explained what it meant, my "good sport" was very proud of himself. And the next time we played a game, my other son deliberately lost just so he could be a good sport, too.

Kids can endure failure. My son understood that he might not win the   10
pumpkin contest. He would have been fine if he hadn't gotten a ribbon; he would have tried again next year. The letdown for him was that no winner was chosen at all. I'm certain there were a lot of hopeful entrants who felt unsatisfied when no one walked away with first prize. Too bad my kindergartner wasn't the judge. The following morning he asked me again, "Mommy, who really won the pumpkin contest?"

"They didn't pick one winner," I explained again.   11

"Well, *I* think the snowman won," he said with a nod. And with this he   12
was satisfied.

[3]**symbiotic:** intimately related, mutually dependent

[4]**foster:** nurture, promote the development of

SUMMARIZE AND RESPOND

In your reading journal or elsewhere, write a brief summary (three to five sentences) of "It's Not Just How We Play That Matters." Next, jot down your initial response to the reading. Do you agree or disagree with Sievert's argument? Why?

CHECK YOUR COMPREHENSION

1. Which of the following would be the best alternative title for this essay?

   a. "In Fairness to All"

   b. "New Game Trend Keeps Children from Learning Important Lessons"

   c. "Why Children's Games Are Unfair"

   d. "No Winners, No Losers"

2. The main idea of this essay is that

   a. children have trouble handling failure when they lose a game or contest.

   b. it is difficult to judge a children's contest.

   c. children should be encouraged to develop a competitive spirit.

   d. children benefit from being allowed to win board games.

3. What does Sievert say about competition?

   a. it is important for children to learn how to lose.

   b. adults should occasionally let their children win board games.

   c. contests with winners and losers stifle children's creativity.

   d. children are too fragile to handle defeat.

4. If you are unfamiliar with the following words, use your dictionary to check their meanings: lugged (para. 1); overzealous, invaluable (8); taunts (9).

READ CRITICALLY

1. In paragraph 4, Sievert asks, "What's the point of having a contest if you're not going to pick a winner?" How do you think the organizers of the pumpkin-decorating contest would answer this question? How would Sievert respond?

2. What reasons does Sievert present to support her argument? What type of evidence does she use?

3. How does Sievert handle competition in her family?

4. What does Sievert say will happen if we eliminate competition from children's lives?

5. How does Sievert link the essay's conclusion to its introduction?

WRITE AN ESSAY

Write an essay that argues for or against competition in college or in the workplace. Does a competitive spirit benefit students or employees, or does it harm them? Support your argument with evidence from your personal experience.

Alfie Kohn

The Case against Competition

Alfie Kohn, a writer and speaker on human behavior and education, was born in 1957 in Miami Beach, Florida. After graduating with a B.A. from Brown University and an M.A. from the University of Chicago, Kohn spent several years teaching before devoting himself to writing full-time. Kohn's books, which often challenge conventional methods of teaching and parenting, include *No Contest: The Case against Competition* (1986); *Punished by Rewards: The Trouble with Gold Stars, Incentive Plans, A's, Praise, and Other Bribes* (1993); and *The Case against Standardized Testing: Raising the Scores, Ruining the Schools* (2000).

In the following essay, first published in *Working Mother* magazine in 1987, Kohn presents an argument that opposes Suzanne Sievert's position in "It's Not Just How We Play That Matters." Kohn presents the reasons why, in his view, "the best amount of competition for our children is none at all."

ESL
Discuss how competition is viewed by various cultures. Include definitions of competition as viewed through the differing lenses of race, social class, gender, religion, and age.

GUIDING QUESTION
Why does Kohn favor cooperation over competition?

TEACHING TIP
Ask students to map or outline the essay, noting the thesis, major support points, and supporting details. Does Kohn's argument contain any gaps, redundancies, or shifts in logic?

When it comes to competition, we Americans typically recognize only   1
two legitimate positions: enthusiastic support and qualified support.

The first view holds that the more we immerse our children (and our-   2
selves) in rivalry, the better. Competition builds character and produces excellence. The second stance admits that our society has gotten carried

away with the need to be Number One, that we push our kids too hard and too fast to become winners—but insists that competition can be healthy and fun if we keep it in perspective.

I used to be in the second camp. But after five years of investigating   3
the topic, looking at research from psychology, sociology, education, and other fields, I'm now convinced that neither position is correct. Competition is bad news all right, but it's not just that we overdo it or misapply it. The trouble lies with competition itself. The best amount of competition for our children is none at all, and the very phrase "healthy competition" is actually a contradiction in terms.

That may sound extreme if not downright un-American. But some   4
things aren't just bad because they're done to excess; some things are inherently[1] destructive. Competition, which simply means that one person can succeed only if others fail, is one of those things. It's always unnecessary and inappropriate at school, at play, and at home.

Think for a moment about the goals you have for your children.   5
Chances are you want them to develop healthy self-esteem, to accept themselves as basically good people. You want them to become successful, to achieve the excellence of which they're capable. You want them to have loving and supportive relationships. And you want them to enjoy themselves.

These are fine goals. But competition not only isn't necessary for   6
reaching them—it actually undermines[2] them.

Competition is to self-esteem as sugar is to teeth. Most people lose in   7
most competitive encounters, and it's obvious why that causes self-doubt. But even winning doesn't build character; it just lets a child gloat temporarily. Studies have shown that feelings of self-worth become dependent on external sources of evaluation as a result of competition: Your value is defined by what you've done. Worse—you're a good person in proportion to the number of people you've beaten.

In a competitive culture, a child is told that it isn't enough to be good—   8
he must triumph over others. Success comes to be defined as victory, even though these are really two very different things. Even when the child manages to win, the whole affair, psychologically speaking, becomes a vicious circle: The more he competes, the more he needs to compete to feel good about himself.

When I made this point on the *Phil Donahue Show* last year, my objec-   9
tions were waved aside by the parents of a seven-year-old tennis champion named Kyle, who appeared on the program with me. Kyle had been used to winning ever since a tennis racket was put in his hands at the age of two.

---

[1]**inherently:** fundamentally and permanently, by nature

[2]**undermines:** weakens

But at the very end of the show, someone in the audience asked him how he felt when he lost. Kyle lowered his head and in a small voice replied, "Ashamed."

This is not to say that children shouldn't learn discipline and tenac- 10
ity,[3] that they shouldn't be encouraged to succeed or even have a nodding acquaintance with failure. But none of these requires winning and losing — that is, having to beat other children and worry about being beaten. When classrooms and playing fields are based on cooperation rather than competition, children feel better about themselves. They work with others instead of against them, and their self-esteem doesn't depend on winning a spelling bee or a Little League game.

Children succeed in spite of competition, not because of it. Most of us 11
were raised to believe that we do our best work when we're in a race — that without competition we would all become fat, lazy, and mediocre.[4] It's a belief that our society takes on faith. It's also false.

There is good evidence that productivity in the workplace suffers as a 12
result of competition. The research is even more compelling in classroom settings. David Johnson, a professor of social psychology at the University of Minnesota, and his colleagues reviewed all the studies they could find on the subject from 1924 to 1980. Sixty-five of the studies found that children learn better when they work cooperatively as opposed to competitively, eight found the reverse, and thirty-six found no significant difference. The more complex the learning task, the worse children in a competitive environment fared.

Brandeis University psychologist Teresa Amabile was more interested 13
in creativity. She asked twenty-two girls, ages seven to eleven, to make "silly collages." Some competed for prizes and some didn't. Seven artists then independently rated the girls' work. It turned out that the children who were trying to win produced collages that were much less creative — less spontaneous, complex, and varied — than the others.

One after another, researchers across the country have concluded that 14
children do not learn better when education is transformed into a competitive struggle. Why? First, competition often makes kids anxious and that interferes with concentration. Second, competition doesn't permit them to share their talents and resources as cooperation does, so they can't learn from one another. Finally, trying to be Number One distracts them from what they're supposed to be learning. It may seem paradoxical,[5] but when a student concentrates on the reward (an A or a gold star or a trophy), she becomes less interested in what she's doing. The result: Performance declines.

[3]**tenacity:** persistence, the ability to pursue a goal despite obstacles

[4]**mediocre:** moderate to inferior in quality, ordinary

[5]**paradoxical:** seemingly contradictory, contrary to common sense but perhaps true

Just because forcing children to try to outdo one another is counter- 15
productive doesn't mean they can't keep track of how they're doing.
There's no problem with comparing their achievements to an objective
standard (how fast they ran, how many questions they got right) or to how
they did yesterday or last year. But any mother who values intellectual
development for her child should realize that turning learning into a race
simply doesn't work.

Competition is a recipe for hostility. By definition, not everyone can 16
win a contest. If one child wins, another cannot. This means that each
child inevitably comes to regard others as obstacles to his or her own success. Forget fractions or home runs; this is the real lesson our children
learn in a competitive environment.

Competition leads children to envy winners, to dismiss losers (there's 17
no nastier epithet[6] in our language than "Loser!"), and to be suspicious of
just about everyone. Competition makes it difficult to regard others as
potential friends or collaborators; even if you're not my rival today, you
could be tomorrow.

This is not to say that competitors will always detest each other. But 18
trying to outdo someone is not conducive[7] to trust — indeed, it would be
irrational to trust someone who gains from your failure. At best, competition leads one to look at others through narrowed eyes; at worst, it invites
outright aggression. Existing relationships are strained to the breaking
point, while new friendships are often nipped in the bud.

Again, the research helps to explain the destructive effect of win/lose 19
arrangements. When children compete, they are less able to take the perspective of others — that is, to see the world from someone else's point of
view. One study demonstrated conclusively that competitive children were
less empathetic[8] than others; another study showed that competitive children were less generous.

Cooperation, on the other hand, is marvelously successful at helping 20
children to communicate effectively, to trust in others and to accept those
who are different from themselves. Competition interferes with these goals
and often results in outright antisocial behavior. The choice is ours: We can
blame the individual children who cheat, turn violent or withdraw, or we
can face the fact that competition itself is responsible for such ugliness.

Studies also show, incidentally, that competition among groups isn't 21
any better than competition among individuals. Kids don't have to work
against a common enemy in order to know the joys of camaraderie[9] or to

[6]**epithet:** a word or phrase (often negative) used to characterize a person or thing

[7]**conducive:** helpful or beneficial

[8]**empathetic:** understanding of another's feelings, situation, or motives

[9]**camaraderie:** comradeship, good fellowship among friends

experience success. Real cooperation doesn't require triumphing over another group.

Having fun doesn't mean turning playing fields into battlefields. It's remarkable, when you stop to think about it, that the way we teach our kids to have a good time is to play highly structured games in which one individual or team must defeat another. 22

Consider one of the first games our children learn to play: musical chairs. Take away one chair and one child in each round until one smug winner is seated and everyone else has been excluded from play. You know that sour birthday party scene; the needle is lifted from the record and someone else is transformed into a loser, forced to sit out the rest of the game with the other unhappy kids on the side. That's how children learn to have fun in America. 23

Terry Orlick, a Canadian expert on games, suggests changing the goal of musical chairs so children are asked to fit on a diminishing number of seats. At the end, seven or eight giggling, happy kids are trying to squish on a single chair. Everyone has fun and there are no winners or losers. 24

What's true of musical chairs is true of all recreation; with a little ingenuity, we can devise games in which the obstacle is something intrinsic[10] to the task itself rather than another person or team. 25

In fact, not one of the benefits attributed to sports or other competitive games actually requires competition. Children can get plenty of exercise without struggling against each other. Teamwork? Cooperative games allow everyone to work together, without creating enemies. Improving skills and setting challenges? Again, an objective standard or one's own earlier performance will do. 26

When Orlick taught a group of children noncompetitive games, two-thirds of the boys and all of the girls preferred them to games that require opponents. If our culture's idea of a good time is competition, it may just be because we haven't tried the alternative. 27

How can parents raise a noncompetitive child in a competitive world? Competition is actually destructive to children's self-esteem. It interferes with learning, sabotages relationships, and isn't necessary for a good time. But how do you raise a child in a culture that hasn't yet caught on to this? 28

There are no easy answers here. But there is one clearly unsatisfactory answer: Make your son or daughter competitive in order to fit into the "real world." That isn't desirable for the child—for all the reasons given here—and it perpetuates[11] the poison of competition in another generation. 29

Children can be taught about competition, prepared for the destructive forces they'll encounter, without being groomed to take part in it 30

---

[10]**intrinsic:** built-in, existing already as a characteristic

[11]**perpetuates:** prolongs the existence of

uncritically. They can be exposed to the case against competition just as they are taught the harms of drug abuse or reckless driving.

You will have to decide how much compromise is appropriate so your   31
child isn't left out or ridiculed in a competitive society. But at least you can make your decision based on knowledge about competition's destructiveness. You can work with other parents and with your child's teachers and coaches to help change the structures that set children against one another. Or you may want to look into cooperative schools and summer camps, which are beginning to catch on around the country.

As for reducing rivalry and competitive attitudes in the home: 32

- Avoid comparing a child's performance to that of a sibling, a classmate, or yourself as a child.

- Don't use contests ("Who can dry the dishes fastest?") around the house. Watch your use of language ("Who's the best little girl in the whole wide world?") that reinforces competitive attitudes.

- Never make your love or acceptance conditional on a child's performance. Some parents give subtle messages; they may say to their child, "As long as you did your best...," but Bobby knows that Mommy really likes him better when he wins. Nothing is more psychologically destructive than making approval dependent on victory.

- Be aware of your power as a model. If you need to beat others, your child will learn that from you regardless of what you say. The lesson will be even stronger if you use your child to provide you with vicarious[12] victories.

Raising healthy, happy, productive children goes hand in hand with   33
creating a better society. The first step to achieving both is recognizing that our belief in the value of competition is built on myths. There are better ways for our children — and for us — to work and play and live.

[12]**vicarious:** felt as if one were taking part in the experiences of another

▨ SUMMARIZE AND RESPOND

In your reading journal or elsewhere, write a brief summary (three to five sentences) of "The Case against Competition." Next, jot down your initial response to the reading. Do you agree with Kohn's argument, or do you think his position is too extreme? Why?

■ **CHECK YOUR COMPREHENSION**

1. Which of the following would be the best alternative title for this essay?

   a. "Why Games Damage Children's Self-Esteem"

   b. "Too Much Too Soon"

   c. "The Vicious Circle"

   d. "Healthy Competition: A Contradiction in Terms"

2. The main idea of this essay is that

   a. competition strengthens the character only of children who win.

   b. competition among children is destructive.

   c. competition can benefit children if we keep it in perspective.

   d. competition is an important part of American society.

3. What does the author say about the link between competition and learning?

   a. Children learn more quickly when they work in groups.

   b. Competition distracts children from what they should be learning.

   c. Rewards encourage children to learn difficult material.

   d. Competition helps children become more interested in learning.

4. If you are unfamiliar with these words or phrases, use your dictionary to check their meanings: immerse, stance (para. 2); gloat, proportion (7); counterproductive (15); irrational (18); smug (23); ingenuity (25); sabotages (28).

■ **READ CRITICALLY**

1. What three major reasons does Kohn give in support of his position? Discuss the types of evidence (facts and statistics, examples, and expert opinions) he uses to back up his points.

2. In paragraph 7 Kohn writes, "Competition is to self-esteem as sugar is to teeth." What does he mean by this statement, and what examples does he use to support this position?

3. Why does Kohn mention his appearance on the *Phil Donahue Show*? How does this detail support his argument?

4. Where in the essay does Kohn acknowledge opposing views? How does he address these opposing positions?

5. Is Kohn's conclusion effective? Why or why not? What suggestions does he make about raising noncompetitive children?

◼ WRITE AN ESSAY

Write an essay that argues for or against children's participation in organized sports programs. Do you think that playing an organized sport, such as Little League baseball, benefits children? Or is it better for children to participate only in noncompetitive sports and games? Remember to consider your opponents' views and provide evidence that supports your position.

Tom Magliozzi and Ray Magliozzi
Protecting Its People: Let Our Government Do Its Job

Better known by their on-air names Click and Clack, Tom Magliozzi and Ray Magliozzi are the hosts of the National Public Radio show *Car Talk.* Once a week, more than 2.3 million listeners tune in as the brothers give humorous advice on car repairs. They also write a weekly newspaper column and have published two books.

Born and raised in East Cambridge, Massachusetts, Tom and Ray both studied at the Massachusetts Institute of Technology. After graduation, they opened their own garage, which Ray continues to operate. Aside from their work as Click and Clack, Tom is also a marketing consultant and Ray has taught adult education automotive courses.

Tom and Ray are currently in charge of "Drive Now, Talk Later," a national campaign to ban cell-phone use while driving. In "Protecting Its People: Let Our Government Do Its Job," which first appeared in slightly different form in a 2001 issue of the *San Jose Mercury News,* Tom and Ray argue for legislation to regulate cell-phone use in cars. They directly respond to the argument Robert W. Hahn and Paul C. Tetlock present in "Driving and Talking Do Mix," which follows this selection.

GUIDING QUESTION
According to the authors, why do we need laws to regulate cell-phone use in cars?

I t's "premature to push for federal legislation" to ban cell-phone use while driving. That's according to Robert Shelton, executive director of the National Highway Traffic Safety Administration, in congressional testimony this spring. To that, we respond with a hearty, "Oh, bullfeathers, Robert!"

Was it premature to push for seat belts in the 1950s? And premature to try to crack down on drinking and driving in the 1980s? Of course not. It was courageous. We guess it's premature for Shelton, the nation's top highway-safety official, to summon up his courage.

But if courage was in short supply at the congressional hearings on driver distraction, hyperbole[1] sure wasn't. According to the cell-phone industry's top lobbyist, Tom Wheeler, "the wireless phone is the greatest safety tool since the development of 911." That self-serving piece of prattle is like saying the twist-off bottle cap cuts down on accidents because drivers don't have to fiddle with openers while changing lanes.

Driving while talking on cell phones is causing accidents, not preventing them.

A short drive around any city or town provides more than enough evidence for most of us that cell-phone use and other forms of driver distraction are threatening the safety of anyone who ventures[2] on or near our roads.

Don't take our word for it. Talk to the relatives and friends of Gregory Davis, Leona Greif, Marcia Nathans, Richard McKeefery, or two-year-old Morgan Pena. Each died at the hands of a driver who was chatting on the phone while steering thousands of pounds of deadly steel.

The list of victims grows ever longer. Supermodel Niki Taylor — the twenty-six-year-old mother of six-year-old twin boys — had the misfortune of being added to the list of the injured last month when the driver of the car she was in leaned down to answer his phone. He plowed into a telephone pole, critically injuring Taylor.

But guys like Robert Hahn at the American Enterprise Institute tell us that the benefits of cell phones far outweigh their costs. And people refer to this organization as a think tank?[3] Listen to their logic and see what you think.

Just what are these benefits that the American Enterprise Institute thinks outweigh accidents and deaths? In a 1999 opinion piece he wrote for the *New York Times,* Hahn said one benefit was the ability to summon help on a lonely highway. But aren't we a little short on logic here? How would a ban on cell-phone use while driving prevent one from using the

[1]**hyperbole:** obvious and intentional exaggeration

[2]**ventures:** takes a risk, braves the dangers of

[3]**think tank:** an institution that researches and reports on social problems

phone from the breakdown lane? Another of the benefits, according to Hahn: the convenience of being able to remind your spouse of your daughter's school play.

Exactly what price do economists plug into their nice, clean economic   10
models to account for the misery and tears that such outright selfishness has wrought? In his *Times* piece, Hahn estimated that cell-phone use in cars that year would cause 10,000 serious accidents, leading to 100 fatalities.

As calls to ban cell-phone use in cars increase, the cell-phone industry   11
is using the innovative[4] delaying tactic of calling for more study. But most driver-distraction research is hopelessly flawed.

Take the recently publicized study by the AAA Foundation for Traffic   12
Safety. The AAA used data that relied in good part on postaccident interviews with drivers. Find us one person who will freely admit that he was stupid enough to be talking to his broker or ordering Chinese food instead of paying attention to the road. The AAA found very few. Big surprise.

It's human nature: You can't count on people to tell you if they've done   13
something stupid. The only study we've seen that didn't make this mistake was published in the *New England Journal of Medicine* more than four years ago. Researchers checked actual phone records. Their findings are well known: Drivers are four times as likely to crash when talking on a phone— about the same chances as a legally drunk driver has—and three times as likely when talking on a "hands-free" phone.

Some cell-phone companies are in favor of a hands-free law. (Now   14
there's a coincidence. Taking this stand gives them a chance to sell new phones to millions of customers.) Some legislators see the hands-free option as a compromise. It's not a compromise. It's a cop-out. When you're talking on a cell phone, it's the brain that's distracted, not the hands.

The cell-phone lobbyists will tell you that using a hands-free phone is   15
the same as talking to a passenger, but it's not. We're not psychologists, but it's clear that talking on the phone while driving somehow drags you away from the here and now. It may have something to do with visualizing the person you're talking to. Drivers talking to a passenger do not stray from lane to lane; cell-phone users do.

Do we trust all drivers to know when enough alcohol is enough? Of   16
course not. Laws are necessary, since we can't trust everybody's judgment.

Our suggestion is that any proposed legislation focus on distraction;   17
that is, the bills should ban any behavior that dangerously distracts a driver's attention. The ban should include talking on cell phones of all kinds, hands-free or not. And to answer the critics who say, "What about other distractions?" the ban should also cover surfing the Web while driving (it's coming); blow-drying one's hair while driving (we've seen it); and build-

[4]**innovative:** creative

ing a model airplane out of balsa wood while driving (just anticipating the next trend).

If we don't take a stand soon on what gadgets ought to be in cars, we will be confronted with distractions beyond our wildest dreams. The automotive and electronics industries have plans for devices in cars that will be far more distracting than cell phones, including built-in computers that can call up e-mail and stock quotes.   18

We can't trust the automotive industry to show any good judgment here, because it has not shown good judgment about design in the past. A classic example is the trend to offer luxury-car buyers touch-sensitive screens to replace all the controls for radios, tape and CD players, and heating and cooling. These devices display myriad[5] controls on a flat screen. Want to adjust the temperature? No problem. Just stare at the screen until you find the right menu selection. Make your choice. Then, on the next screen, adjust the temperature. Bingo, you're done. Too bad you had your eyes off the road for 10 seconds. Now call the wrecker.   19

None of us wants Big Brother controlling what we do, but we must acknowledge that the cell-phone industry's primary interest is increasing sales and, especially, usage of their phones. Our government's primary charge is protecting the well-being of its citizens, not ensuring the future profits of an industry at the expense of injuries and lives.   20

We must insist that our government step in to ensure basic protection for those of us who need to use the roads and sidewalks. We hope that legislators will have the courage not to cave in to the powerful cell-phone lobbyists and to prove to us that the needs of the people who voted them into office far outweigh those of private interests.   21

It's sad to think that our fate—and maybe our lives—is in the hands of politicians, but let's hope they have the guts to do what's right. It's our hope that every newspaper in the country will publish the results in every state where legislation is voted on. We want to know whom to vote for next time.   22

[5]**myriad:** a very large number of

■ SUMMARIZE AND RESPOND

In your reading journal or elsewhere, write a brief summary (three to five sentences) of "Protecting Its People: Let Our Government Do Its Job." Next, jot down your initial response to this reading. Are you familiar with the "Car Talk" program on National Public Radio? Do you agree with the authors' argument? Why, or why not? If you have ever used a cell phone while driving, how did the essay make you feel?

■ **CHECK YOUR COMPREHENSION**

1. Which of the following would be the best alternative title for this essay?

   a. "Car Phones: Annoying but Necessary"

   (b.) "Drive Now, Talk Later: Why the Government Should Regulate Cell-Phone Use"

   c. "The Government Should Mind Its Own Business"

   d. "Phone Industry Tactics"

2. The main idea of this essay is that

   a. the benefits of cell phones outweigh their problems.

   b. it is too early to push for federal legislation that would regulate car-phone use.

   c. in the future, there will be devices in cars that are even more distracting than cell phones.

   (d.) the government should ban all cell-phone use by drivers.

3. According to the authors,

   (a.) driver-distraction studies are often flawed.

   b. driving while talking on cell phones is sometimes justified.

   c. a touch-sensitive screen that controls a car's radio and air is less distracting than traditional control knobs.

   d. using a hands-free phone is less dangerous than having a conversation while driving.

4. If you are unfamiliar with the following words or phrases, use a dictionary to check their meanings: premature (para. 1); prattle (3).

■ **READ CRITICALLY**

1. How do the authors support their argument by acknowledging opposing views? What weakness do they see in points made by the opposing position?

2. Describe the tone of this essay. Find specific sentences or passages that support your description.

3. According to the authors, how is the cell-phone industry responding to the push for the government to regulate car-phone use? How do the authors feel about the industry's response?

4. What do the authors say will happen if we don't push for legislation banning *all* behavior that dangerously distracts a driver? What examples do they use to make their point?

5. What are the authors' attitudes toward congressional legislators and the cell-phone industry? What examples in the essay support your answer?

WRITE AN ESSAY

Write an essay that argues for some ban or requirement that would promote citizens' health, safety, or welfare. Instead of tackling an issue that is frequently debated, consider a small, specific change or a local issue.

Robert W. Hahn and Paul C. Tetlock
Driving and Talking Do Mix

Robert W. Hahn is the director of the AEI-Brookings Joint Center for Regulatory Studies, a group that evaluates governmental regulations based on their economic effects. Hahn, who holds a Ph.D. in economics from the California Institute of Technology, has published several books on regulatory issues. He has also written articles for publications including the *New York Times* and the *Wall Street Journal.*

Paul Tetlock is currently studying economics at Harvard University, where he expects to complete his Ph.D. in 2003. He cowrote "Driving and Talking Do Mix" while working at the AEI-Brookings Joint Center as a research assistant.

In the following essay, which first appeared in a 1999 issue of *Policy Matters,* Hahn and Tetlock argue against legislation that bans the use of cell phones while driving. To support their argument, the authors summarize the controversial findings of their study on the benefits and costs of car-phone use. The study sparked many angry responses, including Tom Magliozzi and Ray Magliozzi's essay "Protecting Its People: Let Our Government Do Its Job."

GUIDING QUESTION

What parts of the authors' argument are convincing to you, and what parts are not particularly effective?

Check out that guy in the next lane—the one with the cell phone glued   1
to his ear, who's weaving wildly. Wow, that was close. So close that Ann
Landers just came out in support of a ban on driving and phoning. And
Click and Clack, the car guys, are giving away bumper stickers that say
"Drive Now, Talk Later."

Legislators are listening. From Victoria, Australia, to Brooklyn, Ohio,   2
total bans on cell-phone calls by drivers have been enacted.[1] England,
Australia, Singapore, and Brazil all restrict the use of car phones to the
hands-free type. And New York City bars cell-phone calls by taxi drivers
(ferrrgetaboutit . . .).

But does a ban make sense? At first blush, it seems a no-brainer if cell   3
phones are indeed causing fatal accidents. But lots of activities—tuning
the radio, drinking double lattes, refereeing the sibling wars in the back
seat—can lead to fatal crashes. No one is banning these, though all told
government numbers suggest that such mundane[2] distractions contribute
to some 4,000 deadly accidents annually. Society chooses not to regulate
where we slurp our Starbucks, at least in part because the social benefits
of regulation may not exceed the costs.

We took a hard look at what society loses from car-phone use—along   4
with what it gains. And while in-car phoning does increase risk, the benefits far outweigh the costs. Moreover, our calculations are conservative
because we did not include the value of using cell phones to report accidents or to alert police to crimes in progress.

Start with the likely costs of not being able to conduct business from   5
the car, or to call home on the fly to find out whether junior's already seen
the Tarzan video. We estimate these costs in lost time and productivity at
about $24 billion—over $200 per household annually.

The benefits of a ban, of course, would include the decrease in   6
injuries, property damage, and fatalities linked to cell-phone use. Our best
estimate is about 10,000 serious accidents and 100 traffic fatalities—less
than one percent of the annual total. Putting a dollar value on these deaths
and injuries is difficult, even for us bloodless economists. But everyone
takes chances in daily life. And using standard measures of how ordinary
people make the trade-off between convenience and small risks of large
disasters, we estimate the cost of car-phone-induced mayhem at about $1
billion annually.

Fiddling with our assumptions—reducing the estimated benefits of   7
car calls, raising the implicit[3] value of lives saved—doesn't change the bottom line. Nor, for that matter, does assuming that cell-phone use is actually as dangerous as driving after drinking a few beers. Thus, on balance,
the safety purchased with a cell-phone ban would simply be too expensive.

---

[1]**enacted:** made into law

[2]**mundane:** ordinary, common

[3]**implicit:** implied or understood, although not stated directly

TEACHING TIP
Have students visit the AEI-Brookings Joint Center for Regulatory Studies Web site at <**www.aei-brookings.org**> and follow some of the links posted there. Then have them write a journal entry comparing and contrasting some of the other articles on the Web site to "Driving and Talking Do Mix."

OK, so a ban does not make sense. But what about requiring drivers   8
to pull off to the side of the road if they want to make calls? As a practical matter, that would come pretty close to a ban. But with a perverse twist: If drivers aren't careful, they could actually cause more accidents this way than they prevent.

The required use of hands-free devices, such as headsets, is a harder call.   9
But we don't know much about the effectiveness of hands-free devices. Some studies say they would have no impact on accidents, while others suggest the reductions could be sizable. Until we know more, it seems imprudent[4] to call for a multibillion-dollar expenditure that may yield little benefit.

Washington and the states should be working hard to find out what   10
really makes a material difference in the safety of on-board calling. But until we know more, governments should let the 77 million Americans who own cellular phones make their own decisions about when and where to use them. The market, in the form of consumers, producers, and insurers, is doing pretty well in developing a technology that Americans are finding they can't live without.

[4]**imprudent:** unwise, not good judgment

SUMMARIZE AND RESPOND

In your reading journal or elsewhere, write a brief summary (three to five sentences) of "Driving and Talking Do Mix." Next, jot down your initial response to the reading. Before reading this essay, what was your position on the use of cell phones while driving? Did this essay support your opinion, or did it make you rethink your position?

CHECK YOUR COMPREHENSION

1. Which of the following would be the best alternative title for this essay?
   a. "Car Phones: More Helpful Than Harmful"
   b. "Multitasking on the Road"
   c. "Keeping It in Perspective"
   d. "Why It's Safe to Drive and Talk"

2. The main idea of this essay is that
   a. cell phones are not responsible for automobile accidents.
   b. banning cell-phone use in cars would not result in fewer accidents.
   c. the benefits of using a car phone outweigh the risks.
   d. cell phones are a vital aid to report car accidents and crimes.

3. According to the author,

   a. more studies should be conducted before the government regulates our use of car phones.

   b. a ban on cell-phone use while driving would have a significant impact on traffic fatality statistics.

   c. hands-free devices lessen the risk of accidents caused by cell phones.

   d. the government should require drivers to pull off the road to use cell phones.

4. If you are unfamiliar with the following words, use a dictionary to check their meanings: mayhem (para. 6); imprudent (9).

READ CRITICALLY

1. In paragraph 7, the authors say that "the safety purchased with a cell-phone ban would simply be too expensive." What do they mean by this, and how do they support this claim?

2. The authors acknowledge that cell phones might indeed cause car accidents. Does this fact undermine their argument, or do they use it to support their position?

3. Describe the authors' tone. Based on their tone and on the reasons they use to support their argument, what can you infer about the way they approach problems in society?

4. According to the authors, the benefits of using cell phones while driving outweigh the risks. What examples do they provide to illustrate the benefits of car-phone use? What other examples would support their point?

5. What do you think are the authors' attitudes toward issues involving civil liberties or fundamental individual rights that are protected from governmental interference? Why?

WRITE AN ESSAY

Write an essay that responds to Hahn and Tetlock, either by adding more points to their argument or by challenging it. You may use ideas you developed for the Summarize and Respond exercise above.

Appendix A

How to Write Email and Memos

Understand and Write Email

DEFINITION: **Email**, the term used for electronic mail, is a form of written communication sent over a computer network. It is fast, and it is not time-dependent: You can send an email anytime, and the recipient can read it anytime. Like any other form of written communication, however, email requires following certain conventions. You might use email to communicate in all sorts of ways, as shown in the following examples.

COLLEGE

- You are assigned a group project, and you and other members of the group communicate by email rather than always having to get together at the same time in the same place.

WORK

- You send a group message to your coworkers by email rather than printing it out, copying it, and distributing it.

EVERYDAY LIFE

- You have a friend or family member who lives far away, and you keep in touch by email.

AUDIENCE: When you are writing an email message, consider your audience and your purpose just as you do when you are writing a paragraph or an essay. People often think of email as very informal, and if you are communicating with a friend or family member for personal reasons, an informal, chatty tone is certainly appropriate. But when you are writing an email that will go out to your instructor, other students, or anyone at work, it should be more formal.

PURPOSE: If you are writing an email to family or friends, your purpose is probably to stay in touch, and you don't need to think too much about it. Be careful, though, about what you say and how you say it. Unlike speech, email is a written document. The recipient can't see your facial expressions or hear your tone of voice. Before sending even an informal email, read it over to make sure that it serves your purpose and doesn't include anything that could be misinterpreted.

If you are writing a formal email, decide what your purpose is before you write. State your purpose clearly at the beginning of the message so that your readers know why you are writing and what they should be looking for. A formal email should have a clear topic and related points just as any other piece of formal writing does.

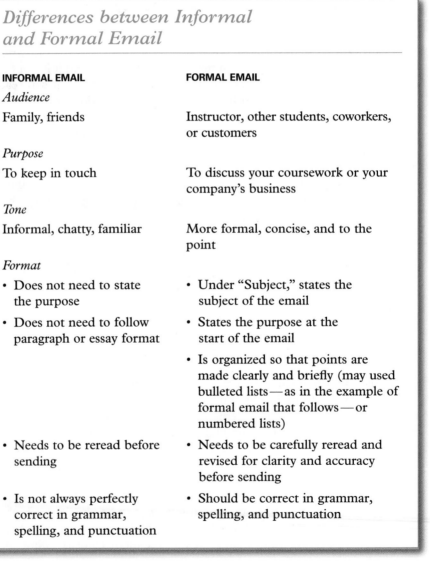

Differences between Informal and Formal Email

INFORMAL EMAIL	FORMAL EMAIL
Audience	
Family, friends	Instructor, other students, coworkers, or customers
Purpose	
To keep in touch	To discuss your coursework or your company's business
Tone	
Informal, chatty, familiar	More formal, concise, and to the point
Format	
• Does not need to state the purpose	• Under "Subject," states the subject of the email
• Does not need to follow paragraph or essay format	• States the purpose at the start of the email
	• Is organized so that points are made clearly and briefly (may used bulleted lists—as in the example of formal email that follows—or numbered lists)
• Needs to be reread before sending	• Needs to be carefully reread and revised for clarity and accuracy before sending
• Is not always perfectly correct in grammar, spelling, and punctuation	• Should be correct in grammar, spelling, and punctuation

EXAMPLE: INFORMAL EMAIL TO A FRIEND

From: Isabel DeSimone
Sent: Thu 10/2/03 9:48 AM
To: Lynn Vargas
Subject: Need a vacation

Hi,
       This week is like never-ending! I just finished a huge data entry project, and my manager handed me this new top-priority research thing two minutes ago. Does she expect me to finish this before I leave for my vacation? Maybe she's forgotten. I sure haven't, though. I can't wait to get on that plane and leave phones, email, filing, and faxing behind for one blessed week! What's going on with you?

EXAMPLE: FORMAL EMAIL TO A MANAGER

From: Robert Sullivan
Sent: Thu 10/2/03 1:52 PM
To: Will Stepney
Subject: Visit to competing test lab ——————————— States topic

Mr. Stepney: ————————————— Formal, businesslike
       My more formal report will follow, but here are my quick
impressions based on a visit to Front Range Testing Services, —— States purpose of
Inc., a new key player in product safety testing: email

- Ample product testing support for manufacturers and distributors of goods to Europe, Canada, and Mexico; no support for South America.
- The Boulder facility has two 3-meter indoor open area test —— Uses a bulleted list to present points briefly sites; one 10-meter indoor open area test site; and three RF Shielded Rooms. All seem to be in good condition.
- The Estes Park facility has an acoustical sound room and two brand-new environmental chambers.
- Rates are high—especially for testing performed at the Estes Park facility.

My complete report, which I will submit to you next week, will —— Has a conclusion
make recommendations for competing against Front Range
and other labs.

Thank you.

Robert Sullivan

■   **PRACTICE 1   WRITING EMAILS FOR DIFFERENT AUDIENCES**

For each of the following topics, write two different emails to the two audiences indicated. Put each email on a separate piece of paper or in a separate computer file. Keep all of the emails brief. Use the list on page 720 to help you.

1. **TOPIC:** A difficult customer

   INFORMAL AUDIENCE: A friend

   FORMAL AUDIENCE: A boss

2. **TOPIC:** Two days without heat in your apartment

   INFORMAL AUDIENCE: A friend

   FORMAL AUDIENCE: Your landlord

SOME CAUTIONS ABOUT EMAIL
- Avoid emailing friends from work. Most companies regard personal use of email in the same way that they regard personal phone calls.
- Do not put anything in an email that you would not want to be seen by anyone else. Deleting an email does not make it disappear altogether, and others may have access to it.
- If you communicate an important message via email, send a hard copy to your reader as well. Also make a file copy. Too often people forget to print out copies of email communications and don't have the information available in their files.
- Do not use email to replace face-to-face or phone communications. Although email is efficient and valuable, it can isolate people from personal contact with customers, coworkers, and even friends and family.

Understand and Write Memos

DEFINITION: Memos are a very common form of internal written communication in the workplace, and you will almost certainly need to know how to write them. Because people at work are busy, effective memos provide accurate information that they can quickly read and understand.

Memos are similar to formal emails. When you have a message to communicate, your choice of either a memo or a formal email will depend on your individual situation. When you write and send a memo, make a file copy of it.

SEVEN BASICS OF A GOOD MEMO

1. It has a businesslike tone: courteous but to the point.
2. It uses the fewest words possible to convey the necessary information to the particular reader(s).
3. It states the purpose clearly.
4. It allows readers to find points of information easily.
5. It presents points in a logical order.
6. It follows standard memo format.
7. It is correct in grammar, spelling, and punctuation.

AUDIENCE: Because memos are used most commonly in the workplace, keeping your audience in mind is essential. Give the information that the reader or group of readers needs, and express it in terms that they will understand. Otherwise, you may be misunderstood, and your memo could result in errors that affect you and your fellow workers.

PURPOSE: Know exactly what your purpose is when you write a memo, and make that purpose clear to your readers from the start. You should also know what information you need to include to fulfill that purpose.

FORMAT: All memos should include the following information, usually in this order. Many companies have preprinted memo forms, and many word-processing programs have a memo-format feature.

Date:
To:
From:
Subject:
cc: (people to whom you are sending copies of the memo)

Depending on their purpose, some memos may be very brief, as in the following example.

Date: June 15, 2003
To: Tamara Shue
From: Susan Anker
Subject: Vacation time
cc: M. Weiser, Human Resources

I would like to take five days of vacation from 7/31/03–8/4/03.
Thank you for your consideration.

Memos can also be longer, but they should be no longer than it takes you to convey necessary information. As with emails, memos often make use of bulleted lists to highlight main points.

MEMORANDUM
Date: October 30, 2003
To: All sales associates
From: Karen Eisenhauer
Subject: Change in employee benefits

Effective January 1, 2004, all full-time sales associates will be eligible for tuition reimbursement benefits. The company recognizes that when comparable training is not available at the corporate training center, employees miss out on advancement opportunities. The company has established a policy with the aim of retaining valuable long-term employees. Brief details of the plan are as follows:

- "Full-time" is considered twenty-eight or more hours in a week.
- Employees are eligible to be reimbursed up to $75 per credit hour.
- Employees are eligible to be reimbursed only for those courses in which they earned a "Pass" grade (Pass/Fail) or "C" or better in a graded course.

I will describe the benefits in greater detail at our regularly scheduled staff meeting next Tuesday, November 4.

PRACTICE 2   WRITING MEMOS

On separate pieces of paper, or in separate computer files, write memos on the following topics. Use the list on page 723 to help you.

1. **TOPIC:** Announcement of a company holiday

   AUDIENCE: Employees

2. **TOPIC:** Process for evacuating the building when the fire alarm sounds

   AUDIENCE: People in this classroom

Appendix B

How to Write a Résumé and a
Letter of Application

DEFINITION: A **résumé** presents your experience and skills in brief written form. When you apply for a job, you should have an up-to-date résumé that you can send to a prospective employer or carry with you to an interview. Because the quality of your résumé will often determine whether you are called for an interview, it is worth your time to put together a good one.

DEFINITION: A **letter of application** is the letter you write to a prospective employer when you are interested in applying for a position. Usually, you will send a letter of application with your résumé.

How to Write a Good Résumé

The following descriptive guide was written by Jill Lee, formerly coordinator of career services at the University of Toledo Community and Technical College.

The appearance of your résumé is very important. Use a good-quality paper, and print copies of your résumé on a laser printer. Spelling and grammar are also important. A spelling error or an obvious grammar error may eliminate you as a job candidate, so proofread your résumé carefully. Emphasize your positive qualities in your résumé, highlighting your skills and accomplishments. Within each section, list the most recent information first and then work back in time. For example, under "Experience" or "Employment" you should list your current or most recent position first, then the one before that, and so on.

A competitive résumé must be concise and well organized. Prospective employers spend an average of six to eight seconds deciding whether to give a résumé serious consideration, so you should be brief and highlight your skills and experience. Try to keep your résumé to one page.

A résumé should include the following categories of information. (See the sample résumé on p. 730.)

IDENTIFYING INFORMATION

At the top of the page, put your identifying information: your full name, address, telephone number (including area code), and email address if you have one. Include your work number if it's all right for someone to contact you there. It's important to include a number where a caller can leave a message. Each piece of information should be on its own line and centered.

CAREER OBJECTIVE

If you have a specific career objective, you can list it under this category. It should be a clearly defined, short-term goal.

OBJECTIVE: To obtain a position as an engineering technician

OBJECTIVE: To obtain an accounting position

Make sure that your objective matches the career opportunities available at the company you are sending your résumé to.

EDUCATION

Under "Education," be sure to correctly identify your degree(s). Include the date you received each degree, or your "anticipated" or "expected" graduation date. Under most circumstances, you should not include your high school. Note: Associate degrees do not have an -s at the end of the word *associate*.

Associate of Applied Business/Science degree in Medical Technology, May 2000

B.A. in Communication, May 2002 (anticipated)

Under the appropriate degree(s), include the complete name of each school you attended, along with the city and state where it is located.

The University of Toledo Community and Technical College, Toledo, Ohio

List any relevant additional information, such as grade point average (GPA) if it was 3.0 or higher, dean's list, honorary society, or other academic honors or awards.

EXPERIENCE

List both paid employment and volunteer work or internships, focusing on the experience that is most relevant to your career objective. If you like, you can create both an "Employment" category listing paid positions and a separate "Related Experience" section listing unpaid positions such as computer-lab tutor, campus guide, or senior mentor.

Each entry in the experience section should include the following information:

Title of position

Company name and location (city, state)

Dates of employment/experience

Summarize the positions you've held, and highlight your accomplishments. Include all of the concrete skills and abilities you have developed, particularly those skills relevant to your current career goals. Remember that a résumé is not the place for undue modesty about your achievements. You need to emphasize your skills to prospective employers. Tell an employer what you can do for the company or organization. Imagine a reader who is asking the question, "Why should I hire you?" and provide reasons. Use action verbs to describe your achievements.

Developed a proposal for marketing career services.

Assisted with legal research.

Analyzed reports and data and *compiled* results.

SKILLS

List any special abilities and skills in this category, such as computer, budgeting, or math skills; language skills; telephone abilities; and equipment skills. Don't skimp on this section. Brainstorm to make a list of everything you can do. Then pare down your list to the skills that may be relevant to an employer.

REFERENCES

References are people who will vouch for you. They should be people who have worked closely with you, such as former employers or instructors, who you think will say positive things about you. Be sure to check with the people you plan to list to make sure it's okay to use them as references.

On your résumé, you may list the names, positions, companies, and telephone numbers of your references, or you may simply write "References available upon request." If you state that references are available, make sure you have people and contact numbers lined up.

OTHER POSSIBLE HEADINGS

You may have qualifications or abilities that you want to include on your résumé but that don't fit neatly into any of the categories. Don't omit them; consider adding categories to fit your qualifications, such as "Special Training" or "Certifications." You want your résumé to include any information that will strengthen your appeal as a potential employee.

■ ASSIGNMENT   **WRITING A RÉSUMÉ**

Using the model résumé and the Checklist: How to Write a Résumé, which follows, write your own résumé.

SAMPLE RÉSUMÉ

Megan Ormsby
2005 Garden Park Drive
Toledo, OH 43612
(419) 555-0622
mormsby@hotmail.net

CAREER OBJECTIVE	To obtain a position as a legal secretary
EDUCATION	Associate degree in Legal Secretarial Technology, June 2002
	The University of Toledo Community and Technical College, Toledo, Ohio
	GPA: 3.5 (A = 4.0)
	• Dean's list
	• Golden Key National Honor Society
EXPERIENCE	**March 2000–present:**
	Legal secretary
	Johnson's Legal Services,
	Perrysburg, Ohio
	• Combined and entered expert testimony into database
	• Drafted distribution and settlement letters
	• Entered and updated claims in Lawtrac
	• Filled out and filed probate forms
	• Attended administrative hearings
	• Helped organize information for spreadsheets
	January 1996–March 2000:
	Secretary
	The University of Toledo, Toledo, Ohio
	• Developed an office procedures manual
	• Typed documents
	• Organized the office
	• Provided courteous, personal service
SKILLS	• Proficient in WordPerfect, Excel, Windows, Lotus Notes, Microsoft Word, PageMaker, QuarkXPress
	• Excellent written and oral communication skills
	• Excellent editing and proofreading skills
	• Certified legal secretary
REFERENCES	Available upon request

■ CHECKLIST   **HOW TO WRITE A RÉSUMÉ**

Check off the items as you write your résumé.

1.   Put your name, address, telephone number, and email address centered at the top of the page.

2.   State your career objective; keep it brief and as specific as possible.

3.   Complete the "Education" category.

_____ List degrees received, the date you received each degree, and the institution for each.

4.   Complete the "Experience" category.

_____ Start with your most recent position.

_____ List the title of each position, the company name and location, and the dates of employment.

_____ For each position, particularly the most recent one, list your achievements and/or responsibilities. Start with an action verb (_Designed_ a brochure using QuarkXPress).

5.   Complete the "Skills" category.

_____ List any skills you have that are relevant to the position you are seeking (computer, language, office machines, and so on).

6.   Provide a list of references, or state "References available upon request."

_____ Check with the people you are listing to make sure that they are willing to give you a reference and that you have their most current contact information.

7.   Revise your draft résumé.

_____ Add any experiences or skills that you overlooked.

_____ Make sure that all information is complete and accurate.

8.   Edit your résumé.

_____ Carefully read your résumé, checking for and correcting errors in grammar, spelling, or punctuation.

(_continued_)

_____   Leave enough space between items so that the résumé looks easy to read and attractive.

9.   Print your résumé.

_____   Use a high-quality printer, or go to a copy shop to print your résumé. It is important that it look clean, crisp, and professional.

How to Write a Letter of Application

Although your résumé provides detailed information about your experience and skills, your letter of application is the first item a prospective employer sees, so it is a very important piece of writing.

SIX BASICS OF A GOOD LETTER OF APPLICATION

1. It considers your audience (the prospective employer), what information that person would value, and the appropriate tone with which to address that person.
2. It keeps your purpose (to become a candidate for employment) in mind.
3. It follows a standard business-letter format.
4. It briefly but specifically summarizes what position(s) you are interested in, what your qualifications are, and why you should be considered for a position.
5. It provides contact information.
6. It is free of grammar, punctuation, and spelling errors.

The letter of application on page 733 uses a correct business format, and its parts are labeled to show you how the letter should be set up and what it should include. Note that the writer tells the prospective employer exactly how to reach her.

■   **ASSIGNMENT**   **WRITING A LETTER OF APPLICATION**

Write a letter of application to a company that you would like to work for. If possible, look up the address and the name of the director of human resources for that company. Use the sample letter of application and the Checklist: How to Write a Letter of Application, which follows, to help you.

Megan Ormsby
2005 Garden Park Drive
Toledo, OH 43612
(419) 555-0622
mormsby@hotmail.net

Letterhead should match heading of résumé.

January 4, 2003

Date of letter

Donna Contini, Manager
Human Resources
Carter, Jonas, and Abrams
1027 Center Drive
Canton, OH 44011

Name and title of person you are writing to

Department

Name of company and address

Dear Ms. Contini:

Uses formal *Mr.*, *Ms.*, or *Mrs.* followed by a colon

I am interested in the position of legal secretary at your firm, which you recently advertised in the *Canton News*. Carter, Jonas, and Abrams is a well-respected, large, and busy law firm, and I would like to be part of just such an organization. I believe that my education, my experience, and my skills fit the requirements for this position.

States position writer is interested in

Makes positive statement about company and writer's fit for position

In June 2002, I received a degree in Legal Secretarial Technology from the University of Toledo Community and Technical College, where I maintained a consistently high grade point average. While pursuing my degree, I worked full-time as a legal secretary at a small firm where I am still employed. During my years there I have had the opportunity to sharpen my computer and communication skills and have learned to organize and keep track of a large number of tasks.

Summarizes experience, education, and skills

I am ready to move to a more challenging atmosphere and am eager to apply myself to a new and demanding position at a dynamic firm such as Carter, Jonas, and Abrams. Because of my experience, I can be productive from my first day on the job, though I know I will have much to learn. I am enthusiastic about that prospect.

Shows benefit of hiring writer and enthusiasm

I have enclosed a résumé that details my education, experience, and skills. I hope you will agree that they are a good match for the position at Carter, Jonas, and Abrams, and I will look forward to hearing from you. Because I am at work during the day, the best way to reach me is to call the number listed above and leave a message letting me know when it would be convenient for me to return your call. Thank you for your consideration.

Lets reader know how to reach writer

Ends with enthusiasm, confidence, and polite thanks

Sincerely,

Megan Ormsby

Megan Ormsby

CHECKLIST   **HOW TO WRITE A LETTER OF APPLICATION**

Check off the items as you write your letter.

1.   **Put your name, address, telephone number, and email address in a letterhead that is centered at the top of the page.**

2.   **Write the date and address of your letter.**

_____   Write the date and skip two or three spaces.

_____   Write the name, title, and address of the person you are writing to. Skip two more spaces.

3.   **Write your salutation.**

_____   Write *Dear Mr./Ms./Mrs./Dr.* and the person's last name. Put a colon (:) after the name.

_____   Skip two spaces.

4.   **Write the body of your letter.**

_____   In the first paragraph, state the position you are interested in.

_____   In the second paragraph, briefly but specifically state your qualifications, skills, and strengths.

_____   In the third paragraph, restate your interest in the position, your enthusiasm, and your confidence in your ability to succeed in the position; indicate how the prospective employer can contact you; and thank him or her for considering you.

_____   Skip two spaces.

5.   **Write your closing.**

_____   Write *Sincerely* followed by a comma (,).

_____   Skip four spaces and type your name.

6.   **Revise your letter.**

_____   Reread what you have written, and add anything that would strengthen your appeal to the prospective employer.

7. **Edit your letter.**

_____ Carefully edit your letter, making sure that it has no errors in spelling, grammar, or punctuation.

_____ Make sure that it follows the standard format for a letter of application and includes all of the elements.

8. **Print and sign your letter.**

_____ Use a high-quality printer, or go to a copy shop to print your letter. It is important that it look clean, crisp, and professional.

_____ Sign your name, neatly, above the typed signature.

_____ Make a copy of your letter for your files.

Appendix C

How to Make an Oral Presentation

Five Surefire Strategies

In college, at work—sometimes even in your everyday life—you will need to make oral presentations. Most people rate public speaking as one of life's most stressful experiences. A number of practical strategies, however, can help you cope with the anxiety that may be caused by this task. Knowing how to prepare for an oral presentation will help you feel confident and in control of the situation.

You have probably witnessed an embarrassing oral presentation, a situation in which the speaker fell apart and the audience felt as uncomfortable as the speaker. The following is an example of such an occurrence.

SITUATION: Jean is in the middle of reviewing her presentation notes when she hears herself being introduced. Startled, she gathers her materials into a messy stack of notes and papers, apologizes for not being ready, and walks quickly to the front of the room.

Obviously flustered, she tries to reorganize her notes, shuffling papers, frowning, and sighing loudly. She begins reading her presentation with her head down, speaking quickly and softly. Several people call out, "I can't hear you" or "Speak up."

Jean clears her throat and starts from the beginning. She's so rattled that her voice quivers and then breaks. She looks up, red in the face, and says, "Sorry. I'm really nervous."

She continues but moves too quickly from one point to the next because she doesn't want to bore people. She forgets to introduce or summarize any of her points, so the audience finds it difficult to follow her speech. People start to tune out.

Aware that she's not doing very well, Jean nervously fiddles with her hair while speaking. She reads quickly and with no emphasis, thinking that the sooner she gets through this, the sooner she can sit down. The words that looked so good when she wrote them sound stupid and awkward when she says them aloud.

As Jean turns to the second page, she realizes that her papers are out of order. There is an awkward silence as she searches desperately for the right page. She finally finds it and begins again. Soon she comes to a word that she can't read, and she has to stop again to figure it out. Still fiddling with her hair, she now looks as if she's about to pull it out.

Jean skips the word and continues. Her only goal now is to finish. But she's run out of time because of her fumbling and because her presentation was too long to begin with. The warning signal goes off, indicating that one minute remains.

This is the last straw for Jean. She looks up, bright red and nearly in tears, and says, "I guess I've run out of time. I only got through one of my points. I don't have time for what I really wanted to say." She grabs her papers and returns to her seat.

Jean sits in total misery, sure that everyone is looking at her. She can't listen to anyone else's presentation. All she can do is stare at the floor and wait impatiently for the moment she can escape from the room.

ANALYSIS: Jean's presentation was not successful because of some common pitfalls she could easily have avoided. She wasn't adequately prepared, she was obviously very nervous, she hadn't structured her presentation to make her points clear to her audience, she hadn't practiced reading her presentation aloud, and she fled at the end. If she had practiced five simple strategies for making an oral presentation, her experience would have been much less painful, and her presentation would have been much better.

Strategy 1. Be Prepared

Jean's first mistake was not being well prepared. She wasn't psychologically ready to speak, and she hadn't organized the materials for her presentation properly. Because she was busy reviewing her notes at the last minute, she was caught off guard. Her papers got messed up, she was startled, and she was off to a bad start.

ORGANIZE YOUR NOTES

Before you go into the room where you are giving your presentation, make sure all of your notes are in order. Number all pages or notecards so you can quickly reorganize them if they get mixed up, and carry all of your materials in a folder.

KEEP YOUR NOTES IN ORDER

If you want to review your key points while waiting to make your presentation, try to run through them in your head. Leave the folder closed. If you need to refresh your memory on a particular point, open the folder and carefully go through your notes until you find the answer.

USE YOUR ENERGY

Be aware of when your turn is coming, and focus on being calm. Tell yourself that you're prepared and you know what you're doing. Breathe deeply. Don't worry if your heart is beating hard and fast; that's normal. Nervous energy before a performance of any sort is natural and can make you a more engaging speaker. You just need to learn to channel that energy and make it work *for* you. Use that adrenaline to fuel your enthusiasm for your topic.

BUILD YOURSELF UP

Keep breathing normally. However silly it may seem, remind yourself of your strengths and repeat them in your head as your turn to speak approaches: "I know what I'm talking about." "I look good today." "I have a good voice." Remember that your audience isn't waiting for you to fail. Most people understand the stress of oral presentations and are sympathetic. Your audience wants you to do well.

CARRY YOURSELF LIKE ROYALTY

When it's your turn, take a deep breath, calmly pick up your folder, and walk to the front of the room. Walk slowly, stand straight, and focus on projecting a confident image. Remember that you're in control.

Strategy 2. Act with Confidence

Jean's second mistake was not acting with confidence and authority. She was visibly upset as she tried to get her notes in order, and when she did start, she spoke too softly to be heard. When her voice broke, she apologized to the audience and announced her nervousness. Practicing several techniques would have made her appear confident and in control.

TAKE YOUR TIME

After you've walked to the front of the room, take a few moments to calmly arrange your notes and papers before you begin. Relax. The timing of your presentation won't start until you begin speaking, so make sure your materials are where you need them before beginning. Remember that even professional speakers need a few moments to lay out their notes and compose themselves.

TAKE COMMAND AND GREET YOUR AUDIENCE

When you're ready to begin, stand up straight and look up and out at the audience. Remember that you are in command of the room. Pause for a few seconds to let people know you're about to begin, and wait for them to give you their attention. When you have their attention, take a deep breath and begin.

Smile and greet the audience, surveying the room as you do so. Your greeting should be simple, like "Good morning and thank you all for coming." If some people in the audience don't know you, be sure to introduce yourself. Don't forget to smile: It will relax you as well as your audience.

SLOW DOWN AND SPEAK UP

Make sure that you speak slowly, clearly, and loudly. If you're nervous, you will tend to speak too quickly, so try to slow down your speech a bit. Try to project your voice so that the people in the last row can hear you. It may feel as if you're shouting, but you won't be. Don't be embarrassed to ask if everyone can hear you. Experienced speakers often break the ice by encouraging an audience to tell them if they need to speak up.

Strategy 3. Structure Your Presentation

Jean's third mistake was not giving her presentation a clear structure, which would have made it easy for her audience to follow her key points. Your presentation should include lots of verbal cues that let people know when you're making a point, what it is, and when you're moving to another point. The structure of an oral presentation must be much more obvious than the structure of a written paper so that people can understand as they are listening.

LIMIT YOUR TOPIC

Choose a manageable topic for the time allotted, and limit the number of points you plan to make. Listening is hard work, and most people can absorb only a few key points from a speech. In any presentation, try to limit yourself to three key points, and be sure to support each of them with concrete examples. When you give more complex presentations, you may need to use visual aids—such as transparencies or slides—that will allow you to illustrate and reinforce your points.

STATE YOUR THESIS AND PREVIEW YOUR KEY POINTS

Let your audience know what your topic is and the main point you are going to make about it. State your thesis (your main point) slowly so that people understand the purpose of your presentation. Tell them: "My topic today is _____," and "I will be arguing [or showing, or explaining] _____."

Tell your audience about the structure of your presentation by giving them a preview of your key points. You might say: "There are three major points I'd like to make about _____. First I'll present _____. Second I'll discuss _____. And my third point will be _____. This presentation should take approximately three minutes, and there will be time for questions at the end."

USE TRANSITIONS TO MOVE FROM POINT TO POINT

Use transitions to let your audience know when you're finished with one point and are about to make another. In your preview, you told the audience what your key points would be. As you speak, you should give clear verbal cues when introducing and summarizing each point. Here is one way to do so.

- My first point is _____.
- Give examples/explanation.
- Repeat or summarize the first point (to remind the audience of what it is and to let them know you're about to move to another point).
- My second point is _____.
- Give examples/explanation.
- Repeat or summarize second point.
- My third and final point is _____.
- Give examples/explanation.
- Repeat or summarize third point.

CONCLUDE BY REVIEWING YOUR KEY POINTS

Let people know when you're coming to the end of your presentation by using a verbal cue such as *in conclusion, to summarize,* or *to review.* Then review your key points. Conclude with a simple, strong sentence that restates the overall purpose of your presentation—the main point you want to make.

Strategy 4. Practice Your Presentation

Like many people, Jean made the mistake of not adequately practicing her presentation. The right kind of practice would have helped her avoid the following problems: fidgeting with her hair, writing a presentation that sounded awkward when presented orally, losing her place in the middle of her talk, being unable to read her handwriting, and running out of time.

Even professional speakers practice their speeches. You should allow plenty of time to practice giving your oral presentation.

PRACTICE ALOUD

Phrases and sentences that sound good in writing often sound awkward when spoken. Read your presentation aloud—several times—to make sure that it sounds right. You'll feel silly, but do it anyway. Stop and make changes when a sentence sounds awkward. Be aware of any distracting habits you may have, such as interrupting your speech with expressions like "uh," or "you know."

Practicing aloud will also help you remember your key points. Practice your speech again and again until you feel comfortable with it. Be sure to practice aloud a final time on the day of your presentation.

PRACTICE IN FRONT OF A MIRROR

You need to see what you look like as you give your presentation, so try practicing in front of a mirror. This may make you feel even sillier than just saying the speech aloud, but it will also make you feel much more confident when you actually give the presentation.

- Stand straight and look up at the mirror frequently. Pretend you are looking out at an audience.

- Be aware of any distracting habits you have while speaking, such as fidgeting with your hair, as Jean did. Some people shift their weight from one leg to another, or sway back and forth, or stand with their legs far apart in a military stance.
- Practice keeping your hands still, except when you want to gesture or point to something for emphasis. You can hold your notes at your side or in front of you, or you can place them on a table or podium.
- Practice keeping your feet slightly apart and your weight evenly distributed. Don't shift back and forth or rock.
- If you know you will be seated when giving your presentation, you should sit in a chair while practicing. Don't jiggle your feet or swing your legs. Keep your feet flat on the floor.

PRACTICE WORKING WITH YOUR MATERIAL

Figure out in advance how you will handle your notes and papers. After you've said your presentation aloud a couple of times to get the wording right, decide whether you will work with the whole presentation written out, an outline, or notecards.

THE WHOLE PRESENTATION: If you think you need the whole presentation—written out word for word—to read from, that's fine, but you still have to practice. You have to be comfortable enough with the written version to be able to deliver it naturally, not as if you're reading, and to look up at your audience without fear of losing your place. If your eyes are glued to the page, you'll lose your audience's attention.

In addition to practicing, you should format your presentation so that it will be easy for you to find your place.

- Highlight your key points in color or by obvious underlining so that you'll be able to find your place quickly if you get lost.
- Double-space between the lines of your presentation so that you won't have trouble reading it.
- Use a large type size. If you must handwrite your presentation, make sure that you can read your handwriting.
- Write the numbers of your key points in the margin (next to the paragraphs where you introduce those points), write "conc." next to your conclusion, and so on.
- Make sure your pages are clearly numbered so that they can easily be put in order if you mix them up.

OUTLINE: Instead of writing out your entire presentation, word for word, you may want to write your key points in outline form. An outline should include all of the major points you want to make, with examples or explanations. It should also include the points to be made in the intro-duction and conclusion.

NOTECARDS: Some people prefer to work from 3″ × 5″ notecards rather than pieces of paper. They prepare a separate notecard for each major point, listing the point and an example. If you use notecards, be sure to number them in the top right corner so that you can easily reassemble them if they get out of order.

TIME YOURSELF

As you practice aloud, time yourself. You need to be sure that you can fin-ish your presentation within the time limit you've been given.

If you find that you don't have enough time to make your major points, don't just speak more quickly. Go back and revise your presenta-tion. Keep the points simple and the examples clear. If necessary, cut back on the number of points you are making, keeping only the strongest ones.

Be sure to time yourself at least twice after you have your presentation in final form.

Strategy 5. Create a Good Final Impression

Jean's last mistake was that when she ran short on time, she panicked and ended on a bad note. Practicing aloud and timing yourself will help you avoid this problem, but if you do run short on time, don't panic.

Usually speakers are given a warning signal of some sort to let them know that they need to finish. If you get a warning signal before you've said all you wanted to, remember that it's a warning. You have a little time left to conclude your presentation.

You may have enough time to finish your speech as planned, but if you know you can't cover all of it in the time remaining, you will need to con-dense it. Reduce the details about your points, and move to a very brief conclusion. You may need to move to your final point and give it without an example. Then say, "Again, here are the major points," repeat them briefly, and conclude.

When the time is over, look up, smile at your audience, thank them for their attention, and ask if they have any questions. Give the audience time to respond. It may take them a while to start asking questions. Wait calmly, and look around the room. If there are no questions, thank the audience again and return to your seat.

Answers to Odd-Numbered Exercises

CHAPTER 22: THE BASIC SENTENCE

Practice 22-1, page 347

Answers: **1.** Subject: thousands; prepositional phrases: of young people; from all over the country; to New York City **3.** Subject: artists; prepositional phrases: with big talent and very little money; of finding an apartment; in New York. **5.** Subject: advice; prepositional phrase: of a real estate broker **7.** Subject: apartment; prepositional phrases: with no closets and no view; on the island of Manhattan **9.** Subject: people; prepositional phrases: without money; with roommates

Practice 22-2, page 350

Answers: **1.** Subject: family; action verb: moved **3.** Subject: Miguel; helping verb + main verb: was learning **5.** Subject: he; linking verb: was **7.** Subject: plan; helping verb + main verb: had been **9.** Subject: family; linking verb: is

Practice 22-3, page 352

Answers and possible edits: **1.** I (incomplete thought); He walked down the red carpet, smiling broadly as the cameras flashed all around him. **3.** I (incomplete thought); The man who lives in the big brick house on Valley Street is my new boss. **5.** C (complete thought) **7.** I (incomplete thought); Sandra had her appendix removed, which explains why she missed class last week. **9.** C (complete thought)

CHAPTER 23: FRAGMENTS

Practice 23-1, page 356

Possible edits: **1.** Fingerprinting must have seemed like magic to the public a hundred years ago. **3.** With the development of techniques for finding and preserving fingerprints, detectives gained an advantage over criminals who did not wear gloves. **5.** Until recently, few people realized that identifying fingerprints was not an exact science. **7.** When two prints were very similar, there have even been a few cases of mistaken fingerprint identification. **9.** DNA evidence has become the new industry standard in the past decade.

Practice 23-2, page 359

Answers and possible edits: **1.** Dependent word: if. If a company mainly sells information, its workers are more likely than employees of other businesses to be allowed to do their jobs at home. **3.** Dependent word: unless. Some companies are reluctant to approve telecommuting, unless their workers already have the necessary computer equipment at home. **5.** Dependent word: while. While going to work in a bathrobe may be appealing, telecommuters sometimes discover that working at home also has drawbacks. **7.** Dependent word: so. A telecommuter needs motivation and discipline so that he or she can concentrate on the job while surrounded by all the distractions of home. **9.** Dependent word: which. Finally, telecommuters may find the pace of their work slowed down by their home Internet connection, which may not be as fast as an office's high-speed line.

Practice 23-3, page 362

Answers and possible edits: **1.** *–ing* verb: living. My grandmother spent her entire life living on a farm in eastern Wyoming. **3.** *–ing* verb: creating. She was a natural seamstress. My grandmother created shirts and dresses more beautiful than anything available in a store. **5.** *–ing* verb: using. The quilting circle made quilts for special occasions using scraps of cloth left over from other sewing projects. **7.** *–ing* verb: celebrating. Celebrating the birth of her first child, my father, the quilting circle gave my grandmother a baby quilt that is now a treasured heirloom. **9.** *–ing* verb: looking. Looking at each bit of cloth in that quilt, my grandmother could still describe, years later, the garment she had made from it.

Practice 23-4, page 364

Answers and possible edits: **1.** *To* + verb: to refuse. In 1976, several oil-producing countries in the Middle East made an agreement to refuse to sell oil to the United States. **3.** *To* + verb: to meet. American automakers increased the fuel efficiency of their cars to meet consumers' demands for vehicles with better gas mileage. **5.** *To* + verb: to stop. Oil and gasoline soon became widely available again, so many Americans made a decision to stop worrying about conserving energy. **7.** *To* + verb: to deal. The nation had to deal with energy shortages in California and rising gas prices across the country in 2001. Some people suggested that Americans needed to consume less energy. **9.** *To* + verb: to consider. Perhaps the booming economy of the 1990s convinced too many Americans that there would never be a need for them to consider a less wasteful lifestyle.

Practice 23-5, page 367
Possible edits: **1.** Many parents believe that they would know if their daughters were being abused, either physically or emotionally. **3.** A young man can be abusive without laying a finger on his girlfriend. He might monitor her actions and keep her from spending time with other friends. **5.** Around her parents, a teenager's boyfriend may act like a perfect gentleman. He may be polite, attentive, and kind to the young woman. **7.** A young woman with an abusive boyfriend may develop psychological problems that will be difficult to treat, such as low self-esteem. **9.** Friends who think that a young woman is involved in an abusive relationship should try to be supportive of her, not turn away even if she will not leave her boyfriend.

Practice 23-6, page 369
Answers and possible edits: **1.** (1/2) Genetically modified foods are being marketed as the foods of the future. (3) Correct (4) Correct (5/6) A gene from a fish may be found to make tomatoes more resistant to disease. (7/8/9) Of course, this genetic modification may have unintended effects, as in the case of genetically modified corn, which may harm monarch butterfly caterpillars. (10/11) Arguing that the long-term effects of genetic modification may not be known for years to come, some scientists urge caution before marketing genetically modified foods. **3.** (1/2) The term *organic* means different things to different people. (3/4) Organic foods are supposed to be grown without pesticides, a method that reduces a farm's impact on the environment. (5) Correct (6) Correct (7/8) They pay premium prices for organic products because they think the food is good for their own well-being, not just that of the environment. (9) Correct (10/11) The label merely means that the ingredients meet a certain government standard, while guaranteeing nothing about the nutritional content or health benefits of the food. **5.** (1) Correct (2/3) Doctors have begun to explain to their patients that antibiotics are useful only for certain kinds of infections and that patients must finish every course of antibiotics they start. (4/5) Antibiotic use in agriculture, however, has continued to increase. (6/7) The government does not even keep records of antibiotic use in farm animals. (8/9) Many cattle, pigs, and chickens get antibiotics for economic reasons, such as to keep them

healthy and to make them grow faster. (10) Correct (11) Correct

CHAPTER 24: RUN-ONS
Practice 24-1, page 376
Answers and possible edits: **1.** FS (fused sentence). The invention of cell phones made telephoning from a car possible. People could telephone for help if they were stranded on the highway. **3.** CS (comma splice). Some communities in the United States have banned drivers from talking on handheld cell phones; a driver must stop the car to place a call legally in those areas. **5.** FS (fused sentence). No one debates that drivers can be distracted by cell phones. Some people wonder, however, whether the problem is really the fact that a driver is holding the phone. **7.** FS (fused sentence). Some people worry that drivers are distracted not by holding the telephone, but by holding a conversation. A tense discussion with the boss or good news from a relative can take the driver's attention from traffic. **9.** CS (comma splice) There are differences, however, between talking on a cell phone and listening to music in the car. The telephone requires interaction from the driver, but the radio calls for passive listening.

Practice 24-2, page 379
Answers and possible edits: **1.** Subjects: penguins; birds. Verbs: live; have been. Fairy penguins, a small breed of penguin, live in Tasmania, and these birds have often been the victims of oil spills. **3.** Subjects: attempts; oil. Verbs: can be; is. Unfortunately, the penguins' attempts to clean off their feathers can be fatal, for crude oil is poisonous to penguins. **5.** Subjects: one; volunteers; Verbs: created; knitted. One of the conservationists created a pattern for a sweater for the penguins, and volunteers from around the world knitted these unusual sweaters. **7.** Subjects: most; some. Verbs: were made; were sent. Most of the sweaters were made by elderly nursing-home residents in Tasmania, but some were sent from as far away as Japan. **9.** Subjects: some; few. Verbs: made; have. Some creative knitters made tuxedo-patterned sweaters, and a few of these penguin suits even have bow ties.

Practice 24-3, page 381
Answers and possible edits: **1.** Subjects: neighbor; children. Verbs: began; were. My neighbor, Mr. Johnson, began his hobby because his children were worried about his ability to keep busy after retirement. **3.** Subjects: he; he. Verbs: made; was. He made the models out of sheet metal because he was used to working with that material. **5.** Subjects: he; Mr. Johnson. Verbs: finished; painted. After he finished the metal work, Mr. Johnson painted the house white with a green roof, just like the original. **7.** Subjects: he; he. Verbs: was working; found. While he was working on the

model courthouse, he found photographs of his childhood home.   **9.** Subjects: he; family. Verbs: finished; began. When he finished his model of the old house, his family began to show the models to other people.

Practice 24-4, page 383
Answers and possible edits: **1.** (1) Correct (2) It's often easy to forget things when you want desperately to remember them. (3) You have probably had the experience of forgetting an acquaintance's name, which comes to your mind only when it's too late. (4) You have also probably been unable to find your keys once in a while because you put them down somewhere without thinking. (5) At other times, however, you may find it difficult to forget some things even though you wish you could never think of them again. (6) Correct (7) Sometimes you may find yourself forced to relive your most embarrassing moment over and over again in your mind; your memory won't let you leave that part of your past behind. (8) Some scholars believe that these annoying habits of memory evolved for a reason. It's hard to imagine, though, any good reason for developing the ability to forget where you left your keys.

CHAPTER 25: PROBLEMS WITH SUBJECT-VERB AGREEMENT
Practice 25-1, page 391
Answers: **1.** Subject: I; verb: was   **3.** Subject: I; verb: have   **5.** Subject: games; verb: are   **7.** Subject: incidents; verb: do   **9.** Subject: children; verb: do

Practice 25-2, page 391
Answers: **1.** Subject: students; verb: are   **3.** Subject: computer; verb: does   **5.** Subject: program; verb: has   **7.** Subject: teachers; verb: are   **9.** Subject: computer; verb: does

Practice 25-3, page 393
Answers: **1.** Prepositional phrase: with hearing loss; verb: have   **3.** Prepositional phrase: with words; verb: comes   **5.** Prepositional phrase: in this country; verb: feel   **7.** Prepositional phrase: in a deaf household; verb: resembles   **9.** Prepositional phrase: to the hearing world and the deaf world; verb: pull

Practice 25-4, page 395
Answers: **1.** Dependent clause: which is a job applicant's first contact with many prospective employers; verb: contains   **3.** Dependent clause: who held a previous job for two months; verb: claims   **5.** Dependent clause: who never completed a college degree; verb is OK   **7.** Dependent clause: who like a résumé; verb: check   **9.** Dependent clause: who invent material on a résumé; verb: forget

Practice 25-5, page 396
Answers: **1.** Subject joined by: and; verb: do   **3.** Subject joined by: or; verb: is   **5.** Subject joined by: and; verb: contain   **7.** Subject joined by: and; verb: contribute   **9.** Subject joined by: nor; verb: are

Practice 25-6, page 398
Answers: **1.** Subject: anyone; verb: needs; dependent clause: who wants to take college courses   **3.** Subject: several; verb: offer; prepositional phrase: of the hundreds of accredited colleges in the United States   **5.** Subject: everyone; verb: has; dependent clause: who takes online courses   **7.** Subject: someone; verb: is; dependent clause: who learns best by listening   **9.** Subject: anybody; verb: needs; dependent clause: who is considering an online class

Practice 25-7, page 400
Answers: **1.** Where are the corporation's main offices located?   **3.** How well does the average employee abroad speak English?   **5.** How many languages is the manual written in?   **7.** There are some machines that can do translation.   **9.** OK

Practice 25-8, page 401
Answers: **1.** (1) School systems around the country are embracing educational standards. (2) The idea of standards sounds reasonable. (3) Correct (4) A national standard for all American students has many supporters, too. (5) If the requirements for graduation in Oregon and Tennessee are the same, everyone with a high school diploma gets a similar education. (6) Correct (7) Correct (8) Mathematics and writing are important, but so are music and physical education. (9) How are parents, teachers, and administrators ever going to find standards that everyone accepts?   **3.** (1) Correct (2) Most school districts that have a testing program use tests that can be scored by a computer. (3) Computers cannot read, so the tests that they grade usually offer multiple-choice questions. (4) A multiple-choice test in science or mathematics does not allow students to demonstrate critical thinking. (5) How do students show their writing ability on such a test? (6) There are tricks to answering multiple-choice questions that many students learn. (7) Correct (8) Nevertheless, the quick results and low cost of a multiple-choice computer-graded test mean that this imperfect testing system is used in many school systems.   **5.** (1) Many parents who send their children to public school fear that the schools are not teaching the students adequately. (2) As these fears increase, the number of states that require tests rises as well. (3) But there have been some teachers and parents willing to resist standardized testing. (4) A few parents have kept their children home on test days. (5) In rare cases, teachers who oppose testing have refused to administer standardized tests to their students. (6) In the

places that require students to pass tests in order to graduate, rebellion against tests has serious consequences for the student. (7) Correct (8) People who believe that standardized testing is not the answer are still trying to change this growing national trend.

CHAPTER 26: VERB PROBLEMS

Practice 26-1, page 407
Answers: **1.** Subject: I; verb: enjoy **3.** Subject: I; verb: work **5.** Subject: he; verb: loves **7.** Subject: they; verb: use **9.** Subject: hospital; verb: allows

Practice 26-2, page 408
Answers: **1.** faced **3.** covered; wanted; realized; involved **5.** called **7.** needed **9.** offered; failed **11.** freed; carried

Practice 26-3, page 409
Answers: **1.** Helping verb: has; verb: forced **3.** Helping verb: had; verb: attended **5.** Helping verb: have; verb: objected **7.** Helping verb: have; verb: traveled **9.** Helping verb: had; verb: hoped

Practice 26-4, page 413
Answers: **1.** am **3.** has **5.** are **7.** has **9.** are

Practice 26-5, page 414
Answers: **1.** were; were **3.** was; were **5.** was; was **7.** was **9.** were; were

Practice 26-6, page 415
Answers: **1.** built **3.** hung **5.** struck **7.** began **9.** left; stood

Practice 26-7, page 416
Answers: **1.** Two years ago, my high school set up a student court to give students a voice in disciplining rule breakers. **3.** Some of us served as members of juries, and others became advocates or even judges. **5.** Then, last spring, my friend Dewayne appeared before the student court after he lost his temper and struck a fellow student. **7.** I told the jury that he knew his violent reaction was a mistake. **9.** After hearing the verdict, Dewayne shook hands with all the jurors and thanked them for their fairness.

Practice 26-8, page 417
Answers: **1.** Helping verb: had; verb: taken **3.** Helping verb: had; verb: begun **5.** Helping verb: had; verb: been **7.** Helping verb: had; verb: bought **9.** Helping verb: had; verb: sold

Practice 26-9, page 419
Answers: **1.** have been **3.** have found **5.** have begun **7.** discovered **9.** have faced; have been

Practice 26-10, page 420
Answers: **1.** got **3.** had heard **5.** had just learned **7.** raised **9.** had warned

Practice 26-11, page 422
Possible edits: **1.** The Senate denied Robert Bork's nomination to the Supreme Court. **3.** Genzyme, Inc., is laying off eighty employees. **5.** I mailed the check last Tuesday.

Practice 26-12, page 423
Answers: **1.** Verbs: love, wanted; corrected verb: want **3.** Verbs: is, counted; corrected verb: counts **5.** Verbs: appear, had; corrected verb: have **7.** Verbs: had, go; corrected verb: went **9.** Verbs: had, can offer; corrected verb: have

Practice 26-13, page 424
Answers: **1.** (1) Since 1835, trapeze artists have considered the triple somersault the most dangerous maneuver. (2) That year, a performer tried to do a triple somersault on a trapeze for the first time and died in the attempt. (3) Only one person managed to do the trick successfully for the next sixty-three years. (4) That man, a trapeze artist named Armor, did a triple somersault in 1860 and was afraid to try it again. (5) According to circus legend, the second person to survive the triple, Ernie Clarke, once did a quadruple somersault in private. (6) Correct (7) Circus historians now believe that Alfredo Codona, a performer in the 1920s and 1930s, was the greatest master of the triple somersault. (8) He has gone down in history as the King of Trapeze. **3.** (1) The Olympic Games first let women compete in swimming events in 1912, and with that, the swimsuit revolution began. (2) Correct (3) Before that year, women had only been able to wade at the beach in bathing costumes with long, baggy legs. (4) The 1913 suits, designed by Carl Jantzen, were ribbed one-piece outfits that allowed actual swimming. (5) An engineer, Louis Réard, came up with the next major development in swimwear in 1946 while working in the lingerie business (6) He called it the "bikini," after a Pacific island used for testing the atomic bomb. (7) In the 1950s, few Americans dared to wear bikinis, which were considered scandalous. (8) Two-piece swimsuits caught on in the 1960s and 1970s. (9) The bikini lost some popularity in the last decades of the twentieth century, but it has made a triumphant return in the new millennium.

CHAPTER 27: PRONOUNS

Practice 27-1, page 431
Answers: **1.** Pronoun: they; noun: people **3.** Pronoun: it; noun: microlending **5.** Pronoun: them; noun: owners **7.** Pronoun: her; noun: woman **9.** Pronoun: his or her; noun: entrepreneur

Practice 27-2, page 434
Answers: **1.** his or her   **3.** their   **5.** himself or herself
7. they need   **9.** their

Practice 27-3, page 436
Answers: **1.** its   **3.** its   **5.** its   **7.** its   **9.** its

Practice 27-4, page 438
Possible edits: **1.** In a psychology study, volunteers who watched a video of two basketball teams had to count the number of passes. **3.** Later, when meeting with the researchers, many of the volunteers asked, "What gorilla?" **5.** The way the human brain processes visual information may keep people from using that information wisely. **7.** A stop sign appearing at an intersection cannot prevent an accident if drivers do not see the sign. **9.** However, the study indicates that drivers make mistakes because they may not see problems ahead.

Practice 27-5, page 439
Answers: **1.** Robots have been part of many science-fiction classics, from *The Jetsons* to *Star Wars*. **3.** In some industries, robots are already part of the workforce. **5.** A factory might use robots to handle substances that are dangerous for humans to touch. **7.** Some children who wanted a robot friend have already gotten their wish. **9.** The robot dog was first on many holiday and birthday gift lists for children in the past few years.

Practice 27-6, page 442
Answers: **1.** I met Jun when we were students in an engineering program, and he and I both decided that we were interested in business careers. **3.** C **5.** He and I were convinced that smart people with master's degrees in engineering would be useful in the business world, with or without an MBA. **7.** C **9.** Nancy said that she and Andrew had learned that people without MBAs perform just as well in corporate America as people who have business degrees.

Practice 27-7, page 443
Answers: **1.** My mother and father had a garden in their backyard, but she spent much more time there than he. **3.** The garden was filled with tomatoes because my mother loved no other vegetable as much as them. **5.** C **7.** He made sure that the leaf of each plant was free of slugs, for few other garden pests are as destructive as they. **9.** I spend just as much time as he working in the garden, however.

Practice 27-8, page 444
Answers: **1.** whom   **3.** whom   **5.** who

Practice 27-9, page 446
Possible edits: **1.** Experts agree that the percentage of people with allergies to foods is rising, but they don't know why. **3.** If a person has a severe allergy to a food and unknowingly eats even a small amount of that food, he or she could die. **5.** When young children have severe allergies, their parents can be extremely cautious. **7.** He carries an adrenaline pen that can save his life if he goes into shock from a food allergy. **9.** My mother will not take my brother to any public place where she can even smell peanuts.

Practice 27-10, page 447
Possible edits: **1.** The picture phone never caught on with consumers, but videoconferencing uses the same idea. (2) Anyone who has a video camera hooked up to a home computer can connect to someone else with a similar setup. (3) A person simply sits in front of the camera and talks; a person or group of people on the other end is able to see and hear him or her. (4) Videoconferencing has been wonderful for both businesses and families. (5) In the new global economy, a company often has its offices all over the world. (6) Once, a businessperson might have had to travel a great deal to keep in touch with his or her clients, suppliers, and fellow employees around the globe. (7) Today, much business can be done with videoconferencing. (8) People can attend a meeting and see their clients face to face while remaining on a different continent. (9) The technology has improved so that anyone can transmit high-quality images and sound, and the cost of videoconferencing continues to drop. (10) And of course, a videoconferencing businessperson with competitors who travel the world will save much more money than they on airfare and accommodations. (11) Correct (12) A family today may find that they often must spend time apart. (13) A parent traveling for business may not see his or her spouse or children for days at a time. (14) People move across the country from where they grew up, leaving parents and siblings behind. (15) Parents sometimes divorce, and sometimes one starts a new job far away from the children. (16) Today, however, people who cannot be present to kiss their children goodnight or wish their sister a happy birthday can see family members across the miles through videoconferencing. (17) Divorced parents whom judges have allowed to move to another state have actually been required by law to buy videoconferencing technology to keep in touch with their children. (18) Most people do not feel that videoconferencing can replace being physically present with family members and clients, but videoconferences cost less than regular visits while offering more intimacy than a telephone call. (19) If the eyes are the windows of the soul, videoconferencing helps people look into those windows and stay connected.

CHAPTER 28: ADJECTIVES AND ADVERBS
Practice 28-1, page 452
Answers: **1.** *Easy* modifies *jobs*. **3.** *Frequent* modifies *employer*. **5.** *Interesting* modifies *work*. **7.** *Responsibly* modifies *behaving*. **9.** *Financially* modifies *independent*.

Practice 28-2, page 454
Answers: **1.** most commonly **3.** longer **5.** smaller **7.** highest **9.** more difficult

Practice 28-3, page 456
Answers: **1.** *Well* modifies *known.* **3.** *Well* modifies *contrasts.* **5.** *Good* modifies *tale.* **7.** *Well* modifies *lives.* **9.** *Well* modifies *jump.*

Practice 28-4, page 457
Answers: **1.** better **3.** worst **5.** worst **7.** best **9.** worse

Practice 28-5, page 458
Answers: **1.** (1) For an average European in the Middle Ages, wearing stripes was not simply a fashion mistake. (2) According to Michel Pastoureau, a scholar of the medieval period, wearing stripes was one of the worst things a European Christian could do in the thirteenth and fourteenth centuries. (3) Stripes might be taken as a sign that the wearer was sillier than other people; jesters, for example, often wore them. (4) Prostitutes also wore striped clothes, so stripes might be seen as an indication that the person was more sinful than others. (5) Wearing stripes was most dangerous for clergymen. (6) At least one clergyman in fourteenth-century France was executed because he had been foolish enough to wear striped clothes. (7) Carmelite monks who wore striped cloaks were frequently attacked, and several popes insisted that the monks change to a simpler costume. (8) People in medieval Europe certainly took their clothing seriously. (9) Correct

CHAPTER 29: MISPLACED AND DANGLING MODIFIERS

Practice 29-1, page 464
Possible edits: **1.** Are there energy fields in a human body that can be touched by trained professionals? **3.** According to believers in therapeutic touch, an energy field that is out of alignment can cause pain and illness. **5.** After a session of therapeutic touch, many patients report that they just felt better without knowing why. **7.** In her experiment, practitioners who could not see Emily were supposed to use the invisible energy field to determine when her hands were near theirs. **9.** Anyone who can demonstrate the ability to detect a human energy field in a similar experiment can claim a million-dollar prize.

Practice 29-2, page 466
Possible edits: **1.** Trading in a used car, a seller will get a better price if the car is clean. **3.** With the used car looking like new, the owner can get the best price for a trade-in or a resale. **5.** Approved as safe and drivable by a reputable mechanic, a used car may still have minor mechanical problems that do not have to be fixed. **7.** By deducting the cost of repairing minor problems from the asking price, the owner can be fair with a buyer. **9.** With higher than usual mileage, a used car might need a reduced asking price.

Practice 29-3, page 467
Possible edits: **1.** (1) Shipping and handling costs can make or break a business that sells online. (2) By charging too much, a site may force customers to abandon their order. (3) A customer who feels that shipping and handling charges are too high may never return to the site. (4) Most people have shipped packages at least occasionally, so they know how much shipping costs. (5) Going too far in the other direction, some online sites offer their customers free shipping and handling. (6) The sites that offer free shipping lose money, and may have to either close down for good or start charging shipping fees. (7) Correct (8) Using these shippers, the online sites must either charge a flat fee, which may be too much or too little, or make the customer wait until the order is complete to find out the shipping fee. (9) Neither option is perfect, so a business that wants to keep expanding its customer base must choose the least unattractive solution.

CHAPTER 30: COORDINATION AND SUBORDINATION

Practice 30-1, page 473
Possible edits: **1.** or **3.** and **5.** so **7.** for **9.** and

Practice 30-2, page 474
Possible edits: **1.** Gasoline prices are lower in the United States than in many other industrialized countries, but most Americans do not find this news comforting. **3.** In 2000, Hong Kong drivers paid over three times as much as Americans paid for gasoline, and Italians and Japanese were buying gas at more than four dollars a gallon. **5.** Few people would argue that gasoline prices in the United States are too low, but the reason for these relatively cheap prices is that gasoline is not heavily taxed. **7.** Gasoline taxes can help to pay for roads, or they can raise money for research into fuel efficiency. **9.** Many Americans do not want to pay gas taxes of even two or three cents per gallon, nor do most want to spend tax money on mass transit systems.

Practice 30-3, page 477
Answers: **1.** Legal differences can cause problems in the global marketplace; businesses from two different countries working together will probably not use the laws of either country when they draw up a contract. **3.** The American legal system is set up to deal with corporations and business interests; it is not surprising that many international businesses choose to follow U.S. laws. **5.** International students can often find good jobs after finishing law school;

they usually know more than one language and understand more than one culture.

Practice 30-4, page 477

Possible edits: **1.** Some high school graduates want to grow up as quickly as possible; however, others want to enjoy a period with limited responsibilities. **3.** Some students are not ready to think about college yet; therefore, they should choose another option. **5.** Many high school graduates have minimal living expenses; as a result, they can experiment with careers and find out what they enjoy doing. **7.** Volunteer work allows many high school graduates to help causes they believe in; in addition, they may get to visit other parts of the world. **9.** Some high school graduates work, volunteer, or join the military as an intermediate step; in fact, they may plan to go to college after spending some time away from school.

Practice 30-5, page 479

Possible edits: **1.** because **3.** after **5.** so that **7.** where **9.** if

Practice 30-6, page 481

Possible edits: **1.** Although toddlers do not get to make many decisions, they want to have some power over their own lives. **3.** If parents want to avoid power struggles with their toddlers, the parents should learn to pick their battles. **5.** Parents should not let a child do anything dangerous even though the child may want to. **7.** Although adolescents need to establish their independence from their parents, they also want their parents to set some limits. **9.** Food, sleep, clothes, and grooming are often battlefields for children and parents unless parents remember their own rebellious phases and try to understand what their children are feeling.

Practice 30-7, page 482

Possible edits: **1.** (1/2) Lyme disease, which is carried by deer ticks, appears most frequently in the northeastern United States. (3) No change (4/5) After people venture into tall grass or brush against other foliage, they should inspect any exposed skin carefully for the minuscule ticks. (6) No change (7/8) Limiting exposed skin by wearing socks, long pants, and long sleeves gives ticks fewer chances to attach themselves; so does washing exposed skin within about ninety minutes of being outdoors. (9) No change

CHAPTER 31: PARALLELISM

Practice 31-1, page 486

Answers and possible edits: **1.** Parts that should be parallel: to remain safe/so that assistance will come quickly. When your car breaks down on the road, you should follow simple rules to remain safe and get assistance quickly. **3.** Parts that should be parallel: open the hood/put on emergency flashers/

you could tie a handkerchief to the antenna. All of the cars in a parking lot look similar, so a mechanic may have trouble finding your car unless you open the hood, put on emergency flashers, or tie a handkerchief to the antenna. **5.** Parts that should be parallel: sees no obviously broken-down car/he or she has other calls to deal with. A mechanic who sees no obviously broken-down car and has other calls to deal with may simply go on to the next customer. **7.** Parts that should be parallel: about problems/if there are delays. Most pay phones nowadays do not receive incoming calls, so the garage may not be able to call you back on a pay phone to let you know about problems or delays. **9.** Parts that should be parallel: sitting in a car/if you stand behind it. Sitting in a car or standing behind it can be very dangerous when a breakdown occurs on the side of the highway.

Practice 31-2, page 488

Answers and possible edits: **1.** Parts that should be parallel: getting the household electric bill/to pay the rent each month. For many people, getting the household electric bill is more worrisome than paying the rent each month. **3.** Parts that should be parallel: saving money/to use less electricity. Saving money appeals to many consumers more than using less electricity. **5.** Parts that should be parallel: running the refrigerator/the use of all other appliances. In most households, running the refrigerator uses more energy than using all other appliances. **7.** Parts that should be parallel: an energy-efficient new refrigerator/running an inefficient older model. However, running an energy-efficient new refrigerator uses much less electricity than running an inefficient older model. **9.** Parts that should be parallel: to buy an efficient new refrigerator/it would take to run the old one for another five years. Householders might spend less money to buy an efficient new refrigerator than to run the old one for another five years.

Practice 31-3, page 489

Answers and possible edits: **1.** Paired words: both/and. Parts that should be parallel: pressed for time/have gotten used to convenient but fattening foods. People in the United States are both pressed for time and used to convenient but fattening foods. **3.** Paired words: rather/than. Parts that should be parallel: look thinner/to stay the same size and get in better shape. Being overweight can be unhealthy, but many Americans would rather look thinner than stay the same size and get in better shape. **5.** Paired words: both/and. Parts that should be parallel: overweight people/it even influences people of normal weight. The idea that thinner is better affects both overweight people and people of normal weight. **7.** Paired words: either/or. Parts that should be parallel: surgical procedures to remove fat/they have died from dangerous diet drugs. Dozens of healthy, average-sized Americans in the past ten years have died from either surgical procedures to remove fat or dangerous diet drugs. **9.** Paired words: not only/but also. Parts that should be parallel: in good health/can be physically fit. Some people who are larger than average are not only in good health but also physically fit.

Practice 31-4, page 491
Possible edits: **1.** but also leadership experience. **3.** nor allows flexibility. **5.** and from other students.

Practice 31-5, page 491
Possible edits: **1.** (1) Some employees who want to advance their careers would rather transfer within their company than look for a new job elsewhere. (2) In-house job changes are possible, but employees should be sure that they both meet the criteria of the job and avoid making their present boss angry. (3) Because businesses invest money in each person they hire, many companies would rather hire from within than bring an outsider into a position. (4) By hiring an employee from another department, a company neither needs to make an investment in a new employee nor loses a current employee. (5) Transfers usually go more smoothly now than in the past; however, an in-house job move can still require diplomacy and honesty. (6) Experts caution employees who are considering an in-house transfer to tell their current manager the truth and to discuss their wish to transfer with the potential new manager. (7) Employees should neither threaten to quit if they do not get the new job nor spread the word around the department that they are anxious to leave their present job. (8) Employees' goals for in-house transfers should be advancing their careers and making sure that they create no bad feelings with the move.

CHAPTER 32: SENTENCE VARIETY

Practice 32-1, page 497
Answers: **1.** Annually, harsh weather takes a toll on sandy beaches. **3.** Eventually, the ocean washed the ground out from under it. **5.** Now it is going to be demolished.

Practice 32-2, page 497
Possible edits: **1.** Once **3.** Overnight, **5.** Later,

Practice 32-4, page 499
Possible edits: **1.** Paying attention to role models, some children learn aggression from people at home, at school, or on television. **3.** Acting violently under stress, his favorite television characters do not model good behavior, either. **5.** Punishing my son for his angry outbursts, I used to take away his toys and privileges. **7.** Giving him something to focus on before lashing out, I taught my son concrete ways to react to his anger. **9.** Counting to ten when he gets angry, Sean now gives himself time to cool off.

Practice 32-5, page 500
Possible edits: **1.** *Staring* **3.** Pounding **5.** Returning

Practice 32-7, page 502
Possible edits: **1.** Many New Yorkers refused to believe in the existence of the alligator spotted in a pond in Central Park in New York City in June of 2001. **3.** Believed by some gullible people, the rumors about giant sewer alligators were untrue. **5.** Reported by several New Yorkers, the Central Park alligator sightings were confirmed when a television news crew filmed a reptile in the pond. **7.** Surrounded by news cameras and curious onlookers, the pond in Central Park was brightly lit just before 11:00 P.M. on June 22. **9.** Surprised to find that the caiman was only two feet long, some New Yorkers may have felt a bit foolish for expecting to see a giant alligator in the park.

Practice 32-8, page 503
Possible edits: **1.** Trained **3.** Treated **5.** Asked

Practice 32-10, page 505
Possible edits: **1.** In the late 1980s, political activists, a rare breed, were almost unknown on many college campuses. **3.** Protests made the news again in 1999, the year activists targeted the Seattle meeting of the World Trade Organization. **5.** But the Seattle protests publicized the idea of social activism, a concept that was out of fashion at the time. **7.** Most social activists share a common goal, to have a positive effect on others' lives. **9.** College courses can provide young activists with a knowledge of history, an essential subject for anyone who hopes to improve society.

Practice 32-11, page 506
Possible edits: **1.** *Love and Desire* **3.** an aging but reliable machine **5.** a pile over two feet high

Practice 32-12, page 507
Possible edits: **1.** Cats produce a protein that keeps their skin soft. **3.** Some cat lovers who are allergic to cats can control their allergies with medication. **5.** Scientists have successfully cloned mice that have been genetically engineered for scientific study. **7.** According to cat experts, more than 10 percent of those people who have allergic reactions to cats are allergic to something other than the skin-softening protein. **9.** However, owning a genetically engineered cat would allow an allergic person to avoid taking allergy medications, which can sometimes cause dangerous side effects.

Practice 32-13, page 509
Possible edits: **1.** that receive hundreds or thousands of hits each day **3.** , which is becoming rarer every day, **5.** , which companies use to target potential customers,

Practice 32-14, page 509
Possible edits: (1) Lotteries, which were illegal until recently in most U.S. states, have now been legalized in most parts of this country. (3) Run by state governments in many places, lotteries allow the governments to raise money without raising taxes. (5) The money can help fund education and other projects that are necessary and expensive. (7) Many citizens who consider lotteries an ideal way to raise funds reason that no one is forced to buy a lottery ticket. (9) No change (10/11) Many experts on gambling worry about the increasing numbers of state lotteries, which are difficult for many people to resist. (12/13) Offering prizes of millions of dollars, lotteries make people fantasize about easy wealth. (14/15) Costing very little, lottery tickets are sold in grocery stores and shops in every neighborhood. (16/17) Unfortunately, the people least able to afford lottery tickets spend the most money on them, convinced that they will strike it rich someday. (18/19) In many impoverished areas, large numbers of people regularly buy several lottery tickets each week, hoping to escape boring, low-paying jobs. (20) No change (21) Many people addicted to gambling do not consider the nearly impossible odds of winning a lottery jackpot. (23/24) Hooked by occasional small payoffs of two or three dollars, addicted gamblers will keep buying tickets until they have no money left. (25/26) Promising a big payoff for a little investment, lotteries bring vast amounts of money into state treasuries. (27/28) But lottery supporters, believing that lotteries save everyone money, seldom think about the victims of lotteries. (29) No change (31) No change

CHAPTER 33: ESL CONCERNS
Practice 33-1, page 516
Answers: **1.** I am a waitress at a restaurant four days a week. **3.** There is a university close by, so many college students eat at my restaurant because it serves cheap food. **5.** They seem to think that it is okay to be rude to the person serving them. **7.** I do not make a high salary, so I need the tips from my customers to make a good living. **9.** However, I think that people who cannot afford to leave a tip should not eat in a restaurant.

Practice 33-2, page 518
Answers: **1.** Marlene and Agnetha wanted to see a certain movie after they saw the advertisement for it in the newspaper. **3.** The two women did not want to miss seeing the film at their neighborhood theater, so they arranged their schedules carefully. **5.** After they saw the movie, they were very angry that they had wasted their time and money. **7.** Then Marlene read in a different newspaper that the movie studio had admitted to inventing David Manning. **9.** Therefore, the studio executives had decided to publish advertisements that contained a made-up quotation saying that the film was wonderful.

Practice 33-3, page 521
Answers: **1.** During World War II, more than 120,000 Japanese Americans were shut up in internment camps. **3.** These soldiers often had to fight against prejudice as well as the enemy. **5.** After the war, many Japanese Americans who had been interned were ashamed of their experience. **7.** They wanted to make other Americans aware of the sacrifices of Japanese Americans during World War II. **9.** For the center of the memorial park, the designers picked out a sculpture by a Japanese American artist, Nina Akamu, featuring two cranes tangled in barbed wire.

Practice 33-4, page 522
Answers: **1.** Students who are anxious about mathematics take fewer math classes and perform worse in them than students who do not have math anxiety. **3.** It turns out that worry prevents students from understanding mathematics as well as they could. **5.** Starting at about the age of twelve, students with math anxiety become less able to compensate for the loss of working memory. **7.** Students who once thought they would never be able to understand math may someday find out that they can conquer their anxiety and cope with numbers.

Practice 33-5, page 524
Answers: **1.** Negative: We will not have to cancel the picnic. Question: Will we have to cancel the picnic? **3.** Negative: The garden does not need water this year. Question: Does the garden need water this year? **5.** Negative: Carrying an umbrella was not a good idea. Question: Was carrying an umbrella a good idea?

Practice 33-6, page 526
Possible edits: **1.** We found a faded lace handkerchief lying in the drawer. **3.** During the restoration, builders added a massive new marble stairway to the entrance. **5.** I put several delicious red New Jersey tomatoes in the salad.

CHAPTER 34: WORD CHOICE
Practice 34-1, page 531
Answers and possible edits: **1.** Vague or abstract words: little; good. My four-year-old sister cleans up her room, puts away her toys and books, and helps my parents and me with simple chores. **3.** Vague or abstract words: fun. My sister and I enjoy playing board games and reading books together. **5.** Vague or abstract words: nicest. My grandmother hugs me enthusiastically and has been encouraging me to try to get a dance scholarship. **7.** Vague or abstract words: one of my uncles; a little crazy. My uncle Mahmoud wears loud purple suits and spikes his hair straight up. **9.** Vague or abstract words: treats me; very young. He pinches my cheeks as if I were a kindergartner instead of a college student.

Practice 34-2, page 532

Answers and possible edits: **1.** Slang: fab. I wanted to express my appreciation for the wonderful new benefits package. **3.** Slang: biggie. Now that my wife and I are starting a family, insurance is a major factor. **5.** Slang: no way. Without the company paying for this leave, I would not be able to afford the time off. **7.** Slang: cake. I know that adjusting to fatherhood will not be easy. **9.** Slang: give me a shout. If I can do anything to make my absence easier on my coworkers, please let me know.

Practice 34-3, page 534

Answers and possible edits: **1.** Wordy language: the fact of the matter is that. Many young people get their first ideas about interesting jobs from watching television. **3.** Wordy language: a great number of. Shows like *L.A. Law* made the legal profession attractive to many future lawyers. **5.** Wordy language: there are some people who. Some believe that declining respect for politicians began with television shows. **7.** Wordy language: in this day and age. Now, however, more young people are becoming interested in careers in government. **9.** Wordy language: due to the fact that. Will the United States have a crop of idealistic young politicians in the next decade because they watched *West Wing* as impressionable teens?

Practice 34-4, page 536

Answers and possible edits: **1.** Cliché: eyes in the back of their heads. People with young children need to be constantly alert. **3.** Cliché: have their heads examined. Parents of a toddler should rethink their safety policies if they do not lock cabinets containing household chemicals. **5.** Cliché: in the nick of time. Parents sometimes recognize dangers moments before a mishap and stop their children from injuring themselves. **7.** Cliché: mortal fears. Parents worry about their young children running into traffic to chase a ball. **9.** Cliché: to keep their hands to themselves. Children must learn not to touch the weapon and to leave the area immediately if they find a gun in someone's home.

Practice 34-5, page 537

Possible edits: (1) Being the chief executive officer at a major American corporation almost always pays extremely well. (3) Even if the company performs poorly and the CEO gets fired, he (and it is almost always a man) often gets a severance package that is worth additional millions. (5) This ratio is enormous compared with the ratios in other industrialized countries. (7) Are American CEOs really exceptional? (9) In fact, highly paid CEOs can rarely do what corporate directors hope. (11) There is no guarantee that these men will be able to make another business succeed. (13) Then the corporation would be able to spend a few million dollars less on its chief officer. (15) The problem with promoting a

CEO from within the company is that few companies want to take risks. (17) Company directors think that their stockholders expect the companies to bring in a highly paid outsider. (19) Of course, most CEOs brought in from elsewhere also fail to satisfy the shareholders, but the corporate boards can at least reassure themselves that their choice has a track record when he arrives. (21) However, few corporate boards of directors are willing to look anywhere other than conventional places for their next leaders.

CHAPTER 35: COMMONLY CONFUSED WORDS

Practice 35-1, page 550

Answers: **1.** their **3.** find **5.** an; except **7.** write **9.** though; effect

Practice 35-2, page 551

Answers: **1.** (1) Most people know that Americans love to drive their cars. (2) However, many people may not be conscious of how much the government does to support our car culture. (3) For instance, the United States would never have had so many good highways without federal and state assistance for road construction and maintenance. (4) New highways are usually paid for mainly by tax money. (5) It is rare for a new road to be paid for with tolls, which would come exclusively from the people driving on it. (6) Americans also expect their roads to be well maintained, and they may write to their representatives to complain about potholes and aging road surfaces. (7) The government is even responsible for keeping gas prices lower here than in most other industrialized nations. (8) Few people mind that the government assists drivers in these ways. (9) Some would argue that it's a government's job to help pay for transportation. (10) However, other forms of transportation in this country are often passed over when Congress hands out funds. (11) Amtrak, the U.S. railroad, will soon lose all government funds, even though many government officials are skeptical of its ability to keep operating without government assistance. (12) Except for a few places like New York and San Francisco, most U.S. cities do not have good mass transit systems. (13) Americans whose travels have taken them to certain parts of the world praise the national train systems and city transit systems they find there. (14) As traffic gets worse in our nation's urban and suburban areas, some people find it odd that the United States does not invest more in transportation that would allow people to leave their cars at home.

CHAPTER 36: SPELLING

Practice 36-2, page 562

Answers: **1.** (1) Anyone interested in weird events should visit New York City on October 31, when the biggest Halloween parade in the country takes place. (2) Everyone in the city, it seems, marches in the parade, yet there are still an estimated two million people watching from the sidewalks. (3) The parade had its beginnings in Greenwich Village, and original parade-goers walked though the small, winding streets of that old New York neighborhood. (4) By now the parade has gotten so large that it has to go down one of the city's broad avenues. (5) The Halloween parade surprises a lot of people who see it for the first time. (6) The merriment begins early in the evening, as costumed paraders line up. (7) You're likely to see a huge group of friends dressed as one hundred and one dalmatians or perhaps some comically exaggerated versions of government officials. (8) Every kind of costume is permitted in the parade, and some people attend skimpily dressed, apparently without embarrassment, in spite of the October chill. (9) For a fascinating look at how strangely people can behave on Halloween, the New York City Halloween parade is the place to be.

CHAPTER 37: COMMAS
Practice 37-1, page 568
Answers: **1.** C   **3.** A recent study of sixty-eight dollar bills found five carrying germs that could infect healthy people, fifty-nine harboring bacteria that could sicken people with depressed immune systems, and only four that were free of dangerous infectious agents.   **5.** Of course, this study involved a very small, localized, and not necessarily representative sample of bills.   **7.** Once, when I was attempting to open my purse, accept a receipt from a cashier, and hold my change at the same time, I stuck some dollar bills in my mouth for a moment.   **9.** Although the study of the sixty-eight dollar bills does not reveal whether germs can transfer from bills to people, survive for long periods on money, or otherwise contribute to human illness, reading about it made me realize that my mother had been right to be worried.

Practice 37-2, page 570
Answers: **1.** Working in a nursing home is a difficult job, for elderly patients can seldom do much for themselves. **3.** Few trained nurses and nurse's aides want nursing-home jobs, for the pay is also usually lower than that offered by hospitals.   **5.** More workers will be needed as the baby boomers become elderly, yet there is already a shortage of people willing to do the tough and often unpleasant work. **7.** C   **9.** Solving these problems will be difficult, for long-term care for the elderly is already very expensive.

Practice 37-3, page 571
Answers: **1.** Along roadsides all across this country, drivers see the bodies of animals hit by cars.   **3.** Of course, hitting a deer is not only disturbing but also potentially harmful or fatal to the occupants of a car.   **5.** On the other hand, drivers in wilderness areas may accidentally kill endangered species.   **7.** Maintaining the world's largest network of roads, the U.S. Forest Service tries to balance the needs of humans and wildlife.   **9.** Unfortunately, wilderness roads may isolate populations of animals that will not cross them and kill animals that make the attempt.

Practice 37-4, page 573
Answers: **1.** Road rage, as most people have heard, occurs when an angry driver overreacts.   **3.** One famous air rage incident, a confrontation between a drunken businessman and a flight attendant, ended with the passenger tied to his seat for the rest of the flight.   **5.** Ground rage, however, occurs in the terminal, not in the air.   **7.** Oversold seats, a common occurrence in air travel, can mean that some passengers are forced to miss a flight.   **9.** Some delayed or bumped passengers take out their anger on the gate agent, a convenient target.

Practice 37-5, page 575
Answers: **1.** C   **3.** C   **5.** C   **7.** Such people, who may never love clowns, will still be able to tolerate having them around.   **9.** Few adults admit to having coulrophobia, which is most effectively treated when the sufferer confronts the fear.

Practice 37-6, page 577
Answers: **1.** My sister asked, "James, do you get a lot of telemarketing calls?"   **3.** She told me that in April 2001, new laws that could help me protect my privacy had taken effect. **5.** My address, which is 21 Highland Road, Binghamton, New York, has now been added to the state registry.   **7.** I simply replied, "No, I have news for you."   **9.** "As you probably know," I told my unwanted callers, "it is illegal for you to contact me in this way."

Practice 37-7, page 578
Answers: **1.** (1) Everyone who uses cleaning products at home has probably seen warning labels on those products, for most household cleaners contain harsh chemicals. (2) The warnings, which are required by law, are so common that many users probably ignore them. (3) However, all cleaning products should be used with care, and some of them can seriously injure children or anyone else who misuses them. (4) Drain cleaners, toilet bowl cleaners, and chlorine bleach can all cause serious damage to skin, eyes, and other sensitive tissue. (5) Glass cleaners can react with bleach to produce toxic fumes. (6) Alternative cleansers, nontoxic products that can be made from items in an average kitchen, are cheaper than brand-name cleaning products and usually work just as well. (7) For most cleaning jobs, a solution of vinegar and water or baking soda

and water is effective. (8) A plunger can often fix a clogged drain as well as a drain cleaner can, and club soda cleans windows nicely. (9) As for air fresheners, one expert advises, "Open your windows." (10) Economy, efficiency, and safety are three excellent reasons for choosing home-made cleansers.

CHAPTER 38: APOSTROPHES
Practice 38-1, page 583
Answers: **1.** A thermometer's indicator mark at 98.6 degrees is supposed to show a person's normal body temperature. **3.** Fevers help the body combat viruses and stimulate the immune system. **5.** A fever's appearance is not necessarily a reason to take fever-reducing medications, which can lower a body's temperature without doing anything to fight the infection. **7.** Many doctors do not recommend using any drugs to treat a fever if it's lower than 102 degrees. **9.** Some parents' fears of fever are so intense that they suffer from "fever phobia" and overreact to their children's symptoms.

Practice 38-2, page 585
Answers: **1.** If you've ever read a book that was so wonderful you wanted all of your friends to read it, you may have considered the question "What makes a book great?" **3.** There's a problem with trying to establish which books are worth reading: Who's going to decide? **5.** This requirement may mean, however, that a book written a hundred years ago is frequently taught and a newer book that's just as good isn't. **7.** In many cases, female and minority writers of the past didn't have the money or connections to get a book published or couldn't find an audience for a book that was ahead of its time. **9.** Others think that it's important to introduce college students to books by female and minority writers because books by dead white men aren't going to interest a large percentage of today's students.

Practice 38-3, page 586
Answers: **1.** Last year, I turned down a summer's worth of beachgoing to stay in town and work at the local movie theater. **3.** I was trying to write *O Brother, Where Art Thou?* and *George Clooney,* but I ran out of *E*'s. **5.** When I discovered that I didn't have two more *o*'s for *Clooney* and turned an *8* on its side instead, the manager told me I would go far in the movie business.

Practice 38-4, page 587
Answers: **1.** (1) Some of the first discussions of global warming focused attention on one of the gases that contributes to the greenhouse effect: methane. (2) Like other greenhouse gases, methane helps to keep the earth's heat trapped in our atmosphere, and the temperature of the earth goes up as a result. (3) Humans aren't the only producers of methane; it's also a by-product of cows' digestion of their food. (4) For a while, many Americans' knowledge of global warming didn't go much further than cow jokes. (5) As scientists have become more convinced that global warming is real and a potential threat to humans, our knowledge of the causes of the greenhouse effect has expanded. (6) Cows aren't completely off the hook, but they're far less guilty of contributing to global warming than humans and cars are. (7) The amount of methane produced by cows adds up to about 3 percent of the total amount of greenhouse gases produced by people. (8) Getting a cow to change its diet won't solve the world's warming problem. **3.** (1) In March of 2001, the keyless entry systems of cars in Bremerton, Washington, suddenly stopped working, and no one knows why. (2) The cars' locks were supposed to respond when their owners pushed a button, and all at once they wouldn't. (3) After a few days' wait, the entry systems began functioning again. (4) Many residents of Bremerton, the home of a Navy shipyard, were convinced that the military's technological activity had affected the cars, but Navy officials denied it. (5) Other people wondered if radio transmissions might have jammed the frequency and prevented the keyless systems from functioning. (6) Fortunately, people whose cars have keyless entry systems weren't locked out for those days. (7) These owners simply had to resort to a backup system to open and lock their cars—it's called a "key."

CHAPTER 39: QUOTATION MARKS
Practice 39-1, page 592
Answers: **1.** Writing about the United States in the nineteenth century, Alexis de Tocqueville noted, "If ever the Supreme Court came to be composed of rash or corrupt men, the confederation would be threatened by anarchy or by civil war." **3.** "Were the justices 'rash or corrupt,'" she continued, "or did they do the right thing when they ended the long election?" **5.** "But," Roberto interrupted, "we can't ever know people's intentions for certain, so the only important question is how the Florida citizens actually voted." **7.** Professor Patel reminded us, "No one has answered my question yet." **9.** "The justices who stopped the recount were motivated by conservative political views," Natalie fumed. "The decision was obviously corrupt!"

Practice 39-2, page 594
Answers: **1.** "I loved the informal office at first," she said. **3.** She admitted, "I have never been a business-suit kind of person, so I liked the fact that every day was casual." **5.** C **7.** C **9.** "I was just starting to send out résumés when I got laid off," she recalled, "and fortunately I found something before my severance pay ended."

Practice 39-3, page 596

Answers: **1.** At the meeting, an outside consultant tried to motivate us by quoting from an article in USA Today called, "How to Get the Job Done."   **3.** Marta looked as if she were taking careful notes, but I knew that she was working on the final draft of an essay she was hoping to publish in Business Review, her favorite magazine.   **5.** When the grueling meeting was over, Marta reminded me that Wallace Stevens, the poet who wrote "Sunday Morning," had found a way to be creative while he spent his days working at an insurance company.

Practice 39-4, page 597

Answers: **1.** (1) After Michael saw an advertisement in his local newspaper for a concert featuring "The Pink Panther Theme," "Charade," and other songs by Henry Mancini, he immediately bought a ticket. (2) He had just finished reading a book about the film composer, and he told me that he couldn't wait to hear the music played live. (3) He said that I should go, too, but I stayed home and watched television. (4) After he went to the show, he told me, "I thought that they saved the best for last." (5) He described the final number, when a young woman stepped onto the stage and sang, "Moon river, wider than a mile, I'm crossing you in style someday." (6) He knew "Moon River" from the movie Breakfast at Tiffany's and as a hit song for Andy Williams in the 1960s, but he had never found the song as beautiful as it seemed that night at the concert. (7) "It was an amazing evening," he told me. (8) His description of the concert was so vivid that I went out and bought a CD called Henry Mancini's Greatest Hits. (9) Now I regret my decision: Why didn't I go to the concert when Michael said, "Come with me; you'll love the music"? (10) As I listen to the CD, I realize that he was right, and next time he tells me about a show that he thinks I'll love, I'm going to go along.

CHAPTER 40: OTHER PUNCTUATION

Practice 40-1, page 604

Possible edits: **1.** (1) The International Olympic Committee met in 2001 to choose the site of the 2008 Olympic Games; the winner was Beijing, China's capital. (2) Beijing (the loser to Sydney, Australia for the 2000 Olympics by just two votes) had campaigned heavily for the honor of hosting the Olympics. (3) The 2001 vote—which had some vocal opponents—granted the Olympic Games to China for the first time in history. (4) Those who objected to the Olympic Committee's choice had several strong reasons: China has a history of environmental problems, including severe smog in Beijing as a result of coal-burning factories, polluting buses, and heavy automobile traffic; and, even more important, the country has been scrutinized for human rights abuses. (5) Chinese officials had announced a twelve-billion-dollar project to cut air pollution in the city before the Olympic Committee made its decision. (6) Human rights abuses are not as easily answered; several members of Congress were among those complaining about China's treatment of political and religious dissidents. (7) Supporters of Beijing's bid to host the Olympics believe that the Games will make China a more open society: Reporters, athletes, and spectators will flood Beijing in 2008. (8) Some members of the Olympic Committee (including the outgoing president, said to be a strong supporter of Beijing's bid) hope the vote will lead to improved human rights situations in China. (9) There are many skeptics; some argue that Beijing will see the Olympics as a reward, not as an opportunity for change. (10) Some even compare the Beijing Olympics to the 1936 Olympics in Hitler's Berlin; one difference, however, is that billions of people will be watching the Games on television in 2008. (11) Whatever happens in China as a result of holding the Games in Beijing, the Chinese people—strong supporters of the Beijing Olympics—are overjoyed at the chance to show off their capital city. (12) Sports fans and freedom-loving people all over the world will be watching China as 2008 approaches.

CHAPTER 41: CAPITALIZATION

Practice 41-1, page 608

Answers: (1) C (3) The same year, audiences thrilled to the story of little Dorothy, who clicked her heels together and chanted, "There's no place like home."

Practice 41-2, page 610

Answers: **1.** Lindsborg is a small town in McPherson County, Kansas, that calls itself "Little Sweden, U.S.A." **3.** The town's most famous resident was probably a Swedish immigrant artist named Birger Sandzen. **5.** Sandzen intended to stay in Kansas for two or three years, but he loved the Great Plains and ended up remaining in Lindsborg for the rest of his life.   **7.** Although Sandzen worked mainly in the Midwest, the Rocky Mountains, and other relatively unpopulated parts of the United States, he exhibited widely.   **9.** Sandzen's use of vivid color showed the beauty of the natural landscapes of the West.

Practice 41-3, page 612

Answers: **1.** The television show *Sesame Street,* which began in 1969, was an innovator in programming for children.   **3.** The popular Muppets Kermit the Frog and Miss Piggy starred in several films, including one based on Charles Dickens's classic *A Christmas Carol* and one based on Robert Louis Stevenson's *Treasure Island.* **5.** "Elmo's World," a segment added to the show in the 1990s, introduced the small red monster who would become one of the most popular toys in history.

Practice 41-4, page 612

Answers: (1) Are pennies necessary? (3) According to the group Americans for Common Cents, however, "Pennies are a part of our culture and our economy." (5) Opponents of the copper coin—which has been made of zinc with a copper coating since 1982—say that people don't like to use pennies. (7) Many stores place penny trays on the counter so that customers can either leave unwanted pennies or pick a few up for the cashier to avoid getting any pennies in change. (9) Yet the penny is undeniably a part of American history. (11) Only four of these original coins survive, and they are valued at more than a quarter of a million dollars each. (13) Fifty years later, the Lincoln Memorial was added to the reverse side, replacing the stalks of wheat on earlier pennies. (15) Everyone has heard, "A penny saved is a penny earned," and that saying is not likely to change even though a penny doesn't buy much today. (17) Finally, unlike the John F. Kennedy half-dollar coin, which is no longer minted, people simply expect pennies to be there. (19) But many U.S. citizens care about the fate of the penny and don't want it to disappear.

Index

Y

Z

Acknowledgments continued from p. iv

Amy L. Beck. "Struggling for Perfection." From the *Harvard Crimson*, March 19, 1998. Reprinted by permission.

Perry W. Buffington. "How to Avoid a Speeding Ticket" and "Get the Raise You Deserve" from *Cheap Psychological Tricks: What to Do When Hard Work, Honesty, and Perseverance Fail* by Perry W. Buffington, Ph.D., illustrated by Mitzi Cartee. Copyright © 1996 by Perry W. Buffington, Ph.D. Published by Peachtree Publishers. Reprinted by permission of Peachtree Publishers, Atlanta, GA.

Consumer Reports. "Laptop Computers" from the June 2001 issue of *Consumer Reports* for educational purposes only. © 2001 by Consumers Union of U.S., Inc., Yonkers, NY 10703–1057, a nonprofit organization. Reprinted with permission. No personal use or photocopying permitted. To learn more about Consumers Union, log onto www.ConsumerReports.org.

Chitra Divakaruni. "Why Don't They Just Leave?" From *Mothers Who Think* by Camille Peri and Kate Moses. This article first appeared in Salon.com, at http://www.Salon.com. An online version remains in the Salon archives. Reprinted with permission.

Bob Greene. "Foul Mouths Are Fair Game in Our Coarsening Culture." © Tribune Media Services, Inc. All rights reserved. Reprinted with permission.

Robert W. Hahn and Paul C. Tetlock. "Driving and Talking Do Mix." From www.cartalk.cars.com, November 12, 1999. Reprinted by permission.

Sidney J. Harris. "A Jerk." From "Strictly Personal" column, *Chicago Daily News*. Published in *Last Things First* by Sidney J. Harris. Copyright © 1961 by Sidney J. Harris. Reprinted with special permission of King Features Syndicate.

Robert L. Heilbroner. "Don't Let Stereotypes Warp Your Judgments." Originally published in *Think* magazine, June 1961. Reprinted by permission of the author.

Alfie Kohn. "The Case against Competition." Copyright © 1987 by Alfie Kohn. Reprinted from *Working Mother* (1987), with the author's permission.

Tom Magliozzi and Ray Magliozzi. "Protecting Its People: Let Our Government Do Its Job." Courtesy www.cartalk.cars.com.

Malcolm X. "My First Conk." Originally titled "Hair" from *The Autobiography of Malcolm X* by Malcolm X and Alex Haley. Copyright © 1964 by Alex Haley and Malcolm X. Copyright © 1965 by Alex Haley and Betty Shabazz. Used by permission of Random House, Inc. and John Hawkins and Associates.

McNeil-PPC, Inc. "Concerta" Web site: www.concerta.net. Courtesy McNeil Consumer & Specialty Pharmaceuticals, a division of McNeil-PPC, Inc.

Microsoft Word screen shots. www.microsoft.com. © 2002 Microsoft Corporation. All rights reserved.

Wesley Morris. "Delay Gives 'Damage' a Fighting Chance." From the *Boston Globe*, February 8, 2002. "Survey Finds Many Firms Monitor Staff." From the *Boston Globe*, April 29, 2001. Staff writer. Courtesy of the Boston Globe.

Kerry Pechter. "Pet Therapy for Heart and Soul." First published in *Prevention*, August 1995. Copyright © 1995 by Kerry Pechter. Reprinted by permission of the author.

Andy Rooney. "How to Put off Doing a Job." From *Word for Word* by Andrew A. Rooney. Copyright © 1984, 1985, 1986 by Essay Production, Inc. Used by permission of G. P. Putnam's Sons, a division of Penguin Putnam, Inc. and the author.

Suzanne Sievert. "It's Not Just How We Play That Matters." From *Newsweek*, March 10, 2001, p. 13. Copyright © 2001 Newsweek, Inc. All rights reserved. Reprinted by permission.

Pamela J. Transue. "A Humbling Experience." From *Community College Journal*, Vol. 72, No. 3, December/January 2002. Reprinted with permission.

Marie Winn. "Cookies or Heroin?" From *The Plug-In Drug*, Revised and Updated-25th Anniversary Edition by Marie Winn. Copyright © 1977, 1985, 2002 by Marie Winn Miller. Used by permission of Viking Penguin, a division of Penguin Putnam, Inc.

Correction Symbols

This chart lists typical symbols that instructors use to point out writing problems. The explanation of each symbol includes a step you can take to revise or edit your writing. Included also are suggested chapters to check for more help and information. If your instructor uses different symbols for some errors, write them in the left-hand column for future reference.

YOUR INSTRUCTOR'S SYMBOL	STANDARD SYMBOL	HOW TO REVISE OR EDIT (NUMBERS IN BOLDFACE ARE CHAPTERS WHERE YOU CAN FIND HELP)
	adj	Use correct adjective form **28**
	adv	Use correct adverb form **28**
	agr	Correct subject-verb agreement or pronoun agreement **25**; **27**
	awk	Awkward expression: edit for clarity **7**
	cap	Use capital letter correctly **41**
	case	Use correct pronoun case **27**
	cliché	Replace overused phrase with fresh words **34**
	coh	Revise paragraph or essay for coherence **7**
	combine	Combine sentences **32**
	con t	Correct the inconsistent verb tense **26**
	coord	Use coordination correctly **30**
	cs	Comma splice: join the two sentences correctly **24**
	d or dic	Diction: edit word choice **34**
	dev	Develop your paragraph or essay more completely **4**; **6**
	dm	Revise to avoid a dangling modifier **29**
	frag	Attach the fragment to a sentence or make it a sentence **23**
	fs	Fused sentence: join the two sentences correctly **24**
	intro	Add or strengthen your introduction **6**
	ital	Use italics **39**
	lc	Use lowercase **41**
	mm	Revise to avoid a misplaced modifier **29**
	pl	Use the correct plural form of the verb **26**
	ref	Make pronoun reference clear **27**
	ro	Run-on sentence: join the two sentences correctly **24**
	sp	Correct the spelling error **35**; **36**
	sub	Use subordination correctly **30**
	sup	Support your point with details, examples, or facts **4**
	tense	Correct the problem with verb tense **26**
	trans	Add a transition **7**
	ts	Add or strengthen your topic sentence or thesis statement **3**
	u	Revise paragraph or essay for unity **7**
	w	Delete unnecessary words **34**
	?	Make your meaning clearer **7**
	,	Use comma correctly **37**
	; : ( ) - —	Use semicolon/colon/parentheses/hyphen/dash correctly **40**
	" "	Use quotation marks correctly **39**

Useful Lists, Checklists, and Charts